The Crowd
by Gustave Le Bon

Extraordinary Popular Delusions and the Madness of Crowds
by Charles Mackay

The Crowd
by Gustave Le Bon

TABLE OF CONTENTS

Preface.

The following work is devoted to an account of the characteristics of crowds.

The whole of the common characteristics with which heredity endows the individuals of a race constitute the genius of the race. When, however, a certain number of these individuals are gathered together in a crowd for purposes of action, observation proves that, from the mere fact of their being assembled, there result certain new psychological characteristics, which are added to the racial characteristics and differ from them at times to a very considerable degree.

Organised crowds have always played an important part in the life of peoples, but this part has never been of such moment as at present. The substitution of the unconscious action of crowds for the conscious activity of individuals is one of the principal characteristics of the present age.

I have endeavoured to examine the difficult problem presented by crowds in a purely scientific manner — that is, by making an effort to proceed with method, and without being influenced by opinions, theories, and doctrines. This, I believe, is the only mode of arriving at the discovery of some few particles of truth, especially when dealing, as is the case here, with a question that is the subject of impassioned controversy. A man of science bent on verifying a phenomenon is not called upon to concern himself with the interests his verifications may hurt. In a recent publication an eminent thinker,
M. Goblet d'Alviela, made the remark that, belonging to none of the contemporary schools, I am occasionally found in opposition of sundry of the conclusions of all of them. I hope this new work will merit a similar observation. To belong to a school is necessarily to espouse its prejudices and preconceived opinions.

Still I should explain to the reader why he will find me draw conclusions from my investigations which it might be thought at first sight they do not bear; why, for instance, after noting the extreme mental inferiority of crowds, picked assemblies included, I yet affirm it would be dangerous to meddle with their organisation, notwithstanding this inferiority.

The reason is, that the most attentive observation of the facts of history has invariably demonstrated to me that social organisms being every whit as complicated as those of all beings, it is in no wise in our power to force them to undergo on a sudden far-reaching transformations. Nature has recourse at times to radical measures, but never after our fashion, which explains how it is that nothing is more fatal to a people than the mania for great reforms, however excellent these reforms may appear theoretically. They would only be useful were it possible to change instantaneously the genius of nations. This power, however, is onlypossessed bytime. Men are ruled by ideas, sentiments, and customs — matters which are of the essence of ourselves. Institutions and laws are the outward manifestation of our character, the expression of its needs. Being its outcome, institutions and laws cannot change this character.

The study of social phenomena cannot be separated from that of the peoples among whom they have come into existence. From the philosophic point of view these phenomena may have an absolute value; in practice they have only a relative value.

It is necessary, in consequence, when studying a social phenomenon, to consider it successively under two very different aspects. It will then be seen that the teachings of pure reason are very often contrary to those of practical reason. There are scarcely any data, even physical, to which this distinction is not applicable. From the point of view of absolute truth a cube or a circle are invariable geometrical figures, rigorously defined by certain formulas. From the point of view of the impression they make on our eye these geometrical figures may assume very varied shapes. By perspective the cube may be transformed into a pyramid or a square, the circle into an ellipse or a straight line. Moreover, the consideration of these fictitious shapes is far more important than that of the real shapes, for it is they and they alone that we see and that can be reproduced by photography or in pictures. In certain cases there is more truth in the unreal than in the real. To present objects with their exact geometrical forms would be to distort nature and render it unrecognisable. If we imagine a world whose inhabitants could only copy or photograph objects, but were unable to touch them, it would be very difficult for such persons to attain to an exact idea of their form. Moreover, the knowledge of this form, accessible only to a small number of learned men, would present but a very minor interest.

The philosopher who studies social phenomena should bear in mind that side by side with their theoretical value they possess a practical value, and that this latter, so far as the evolution of civilisation is concerned, is alone of importance. The recognition of this fact should render him very circumspect with regard to the conclusions that logic would seem at first to enforce upon him.

There are other motives that dictate to him a like reserve. The complexity of social facts is such, that it is impossible to grasp them as a whole and to foresee the effects of their reciprocal influence. It seems, too, that behind the visible facts are hidden at times thousands of invisible causes. Visible social phenomena appear to be the result of an immense, unconscious working, that as a rule is beyond the reach of our analysis. Perceptible phenomena may be compared to the waves, which are the expression on the surface of the ocean of deep-lying disturbances of which we know nothing. So far as the majority of their acts are considered, crowds display a singularly inferior mentality; yet there are other acts in which they appear to be guided by those mysterious forces which the ancients denominated destiny, nature, or providence, which we call the voices of the dead, and whose power it is impossible to overlook, although we ignore their essence. It would seem, at times, as if there were latent forces in the inner being of nations which serve to guide them. What, for instance, can be more complicated, more logical, more marvellous than a language? Yet whence can this admirably organised production have arisen, except it be the outcome of the unconscious genius of crowds? The most learned academics, the most esteemed grammarians can do no more than note down the laws that govern languages; they would be utterly incapable of creating them. Even with respect to the ideas of great men are we certain that they are exclusively the offspring of their brains? No doubt such ideas are always created by solitary minds, but is it not the genius of crowds that has furnished the thousands of grains of dust forming the soil in which they have sprung up?

Crowds, doubtless, are always unconscious, but this very unconsciousness is perhaps one of the secrets of their strength. In the natural world beings exclusively governed by instinct accomplish acts whose marvellous complexity astounds us. Reason is an attribute of humanity of too recent date and still too imperfect to reveal to us the laws of the unconscious, and still more to take its place. The part played by the unconscious in all our acts is immense, and that played by reason very small. The unconscious acts like a force still unknown.

If we wish, then, to remain within the narrow but safe limits within which science can attain to knowledge, and not to wander in the domain of vague conjecture and vain hypothesis, all we must do is simply to take note of such phenomena as are accessible to us, and confine ourselves to their consideration. Every conclusion drawn from our observation is, as a rule, premature, for behind the phenomena which we see clearly are other phenomena that we see indistinctly, and perhaps behind these latter, yet others which we do not see at all.

Introduction. The Era of Crowds.

The great upheavals which precede changes of civilisations such as the fall of the Roman Empire and the foundation of the Arabian Empire, seem at first sight determined more especially by political transformations, foreign invasion, or the overthrow of dynasties. But a more attentive study of these events shows that behind their apparent causes the real cause is generally seen to be a profound modification in the ideas of the peoples. The true historical upheavals are not those which astonish us by their grandeur and violence. The only important changes whence the renewal of civilisations results, affect ideas, conceptions, and beliefs. The memorable events of history are the visible effects of the invisible changes of human thought. The reason these great events are so rare is that there is nothing so stable in a race as the inherited groundwork of its thoughts.

The present epoch is one of these critical moments in which the thought of mankind is undergoing a process of transformation.

Two fundamental factors are at the base of this transformation. The first is the destruction of those religious, political, and social beliefs in which all the elements of our civilisation are rooted. The second is the creation of entirely new conditions of existence and thought as the result of modern scientific and industrial discoveries.

The ideas of the past, although half destroyed, being still very powerful, and the ideas which are to replace them being still in process of formation, the modern age represents a period of transition and anarchy.

It is not easy to say as yet what will one day be evolved from this necessarily somewhat chaotic period. What will be the fundamental ideas on which the societies that are to succeed our own will be built up? We do not at present know. Still it is already clear that on whatever lines the societies of the future are organised, they will have to count with a new power, with the last surviving sovereign force of modern times, the power of crowds. On the ruins of so many ideas formerly considered beyond discussion, and to-day decayed or decaying, of so many sources of authority that successive revolutions have destroyed, this power, which alone has arisen in their stead, seems soon destined to absorb the others. While all our ancient beliefs are tottering and disappearing, while the old pillars of society are giving way one by one, the power of the crowd is the only force that nothing menaces, and of which the prestige is continually on the increase. The age we are about to enter will in truth be the *Era of Crowds*.

Scarcely a century ago the traditional policy of European states and the rivalries of sovereigns were the principal factors that shaped events. The opinion of the masses scarcely counted, and most frequently indeed did not count at all. To-day it is the traditions which used to obtain in politics, and the individual tendencies and rivalries of rulers which do not count; while, on the contrary, the voice of the masses has become preponderant. It is this voice that dictates their conduct to kings, whose endeavour is to take note of its utterances. The destinies of nations are elaborated at present in the heart of the masses, and no longer in the councils of princes.

The entry of the popular classes into political life — that is to say, in reality, their progressive transformation into governing classes — is one of the most striking characteristics of our epoch of transition. The introduction of universal suffrage, which exercised for a long time but little influence, is not, as might be thought, the distinguishing feature of this transference of political power. The progressive growth of the power of the masses took place at first by the propagation of certain ideas, which have slowly implanted themselves in men's minds, and afterwards by the gradual association of individuals bent on bringing about the realisation of theoretical

13

conceptions. It is by association that crowds have come to procure ideas with respect to their interests which are very clearly defined if not particularly just, and have arrived at a consciousness of their strength. The masses are founding syndicates before which the authorities capitulate one after the other; they are also founding labour unions, which in spite of all economic laws tend to regulate the conditions of labour and wages. They return to assemblies in which the Government is vested, representatives utterly lacking initiative and independence, and reduced most often to nothing else than the spokesmen of the committees that have chosen them.

To-day the claims of the masses are becoming more and more sharply defined, and amount to nothing less than a determination to utterly destroy society as it now exists, with a view to making it hark back to that primitive communism which was the normal condition of all human groups before the dawn of civilisation. Limitations of the hours of labour, the nationalisation of mines, railways, factories, and the soil, the equal distribution of all products, the elimination of all the upper classes for the benefit of the popular classes, &c., such are these claims.

Little adapted to reasoning, crowds, on the contrary, are quick to act. As the result of their present organisation their strength has become immense. The dogmas whose birth we are witnessing will soon have the force of the old dogmas; that is to say, the tyrannical and sovereign force of being above discussion. The divine right of the masses is about to replace the divine right of kings.

The writers who enjoy the favour of our middle classes, those who best represent their rather narrow ideas, their somewhat prescribed views, their rather superficial scepticism, and their at times somewhat excessive egoism, display profound alarm at this new power which they see growing; and to combat the disorder in men's minds they are addressing despairing appeals to those moral forces of the Church for which they formerly professed so much disdain. They talk to us of the bankruptcy of science, go back in penitence to Rome, and remind us of the teachings of revealed truth. These new converts forget that it is too late. Had they been really touched by grace, a like operation could not have the same influence on minds less concerned with the preoccupations which beset these recent adherents to religion. The masses repudiate to-day the gods which their admonishers repudiated yesterday and helped to destroy. There is no power, Divine or human, that can oblige a stream to flow back to its source.

There has been no bankruptcy of science, and science has had no share in the present intellectual anarchy, nor in the making of the new power which is springing up in the midst of this anarchy. Science promised us truth, or at least a knowledge of such relations as our intelligence can seize: it never promised us peace or happiness. Sovereignly indifferent to our feelings, it is deaf to our lamentations. It is for us to endeavour to live with science, since nothing can bring back the illusions it has destroyed.

Universal symptoms, visible in all nations, show us the rapid growth of the power of crowds, and do not admit of our supposing that it is destined to cease growing at an early date. Whatever fate it may reserve for us, we shall have to submit to it. All reasoning against it is a mere vain war of words. Certainly it is possible that the advent to power of the masses marks one of the last stages of Western civilisation, a complete return to those periods of confused anarchy which seem always destined to precede the birth of every new society. But may this result be prevented?

Up to now these thoroughgoing destructions of a worn-out civilisation have constituted the most obvious task of the masses. It is not indeed to-day merely that this can be traced. History tells us, that from the moment when the moral forces on which a civilisation rested have lost their strength, its final dissolution is brought about by those unconscious and brutal crowds known, justifiably enough, as barbarians. Civilisations as yet have only been created and directed by a small intellectual aristocracy, never by crowds. Crowds are only powerful for destruction. Their rule is always tantamount to a barbarian phase. A civilisation involves fixed rules, discipline, a passing from the instinctive to the rational state, forethought for the future, an elevated degree of culture — all of them conditions that crowds, left to themselves, have invariably shown themselves incapable of realising. In consequence of the purely destructive nature of their power crowds act like those microbes which hasten the dissolution of enfeebled or dead bodies. When the structure of a civilisation is rotten, it is always the masses that bring about its downfall. It is at such a juncture that their chief mission is plainly visible, and that for a while the philosophy of number seems the only philosophy of history.

Is the same fate in store for our civilisation? There is ground to fear that this is the case, but we are not as yet in a position to be certain of it.

However this may be, we are bound to resign ourselves to the reign of the masses, since want of foresight has in succession overthrown all the barriers that might have kept the crowd in check.

We have a very slight knowledge of these crowds which are beginning to be the object of so much discussion. Professional students of psychology, having lived far from them, have always ignored them, and when, as of late, they have turned their attention in this direction it has only been to consider the crimes crowds are capable of committing. Without a doubt criminal crowds exist, but virtuous and heroic crowds, and crowds of many other kinds, are also to be met with. The crimes of crowds only constitute a particular phase of their psychology. The mental constitution of crowds is not to be learnt merely by a study of their crimes, any more than that of an individual by a mere description of his vices.

However, in point of fact, all the world's masters, all the founders of religions or empires, the apostles of all beliefs, eminent statesmen, and, in a more modest sphere, the mere chiefs of small groups of men have always been unconscious psychologists, possessed of an instinctive and often very sure knowledge of the character of crowds, and it is their accurate knowledge of this character that has enabled them to so easily establish their mastery. Napoleon had a marvellous insight into the psychology of the masses of the country over which he reigned, but he, at times, completely misunderstood the psychology of crowds belonging to other races[1]; and it is because he thus misunderstood it that he engaged in Spain, and notably in Russia, in conflicts in which his power received blows which were destined within a brief space of time to ruin it. A knowledge of the psychology of crowds is to-day the last resource of the statesman who wishes not to govern them — that is becoming a very difficult matter — but at any rate not to be too much governed by them.

It is only by obtaining some sort of insight into the psychology of crowds that it can be understood how slight is the action upon them of laws and institutions, how powerless they are to hold any opinions other than those which are imposed upon them, and that it is not with rules based on theories of pure equity that they are to be led, but by seeking what produces an impression on them and what seduces them. For instance, should a legislator, wishing to impose a new tax, choose that which would be theoretically the most just? By no means. In practice the most unjust may be the best for the masses. Should it at the same time be the least obvious, and apparently the least burdensome, it will be the most easily tolerated. It is for this reason that an indirect tax, however exorbitant it be, will always be accepted by the crowd, because, being paid

---

[1] His most subtle advisers, moreover, did not understand this psychology any better. Talleyrand wrote him that "Spain would receive his soldiers as liberators." It received them as beasts of prey. A psychologist acquainted with the hereditary instincts of the Spanish race would have easily foreseen this reception.

daily in fractions of a farthing on objects of consumption, it will not interfere with the habits of the crowd, and will pass unperceived. Replace it by a proportional tax on wages or income of any other kind, to be paid in a lump sum, and were this new imposition theoretically ten times less burdensome than the other, it would give rise to unanimous protest. This arises from the fact that a sum relatively high, which will appear immense, and will in consequence strike the imagination, has been substituted for the unperceived fractions of a farthing. The new tax would only appear light had it been saved farthing by farthing, but this economic proceeding involves an amount of foresight of which the masses are incapable.

The example which precedes is of the simplest. Its appositeness will be easily perceived. It did not escape the attention of such a psychologist as Napoleon, but our modern legislators, ignorant as they are of the characteristics of a crowd, are unable to appreciate it. Experience has not taught them as yet to a sufficient degree that men never shape their conduct upon the teaching of pure reason.

Many other practical applications might be made of the psychology of crowds. A knowledge of this science throws the most vivid light on a great number of historical and economic phenomena totally incomprehensible without it. I shall have occasion to show that the reason why the most remarkable of modern historians, Taine, has at times so imperfectly understood the events of the great French Revolution is, that it never occurred to him to study the genius of crowds. He took as his guide in the study of this complicated period the descriptive method resorted to by naturalists; but the moral forces are almost absent in the case of the phenomena which naturalists have to study. Yet it is precisely these forces that constitute the true mainsprings of history.

In consequence, merely looked at from its practical side, the study of the psychology of crowds deserved to be attempted. Were its interest that resulting from pure curiosity only, it would still merit attention. It is as interesting to decipher the motives of the actions of men as to determine the characteristics of a mineral or a plant. Our study of the genius of crowds can merely be a brief synthesis, a simple summary of our investigations. Nothing more must be demanded of it than a few suggestive views. Others will work the ground more thoroughly. To-day we only touch the surface of a still almost virgin soil.

Book I. The Mind of Crowds.
Chapter I. General Characteristics of Crowds. — Psychological Law of Their Mental Unity.

In its ordinary sense the word "crowd" means a gathering of individuals of whatever nationality, profession, or sex, and whatever be the chances that have brought them together. From the psychological point of view the expression "crowd" assumes quite a different signification. Under certain given circumstances, and only under those circumstances, an agglomeration of men presents new characteristics very different from those of the individuals composing it. The sentiments and ideas of all the persons in the gathering take one and the same direction, and their conscious personality vanishes. A collective mind is formed, doubtless transitory, but presenting very clearly defined characteristics. The gathering has thus become what, in the absence of a better expression, I will call an organised crowd, or, if the term is considered preferable, a psychological crowd. It forms a single being, and is subjected to the law of the mental unity of crowds.

It is evident that it is not by the mere fact of a number of individuals finding themselves accidentally side by side that they acquire the character of an organised crowd. A thousand individuals accidentally gathered in a public place without any determined object in no way constitute a crowd from the psychological point of view. To acquire the special characteristics of such a crowd, the influence is necessary of certain predisposing causes of which we shall have to determine the nature.

The disappearance of conscious personality and the turning of feelings and thoughts in a definite direction, which are the primary characteristics of a crowd about to become organised, do not always involve the simultaneous presence of a number of individuals on one spot. Thousands of isolated individuals may acquire at certain moments, and under the influence of certain violent emotions — such, for example, as a great national event — the characteristics of a psychological crowd. It will be sufficient in that case that a mere chance should bring them together for their acts to at once assume the characteristics peculiar to the acts of a crowd. At certain moments half a dozen men might constitute a psychological crowd, which may not happen in the case of hundreds of men gathered together by accident. On the other hand, an entire nation, though there may be no visible agglomeration, may become a crowd under the action of certain influences.

A psychological crowd once constituted, it acquires certain provisional but determinable general characteristics. To these general characteristics there are adjoined particular characteristics which vary according to the elements of which the crowd is composed, and may modify its mental constitution. Psychological crowds, then, are susceptible of classification; and when we come to occupy ourselves with this matter, we shall see that a heterogeneous crowd — that is, a crowd composed of dissimilar elements — presents certain characteristics in common with homogeneous crowds — that is, with crowds composed of elements more or less akin (sects, castes, and classes) — and side by side with these common characteristics particularities which permit of the two kinds of crowds being differentiated.

But before occupying ourselves with the different categories of crowds, we must first of all examine the characteristics common to them all. We shall set to work like the naturalist, who begins by describing the general characteristics common to all the members of a family before concerning himself with the particular characteristics which allow the differentiation of the genera and species that the family includes.

It is not easy to describe the mind of crowds with exactness, because its organisation varies not only according to race and composition, but also according to the nature and intensity of the exciting causes to which crowds are subjected. The same difficulty, however, presents itself in the psychological study of an individual. It is only in novels that individuals are found to traverse their whole life with an unvarying character. It is only the uniformity of the environment that creates the apparent uniformity of characters. I have shown elsewhere that all mental constitutions contain possibilities of character which may be manifested in consequence of a sudden change of environment. This explains how it was that among the most savage members of the French Convention were to be found inoffensive citizens who, under ordinary circumstances, would have been peaceable notaries or virtuous magistrates. The storm past, they resumed their normal character of quiet, law-abiding citizens. Napoleon found amongst them his most docile servants.

It being impossible to study here all the successive degrees of organisation of crowds, we shall concern ourselves more especially with such crowds as have attained to the phase of complete organisation. In this way we shall see what crowds may become, but not what they invariably are. It is only in this advanced phase of organisation that certain new and special characteristics are superposed on the unvarying and dominant character of the race; then takes place that turning already alluded to of all the feelings and thoughts of the collectivity in an identical direction. It is only under such circumstances, too, that what I have called above the psychological law of the mental unity of crowds comes into play.

Among the psychological characteristics of crowds there are some that they may present in common with isolated individuals, and others, on the contrary, which are absolutely peculiar to them and are only to be met with in collectivities. It is these special characteristics that we shall study, first of all, in order to show their importance.

The most striking peculiarity presented by a psychological crowd is the following: Whoever be the individuals that compose it, however like or unlike be their mode of life, their occupations, their character, or their intelligence, the fact that they have been transformed into a crowd puts them in possession of a sort of collective mind which makes them feel, think, and act in a manner quite different from that in which each individual of them would feel, think, and act were he in a state of isolation. There are certain ideas and feelings which do not come into being, or do not transform themselves into acts except in the case of individuals forming a crowd. The psychological crowd is a provisional being formed of heterogeneous elements, which for a moment are combined, exactly as the cells which constitute a living body form by their reunion a new being which displays characteristics very different from those possessed by each of the cells singly.

Contrary to an opinion which one is astonished to find coming from the pen of so acute a philosopher as Herbert Spencer, in the aggregate which constitutes a crowd there is in no sort a summing-up of or an average struck between its elements. What really takes place is a combination followed by the creation of new characteristics, just as in chemistry certain elements, when brought into contact — bases and acids, for example — combine to form a new body possessing properties quite different from those of the bodies that have served to form it.

It is easy to prove how much the individual forming part of a crowd differs from the isolated individual, but it is less easy to discover the causes of this difference.

To obtain at any rate a glimpse of them it is necessary in the first place to call to mind the truth established by modern psychology, that unconscious phenomena play an altogether preponderating part not only in organic life, but also in the operations of the intelligence. The conscious life of the mind is of small importance in comparison with its unconscious life. The most subtle analyst, the most acute observer, is scarcely successful in discovering more than a very small number of the unconscious motives that determine his conduct. Our conscious acts are the outcome of an unconscious substratum created in the mind in the main by hereditary influences. This substratum consists of the innumerable common characteristics handed down from generation to generation, which constitute the genius of a race. Behind the avowed causes of our acts there undoubtedly lie secret causes that we do not avow, but behind these secret causes there are many others more secret still which we ourselves ignore. The greater part of our daily actions are the result of hidden motives which escape our observation.

It is more especially with respect to those unconscious elements which constitute the genius of a race that all the individuals belonging to it resemble each other, while it is principally in respect to the conscious elements of their character — the fruit of education, and yet more of exceptional hereditary conditions — that they differ from each other. Men the most unlike in the matter of their intelligence possess instincts, passions, and feelings that are very similar. In the case of every thing that belongs to the realm of sentiment
— religion, politics, morality, the affections and antipathies, &c. — the most eminent men seldom surpass the standard of the most ordinary individuals. From the intellectual point of view an abyss may exist between a great mathematician and his boot maker, but from the point of view of character the difference is most often slight or non-existent.

It is precisely these general qualities of character, governed by forces of which we are unconscious, and possessed by the majority of the normal individuals of a race in much the same degree — it is precisely these qualities, I say, that in crowds become common property. In the collective mind the intellectual aptitudes of the individuals, and in consequence their individuality, are weakened. The heterogeneous is swamped by the homogeneous, and the unconscious qualities obtain the upper hand.

This very fact that crowds possess in common ordinary qualities explains why they can never accomplish acts demanding a high degree of intelligence. The decisions affecting matters of general interest come to by an assembly of men of distinction, but specialists in different walks of life, are not sensibly superior to the decisions that would be adopted by a gathering of imbeciles. The truth is, they can only bring to bear in common on the work in hand those mediocre qualities which are the birthright of every average individual. In crowds it is stupidity and not mother-wit that is accumulated. It is not all the world, as is so often repeated, that has more wit than Voltaire, but assuredly Voltaire that has more wit than all the world, if by "all the world" crowds are to be understood.

If the individuals of a crowd confined themselves to putting in common the ordinary qualities of which each of them has his share, there would merely result the striking of an average, and not, as we have said is actually the case, the creation of new characteristics. How is it that these new characteristics are created? This is what we are now to investigate.

Different causes determine the appearance of these characteristics peculiar to crowds, and not possessed by isolated individuals. The first is that the individual forming part of a crowd acquires, solely from numerical considerations, a sentiment of invincible power which allows him to yield to instincts which, had he been alone, he would perforce have kept under restraint. He will be the less disposed to check himself from the consideration that, a crowd being anonymous, and in consequence irresponsible, the sentiment of responsibility which always controls individuals disappears entirely.

The second cause, which is contagion, also intervenes to determine the manifestation in crowds of their special characteristics, and at the same time the trend they are to take. Contagion is a phenomenon of which it is easy to establish the presence, but that it is not easy to explain. It must be classed among those phenomena of a hypnotic order, which we shall shortly study. In a crowd every sentiment and act is contagious, and contagious to such a degree that an individual readily sacrifices his personal interest to the collective interest. This is an aptitude very contrary to his nature, and of which a man is scarcely capable, except when he makes part of a crowd.

A third cause, and by far the most important, determines in the individuals of a crowd special characteristics which are quite contrary at times to those presented by the isolated individual. I allude to that suggestibility of which, moreover, the contagion mentioned above is neither more nor less than an effect.

To understand this phenomenon it is necessary to bear in mind certain recent physiological discoveries. We know to-day that by various processes an individual may be brought into such a condition that, having entirely lost his conscious personality, he obeys all the suggestions of the operator who has deprived him of it, and commits acts in utter contradiction with his character and habits. The most careful observations seem to prove that an individual immerged for some length of time in a crowd in action soon finds himself — either in consequence of the magnetic influence given out by the crowd, or from some other cause of which we are ignorant — in a special state, which much resembles the state of fascination in which the hypnotised individual finds himself in the hands of the hypnotiser. The activity of the brain being paralysed in the case of the hypnotised subject, the latter becomes the slave of all the unconscious activities of his spinal cord, which the hypnotiser directs at will. The conscious personality has entirely vanished; will and discernment are lost. All feelings and thoughts are bent in the direction determined by the hypnotiser.

Such also is approximately the state of the individual forming part of a psychological crowd. He is no longer conscious of his acts. In his case, as in the case of the hypnotised subject, at the same time that certain faculties are destroyed, others may be brought to a high degree of exaltation. Under the influence of a suggestion, he will undertake the accomplishment of certain acts with irresistible impetuosity. This impetuosity is the more irresistible in the case of crowds than in that of the hypnotised subject, from the fact that, the suggestion being the same for all the individuals of the crowd, it gains in strength by reciprocity. The individualities in the crowd who might possess a personality sufficiently strong to resist the suggestion are too few in number to struggle against the current. At the utmost, they may be able to attempt a diversion by means of different suggestions. It is in this way, for instance, that a happy expression, an image opportunely evoked, have occasionally deterred crowds from the most bloodthirsty acts.

We see, then, that the disappearance of the conscious personality, the predominance of the unconscious personality, the turning by means of suggestion and contagion of feelings and ideas in an identical direction, the tendency to immediately transform the suggested ideas into acts; these, we see, are the principal characteristics of the individual forming part of a crowd. He is no longer himself, but has become an automaton who has ceased to be guided by his will.

Moreover, by the mere fact that he forms part of an organised crowd, a man descends several rungs in the ladder of civilisation. Isolated, he may be a cultivated individual; in a crowd, he is a barbarian — that is, a creature acting by instinct. He possesses the spontaneity, the violence, the ferocity, and also the enthusiasm and heroism of primitive beings, whom he further tends to resemble by the facility with which he allows himself to be impressed by words and images — which would be entirely without action on each of the isolated individuals composing the crowd

— and to be induced to commit acts contrary to his most obvious interests and his best-known habits. An individual in a crowd is a grain of sand amid other grains of sand, which the wind stirs up at will.

It is for these reasons that juries are seen to deliver verdicts of which each individual juror would disapprove, that parliamentary assemblies adopt laws and measures of which each of their members would disapprove in his own person. Taken separately, the men of the Convention were enlightened citizens of peaceful habits. United in a crowd, they did not hesitate to give their adhesion to the most savage proposals, to guillotine individuals most clearly innocent, and, contrary to their interests, to renounce their inviolability and to decimate themselves.

It is not only by his acts that the individual in a crowd differs essentially from himself. Even before he has entirely lost his independence, his ideas and feelings have undergone a transformation, and the transformation is so profound as to change the miser into a spendthrift, the sceptic into a believer, the honest man into a criminal, and the coward into a hero. The renunciation of all its privileges which the nobility voted in a moment of enthusiasm during the celebrated night of August 4, 1789, would certainly never have been consented to by any of its members taken singly.

The conclusion to be drawn from what precedes is, that the crowd is always intellectually inferior to the isolated individual, but that, from the point of view of feelings and of the acts these feelings provoke, the crowd may, according to circumstances, he better or worse than the individual. All depends on the nature of the suggestion to which the crowd is exposed. This is the point that has been completely misunderstood by writers who have only studied crowds from the criminal point of view. Doubtless a crowd is often criminal, but also it is often heroic. It is crowds rather than isolated individuals that may be induced to run the risk of death to secure the triumph of a creed or an idea, that may be fired with enthusiasm for glory and honour, that are led on — almost without bread and without arms, as in the age of the Crusades — to deliver the tomb of Christ from the infidel, or, as in '93, to defend the fatherland. Such heroism is without doubt somewhat unconscious, but it is of such heroism that history is made. Were peoples only to be credited with the great actions performed in cold blood, the annals of the world would register but few of them.

Chapter II. The Sentiments and Morality of Crowds.

Having indicated in a general way the principal characteristics of crowds, it remains to study these characteristics in detail.

It will be remarked that among the special characteristics of crowds there are several — such as impulsiveness, irritability, incapacity to reason, the absence of judgment and of the critical spirit, the exaggeration of the sentiments, and others besides — which are almost always observed in beings belonging to inferior forms of evolution — in women, savages, and children, for instance. However, I merely indicate this analogy in passing; its demonstration is outside the scope of this work. It would, moreover, be useless for persons acquainted with the psychology of primitive beings, and would scarcely carry conviction to those in ignorance of this matter.

I now proceed to the successive consideration of the different characteristics that may be observed in the majority of crowds.

1. Impulsiveness, Mobility, and Irritability of Crowds.

When studying the fundamental characteristics of a crowd we stated that it is guided almost exclusively by unconscious motives. Its acts are far more under the influence of the spinal cord than of the brain. In this respect a crowd is closely akin to quite primitive beings. The acts performed may be perfect so far as their execution is concerned, but as they are not directed by the brain, the individual conducts himself according as the exciting causes to which he is submitted may happen to decide. A crowd is at the mercy of all external exciting causes, and reflects their incessant variations. It is the slave of the impulses which it receives. The isolated individual may be submitted to the same exciting causes as the man in a crowd, but as his brain shows him the inadvisability of yielding to them, he refrains from yielding. This truth may be physiologically expressed by saying that the isolated individual possesses the capacity of dominating his reflex actions, while a crowd is devoid of this capacity.

The varying impulses to which crowds obey may be, according to their exciting causes, generous or cruel, heroic or cowardly, but they will always be so imperious that the interest of the individual, even the interest of self-preservation, will not dominate them. The exciting causes that may act on crowds being so varied, and crowds always obeying them, crowds are in consequence extremely mobile. This explains how it is that we see them pass in a moment from the most bloodthirsty ferocity to the most extreme generosity and heroism. A crowd may easily enact the part of an executioner, but not less easily that of a martyr. It is crowds that have furnished the torrents of blood requisite for the triumph of every belief. It is not necessary to go back to the heroic ages to see what crowds are capable of in this latter direction. They are never sparing of their life in an insurrection, and not long since a general[2], becoming suddenly popular, might easily have found a hundred thousand men ready to sacrifice their lives for his cause had he demanded it.

Any display of premeditation by crowds is in consequence out of the question. They may be animated in succession by the most contrary sentiments, but they will always be under the influence of the exciting causes of the moment. They are like the leaves which a tempest whirls up and scatters in every direction and then allows to fall. When studying later on certain

---
[2] General Boulanger.

revolutionary crowds we shall give some examples of the variability of their sentiments.

This mobility of crowds renders them very difficult to govern, especially when a measure of public authority has fallen into their hands. Did not the necessities of everyday life constitute a sort of invisible regulator of existence, it would scarcely be possible for democracies to last. Still, though the wishes of crowds are frenzied they are not durable. Crowds are as incapable of willing as of thinking for any length of time.

A crowd is not merely impulsive and mobile. Like a savage, it is not prepared to admit that anything can come between its desire and the realisation of its desire. It is the less capable of understanding such an intervention, in consequence of the feeling of irresistible power given it by its numerical strength. The notion of impossibility disappears for the individual in a crowd. An isolated individual knows well enough that alone he cannot set fire to a palace or loot a shop, and should he be tempted to do so, he will easily resist the temptation. Making part of a crowd, he is conscious of the power given him by number, and it is sufficient to suggest to him ideas of murder or pillage for him to yield immediately to temptation. An unexpected obstacle will be destroyed with frenzied rage. Did the human organism allow of the perpetuity of furious passion, it might be said that the normal condition of a crowd baulked in its wishes is just such a state of furious passion.

The fundamental characteristics of the race, which constitute the unvarying source from which all our sentiments spring, always exert an influence on the irritability of crowds, their impulsiveness and their mobility, as on all the popular sentiments we shall have to study. All crowds are doubtless always irritable and impulsive, but with great variations of degree. For instance, the difference between a Latin and an Anglo-Saxon crowd is striking. The most recent facts in French history throw a vivid light on this point. The mere publication, twenty-five years ago, of a telegram, relating an insult supposed to have been offered an ambassador, was sufficient to determine an explosion of fury, whence followed immediately a terrible war. Some years later the telegraphic announcement of an insignificant reverse at Langson provoked a fresh explosion which brought about the instantaneous overthrow of the government. At the same moment a much more serious reverse undergone by the English expedition to Khartoum produced only a slight emotion in England, and no ministry was overturned. Crowds are everywhere distinguished by feminine characteristics, but Latin crowds are the most feminine of all. Whoever trusts in them may rapidly attain a lofty destiny, but to do so is to be perpetually skirting the brink of a Tarpeian rock, with the certainty of one day being precipitated from it.

2. The Suggestibility and Credulity of Crowds.

When defining crowds, we said that one of their general characteristics was an excessive suggestibility, and we have shown to what an extent suggestions are contagious in every human agglomeration; a fact which explains the rapid turning of the sentiments of a crowd in a definite direction. However indifferent it may be supposed, a crowd, as a rule, is in a state of expectant attention, which renders suggestion easy. The first suggestion formulated which arises implants itself immediately by a process of contagion in the brains of all assembled, and the identical bent of the sentiments of the crowd is immediately an accomplished fact.

As is the case with all persons under the influence of suggestion, the idea which has entered the brain tends to transform itself into an act. Whether the act is that of setting fire to a palace, or involves self-sacrifice, a crowd lends itself to it with equal facility. All will depend on the nature of the exciting cause, and no longer, as in the case of the isolated individual, on the relations existing between the act suggested and the sum total of the reasons which may be urged against its realisation.

In consequence, a crowd perpetually hovering on the borderland of unconsciousness, readily yielding to all suggestions, having all the violence of feeling peculiar to beings who cannot appeal to the influence of reason, deprived of all critical faculty, cannot be otherwise than excessively credulous. The improbable does not exist for a crowd, and it is necessary to bear this circumstance well in mind to understand the facility with which are created and propagated the most improbable legends and stories[3].

The creation of the legends which so easily obtain circulation in crowds is not solely the consequence of their extreme credulity. It is also the result of the prodigious perversions that events undergo in the imagination of a throng. The simplest event that comes under the observation of a crowd is soon totally transformed. A crowd thinks in images, and the image itself immediately calls up a series of other images, having no logical connection with the first. We can easily conceive this state by thinking of the fantastic succession of ideas to which we are sometimes led by calling up in our minds any fact. Our reason shows us the incoherence there is in these images, but a crowd is almost blind to this truth, and confuses with the real event the deforming action of its imagination has superimposed thereon. A crowd scarcely distinguishes between the subjective and the objective. It accepts as real the images evoked in its mind, though they most often have only a very distant relation with the observed fact.

The ways in which a crowd perverts any event of which it is a witness ought, it would seem, to be innumerable and unlike each other, since the individuals composing the gathering are of very different temperaments. But this is not the case. As the result of contagion the perversions are of the same kind, and take the same shape in the case of all the assembled individuals.

The first perversion of the truth effected by one of the individuals of the gathering is the starting-point of the contagious suggestion. Before St. George appeared on the walls of Jerusalem to all the Crusaders he was certainly perceived in the first instance by one of those present. By dint of suggestion and contagion the miracle signalised by a single person was immediately accepted by all.

Such is always the mechanism of the collective hallucinations so frequent in history — hallucinations which seem to have all the recognised characteristics of authenticity, since they are phenomena observed by thousands of persons.

To combat what precedes, the mental quality of the individuals composing a crowd must not be brought into consideration. This quality is without importance. From the moment that they form part of a crowd the learned man and the ignoramus are equally incapable of observation.

This thesis may seem paradoxical. To demonstrate it beyond doubt it would be necessary to investigate a great number of historical facts, and several volumes would be insufficient for the purpose.

Still, as I do not wish to leave the reader under the impression of unproved assertions, I shall give him some examples taken at hazard from the immense number of those that might be quoted.

The following fact is one of the most typical, because chosen from among collective hallucinations of which a crowd is the victim, in which are to be found individuals of every kind, from the most ignorant to the most highly educated. It is related incidentally by Julian Felix, a naval lieutenant, in his book on "Sea Currents," and has been previously cited by the *Revue Scientique*.

The frigate, the *Belle Poule*, was cruising in the open sea for the purpose of finding the cruiser

---

[3] Persons who went through the siege of Paris saw numerous examples of this credulity of crowds. A candle alight in an upper story was immediately looked upon as a signal given the besiegers, although it was evident, after a moment of reflection, that it was utterly impossible to catch sight of the light of the candle at a distance of several miles.

Le Berceau, from which she had been separated by a violent storm. It was broad daylight and in full sunshine. Suddenly the watch signalled a disabled vessel; the crew looked in the direction signalled, and every one, officers and sailors, clearly perceived a raft covered with men towed by boats which were displaying signals of distress. Yet this was nothing more than a collective hallucination. Admiral Desfosses lowered a boat to go to the rescue of the wrecked sailors. On nearing the object sighted, the sailors and officers on board the boat saw "masses of men in motion, stretching out their hands, and heard the dull and confused noise of a great number of voices." When the object was reached those in the boat found themselves simply and solely in the presence of a few branches of trees covered with leaves that had been swept out from the neighbouring coast. Before evidence so palpable the hallucination vanished.

The mechanism of a collective hallucination of the kind we have explained is clearly seen at work in this example. On the one hand we have a crowd in a state of expectant attention, on the other a suggestion made by the watch signalling a disabled vessel at sea, a suggestion which, by a process of contagion, was accepted by all those present, both officers and sailors.

It is not necessary that a crowd should be numerous for the faculty of seeing what is taking place before its eyes to be destroyed and for the real facts to be replaced by hallucinations unrelated to them. As soon as a few individuals are gathered together they constitute a crowd, and, though they should be distinguished men of learning, they assume all the characteristics of crowds with regard to matters outside their speciality. The faculty of observation and the critical spirit possessed by each of them individually at once disappears. An ingenious psychologist, Mr. Davey, supplies us with a very curious example in point, recently cited in the *Annales des Sciences Psychiques*, and deserving of relation here. Mr. Davey, having convoked a gathering of distinguished observers, among them one of the most prominent of English scientific men, Mr. Wallace, executed in their presence, and after having allowed them to examine the objects and to place seals where they wished, all the regulation spiritualistic phenomena, the materialisation of spirits, writing on slates, &c. Having subsequently obtained from these distinguished observers written reports admitting that the phenomena observed could only have been obtained by supernatural means, he revealed to them that they were the result of very simple tricks. "The most astonishing feature of Monsieur Davey's investigation," writes the author of this account, "is not the marvellousness of the tricks themselves, but the extreme weakness of the reports made with respect to them by the non-initiated witnesses. It is clear, then," he says, "that witnesses even in number may give circumstantial relations which are completely erroneous, but whose result is that, if their descriptions are accepted as exact, the phenomena they describe are inexplicable by trickery. The methods invented by Mr. Davey were so simple that one is astonished that he should have had the boldness to employ them; but he had such a power over the mind of the crowd that he could persuade it that it saw what it did not see." Here, as always, we have the power of the hypnotiser over the hypnotised. Moreover, when this power is seen in action on minds of a superior order and previously invited to be suspicious, it is understandable how easy it is to deceive ordinary crowds.

Analogous examples are innumerable. As I write these lines the papers are full of the story of two little girls found drowned in the Seine. These children, to begin with, were recognised in the most unmistakable manner by half a dozen witnesses. All the affirmations were in such entire concordance that no doubt remained in the mind of the *juge d'instruction*. He had the certificate of death drawn up, but just as the burial of the children was to have been proceeded with, a mere chance brought about the discovery that the supposed victims were alive, and had, moreover, but a remote resemblance to the drowned girls. As in several of the examples previously cited, the affirmation of the first witness, himself a victim of illusion, had sufficed to influence the other witnesses.

In parallel cases the starting-point of the suggestion is always the illusion produced in an individual by more or less vague reminiscences, contagion following as the result of the affirmation of this initial illusion. If the first observer be very impressionable, it will often be sufficient that the corpse he believes he recognises should present — apart from all real resemblance — some peculiarity, a scar, or some detail of toilet which may evoke the idea of another person. The idea evoked may then become the nucleus of a sort of crystallisation which invades the understanding and paralyses all critical faculty. What the observer then sees is no longer the object itself, but the image-evoked in his mind. In this way are to be explained erroneous recognitions of the dead bodies of children by their own mother, as occurred in the following case, already old, but which has been recently recalled by the newspapers. In it are to be traced precisely the two kinds of suggestion of which I have just pointed out the mechanism.

"The child was recognised by another child, who was mistaken. The series of unwarranted recognitions then began.

"An extraordinary thing occurred. The day after a schoolboy had recognised the corpse a woman exclaimed, `Good Heavens, it is my child!'

"She was taken up to the corpse; she examined the clothing, and noted a scar on the forehead. `It is certainly,' she said, `my son who disappeared last July. He has been stolen from me and murdered.'

"The woman was concierge in the Rue du Four; her name was Chavandret. Her brother-in-law was summoned, and when questioned he said, `That is the little Filibert.' Several persons living in the street recognised the child found at La Villette as Filibert Chavandret, among them being the boy's schoolmaster, who based his opinion on a medal worn by the lad.

"Nevertheless, the neighbours, the brother-in-law, the schoolmaster, and the mother were mistaken. Six weeks later the identity of the child was established. The boy, belonging to Bordeaux, had been murdered there and brought by a carrying company to Paris.[4]"

It will be remarked that these recognitions are most often made by women and children — that is to say, by precisely the most impressionable persons. They show us at the same time what is the worth in law courts of such witnesses. As far as children, more especially, are concerned, their statements ought never to be invoked. Magistrates are in the habit of repeating that children do not lie. Did they possess a psychological culture a little less rudimentary than is the case they would know that, on the contrary, children invariably lie; the lie is doubtless innocent, but it is none the less a lie. It would be better to decide the fate of an accused person by the toss of a coin than, as has been so often done, by the evidence of a child.

To return to the faculty of observation possessed by crowds, our conclusion is that their collective observations are as erroneous as possible, and that most often they merely represent the illusion of an individual who, by a process of contagion, has suggested his fellows. Facts proving that the most utter mistrust of the evidence of crowds is advisable might be multiplied to any extent. Thousands of men were present twenty-five years ago at the celebrated cavalry charge during the battle of Sedan, and yet it is impossible, in the face of the most contradictory ocular testimony, to decide by whom it was commanded. The English general, Lord Wolseley, has proved in a recent book
that up to now the gravest errors of fact have been committed with regard to the most important

---

[4] *L'Eclair*, April 21, 1895.

incidents of the battle of Waterloo — facts that hundreds of witnesses had nevertheless attested[5].

Such facts show us what is the value of the testimony of crowds. Treatises on logic include the unanimity of numerous witnesses in the category of the strongest proofs that can be invoked in support of the exactness of a fact. Yet what we know of the psychology of crowds shows that treatises on logic need on this point to be rewritten. The events with regard to which there exists the most doubt are certainly those which have been observed by the greatest number of persons. To say that a fact has been simultaneously verified by thousands of witnesses is to say, as a rule, that the real fact is very different from the accepted account of it.

It clearly results from what precedes that works of history must be considered as works of pure imagination. They are fanciful accounts of ill-observed facts, accompanied by explanations the result of reflection. To write such books is the most absolute waste of time. Had not the past left us its literary, artistic, and monumental works, we should know absolutely nothing in reality with regard to bygone times. Are we in possession of a single word of truth concerning the lives of the great men who have played preponderating parts in the history of humanity — men such as Hercules, Buddha, or Mahomet? In all probability we are not. In point of fact, moreover, their real lives are of slight importance to us. Our interest is to know what our great men were as they are presented by popular legend. It is legendary heroes, and not for a moment real heroes, who have impressed the minds of crowds.

Unfortunately, legends — even although they have been definitely put on record by books — have in themselves no stability. The imagination of the crowd continually transforms them as the result of the lapse of time and especially in consequence of racial causes. There is a great gulf fixed between the sanguinary Jehovah of the Old Testament and the God of Love of Sainte Thérèse, and the Buddha worshipped in China has no traits in common with that venerated in India.

It is not even necessary that heroes should be separated from us by centuries for their legend to be transformed by the imagination of the crowd. The transformation occasionally takes place within a few years. In our own day we have seen the legend of one of the greatest heroes of history modified several times in less than fifty years. Under the Bourbons Napoleon became a sort of idyllic and liberal philanthropist, a friend of the humble who, according to the poets, was destined to be long remembered in the cottage. Thirty years afterwards this easy-going hero had become a sanguinary despot, who, after having usurped power and destroyed liberty, caused the slaughter of three million men solely to satisfy his ambition. At present we are witnessing a fresh transformation of the legend. When it has undergone the influence of some dozens of centuries the learned men of the future, face to face with these contradictory accounts, will perhaps doubt the very existence of the hero, as some of them now doubt that of Buddha, and will see in him nothing more than a solar myth or a development of the legend of Hercules. They will doubtless console themselves easily for this uncertainty, for, better initiated than we are to-day in the characteristics and psychology of crowds, they will know that history is scarcely capable of preserving the memory of anything except myths.

---

[5] Do we know in the case of one single battle exactly how it took place? I am very doubtful on the point. We know who were the conquerors and the conquered, but this is probably all. What M. D'Harcourt has said with respect to the battle of Solferino, which he witnessed and in which he was personally engaged, may be applied to all battles — "The generals (informed, of course,

by the evidence of hundreds of witnesses) forward their official reports; the orderly officers modify these documents and draw up a definite narrative; the chief of the staff raises objections and re-writes the whole on a fresh basis. It is carried to the Marshal, who exclaims, 'You are entirely in error,' and he substitutes a fresh edition. Scarcely anything remains of the original report."

M. D'Harcourt relates this fact as proof of the impossibility of establishing the truth in connection with the most striking, the best observed events.

3. The Exaggeration and Ingenuousness of the Sentiments of Crowds.

Whether the feelings exhibited by a crowd be good or bad, they present the double character of being very simple and very exaggerated. On this point, as on so many others, an individual in a crowd resembles primitive beings. Inaccessible to fine distinctions, he sees things as a whole, and is blind to their intermediate phases. The exaggeration of the sentiments of a crowd is heightened by the fact that any feeling when once it is exhibited communicating itself very quickly by a process of suggestion and contagion, the evident approbation of which it is the object considerably increases its force.

The simplicity and exaggeration of the sentiments of crowds have for result that a throng knows neither doubt nor uncertainty. Like women, it goes at once to extremes. A suspicion transforms itself as soon as announced into incontrovertible evidence. A commencement of antipathy or disapprobation, which in the case of an isolated individual would not gain strength, becomes at once furious hatred in the case of an individual in a crowd.

The violence of the feelings of crowds is also increased, especially in heterogeneous crowds, by the absence of all sense of responsibility. The certainty of impunity, a certainty the stronger as the crowd is more numerous, and the notion of a considerable momentary force due to number, make possible in the case of crowds sentiments and acts impossible for the isolated individual. In crowds the foolish, ignorant, and envious persons are freed from the sense of their insignificance and powerlessness, and are possessed instead by the notion of brutal and temporary but immense strength.

Unfortunately, this tendency of crowds towards exaggeration is often brought to bear upon bad sentiments. These sentiments are atavistic residuum of the instincts of the primitive man, which the fear of punishment obliges the isolated and responsible individual to curb. Thus it is that crowds are so easily led into the worst excesses.

Still this does not mean that crowds, skilfully influenced, are not capable of heroism and devotion and of evincing the loftiest virtues; they are even more capable of showing these qualities than the isolated individual. We shall soon have occasion to revert to this point when we come to study the morality of crowds.

Given to exaggeration in its feelings, a crowd is only impressed by excessive sentiments. An orator wishing to move a crowd must make an abusive use of violent affirmations. To exaggerate, to affirm, to resort to repetitions, and never to attempt to prove anything by reasoning are methods of argument well known to speakers at public meetings.

Moreover, a crowd exacts a like exaggeration in the sentiments of its heroes. Their apparent qualities and virtues must always be amplified. It has been justly remarked that on the stage a crowd demands from the hero of the piece a degree of courage, morality, and virtue that is never to be found in real life.

Quite rightly importance has been laid on the special standpoint from which matters are viewed in the theatre. Such a standpoint exists no doubt, but its rules for the most part have nothing to do with common sense and logic. The art of appealing to crowds is no doubt of an inferior order, but it demands quite special aptitudes. It is often impossible on reading plays to explain their success. Managers of theatres when accepting pieces are themselves, as a rule, very uncertain of their success, because to judge the matter it would be necessary that they should be able to transform themselves into a crowd [6].

---

[6] It is understandable for this reason why it sometimes happens that pieces refused by all theatrical managers obtain a prodigious success when by a stroke of chance they are put on the stage. The recent success of Francois Coppée's play "Pour la Couronne" is well known, and yet, in spite of the name of its author, it was refused during ten years by the managers of the principal Parisian theatres.

Here, once more, were we able to embark on more extensive explanations, we should show the preponderating influence of racial considerations. A play which provokes the enthusiasm of the crowd in one country has sometimes no success in another, or has only a partial and conventional success, because it does not put in operation influences capable of working on an altered public.

I need not add that the tendency to exaggeration in crowds is only present in the case of sentiments and not at all in the matter of intelligence. I have already shown that, by the mere fact that an individual forms part of a crowd, his intellectual standard is immediately and considerably lowered. A learned magistrate, M. Tarde, has also verified this fact in his researches on the crimes of crowds. It is only, then, with respect to sentiment that crowds can rise to a very high or, on the contrary, descend to a very low level.

4. The Intolerance, Dictatorialness and Conservatism of Crowds.

Crowds are only cognizant of simple and extreme sentiments; the opinions, ideas, and beliefs suggested to them are accepted or rejected as a whole, and considered as absolute truths or as not less absolute errors. This is always the case with beliefs induced by a process of suggestion instead of engendered by reasoning. Every one is aware of the intolerance that accompanies religious beliefs, and of the despotic empire they exercise on men's minds.

Being in doubt as to what constitutes truth or error, and having, on the other hand, a clear notion of its strength, a crowd is as disposed to give authoritative effect to its inspirations as it is intolerant. An individual may accept contradiction and discussion; a crowd will never do so. At public meetings the slightest contradiction on the part of an orator is immediately received with howls of fury and violent invective, soon followed by blows, and expulsion should the orator stick to his point. Without the restraining presence of the representatives of authority the contradictor, indeed, would often be done to death.

Dictatorialness and intolerance are common to all categories of crowds, but they are met with in a varying degree of intensity. Here, once more, reappears that fundamental notion of race which dominates all the feelings and all the thoughts of men. It is more especially in Latin crowds that authoritativeness and intolerance are found developed in the highest measure. In fact, their development is such in crowds of Latin origin that they have entirely destroyed that sentiment of the independence of the individual so powerful in the Anglo-Saxon. Latin crowds are only concerned with the collective independence of the sect to which they belong, and the characteristic feature of their conception of independence is the need they experience of bringing those who are in disagreement with themselves into immediate and violent subjection to their beliefs. Among the Latin races the Jacobins of every epoch, from those of the Inquisition downwards, have never been able to attain to a different conception of liberty.

Authoritativeness and intolerance are sentiments of which crowds have a very clear notion, which they easily conceive and which they entertain as readily as they put them in practice when once they are imposed upon them. Crowds exhibit a docile respect for force, and are but slightly impressed by kindness, which for them is scarcely other than a form of weakness. Their sympathies have never been bestowed on easy-going masters, but on tyrants who vigorously oppressed them. It is to these latter that they always erect the loftiest statues. It is true that they

---

"Charley's Aunt," refused at every theatre, and finally staged at the expense of a stockbroker, has had two hundred representations in France, and more than a thousand in London. Without the explanation given above of the impossibility for theatrical managers to mentally substitute themselves for a crowd, such mistakes in judgment on the part of competent individuals, who are most interested not to commit such grave blunders, would be inexplicable.

This is a subject that I cannot deal with here, but it might worthily tempt the pen of a writer acquainted with theatrical matters, and at the same time a subtle psychologist — of such a writer, for instance, as M. Francisque Sarcey.

willingly trample on the despot whom they have stripped of his power, but it is because, having lost his strength, he has resumed his place among the feeble, who are to be despised because they are not to be feared. The type of hero dear to crowds will always have the semblance of a Caesar. His insignia attracts them, his authority overawes them, and his sword instils them with fear.

A crowd is always ready to revolt against a feeble, and to bow down servilely before a strong authority. Should the strength of an authority be intermittent, the crowd, always obedient to its extreme sentiments, passes alternately from anarchy to servitude, and from servitude to anarchy.

However, to believe in the predominance among crowds of revolutionary instincts would be to entirely misconstrue their psychology. It is merely their tendency to violence that deceives us on this point. Their rebellious and destructive outbursts are always very transitory. Crowds are too much governed by unconscious considerations, and too much subject in consequence to secular hereditary influences not to be extremely conservative. Abandoned to themselves, they soon weary of disorder, and instinctively turn to servitude. It was the proudest and most untractable of the Jacobins who acclaimed Bonaparte with greatest energy when he suppressed all liberty and made his hand of iron severely felt.

It is difficult to understand history, and popular revolutions in particular, if one does not take sufficiently into account the profoundly conservative instincts of crowds. They may be desirous, it is true, of changing the names of their institutions, and to obtain these changes they accomplish at times even violent revolutions, but the essence of these institutions is too much the expression of the hereditary needs of the race for them not invariably to abide by it. Their incessant mobility only exerts its influence on quite superficial matters. In fact they possess conservative instincts as indestructible as those of all primitive beings. Their fetish like respect for all traditions is absolute; their unconscious horror of all novelty capable of changing the essential conditions of their existence is very deeply rooted. Had democracies possessed the power they wield to-day at the time of the invention of mechanical looms or of the introduction of steam-power and of railways, the realisation of these inventions would have been impossible, or would have been achieved at the cost of revolutions and repeated massacres. It is fortunate for the progress of civilisation that the power of crowds only began to exist when the great discoveries of science and industry had already been effected.

5. The Morality of Crowds.

Taking the word "morality" to mean constant respect for certain social conventions, and the permanent repression of selfish impulses, it is quite evident that crowds are too impulsive and too mobile to be moral. If, however, we include in the term morality the transitory display of certain qualities such as abnegation, self-sacrifice, disinterestedness, devotion, and the need of equity, we may say, on the contrary, that crowds may exhibit at times a very lofty morality.

The few psychologists who have studied crowds have only considered them from the point of view of their criminal acts, and noticing how frequent these acts are, they have come to the conclusion that the moral standard of crowds is very low.

Doubtless this is often the case; but why? Simply because our savage, destructive instincts are the inheritance left dormant in all of us from the primitive ages. In the life of the isolated individual it would be dangerous for him to gratify these instincts, while his absorption in an irresponsible crowd, in which in consequence he is assured of impunity, gives him entire liberty to follow them. Being unable, in the ordinary course of events, to exercise these destructive instincts on our fellow-men, we confine ourselves to exercising them on animals. The passion, so widespread, for the chase and the acts of ferocity of crowds proceed from one and the same source. A crowd which slowly slaughters a defenceless victim displays a very cowardly ferocity; but for the philosopher this ferocity is very closely related to that of the huntsmen who gather in dozens for the pleasure of taking part in the pursuit and killing of a luckless stag by their hounds.

A crowd may be guilty of murder, incendiarism, and every kind of crime, but it is also capable of very lofty acts of devotion, sacrifice, and disinterestedness, of acts much loftier indeed than those of which the isolated individual is capable. Appeals to sentiments of glory, honour, and patriotism are particularly likely to influence the individual forming part of a crowd, and often to the extent of obtaining from him the sacrifice of his life. History is rich in examples analogous to those furnished by the Crusaders and the volunteers of 1793. Collectivities alone are capable of great disinterestedness and great devotion. How numerous are the crowds that have heroically faced death for beliefs, ideas, and phrases that they scarcely understood! The crowds that go on strike do so far more in obedience to an order than to obtain an increase of the slender salary with which they make shift. Personal interest is very rarely a powerful motive force with crowds, while it is almost the exclusive motive of the conduct of the isolated individual. It is assuredly not self-interest that has guided crowds in so many wars, incomprehensible as a rule to their intelligence — wars in which they have allowed themselves to be massacred as easily as the larks hypnotised by the mirror of the hunter.

Even in the case of absolute scoundrels it often happens that the mere fact of their being in a crowd endows them for the moment with very strict principles of morality. Taine calls attention to the fact that the perpetrators of the September massacres deposited on the table of the committees the pocket-books and jewels they had found on their victims, and with which they could easily have been able to make away. The howling, swarming, ragged crowd which invaded the Tuileries during the revolution of 1848 did not lay hands on any of the objects that excited its astonishment, and one of which would have meant bread for many days.

This moralisation of the individual by the crowd is not certainly a constant rule, but it is a rule frequently observed. It is even observed in circumstances much less grave than those I have just cited. I have remarked that in the theatre a crowd exacts from the hero of the piece exaggerated virtues, and it is a commonplace observation that an assembly, even though composed of inferior elements, shows itself as a rule very prudish. The debauchee, the souteneur, the rough often break out into murmurs at a slightly risky scene or expression, though they be very harmless in comparison with their customary conversation.

If, then, crowds often abandon themselves to low instincts, they also set the example at times of acts of lofty morality. If disinterestedness, resignation, and absolute devotion to a real or chimerical ideal are moral virtues, it may be said that crowds often possess these virtues to a degree rarely attained by the wisest philosophers. Doubtless they practice them unconsciously, but that is of small import. We should not complain too much that crowds are more especially guided by unconscious considerations and are not given to reasoning. Had they, in certain cases, reasoned and consulted their immediate interests, it is possible that no civilisation would have grown up on our planet and humanity would have had no history.

Chapter III. The Ideas, Reasoning Power, and Imagination of Crowds.

1. The Ideas of Crowds.

When studying in a preceding work the part played by ideas in the evolution of nations, we showed that every civilisation is the outcome of a small number of fundamental ideas that are very rarely renewed. We showed how these ideas are implanted in the minds of crowds, with what difficulty the process is effected, and the power possessed by the ideas in question when once it has been accomplished. Finally we saw that great historical perturbations are the result, as a rule, of changes in these fundamental ideas.

Having treated this subject at sufficient length, I shall not return to it now, but shall confine myself to saying a few words on the subject of such ideas as are accessible to crowds, and of the forms under which they conceive them.

They may be divided into two classes. In one we shall place accidental and passing ideas created by the influences of the moment: infatuation for an individual or a doctrine, for instance. In the other will be classed the fundamental ideas, to which the environment, the laws of heredity and public opinion give a very great stability; such ideas are the religious beliefs of the past and the social and democratic ideas of to-day.

These fundamental ideas resemble the volume of the water of a stream slowly pursuing its course; the transitory ideas are like the small waves, for ever changing, which agitate its surface, and are more visible than the progress of the stream itself although without real importance.

At the present day the great fundamental ideas which were the mainstay of our fathers are tottering more and more. They have lost all solidity, and at the same time the institutions resting upon them are severely shaken. Every day there are formed a great many of those transitory minor ideas of which I have just been speaking; but very few of them to all appearance seem endowed with vitality and destined to acquire a preponderating influence.

Whatever be the ideas suggested to crowds they can only exercise effective influence on condition that they assume a very absolute, uncompromising, and simple shape. They present themselves then in the guise of images, and are only accessible to the masses under this form. These imagelike ideas are not connected by any logical bond of analogy or succession, and may take each other's place like the slides of a magic-lantern which the operator withdraws from the groove in which they were placed one above the other. This explains how it is that the most contradictory ideas may be seen to be simultaneously current in crowds. According to the chances of the moment, a crowd will come under the influence of one of the various ideas stored up in its understanding, and is capable, in consequence, of committing the most dissimilar acts. Its complete lack of the critical spirit does not allow of its perceiving these contradictions.

This phenomenon is not peculiar to crowds. It is to be observed in many isolated individuals, not only among primitive beings, but in the case of all those — the fervent sectaries of a religious faith, for instance — who by one side or another of their intelligence are akin to primitive beings. I have observed its presence to a curious extent in the case of educated Hindoos brought up at our European universities and having taken their degree. A number of

Western ideas had been superposed on their unchangeable and fundamental hereditary or social ideas. According to the chances of the moment, the one or the other set of ideas showed themselves each with their special accompaniment of acts or utterances, the same individual presenting in this way the most flagrant contradictions. These contradictions are more apparent than real, for it is only hereditary ideas that have sufficient influence over the isolated individual to become motives of conduct. It is only when, as the result of the intermingling of different races, a man is placed between different hereditary tendencies that his acts from one moment to another may be really entirely contradictory. It would be useless to insist here on these phenomena, although their psychological importance is capital. I am of opinion that at least ten years of travel and observation would be necessary to arrive at a comprehension of them.

Ideas being only accessible to crowds after having assumed a very simple shape must often undergo the most thoroughgoing transformations to become popular. It is especially when we are dealing with somewhat lofty philosophic or scientific ideas that we see how far-reaching are the modifications they require in order to lower them to the level of the intelligence of crowds. These modifications are dependent on the nature of the crowds, or of the race to which the crowds belong, but their tendency is always belittling and in the direction of simplification. This explains the fact that, from the social point of view, there is in reality scarcely any such thing as a hierarchy of ideas — that is to say, as ideas of greater or less elevation. However great or true an idea may have been to begin with, it is deprived of almost all that which constituted its elevation and its greatness by the mere fact that it has come within the intellectual range of crowds and exerts an influence upon them.

Moreover, from the social point of view the hierarchical value of an idea, its intrinsic worth, is without importance. The necessary point to consider is the effects it produces. The Christian ideas of the Middle Ages, the democratic ideas of the last century, or the social ideas of to-day are assuredly not very elevated. Philosophically considered, they can only be regarded as somewhat sorry errors, and yet their power has been and will be immense, and they will count for a long time to come among the most essential factors that determine the conduct of States.

Even when an idea has undergone the transformations which render it accessible to crowds, it only exerts influence when, by various processes which we shall examine elsewhere, it has entered the domain of the unconscious, when indeed it has become a sentiment, for which much time is required.

For it must not be supposed that merely because the justness of an idea has been proved it can be productive of effective action even on cultivated minds. This fact may be quickly appreciated by noting how slight is the influence of the clearest demonstration on the majority of men. Evidence, if it be very plain, may be accepted by an educated person, but the convert will be quickly brought back by his unconscious self to his original conceptions. See him again after the lapse of a few days and he will put forward afresh his old arguments in exactly the same terms. He is in reality under the influence of anterior ideas, that have become sentiments, and it is such ideas alone that influence the more recondite motives of our acts and utterances. It cannot be otherwise in the case of crowds.

When by various processes an idea has ended by penetrating into the minds of crowds, it possesses an irresistible power, and brings about a series of effects, opposition to which is bootless. The philosophical ideas which resulted in the French Revolution took nearly a century to implant themselves in the mind of the crowd. Their irresistible force, when once they had taken root, is known. The striving of an entire nation towards the conquest of social equality, and the realisation of abstract rights and ideal liberties, caused the tottering of all thrones and profoundly disturbed the Western world. During twenty years the nations were engaged in internecine conflict, and Europe witnessed hecatombs that would have terrified Ghengis Khan and Tamerlane. The world had never seen on such a scale what may result from the promulgation of an idea.

A long time is necessary for ideas to establish themselves in the minds of crowds, but just as long a time is needed for them to be eradicated. For this reason crowds, as far as ideas are concerned, are always several generations behind learned men and philosophers. All statesmen are well aware to-day of the admixture of error contained in the fundamental ideas I referred to a short while back, but as the influence of these ideas is still very powerful they are obliged to govern in accordance with principles in the truth of which they have ceased to believe.

2. The Reasoning Power of Crowds.

It cannot absolutely be said that crowds do not reason and are not to be influenced by reasoning.

However, the arguments they employ and those which are capable of influencing them are, from a logical point of view, of such an inferior kind that it is only by way of analogy that they can be described as reasoning.

The inferior reasoning of crowds is based, just as is reasoning of a high order, on the association of ideas, but between the ideas associated by crowds there are only apparent bonds of analogy or succession. The mode of reasoning of crowds resembles that of the Esquimaux who, knowing from experience that ice, a transparent body, melts in the mouth, concludes that glass, also a transparent body, should also melt in the mouth; or that of the savage who imagines that by eating the heart of a courageous foe he acquires his bravery; or of the workman who, having been exploited by one employer of labour, immediately concludes that all employers exploit their men.

The characteristics of the reasoning of crowds are the association of dissimilar things possessing a merely apparent connection between each other, and the immediate generalisation of particular cases. It is arguments of this kind that are always presented to crowds by those who know how to manage them. They are the only arguments by which crowds are to be influenced. A chain of logical argumentation is totally incomprehensible to crowds, and for this reason it is permissible to say that they do not reason or that they reason falsely and are not to be influenced by reasoning. Astonishment is felt at times on reading certain speeches at their weakness, and yet they had an enormous influence on the crowds which listened to them, but it is forgotten that they were intended to persuade collectivities and not to be read by philosophers. An orator in intimate communication with a crowd can evoke images by which it will be seduced. If he is successful his object has been attained, and twenty volumes of harangues — always the outcome of reflection — are not worth the few phrases which appealed to the brains it was required to convince.

It would be superfluous to add that the powerlessness of crowds to reason aright prevents them displaying any trace of the critical spirit, prevents them, that is, from being capable of discerning truth from error, or of forming a precise judgment on any matter. Judgments accepted by crowds are merely judgments forced upon them and never judgments adopted after discussion. In regard to this matter the individuals who do not rise above the level of a crowd are numerous. The ease with which certain opinions obtain general acceptance results more especially from the impossibility experienced by the majority of men of forming an opinion peculiar to themselves and based on reasoning of their own.

3. The Imagination of Crowds.

Just as is the case with respect to persons in whom the reasoning power is absent, the figurative imagination of crowds is very powerful, very active and very susceptible of being keenly impressed. The images evoked in their mind by a personage, an event, an accident, are almost as lifelike as the reality. Crowds are to some extent in the position of the sleeper whose reason, suspended for the time being, allows the arousing in his mind of images of extreme intensity which would quickly be dissipated could they be submitted to the action of reflection. Crowds, being incapable both of reflection and of reasoning, are devoid of the notion of improbability; and it is to be noted that in a general way it is the most improbable things that are the most striking.

This is why it happens that it is always the marvellous and legendary side of events that more specially strike crowds. When a civilisation is analysed it is seen that, in reality, it is the marvellous and the legendary that are its true supports. Appearances have always played a much more important part than reality in history, where the unreal is always of greater moment than the real.

Crowds being only capable of thinking in images are only to be impressed by images. It is only images that terrify or attract them and become motives of action.

For this reason theatrical representations, in which the image is shown in its most clearly visible shape, always have an enormous influence on crowds. Bread and spectacular shows constituted for the plebeians of ancient Rome the ideal of happiness, and they asked for nothing more. Throughout the successive ages this ideal has scarcely varied. Nothing has a greater effect on the imagination of crowds of every category than theatrical representations. The entire audience experiences at the same time the same emotions, and if these emotions are not at once transformed into acts, it is because the most unconscious spectator cannot ignore that he is the victim of illusions, and that he has laughed or wept over imaginary adventures. Sometimes, however, the sentiments suggested by the images are so strong that they tend, like habitual suggestions, to transform themselves into acts. The story has often been told of the manager of a popular theatre who, in consequence of his only playing sombre dramas, was obliged to have the actor who took the part of the traitor protected on his leaving the theatre, to defend him against the violence of the spectators, indignant at the crimes, imaginary though they were, which the traitor had committed. We have here, in my opinion, one of the most remarkable indications of the mental state of crowds, and especially of the facility with which they are suggestioned. The unreal has almost as much influence on them as the real. They have an evident tendency not to distinguish between the two.

The power of conquerors and the strength of States is based on the popular imagination. It is more particularly by working upon this imagination that crowds are led. All great historical facts, the rise of Buddhism, of Christianity, of Islamism, the Reformation, the French Revolution, and, in our own time, the threatening invasion of Socialism are the direct or indirect consequences of strong impressions produced on the imagination of the crowd.

Moreover, all the great statesmen of every age and every country, including the most absolute despots, have regarded the popular imagination as the basis of their power, and they have never attempted to govern in opposition to it "It was by becoming a Catholic," said Napoleon to the Council of State, "that I terminated the Vendéen war. By becoming a Mussulman that I obtained a footing in Egypt. By becoming an Ultramontane that I won over the Italian priests, and had I to govern a nation of Jews I would rebuild Solomon's temple." Never perhaps since Alexander and Caesar has any great man better understood how the imagination of the crowd should be impressed. His constant preoccupation was to strike it. He bore it in mind in his victories, in his harangues, in his speeches, in all his acts. On his deathbed it was still in his thoughts.

How is the imagination of crowds to be impressed? We shall soon see. Let us confine ourselves for the moment to saying that the feat is never to be achieved by attempting to work upon the intelligence or reasoning faculty, that is to say, by way of demonstration. It was not by means of cunning rhetoric that Antony succeeded in making the populace rise against the murderers of Cæsar; it was by reading his will to the multitude and pointing to his corpse.

Whatever strikes the imagination of crowds presents itself under the shape of a startling and very clear image, freed from all accessory explanation, or merely having as accompaniment a few marvellous or mysterious facts: examples in point are a great victory, a great miracle, a great crime, or a great hope. Things must be laid before the crowd as a whole, and their genesis must never be indicated. A hundred petty crimes or petty accidents will not strike the imagination of crowds in the least, whereas a single great crime or a single great accident will profoundly impress them, even though the results be infinitely less disastrous than those of the hundred small accidents put together. The epidemic of influenza, which caused the death but a few years ago of five thousand persons in Paris alone, made very little impression on the popular imagination. The reason was that this veritable hecatomb was not embodied in any visible image, but was only learnt from statistical information furnished weekly. An accident which should have caused the death of only five hundred instead of five thousand persons, but on the same day and in public, as the outcome of an accident appealing strongly to the eye, by the fall, for instance, of the Eiffel Tower, would have produced, on the contrary, an immense impression on the imagination of the crowd. The probable loss of a transatlantic steamer that was supposed, in the absence of news, to have gone down in mid-ocean profoundly impressed the imagination of the crowd for a whole week. Yet official statistics show that 850 sailing vessels and 203 steamers were lost in the year 1894 alone. The crowd, however, was never for a moment concerned by these successive losses, much more important though they were as far as regards the destruction of life and property, than the loss of the Atlantic liner in question could possibly have been.

It is not, then, the facts in themselves that strike the popular imagination, but the way in which they take place and are brought under notice. It is necessary that by their condensation, if I may thus express myself, they should produce a startling image which fills and besets the mind. To know the art of impressing the imagination of crowds is to know at the same time the art of governing them.

Chapter IV. A Religious Shape Assumed by All the Convictions of Crowds.

We have shown that crowds do not reason, that they accept or reject ideas as a whole, that they tolerate neither discussion nor contradiction, and that the suggestions brought to bear on them invade the entire field of their understanding and tend at once to transform themselves into acts. We have shown that crowds suitably influenced are ready to sacrifice themselves for the ideal with which they have been inspired. We have also seen that they only entertain violent and extreme sentiments, that in their case sympathy quickly becomes adoration, and antipathy almost as soon as it is aroused is transformed into hatred. These general indications furnish us already with a presentiment of the nature of the convictions of crowds.

When these convictions are closely examined, whether at epochs marked by fervent religious faith, or by great political upheavals such as those of the last century, it is apparent that they always assume a peculiar form which I cannot better define than by giving it the name of a religious sentiment.

This sentiment has very simple characteristics, such as worship of a being supposed superior, fear of the power with which the being is credited, blind submission to its commands, inability to discuss its dogmas, the desire to spread them, and a tendency to consider as enemies all by whom they are not accepted. Whether such a sentiment apply to an invisible God, to a wooden or stone idol, to a hero or to a political conception, provided that it presents the preceding characteristics, its essence always remains religious. The supernatural and the miraculous are found to be present to the same extent. Crowds unconsciously accord a mysterious power to the political formula or the victorious leader that for the moment arouses their enthusiasm.

A person is not religious solely when he worships a divinity, but when he puts all the resources of his mind, the complete submission of his will, and the whole-souled ardour of fanaticism at the service of a cause or an individual who becomes the goal and guide of his thoughts and actions.

Intolerance and fanaticism are the necessary accompaniments of the religious sentiment. They are inevitably displayed by those who believe themselves in the possession of the secret of earthly or eternal happiness. These two characteristics are to be found in all men grouped together when they are inspired by a conviction of any kind. The Jacobins of the Reign of Terror were at bottom as religious as the Catholics of the Inquisition, and their cruel ardour proceeded from the same source.

The convictions of crowds assume those characteristics of blind submission, fierce intolerance, and the need of violent propaganda which are inherent in the religious sentiment, and it is for this reason that it may be said that all their beliefs have a religious form. The hero acclaimed by a crowd is a veritable god for that crowd. Napoleon was such a god for fifteen years, and a divinity never had more fervent worshippers or sent men to their death with greater ease. The Christian and Pagan Gods never exercised a more absolute empire over the minds that had fallen under their sway.

All founders of religious or political creeds have established them solely because they were successful in inspiring crowds with those fanatical sentiments which have as result that men find their happiness in worship and obedience and are ready to lay down their lives for their idol.

This has been the case at all epochs. Fustel de Coulanges, in his excellent work on Roman Gaul, justly remarks that the Roman Empire was in no wise maintained by force, but by the religious admiration it inspired. "It would be without a parallel in the history of the world," he observes rightly, "that a form of government held in popular detestation should have lasted for five centuries.... It would be inexplicable that the thirty legions of the Empire should have constrained a hundred million men to obedience." The reason of their obedience was that the Emperor, who personified the greatness of Rome, was worshipped like a divinity by unanimous consent. There were altars in honour of the Emperor in the smallest townships of his realm. "From one end of the Empire to the other a new religion was seen to arise in those days which had for its divinities the emperors themselves. Some years before the Christian era the whole of Gaul, represented by sixty cities, built in common a temple near the town of Lyons in honour of Augustus.... Its priests, elected by the united Gallic cities, were the principal personages in their country.... It is impossible to attribute all this to fear and servility. Whole nations are not servile, and especially for three centuries. It was not the courtiers who worshipped the prince, it was Rome, and it was not Rome merely, but it was Gaul, it was Spain, it was Greece and Asia."

To-day the majority of the great men who have swayed men's minds no longer have altars, but they have statues, or their portraits are in the hands of their admirers, and the cult of which they are the object is not notably different from that accorded to their predecessors. An understanding of the philosophy of history is only to be got by a thorough appreciation of this fundamental point of the psychology of crowds. The crowd demands a god before everything else.

It must not be supposed that these are the superstitions of a bygone age which reason has definitely banished. Sentiment has never been vanquished in its eternal conflict with reason. Crowds will hear no more of the words divinity and religion, in whose name they were so long enslaved; but they have never possessed so many fetishes as in the last hundred years, and the old divinities have never had so many statues and altars raised in their honour. Those who in recent years have studied the popular movement known under the name of Boulangism have been able to see with what ease the religious instincts of crowds are ready to revive. There was not a country inn that did not possess the hero's portrait. He was credited with the power of remedying all injustices and all evils, and thousands of men would have given their lives for him. Great might have been his place in history had his character been at all on a level with his legendary reputation.

It is thus a very useless commonplace to assert that a religion is necessary for the masses, because all political, divine, and social creeds only take root among them on the condition of always assuming the religious shape — a shape which obviates the danger of discussion. Were it possible to induce the masses to adopt atheism, this belief would exhibit all the intolerant ardour of a religious sentiment, and in its exterior forms would soon become a cult. The evolution of the small Positivist sect furnishes us a curious proof in point. What happened to the Nihilist whose story is related by that profound thinker Dostoïewsky has quickly happened to the Positivists. Illumined one day by the light of reason he broke the images of divinities and saints that adorned the altar of a chapel, extinguished the candles, and, without losing a moment, replaced the destroyed objects by the works of atheistic philosophers such as Büchner and Moleschott, after which he piously relighted the candles. The object of his religious beliefs had been transformed, but can it be truthfully said that his religious sentiments had changed?

Certain historical events — and they are precisely the most important — I again repeat, are not to be understood unless one has attained to an appreciation of the religious form which the convictions of crowds always assume in the long run. There are social phenomena that need to be studied far more from the point of view of the psychologist than from that of the naturalist.

The great historian Taine has only studied the Revolution as a naturalist, and on this account the real genesis of events has often escaped him. He has perfectly observed the facts, but from want of having studied the psychology of crowds he has not always been able to trace their causes. The facts having appalled him by their bloodthirsty, anarchic, and ferocious side, he has scarcely seen in the heroes of the great drama anything more than a horde of epileptic savages abandoning themselves without restraint to their instincts. The violence of the Revolution, its massacres, its need of propaganda, its declarations of war upon all things, are only to be properly explained by reflecting that the Revolution was merely the establishment of a new religious belief in the mind of the masses. The Reformation, the massacre of Saint Bartholomew, the French religious wars, the Inquisition, the Reign of Terror are phenomena of an identical kind, brought about by crowds animated by those religious sentiments which necessarily lead those imbued with them to pitilessly extirpate by fire and sword whoever is opposed to the establishment of the new faith. The methods of the Inquisition are those of all whose convictions are genuine and sturdy. Their convictions would not deserve these epithets did they resort to other methods.

Upheavals analogous to those I have just cited are only possible when it is the soul of the masses that brings them about. The most absolute despots could not cause them. When historians tell us that the massacre of Saint Bartholomew was the work of a king, they show themselves as ignorant of the psychology of crowds as of that of sovereigns. Manifestations of this order can only proceed from the soul of crowds. The most absolute power of the most despotic monarch can scarcely do more than hasten or retard the moment of their apparition. The massacre of Saint Bartholomew or the religious wars were no more the work of kings than the Reign of Terror was the work of Robespierre, Danton, or Saint Just. At the bottom of such events is always to be found the working of the soul of the masses, and never the power of potentates.

44

Book II. The Opinions and Beliefs of Crowds. Chapter I. Remote Factors of the Opinions and Beliefs of Crowds.

Having studied the mental constitution of crowds and become acquainted with their modes of feeling, thinking, and reasoning, we shall now proceed to examine how their opinions and beliefs arise and become established.

The factors which determine these opinions and beliefs are of two kinds: remote factors and immediate factors.

The remote factors are those which render crowds capable of adopting certain convictions and absolutely refractory to the acceptance of others. These factors prepare the ground in which are suddenly seen to germinate certain new ideas whose force and consequences are a cause of astonishment, though they are only spontaneous in appearance. The outburst and putting in practice of certain ideas among crowds present at times a startling suddenness. This is only a superficial effect, behind which must be sought a preliminary and preparatory action of long duration.

The immediate factors are those which, coming on the top of this long, preparatory working, in whose absence they would remain without effect, serve as the source of active persuasion on crowds; that is, they are the factors which cause the idea to take shape and set it loose with all its consequences. The resolutions by which collectivities are suddenly carried away arise out of these immediate factors; it is due to them that a riot breaks out or a strike is decided upon, and to them that enormous majorities invest one man with power to overthrow a government.

The successive action of these two kinds of factors is to be traced in all great historical events. The French Revolution — to cite but one of the most striking of such events — had among its remote factors the writings of the philosophers, the exactions of the nobility, and the progress of scientific thought. The mind of the masses, thus prepared, was then easily roused by such immediate factors as the speeches of orators, and the resistance of the court party to insignificant reforms.

Among the remote factors there are some of a general nature, which are found to underlie all the beliefs and opinions of crowds. They are race, traditions, time, institutions, and education.

We now proceed to study the influence of these different factors.

1. Race.

This factor, race, must be placed in the first rank, for in itself it far surpasses in importance all the others. We have sufficiently studied it in another work; it is therefore needless to deal with it again.

We showed, in a previous volume, what an historical race is, and how, its character once formed, it possesses, as the result of the laws of heredity such power that its beliefs, institutions, and arts — in a word, all the elements of its civilisation — are merely the outward expression of its genius. We showed that the power of the race is such that no element can pass from one people to another without undergoing the most profound transformations[7].

Environment, circumstances, and events represent the social suggestions of the moment. They may have a considerable influence, but this influence is always momentary if it be contrary to the suggestions of the race; that is, to those which are inherited by a nation from the entire series of its ancestors.

We shall have occasion in several of the chapters of this work to touch again upon racial influence, and to show that this influence is so great that it dominates the characteristics peculiar to the genius of crowds. It follows from this fact that the crowds of different countries offer very considerable differences of beliefs and conduct and are not to be influenced in the same manner.

2. Traditions.

Traditions represent the ideas, the needs, and the sentiments of the past. They are the synthesis of the race, and weigh upon us with immense force.

The biological sciences have been transformed since embryology has shown the immense influence of the past on the evolution of living beings; and the historical sciences will not undergo a less change when this conception has become more widespread. As yet it is not sufficiently general, and many statesmen are still no further advanced than the theorists of the last century, who believed that a society could break off with its past and be entirely recast on lines suggested solely by the light of reason.

A people is an organism created by the past, and, like every other organism, it can only be modified by slow hereditary accumulations.

It is tradition that guides men, and more especially so when they are in a crowd. The changes they can effect in their traditions with any ease, merely bear, as I have often repeated, upon names and outward forms.

This circumstance is not to be regretted. Neither a national genius nor civilisation would be possible without traditions. In consequence man's two great concerns since he has existed have been to create a network of traditions which he afterwards endeavours to destroy when their beneficial effects have worn themselves out. Civilisation is impossible without traditions, and progress impossible without the destruction of those traditions. The difficulty, and it is an immense difficulty, is to find a proper equilibrium between stability and variability. Should a people allow its customs to become too firmly rooted, it can no longer change, and becomes, like China, incapable of improvement. Violent revolutions are in this case of no avail; for what happens is that either the broken fragments of the chain are pieced together again and the past resumes its empire without change, or the fragments remain apart and decadence soon succeeds

---

[7] The novelty of this proposition being still considerable and history being quite unintelligible without it, I devoted four chapters to its demonstration in my last book ("The Psychological Laws of the Evolution of Peoples"). From it the reader will see that, in spite of fallacious appearances, neither language, religion, arts, or, in a word, any element of civilisation, can pass, intact, from one people to another.

anarchy.

The ideal for a people is in consequence to preserve the institutions of the past, merely changing them insensibly and little by little. This ideal is difficult to realise. The Romans in ancient and the English in modern times are almost alone in having realised it.

It is precisely crowds that cling the most tenaciously to traditional ideas and oppose their being changed with the most obstinacy. This is notably the case with the category of crowds constituting castes. I have already insisted upon the conservative spirit of crowds, and shown that the most violent rebellions merely end in a changing of words and terms. At the end of the last century, in the presence of destroyed churches, of priests expelled the country or guillotined, it might have been thought that the old religious ideas had lost all their strength, and yet a few years had barely lapsed before the abolished system of public worship had to be re-established in deference to universal demands[8].

Blotted out for a moment, the old traditions had resumed their sway.

No example could better display the power of tradition on the mind of crowds. The most redoubtable idols do not dwell in temples, nor the most despotic tyrants in palaces; both the one and the other can be broken in an
instant. But the invisible masters that reign in our innermost selves are safe from every effort at revolt, and only yield to the slow wearing away of centuries.

3. Time.

In social as in biological problems time is one of the most energetic factors. It is the sole real creator and the sole great destroyer. It is time that has made mountains with grains of sand and raised the obscure cell of geological eras to human dignity. The action of centuries is sufficient to transform any given phenomenon. It has been justly observed that an ant with enough time at its disposal could level Mount Blanc. A being possessed of the magical force of varying time at his will would have the power attributed by believers to God.

In this place, however, we have only to concern ourselves with the influence of time on the genesis of the opinions of crowds. Its action from this point of view is still immense. Dependent upon it are the great forces such as race, which cannot form themselves without it. It causes the birth, the growth, and the death of all beliefs. It is by the aid of time that they acquire their strength and also by its aid that they lose it.

It is time in particular that prepares the opinions and beliefs of crowds, or at least the soil on which they will germinate. This is why certain ideas are realisable at one epoch and not at another. It is time that accumulates that immense detritus of beliefs and thoughts on which the ideas of a given period spring up. They do not grow at hazard and by chance; the roots of each of them strike down into a long past. When they blossom it is time that has prepared their blooming; and to arrive at a notion of their genesis it is always back in the past that it is necessary to search. They are the daughters of the past and the mothers of the future, but throughout the slaves of time.

Time, in consequence, is our veritable master, and it suffices to leave it free to act to see all things transformed. At the present day we are very uneasy with regard to the threatening

---

[8] The report of the ex-Conventionist, Fourcroy, quoted by Taine, is very clear on this point.

"What is everywhere seen with respect to the keeping of Sunday and attendance at the churches proves that the majority of Frenchmen desire to return to their old usages and that it is no longer opportune to resist this natural tendency.... The great majority of men stand in need of religion, public worship, and priests. It is an error of some modern philosophers, by which I myself have been led away, to believe in the possibility of instruction being so general as to destroy religious prejudices, which for a great number of unfortunate persons are a source of consolation.... The mass of the people, then, must be allowed its priests, its altars, and its public worship."

aspirations of the masses and the destructions and upheavals foreboded thereby. Time, without other aid, will see to the restoration of equilibrium. "No form of government," M. Lavisse very properly writes, "was founded in a day. Political and social organisations are works that demand centuries. The feudal system existed for centuries in a shapeless, chaotic state before it found its laws; absolute monarchy also existed for centuries before arriving at regular methods of government, and these periods of expectancy were extremely troubled."

4. *Political and Social Institutions.*

The idea that institutions can remedy the defects of societies, that national progress is the consequence of the improvement of institutions and governments, and that social changes can be effected by decrees — this idea, I say, is still generally accepted. It was the starting-point of the French Revolution, and the social theories of the present day are based upon it.

The most continuous experience has been unsuccessful in shaking this grave delusion. Philosophers and historians have endeavoured in vain to prove its absurdity, but yet they have had no difficulty in demonstrating that institutions are the outcome of ideas, sentiments, and customs, and that ideas, sentiments, and customs are not to be recast by recasting legislative codes. A nation does not choose its institutions at will any more than it chooses the colour of its hair or its eyes. Institutions and governments are the product of the race. They are not the creators of an epoch, but are created by it. Peoples are not governed in accordance with their caprices of the moment, but as their character determines that they shall be governed. Centuries are required to form a political system and centuries needed to change it. Institutions have no intrinsic virtue: in themselves they are neither good nor bad. Those which are good at a given moment for a given people may be harmful in the extreme for another nation.

Moreover, it is in no way in the power of a people to really change its institutions. Undoubtedly, at the cost of violent revolutions, it can change their name, but in their essence they remain unmodified. The names are mere futile labels with which an historian who goes to the bottom of things need scarcely concern himself. It is in this way, for instance, that England[9], the most democratic country in the world, lives, nevertheless, under a monarchical régime, whereas the countries in which the most oppressive despotism is rampant are the Spanish-American Republics, in spite of their republican constitutions. The destinies of peoples are determined by their character and not by their government. I have endeavoured to establish this view in my previous volume by setting forth categorical examples.

To lose time in the manufacture of cut-and-dried constitutions is, in consequence, a puerile task, the useless labour of an ignorant rhetorician. Necessity and time undertake the charge of elaborating constitutions when we are wise enough to allow these two factors to act. This is the plan the Anglo-Saxons have adopted, as their great historian, Macaulay, teaches us in a passage that the politicians of all Latin countries ought to learn by heart. After having shown all the good that can be accomplished by laws which appear from the point of view of pure reason a chaos of absurdities and contradictions, he compares the scores of constitutions that have been engulphed in the convulsions of the Latin peoples with that of England, and points out that the latter has only been very slowly changed part by part, under the influence of immediate necessities and never of speculative reasoning.

---

[9] The most advanced republicans, even of the United States, recognise this fact. The American magazine, The Forum, recently gave categorical expression to the opinion in terms which I reproduce here from the Review of Reviews for December, 1894: —

"It should never be forgotten, even by the most ardent enemies of an aristocracy, that England is to-day the most democratic country of the universe, the country in which the rights of the individual are most respected, and in which the individual possesses the most liberty."

"To think nothing of symmetry and much of convenience; never to remove an anomaly merely because it is an anomaly; never to innovate except when some grievance is felt; never to innovate except so far as to get rid of the grievance; never to lay down any proposition of wider extent than the particular case for which it is necessary to provide; these are the rules which have, from the age of John to the age of Victoria, generally guided the deliberations of our two hundred and fifty Parliaments."

It would be necessary to take one by one the laws and institutions of each people to show to what extent they are the expression of the needs of each race and are incapable, for that reason, of being violently transformed. It is possible, for, instance, to indulge in philosophical dissertations on the advantages and disadvantages of centralisation; but when we see a people composed of very different races devote a thousand years of efforts to attaining to this centralisation; when we observe that a great revolution, having for object the destruction of all the institutions of the past, has been forced to respect this centralisation, and has even strengthened it; under these circumstances we should admit that it is the outcome of imperious needs, that it is a condition of the existence of the nation in question, and we should pity the poor mental range of politicians who talk of destroying it. Could they by chance succeed in this attempt, their success would at once be the signal for a frightful civil war[10], which, moreover, would immediately bring back a new system of centralisation much more oppressive than the old.

The conclusion to be drawn from what precedes is, that it is not in institutions that the means is to be sought of profoundly influencing the genius of the masses. When we see certain countries, such as the United States, reach a high degree of prosperity under democratic institutions, while others, such as the Spanish-American Republics, are found existing in a pitiable state of anarchy under absolutely similar institutions, we should admit that these institutions are as foreign to the greatness of the one as to the decadence of the others. Peoples are governed by their character, and all institutions which are not intimately modelled on that character merely represent a borrowed garment, a transitory disguise. No doubt sanguinary wars and violent revolutions have been undertaken, and will continue to be undertaken, to impose institutions to which is attributed, as to the relics of saints, the supernatural power of creating welfare. It may be said, then, in one sense, that institutions react on the mind of the crowd inasmuch as they engender such upheavals. But in reality it is not the institutions that react in this manner, since we know that, whether triumphant or vanquished, they possess in themselves no virtue. It is illusions and words that have influenced the mind of the crowd, and especially words
— words which are as powerful as they are chimerical, and whose astonishing sway we shall shortly demonstrate.

5. Instruction and Education.

Foremost among the dominant ideas of the present epoch is to be found the notion that instruction is capable of considerably changing men, and has for its unfailing consequence to improve them and even to make them equal. By the mere fact of its being constantly repeated,

---

[10] If a comparison be made between the profound religious and political dissensions which separate the various parties in France, and are more especially the result of social questions, and the separatist tendencies which were manifested at the time of the Revolution, and began to again display themselves towards the close of the Franco-German war, it will be seen that the different races represented in France are still far from being completely blended. The vigorous centralisation of the Revolution and the creation of artificial departments destined to bring about the fusion of the ancient provinces was certainly its most useful work. Were it possible to bring about the decentralisation which is to-day preoccupying minds lacking in foresight, the achievement would promptly have for consequence the most sanguinary disorders. To overlook this fact is to leave out of account the entire history of France.

this assertion has ended by becoming one of the most steadfast democratic dogmas. It would be as difficult now to attack it as it would have been formerly to have attacked the dogmas of the Church.

On this point, however, as on many others, democratic ideas are in profound disagreement with the results of psychology and experience. Many eminent philosophers, among them Herbert Spencer, have had no difficulty in showing that instruction neither renders a man more moral nor happier, that it changes neither his instincts nor his hereditary passions, and that at times — for this to happen it need only be badly directed — it is much more pernicious than useful. Statisticians have brought confirmation of these views by telling us that criminality increases with the generalisation of instruction, or at any rate of a certain kind of instruction, and that the worst enemies of society, the anarchists, are recruited among the prize-winners of schools; while in a recent work a distinguished magistrate, M. Adolphe Guillot, made the observation that at present 3,000 educated criminals are met with for every 1,000 illiterate delinquents, and that in fifty years the criminal percentage of the population has passed from 227 to 552 for every 100,000 inhabitants, an increase of 133 per cent. He has also noted in common with his colleagues that criminality is particularly on the increase among young persons, for whom, as is known, gratuitous and obligatory schooling has — in France — replaced apprenticeship.

It is not assuredly — and nobody has ever maintained this proposition — that well-directed instruction may not give very useful practical results, if not in the sense of raising the standard of morality, at least in that of developing professional capacity. Unfortunately the Latin peoples, especially in the last twenty-five years, have based their systems of instruction on very erroneous principles, and in spite of the observations of the most eminent minds, such as Bréal, Fustel de Coulanges, Taine, and many others, they persist in their lamentable mistakes. I have myself shown, in a work published some time ago, that the French system of education transforms the majority of those who have undergone it into enemies of society, and recruits numerous disciples for the worst forms of socialism.

The primary danger of this system of education — very properly qualified as Latin — consists in the fact that it is based on the fundamental psychological error that the intelligence is developed by the learning by heart of text-books. Adopting this view, the endeavour has been made to enforce a knowledge of as many hand-books as possible. From the primary school till he leaves the university a young man does nothing but acquire books by heart without his judgment or personal initiative being ever called into play. Education consists for him in reciting by heart and obeying.

"Learning lessons, knowing by heart a grammar or a compendium, repeating well and imitating well — that," writes a former Minister of Public Instruction,
M. Jules Simon, "is a ludicrous form of education whose every effort is an act of faith tacitly admitting the infallibility of the master, and whose only results are a belittling of ourselves and a

rendering of us impotent."

Were this education merely useless, one might confine one's self to expressing compassion for the unhappy children who, instead of making needful studies at the primary school, are instructed in the genealogy of the sons of Clotaire, the conflicts between Neustria and Austrasia, or zoological classifications. But the system presents a far more serious danger. It gives those who have been submitted to it a violent dislike to the state of life in which they were born, and an intense desire to escape from it. The working man no longer wishes to remain a working man, or the peasant to continue a peasant, while the most humble members of the middle classes admit of no possible career for their sons except that of State-paid functionaries. Instead of preparing men for life French schools solely prepare them to occupy public functions, in which success can be attained without any necessity for self-direction or the exhibition of the least glimmer of personal initiative. At the bottom of the social ladder the system creates an army of proletarians discontented with their lot and always ready to revolt, while at the summit it brings into being a frivolous bourgeoisie, at once sceptical and credulous, having a superstitious confidence in the State, whom it regards as a sort of Providence, but without forgetting to display towards it a ceaseless hostility, always laying its own faults to the door of the Government, and incapable of the least enterprise without the intervention of the authorities.

The State, which manufactures by dint of textbooks all these persons possessing diplomas, can only utilise a small number of them, and is forced to leave the others without employment. It is obliged in consequence to resign itself to feeding the first mentioned and to having the others as its enemies. From the top to the bottom of the social pyramid, from the humblest clerk to the professor and the prefect, the immense mass of persons boasting diplomas besiege the professions. While a business man has the greatest difficulty in finding an agent to represent him in the colonies, thousands of candidates solicit the most modest official posts. There are 20,000 schoolmasters and mistresses without employment in the department of the Seine alone, all of them persons who, disdaining the fields or the workshops, look to the State for their livelihood. The number of the chosen being restricted, that of the discontented is perforce immense. The latter are ready for any revolution, whoever be its chiefs and whatever the goal they aim at. The acquisition of knowledge for which no use can be found is a sure method of driving a man to revolt[11].

It is evidently too late to retrace our steps. Experience alone, that supreme educator of peoples, will be at pains to show us our mistake. It alone will be powerful enough to prove the necessity of replacing our odious text-books and our pitiable examinations by industrial instruction capable of inducing our young men to return to the fields, to the workshop, and to the colonial enterprise which they avoid to-day at all costs.

The professional instruction which all enlightened minds are now demanding was the instruction received in the past by our forefathers. It is still in vigour at the present day among

---

[11] This phenomenon, moreover, is not peculiar to the Latin peoples. It is also to be observed in China, which is also a country in the hands of a solid hierarchy of mandarins or functionaries, and where a function is obtained, as in France, by competitive examination, in which the only test is the imperturbable recitation of bulky manuals.
The army of educated persons without employment is considered in China at the present day as a veritable national calamity. It is the same in India where, since the English have opened schools, not for educating purposes, as is the case in England itself, but simply to furnish the indigenous inhabitants with instruction, there
has been formed a special class of educated persons, the Baboos, who, when they do not obtain employment, become the irreconcilable enemies of the English rule. In the case of all the Baboos, whether provided with employment or not, the first effect of their instruction has been to lower their standard of morality. This is a fact on which I have insisted at length in my book, "The Civilisations of India" — a fact, too, which has been observed
by all authors who have visited the great peninsula.

the nations who rule the world by their force of will, their initiative, and their spirit of enterprise. In a series of remarkable pages, whose principal passages I reproduce further on, a great thinker, M. Taine, has clearly shown that our former system of education was approximately that in vogue to-day in England and America, and in a remarkable parallel between the Latin and Anglo-Saxon systems he has plainly pointed out the consequences of the two methods.

One might consent, perhaps, at a pinch, to continue to accept all the disadvantages of our classical education, although it produced nothing but discontented men, and men unfitted for their station in life, did the superficial acquisition of so much knowledge, the faultless repeating by heart of so many text-books, raise the level of intelligence. But does it really raise this level? Alas, no! The conditions of success in life are the possession of judgment, experience, initiative, and character — qualities which are not bestowed by books. Books are dictionaries, which it is useful to consult, but of which it is perfectly useless to have lengthy portions in one's head.

How is it possible for professional instruction to develop the intelligence in a measure quite beyond the reach of classical instruction? This has been well shown by M. Taine.

"Ideas, he says, are only formed in their natural and normal surroundings; the promotion of the growth is effected by the innumerable impressions appealing to the senses which a young man receives daily in the workshop, the mine, the law court, the study, the builder's yard, the hospital; at the sight of tools, materials, and operations; in the presence of customers, workers, and labour, of work well or ill done, costly or lucrative. In such a way are obtained those trifling perceptions of detail of the eyes, the ear, the hands, and even the sense of smell, which, picked up involuntarily, and silently elaborated, take shape within the learner, and suggest to him sooner or, later this or that new combination, simplification, economy, improvement, or invention. The young Frenchman is deprived, and precisely at the age when they are most fruitful, of all these precious contacts, of all these indispensable elements of assimilation. For seven or eight years on end he is shut up in a school, and is cut off from that direct personal experience which would give him a keen and exact notion of men and things and of the various ways of handling them."

"... At least nine out of ten have wasted their time and pains during several years of their life — telling, important, even decisive years. Among such are to be counted, first of all, the half or two-thirds of those who present themselves for examination — I refer to those who are rejected; and then among those who are successful, who obtain a degree, a certificate, a diploma, there is still a half or two-thirds — I refer to the overworked. Too much has been demanded of them by exacting that on a given day, on a chair or before a board, they should, for two hours in succession, and with respect to a group of sciences, be living repertories of all human knowledge. In point of fact they were that, or nearly so, for two hours on that particular day, but a month later they are so no longer. They could not go through the examination again. Their too numerous and too burdensome acquisitions slip incessantly from their mind, and are not replaced. Their mental vigour has declined, their fertile capacity for growth has dried up, the fully-developed man appears, and he is often a used up man. Settled down, married, resigned to turning in a circle, and indefinitely in the same circle, he shuts himself up in his confined function, which he fulfils adequately, but nothing more. Such is the average yield: assuredly the receipts do not balance the expenditure. In England or America, where, as in France previous to 1789, the contrary proceeding is adopted, the outcome obtained is equal or superior."

The illustrious psychologist subsequently shows us the difference between our system and that of the Anglo-Saxons. The latter do not possess our innumerable special schools. With them instruction is not based on book-learning, but on object lessons. The engineer, for example, is trained in a workshop, and never at a school; a method which allows of each individual reaching the level his intelligence permits of. He becomes a workman or a foreman if he can get no further, an engineer if his aptitudes take him as far. This manner of proceeding is much more democratic and of much greater benefit to society than that of making the whole career of an individual depend on an examination, lasting a few hours, and undergone at the age of nineteen or twenty.

"In the hospital, the mine, the factory, in the architect's or the lawyer's office, the student, who makes a start while very young, goes through his apprenticeship, stage by stage, much as does with us a law clerk in his office, or an artist in his studio. Previously, and before making a practical beginning, he has had an opportunity of following some general and summary course of instruction, so as to have a framework ready prepared in which to store the observations he is shortly to make. Furthermore he is able, as a rule, to avail himself of sundry technical courses which he can follow in his leisure hours, so as to co-ordinate step by step the daily experience he is gathering. Under such a system the practical capabilities increase and develop of themselves in exact proportion to the faculties of the student, and in the direction requisite for his future task and the special work for which from now onwards he desires to fit himself. By this means in England or the United States a young man is quickly in a position to develop his capacity to the utmost. At twenty-five years of age, and much sooner if the material and the parts are there, he is not merely a useful performer, he is capable also of spontaneous enterprise; he is not only a part of a machine, but also a motor. In France, where the contrary system prevails — in France, which with each succeeding generation is falling more and more into line with China — the sum total of the wasted forces is enormous."

The great philosopher arrives at the following conclusion with respect to the growing incongruity between our Latin system of education and the requirements of practical life: —

"In the three stages of instruction, those of childhood, adolescence and youth, the theoretical and pedagogic preparation by books on the school benches has lengthened out and become overcharged in view of the examination, the degree, the diploma, and the certificate, and solely in this view, and by the worst methods, by the application of an unnatural and anti-social régime, by the excessive postponement of the practical apprenticeship, by our boarding-school system, by artificial training and mechanical cramming, by overwork, without thought for the time that is to follow, for the adult age and the functions of the man, without regard for the real world on which the young man will shortly be thrown, for the society in which we move and to which he must be adapted or be taught to resign himself in advance, for the struggle in which humanity is engaged, and in which to defend himself and to keep his footing he ought previously to have been equipped, armed, trained, and hardened. This indispensable equipment, this acquisition of more importance than any other, this sturdy common sense and nerve and will-power our schools do not procure the young Frenchman; on the contrary, far from qualifying him for his approaching and definite state, they disqualify him. In consequence, his entry into the world and his first steps in the field of action are most often merely a succession of painful falls, whose effect is that he long remains wounded and bruised, and sometimes disabled for life. The test is severe and dangerous. In the course of it the mental and moral equilibrium is affected, and runs the risk of not being re-established. Too sudden and complete disillusion has supervened. The deceptions have been too great, the disappointments too keen[12]."

Have we digressed in what precedes from the psychology of crowds? Assuredly not. If we desire to understand the ideas and beliefs that are germinating to-day in the masses, and will spring up to-morrow, it is necessary to know how the ground has been prepared. The instruction given the youth of a country allows of a knowledge of what that country will one day be. The education accorded the present generation justifies the most gloomy previsions. It is in part by instruction and education that the mind of the masses is improved or deteriorated. It was necessary in consequence to show how this mind has been fashioned by the system in vogue,

_____

[12] Taine, "Le Regime moderne," vol. ii., 1894. These pages are almost the last that Taine wrote. They resume admirably the results of the great philosopher's long experience. Unfortunately they are in my opinion totally incomprehensible for such of our university professors who have not lived abroad. Education is the only means at our disposal of influencing to some extent the mind of a nation, and it is profoundly saddening to have to think
that there is scarcely any one in France who can arrive at understanding that our present system of teaching is a
grave cause of rapid decadence, which instead of elevating our youth, lowers and perverts it.
A useful comparison may be made between Taine's pages and the observations on American education recently
made by M. Paul Bourget in his excellent book, "Outre-Mer." He, too, after having noted that our education merely produces narrow-minded bourgeois, lacking in initiative and will-power, or anarchists — "those two equally harmful types of the civilised man, who degenerates into impotent platitude or insane destructiveness" — he too, I say, draws a comparison that cannot be the object of too much reflection between our French lycées
(public schools), those factories of degeneration, and the American schools, which prepare a man admirably for
life. The gulf existing between truly democratic nations and those who have democracy in their speeches, but in
no wise in their thoughts, is clearly brought out in this comparison.

and how the mass of the indifferent and the neutral has become progressively an army of the discontented ready to obey all the suggestions of utopians and rhetoricians. It is in the schoolroom that socialists and anarchists are found nowadays, and that the way is being paved for the approaching period of decadence for the Latin peoples.

Chapter II. The Immediate Factors of the Opinions of Crowds.

We have just investigated the remote and preparatory factors which give the mind of crowds a special receptivity, and make possible therein the growth of certain sentiments and certain ideas. It now remains for us to study the factors capable of acting in a direct manner. We shall see in a forthcoming chapter how these factors should be put in force in order that they may produce their full effect.

In the first part of this work we studied the sentiments, ideas, and methods of reasoning of collective bodies, and from the knowledge thus acquired it would evidently be possible to deduce in a general way the means of making an impression on their mind. We already know what strikes the imagination of crowds, and are acquainted with the power and contagiousness of suggestions, of those especially that are presented under the form of images. However, as suggestions may proceed from very different sources, the factors capable of acting on the minds of crowds may differ considerably. It is necessary, then, to study them separately. This is not a useless study. Crowds are somewhat like the sphinx of ancient fable: it is necessary to arrive at a solution of the problems offered by their psychology or to resign ourselves to being devoured by them.

1. Images, Words, and Formulas.

When studying the imagination of crowds we saw that it is particularly open to the impressions produced by images. These images do not always lie ready to hand, but it is possible to evoke them by the judicious employment of words and formulas. Handled with art, they possess in sober truth the mysterious power formerly attributed to them by the adepts of magic. They cause the birth in the minds of crowds of the most formidable tempests, which in turn they are capable of stilling. A pyramid far loftier than that of old Cheops could be raised merely with the bones of men who have been victims of the power of words and formulas.

The power of words is bound up with the images they evoke, and is quite independent of their real significance. Words whose sense is the most ill-defined are sometimes those that possess the most influence. Such, for example, are the terms democracy, socialism, equality, liberty, &c., whose meaning is so vague that bulky volumes do not suffice to precisely fix it. Yet it is certain that a truly magical power is attached to those short syllables, as if they contained the solution of all problems. They synthesise the most diverse unconscious aspirations and the hope of their realisation.

Reason and arguments are incapable of combatting certain words and formulas. They are uttered with solemnity in the presence of crowds, and as soon as they have been pronounced an expression of respect is visible on every countenance, and all heads are bowed. By many they are considered as natural forces, as supernatural powers. They evoke grandiose and vague images in men's minds, but this very vagueness that wraps them in obscurity augments their mysterious power. They are the mysterious divinities hidden behind the tabernacle, which the devout only approach in fear and trembling.

The images evoked by words being independent of their sense, they vary from age to age and from people to people, the formulas remaining identical. Certain transitory images are attached to certain words: the word is merely as it were the button of an electric bell that calls them up.

All words and all formulas do not possess the power of evoking images, while there are some which have once had this power, but lose it in the course of use, and cease to waken any response in the mind. They then become vain sounds, whose principal utility is to relieve the person who employs them of the obligation of thinking. Armed with a small stock of formulas and commonplaces learnt while we are young, we possess all that is needed to traverse life without the tiring necessity of having to reflect on anything whatever.

If any particular language be studied, it is seen that the words of which it is composed change rather slowly in the course of ages, while the images these words evoke or the meaning attached to them changes ceaselessly. This is the reason why, in another work, I have arrived at the conclusion that the absolute translation of a language, especially of a dead language, is totally impossible. What do we do in reality when we substitute a French for a Latin, Greek, or Sanscrit expression, or even when we endeavour to understand a book written in our own tongue two or three centuries back? We merely put the images and ideas with which modern life has endowed our intelligence in the place of absolutely distinct notions and images which ancient life had brought into being in the mind of races submitted to conditions of existence having no analogy with our own. When the men of the Revolution imagined they were copying the Greeks and Romans, what were they doing except giving to ancient words a sense the latter had never had? What resemblance can possibly exist between the institutions of the Greeks and those designated to-day by corresponding words? A republic at that epoch was an essentially aristocratic institution, formed of a reunion of petty despots ruling over a crowd of slaves kept in the most absolute subjection. These communal aristocracies, based on slavery, could not have existed for a moment without it.

The word "liberty," again, what signification could it have in any way resembling that we attribute to it to-day at a period when the possibility of the liberty of thought was not even suspected, and when there was no greater and more exceptional crime than that of discussing the gods, the laws and the customs of the city? What did such a word as "fatherland" signify to an Athenian or Spartan unless it were the cult of Athens or Sparta, and in no wise that of Greece, composed of rival cities always at war with each other? What meaning had the same word "fatherland" among the ancient Gauls, divided into rival tribes and races, and possessing different languages and religions, and who were easily vanquished by Caesar because he always found allies among them? It was Rome that made a country of Gaul by endowing it with political and religious unity. Without going back so far, scarcely two centuries ago, is it to be believed that this same notion of a fatherland was conceived to have the same meaning as at present by French princes like the great Condé, who allied themselves with the foreigner against their sovereign? And yet again, the same word had it not a sense very different from the modern for the French royalist emigrants, who thought they obeyed the laws of honour in fighting against France, and who from their point of view did indeed obey them, since the feudal law bound the vassal to the lord and not to the soil, so that where the sovereign was there was the true fatherland?

Numerous are the words whose meaning has thus profoundly changed from age to age — words which we can only arrive at understanding in the sense in which they were formerly understood after a long effort. It has been said with truth that much study is necessary merely to arrive at conceiving what was signified to our great grandfathers by such words as the "king" and the "royal family." What, then, is likely to be the case with terms still more complex?

Words, then, have only mobile and transitory significations which change from age to age and people to people; and when we desire to exert an influence by their means on the crowd what it is requisite to know is the meaning given them by the crowd at a given moment, and not the meaning which they formerly had or may yet have for individuals of a different mental constitution.

Thus, when crowds have come, as the result of political upheavals or changes of belief, to acquire a profound antipathy for the images evoked by certain words, the first duty of the true statesman is to change the words without, of course, laying hands on the things themselves, the latter being too intimately bound up with the inherited constitution to be transformed. The judicious Tocqueville long ago made the remark that the work of the consulate and the empire consisted more particularly in the clothing with new words of the greater part of the institutions of the past — that is to say, in replacing words evoking disagreeable images in the imagination of the crowd by other words of which the novelty prevented such evocations. The "taille" or tallage has become the land tax; the "gabelle," the tax on salt; the "aids," the indirect contributions and the consolidated duties; the tax on trade companies and guilds, the license, &c.

One of the most essential functions of statesmen consists, then, in baptizing with popular or, at any rate, indifferent words things the crowd cannot endure under their old names. The power of words is so great that it suffices to designate in well-chosen terms the most odious things to make them acceptable to crowds. Taine justly observes that it was by invoking liberty and fraternity — words very popular at the time — that the Jacobins were able "to install a despotism worthy of Dahomey, a tribunal similar to that of the Inquisition, and to accomplish human hecatombs akin to those of ancient Mexico." The art of those who govern, as is the case with the art of advocates, consists above all in the science of employing words. One of the greatest difficulties of this art is, that in one and the same society the same words most often have very different meanings for the different social classes, who employ in appearance the same words, but never speak the same language.

In the preceding examples it is especially time that has been made to intervene as the principal factor in the changing of the meaning of words. If, however, we also make race intervene, we shall then see that, at the same period, among peoples equally civilised but of different race, the same words very often correspond to extremely dissimilar ideas. It is impossible to understand these differences without having travelled much, and for this reason I shall not insist upon them. I shall confine myself to observing that it is precisely the words most often employed by the masses which among different peoples possess the most different meanings. Such is the case, for instance, with the words "democracy" and "socialism" in such frequent use nowadays.

In reality they correspond to quite contrary ideas and images in the Latin and Anglo-Saxon mind. For the Latin peoples the word "democracy" signifies more especially the subordination of the will and the initiative of the individual to the will and the initiative of the community represented by the State. It is the State that is charged, to a greater and greater degree, with the direction of everything, the centralisation, the monopolisation, and the manufacture of everything. To the State it is that all parties without exception, radicals, socialists, or monarchists, constantly appeal. Among the Anglo-Saxons and notably in America this same word "democracy" signifies, on the contrary, the intense development of the will of the individual, and as complete a subordination as possible of the State, which, with the exception of the police, the army, and diplomatic relations, is not allowed the direction of anything, not even of public instruction. It is seen, then, that the same word which signifies for one people the subordination of the will and the initiative of the individual and the preponderance of the State, signifies for another the excessive development of the will and the initiative of the individual and the complete subordination of the State[13].

---

[13]   In my book, "The Psychological Laws of the Evolution of Peoples," I have insisted at length on the differences which distinguish the Latin democratic ideal from the Anglo-Saxon democratic ideal. Independently, and as the result of his travels, M. Paul Bourget has arrived, in his quite recent book, "Outre-Mer," at conclusions almost

2. Illusions.

From the dawn of civilisation onwards crowds have always undergone the influence of illusions. It is to the creators of illusions that they have raised more temples, statues, and altars than to any other class of men. Whether it be the religious illusions of the past or the philosophic and social illusions of the present, these formidable sovereign powers are always found at the head of all the civilisations that have successively flourished on our planet. It is in their name that were built the temples of Chaldea and Egypt and the religious edifices of the Middle Ages, and that a vast upheaval shook the whole of Europe a century ago, and there is not one of our political, artistic, or social conceptions that is free from their powerful impress. Occasionally, at the cost of terrible disturbances, man overthrows them, but he seems condemned to always set them up again. Without them he would never have emerged from his primitive barbarian state, and without them again he would soon return to it. Doubtless they are futile shadows; but these children of our dreams have forced the nations to create whatever the arts may boast of splendour or civilisation of greatness.

"If one destroyed in museums and libraries, if one hurled down on the flagstones before the churches all the works and all the monuments of art that religions have inspired, what would remain of the great dreams of humanity? To give to men that portion of hope and illusion without which they cannot live, such is the reason for the existence of gods, heroes, and poets. During fifty years science appeared to undertake this task. But science has been compromised in hearts hungering after the ideal, because it does not dare to be lavish enough of promises, because it cannot lie[14]."

The philosophers of the last century devoted themselves with fervour to the destruction of the religious, political, and social illusions on which our forefathers had lived for a long tale of centuries. By destroying them they have dried up the springs of hope and resignation. Behind the immolated chimeras they came face to face with the blind and silent forces of nature, which are inexorable to weakness and ignore pity.

Notwithstanding all its progress, philosophy has been unable as yet to offer the masses any ideal that can charm them; but, as they must have their illusions at all cost, they turn instinctively, as the insect seeks the light, to the rhetoricians who accord them what they want. Not truth, but error has always been the chief factor in the evolution of nations, and the reason why socialism is so powerful to-day is that it constitutes the last illusion that is still vital. In spite of all scientific demonstrations it continues on the increase. Its principal strength lies in the fact that it is championed by minds sufficiently ignorant of things as they are in reality to venture boldly to promise mankind happiness. The social illusion reigns to-day upon all the heaped-up ruins of the past, and to it belongs the future. The masses have never thirsted after truth. They turn aside from evidence that is not to their taste, preferring to deify error, if error seduce them. Whoever can supply them with illusions is easily their master; whoever attempts to destroy their illusions is always their victim.

3. Experience.

Experience constitutes almost the only effective process by which a truth may be solidly established in the mind of the masses, and illusions grown too dangerous be destroyed. To this end, however, it is necessary that the experience should take place on a very large scale, and be very frequently repeated. The experiences undergone by one generation are useless, as a rule, for the generation that follows, which is the reason why historical facts, cited with a view to

---

identical with mine.

[14]   Daniel Lesueur.

demonstration, serve no purpose. Their only utility is to prove to what an extent experiences need to be repeated from age to age to exert any influence, or to be successful in merely shaking an erroneous opinion when it is solidly implanted in the mind of the masses.

Our century and that which preceded it will doubtless be alluded to by historians as an era of curious experiments, which in no other age have been tried in such number.

The most gigantic of these experiments was the French Revolution. To find out that a society is not to be refashioned from top to bottom in accordance with the dictates of pure reason, it was necessary that several millions of men should be massacred and that Europe should be profoundly disturbed for a period of twenty years. To prove to us experimentally that dictators cost the nations who acclaim them dear, two ruinous experiences have been required in fifty years, and in spite of their clearness they do not seem to have been sufficiently convincing. The first, nevertheless, cost three millions of men and an invasion, the second involved a loss of territory, and carried in its wake the necessity for permanent armies. A third was almost attempted not long since, and will assuredly be attempted one day. To bring an entire nation to admit that the huge German army was not, as was currently alleged thirty years ago, a sort of harmless national guard[15], the terrible war which cost us so dear had to take place. To bring about the recognition that Protection ruins the nations who adopt it, at least twenty years of disastrous experience will be needful. These examples might be indefinitely multiplied.

4. *Reason.*

In enumerating the factors capable of making an impression on the minds of crowds all mention of reason might be dispensed with, were it not necessary to point out the negative value of its influence.

We have already shown that crowds are not to be influenced by reasoning, and can only comprehend rough-and-ready associations of ideas. The orators who know how to make an impression upon them always appeal in consequence to their sentiments and never to their reason. The laws of logic have no action on crowds[16]. To bring home conviction to crowds it is

---

[15]   The opinion of the crowd was formed in this case by those rough-and-ready associations of dissimilar things, the mechanism of which I have previously explained. The French national guard of that period, being composed
of peaceable shopkeepers, utterly lacking in discipline and quite incapable of being taken seriously, whatever bore a similar name, evoked the same conception and was considered in consequence as harmless. The error of the crowd was shared at the time by its leaders, as happens so often in connection with opinions dealing with
generalisations. In a speech made in the Chamber on the 31st of December, 1867, and quoted in a book by M. E. Ollivier that has appeared recently, a statesman who often followed the opinion of the crowd but was never in
advance of it — I allude to M. Thiers — declared that Prussia only possessed a national guard analogous to that
of France, and in consequence without importance, in addition to a regular army about equal to the French regular army; assertions about as accurate as the predictions of the same statesman as to the insignificant future reserved for railways.

[16]   My first observations with regard to the art of impressing crowds and touching the slight assistance to be derived in this connection from the rules of logic date back to the seige of Paris, to the day when I saw conducted to the Louvre, where the Government was then sitting, Marshal V ——, whom a furious crowd asserted they had surprised in the act of taking the plans of the fortifications to sell them to the Prussians. A member of the Government (G. P ——), a very celebrated orator, came out to harangue the crowd, which was demanding the immediate execution of the prisoner. I had expected that the speaker would point out the absurdity of the accusation by remarking that the accused Marshal was positively one of those who had constructed the fortifications, the plan of which, moreover, was on sale at every booksellers.
To my immense stupefaction — I was very young then — the speech was on quite different lines. "Justice shall be done," exclaimed the orator, advancing towards the prisoner, "and pitiless justice. Let the Government of the

necessary first of all to thoroughly comprehend the sentiments by which they are animated, to pretend to share these sentiments, then to endeavour to modify them by calling up, by means of rudimentary associations, certain eminently suggestive notions, to be capable, if need be, of going back to the point of view from which a start was made, and, above all, to divine from instant to instant the sentiments to which one's discourse is giving birth. This necessity of ceaselessly varying one's language in accordance with the effect produced at the moment of speaking deprives from the outset a prepared and studied harangue of all efficaciousness. In such a speech the orator follows his own line of thought, not that of his hearers, and from this fact alone his influence is annihilated.

Logical minds, accustomed to be convinced by a chain of somewhat close reasoning, cannot avoid having recourse to this mode of persuasion when addressing crowds, and the inability of their arguments always surprises them. "The usual mathematical consequences based on the syllogism — that is, on associations of identities — are imperative ..." writes a logician. "This imperativeness would enforce the assent even of an inorganic mass were it capable of following associations of identities." This is doubtless true, but a crowd is no more capable than an inorganic mass of following such associations, nor even of understanding them. If the attempt be made to convince by reasoning primitive minds — savages or children, for instance — the slight value possessed by this method of arguing will be understood.

It is not even necessary to descend so low as primitive beings to obtain an insight into the utter powerlessness of reasoning when it has to fight against sentiment. Let us merely call to mind how tenacious, for centuries long, have been religious superstitions in contradiction with the simplest logic. For nearly two thousand years the most luminous geniuses have bowed before their laws, and modern times have to be reached for their veracity to be merely contested. The Middle Ages and the Renaissance possessed many enlightened men, but not a single man who attained by reasoning to an appreciation of the childish side of his superstitions, or who promulgated even a slight doubt as to the misdeeds of the devil or the necessity of burning sorcerers.

Should it be regretted that crowds are never guided by reason? We would not venture to affirm it. Without a doubt human reason would not have availed to spur humanity along the path of civilisation with the ardour and hardihood its illusions have done. These illusions, the offspring of those unconscious forces by which we are led, were doubtless necessary. Every race carries in its mental constitution the laws of its destiny, and it is, perhaps, these laws that it obeys with a resistless impulse, even in the case of those of its impulses which apparently are the most unreasoned. It seems at times as if nations were submitted to secret forces analogous to those which compel the acorn to transform itself into an oak or a comet to follow its orbit.

What little insight we can get into these forces must be sought for in the general course of the evolution of a people, and not in the isolated facts from which this evolution appears at times to proceed. Were these facts alone to be taken into consideration, history would seem to be the result of a series of improbable chances. It was improbable that a Galilean carpenter should become for two thousand years an all-powerful God in whose name the most important civilisations were founded; improbable, too, that a few bands of Arabs, emerging from their deserts, should conquer the greater part of the old Graco-Roman world, and establish an empire greater than that of Alexander; improbable, again, that in Europe, at an advanced period of its development, and when authority throughout it had been systematically hierarchised, an obscure lieutenant of artillery should have succeeded in reigning over a multitude of peoples and kings.

Let us leave reason, then, to philosophers, and not insist too strongly on its intervention in the governing of men. It is not by reason, but most often in spite of it, that are created those sentiments that are the mainsprings of all civilisation — sentiments such as honour, self-sacrifice, religious faith, patriotism, and the love of glory.

Chapter III. The Leaders of Crowds and Their Means of Persuasion.

We are now acquainted with the mental constitution of crowds, and we also know what are the motives capable of making an impression on their mind. It remains to investigate how these motives may be set in action, and by whom they may usefully be turned to practical account.

1. The Leaders of Crowds.

As soon as a certain number of living beings are gathered together, whether they be animals or men, they place themselves instinctively under the authority of a chief.

In the case of human crowds the chief is often nothing more than a ringleader or agitator, but as such he plays a considerable part. His will is the nucleus around which the opinions of the crowd are grouped and attain to identity. He constitutes the first element towards the organisation of heterogeneous crowds, and paves the way for their organisation in sects; in the meantime he directs them. A crowd is a servile flock that is incapable of ever doing without a master.

The leader has most often started as one of the led. He has himself been hypnotised by the idea, whose apostle he has since become. It has taken possession of him to such a degree that everything outside it vanishes, and that every contrary opinion appears to him an error or a superstition. An example in point is Robespierre, hypnotised by the philosophical ideas of Rousseau, and employing the methods of the Inquisition to propagate them.

The leaders we speak of are more frequently men of action than thinkers. They are not gifted with keen foresight, nor could they be, as this quality generally conduces to doubt and inactivity. They are especially recruited from the ranks of those morbidly nervous, excitable, half-deranged persons who are bordering on madness. However absurd may be the idea they uphold or the goal they pursue, their convictions are so strong that all reasoning is lost upon them. Contempt and persecution do not affect them, or only serve to excite them the more. They sacrifice their personal interest, their family — everything. The very instinct of self-preservation is entirely obliterated in them, and so much so that often the only recompense they solicit is that of martyrdom. The intensity of their faith gives great power of suggestion to their words. The multitude is always ready to listen to the strong-willed man, who knows how to impose himself upon it. Men gathered in a crowd lose all force of will, and turn instinctively to the person who possesses the quality they lack.

Nations have never lacked leaders, but all of the latter have by no means been animated by those strong convictions proper to apostles. These leaders are often subtle rhetoricians, seeking only their own personal interest, and endeavouring to persuade by flattering base instincts. The influence they can assert in this manner may be very great, but it is always ephemeral. The men of ardent convictions who have stirred the soul of crowds, the Peter the Hermits, the Luthers, the Savonarolas, the men of the French Revolution, have only exercised their fascination after having been themselves fascinated first of all by a creed. They are then able to call up in the souls of their fellows that formidable force known as faith, which renders a man the absolute slave of his dream.

The arousing of faith — whether religious, political, or social, whether faith in a work, in a person, or an idea — has always been the function of the great leaders of crowds, and it is on this account that their influence is always very great. Of all the forces at the disposal of humanity, faith has always been one of the most tremendous, and the gospel rightly attributes to it the power of moving mountains. To endow a man with faith is to multiply his strength tenfold. The great events of history have been brought about by obscure believers, who have had little beyond their faith in their favour. It is not by the aid of the learned or of philosophers, and still less of sceptics, that have been built up the great religions which have swayed the world, or the vast empires which have spread from one hemisphere to the other.

In the cases just cited, however, we are dealing with great leaders, and they are so few in number that history can easily reckon them up. They form the summit of a continuous series, which extends from these powerful masters of men down to the workman who, in the smoky atmosphere of an inn, slowly fascinates his comrades by ceaselessly drumming into their ears a few set phrases, whose purport he scarcely comprehends, but the application of which, according to him, must surely bring about the realisation of all dreams and of every hope.

In every social sphere, from the highest to the lowest, as soon as a man ceases to be isolated he speedily falls under the influence of a leader. The majority of men, especially among the masses, do not possess clear and reasoned ideas on any subject whatever outside their own speciality. The leader serves them as guide. It is just possible that he may be replaced, though very inefficiently, by the periodical publications which manufacture opinions for their readers and supply them with ready-made phrases which dispense them of the trouble of reasoning.

The leaders of crowds wield a very despotic authority, and this despotism indeed is a condition of their obtaining a following. It has often been remarked how easily they extort obedience, although without any means of backing up their authority, from the most turbulent section of the working classes. They fix the hours of labour and the rate of wages, and they decree strikes, which are begun and ended at the hour they ordain.

At the present day these leaders and agitators tend more and more to usurp the place of the public authorities in proportion as the latter allow themselves to be called in question and shorn of their strength. The tyranny of these new masters has for result that the crowds obey them much more docilely than they have obeyed any government. If in consequence of some accident or other the leaders should be removed from the scene the crowd returns to its original state of a collectivity without cohesion or force of resistance. During the last strike of the Parisian omnibus employés the arrest of the two leaders who were directing it was at once sufficient to bring it to an end. It is the need not of liberty but of servitude that is always predominant in the soul of crowds. They are so bent on obedience that they instinctively submit to whoever declares himself their master.

These ringleaders and agitators may be divided into two clearly defined classes. The one includes the men who are energetic and possess, but only intermittently, much strength of will, the other the men, far rarer than the preceding, whose strength of will is enduring. The first mentioned are violent, brave, and audacious. They are more especially useful to direct a violent enterprise suddenly decided on, to carry the masses with them in spite of danger, and to transform into heroes the men who but yesterday were recruits. Men of this kind were Ney and Murat under the First Empire, and such a man in our own time was Garibaldi, a talentless but energetic adventurer who succeeded with a handful of men in laying hands on the ancient kingdom of Naples, defended though it was by a disciplined army.

Still, though the energy of leaders of this class is a force to be reckoned with, it is transitory, and scarcely outlasts the exciting cause that has brought it into play. When they have returned to their ordinary course of life the heroes animated by energy of this description often evince, as was the case with those I have just cited, the most astonishing weakness of character. They seem incapable of reflection and of conducting themselves under the simplest circumstances, although they had been able to lead others. These men are leaders who cannot exercise their function except on the condition that they be led themselves and continually stimulated, that they have always as their beacon a man or an idea, that they follow a line of conduct clearly traced. The second category of leaders, that of men of enduring strength of will, have, in spite of a less brilliant aspect, a much more considerable influence. In this category are to be found the true founders of religions and great undertakings: St. Paul, Mahomet, Christopher Columbus, and de Lesseps, for example. Whether they be intelligent or narrow-minded is of no importance: the world belongs to them. The persistent will-force they possess is an immensely rare and immensely powerful faculty to which everything yields. What a strong and continuous will is capable of is not always properly appreciated. Nothing resists it; neither nature, gods, nor man.

The most recent example of what can be effected by a strong and continuous will is afforded us by the illustrious man who separated the Eastern and Western worlds, and accomplished a task that during three thousand years had been attempted in vain by the greatest sovereigns. He failed later in an identical enterprise, but then had intervened old age, to which everything, even the will, succumbs.

When it is desired to show what may be done by mere strength of will, all that is necessary is to relate in detail the history of the difficulties that had to be surmounted in connection with the cutting of the Suez Canal. An ocular witness, Dr. Cazalis, has summed up in a few striking lines the entire story of this great work, recounted by its immortal author.

"From day to day, episode by episode, he told the stupendous story of the canal. He told of all he had had to vanquish, of the impossible he had made possible, of all the opposition he encountered, of the coalition against him, and the disappointments, the reverses, the defeats which had been unavailing to discourage or depress him. He recalled how England had combatted him, attacking him without cessation, how Egypt and France had hesitated, how the French Consul had been foremost in his opposition to the early stages of the work, and the nature of the opposition he had met with, the attempt to force his workmen to desert from thirst by refusing them fresh water; how the Minister of Marine and the engineers, all responsible men of experienced and scientific training, had naturally all been hostile, were all certain on scientific grounds that disaster was at hand, had calculated its coming, foretelling it for such a day and hour as an eclipse is foretold."

The book which relates the lives of all these great leaders would not contain many names, but these names have been bound up with the most important events in the history of civilisation.

2. The Means of Action of the Leaders: Affirmation, Repetition, Contagion.

When it is wanted to stir up a crowd for a short space of time, to induce it to commit an act of any nature — to pillage a palace, or to die in defence of a stronghold or a barricade, for instance — the crowd must be acted upon by rapid suggestion, among which example is the most powerful in its effect. To attain this end, however, it is necessary that the crowd should have been previously prepared by certain circumstances, and, above all, that he who wishes to work upon it should possess the quality to be studied farther on, to which I give the name of prestige.

When, however, it is proposed to imbue the mind of a crowd with ideas and beliefs — with modern social theories, for instance — the leaders have recourse to different expedients. The principal of them are three in number and clearly defined — affirmation, repetition, and contagion. Their action is somewhat slow, but its effects, once produced, are very lasting.

Affirmation pure and simple, kept free of all reasoning and all proof, is one of the surest means of making an idea enter the mind of crowds. The conciser an affirmation is, the more destitute of every appearance of proof and demonstration, the more weight it carries. The religious books and the legal codes of all ages have always resorted to simple affirmation. Statesmen called upon to defend a political cause, and commercial men pushing the sale of their products by means of advertising are acquainted with the value of affirmation.

Affirmation, however, has no real influence unless it be constantly repeated, and so far as possible in the same terms. It was Napoleon, I believe, who said that there is only one figure in rhetoric of serious importance, namely, repetition. The thing affirmed comes by repetition to fix itself in the mind in such a way that it is accepted in the end as a demonstrated truth.

The influence of repetition on crowds is comprehensible when the power is seen which it exercises on the most enlightened minds. This power is due to the fact that the repeated statement is embedded in the long run in those profound regions of our unconscious selves in which the motives of our actions are forged. At the end of a certain time we have forgotten who is the author of the repeated assertion, and we finish by believing it. To this circumstance is due the astonishing power of advertisements. When we have read a hundred, a thousand, times that X's chocolate is the best, we imagine we have heard it said in many quarters, and we end by acquiring the certitude that such is the fact. When we have read a thousand times that Y's flour has cured the most illustrious persons of the most obstinate maladies, we are tempted at last to try it when suffering from an illness of a similar kind. If we always read in the same papers that A is an arrant scamp and B a most honest man we finish by being convinced that this is the truth, unless, indeed, we are given to reading another paper of the contrary opinion, in which the two qualifications are reversed. Affirmation and repetition are alone powerful enough to combat each other. When an affirmation has been sufficiently repeated and there is unanimity in this repetition — as has occurred in the case of certain famous financial undertakings rich enough to purchase every assistance — what is called a current of opinion is formed and the powerful mechanism of contagion intervenes. Ideas, sentiments, emotions, and beliefs possess in crowds a contagious power as intense as that of microbes. This phenomenon is very natural, since it is observed even in animals when they are together in number. Should a horse in a stable take to biting his manger the other horses in the stable will imitate him. A panic that has seized on a few sheep will soon extend to the whole flock. In the case of men collected in a crowd all emotions are very rapidly contagious, which explains the suddenness of panics. Brain disorders, like madness, are themselves contagious. The frequency of madness among doctors who are specialists for the mad is notorious. Indeed, forms of madness have recently been cited — agoraphobia, for instance — which are communicable from men to animals.

For individuals to succumb to contagion their simultaneous presence on the same spot is not indispensable. The action of contagion may be felt from a distance under the influence of events which give all minds an individual trend and the characteristics peculiar to crowds. This is especially the case when men's minds have been prepared to undergo the influence in question by those remote factors of which I have made a study above. An example in point is the revolutionary movement of 1848, which, after breaking out in Paris, spread rapidly over a great part of Europe and shook a number of thrones.

Imitation, to which so much influence is attributed in social phenomena, is in reality a mere effect of contagion. Having shown its influence elsewhere, I shall confine myself to reproducing what I said on the subject fifteen years ago. My remarks have since been developed by other writers in recent publications.

"Man, like animals, has a natural tendency to imitation. Imitation is a necessity for him, provided always that the imitation is quite easy. It is this necessity that makes the influence of what is called fashion so powerful. Whether in the matter of opinions, ideas, literary manifestations, or merely of dress, how many persons are bold enough to run counter to the fashion? It is by examples not by arguments that crowds are guided. At every period there exists a small number of individualities which react upon the remainder and are imitated by the unconscious mass. It is needful however, that these individualities should not be in too pronounced disagreement with received ideas. Were they so, to imitate them would be too difficult and their influence would be nil. For this very reason men who are too superior to their epoch are generally without influence upon it. The line of separation is too strongly marked. For the same reason too Europeans, in spite of all the advantages of their civilisation, have so insignificant an influence on Eastern people; they differ from them to too great an extent.

"The dual action of the past and of reciprocal imitation renders, in the long run, all the men of the same country and the same period so alike that even in the case of individuals who would seem destined to escape this double influence, such as philosophers, learned men, and men of letters, thought and style have a family air which enables the age to which they belong to be immediately recognised. It is not necessary to talk for long with an individual to attain to a thorough knowledge of what he reads, of his habitual occupations, and of the surroundings amid which he lives[17]."

Contagion is so powerful that it forces upon individuals not only certain opinions, but certain modes of feeling as well. Contagion is the cause of the contempt in which, at a given period, certain works are held — the example of "Tannhaüser" may be cited — which, a few years later, for the same reason are admired by those who were foremost in criticising them.

The opinions and beliefs of crowds are specially propagated by contagion, but never by reasoning. The conceptions at present rife among the working classes have been acquired at the public-house as the result of affirmation, repetition, and contagion, and indeed the mode of creation of the beliefs of crowds of every age has scarcely been different. Renan justly institutes a comparison between the first founders of Christianity and "the socialist working men spreading their ideas from public-house to public-house"; while Voltaire had already observed in connection with the Christian religion that "for more than a hundred years it was only embraced by the vilest riff-raff."

It will be noted that in cases analogous to those I have just cited, contagion, after having been at work among the popular classes, has spread to the higher classes of society. This is what we see happening at the present day with regard to the socialist doctrines which are beginning to be held by those who will yet be their first victims. Contagion is so powerful a force that even the

---

17 Gustave le Bon, "L'Homme et les Sociétés," vol. ii. p. 116. 1881.

sentiment of personal interest disappears under its action.

This is the explanation of the fact that every opinion adopted by the populace always ends in implanting itself with great vigour in the highest social strata, however obvious be the absurdity of the triumphant opinion. This reaction of the lower upon the higher social classes is the more curious, owing to the circumstance that the beliefs of the crowd always have their origin to a greater or less extent in some higher idea, which has often remained without influence in the sphere in which it was evolved. Leaders and agitators, subjugated by this higher idea, take hold of it, distort it and create a sect which distorts it afresh, and then propagates it amongst the masses, who carry the process of deformation still further. Become a popular truth the idea returns, as it were, to its source and exerts an influence on the upper classes of a nation. In the long run it is intelligence that shapes the destiny of the world, but very indirectly. The philosophers who evolve ideas have long since returned to dust, when, as the result of the process I have just described, the fruit of their reflection ends by triumphing.

3. Prestige.

Great power is given to ideas propagated by affirmation, repetition, and contagion by the circumstance that they acquire in time that mysterious force known as prestige.

Whatever has been a ruling power in the world, whether it be ideas or men, has in the main enforced its authority by means of that irresistible force expressed by the word "prestige." The term is one whose meaning is grasped by everybody, but the word is employed in ways too different for it to be easy to define it. Prestige may involve such sentiments as admiration or fear. Occasionally even these sentiments are its basis, but it can perfectly well exist without them. The greatest measure of prestige is possessed by the dead, by beings, that is, of whom we do not stand in fear — by Alexander, Cæsar, Mahomet, and Buddha, for example. On the other hand, there are fictive beings whom we do not admire — the monstrous divinities of the subterranean temples of India, for instance — but who strike us nevertheless as endowed with a great prestige.

Prestige in reality is a sort of domination exercised on our mind by an individual, a work, or an idea. This domination entirely paralyses our critical faculty, and fills our soul with astonishment and respect. The sentiment provoked is inexplicable, like all sentiments, but it would appear to be of the same kind as the fascination to which a magnetised person is subjected. Prestige is the mainspring of all authority. Neither gods, kings, nor women have ever reigned without it.

The various kinds of prestige may be grouped under two principal heads: acquired prestige and personal prestige. Acquired prestige is that resulting from name, fortune, and reputation. It may be independent of personal prestige. Personal prestige, on the contrary, is something essentially peculiar to the individual; it may coexist with reputation, glory, and fortune, or be strengthened by them, but it is perfectly capable of existing in their absence.

Acquired or artificial prestige is much the most common. The mere fact that an individual occupies a certain position, possesses a certain fortune, or bears certain titles, endows him with prestige, however slight his own personal worth. A soldier in uniform, a judge in his robes, always enjoys prestige. Pascal has very properly noted the necessity for judges of robes and wigs. Without them they would be stripped of half their authority. The most unbending socialist is always somewhat impressed by the sight of a prince or a marquis; and the assumption of such titles makes the robbing of tradesmen an easy matter[18].

---

[18]   The influence of titles, decorations, and uniforms on crowds is to be traced in all countries, even in those in which the sentiment of personal independence is the most strongly developed. I quote in this connection a

The prestige of which I have just spoken is exercised by persons; side by side with it may be placed that exercised by opinions, literary and artistic works, &c. Prestige of the latter kind is most often merely the result of accumulated repetitions. History, literary and artistic history especially, being nothing more than the repetition of identical judgments, which nobody endeavours to verify, every one ends by repeating what he learnt at school, till there come to be names and things which nobody would venture to meddle with. For a modern reader the perusal of Homer results incontestably in immense boredom; but who would venture to say so? The Parthenon, in its present state, is a wretched ruin, utterly destitute of interest, but it is endowed with such prestige that it does not appear to us as it really is, but with all its accompaniment of historic memories. The special characteristic of prestige is to prevent us seeing things as they are and to entirely paralyse our judgment. Crowds always, and individuals as a rule, stand in need of ready-made opinions on all subjects. The popularity of these opinions is independent of the measure of truth or error they contain, and is solely regulated by their prestige.

I now come to personal prestige. Its nature is very different from that of artificial or acquired prestige, with which I have just been concerned. It is a faculty independent of all titles, of all authority, and possessed by a small number of persons whom it enables to exercise a veritably magnetic fascination on those around them, although they are socially their equals, and lack all ordinary means of domination. They force the acceptance of their ideas and sentiments on those about them, and they are obeyed as is the tamer of wild beasts by the animal that could easily devour him.

The great leaders of crowds, such as Buddha, Jesus, Mahomet, Joan of Arc, and Napoleon, have possessed this form of prestige in a high degree, and to this endowment is more particularly due the position they attained. Gods, heroes, and dogmas win their way in the world of their own inward strength. They are not to be discussed: they disappear, indeed, as soon as discussed.

The great personages I have just cited were in possession of their power of fascination long before they became illustrious, and would never have become so without it. It is evident, for instance, that Napoleon at the zenith of his glory enjoyed an immense prestige by the mere fact of his power, but he was already endowed in part with this prestige when he was without power and completely unknown. When, an obscure general, he was sent, thanks to influential protection, to command the army of Italy, he found himself among rough generals who were of a mind to give a hostile reception to the young intruder dispatched them by the Directory. From the very beginning, from the first interview, without the aid of speeches, gestures, or threats, at the first sight of the man who was to become great they were vanquished. Taine furnishes a curious account of this interview taken from contemporary memoirs.

"The generals of division, amongst others Augereau, a sort of swashbuckler, uncouth and heroic, proud of his height and his bravery, arrive at the staff quarters very badly disposed towards the little upstart dispatched them from Paris. On the strength of the description of him

curious passage from a recent book of travel, on the prestige enjoyed in England by great persons.
"I had observed, under various circumstances, the peculiar sort of intoxication produced in the most reasonable
Englishmen by the contact or sight of an English peer.
"Provided his fortune enables him to keep up his rank, he is sure of their affection in advance, and brought into contact with him they are so enchanted as to put up with anything at his hands. They may be seen to redden with pleasure at his approach, and if he speaks to them their suppressed joy increases their redness, and causes their eyes to gleam with unusual brilliance.
Respect for nobility is in their blood, so to speak, as with Spaniards the love of dancing, with Germans that of music, and with Frenchmen the liking for revolutions. Their passion for horses and Shakespeare is less violent, the satisfaction and pride they derive from these sources a less integral part of their being. There is a considerable sale for books dealing with the peerage, and go where one will they are to be found, like the Bible,
in all hands."

that has been given them, Augereau is inclined to be insolent and insubordinate; a favourite of Barras, a general who owes his rank to the events of Vendémiaire who has won his grade by street-fighting, who is looked upon as bearish, because he is always thinking in solitude, of poor aspect, and with the reputation of a mathematician and dreamer. They are introduced, and Bonaparte keeps them waiting. At last he appears, girt with his sword; he puts on his hat, explains the measures he has taken, gives his orders, and dismisses them. Augereau has remained silent; it is only when he is outside that he regains his self-possession and is able to deliver himself of his customary oaths. He admits with Masséna that this little devil of a general has inspired him with awe; he cannot understand the ascendency by which from the very first he has felt himself overwhelmed."

Become a great man, his prestige increased in proportion as his glory grew, and came to be at least equal to that of a divinity in the eyes of those devoted to him. General Vandamme, a rough, typical soldier of the Revolution, even more brutal and energetic than Augereau, said of him to Marshal d'Arnano in 1815, as on one occasion they mounted together the stairs of the Tuileries: "That devil of a man exercises a fascination on me that I cannot explain even to myself, and in such a degree that, though I fear neither God nor devil, when I am in his presence I am ready to tremble like a child, and he could make me go through the eye of a needle to throw myself into the fire." Napoleon exercised a like fascination on all who came into contact with him[19].

Davoust used to say, talking of Maret's devotion and of his own: "Had the Emperor said to us, `It is important in the interest of my policy that Paris should be destroyed without a single person leaving it or escaping,' Maret I am sure would have kept the secret, but he could not have abstained from compromising himself by seeing that his family got clear of the city. On the other hand, I, for fear of letting the truth leak out, would have let my wife and children stay."

It is necessary to bear in mind the astounding power exerted by fascination of this order to understand that marvellous return from the Isle of Elba, that lightning-like conquest of France by an isolated man confronted by all the organised forces of a great country that might have been supposed weary of his tyranny. He had merely to cast a look at the generals sent to lay hands on him, and who had sworn to accomplish their mission. All of them submitted without discussion.

"Napoleon," writes the English General Wolseley, "lands in France almost alone, a fugitive from the small island of Elba which was his kingdom, and succeeded in a few weeks, without bloodshed, in upsetting all organised authority in France under its legitimate king; is it possible for the personal ascendency of a man to affirm itself in a more astonishing manner? But from the beginning to the end of this campaign, which was his last, how remarkable too is the ascendency he exercised over the Allies, obliging them to follow his initiative, and how near he came to crushing them!"

His prestige outlived him and continued to grow. It is his prestige that made an emperor of his obscure nephew. How powerful is his memory still is seen in the resurrection of his legend in progress at the present day. Ill-treat men as you will, massacre them by millions, be the cause of invasion upon invasion, all is permitted you if you possess prestige in a sufficient degree and the talent necessary to uphold it. I have invoked, no doubt, in this case a quite exceptional example

---

[19] Thoroughly conscious of his prestige, Napoleon was aware that he added to it by treating rather worse than stable lads the great personages around him, and among whom figured some of those celebrated men of the Convention of whom Europe had stood in dread. The gossip of the period abounds in illustrations of this fact. One day, in the midst of a Council of State, Napoleon grossly insults Beugnot, treating him as one might an unmannerly valet. The effect produced, he goes up to him and says, "Well, stupid, have you found your head again?" Whereupon Beugnot, tall as a drum-major, bows very low, and the little man raising his hand, takes the tall one by the ear, "an intoxicating sign of favour," writes Beugnot, "the familiar gesture of the master who waxes gracious." Such examples give a clear idea of the degree of base platitude that prestige can provoke. They enable us to understand the immense contempt of the great despot for the men surrounding him — men whom he merely looked upon as "food for powder."

of prestige, but one it was useful to cite to make clear the genesis of great religions, great doctrines, and great empires. Were it not for the power exerted on the crowd by prestige, such growths would be incomprehensible.

Prestige, however, is not based solely on personal ascendency, military glory, and religious terror; it may have a more modest origin and still be considerable. Our century furnishes several examples. One of the most striking ones that posterity will recall from age to age will be supplied by the history of the illustrious man who modified the face of the globe and the commercial relations of the nations by separating two continents. He succeeded in his enterprise owing to his immense strength of will, but also owing to the fascination he exercised on those surrounding him. To overcome the unanimous opposition he met with, he had only to show himself. He would speak briefly, and in face of the charm he exerted his opponents became his friends. The English in particular strenuously opposed his scheme; he had only to put in an appearance in England to rally all suffrages. In later years, when he passed Southampton, the bells were rung on his passage; and at the present day a movement is on foot in England to raise a statue in his honour.

"Having vanquished whatever there is to vanquish, men and things, marshes, rocks, and sandy wastes," he had ceased to believe in obstacles, and wished to begin Suez over again at Panama. He began again with the same methods as of old; but he had aged, and, besides, the faith that moves mountains does not move them if they are too lofty. The mountains resisted, and the catastrophe that ensued destroyed the glittering aureole of glory that enveloped the hero. His life teaches how prestige can grow and how it can vanish. After rivalling in greatness the most famous heroes of history, he was lowered by the magistrates of his country to the ranks of the vilest criminals. When he died his coffin, unattended, traversed an indifferent crowd. Foreign sovereigns are alone in rendering homage to his memory as to that of one of the greatest men that history has known[20].

Still, the various examples that have just been cited represent extreme cases. To fix in detail the psychology of prestige, it would be necessary to place them at the extremity of a series, which would range from the founders of religions and empires to the private individual who endeavours to dazzle his neighbours by a new coat or a decoration.

Between the extreme limits of this series would find a place all the forms of prestige resulting

---

[20] An Austrian paper, the Neue Freie Presse, of Vienna, has indulged on the subject of the destiny of de Lesseps in reflections marked by a most judicious psychological insight. I therefore reproduce them here: —
"After the condemnation of Ferdinand de Lesseps one has no longer the right to be astonished at the sad end of Christopher Columbus. If Ferdinand de Lesseps were a rogue every noble illusion is a crime. Antiquity World have crowned the memory of de Lesseps with an aureole of glory, and would have made him drink from the bowl of nectar in the midst of Olympus, for he has altered the face of the earth and accomplished works which make the creation more perfect. The President of the Court of Appeal has immortalised himself by condemning Ferdinand de Lesseps, for the nations will always demand the name of the man who was not afraid to debase his century by investing with the convict's cap an aged man, whose life redounded to the glory of his contemporaries.
"Let there be no more talk in the future of inflexible justice, there where reigns a bureaucratic hatred of audacious feats. The nations have need of audacious men who believe in themselves and overcome every obstacle without concern for their personal safety. Genius cannot he prudent; by dint of prudence it could never enlarge the sphere of human activity "... Ferdinand de Lesseps has known the intoxication of triumph and the bitterness of disappointment — Suez and Panama. At this point the heart revolts at the morality of success. When de Lesseps had succeeded in joining two seas princes and nations rendered him their homage; to-day, when he meets with failure among the rocks of the Cordilleras, he is nothing but a vulgar rogue.... In this result we see a war between the classes of society, the discontent of bureaucrats and employés, who take their revenge with the aid of the criminal code on those who would raise themselves above their fellows.
... Modern legislators are filled with embarrassment when confronted by the lofty ideas due to human genius; the public comprehends such ideas still less, and it is easy for an advocate-general to prove that Stanley is a murderer and de Lesseps a deceiver."

from the different elements composing a civilisation — sciences, arts, literature, &c. — and it would be seen that prestige constitutes the fundamental element of persuasion. Consciously or not, the being, the idea, or the thing possessing prestige is immediately imitated in consequence of contagion, and forces an entire generation to adopt certain modes of feeling and of giving expression to its thought. This imitation, moreover, is, as a rule, unconscious, which accounts for the fact that it is perfect. The modern painters who copy the pale colouring and the stiff attitudes of some of the Primitives are scarcely alive to the source of their inspiration. They believe in their own sincerity, whereas, if an eminent master had not revived this form of art, people would have continued blind to all but its naïve and inferior sides. Those artists who, after the manner of another illustrious master, inundate their canvasses with violet shades do not see in nature more violet than was detected there fifty years ago; but they are influenced, "suggestioned," by the personal and special impressions of a painter who, in spite of this eccentricity, was successful in acquiring great prestige. Similar examples might be brought forward in connection with all the elements of civilisation.

It is seen from what precedes that a number of factors may be concerned in the genesis of prestige; among them success was always one of the most important. Every successful man, every idea that forces itself into recognition, ceases, ipso facto, to be called in question. The proof that success is one of the principal stepping-stones to prestige is that the disappearance of the one is almost always followed by the disappearance of the other. The hero whom the crowd acclaimed yesterday is insulted to-day should he have been overtaken by failure. The re-action, indeed, will be the stronger in proportion as the prestige has been great. The crowd in this case considers the fallen hero as an equal, and takes its revenge for having bowed to a superiority whose existence it no longer admits. While Robespierre was causing the execution of his colleagues and of a great number of his contemporaries, he possessed an immense prestige. When the transposition of a few votes deprived him of power, he immediately lost his prestige, and the crowd followed him to the guillotine with the self-same imprecations with which shortly before it had pursued his victims. Believers always break the statues of their former gods with every symptom of fury.

Prestige lost by want of success disappears in a brief space of time. It can also be worn away, but more slowly by being subjected to discussion.

This latter power, however, is exceedingly sure. From the moment prestige is called in question it ceases to be prestige. The gods and men who have kept their prestige for long have never tolerated discussion. For the crowd to admire, it must be kept at a distance.

Chapter IV. Limitations of the Variability of the Beliefs and Opinions of Crowds.

1. Fixed Beliefs.

A close parallel exists between the anatomical and psychological characteristics of living beings.

In these anatomical characteristics certain invariable, or slightly variable, elements are met with, to change which the lapse is necessary of geological ages. Side by side with these fixed, indestructible features are to be found others extremely changeable, which the art of the breeder or horticulturist may easily modify, and at times to such an extent as to conceal the fundamental characteristics from an observer at all inattentive.

The same phenomenon is observed in the case of moral characteristics. Alongside the unalterable psychological elements of a race, mobile and changeable elements are to be encountered. For this reason, in studying the beliefs and opinions of a people, the presence is always detected of a fixed groundwork on which are engrafted opinions as changing as the surface sand on a rock.

The opinions and beliefs of crowds may be divided, then, into two very distinct classes. On the one hand we have great permanent beliefs, which endure for several centuries, and on which an entire civilisation may rest. Such, for instance, in the past were feudalism, Christianity, and Protestantism; and such, in our own time, are the nationalist principle and contemporary democratic and social ideas. In the second place, there are the transitory, changing opinions, the outcome, as a rule, of general conceptions, of which every age sees the birth and disappearance; examples in point are the theories which mould literature and the arts — those, for instance, which produced romanticism, naturalism, mysticism, &c. Opinions of this order are as superficial, as a rule, as fashion, and as changeable. They may be compared to the ripples which ceaselessly arise and vanish on the surface of a deep lake.

The great generalised beliefs are very restricted in number. Their rise and fall form the culminating points of the history of every historic race. They constitute the real framework of civilisation.

It is easy to imbue the mind of crowds with a passing opinion, but very difficult to implant therein a lasting belief. However, a belief of this latter description once established, it is equally difficult to uproot it. It is usually only to be changed at the cost of violent revolutions. Even revolutions can only avail when the belief has almost entirely lost its sway over men's minds. In that case revolutions serve to finally sweep away what had already been almost cast aside, though the force of habit prevented its complete abandonment. The beginning of a revolution is in reality the end of a belief.

The precise moment at which a great belief is doomed is easily recognisable; it is the moment when its value begins to be called in question. Every general belief being little else than a fiction, it can only survive on the condition that it be not subjected to examination.

But even when a belief is severely shaken, the institutions to which it has given rise retain their strength and disappear but slowly. Finally, when the belief has completely lost its force, all that rested upon it is soon involved in ruin. As yet a nation has never been able to change its beliefs without being condemned at the same time to transform all the elements of its civilisation. The nation continues this process of transformation until it has alighted on and accepted a new general belief: until this juncture it is perforce in a state of anarchy. General beliefs are the indispensable pillars of civilisations; they determine the trend of ideas. They alone are capable of inspiring faith and creating a sense of duty.

Nations have always been conscious of the utility of acquiring general beliefs, and have instinctively understood that their disappearance would be the signal for their own decline. In the case of the Romans, the fanatical cult of Rome was the belief that made them masters of the world, and when the belief had died out Rome was doomed to die. As for the barbarians who destroyed the Roman civilisation, it was only when they had acquired certain commonly accepted beliefs that they attained a measure of cohesion and emerged from anarchy.

Plainly it is not for nothing that nations have always displayed intolerance in the defence of their opinions. This intolerance, open as it is to criticism from the philosophic standpoint, represents in the life of a people the most necessary of virtues. It was to found or uphold general beliefs that so many victims were sent to the stake in the Middle Ages and that so many inventors and innovators have died in despair even if they have escaped martyrdom. It is in defence, too, of such beliefs that the world has been so often the scene of the direst disorder, and that so many millions of men have died on the battlefield, and will yet die there.

There are great difficulties in the way of establishing a general belief, but when it is definitely implanted its power is for a long time to come invincible, and however false it be philosophically it imposes itself upon the most luminous intelligence. Have not the European peoples regarded as incontrovertible for more than fifteen centuries religious legends which, closely examined, are as barbarous[21] as those of Moloch? The frightful absurdity of the legend of a God who revenges himself for the disobedience of one of his creatures by inflicting horrible tortures on his son remained unperceived during many centuries. Such potent geniuses as a Galileo, a Newton, and a Leibnitz never supposed for an instant that the truth of such dogmas could be called in question. Nothing can be more typical than this fact of the hypnotising effect of general beliefs, but at the same time nothing can mark more decisively the humiliating limitations of our intelligence.

As soon as a new dogma is implanted in the mind of crowds it becomes the source of inspiration whence are evolved its institutions, arts, and mode of existence. The sway it exerts over men's minds under these circumstances is absolute. Men of action have no thought beyond realising the accepted belief, legislators beyond applying it, while philosophers, artists, and men of letters are solely preoccupied with its expression under various shapes.

From the fundamental belief transient accessory ideas may arise, but they always bear the impress of the belief from which they have sprung. The Egyptian civilisation, the European civilisation of the Middle Ages, the Mussulman civilisation of the Arabs are all the outcome of a small number of religious beliefs which have left their mark on the least important elements of these civilisations and allow of their immediate recognition.

Thus it is that, thanks to general beliefs, the men of every age are enveloped in a network of traditions, opinions, and customs which render them all alike, and from whose yoke they cannot extricate themselves. Men are guided in their conduct above all by their beliefs and by the customs that are the consequence of those beliefs. These beliefs and customs regulate the smallest acts of our existence, and the most independent spirit cannot escape their influence. The tyranny exercised unconsciously on men's minds is the only real tyranny, because it cannot be fought against. Tiberius, Ghengis Khan, and Napoleon were assuredly redoubtable tyrants, but from the depth of their graves Moses, Buddha, Jesus, and Mahomet have exerted on the human soul a far profounder despotism. A conspiracy may overthrow a tyrant, but what can it avail

---

21 Barbarous, philosophically speaking, I mean. In practice they have created an entirely new civilisation, and for fifteen centuries have given mankind a glimpse of those enchanted realms of generous dreams and of hope which he will know no more.

against a firmly established belief? In its violent struggle with Roman Catholicism it is the French Revolution that has been vanquished, and this in spite of the fact that the sympathy of the crowd was apparently on its side, and in spite of recourse to destructive measures as pitiless as those of the Inquisition. The only real tyrants that humanity has known have always been the memories of its dead or the illusions it has forged itself.

The philosophic absurdity that often marks general beliefs has never been an obstacle to their triumph. Indeed the triumph of such beliefs would seem impossible unless on the condition that they offer some mysterious absurdity. In consequence, the evident weakness of the socialist beliefs of to-day will not prevent them triumphing among the masses. Their real inferiority to all religious beliefs is solely the result of this consideration, that the ideal of happiness offered by the latter being realisable only in a future life, it was beyond the power of anybody to contest it. The socialist ideal of happiness being intended to be realised on earth, the vanity of its promises will at once appear as soon as the first efforts towards their realisation are made, and simultaneously the new belief will entirely lose its prestige. Its strength, in consequence, will only increase until the day when, having triumphed, its practical realisation shall commence. For this reason, while the new religion exerts to begin with, like all those that have preceded it, a destructive influence, it will be unable, in the future, to play a creative part.

2. The Changeable Opinions of Crowds.

Above the substratum of fixed beliefs, whose power we have just demonstrated, is found an overlying growth of opinions, ideas, and thoughts which are incessantly springing up and dying out. Some of them exist but for a day, and the more important scarcely outlive a generation. We have already noted that the changes which supervene in opinions of this order are at times far more superficial than real, and that they are always affected by racial considerations. When examining, for instance, the political institutions of France we showed that parties to all appearance utterly distinct — royalists, radicals, imperialists, socialists, &c. — have an ideal absolutely identical, and that this ideal is solely dependent on the mental structure of the French race, since a quite contrary ideal is found under analogous names among other races. Neither the name given to opinions nor deceptive adaptations alter the essence of things. The men of the Great Revolution, saturated with Latin literature, who (their eyes fixed on the Roman Republic), adopted its laws, its fasces, and its togas, did not become Romans because they were under the empire of a powerful historical suggestion. The task of the philosopher is to investigate what it is which subsists of ancient beliefs beneath their apparent changes, and to identify amid the moving flux of opinions the part determined by general beliefs and the genius of the race.

In the absence of this philosophic test it might be supposed that crowds change their political or religious beliefs frequently and at will. All history, whether political, religious, artistic, or literary, seems to prove that such is the case. As an example, let us take a very short period of French history, merely that from 1790 to 1820, a period of thirty years' duration, that of a generation. In the course of it we see the crowd at first monarchical become very revolutionary, then very imperialist, and again very monarchical. In the matter of religion it gravitates in the same lapse of time from Catholicism to atheism, then towards deism, and then returns to the most pronounced forms of Catholicism. These changes take place not only amongst the masses, but also amongst those who direct them. We observe with astonishment the prominent men of the Convention, the sworn enemies of kings, men who would have neither gods nor masters, become the humble servants of Napoleon, and afterwards, under Louis XVIII, piously carry candles in religious processions.

Numerous, too, are the changes in the opinions of the crowd in the course of the following seventy years. The "Perfidious Albion" of the opening of the century is the ally of France under Napoleon's heir; Russia, twice invaded by France, which looked on with satisfaction at French reverses, becomes its friend.

In literature, art, and philosophy the successive evolutions of opinion are more rapid still. Romanticism, naturalism, mysticism, &c., spring up and die out in turn. The artist and the writer applauded yesterday are treated on the morrow with profound contempt.

When, however, we analyse all these changes in appearance so far reaching, what do we find? All those that are in opposition with the general beliefs and sentiments of the race are of transient duration, and the diverted stream soon resumes its course. The opinions which are not linked to any general belief or sentiment of the race, and which in consequence cannot possess stability, are at the mercy of every chance, or, if the expression be preferred, of every change in the surrounding circumstances. Formed by suggestion and contagion, they are always momentary; they crop up and disappear as rapidly on occasion as the sandhills formed by the wind on the sea-coast.

At the present day the changeable opinions of crowds are greater in number than they ever were, and for three different reasons.

The first is that as the old beliefs are losing their influence to a greater and greater extent, they are ceasing to shape the ephemeral opinions of the moment as they did in the past. The weakening of general beliefs clears the ground for a crop of haphazard opinions without a past or a future.

The second reason is that the power of crowds being on the increase, and this power being less and less counterbalanced, the extreme mobility of ideas, which we have seen to be a peculiarity of crowds, can manifest itself without let or hindrance.

Finally, the third reason is the recent development of the newspaper press, by whose agency the most contrary opinions are being continually brought before the attention of crowds. The suggestions that might result from each individual opinion are soon destroyed by suggestions of an opposite character. The consequence is that no opinion succeeds in becoming widespread, and that the existence of all of them is ephemeral. An opinion nowadays dies out before it has found a sufficiently wide acceptance to become general.

A phenomenon quite new in the world's history, and most characteristic of the present age, has resulted from these different causes; I allude to the powerlessness of governments to direct opinion.

In the past, and in no very distant past, the action of governments and the influence of a few writers and a very small number of newspapers constituted the real reflectors of public opinion. To-day the writers have lost all influence, and the newspapers only reflect opinion. As for statesmen, far from directing opinion, their only endeavour is to follow it. They have a dread of opinion, which amounts at times to terror, and causes them to adopt an utterly unstable line of conduct.

The opinion of crowds tends, then, more and more to become the supreme guiding principle in politics. It goes so far to-day as to force on alliances, as has been seen recently in the case of the Franco-Russian alliance, which is solely the outcome of a popular movement. A curious symptom of the present time is to observe popes, kings, and emperors consent to be interviewed as a means of submitting their views on a given subject to the judgment of crowds. Formerly it might have been correct to say that politics were not a matter of sentiment. Can the same be said toÄday, when politics are more and more swayed by the impulse of changeable crowds, who are uninfluenced by reason and can only be guided by sentiment?

As to the press, which formerly directed opinion, it has had, like governments, to humble itself before the power of crowds. It wields, no doubt, a considerable influence, but only because it is exclusively the reflection of the opinions of crowds and of their incessant variations. Become a mere agency for the supply of information, the press has renounced all endeavour to enforce an idea or a doctrine. It follows all the changes of public thought, obliged to do so by the necessities of competition under pain of losing its readers. The old staid and influential organs of the past, such as the Constitutionnel, the Débats, or the Siécle, which were accepted as oracles by the preceding generation, have disappeared or have become typical modern papers, in which a maximum of news is sandwiched in between light articles, society gossip, and financial puffs. There can be no question to-day of a paper rich enough to allow its contributors to air their personal opinions, and such opinions would be of slight weight with readers who only ask to be kept informed or to be amused, and who suspect every affirmation of being prompted by motives of speculation. Even the critics have ceased to be able to assure the success of a book or a play. They are capable of doing harm, but not of doing a service. The papers are so conscious of the uselessness of everything in the shape of criticism or personal opinion, that they have reached the point of suppressing literary criticism, confining themselves to citing the title of a book, and appending a "puff" of two or three lines[22]. In twenty years' time the same fate will probably have overtaken theatrical criticism.

The close watching of the course of opinion has become to-day the principal preoccupation of the press and of governments. The effect produced by an event, a legislative proposal, a speech, is without intermission what they require to know, and the task is not easy, for nothing is more mobile and changeable than the thought of crowds, and nothing more frequent than to see them execrate to-day what they applauded yesterday.

This total absence of any sort of direction of opinion, and at the same time the destruction of general beliefs, have had for final result an extreme divergency of convictions of every order, and a growing indifference on the part of crowds to everything that does not plainly touch their immediate interests. Questions of doctrine, such as socialism, only recruit champions boasting genuine convictions among the quite illiterate classes, among the workers in mines and factories, for instance. Members of the lower middle class, and working men possessing some degree of instruction, have either become utterly sceptical or extremely unstable in their opinions.

The evolution which has been effected in this direction in the last twenty-five years is striking. During the preceding period, comparatively near us though it is, opinions still had a certain general trend; they had their origin in the acceptance of some fundamental belief. By the mere fact that an individual was a monarchist he possessed inevitably certain clearly defined ideas in history as well as in science, while by the mere fact that he was a republican, his ideas were quite contrary. A monarchist was well aware that men are not descended from monkeys, and a republican was not less well aware that such is in truth their descent. It was the duty of the monarchist to speak with horror, and of the republican to speak with veneration, of the great Revolution. There were certain names, such as those of Robespierre and Marat, that had to be uttered with an air of religious devotion, and other names, such as those of Cæsar, Augustus, or Napoleon, that ought never to be mentioned unaccompanied by a torrent of invective. Even in the French Sorbonne this ingenuous fashion of conceiving history was general[23].

---

22 These remarks refer to the French newspaper press. — Note of the Translator.
23 There are pages in the books of the French official professors of history that are very curious from this point of view. They prove too how little the critical spirit is developed by the system of university education in vogue in France. I cite as an example the following extracts from the "French Revolution" of M. Rambaud, professor of history at the Sorbonne:
"The taking of the Bastille was a culminating event in the history not only of France, but of all Europe; and inaugurated a new epoch in the history of the world!"
With respect to Robespierre, we learn with stupefaction that "his dictatorship was based more especially on

At the present day, as the result of discussion and analysis, all opinions are losing their prestige; their distinctive features are rapidly worn away, and few survive capable of arousing our enthusiasm. The man of modern times is more and more a prey to indifference.

The general wearing away of opinions should not be too greatly deplored. That it is a symptom of decadence in the life of a people cannot be contested. It is certain that men of immense, of almost supernatural insight, that apostles, leaders of crowds — men, in a word, of genuine and strong convictions — exert a far greater force than men who deny, who criticise, or who are indifferent, but it must not be forgotten that, given the power possessed at present by crowds, were a single opinion to acquire sufficient prestige to enforce its general acceptance, it would soon be endowed with so tyrannical a strength that everything would have to bend before it, and the era of free discussion would be closed for a long time. Crowds are occasionally easy-going masters, as were Heliogabalus and Tiberius, but they are also violently capricious. A civilisation, when the moment has come for crowds to acquire a high hand over it, is at the mercy of too many chances to endure for long. Could anything postpone for a while the hour of its ruin, it would be precisely the extreme instability of the opinions of crowds and their growing indifference with respect to all general beliefs.

opinion, persuasion, and moral authority; it was a sort of pontificate in the hands of a virtuous man!" (pp. 91 and
220.)

Book III. The Classification and Description of the Different Kinds of Crowds.

Chapter I. The Classification of Crowds.

We have sketched in this work the general characteristics common to psychological crowds. It remains to point out the particular characteristics which accompany those of a general order in the different categories of collectivities, when they are transformed into a crowd under the influences of the proper exciting causes. We will, first of all, set forth in a few words a classification of crowds.

Our starting-point will be the simple multitude. Its most inferior form is met with when the multitude is composed of individuals belonging to different races. In this case its only common bond of union is the will, more or less respected of a chief. The barbarians of very diverse origin who during several centuries invaded the Roman Empire, may be cited as a specimen of multitudes of this kind.

On a higher level than these multitudes composed of different races are those which under certain influences have acquired common characteristics, and have ended by forming a single race. They present at times characteristics peculiar to crowds, but these characteristics are overruled to a greater or less extent by racial considerations.

These two kinds of multitudes may, under certain influences investigated in this work, be transformed into organised or psychological crowds. We shall break up these organised crowds into the following divisions: —

A. Heterogeneous crowds.
1 Anonymous crowds (street crowds, for example).
2 Crowds not anonymous (juries, parliamentary assemblies, &c.).

B. Homogeneous crowds.
1 Sects (political sects, religious sects, &c.).
2 Castes (the military caste, the priestly caste, the working caste, &c.).
3 Classes (the middle classes, the peasant classes, &c.).

We will point out briefly the distinguishing characteristics of these different categories of crowds.

1. Heterogeneous Crowds.

It is these collectivities whose characteristics have been studied in this volume. They are composed of individuals of any description, of any profession, and any degree of intelligence.

We are now aware that by the mere fact that men form part of a crowd engaged in action, their collective psychology differs essentially from their individual psychology, and their intelligence is affected by this differentiation. We have seen that intelligence is without influence in collectivities, they being solely under the sway of unconscious sentiments.

A fundamental factor, that of race, allows of a tolerably thorough differentiation of the various heterogeneous crowds.

We have often referred already to the part played by race, and have shown it to be the most powerful of the factors capable of determining men's actions. Its action is also to be traced in the character of crowds. A crowd composed of individuals assembled at haphazard, but all of them Englishmen or Chinamen, will differ widely from another crowd also composed of individuals of any and every description, but of other races — Russians, Frenchmen, or Spaniards, for example.

The wide divergencies which their inherited mental constitution creates in men's modes of feeling and thinking at once come into prominence when, which rarely happens, circumstances gather together in the same crowd and in fairly equal proportions individuals of different nationality, and this occurs, however identical in appearance be the interests which provoked the gathering. The efforts made by the socialists to assemble in great congresses the representatives of the working-class populations of different countries, have always ended in the most pronounced discord. A Latin crowd, however revolutionary or however conservative it be supposed, will invariably appeal to the intervention of the State to realise its demands. It is always distinguished by a marked tendency towards centralisation and by a leaning, more or less pronounced, in favour of a dictatorship. An English or an American crowd, on the contrary, sets no store on the State, and only appeals to private initiative. A French crowd lays particular weight on equality and an English crowd on liberty. These differences of race explain how it is that there are almost as many different forms of socialism and democracy as there are nations.

The genius of the race, then, exerts a paramount influence upon the dispositions of a crowd. It is the powerful underlying force that limits its changes of humour. It should be considered as an essential law that the inferior characteristics of crowds are the less accentuated in proportion as the spirit of the race is strong. The crowd state and the domination of crowds is equivalent to the barbarian state, or to a return to it. It is by the acquisition of a solidly constituted collective spirit that the race frees itself to a greater and greater extent from the unreflecting power of crowds, and emerges from the barbarian state. The only important classification to be made of heterogeneous crowds, apart from that based on racial considerations, is to separate them into anonymous crowds, such as street crowds, and crowds not anonymous — deliberative assemblies and juries, for example. The sentiment of responsibility absent from crowds of the first description and developed in those of the second often gives a very different tendency to their respective acts.

2. Homogeneous Crowds.

Homogeneous crowds include: 1. Sects; 2. Castes; 3. Classes.

The *sect* represents the first step in the process of organisation of homogeneous crowds. A sect includes individuals differing greatly as to their education, their professions, and the class of society to which they belong, and with their common beliefs as the connecting link. Examples in point are religious and political sects.

The *caste* represents the highest degree of organisation of which the crowd is susceptible. While the sect includes individuals of very different professions, degrees of education and social surrounding, who are only linked together by the beliefs they hold in common, the caste is composed of individuals of the same profession, and in consequence similarly educated and of much the same social status. Examples in point are the military and priestly castes.

The *class* is formed of individuals of diverse origin, linked together not by a community of beliefs, as are the members of a sect, or by common professional occupations, as are the members of a caste, but by certain interests and certain habits of life and education almost identical. The middle class and the agricultural class are examples.

Being only concerned in this work with heterogeneous crowds, and reserving the study of homogeneous crowds (sects, castes, and classes) for another volume, I shall not insist here on the characteristics of crowds of this latter kind. I shall conclude this study of heterogeneous crowds by the examination of a few typical and distinct categories of crowds.

Chapter II. Crowds Termed Criminal Crowds.

Owing to the fact that crowds, after a period of excitement, enter upon a purely automatic and unconscious state, in which they are guided by suggestion, it seems difficult to qualify them in any case as criminal. I only retain this erroneous qualification because it has been definitely brought into vogue by recent psychological investigations. Certain acts of crowds are assuredly criminal, if considered merely in themselves, but criminal in that case in the same way as the act of a tiger devouring a Hindoo, after allowing its young to maul him for their amusement.

The usual motive of the crimes of crowds is a powerful suggestion, and the individuals who take part in such crimes are afterwards convinced that they have acted in obedience to duty, which is far from being the case with the ordinary criminal.

The history of the crimes committed by crowds illustrates what precedes.

The murder of M. de Launay, the governor of the Bastille, may be cited as a typical example. After the taking of the fortress the governor, surrounded by a very excited crowd, was dealt blows from every direction. It was proposed to hang him, to cut off his head, to tie him to a horse's tail. While struggling, he accidently kicked one of those present. Some one proposed, and his suggestion was at once received with acclamation by the crowd, that the individual who had been kicked should cut the governor's throat.

"The individual in question, a cook out of work, whose chief reason for being at the Bastille was idle curiosity as to what was going on, esteems, that since such is the general opinion, the action is patriotic and even believes he deserves a medal for having destroyed a monster. With a sword that is lent him he strikes the bared neck, but the weapon being somewhat blunt and not cutting, he takes from his pocket a small black-handled knife and (in his capacity of cook he would be experienced in cutting up meat) successfully effects the operation."

The working of the process indicated above is clearly seen in this example. We have obedience to a suggestion, which is all the stronger because of its collective origin, and the murderer's conviction that he has committed a very meritorious act, a conviction the more natural seeing that he enjoys the unanimous approval of his fellow-citizens. An act of this kind may be considered crime legally but not psychologically.

The general characteristics of criminal crowds are precisely the same as those we have met with in all crowds: openness to suggestion, credulity, mobility, the exaggeration of the sentiments good or bad, the manifestation of certain forms of morality, &c.

We shall find all these characteristics present in a crowd which has left behind it in French history the most sinister memories — the crowd which perpetrated the September massacres. In point of fact it offers much similarity with the crowd that committed the Saint Bartholomew massacres. I borrow the details from the narration of M. Taine, who took them from contemporary sources.

It is not known exactly who gave the order or made the suggestion to empty the prisons bymassacring the prisoners. Whether it was Danton, as is probable, or another does not matter; the one interesting fact for us is the powerful suggestion received by the crowd charged with the massacre.

The crowd of murderers numbered some three hundred persons, and was a perfectly typical heterogeneous crowd. With the exception of a very small number of professional scoundrels, it was composed in the main of shopkeepers and artisans of every trade: bootmakers, locksmiths, hairdressers, masons, clerks, messengers, &c. Under the influence of the suggestion received they are perfectly convinced, as was the cook referred to above, that they are accomplishing a patriotic duty. They fill a double office, being at once judge and executioner, but they do not for a moment regard themselves as criminals.

Deeply conscious of the importance of their duty, they begin by forming a sort of tribunal, and in connection with this act the ingenuousness of crowds and their rudimentary conception of justice are seen immediately. In consideration of the large number of the accused, it is decided that, to begin with, the nobles, priests, officers, and members of the king's household — in a word, all the individuals whose mere profession is proof of their guilt in the eyes of a good patriot — shall be slaughtered in a body, there being no need for a special decision in their case. The remainder shall be judged on their personal appearance and their reputation. In this way the rudimentary conscience of the crowd is satisfied. It will now be able to proceed legally with the massacre, and to give free scope to those instincts of ferocity whose genesis I have set forth elsewhere, they being instincts which collectivities always have it in them to develop to a high degree. These instincts, however — as is regularly the case in crowds — will not prevent the manifestation of other and contrary sentiments, such as a tenderheartedness often as extreme as the ferocity.

"They have the expansive sympathy and prompt sensibility of the Parisian working man. At the Abbaye, one of the federates, learning that the prisoners had been left without water for twenty-six hours, was bent on putting the gaoler to death, and would have done so but for the prayers of the prisoners themselves. When a prisoner is acquitted (by the improvised tribunal) every one, guards and slaughterers included, embraces him with transports of joy and applauds frantically," after which the wholesale massacre is recommenced. During its progress a pleasant gaiety never ceases to reign. There is dancing and singing around the corpses, and benches are arranged "for the ladies," delighted to witness the killing of aristocrats. The exhibition continues, moreover, of a special description of justice.

A slaughterer at the Abbaye having complained that the ladies placed at a little distance saw badly, and that only a few of those present had the pleasure of striking the aristocrats, the justice of the observation is admitted, and it is decided that the victims shall be made to pass slowly between two rows of slaughterers, who shall be under the obligation to strike with the back of the sword only so as to prolong the agony. At the prison de la Force the victims are stripped stark naked and literally "carved" for half an hour, after which, when every one has had a good view, they are finished off by a blow that lays bare their entrails.

The slaughterers, too, have their scruples and exhibit that moral sense whose existence in crowds we have already pointed out. They refuse to appropriate the money and jewels of the victims, taking them to the table of the committees.

Those rudimentary forms of reasoning, characteristic of the mind of crowds, are always to be traced in all their acts. Thus, after the slaughter of the 1,200 or 1,500 enemies of the nation, some one makes the remark, and his suggestion is at once adopted, that the other prisons, those containing aged beggars, vagabonds, and young prisoners, hold in reality useless mouths, of which it would be well on that account to get rid. Besides, among them there should certainly be enemies of the people, a woman of the name of Delarue, for instance, the widow of a poisoner:

"She must be furious at being in prison, if she could she would set fire to Paris: she must have said so, she has said so. Another good riddance." The demonstration appears convincing, and the prisoners are massacred without exception, included in the number being some fifty children of from twelve to seventeen years of age, who, of course, might themselves have become enemies of the nation, and of whom in consequence it was clearly well to be rid.

At the end of a week's work, all these operations being brought to an end, the slaughterers can think of reposing themselves. Profoundly convinced that they have deserved well of their country, they went to the authorities and demanded a recompense. The most zealous went so far as to claim a medal.

The history of the Commune of 1871 affords several facts analogous to those which precede. Given the growing influence of crowds and the successive capitulations before them of those in authority, we are destined to witness many others of a like nature.

Chapter III. Criminal Juries.

Being unable to study here every category of jury, I shall only examine the most important — that of the juries of the Court of Assize. These juries afford an excellent example of the heterogeneous crowd that is not anonymous. We shall find them display suggestibility and but slight capacity for reasoning, while they are open to the influence of the leaders of crowds, and they are guided in the main by unconscious sentiments. In the course of this investigation we shall have occasion to observe some interesting examples of the errors that may be made by persons not versed in the psychology of crowds.

Juries, in the first place, furnish us a good example of the slight importance of the mental level of the different elements composing a crowd, so far as the decisions it comes to are concerned. We have seen that when a deliberative assembly is called upon to give its opinion on a question of a character not entirely technical, intelligence stands for nothing. For instance, a gathering of scientific men or of artists, owing to the mere fact that they form an assemblage, will not deliver judgments on general subjects sensibly different from those rendered by a gathering of masons or grocers. At various periods, and in particular previous to 1848, the French administration instituted a careful choice among the persons summoned to form a jury, picking the jurors from among the enlightened classes; choosing professors, functionaries, men of letters, &c. At the present day jurors are recruited for the most part from among small tradesmen, petty capitalists, and employés. Yet, to the great astonishment of specialist writers, whatever the composition of the jury has been, its decisions have been identical. Even the magistrates, hostile as they are to the institution of the jury, have had to recognise the exactness of the assertion. M. Bérard des Glajeux, a former President of the Court of Assizes, expresses himself on the subject in his "Memoirs" in the following terms: —

"The selection of jurymen is to-day in reality in the hands of the municipal councillors, who put people down on the list or eliminate them from it in accordance with the political and electoral preoccupations inherent in their situation.... The majority of the jurors chosen are persons engaged in trade, but persons of less importance than formerly, and employés belonging to certain branches of the administration.... Both opinions and professions counting for nothing once the rôle of judge assumed, many of the jurymen having the ardour of neophytes, and men of the best intentions being similarly disposed in humble situations, the spirit of the jury has not changed: its verdicts have remained the same."

Of the passage just cited the conclusions, which are just, are to be borne in mind and not the explanations, which are weak. Too much astonishment should not be felt at this weakness, for, as a rule, counsel equally with magistrates seem to be ignorant of the psychology of crowds and, in consequence, of juries. I find a proof of this statement in a fact related by the author just quoted. He remarks that Lachaud, one of the most illustrious barristers practising in the Court of Assize, made systematic use of his right to object to a juror in the case of all individuals of intelligence on the list. Yet experience — and experience alone — has ended by acquainting us with the utter uselessness of these objections. This is proved by the fact that at the present day public prosecutors and barristers, at any rate those belonging to the Parisian bar, have entirely renounced their right to object to a juror; still, as M. des Glajeux remarks, the verdicts have not changed, "they are neither better nor worse."

Like all crowds, juries are very strongly impressed by sentimental considerations, and very slightly by argument. "They cannot resist the sight," writes a barrister, "of a mother giving its

child the breast, or of orphans." "It is
sufficient that a woman should be of agreeable appearance," says M. des Glajeux, "to win the benevolence of the jury."

Without pity for crimes of which it appears possible they might themselves be the victims — such crimes, moreover, are the most dangerous for society

— juries, on the contrary, are very indulgent in the case of breaches of the law whose motive is passion. They are rarely severe on infanticide by girl-mothers, or hard on the young woman who throws vitriol at the man who has seduced and deserted her, for the reason that they feel instinctively that society runs but slight danger from such crimes[24], and that in a country in which the law does not protect deserted girls the crime of the girl who avenges herself is rather useful than harmful, inasmuch as it frightens future seducers in advance.

Juries, like all crowds, are profoundly impressed by prestige, and President des Glajeux very properly remarks that, very democratic as juries are in their composition, they are very aristocratic in their likes and dislikes: "Name, birth, great wealth, celebrity, the assistance of an illustrious counsel, everything in the nature of distinction or that lends brilliancy to the accused, stands him in extremely good stead."

The chief concern of a good counsel should be to work upon the feelings of the jury, and, as with all crowds, to argue but little, or only to employ rudimentary modes of reasoning. An English barrister, famous for his successes in the assize courts, has well set forth the line of action to be followed: —

"While pleading he would attentively observe the jury. The most favourable opportunity has been reached. By dint of insight and experience the counsel reads the effect of each phrase on the faces of the jurymen, and draws his conclusions in consequence. His first step is to be sure which members of the jury are already favourable to his cause. It is short work to definitely gain their adhesion, and having done so he turns his attention to the members who seem, on the contrary, ill-disposed, and endeavours to discover why they are hostile to the accused. This is the delicate part of his task, for there may be an infinity of reasons for condemning a man, apart from the sentiment of justice."

These few lines résumé the entire mechanism of the art of oratory, and we see why the speech prepared in advance has so slight an effect, it being necessary to be able to modify the terms employed from moment to moment in accordance with the impression produced.

The orator does not require to convert to his views all the members of a jury, but only the leading spirits among it who will determine the general opinion. As in all crowds, so in juries there are a small number of individuals who serve as guides to the rest. "I have found by experience," says the counsel cited above, "that one or two energetic men suffice to carry the

---

[24] It is to be remarked, in passing, that this division of crimes into those dangerous and those not dangerous for society, which is well and instinctively made by juries is far from being unjust. The object of criminal laws is evidently to protect society against dangerous criminals and not to avenge it.
On the other hand, the French code, and above all the minds of the French magistrates, are still deeply imbued
with the spirit of vengeance characteristic of the old primitive law, and the term "vindicte " (prosecution, from the
Latin vindicta, vengeance) is still in daily use. A proof of this tendency on the part of the magistrates is found in the refusal by many of them to apply Bérenger's law, which allows of a condemned person not undergoing his sentence unless he repeats his crime. Yet no magistrate can be ignorant, for the fact is proved by statistics, that
the application of a punishment inflicted for the first time infallibly leads to further crime on the part of the person
punished. When judges set free a sentenced person it always seems to them that society has not been avenged.
Rather than not avenge it they prefer to create a dangerous, confirmed criminal.

rest of the jury with them." It is those two or three whom it is necessary to convince by skilful suggestions. First of all, and above all, it is necessary to please them. The man forming part of a crowd whom one has succeeded in pleasing is on the point of being convinced, and is quite disposed to accept as excellent any arguments that may be offered him. I detach the following anecdote from an interesting account of M. Lachaud, alluded to above: —

"It is well known that during all the speeches he would deliver in the course of an assize sessions, Lachaud never lost sight of the two or three jurymen whom he knew or felt to be influential but obstinate. As a rule he was successful in winning over these refractory jurors. On one occasion, however, in the provinces, he had to deal with a juryman whom he plied in vain for three-quarters of an hour with his most cunning arguments; the man was the seventh juryman, the first on the second bench. The case was desperate. Suddenly, in the middle of a passionate demonstration, Lachaud stopped short, and addressing the President of the court said: 'Would you give instructions for the curtain there in front to be drawn? The seventh juryman is blinded by the sun.' The juryman in question reddened, smiled, and expressed his thanks. He was won over for the defence."

Many writers, some of them most distinguished, have started of late a strong campaign against the institution of the jury, although it is the only protection we have against the errors, really very frequent, of a caste that is under no control[25]. A portion of these writers advocate a jury recruited solely from the ranks of the enlightened classes; but we have already proved that even in this case the verdicts would be identical with those returned under the present system. Other writers, taking their stand on the errors committed by juries, would abolish the jury and replace it by judges. It is difficult to see how these would-be reformers can forget that the errors for which the jury is blamed were committed in the first instance by judges, and that when the accused person comes before a jury he has already been held to be guilty by several magistrates, by the *juge d'instruction*, the public prosecutor, and the Court of Arraignment. It should thus be clear that were the accused to be definitely judged by magistrates instead of by jurymen, he would lose his only chance of being admitted innocent. The errors of juries have always been first of all the errors of magistrates. It is solely the magistrates, then, who should be blamed when particularly monstrous judicial errors crop up, such, for instance, as the quite recent condemnation of Dr. L —— who, prosecuted by a *juge d'instruction*, of excessive stupidity, on the strength of the denunciation of a half-idiot girl, who accused the doctor of having performed an illegal operation upon her for thirty francs, would have been sent to penal servitude but for an explosion of public indignation, which had for result that he was immediately set at liberty by the Chief of the State. The honourable character given the condemned man by all his fellow-citizens made the grossness of the blunder self-evident. The magistrates themselves admitted it, and yet out of caste considerations they did all they could to prevent the pardon being signed. In all similar affairs the jury, confronted with technical details it is unable to understand, naturally hearkens to the public prosecutor, arguing that, after all, the affair has been investigated by

---

[25] The magistracy is, in point of fact, the only administration whose acts are under no control. In spite of all its revolutions, democratic France does not possess that right of habeas corpus of which England is so proud. We have banished all the tyrants, but have set up a magistrate in each city who disposes at will of the honour and liberty of the citizens. An insignificant juge d'instruction (an examining magistrate who has no exact counterpart in England. — Trans.), fresh from the university, possesses the revolting power of sending to prison at will persons of the most considerable standing, on a simple supposition on his part of their guilt, and without being obliged to justify his act to any one. Under the pretext of pursuing his investigation he can keep these persons in prison for six months or even a year, and free them at last without owing them either an indemnity or excuses. The warrant in France is the exact equivalent of the lettre de cachet, with this difference, that the latter, with the use of which the monarchy was so justly reproached, could only be resorted to by persons occupying a very high position, while the warrant is an instrument in the hands of a whole class of citizens which is far from passing for being very enlightened or very independent.

magistrates trained to unravel the most intricate situations. Who, then, are the real authors of the error — the jurymen or the magistrates? We should cling vigorously to the jury. It constitutes, perhaps, the only category of crowd that cannot be replaced by any individuality. It alone can temper the severity of the law, which, equal for all, ought in principle to be blind and to take no cognisance of particular cases. Inaccessible to pity, and heeding nothing but the text of the law, the judge in his professional severity would visit with the same penalty the burglar guilty of murder and the wretched girl whom poverty and her abandonment by her seducer have driven to infanticide. The jury, on the other hand, instinctively feels that the seduced girl is much less guilty than the seducer, who, however, is not touched by the law, and that she deserves every indulgence.

Being well acquainted with the psychology of castes, and also with the psychology of other categories of crowds, I do not perceive a single case in which, wrongly accused of a crime, I should not prefer to have to deal with a jury rather than with magistrates. I should have some chance that my innocence would be recognised by the former and not the slightest chance that it would be admitted by the latter. The power of crowds is to be dreaded, but the power of certain castes is to be dreaded yet more. Crowds are open to conviction; castes never are.

Chapter IV. Electoral Crowds.

Electoral crowds — that is to say, collectivities invested with the power of electing the holders of certain functions — constitute heterogeneous crowds, but as their action is confined to a single clearly determined matter, namely, to choosing between different candidates, they present only a few of the characteristics previously described. Of the characteristics peculiar to crowds, they display in particular but slight aptitude for reasoning, the absence of the critical spirit, irritability, credulity, and simplicity. In their decision, moreover, is to be traced the influence of the leaders of crowds and the part played by the factors we have enumerated: affirmation, repetition, prestige, and contagion.

Let us examine by what methods electoral crowds are to be persuaded. It will be easy to deduce their psychology from the methods that are most successful.

It is of primary importance that the candidate should possess prestige. Personal prestige can only be replaced by that resulting from wealth. Talent and even genius are not elements of success of serious importance.

Of capital importance, on the other hand, is the necessity for the candidate of possessing prestige, of being able, that is, to force himself upon the electorate without discussion. The reason why the electors, of whom a majority are working men or peasants, so rarely choose a man from their own ranks to represent them is that such a person enjoys no prestige among them. When, by chance, they do elect a man who is their equal, it is as a rule for subsidiary reasons — for instance, to spite an eminent man, or an influential employer of labour on whom the elector is in daily dependence, and whose master he has the illusion he becomes in this way for a moment.

The possession of prestige does not suffice, however, to assure the success of a candidate. The elector stickles in particular for the flattery of his greed and vanity. He must be overwhelmed with the most extravagant blandishments, and there must be no hesitation in making him the most fantastic promises. If he is a working man it is impossible to go too far in insulting and stigmatising employers of labour. As for the rival candidate, an effort must be made to destroy his chance by establishing by dint of affirmation, repetition, and contagion that he is an arrant scoundrel, and that it is a matter of common knowledge that he has been guilty of several crimes. It is, of course, useless to trouble about any semblance of proof. Should the adversary be ill-acquainted with the psychology of crowds he will try to justify himself by arguments instead of confining himself to replying to one set of affirmations by another; and he will have no chance whatever of being successful.

The candidate's written programme should not be too categorical, since later on his adversaries might bring it up against him; in his verbal programme, however, there cannot be too much exaggeration. The most important reforms may be fearlessly promised. At the moment they are made these exaggerations produce a great effect, and they are not binding for the future, it being a matter of constant observation that the elector never troubles himself to know how far the candidate he has returned has followed out the electoral programme he applauded, and in virtue of which the election was supposed to have been secured.

In what precedes, all the factors of persuasion which we have described are to be recognised. We shall come across them again in the action exerted by words and formulas, whose magical sway we have already insisted upon. An orator who knows how to make use of these means of persuasion can do what he will with a crowd. Expressions such as infamous capital, vile exploiters, the admirable working man, the socialisation of wealth, &c., always produce the same effect, although already somewhat worn by use. But the candidate who hits on a new formula as devoid as possible of precise meaning, and apt in consequence to flatter the most varied aspirations, infallibly obtains a success. The sanguinary Spanish revolution of 1873 was brought about by one of these magical phrases of complex meaning on which everybody can put his own interpretation. A contemporary writer has described the launching of this phrase in terms that deserve to be quoted: —

"The radicals have made the discovery that a centralised republic is a monarchy in disguise, and to humour them the Cortes had unanimously proclaimed a federal republic, though none of the voters could have explained what it was he had just voted for. This formula, however, delighted everybody; the joy was intoxicating, delirious. The reign of virtue and happiness had just been inaugurated on earth. A republican whose opponent refused him the title of federalist considered himself to be mortally insulted. People addressed each other in the streets with the words: `Long live the federal republic!' After which the praises were sung of the mystic virtue of the absence of discipline in the army, and of the autonomy of the soldiers. What was understood by the `federal republic?' There were those who took it to mean the emancipation of the provinces, institutions akin to those of the United States and administrative decentralisation; others had in view the abolition of all authority and the speedy commencement of the great social liquidation. The socialists of Barcelona and Andalusia stood out for the absolute sovereignty of the communes; they proposed to endow Spain with ten thousand independent municipalities, to legislate on their own account, and their creation to be accompanied by the suppression of the police and the army. In the southern provinces the insurrection was soon seen to spread from town to town and village to village.

Directly a village had made its pronunciamento its first care was to destroy the telegraph wires and the railway lines so as to cut off all communication with its neighbours and Madrid. The sorriest hamlet was determined to stand on its own bottom. Federation had given place to cantonalism, marked by massacres, incendiarism, and every description of brutality, and bloody saturnalia were celebrated throughout the length and breadth of the land."

With respect to the influence that may be exerted by reasoning on the minds of electors, to harbour the least doubt on this subject can only be the result of never having read the reports of an electioneering meeting. In such a gathering affirmations, invectives, and sometimes blows are exchanged, but never arguments. Should silence be established for a moment it is because some one present, having the reputation of a "tough customer," has announced that he is about to heckle the candidate by putting him one of those embarrassing questions which are always the joy of the audience. The satisfaction, however, of the opposition party is shortlived, for the voice of the questioner is soon drowned in the uproar made by his adversaries. The following reports of public meetings, chosen from hundreds of similar examples, and taken from the daily papers, may be considered as typical: —

"One of the organisers of the meeting having asked the assembly to elect a president, the storm bursts. The anarchists leap on to the platform to take the committee table by storm. The socialists make an energetic defence; blows are exchanged, and each party accuses the other of being spies in the pay of the Government, &c.... A citizen leaves the hall with a black eye.

"The committee is at length installed as best it may be in the midst of the tumult, and the right to speak devolves upon `Comrade' X.

"The orator starts a vigorous attack on the socialists, who interrupt him with shouts of `Idiot, scoundrel, blackguard!' &c., epithets to which Comrade X. replies by setting forth a theory according to which the socialists are `idiots' or `jokers.'"

"The Allemanist party had organised yesterday evening, in the Hall of Commerce, in the Rue du Faubourg-du-Temple, a great meeting, preliminary to the workers' fête of the 1st of May. The watchword of the meeting was 'Calm and Tranquillity!'

"Comrade G — — alludes to the socialists as 'idiots' and 'humbugs.'

"At these words there is an exchange of invectives and orators and audience come to blows. Chairs, tables, and benches are converted into weapons," &c., &c.

It is not to be imagined for a moment that this description of discussion is peculiar to a determined class of electors and dependent on their social position. In every anonymous assembly whatever, though it be composed exclusively of highly educated persons, discussion always assumes the same shape. I have shown that when men are collected in a crowd there is a tendency towards their mental levelling at work, and proof of this is to be found at every turn. Take, for example, the following extract from a report of a meeting composed exclusively of students, which I borrow from the Temps of 13th of February, 1895: —

"The tumult only increased as the evening went on; I do not believe that a single orator succeeded in uttering two sentences without being interrupted. At every instant there came shouts from this or that direction or from every direction at once. Applause was intermingled with hissing, violent discussions were in progress between individual members of the audience, sticks were brandished threateningly, others beat a tattoo on the floor, and the interrupters were greeted with yells of 'Put him out!' or 'Let him speak!'

"M. C — — lavished such epithets as odious and cowardly, monstrous, vile, venal and vindictive, on the Association, which he declared he wanted to destroy," &c., &c.

How, it may be asked, can an elector form an opinion under such conditions? To put such a question is to harbour a strange delusion as to the measure of liberty that may be enjoyed by a collectivity. Crowds have opinions that have been imposed upon them, but they never boast reasoned opinions. In the case under consideration the opinions and votes of the electors are in the hands of the election committees, whose leading spirits are, as a rule, publicans, their influence over the working men, to whom they allow credit, being great. "Do you know what an election committee is?" writes M. Schérer, one of the most

valiant champions of present-day democracy. "It is neither more nor less than the corner-stone of our institutions, the masterpiece of the political machine. France is governed to-day by the election committees[26]."

To exert an influence over them is not difficult, provided the candidate be in himself acceptable and possess adequate financial resources. According to the admissions of the donors, three millions of francs sufficed to secure the repeated elections of General Boulanger.

Such is the psychology of electoral crowds. It is identical with that of other crowds: neither better nor worse.

In consequence I draw no conclusion against universal suffrage from what precedes. Had I to settle its fate, I should preserve it as it is for practical reasons, which are to be deduced in point of fact from our investigation of the psychology of crowds. On this account I shall proceed to set them forth.

---

[26] Committees under whatever name, clubs, syndicates, &c., constitute perhaps the most redoubtable danger resulting from the power of crowds. They represent in reality the most impersonal and, in consequence, the most oppressive form of tyranny. The leaders who direct the committees being supposed to speak and act in the name of a collectivity, are freed from all responsibility, and are in a position to do just as they choose. The most savage tyrant has never ventured even to dream of such proscriptions as those ordained by the committees of the Revolution. Barras has declared that they decimated the convention, picking off its members at their pleasure. So long as he was able to speak in their name, Robespierre wielded absolute power. The moment this frightful dictator separated himself from them, for reasons of personal pride, he was lost. The reign of crowds is the reign of committees, that is, of the leaders of crowds. A severer despotism cannot be imagined.

No doubt the weak side of universal suffrage is too obvious to be overlooked. It cannot be gainsaid that civilisation has been the work of a small minority of superior intelligences constituting the culminating point of a pyramid, whose stages, widening in proportion to the decrease of mental power, represent the masses of a nation. The greatness of a civilisation cannot assuredly depend upon the votes given by inferior elements boasting solely numerical strength. Doubtless, too, the votes recorded by crowds are often very dangerous. They have already cost us several invasions, and in view of the triumph of socialism, for which they are preparing the way, it is probable that the vagaries of popular sovereignty will cost us still more dearly.

Excellent, however, as these objections are in theory, in practice they lose all force, as will be admitted if the invincible strength be remembered of ideas transformed into dogmas. The dogma of the sovereignty of crowds is as little defensible, from the philosophical point of view, as the religious dogmas of the Middle Ages, but it enjoys at present the same absolute power they formerly enjoyed. It is as unattackable in consequence as in the past were our religious ideas. Imagine a modern freethinker miraculously transported into the midst of the Middle Ages. Do you suppose that, after having ascertained the sovereign power of the religious ideas that were then in force, he would have been tempted to attack them? Having fallen into the hands of a judge disposed to send him to the stake, under the imputation of having concluded a pact with the devil, or of having been present at the witches sabbath, would it have occurred to him to call in question the existence of the devil or of the sabbath? It were as wise to oppose cyclones with discussion as the beliefs of crowds. The dogma of universal suffrage possesses to-day the power the Christian dogmas formerly possessed. Orators and writers allude to it with a respect and adulation that never fell to the share of Louis XIV. In consequence the same position must be taken up with regard to it as with regard to all religious dogmas. Time alone can act upon them.

Besides, it would be the more useless to attempt to undermine this dogma, inasmuch as it has an appearance of reasonableness in its favour. "In an era of equality," Tocqueville justly remarks, "men have no faith in each other on account of their being all alike; yet this same similitude gives them an almost limitless confidence in the judgment of the public, the reason being that it does not appear probable that, all men being equally enlightened, truth and numerical superiority should not go hand in hand."

Must it be believed that with a restricted suffrage — a suffrage restricted to those intellectually capable if it be desired — an improvement would be effected in the votes of crowds? I cannot admit for a moment that this would be the case, and that for the reasons I have already given touching the mental inferiority of all collectivities, whatever their composition. In a crowd men always tend to the same level, and, on general questions, a vote, recorded by forty academicians is no better than that of forty water-carriers. I do not in the least believe that any of the votes for which universal suffrage is blamed — the re-establishment of the Empire, for instance — would have fallen out differently had the voters been exclusively recruited among learned and liberally educated men. It does not follow because an individual knows Greek or mathematics, is an architect, a veterinary surgeon, a doctor, or a barrister, that he is endowed with a special intelligence of social questions. All our political economists are highly educated, being for the most part professors or academicians, yet is there a single general question — protection, bimetallism, &c. — on which they have succeeded in agreeing? The explanation is that their science is only a very attenuated form of our universal ignorance. With regard to social problems, owing to the number of unknown quantities they offer, men are substantially, equally ignorant.

In consequence, were the electorate solely composed of persons stuffed with sciences their votes would be no better than those emitted at present. They would be guided in the main by their sentiments and by party spirit. We should be spared none of the difficulties we now have to contend with, and we should certainly be subjected to the oppressive tyranny of castes.

Whether the suffrage of crowds be restricted or general, whether it be exercised under a republic or a monarchy, in France, in Belgium, in Greece, in Portugal, or in Spain, it is everywhere identical; and, when all is said and done, it is the expression of the unconscious aspirations and needs of the race.

In each country the average opinions of those elected represent the genius of the race, and they will be found not to alter sensibly from one generation to another.

It is seen, then, that we are confronted once more by the fundamental notion of race, which we have come across so often, and on this other notion, which is the outcome of the first, that institutions and governments play but a small part in the life of a people. Peoples are guided in the main by the genius of their race, that is, by that inherited residue of qualities of which the genius is the sum total. Race and the slavery of our daily necessities are the mysterious master-causes that rule our destiny.

Chapter V. Parliamentary Assemblies.

In parliamentary assemblies we have an example of heterogeneous crowds that are not anonymous. Although the mode of election of their members varies from epoch to epoch, and from nation to nation, they present very similar characteristics. In this case the influence of the race makes itself felt to weaken or exaggerate the characteristics common to crowds, but not to prevent their manifestation. The parliamentary assemblies of the most widely different countries, of Greece, Italy, Portugal, Spain, France, and America present great analogies in their debates and votes, and leave the respective governments face to face with identical difficulties.

Moreover, the parliamentary system represents the ideal of all modern civilised peoples. The system is the expression of the idea, psychologically erroneous, but generally admitted, that a large gathering of men is much more capable than a small number of coming to a wise and independent decision on a given subject.

The general characteristics of crowds are to be met with in parliamentary assemblies: intellectual simplicity, irritability, suggestibility, the exaggeration of the sentiments and the preponderating influence of a few leaders. In consequence, however, of their special composition parliamentary crowds offer some distinctive features, which we shall point out shortly.

Simplicity in their opinions is one of their most important characteristics. In the case of all parties, and more especially so far as the Latin peoples are concerned, an invariable tendency is met with in crowds of this kind to solve the most complicated social problems by the simplest abstract principles and general laws applicable to all cases. Naturally the principles vary with the party; but owing to the mere fact that the individual members are a part of a crowd, they are always inclined to exaggerate the worth of their principles, and to push them to their extreme consequences. In consequence parliaments are more especially representative of extreme opinions.

The most perfect example of the ingenuous simplification of opinions peculiar to assemblies is offered by the Jacobins of the French Revolution. Dogmatic and logical to a man, and their brains full of vague generalities, they busied themselves with the application of fixed-principles without concerning themselves with events. It has been said of them, with reason, that they went through the Revolution without witnessing it. With the aid of the very simple dogmas that served them as guide, they imagined they could recast society from top to bottom, and cause a highly refined civilisation to return to a very anterior phase of the social evolution. The methods they resorted to to realise their dream wore the same stamp of absolute ingenuousness. They confined themselves, in reality, to destroying what stood in their way.

All of them, moreover — Girondists, the Men of the Mountain, the Thermidorians, &c. — were alike animated by the same spirit.

Parliamentary crowds are very open to suggestion; and, as in the case of all crowds, the suggestion comes from leaders possessing prestige; but the suggestibility of parliamentary assemblies has very clearly defined limits, which it is important to point out.

On all questions of local or regional interest every member of an assembly has fixed, unalterable opinions, which no amount of argument can shake. The talent of a Demosthenes would be powerless to change the vote of a Deputy on such questions as protection or the privilege of distilling alcohol, questions in which the interests of influential electors are involved. The suggestion emanating from these electors and undergone before the time to vote arrives, sufficiently outweighs suggestions from any other source to annul them and to maintain an absolute fixity of opinion[27].

On general questions — the overthrow of a Cabinet, the imposition of a tax, &c. — there is no longer any fixity of opinion, and the suggestions of leaders can exert an influence, though not in quite the same way as in an ordinary crowd. Every party has its leaders, who possess occasionally an equal influence. The result is that the Deputy finds himself placed between two contrary suggestions, and is inevitably made to hesitate. This explains how it is that he is often seen to vote in contrary fashion in an interval of a quarter of an hour or to add to a law an article which nullifies it; for instance, to withdraw from employers of labour the right of choosing and dismissing their workmen, and then to very nearly annul this measure by an amendment.

It is for the same reason that every Chamber that is returned has some very stable opinions, and other opinions that are very shifting. On the whole, the general questions being the more numerous, indecision is predominant in the Chamber — the indecision which results from the ever-present fear of the elector, the suggestion received from whom is always latent, and tends to counterbalance the influence of the leaders.

Still, it is the leaders who are definitely the masters in those numerous discussions, with regard to the subject-matter of which the members of an assembly are without strong preconceived opinions.

The necessity for these leaders is evident, since, under the name of heads of groups, they are met with in the assemblies of every country. They are the real rulers of an assembly. Men forming a crowd cannot do without a master, whence it results that the votes of an assembly only represent, as a rule, the opinions of a small minority.

The influence of the leaders is due in very small measure to the arguments they employ, but in a large degree to their prestige. The best proof of this is that, should they by any circumstance lose their prestige, their influence disappears.

The prestige of these political leaders is individual, and independent of name or celebrity: a fact of which M. Jules Simon gives us some very curious examples in his remarks on the prominent men of the Assembly of 1848, of which he was a member: —

"Two months before he was all-powerful, Louis Napoleon was entirely without the least importance.

"Victor Hugo mounted the tribune. He failed to achieve success. He was listened to as Félix Pyat was listened to, but he did not obtain as much applause. `I don't like his ideas,' Vaulabelle said to me, speaking of Félix Pyat,' but he is one of the greatest writers and the greatest orator of France.' Edgar Quinet, in spite of his exceptional and powerful intelligence, was held in no esteem whatever. He had been popular for awhile before the opening of the Assembly; in the Assembly he had no popularity.

"The splendour of genius makes itself less felt in political assemblies than anywhere else. They only give heed to eloquence appropriate to the time and place and to party services, not to services rendered the country. For homage to be rendered Lamartine in 1848 and Thiers in 1871, the stimulant was needed of urgent, inexorable interest. As soon as the danger was passed the

---

[27]The following reflection of an English parliamentarian of long experience doubtless applies to these opinions, fixed beforehand, and rendered unalterable by electioneering necessities: "During the fifty years that I have sat at Westminster, I have listened to thousands of speeches; but few of them have changed my opinion, not one of them has changed my vote."

parliamentary world forgot in the same instant its gratitude and its fright."

I have quoted the preceding passage for the sake of the facts it contains, not of the explanations it offers, their psychology being somewhat poor. A crowd would at once lose its character of a crowd were it to credit its leaders with their services, whether of a party nature or rendered their country. The crowd that obeys a leader is under the influence of his prestige, and its submission is not dictated by any sentiment of interest or gratitude.

In consequence the leader endowed with sufficient prestige wields almost absolute power. The immense influence exerted during a long series of years, thanks to his prestige, by a celebrated Deputy[28], beaten at the last general election in consequence of certain financial events, is well known. He had only to give the signal and Cabinets were overthrown. A writer has clearly indicated the scope of his action in the following lines: —

"It is due, in the main, to M. X —— that we paid three times as dearly as we should have done for Tonkin, that we remained so long on a precarious footing in Madagascar, that we were defrauded of an empire in the region of the Lower Niger, and that we have lost the preponderating situation we used to occupy in Egypt. The theories of M. X —— have cost us more territories than the disasters of Napoleon I."

We must not harbour too bitter a grudge against the leader in question. It is plain that he has cost us very dear; but a great part of his influence was due to the fact that he followed public opinion, which, in colonial matters, was far from being at the time what it has since become. A leader is seldom in advance of public opinion; almost always all he does is to follow it and to espouse all its errors.

The means of persuasion of the leaders we are dealing with, apart from their prestige, consist in the factors we have already enumerated several times. To make a skilful use of these resources a leader must have arrived at a comprehension, at least in an unconscious manner, of the psychology of crowds, and must know how to address them. He should be aware, in particular, of the fascinating influence of words, phrases, and images. He should possess a special description of eloquence, composed of energetic affirmations — unburdened with proofs — and impressive images, accompanied by very summary arguments. This is a kind of eloquence that is met with in all assemblies, the English Parliament included, the most serious though it is of all.

"Debates in the House of Commons," says the English philosopher Maine, "may be constantly read in which the entire discussion is confined to an exchange of rather weak generalities and rather violent personalities. General formulas of this description exercise a prodigious influence on the imagination of a pure democracy. It will always be easy to make a crowd accept general assertions, presented in striking terms, although they have never been verified, and are perhaps not susceptible of verification."

Too much importance cannot be attached to the "striking terms" alluded to in the above quotation. We have already insisted, on several occasions, on the special power of words and formulas. They must be chosen in such a way as to evoke very vivid images. The following phrase, taken from a speech by one of the leaders of our assemblies, affords an excellent example: —

"When the same vessel shall bear away to the fever-haunted lands of our penitentiary settlements the politician of shady reputation and the anarchist guilty of murder, the pair will be able to converse together, and they will appear to each other as the two complementary aspects of one and the same state of society."

The image thus evoked is very vivid, and all the adversaries of the speaker felt themselves threatened by it. They conjured up a double vision of the fever-haunted country and the vessel

---

28   M. Clemenceau. — Note of the Translator.

that may carry them away; for is it not possible that they are included in the somewhat ill-defined category of the politicians menaced? They experienced the lurking fear that the men of the Convention must have felt whom the vague speeches of Robespierre threatened with the guillotine, and who, under the influence of this fear, invariably yielded to him.

It is all to the interest of the leaders to indulge in the most improbable exaggerations. The speaker of whom I have just cited a sentence was able to affirm, without arousing violent protestations, that bankers and priests had subsidised the throwers of bombs, and that the directors of the great financial companies deserve the same punishment as anarchists. Affirmations of this kind are always effective with crowds. The affirmation is never too violent, the declamation never too threatening. Nothing intimidates the audience more than this sort of eloquence. Those present are afraid that if they protest they will be put down as traitors or accomplices.

As I have said, this peculiar style of eloquence has ever been of sovereign effect in all assemblies. In times of crisis its power is still further accentuated. The speeches of the great orators of the assemblies of the French Revolution are very interesting reading from this point of view. At every instant they thought themselves obliged to pause in order to denounce crime and exalt virtue, after which they would burst forth into imprecations against tyrants, and swear to live free men or perish. Those present rose to their feet, applauded furiously, and then, calmed, took their seats again.

On occasion, the leader may be intelligent and highly educated, but the possession of these qualities does him, as a rule, more harm than good. By showing how complex things are, by allowing of explanation and promoting comprehension, intelligence always renders its owner indulgent, and blunts, in a large measure, that intensity and violence of conviction needful for apostles. The great leaders of crowds of all ages, and those of the Revolution in particular, have been of lamentably narrow intellect; while it is precisely those whose intelligence has been the most restricted who have exercised the greatest influence.

The speeches of the most celebrated of them, of Robespierre, frequently astound one by their incoherence: by merely reading them no plausible explanation is to be found of the great part played by the powerful dictator: —

"The commonplaces and redundancies of pedagogic eloquence and Latin culture at the service of a mind childish rather than undistinguished, and limited in its notions of attack and defence to the defiant attitude of schoolboys. Not an idea, not a happy turn of phrase, or a telling hit: a storm of declamation that leaves us bored. After a dose of this unexhilarating reading one is attempted to exclaim 'Oh!' with the amiable Camille Desmoulins."

It is terrible at times to think of the power that strong conviction combined with extreme narrowness of mind gives a man possessing prestige. It is none the less necessary that these conditions should be satisfied for a man to ignore obstacles and display strength of will in a high measure.

Crowds instinctively recognise in men of energy and conviction the masters they are always in need of.

In a parliamentary assembly the success of a speech depends almost solely on the prestige possessed by the speaker, and not at all on the arguments he brings forward. The best proof of this is that when for one cause or another a speaker loses his prestige, he loses simultaneously all his influence, that is, his power of influencing votes at will.

When an unknown speaker comes forward with a speech containing good arguments, but only arguments, the chances are that he will only obtain a hearing. A Deputy who is a psychologist of insight, M. Desaubes, has recently traced in the following lines the portrait of the Deputy who lacks prestige: —

"When he takes his place in the tribune he draws a document from his portfolio, spreads it out methodically before him, and makes a start with assurance.

"He flatters himself that he will implant in the minds of his audience the conviction by which he is himself animated. He has weighed and reweighed his arguments; he is well primed with figures and proofs; he is certain he will convince his hearers. In the face of the evidence he is to adduce all resistance would be futile. He begins, confident in the justice of his cause, and relying upon the attention of his colleagues, whose only anxiety, of course, is to subscribe to the truth.

"He speaks, and is at once surprised at the restlessness of the House, and a little annoyed by the noise that is being made.

"How is it silence is not kept? Why this general inattention? What are those Deputies thinking about who are engaged in conversation? What urgent motive has induced this or that Deputy to quit his seat?

"An expression of uneasiness crosses his face; he frowns and stops. Encouraged by the Presisident, he begins again, raising his voice. He is only listened to all the less. He lends emphasis to his words, and gesticulates: the noise around him increases. He can no longer hear himself, and again stops; finally, afraid that his silence may provoke the dreaded cry, 'The Closure!' he starts off again. The clamour becomes unbearable."

When parliamentary assemblies reach a certain pitch of excitement they become identical with ordinary heterogeneous crowds, and their sentiments in consequence present the peculiarity of being always extreme. They will be seen to commit acts of the greatest heroism or the worst excesses. The individual is no longer himself, and so entirely is this the case that he will vote measures most adverse to his personal interests.

The history of the French Revolution shows to what an extent assemblies are capable of losing their self-consciousness, and of obeying suggestions most contrary to their interests. It was an enormous sacrifice for the nobility to renounce its privileges, yet it did so without hesitation on a famous night during the sittings of the Constituant Assembly. By renouncing their inviolability the men of the Convention placed themselves under a perpetual menace of death and yet they took this step, and were not afraid to decimate their own ranks, though perfectly aware that the scaffold to which they were sending their colleagues to-day might be their own fate to-morrow. The truth is they had attained to that completely automatic state which I have described elsewhere, and no consideration would hinder them from yielding to the suggestions by which they were hypnotised. The following passage from the memoirs of one of them, Billaud-Varennes, is absolutely typical on this score: "The decisions with which we have been so reproached," he says, "were not desired by us two days, a single day before they were taken: it was the crisis and nothing else that gave rise to them." Nothing can be more accurate.

The same phenomena of unconsciousness were to be witnessed during all the stormy sittings of the Convention.

"They approved and decreed measures," says Taine, "which they held in horror — measures which were not only stupid and foolish, but measures that were crimes — the murder of innocent men, the murder of their friends. The Left, supported by the Right, unanimously and amid loud applause, sent to the scaffold Danton, its natural chief, and the great promoter and leader of the Revolution. Unanimously and amid the greatest applause the Right, supported by the Left, votes the worst decrees of the revolutionary government. Unanimously and amid cries of admiration and enthusiasm, amid demonstrations of passionate sympathy for Collot d'Herbois, Couthon, and Robespierre, the Convention by spontaneous and repeated re-elections keeps in office the homicidal government which the Plain detests because it is homicidal, and

103

the Mountain detests because it is decimated by it. The Plain and the Mountain, the majority and the minority, finish by consenting to help on their own suicide. The 22 Prairial the entire Convention offered itself to the executioner; the 8 Thermidor, during the first quarter of an hour that followed Robespierre's speech, it did the same thing again."

This picture may appear sombre. Yet it is accurate. Parliamentary assemblies, sufficiently excited and hypnotised, offer the same characteristics. They become an unstable flock, obedient to every impulsion. The following description of the Assembly of 1848 is due to M. Spuller, a parliamentarian whose faith in democracy is above suspicion. I reproduce it from the *Revue littéraire*, and it is thoroughly typical. It offers an example of all the exaggerated sentiments which I have described as characteristic of crowds, and of that excessive changeableness which permits of assemblies passing, from moment to moment, from one set of sentiments to another entirely opposite.

"The Republican party was brought to its perdition by its divisions, its jealousies, its suspicions, and, in turn, its blind confidence and its limitless hopes. Its ingenuousness and candour were only equalled by its universal mistrust. An absence of all sense of legality, of all comprehension of discipline, together with boundless terrors and illusions; the peasant and the child are on a level in these respects. Their calm is as great as their impatience; their ferocity is equal to their docility. This condition is the natural consequence of a temperament that is not formed and of the lack of education. Nothing astonishes such persons, and everything disconcerts them. Trembling with fear or brave to the point of heroism, they would go through fire and water or fly from a shadow.

"They are ignorant of cause and effect and of the connecting links between events. They are as promptly discouraged as they are exalted, they are subject to every description of panic, they are always either too highly strung or too downcast, but never in the mood or the measure the situation would require. More fluid than water they reflect every line and assume every shape. What sort of a foundation for a government can they be expected to supply?"

Fortunately all the characteristics just described as to be met with in parliamentary assemblies are in no wise constantly displayed. Such assemblies only constitute crowds at certain moments. The individuals composing them retain their individuality in a great number of cases, which explains how it is that an assembly is able to turn out excellent technical laws. It is true that the author of these laws is a specialist who has prepared them in the quiet of his study, and that in reality the law voted is the work of an individual and not of an assembly. These laws are naturally the best. They are only liable to have disastrous results when a series of amendments has converted them into the outcome of a collective effort. The work of a crowd is always inferior, whatever its nature, to that of an isolated individual. It is specialists who safeguard assemblies from passing ill-advised or unworkable measures. The specialist in this case is a temporary leader of crowds. The Assembly is without influence on him, but he has influence over the Assembly.

In spite of all the difficulties attending their working, parliamentary assemblies are the best form of government mankind has discovered as yet, and more especially the best means it has found to escape the yoke of personal tyrannies. They constitute assuredly the ideal government at any rate for philosophers, thinkers, writers, artists, and learned men — in a word, for all those who form the cream of a civilisation.

Moreover, in reality they only present two serious dangers, one being inevitable financial waste, and the other the progressive restriction of the liberty of the individual.

The first of these dangers is the necessary consequence of the exigencies and want of foresight of electoral crowds. Should a member of an assembly propose a measure giving apparent satisfaction to democratic ideas, should he bring in a Bill, for instance, to assure old-age pensions to all workers, and to increase the wages of any class of State employés, the other Deputies, victims of suggestion in their dread of their electors, will not venture to seem to disregard the interests of the latter by rejecting the proposed measure, although well aware they are imposing a fresh strain on the Budget and necessitating the creation of new taxes. It is impossible for them to hesitate to give their votes. The consequences of the increase of expenditure are remote and will not entail disagreeable consequences for them personally, while the consequences of a negative vote might clearly come to light when they next present themselves for re-election.

In addition to this first cause of an exaggerated expenditure there is another not less imperative — the necessity of voting all grants for local purposes. A Deputy is unable to oppose grants of this kind because they represent once more the exigencies of the electors, and because each individual Deputy can only obtain what he requires for his own constituency on the condition of acceding to similar demands on the part of his colleagues[29].

The second of the dangers referred to above — the inevitable restrictions on liberty consummated by parliamentary assemblies — is apparently less obvious, but is, nevertheless, very real. It is the result of the innumerable laws

---

[29]   In its issue of April 6, 1895, the Economiste published a curious review of the figures that may be reached by expenditure caused solely by electoral considerations, and notably of the outlay on railways. To put Langayes (a town of 3,000 inhabitants, situated on a mountain) in communication with Puy, a railway is voted that will cost 15 millions of francs. Seven millions are to be spent to put Beaumont (3,500 inhabitants) in communication with Castel-Sarrazin; 7 millions to put Oust (a village of 523 inhabitants) in communication with Seix (1,200 inhabitants); 6 millions to put Prade in communication with the hamlet of Olette (747 inhabitants), &c. In 1895 alone 90 millions of francs were voted for railways of only local utility. There is other no less important expenditure necessitated also by electioneering considerations. The law instituting workingmen's pensions will soon involve a minimum annual outlay of 165 millions, according to the Minister of Finance, and of 800 millions according to the academician M. Leroy-Beaulieu.

It is evident that the continued growth of expenditure of this kind must end in bankruptcy. Many European countries — Portugal, Greece, Spain, Turkey — have reached this stage, and others, such as Italy, will soon be reduced to the same extremity. Still too much alarm need not be felt at this state of things, since the public has successively consented to put up with the reduction of four-fifths in the payment of their coupons by these different countries.

Bankruptcy under these ingenious conditions allows the equilibrium of Budgets difficult to balance to be instantly restored. Moreover, wars, socialism, and economic conflicts hold in store for us a profusion of other catastrophes in the period of universal disintegration we are traversing, and it is necessary to be resigned to living from hand to mouth without too much concern for a future we cannot control.

— having always a restrictive action — which parliaments consider themselves obliged to vote and to whose consequences, owing to their shortsightedness, they are in a great measure blind.

The danger must indeed be most inevitable, since even England itself, which assuredly offers the most popular type of the parliamentary régime, the type in which the representative is most independent of his elector, has been unable to escape it. Herbert Spencer has shown, in a work already old, that the increase of apparent liberty must needs be followed by the decrease of real liberty. Returning to this contention in his recent book, "The Individual versus the State," he thus expresses himself with regard to the English Parliament: —

"Legislation since this period has followed the course, I pointed out. Rapidly multiplying dictatorial measures have continually tended to restrict individual liberties, and this in two ways. Regulations have been established every year in greater number, imposing a constraint on the citizen in matters in which his acts were formerly completely free, and forcing him to accomplish acts which he was formerly at liberty to accomplish or not to accomplish at will. At the same time heavier and heavier public, and especially local, burdens have still further restricted his liberty by diminishing the portion of his profits he can spend as he chooses, and by augmenting the portion which is taken from him to be spent according to the good pleasure of the public authorities."

This progressive restriction of liberties shows itself in every country in a special shape which Herbert Spencer has not pointed out; it is that the passing of these innumerable series of legislative measures, all of them in a general way of a restrictive order, conduces necessarily to augment the number, the power, and the influence of the functionaries charged with their application. These functionaries tend in this way to become the veritable masters of civilised countries. Their power is all the greater owing to the fact that, amidst the incessant transfer of authority, the administrative caste is alone in being untouched by these changes, is alone in possessing irresponsibility, impersonality, and perpetuity. There is no more oppressive despotism than that which presents itself under this triple form.

This incessant creation of restrictive laws and regulations, surrounding the pettiest actions of existence with the most complicated formalities, inevitably has for its result the confining within narrower and narrower limits of the sphere in which the citizen may move freely. Victims of the delusion that equality and liberty are the better assured by the multiplication of laws, nations daily consent to put up with trammels increasingly burdensome. They do not accept this legislation with impunity. Accustomed to put up with every yoke, they soon end by desiring servitude, and lose all spontaneousness and energy. They are then no more than vain shadows, passive, unresisting and powerless automata.

Arrived at this point, the individual is bound to seek outside himself the forces he no longer finds within him. The functions of governments necessarily increase in proportion as the indifference and helplessness of the citizens grow. They it is who must necessarily exhibit the initiative, enterprising, and guiding spirit in which private persons are lacking. It falls on them to undertake everything, direct everything, and take everything under their protection. The State becomes an all-powerful god. Still experience shows that the power of such gods was never either very durable or very strong.

This progressive restriction of all liberties in the case of certain peoples, in spite of an outward license that gives them the illusion that these liberties are still in their possession, seems at least as much a consequence of their old age as of any particular system. It constitutes one of the precursory symptoms of that decadent phase which up to now no civilisation has escaped.

Judging by the lessons of the past, and by the symptoms that strike the attention on every side, several of our modern civilisations have reached that phase of extreme old age which precedes decadence. It seems inevitable that all peoples should pass through identical phases of existence, since history is so often seen to repeat its course.

It is easy to note briefly these common phases of the evolution of civilisations, and I shall terminate this work with a summary of them. This rapid sketch will perhaps throw some gleams of light on the causes of the power at present wielded by crowds.

If we examine in their main lines the genesis of the greatness and of the fall of the civilisations that preceded our own, what do we see?

At the dawn of civilisation a swarm of men of various origin, brought together by the chances of migrations, invasions, and conquests. Of different blood, and of equally different languages and beliefs, the only common bond of union between these men is the half-recognised law of a chief. The psychological characteristics of crowds are present in an eminent degree in these confused agglomerations. They have the transient cohesion of crowds, their heroism, their weaknesses, their impulsiveness, and their violence. Nothing is stable in connection with them. They are barbarians.

At length time accomplishes its work. The identity of surroundings, the repeated intermingling of races, the necessities of life in common exert their influence. The assemblage of dissimilar units begins to blend into a whole, to form a race; that is, an aggregate possessing common characteristics and sentiments to which heredity will give greater and greater fixity. The crowd has become a people, and this people is able to emerge from its barbarous state. However, it will only entirely emerge therefrom when, after long efforts, struggles necessarily repeated, and innumerable recommencements, it shall have acquired an ideal. The nature of this ideal is of slight importance; whether it be the cult of Rome, the might of Athens, or the triumph of Allah, it will suffice to endow all the individuals of the race that is forming with perfect unity of sentiment and thought.

At this stage a new civilisation, with its institutions, its beliefs, and its arts, may be born. In pursuit of its ideal, the race will acquire in succession the qualities necessary to give it splendour, vigour, and grandeur. At times no doubt it will still be a crowd, but henceforth, beneath the mobile and changing characteristics of crowds, is found a solid substratum, the genius of the race which confines within narrow limits the transformations of a nation and overrules the play of chance.

After having exerted its creative action, time begins that work of destruction from which neither gods nor men escape. Having reached a certain level of strength and complexity a civilisation ceases to grow, and having ceased to grow it is condemned to a speedy decline. The hour of its old age has struck.

This inevitable hour is always marked by the weakening of the ideal that was the mainstay of the race. In proportion as this ideal pales all the religious, political, and social structures inspired by it begin to be shaken.

With the progressive perishing of its ideal the race loses more and more the qualities that lent it its cohesion, its unity, and its strength. The personality and intelligence of the individual may increase, but at the same time this collective egoism of the race is replaced by an excessive development of the egoism of the individual, accompanied by a weakening of character and a lessening of the capacity for action. What constituted a people, a unity, a whole, becomes in the end an agglomeration of individualities lacking cohesion, and artificially held together for a time by its traditions and institutions. It is at this stage that men, divided by their interests and aspirations, and incapable any longer of self-government, require directing in their pettiest acts, and that the State exerts an absorbing influence.

With the definite loss of its old ideal the genius of the race entirely disappears; it is a mere

swarm of isolated individuals and returns to its original state
— that of a crowd. Without consistency and without a future, it has all the transitory characteristics of crowds. Its civilisation is now without stability, and at the mercy of every chance. The populace is sovereign, and the tide of barbarism mounts. The civilisation may still seem brilliant because it possesses an outward front, the work of a long past, but it is in reality an edifice crumbling to ruin, which nothing supports, and destined to fall in at the first storm.

To pass in pursuit of an ideal from the barbarous to the civilised state, and then, when this ideal has lost its virtue, to decline and die, such is the cycle of the life of a people.

Extraordinary Popular Delusions and the Madness of Crowds
by Charles Mackay

TABLE OF CONTENTS

Preface to 1852 Edition

NATIONAL DELUSIONS.

N'en deplaise a ces fous nommes sages de Grece;
En ce monde il n'est point de parfaite sagesse;
Tous les hommes sont fous, et malgre tous leurs soins,
Ne different entre eux que du plus ou du moins. -- *Boileau.*

In reading the history of nations, we find that, like individuals, they have their whims and their peculiarities; their seasons of excitement and recklessness, when they care not what they do. We find that whole communities suddenly fix their minds upon one object, and go mad in its pursuit; that millions of people become simultaneously impressed with one delusion, and run after it, till their attention is caught by some new folly more captivating than the first. We see one nation suddenly seized, from its highest to its lowest members, with a fierce desire of military glory; another as suddenly becoming crazed upon a religious scruple, and neither of them recovering its senses until it has shed rivers of blood and sowed a harvest of groans and tears, to be reaped by its posterity. At an early age in the annals of Europe its population lost their wits about the Sepulchre of Jesus, and crowded in frenzied multitudes to the Holy Land: another age went mad for fear of the Devil, and offered up hundreds of thousands of victims to the delusion of witchcraft. At another time, the many became crazed on the subject of the Philosopher's Stone, and committed follies till then unheard of in the pursuit. It was once thought a venial offence in very many countries of Europe to destroy an enemy by slow poison. Persons who would have revolted at the idea of stabbing a man to the heart, drugged his pottage without scruple. Ladies of gentle birth and manners caught the contagion of murder, until poisoning, under their auspices, became quite fashionable. Some delusions, though notorious to all the world, have subsisted for ages, flourishing as widely among civilized and polished nations as among the early barbarians with whom they originated, -- that of duelling, for instance, and the belief in omens and divination of the future, which seem to defy the progress of knowledge to eradicate entirely from the popular mind. Money, again, has often been a cause of the delusion of multitudes. Sober nations have all at once become desperate gamblers, and risked almost their existence upon the turn of a piece of paper. To trace the history of the most prominent of these delusions is the object of the present pages. Men, it has been well said, think in herds; it will be seen that they go mad in herds, while they only recover their senses slowly, and one by one.

In the present state of civilization, society has often shown itself very prone to run a career of folly from the last-mentioned cases. This infatuation has seized upon whole nations in a most extraordinary manner. France, with her Mississippi madness, set the first great example, and was very soon imitated by England with her South Sea Bubble. At an earlier period, Holland made herself still more ridiculous in the eyes of the world, by the frenzy which came over her people for the love of Tulips. Melancholy as all these delusions were in their ultimate results, their history is most amusing. A more ludicrous and yet painful spectacle, than that which Holland presented in the years 1635 and 1636, or France in 1719 and 1720, can hardly be imagined. Taking them in the order of their importance, we shall commence our history with John Law and the famous Mississippi scheme of the years above mentioned.

The Mississippi Scheme

Some in clandestine companies combine;
Erect new stocks to trade beyond the line;
With air and empty names beguile the town,
And raise new credits first, then cry 'em down;
Divide the empty nothing into shares,
And set the crowd together by the ears. --*Defoe.*

The personal character and career of one man are so intimately connected with the great scheme of the years 1719 and 1720, that a history of the Mississippi madness can have no fitter introduction than a sketch of the life of its great author, John Law. Historians are divided in opinion as to whether they should designate him a knave or a madman. Both epithets were unsparingly applied to him in his lifetime, and while the unhappy consequences of his projects were still deeply felt. Posterity, however, has found reason to doubt the justice of the accusation, and to confess that John Law was neither knave nor madman, but one more deceived than deceiving; more sinned against than sinning. He was thoroughly acquainted with the philosophy and true principles of credit. He understood the monetary question better than any man of his day; and if his system fell with a crash so tremendous, it was not so much his fault as that of the people amongst whom he had erected it. He did not calculate upon the avaricious frenzy of a whole nation; he did not see that confidence, like mistrust, could be increased, almost ad infinitum, and that hope was as extravagant as fear. How was he to foretell that the French people, like the man in the fable, would kill, in their frantic eagerness, the fine goose he had brought to lay them so many golden eggs? His fate was like that which may be supposed to have overtaken the first adventurous boatman who rowed from Erie to Ontario. Broad and smooth was the river on which he embarked; rapid and pleasant was his progress; and who was to stay him in his career? Alas for him! the cataract was nigh. He saw, when it was too late, that the tide which wafted him so joyously along was a tide of destruction; and when he endeavoured to retrace his way, he found that the current was too strong for his weak efforts to stem, and that he drew nearer every instant to the tremendous falls. Down he went over the sharp rocks, and the waters with him. He was dashed to pieces with his bark, but the waters, maddened and turned to foam by the rough descent, only boiled and bubbled for a time, and then flowed on again as smoothly as ever. Just so it was with Law and the French people. He was the boatman and they were the waters.

John Law was born at Edinburgh in the year 1671. His father was the younger son of an ancient family in Fife, and carried on the business of a goldsmith and banker. He amassed considerable wealth in his trade, sufficient to enable him to gratify the wish, so common among his countrymen, of adding a territorial designation to his name. He purchased with this view the estates of Lauriston and Randleston, on the Frith of Forth on the borders of West and Mid Lothian, and was thenceforth known as Law of Lauriston. The subject of our memoir, being the eldest son, was received into his father's counting-house at the age of fourteen, and for three years laboured hard to acquire an insight into the principles of banking, as then carried on in Scotland. He had always manifested great love for the study of numbers, and his proficiency in the mathematics was considered extraordinary in one of his tender years. At the age of seventeen he was tall, strong, and well made; and his face, although deeply scarred with the small-pox, was agreeable in its expression, and full of intelligence. At this time he began to neglect his business, and becoming vain of his person, indulged in considerable extravagance of attire. He was a great favourite with the ladies, by whom he was called Beau Law, while the other sex, despising his foppery, nicknamed him Jessamy John. At the death of his father, which happened in 1688, he withdrew entirely from the desk, which had become so irksome, and being possessed of the revenues of the paternal estate of Lauriston, he proceeded to London, to see the world.

He was now very young, very vain, good-looking, tolerably rich, and quite uncontrolled. It is no wonder that, on his arrival in the capital, he should launch out into extravagance. He soon became a regular frequenter of the gaming-houses, and by pursuing a certain plan, based upon some abstruse calculation of chances, he contrived to gain considerable sums. All the gamblers envied him his luck, and many made it a point to watch his play, and stake their money on the same chances. In affairs of gallantry he was equally fortunate; ladies of the first rank smiled graciously upon the handsome Scotchman -- the young, the rich, the witty, and the obliging. But all these successes only paved the way for reverses. After he had been for nine years exposed to the dangerous attractions of the gay life he was leading, he became an irrecoverable gambler. As his love of play increased in violence, it diminished in prudence. Great losses were only to be repaired by still greater ventures, and one unhappy day he lost more than he could repay without mortgaging his family estate. To that step he was driven at last. At the same time his gallantry brought him into trouble. A love affair, or slight flirtation, with a lady of the name of Villiers [Miss Elizabeth Villiers, afterwards Countess of Orkney] exposed him to the resentment of a Mr. Wilson, by whom he was challenged to fight a duel. Law accepted, and had the ill fortune to shoot his antagonist dead upon the spot. He was arrested the same day, and brought to trial for murder by the relatives of Mr. Wilson. He was afterwards found guilty, and sentenced to death. The sentence was commuted to a fine, upon the ground that the offence only amounted to manslaughter. An appeal being lodged by a brother of the deceased, Law was detained in the King's Bench, whence, by some means or other, which he never explained, he contrived to escape; and an action being instituted against the sheriffs, he was advertised in the Gazette, and a reward offered for his apprehension. He was described as "Captain John Law, a Scotchman, aged twenty-six; a very tall, black, lean man; well shaped, above six feet high, with large pockholes in his face; big nosed, and speaking broad and loud." As this was rather a caricature than a description of him, it has been supposed that it was drawn up with a view to favour his escape. He succeeded in reaching the Continent, where he travelled for three years, and devoted much of his attention to the monetary and banking affairs of the countries through which he passed. He stayed a few months in Amsterdam, and speculated to some extent in the funds. His mornings were devoted to the study of finance and the principles of trade, and his evenings to the gaming-house. It is generally believed that he returned to Edinburgh in the year 1700. It is certain that he published in that city his "Proposals and Reasons for constituting a Council of Trade." This pamphlet did not excite much attention.

In a short time afterwards he published a project for establishing what he called a Land-bank [The wits of the day called it a sand-bank, which would wreck the vessel of the state.], the notes issued by which were never to exceed the value of the entire lands of the state, upon ordinary interest, or were to be equal in value to the land, with the right to enter into possession at a certain time. The project excited a good deal of discussion in the Scottish parliament, and a motion for the establishment of such a bank was brought forward by a neutral party, called the Squadrone, whom Law had interested in his favour. The Parliament ultimately passed a resolution to the effect, that, to establish any kind of paper credit, so as to force it to pass, was an improper expedient for the nation.

Upon the failure of this project, and of his efforts to procure a pardon for the murder of Mr. Wilson, Law withdrew to the Continent, and resumed his old habits of gaming. For fourteen years he continued to roam about, in Flanders, Holland, Germany, Hungary, Italy, and France. He soon became intimately acquainted with the extent of the trade and resources of each, and daily more confirmed in his opinion that no country could prosper without a paper currency. During the whole of this time he appears to have chiefly supported himself by successful play. At every gambling-house of note in the capitals of Europe,

8

he was known and appreciated as one better skilled in the intricacies of chance than any other man of the day. It is stated in the "Biographie Universelle" that he was expelled, first from Venice, and afterwards from Genoa, by the magistrates, who thought him a visitor too dangerous for the youth of those cities. During his residence in Paris he rendered himself obnoxious to D'Argenson, the lieutenant-general of the police, by whom he was ordered to quit the capital. This did not take place, however, before he had made the acquaintance in the saloons, of the Duke de Vendome, the Prince de Conti, and of the gay Duke of Orleans, the latter of whom was destined afterwards to exercise so much influence over his fate. The Duke of Orleans was pleased with the vivacity and good sense of the Scottish adventurer, while the latter was no less pleased with the wit and amiability of a prince who promised to become his patron. They were often thrown into each other's society, and Law seized every opportunity to instil his financial doctrines into the mind of one whose proximity to the throne pointed him out as destined, at no very distant date, to play an important part in the government.

Shortly before the death of Louis XIV, or, as some say, in 1708, Law proposed a scheme of finance to Desmarets, the Comptroller. Louis is reported to have inquired whether the projector were a Catholic, and, on being answered in the negative, to have declined having anything to do with him. [This anecdote, which is related in the correspondence of Madame de Baviere, Duchess of Orleans, and mother of the Regent, is discredited by Lord John Russell, in his "History of the principal States of Europe, from the Peace of Utrecht;" for what reason he does not inform us. There is no doubt that Law proposed his scheme to Desmarets, and that Louis refused to hear of it. The reason given for the refusal is quite consistent with the character of that bigoted and tyrannical monarch.]

It was after this repulse that he visited Italy. His mind being still occupied with schemes of finance, he proposed to Victor Amadeus, Duke of Savoy, to establish his land-bank in that country. The Duke replied that his dominions were too circumscribed for the execution of so great a project, and that he was by far too poor a potentate to be ruined. He advised him, however, to try the King of France once more; for he was sure, if he knew anything of the French character, that the people would be delighted with a plan, not only so new, but so plausible.

Louis XIV died in 1715, and the heir to the throne being an infant only seven years of age, the Duke of Orleans assumed the reins of government, as Regent, during his minority. Law now found himself in a more favourable position. The tide in his affairs had come, which, taken at the flood, was to waft him on to fortune. The Regent was his friend, already acquainted with his theory and pretensions, and inclined, moreover, to aid him in any efforts to restore the wounded credit of France, bowed down to the earth by the extravagance of the long reign of Louis XIV.

Hardly was that monarch laid in his grave ere the popular hatred, suppressed so long, burst forth against his memory. He who, during his life, had been flattered with an excess of adulation, to which history scarcely offers a parallel, was now cursed as a tyrant, a bigot, and a plunderer. His statues were pelted and disfigured; his effigies torn down, amid the execrations of the populace, and his name rendered synonymous with selfishness and oppression. The glory of his arms was forgotten, and nothing was remembered but his reverses, his extravagance, and his cruelty.

The finances of the country were in a state of the utmost disorder. A profuse and corrupt monarch, whose profuseness and corruption were imitated by almost every functionary, from the highest to the lowest grade, had brought France to the verge of ruin. The national debt amounted to 3000 millions of livres, the revenue to 145 millions, and the expenditure to 142 millions per annum; leaving only three millions to pay the interest upon 3000 millions. The first care of the Regent was to discover a remedy for an evil of such magnitude, and a council was early summoned to take the matter into consideration. The Duke de St. Simon was of opinion that nothing could save the country from revolution but a remedy at once bold and dangerous. He advised the Regent to convoke the States-General, and declare a national bankruptcy. The Duke de Noailles, a man of accommodating principles, an accomplished courtier, and totally averse from giving himself any trouble or annoyance that ingenuity could escape from, opposed the project of St. Simon with all his influence. He represented the expedient as alike dishonest and ruinous. The Regent was of the same opinion, and this desperate remedy fell to the ground.

The measures ultimately adopted, though they promised fair, only aggravated the evil. The first, and most dishonest measure, was of no advantage to the state. A recoinage was ordered, by which the currency was depreciated one-fifth; those who took a thousand pieces of gold or silver to the mint received back an amount of coin of the same nominal value, but only four-fifths of the weight of metal. By this contrivance the treasury gained seventy-two millions of livres, and all the commercial operations of the country were disordered. A trifling diminution of the taxes silenced the clamours of the people, and for the slight present advantage the great prospective evil was forgotten.

A chamber of justice was next instituted, to inquire into the malversations of the loan-contractors and the farmers of the revenues. Tax collectors are never very popular in any country, but those of France at this period deserved all the odium with which they were loaded. As soon as these farmers-general, with all their hosts of subordinate agents, called maltotiers [From maltote, an oppressive tax.], were called to account for their misdeeds, the most extravagant joy took possession of the nation. The Chamber of Justice, instituted chiefly for this purpose, was endowed with very extensive powers. It was composed of the presidents and councils of the parliament, the judges of the Courts of Aid and of Requests, and the officers of the Chamber of Account, under the general presidence of the minister of finance. Informers were encouraged to give evidence against the offenders by the promise of one-fifth part of the fines and confiscations. A tenth of all concealed effects belonging to the guilty was promised to such as should furnish the means of discovering them.

The promulgation of the edict constituting this court caused a degree of consternation among those principally concerned which can only be accounted for on the supposition that their peculation had been enormous. But they met with no sympathy. The proceedings against them justified their terror. The Bastile was soon unable to contain the prisoners that were sent to it, and the gaols all over the country teemed with guilty or suspected persons. An order was issued to all innkeepers and postmasters to refuse horses to such as endeavoured to seek safety in flight; and all persons were forbidden, under heavy fines, to harbour them or favour their evasion. Some were condemned to the pillory, others to the gallies, and the least guilty to fine and imprisonment. One only, Samuel Bernard, a rich banker, and farmer-general of a province remote from the capital, was sentenced to death. So great had been the illegal profits of this man, -- looked upon as the tyrant and oppressor of his district, -- that he offered six millions of livres, or 250,000 pounds sterling, to be allowed to escape.

His bribe was refused, and he suffered the penalty of death. Others, perhaps more guilty, were more fortunate. Confiscation, owing to the concealment of their treasures by the delinquents, often produced less money than a fine. The severity of the government relaxed, and fines, under the denomination of taxes, were indiscriminately levied upon all offenders. But so corrupt was every department of the administration, that the country benefited but little by the sums which thus flowed into the treasury. Courtiers, and courtiers' wives and mistresses, came in for the chief share of the spoils. One contractor had been taxed in proportion to his wealth and guilt, at the sum of twelve millions of livres. The Count *

* *, a man of some weight in the government, called upon him, and offered to procure a remission of the fine, if he would give him a hundred thousand crowns. "Vous etes trop tard, mon ami," replied the financier; "I have already made a bargain with your wife for fifty thousand." [This anecdote is related by M. de la Hode, in his Life of Philippe of Orleans. It would have looked more authentic if he had given the names of the dishonest contractor and the still more dishonest minister. But M. de la Hode's book is liable to the same objection as most of the French memoirs of that and of subsequent periods. It is sufficient with most of them that an anecdote be ben trovato; the veto is but matter of secondary consideration.]

About a hundred and eighty millions of livres were levied in this manner, of which eighty were applied in payment of the debts contracted by the government. The remainder found its way into the pockets of the courtiers. Madame de Maintenon, writing on this subject, says, "We hear every day of some new grant of the Regent; the people murmur very much at this mode of employing the money taken from the peculators." The people, who, after the first burst of their resentment is over, generally express a sympathy for the weak, were indignant that so much severity should be used to so little purpose. They did not see the justice of robbing one set of rogues to fatten another. In a few months all the more guilty had been brought to punishment, and the chamber of justice looked for victims in humbler walks of life. Charges of fraud and extortion were brought against tradesmen of good character, in consequence of the great inducements held out to common informers. They were compelled to lay open their affairs before this tribunal in order to establish their innocence. The voice of complaint resounded from every side, and at the expiration of a year the government found it advisable to discontinue further proceedings. The chamber of justice was suppressed, and a general amnesty granted to all against whom no charges had yet been preferred.

In the midst of this financial confusion Law appeared upon the scene. No man felt more deeply than the Regent the deplorable state of the country, but no man could be more averse from putting his shoulders manfully to the wheel. He disliked business; he signed official documents without proper examination, and trusted to others what he should have undertaken himself. The cares inseparable from his high office were burdensome to him; he saw that something was necessary to be done, but he lacked the energy to do it, and had not virtue enough to sacrifice his case and his pleasures in the attempt. No wonder that, with this character, he listened favourably to the mighty projects, so easy of execution, of the clever adventurer whom he had formerly known, and whose talents he appreciated.

When Law presented himself at court, he was most cordially received. He offered two memorials to the Regent, in which he set forth the evils that had befallen France, owing to an insufficient currency, at different times depreciated. He asserted that a metallic currency, unaided by a paper money, was wholly inadequate to the wants of a commercial country, and particularly cited the examples of Great Britain and Holland to show the advantages of paper. He used many sound arguments on the subject of credit, and proposed, as a means of restoring that of France, then at so low an ebb among the nations, that he should be allowed to set up a bank, which should have the management of the royal revenues, and issue notes, both on that and on landed security. He further proposed that this bank should be administered in the King's name, but subject to the control of commissioners, to be named by the States-General.

While these memorials were under consideration, Law translated into French his essay on money and trade, and used every means to extend through the nation his renown as a financier. He soon became talked of. The confidants of the Regent spread abroad his praise, and every one expected great things of Monsieur Lass. [The French pronounced his name in this manner to avoid the ungallic sound, aw. After the failure of his scheme, the wags said the nation was lasse de lui, and proposed that he should in future be known by the name of Monsieur Helas!]

On the 5th of May, 1716, a royal edict was published, by which Law was authorised, in conjunction with his brother, to establish a bank, under the name of Law and Company, the notes of which should be received in payment of the taxes. The capital was fixed at six millions of livres, in twelve thousand shares of five hundred livres each, purchasable one-fourth in specie and the remainder in billets d'etat. It was not thought expedient to grant him the whole of the privileges prayed for in his memorials until experience should have shown their safety and advantage.

Law was now on the high road to fortune. The study of thirty years was brought to guide him in the management of his bank. He made all his notes payable at sight, and in the coin current at the time they were issued. This last was a master-stroke of policy, and immediately rendered his notes more valuable than the precious metals. The latter were constantly liable to depreciation by the unwise tampering of the government. A thousand livres of silver might be worth their nominal value one day and be reduced one-sixth the next, but a note of Law's bank retained its original value. He publicly declared at the same time that a banker deserved death if he made issues without having sufficient security to answer all demands. The consequence was, that his notes advanced rapidly in public estimation, and were received at one per cent. more than specie. It was not long before the trade of the country felt the benefit. Languishing commerce began to lift up her head; the taxes were paid with greater regularity and less murmuring, and a degree of confidence was established that could not fail, if it continued, to become still more advantageous. In the course of a year Law's notes rose to fifteen per cent. premium, while the billets d'etat, or notes issued by the government, as security for the debts contracted by the extravagant Louis XIV, were at a discount of no less than seventy-eight and a half per cent. The comparison was too great in favour of Law not to attract the attention of the whole kingdom, and his credit extended itself day by day. Branches of his bank were almost simultaneously established at Lyons, Rochelle, Tours, Amiens, and Orleans.

The Regent appears to have been utterly astonished at his success, and gradually to have conceived the idea, that paper, which could so aid a metallic currency, could entirely supersede it. Upon this fundamental error he afterwards acted. In the mean time, Law commenced the famous project which has handed his name down to posterity. He proposed to the Regent, who could refuse him nothing, to establish a company, that should have the exclusive privilege of trading to the great river Mississippi and the province of Louisiana, on its western bank. The country was supposed to abound in the precious metals, and the company, supported by the profits of their exclusive commerce, were to be the sole farmers of the taxes, and sole coiners of money. Letters patent were issued, incorporating the company, in August 1717. The capital was divided into two hundred thousand shares of five hundred livres each, the whole of which might be paid in billets d'etat, at their nominal value, although worth no more than 160 livres in the market.

It was now that the frenzy of speculating began to seize upon the nation. Law's bank had effected so much good, that any promises for the future which he thought proper to make were readily believed. The Regent every day conferred new privileges upon the fortunate projector. The bank obtained the monopoly of the sale of tobacco; the sole right of refinage of gold and silver, and was finally erected into the Royal Bank of France. Amid the intoxication of success, both Law and the Regent forgot the maxim so loudly proclaimed by the former, that a banker deserved death who made issues of paper without the necessary funds to provide for them. As soon as the bank, from a private, became a public institution, the Regent caused a fabrication of notes to the amount of one thousand millions of livres. This was the first departure from sound principles, and one for which Law is not justly blameable. While the affairs of the bank were under his control, the issues had never exceeded sixty millions. Whether Law opposed the inordinate increase is not known, but as it took place as soon as the bank was made a royal establishment, it is but fair to lay the blame of the change of system upon the Regent.

Law found that he lived under a despotic government, but he was not yet aware of the pernicious influence which such a government could exercise upon so delicate a framework as that of credit. He discovered it afterwards to his cost, but in the mean time suffered himself to be impelled by the Regent into courses which his own reason must have disapproved. With a weakness most culpable, he lent his aid in inundating the country with paper money, which, based upon no solid foundation, was sure to fall, sooner or later. The extraordinary present fortune dazzled his eyes, and prevented him from seeing the evil day that would burst over his head, when once, from any cause or other, the alarm was sounded. The Parliament were from the first jealous of his influence as a foreigner, and had, besides, their misgivings as to the safety of his projects. As his influence extended, their animosity increased. D'Aguesseau, the Chancellor, was unceremoniously dismissed by the Regent for his opposition to the vast increase of paper money, and the constant depreciation of the gold and silver coin of the realm. This only served to augment the enmity of the Parliament, and when D'Argenson, a man devoted to the interests of the Regent, was appointed to the vacant chancellorship, and made at the same time minister of finance, they became more violent than ever. The first measure of the new minister caused a further depreciation of the coin. In order to extinguish the billets d'etat, it was ordered that persons bringing to the mint four thousand livres in specie and one thousand livres in billets d'etat, should receive back coin to the amount of five thousand livres. D'Argenson plumed himself mightily upon thus creating five thousand new and smaller livres out of the four thousand old and larger ones, being too ignorant of the true principles of trade and credit to be aware of the immense injury he was inflicting upon both.

The Parliament saw at once the impolicy and danger of such a system, and made repeated remonstrances to the Regent. The latter refused to entertain their petitions, when the Parliament, by a bold, and very unusual stretch of authority, commanded that no money should be received in payment but that of the old standard. The Regent summoned a lit de justice, and annulled the decree. The Parliament resisted, and issued another. Again the Regent exercised his privilege, and annulled it, till the Parliament, stung to fiercer opposition, passed another decree, dated August 12th, 1718, by which they forbade the bank of Law to have any concern, either direct or indirect, in the administration of the revenue; and prohibited all foreigners, under heavy penalties, from interfering, either in their own names, or in that of others, in the management of the finances of the state. The Parliament considered Law to be the author of all the evil, and some of the counsellors, in the virulence of their enmity, proposed that he should be brought to trial, and, if found guilty, be hung at the gates of the Palais de Justice.

Law, in great alarm, fled to the Palais Royal, and threw himself on the protection of the Regent, praying that measures might be taken to reduce the Parliament to obedience. The Regent had nothing so much at heart, both on that account and because of the disputes that had arisen relative to the legitimation of the Duke of Maine and the Count of Thoulouse, the sons of the late King. The Parliament was ultimately overawed by the arrest of their president and two of the counsellors, who were sent to distant prisons.

Thus the first cloud upon Law's prospects blew over: freed from apprehension of personal danger, he devoted his attention to his famous Mississippi project, the shares of which were rapidly rising, in spite of the Parliament. At the commencement of the year 1719 an edict was published, granting to the Mississippi Company the exclusive privilege of trading to the East Indies, China, and the South Seas, and to all the possessions of the French East India Company, established by Colbert. The Company, in consequence of this great increase of their business, assumed, as more appropriate, the title of Company of the Indies, and created fifty thousand new shares. The prospects now held out by Law were most magnificent. He promised a yearly dividend of two hundred livres upon each share of five hundred, which, as the shares were paid for in billets d'etat, at their nominal value, but worth only 100 livres, was at the rate of about 120 per cent. profit.

The public enthusiasm, which had been so long rising, could not resist a vision so splendid. At least three hundred thousand applications were made for the fifty thousand new shares, and Law's house in the Rue de Quincampoix was beset from morning to night by the eager applicants. As it was impossible to satisfy them all, it was several weeks before a list of the fortunate new stockholders could be made out, during which time the public impatience rose to a pitch of frenzy. Dukes, marquises, counts, with their duchesses, marchionesses, and countesses, waited in the streets for hours every day before Mr. Law's door to know the result. At last, to avoid the jostling of the plebeian crowd, which, to the number of thousands, filled the whole thoroughfare, they took apartments in the adjoining houses, that they might be continually near the temple whence the new Plutus was diffusing wealth. Every day the value of the old shares increased, and the fresh applications, induced by the golden dreams of the whole nation, became so numerous that it was deemed advisable to create no less than three hundred thousand new shares, at five thousand livres each, in order that the Regent might take advantage of the popular enthusiasm to pay off the national debt. For this purpose, the sum of fifteen hundred millions of livres was necessary. Such was the eagerness of the nation, that thrice the sum would have been subscribed if the government had authorised it.

Law was now at the zenith of his prosperity, and the people were rapidly approaching the zenith of their infatuation. The highest and the lowest classes were alike filled with a vision of boundless wealth. There was not a person of note among the aristocracy, with the exception of the Duke of St. Simon and Marshal Villars, who was not engaged in buying or selling stock. People of every age and sex, and condition in life, speculated in the rise and fall of the Mississippi bonds. The Rue de Quincampoix was the grand resort of the jobbers, and it being a narrow, inconvenient street, accidents continually occurred in it, from the tremendous pressure of the crowd. Houses in it, worth, in ordinary times, a thousand livres of yearly rent, yielded as much as twelve or sixteen thousand. A cobbler, who had a stall in it, gained about two hundred livres a day by letting it out, and furnishing writing materials to brokers and their clients. The story goes, that a hump-backed man who stood in the street gained considerable sums by lending his hump as a writing-desk to the eager speculators! The great concourse of persons who assembled to do business brought a still greater concourse of spectators. These again drew all the thieves and immoral characters of Paris to the spot, and constant riots and disturbances took place. At nightfall, it was often found necessary to send a troop of soldiers to clear the street.

Law, finding the inconvenience of his residence, removed to the Place Vendome, whither the crowd of agioteurs followed him. That spacious square soon became as thronged as the Rue de Quincampoix : from morning to night it presented the appearance of a fair. Booths and tents were erected for the transaction of business and the sale of refreshments, and gamblers with their roulette tables stationed themselves in the very middle of the place, and reaped a golden, or rather a paper, harvest from the throng. The Boulevards and public gardens were forsaken; parties of pleasure took their walks in preference in the Place Vendome, which became the fashionable lounge of the idle, as well as the general rendezvous of the busy. The noise was so great all day, that the Chancellor, whose court was situated in the square, complained to the Regent and the municipality, that he could not hear the advocates. Law, when applied to, expressed his willingness to aid in the removal of the nuisance, and for this purpose entered into a treaty with the Prince de Carignan for the Hotel de Soissons, which had a garden of several acres in the rear. A bargain was concluded, by which Law became the purchaser of the hotel, at an enormous price, the Prince reserving to himself the magnificent gardens as a new source of profit. They contained some fine statues and several fountains, and were altogether laid out with much taste. As soon as Law was installed in his new abode, an edict was published, forbidding all persons to buy or sell stock anywhere but in the gardens of the Hotel de Soissons. In the midst among the trees, about five hundred small tents and pavilions were erected, for the convenience of the stock-jobbers. Their various colours, the gay ribands and banners which floated from them, the busy crowds which passed continually in and out--the incessant hum of voices, the noise, the music, and the strange mixture of business and pleasure on the countenances of the throng, all combined to give the place an air of enchantment that quite enraptured the Parisians. The Prince de Carignan made enormous profits while the delusion lasted. Each tent was let at the rate of five hundred livres a month; and, as there were at least five hundred of them, his monthly revenue from this source alone must have amounted to 250,000 livres, or upwards of 10,000 pounds sterling.

The honest old soldier, Marshal Villars, was so vexed to see the folly which had smitten his countrymen, that he never could speak with temper on the subject. Passing one day through the Place Vendome in his carriage, the choleric gentleman was so annoyed at the infatuation of the people, that he abruptly ordered his coachman to stop, and, putting his head out of the carriage window, harangued them for full half an hour on their "disgusting avarice." This was not a very wise proceeding on his part. Hisses and shouts of laughter resounded from every side, and jokes without number were aimed at him. There being at last strong symptoms that something more tangible was flying through the air in the direction of his head, Marshal was glad to drive on. He never again repeated the experiment.

Two sober, quiet, and philosophic men of letters, M. de la Motte and the Abbe Terrason, congratulated each other, that they, at least, were free from this strange infatuation. A few days afterwards, as the worthy Abbe was coming out of the Hotel de Soissons, whither he had gone to buy shares in the Mississippi, whom should he see but his friend La Motte entering for the same purpose. "Ha!" said the Abbe, smiling, "is that you?" "Yes," said La Motte, pushing past him as fast as he was able; "and can that be you?" The next time the two scholars met, they talked of philosophy, of science, and of religion, but neither had courage for a long time to breathe one syllable about the Mississippi. At last, when it was mentioned, they agreed that a man ought never to swear against his doing any one thing, and that there was no sort of extravagance of which even a wise man was not capable.

During this time, Law, the new Plutus, had become all at once the most important personage of the state. The ante-chambers of the Regent were forsaken by the courtiers. Peers, judges, and bishops thronged to the Hotel de Soissons; officers of the army and navy, ladies of title and fashion, and every one to whom hereditary rank or public employ gave a claim to precedence, were to be found waiting in his ante-chambers to beg for a portion of his India stock. Law was so pestered that he was unable to see one-tenth part of the applicants, and every manoeuvre that ingenuity could suggest was employed to gain access to him. Peers, whose dignity would have been outraged if the Regent had made them wait half an hour for an interview, were content to wait six hours for the chance of seeing Monsieur Law. Enormous fees were paid to his servants, if they would merely announce their names. Ladies of rank employed the blandishments of their smiles for the same object; but many of them came day after day for a fortnight before they could obtain an audience. When Law accepted an invitation, he was sometimes so surrounded by ladies, all asking to have their names put down in his lists as shareholders in the new stock, that, in spite of his well-known and habitual gallantry, he was obliged to tear himself away par force. The most ludicrous stratagems were employed to have an opportunity of speaking to him. One lady, who had striven in vain during several days, gave up in despair all attempts to see him at his own house, but ordered her coachman to keep a strict watch whenever she was out in her carriage, and if he saw Mr. Law coming, to drive against a post, and upset her. The coachman promised obedience, and for three days the lady was driven incessantly through the town, praying inwardly for the opportunity to be overturned. At last she espied Mr. Law, and, pulling the string, called out to the coachman, "Upset us now! for God's sake, upset us now!" The coachman drove against a post, the lady screamed, the coach was overturned, and Law, who had seen the accident, hastened to the spot to render assistance. The cunning dame was led into the Hotel de Soissons, where she soon thought it advisable to recover from her fright, and, after apologizing to Mr. Law, confessed her stratagem. Law smiled, and entered the lady in his books as the purchaser of a quantity of India stock. Another story is told of a Madame de Boucha, who, knowing that Mr. Law was at dinner at a certain house, proceeded thither in her carriage, and gave the alarm of fire. The company started from table, and Law among the rest; but, seeing one lady making all haste into the house towards him, while everybody else was scampering away, he suspected the trick, and ran off in another direction.

Many other anecdotes are related, which even, though they may be a little exaggerated, are nevertheless worth preserving, as showing the spirit of that singular period. [The curious reader may find an anecdote of the eagerness of the French ladies to retain Law in their company, which will make him blush or smile according as he happens to be very modest or the reverse. It is related in the Letters of Madame Charlotte Elizabeth de Baviere, Duchess of Orleans, vol. ii. p. 274.] The Regent was one day mentioning, in the presence of D'Argenson, the Abbe Dubois, and some other persons, that he was desirous of deputing some lady, of the rank at least of a Duchess, to attend upon his daughter at Modena; "but," added he, "I do not exactly know where to find one." "No!" replied one, in affected surprise; "I can tell you where to find every Duchess in France :--you have only to go to Mr. Law's; you will see them every one in his ante-chamber."

M. de Chirac, a celebrated physician, had bought stock at an unlucky period, and was very anxious to sell out. Stock, however continued to fall for two or three days, much to his alarm. His mind was filled with the subject, when he was suddenly called upon to attend a lady, who imagined herself unwell. He arrived, was shown up stairs, and felt the lady's pulse. "It falls! it falls! good God! it falls continually!" said he, musingly, while the lady looked up in his face, all anxiety for his opinion. "Oh! M. de Chirac," said she, starting to her feet, and ringing the bell for assistance; "I am dying! I am dying! it falls! it falls! it falls!" "What falls?" inquired the doctor, in amazement. "My pulse! my pulse!" said the lady; "I must be dying." "Calm your apprehensions, my dear Madam," said M. de Chirac; "I was speaking of the stocks. The truth is, I have been a great loser, and my mind is so disturbed, I hardly know what I have been saying."

The price of shares sometimes rose ten or twenty per cent. in the course of a few hours, and many persons in the humbler walks of life, who had risen poor in the morning, went to bed in affluence. An extensive holder of stock, being taken ill, sent his servant to sell two hundred and fifty shares, at eight thousand livres each, the price at which they were then quoted. The servant went, and, on his arrival in the Jardin de Soissons, found that in the interval the price had risen to ten thousand livres. The difference of two thousand livres on the two hundred and fifty shares, amounting to 500,000 livres, or 2O,000 pounds sterling, he very coolly transferred to his own use, and, giving the remainder to his master, set out the same evening for another country. Law's coachman in a very short time made money enough to set up a carriage of his own, and requested permission to leave his service. Law, who esteemed the man, begged of him as a favour, that he would endeavour, before he went, to find a substitute as good as himself. The coachman consented, and in the evening brought two of his former comrades, telling Mr. Law to choose between them, and he would take the other. Cookmaids and footmen were now and then as lucky, and, in the full-blown pride of their easily-acquired wealth, made the most ridiculous mistakes. Preserving the language and manners of their old, with the finery of their new station, they afforded continual subjects for the pity of the sensible, the contempt of the sober, and the laughter of everybody. But the folly and meanness of the higher ranks of society were still more disgusting. One instance alone, related by the Duke de St. Simon, will show the unworthy avarice which infected the whole of society. A man of the name of Andre, without character or education, had, by a series of well-timed speculations in Mississippi bonds, gained enormous wealth, in an incredibly short space of time. As St. Simon expresses it, "he had amassed mountains of gold." As he became rich, he grew ashamed of the lowness of his birth, and anxious above all things to be allied to nobility. He had a daughter, an infant only three years of age, and he opened a negotiation with the aristocratic and needy family of D'Oyse, that this child should, upon certain conditions, marry a member of that house. The Marquis d'Oyse, to his shame, consented, and promised to marry her himself on her attaining the age of twelve, if the father would pay him down the sum of a hundred thousand crowns, and twenty thousand livres every year, until the celebration of the marriage. The Marquis was himself in his thirty-third year. This scandalous bargain was duly signed and sealed, the stockjobber furthermore agreeing to settle upon his daughter, on the marriage-day, a fortune of several millions. The Duke of Brancas, the head of the family, was present throughout the negotiation, and shared in all the profits. St. Simon, who treats the matter with the levity becoming what he thought so good a joke, adds, "that people did not spare their animadversions on this beautiful marriage," and further informs us, "that the project fell to the ground some months afterwards by the overthrow of Law, and the ruin of the ambitious Monsieur Andre." It would appear, however, that the noble family never had the honesty to return the hundred thousand crowns.

Amid events like these, which, humiliating though they be, partake largely of the ludicrous, others occurred of a more serious nature. Robberies in the streets were of daily occurrence, in consequence of the immense sums, in paper, which people carried about with them. Assassinations were also frequent. One case in particular fixed the attention of the whole of France, not only on account of the enormity of the offence, but of the rank and high connexions of the criminal.

The Count d'Horn, a younger brother of the Prince d'Horn, and related to the noble families of D'Aremberg, De Ligne, and De Montmorency, was a young man of dissipated character, extravagant to a degree, and unprincipled as he was extravagant. In connexion with two other young men as reckless as himself, named Mille, a Piedmontese captain, and one Destampes, or Lestang, a Fleming, he formed a design to rob a very rich broker, who was known, unfortunately for himself, to carry great sums about his person. The Count pretended a desire to purchase of him a number of shares in the Company of the Indies, and for that purpose appointed to meet him in a cabaret, or low public-house, in the neighbourhood of the Place Vendome. The unsuspecting broker was punctual to his appointment; so were the Count d'Horn and his two associates, whom he introduced as his particular friends. After a few moments' conversation, the Count d'Horn suddenly sprang upon his victim, and stabbed him three times in the breast with a poniard. The man fell heavily to the ground, and, while the Count was employed in rifling his portfolio of bonds in the Mississippi and Indian schemes to the amount of one hundred thousand crowns, Mille, the Piedmontese, stabbed the unfortunate broker again and again, to make sure of his death. But the broker did not fall without a struggle, and his cries brought the people of the cabaret to his assistance. Lestang, the other assassin, who had been set to keep watch at a staircase, sprang from a window and escaped; but Mille and the Count d'Horn were seized in the very act.

This crime, committed in open day, and in so public a place as a cabaret, filled Paris with consternation. The trial of the assassins commenced on the following day, and the evidence being so clear, they were both found guilty and condemned to be broken alive on the wheel. The noble relatives of the Count d'Horn absolutely blocked up the ante-chambers of the Regent, praying for mercy on the misguided youth, and alleging that he was insane. The Regent avoided them as long as possible, being determined that, in a case so atrocious, justice should take its course; but the importunity of these influential suitors was not to be overcome so silently, and they at last forced themselves into the presence of the Regent, and prayed him to save their house the shame of a public execution. They hinted that the Princes d'Horn were allied to the illustrious family of Orleans, and added that the Regent himself would be disgraced if a kinsman of his should die by the hands of a common executioner. The Regent, to his credit, was proof against all their solicitations, and replied to their last argument in the words of Corneille,- "Le crime fait la honte, et non pas l'echafaud:" adding, that whatever shame there might be in the punishment he would very willingly share with the other relatives. Day after day they renewed their entreaties, but always with the same result. At last they thought that if they could interest the Duke de St. Simon in their layout, a man for whom the Regent felt sincere esteem, they might succeed in their object. The Duke, a thorough aristocrat, was as shocked as they were, that a noble assassin should die by the same death as a plebeian felon, and represented to the Regent the impolicy of making enemies of so numerous, wealthy, and powerful a family. He urged, too, that in Germany, where the family of D'Aremberg had large possessions, it was the law, that no relative of a person broken on the wheel could succeed to any public office or employ until a whole generation had passed away. For this reason he thought the punishment of the guilty Count might be transmuted into beheading, which was considered all over Europe as much less infamous. The Regent was moved by this argument, and was about to consent, when Law, who felt peculiarly interested in the fate of the murdered man, confirmed him in his former resolution, to let the law take its course.

The relatives of D'Horn were now reduced to the last extremity. The Prince de Robec Montmorency, despairing of other methods, found means to penetrate into the dungeon of the criminal, and offering him a cup of poison, implored him to save them from disgrace. The Count d'Horn turned away his head, and refused to take it. Montmorency pressed him once more, and losing all patience at his continued refusal, turned on his heel, and exclaiming, "Die, then, as thou wilt, mean-spirited wretch! thou art fit only to perish by the hands of the hangman!" left him to his fate.

D'Horn himself petitioned the Regent that he might be beheaded, but Law, who exercised more influence over his mind than any other person, with the exception of the notorious Abbe Dubois, his tutor, insisted that he could not in justice succumb to the self-interested views of the D'Horns. The Regent had from the first been of the same opinion, and within six days after the commission of their crime, D'Horn and Mille were broken on the wheel in the Place de Greve. The other assassin, Lestang, was never apprehended.

This prompt and severe justice was highly pleasing to the populace of Paris; even M. de Quincampoix, as they called Law, came in for a share of their approbation for having induced the Regent to show no favour to a patrician. But the number of robberies and assassinations did not diminish. No sympathy was shown for rich jobbers when they were plundered: the general laxity of public morals, conspicuous enough before, was rendered still more so by its rapid pervasion of the middle classes, who had hitherto remained comparatively pure, between the open vices of the class above and the hidden crimes of the class below them. The pernicious love of gambling diffused itself through society, and bore all public, and nearly all private, virtue before it.

For a time, while confidence lasted, an impetus was given to trade, which could not fail to be beneficial. In Paris, especially, the good results were felt. Strangers flocked into the capital from every part, bent, not only upon making money, but on spending it. The Duchess of Orleans, mother of the Regent, computes the increase of the population during this time, from the great influx of strangers from all parts of the world, at 305,000 souls. The housekeepers were obliged to make up beds in garrets, kitchens, and even stables, for the accommodation of lodgers; and the town was so full of carriages and vehicles of every description, that they were obliged in the principal streets to drive at a foot-pace for fear of accidents. The looms of the country worked with unusual activity, to supply rich laces, silks, broad-cloth, and velvets, which being paid for in abundant paper, increased in price four-fold. Provisions shared the general advance; bread, meat, and vegetables were sold at prices greater than had ever before been known; while the wages of labour rose in exactly the same proportion. The artisan, who formerly gained fifteen sous per diem, now gained sixty. New houses were built in every direction; an illusory prosperity shone over the land, and so dazzled the eyes of the whole nation that none could see the dark cloud on the horizon, announcing the storm that was too rapidly approaching.

Law himself, the magician whose wand had wrought so surprising a change, shared, of course, in the general prosperity. His wife and daughter were courted by the highest nobility, and their alliance sought by the heirs of ducal and princely houses. He bought two splendid estates in different parts of France, and entered into a negotiation with the family of the Duke de Sully for the purchase of the Marquisate of Rosny. His religion being an obstacle to his advancement, the Regent promised, if he would publicly conform to the Catholic faith, to make him comptroller-general of the finances. Law, who had no more real religion than any other professed gambler, readily agreed, and was confirmed by the Abbe de Tencin in the cathedral of Melun, in presence of a great crowd of spectators. [The following squib was circulated on the occasion :--

"Foin de ton zele seraphique,
Malheureux Abbe de Tencin,
Depuis que Law est Catholique,
Tout le royaume est Capucin!"

Thus, somewhat weakly and paraphrastically rendered by Justansond, in his translation of the *Memoirs of Louis XV*:--

"Tencin, a curse on thy seraphic zeal,
Which by persuasion hath contrived the means
To make the Scotchman at our altars kneel,
Since which we all are poor as Capucines?"]

On the following day he was elected honorary churchwarden of the parish of St. Roch, upon which occasion he made it a present of the sum of five hundred thousand livres. His charities, always magnificent, were not always so ostentatious. He gave away great sums privately, and no tale of real distress ever reached his ears in vain.

At this time, he was by far the most influential person of the state. The Duke of Orleans had so much confidence in his sagacity, and the success of his plans, that he always consulted him upon every matter of moment. He was by no means unduly elevated by his prosperity, but remained the same simple, affable, sensible man that he had shown himself in adversity. His gallantry, which was always delightful to the fair objects of it, was of a nature, so kind, so gentlemanly, and so respectful, that not even a lover could have taken offence at it. If upon any occasion he showed any symptoms of haughtiness, it was to the cringing nobles, who lavished their adulation upon him till it became fulsome. He often took pleasure in seeing how long he could make them dance attendance upon him for a single favour. To such of his own countrymen as by chance visited Paris, and sought an interview with him, he was, on the contrary, all politeness and attention. When Archibald Campbell, Earl of Islay, and afterwards Duke of Argyle, called upon him in the Place Vendome, he had to pass through an ante-chamber crowded with persons of the first distinction, all anxious to see the great financier, and have their names put down as first on the list of some new subscription. Law himself was quietly sitting in his library, writing a letter

19

to the gardener at his paternal estate of Lauriston about the planting of some cabbages! The Earl stayed for a considerable time, played a game of piquet with his countryman, and left him, charmed with his ease, good sense, and good breeding.

Among the nobles who, by means of the public credulity at this time, gained sums sufficient to repair their ruined fortunes, may be mentioned the names of the Dukes de Bourbon, de Guiche, de la Force [The Duke de la Force gained considerable sums, not only by jobbing in the stocks, but in dealing in porcelain, spices, &c. It was debated for a length of time in the Parliament of Paris whether he had not, in his quality of spice-merchant, forfeited his rank in the peerage. It was decided in the negative. A caricature of him was made, dressed as a street porter, carrying a large bale of spices on his back, with the inscription, "Admirez La Force."], de Chaulnes, and d'Antin; the Marechal d'Estrees, the Princes de Rohan, de Poix, and de Leon. The Duke de Bourbon, son of Louis XIV by Madame de Montespan, was peculiarly fortunate in his speculations in Mississippi paper. He rebuilt the royal residence of Chantilly in a style of unwonted magnificence, and, being passionately fond of horses, he erected a range of stables, which were long renowned throughout Europe, and imported a hundred and fifty of the finest racers from England, to improve the breed in France. He bought a large extent of country in Picardy, and became possessed of nearly all the valuable lands lying between the Oise and the Somme.

When fortunes such as these were gained, it is no wonder that Law should have been almost worshipped by the mercurial population. Never was monarch more flattered than he was. All the small poets and litterateurs of the day poured floods of adulation upon him. According to them he was the saviour of the country, the tutelary divinity of France; wit was in all his words, goodness in all his looks, and wisdom in all his actions. So great a crowd followed his carriage whenever he went abroad, that the Regent sent him a troop of horse as his permanent escort, to clear the streets before him.

It was remarked at this time, that Paris had never before been so full of objects of elegance and luxury. Statues, pictures, and tapestries were imported in great quantities from foreign countries, and found a ready market. All those pretty trifles in the way of furniture and ornament which the French excel in manufacturing, were no longer the exclusive play-things of the aristocracy, but were to be found in abundance in the houses of traders and the middle classes in general. Jewellery of the most costly description was brought to Paris as the most favourable mart. Among the rest, the famous diamond, bought by the Regent, and called by his name, and which long adorned the crown of France. It was purchased for the sum of two millions of livres, under circumstances which show that the Regent was not so great a gainer as some of his subjects, by the impetus which trade had received. When the diamond was first offered to him, he refused to buy it, although he desired, above all things, to possess it, alleging as his reason, that his duty to the country he governed would not allow him to spend so large a sum of the public money for a mere jewel. This valid and honourable excuse threw all the ladies of the court into alarm, and nothing was heard for some days but expressions of regret, that so rare a gem should be allowed to go out of France; no private individual being rich enough to buy it. The Regent was continually importuned about it; but all in vain, until the Duke de St. Simon, who, with all his ability, was something of a twaddler, undertook the weighty business. His entreaties, being seconded by Law, the good-natured Regent gave his consent, leaving to Law's ingenuity to find the means to pay for it. The owner took security for the payment of the sum of two millions of livres within a stated period, receiving, in the mean time, the interest of five per cent. upon that amount, and being allowed, besides, all the valuable clippings of the gem. St. Simon, in his Memoirs, relates, with no little complacency, his share in this transaction. After describing the diamond to be as large as a greengage, of a form nearly round, perfectly white, and without flaw, and weighing more than five hundred grains, he concludes with a chuckle, by telling the world, "that he takes great credit to himself for having induced the Regent to make so illustrious a purchase." In other words, he was proud that he had induced him to sacrifice his duty, and buy a bauble for himself, at an extravagant price, out of the public money.

Thus the system continued to flourish till the commencement of the year 1720. The warnings of the Parliament, that too great a creation of paper money would, sooner or later, bring the country to bankruptcy, were disregarded. The Regent, who knew nothing whatever of the philosophy of finance, thought that a system which had produced such good effects could never be carried to excess. If five hundred millions of paper had been of such advantage, five hundred millions additional would be of still greater advantage. This was the grand error of the Regent, and which Law did not attempt to dispel. The extraordinary avidity of the people kept up the delusion; and the higher the price of Indian and Mississippi stock, the more billets de banque were issued to keep pace with it. The edifice thus reared might not unaptly be compared to the gorgeous palace erected by Potemkin, that princely barbarian of Russia, to surprise and please his imperial mistress: huge blocks of ice were piled one upon another; ionic pillars, of chastest workmanship, in ice, formed a noble portico; and a dome, of the same material, shone in the sun, which had just strength enough to gild, but not to melt it. It glittered afar, like a palace of crystals and diamonds; but there came one warm breeze from the south, and the stately building dissolved away, till none were able even to gather up the fragments. So with Law and his paper system. No sooner did the breath of popular mistrust blow steadily upon it, than it fell to ruins, and none could raise it up again.

The first slight alarm that was occasioned was early in 1720. The Prince de Conti, offended that Law should have denied him fresh shares in India stock, at his own price, sent to his bank to demand payment in specie of so enormous a quantity of notes, that three waggons were required for its transport. Law complained to the Regent, and urged on his attention the mischief that would be done, if such an example found many imitators. The Regent was but too well aware of it, and, sending for the Prince de Conti, ordered him, under penalty of his high displeasure, to refund to the Bank two-thirds of the specie which he had withdrawn from it. The Prince was forced to obey the despotic mandate. Happily for Law's credit, De Conti was an unpopular man: everybody condemned his meanness and cupidity, and agreed that Law had been hardly treated. It is strange, however, that so narrow an escape should not have made both Law and the Regent more anxious to restrict their issues. Others were soon found who imitated, from motives of distrust, the example which had been set by De Conti in revenge. The more acute stockjobbers imagined justly that prices could not continue to rise for ever. Bourdon and La Richardiere, renowned for their extensive operations in the funds, quietly and in small quantities at a time, converted their notes into specie, and sent it away to foreign countries. They also bought as much as they could conveniently carry of plate and expensive jewellery, and sent it secretly away to England or to Holland. Vermalet, a jobber, who sniffed the coming storm, procured gold and silver coin to the amount of nearly a million of livres, which he packed in a farmer's cart, and covered over with hay and cow-dung. He then disguised himself in the dirty smock-frock, or blouse, of a peasant, and drove his precious load in safety into Belgium. From thence he soon found means to transport it to Amsterdam.

Hitherto no difficulty had been experienced by any class in procuring specie for their wants. But this system could not long be carried on without causing a scarcity. The voice of complaint was heard on every side, and inquiries being instituted, the cause was soon discovered. The council debated long on the remedies to be taken, and Law, being called on for his advice, was of opinion, that an edict should be published, depreciating the value of coin five per cent. below that of paper. The edict was published accordingly; but, failing of its intended effect, was followed by another, in which the depreciation was increased to ten per cent. The payments of the bank were at the same time restricted to one hundred livres in gold, and ten in silver. All these measures were nugatory to restore confidence in the paper, though the restriction of cash payments within limits so extremely narrow kept up the credit of the Bank.

21

Notwithstanding every effort to the contrary, the precious metals continued to be conveyed to England and Holland. The little coin that was left in the country was carefully treasured, or hidden until the scarcity became so great, that the operations of trade could no longer be carried on. In this emergency, Law hazarded the bold experiment of forbidding the use of specie altogether. In February 1720 an edict was published, which, instead of restoring the credit of the paper, as was intended, destroyed it irrecoverably, and drove the country to the very brink of revolution. By this famous edict it was forbidden to any person whatever to have more than five hundred livres (20 pounds sterling) of coin in his possession, under pain of a heavy fine, and confiscation of the sums found. It was also forbidden to buy up jewellery, plate, and precious stones, and informers were encouraged to make search for offenders, by the promise of one-half the amount they might discover. The whole country sent up a cry of distress at this unheard-of tyranny. The most odious persecution daily took place. The privacy of families was violated by the intrusion of informers and their agents. The most virtuous and honest were denounced for the crime of having been seen with a louis d'or in their possession. Servants betrayed their masters, one citizen became a spy upon his neighbour, and arrests and confiscations so multiplied, that the courts found a difficulty in getting through the immense increase of business thus occasioned. It was sufficient for an informer to say that he suspected any person of concealing money in his house, and immediately a search-warrant was granted. Lord Stair, the English ambassador, said, that it was now impossible to doubt of the sincerity of Law's conversion to the Catholic religion; he had established the inquisition, after having given abundant evidence of his faith in transubstantiation, by turning so much gold into paper.

Every epithet that popular hatred could suggest was showered upon the Regent and the unhappy Law. Coin, to any amount above five hundred livres, was an illegal tender, and nobody would take paper if he could help it. No one knew to-day what his notes would be worth to-morrow. "Never," says Duclos, in his Secret Memoirs of the Regency, "was seen a more capricious government-never was a more frantic tyranny exercised by hands less firm. It is inconceivable to those who were witnesses of the horrors of those times, and who look back upon them now as on a dream, that a sudden revolution did not break out--that Law and the Regent did not perish by a tragical death. They were both held in horror, but the people confined themselves to complaints; a sombre and timid despair, a stupid consternation, had seized upon all, and men's minds were too vile even to be capable of a courageous crime." It would appear that, at one time, a movement of the people was organised. Seditious writings were posted up against the walls, and were sent, in hand-bills, to the houses of the most conspicuous people. One of them, given in the "Memoires de la Regence," was to the following effect :--" Sir and Madam,--This is to give you notice that a St. Bartholomew's Day will be enacted again on Saturday and Sunday, if affairs do not alter. You are desired not to stir out, nor you, nor your servants. God preserve you from the flames! Give notice to your neighbours. Dated Saturday, May 25th, 1720." The immense number of spies with which the city was infested rendered the people mistrustful of one another, and beyond some trifling disturbances made in the evening by an insignificant group, which was soon dispersed, the peace of the capital was not compromised.

The value of shares in the Louisiana, or Mississippi stock, had fallen very rapidly, and few indeed were found to believe the tales that had once been told of the immense wealth of that region. A last effort was therefore tried to restore the public confidence in the Mississippi project. For this purpose, a general conscription of all the poor wretches in Paris was made by order of government. Upwards of six thousand of the very refuse of the population were impressed, as if in time of war, and were provided with clothes and tools to be embarked for New Orleans, to work in the gold mines alleged to abound there. They were paraded day after day through the streets with their pikes and shovels, and then sent off in small detachments to the out-ports to be shipped for America. Two-thirds of them never reached their destination, but dispersed themselves over the country, sold their tools for what they could get, and returned to their old course of life. In less than three weeks afterwards, one-half of them were to be found again in Paris. The manoeuvre, however, caused a trifling advance in Mississippi stock. Many persons of superabundant gullibility believed that operations had begun in earnest in the new Golconda, and that gold and silver ingots would again be found in France.

In a constitutional monarchy some surer means would have been found for the restoration of public credit. In England, at a subsequent period, when a similar delusion had brought on similar distress, how different were the measures taken to repair the evil; but in France, unfortunately, the remedy was left to the authors of the mischief. The arbitrary will of the Regent, which endeavoured to extricate the country, only plunged it deeper into the mire. All payments were ordered to be made in paper, and between the 1st of February and the end of May, notes were fabricated to the amount of upwards of 1500 millions of livres, or 60,000,000 pounds sterling. But the alarm once sounded, no art could make the people feel the slightest confidence in paper which was not exchangeable into metal. M. Lambert, the President of the Parliament of Paris, told the Regent to his face that he would rather have a hundred thousand livres in gold or silver than five millions in the notes of his bank. When such was the general feeling, the superabundant issues of paper but increased the evil, by rendering still more enormous the disparity between the amount of specie and notes in circulation. Coin, which it was the object of the Regent to depreciate, rose in value on every fresh attempt to diminish it. In February, it was judged advisable that the Royal Bank should be incorporated with the Company of the Indies. An edict to that effect was published and registered by the Parliament. The state remained the guarantee for the notes of the bank, and no more were to be issued without an order in council. All the profits of the bank, since the time it had been taken out of Law's hands and made a national institution, were given over by the Regent to the Company of the Indies. This measure had the effect of raising for a short time the value of the Louisiana and other shares of the company, but it failed in placing public credit on any permanent basis.

A council of state was held in the beginning of May, at which Law, D'Argenson (his colleague in the administration of the finances), and all the ministers were present. It was then computed that the total amount of notes in circulation was 2600 millions of livres, while the coin in the country was not quite equal to half that amount. It was evident to the majority of the council that some plan must be adopted to equalise the currency. Some proposed that the notes should be reduced to the value of the specie, while others proposed that the nominal value of the specie should be raised till it was on an equality with the paper. Law is said to have opposed both these projects, but failing in suggesting any other, it was agreed that the notes should be depreciated one-half. On the 21st of May, an edict was accordingly issued, by which it was decreed that the shares of the Company of the Indies, and the notes of the bank, should gradually diminish in value, till at the end of a year they should only pass current for one half of their nominal worth. The Parliament refused to register the edict--the greatest outcry was excited, and the state of the country became so alarming, that, as the only means of preserving tranquillity, the council of the regency was obliged to stultify its own proceedings, by publishing within seven days another edict, restoring the notes to their original value.

On the same day (the 27th of May) the bank stopped payment in specie. Law and D'Argenson were both dismissed from the ministry. The weak, vacillating, and cowardly Regent threw the blame of all the mischief upon Law, who, upon presenting himself at the Palais Royal, was refused admitance. At nightfall, however, he was sent for, and admitted into the palace by a secret door,[Duclos, Memoires Secrets de la Regence.] when the Regent endeavoured to console him, and made all manner of excuses for the severity with which in public he had been compelled to treat him. So capricious was his conduct, that, two days afterwards, he took him publicly to the opera, where he sat in the royal box, alongside of the Regent, who treated him with marked consideration in face of all the people. But such was the hatred against Law that the experiment had well nigh proved fatal to him. The mob assailed his carriage with stones just as he was entering his own door; and if the coachman had not made a sudden jerk into the court-yard, and the domestics closed the gate immediately, he would, in all probability, have been dragged out and torn to pieces. On the following day, his wife and daughter were also assailed by the mob as they were returning in their carriage from the races. When the Regent was informed of these occurrences he sent Law a strong detachment of Swiss guards, who were stationed night and day in the court of his residence. The public indignation at last increased so much, that Law, finding his own house, even with this guard, insecure, took refuge in the Palais Royal, in the apartments of the Regent.

The Chancellor, D'Aguesseau, who had been dismissed in 1718 for his opposition to the projects of Law, was now recalled to aid in the restoration of credit. The Regent acknowledged too late, that he had treated with unjustifiable harshness and mistrust one of the ablest, and perhaps the sole honest public man of that corrupt period. He had retired ever since his disgrace to his country-house at Fresnes, where, in the midst of severe but delightful philosophic studies, he had forgotten the intrigues of an unworthy court. Law himself, and the Chevalier de Conflans, a gentleman of the Regent's household, were despatched in a post-chaise, with orders to bring the ex-chancellor to Paris along with them. D'Aguesseau consented to render what assistance he could, contrary to the advice of his friends, who did not approve that he should accept any recall to office of which Law was the bearer. On his arrival in Paris, five counsellors of the Parliament were admitted to confer with the Commissary of Finance, and on the 1st of June an order was published, abolishing the law which made it criminal to amass coin to the amount of more than five hundred livres. Every one was permitted to have as much specie as he pleased. In order that the bank-notes might be withdrawn, twenty-five millions of new notes were created, on the security of the revenues of the city of Paris, at two-and-a-half per cent. The bank-notes withdrawn were publicly burned in front of the Hotel de Ville. The new notes were principally of the value of ten livres each; and on the 10th of June the bank was re-opened, with a sufficiency of silver coin to give in change for them.

These measures were productive of considerable advantage. All the population of Paris hastened to the bank, to get coin for their small notes; and silver becoming scarce, they were paid in copper. Very few complained that this was too heavy, although poor fellows might be continually seen toiling and sweating along the streets, laden with more than they could comfortably carry, in the shape of change for fifty livres. The crowds around the bank were so great, that hardly a day passed that some one was not pressed to death. On the 9th of July, the multitude was so dense and clamorous that the guards stationed at the entrance of the Mazarin Gardens closed the gate, and refused to admit any more. The crowd became incensed, and flung stones through the railings upon the soldiers. The latter, incensed in their turn, threatened to fire upon the people. At that instant one of them was hit by a stone, and, taking up his piece, he fired into the crowd. One man fell dead immediately, and another was severely wounded. It was every instant expected that a general attack would have been commenced upon the bank; but the gates of the Mazarin Gardens being opened to the crowd, who saw a whole troop of soldiers, with their bayonets fixed, ready to receive them, they contented themselves by giving vent to their indignation in groans and hisses.

Eight days afterwards the concourse of people was so tremendous, that fifteen persons were squeezed to death at the doors of the bank. The people were so indignant that they took three of the bodies on stretchers before them, and proceeded, to the number of seven or eight thousand, to the gardens of the Palais Royal, that they might show the Regent the misfortunes that he and Law had brought upon the country. Law's coachman, who was sitting on the box of his master's carriage, in the court-yard of the palace, happened to have more zeal than discretion, and, not liking that the mob should abuse his master, he said, loud enough to be overheard by several persons, that they were all blackguards, and deserved to be hanged. The mob immediately set upon him, and, thinking that Law was in the carriage, broke it to pieces. The imprudent coachman narrowly escaped with his life. No further mischief was done; a body of troops making their appearance, the crowd quietly dispersed, after an assurance had been given by the Regent that the three bodies they had brought to show him should be decently buried at his own expense. The Parliament was sitting at the time of this uproar, and the President took upon himself to go out and see what was the matter. On his return he informed the councillors, that Law's carriage had been broken by the mob. All the members rose simultaneously, and expressed their joy by a loud shout, while one man, more zealous in his hatred than the rest, exclaimed, "And Law himself, is he torn to pieces ?" [The Duchess of Orleans gives a different version of this story; but whichever be the true one, the manifestation of such feeling in a legislative assembly was not very creditable. She says, that the President was so transported with joy, that he was seized with a rhyming fit, and, returning into the hall, exclaimed to the members :--

"Messieurs ! Messieurs ! bonne nouvelle !
Le carfosse de Lass est reduit en canelle !"]

Much undoubtedly depended on the credit of the Company of the Indies, which was answerable for so great a sum to the nation. It was, therefore, suggested in the council of the ministry, that any privileges which could be granted to enable it to fulfil its engagements, would be productive of the best results. With this end in view, it was proposed that the exclusive privilege of all maritime commerce should be secured to it, and an edict to that effect was published. But it was unfortunately forgotten that by such a measure all the merchants of the country would be ruined. The idea of such an immense privilege was generally scouted by the nation, and petition on petition was presented to the Parliament, that they would refuse to register the decree. They refused accordingly, and the Regent, remarking that they did nothing but fan the flame of sedition, exiled them to Blois. At the intercession of D'Aguesseau, the place of banishment was changed to Pontoise, and thither accordingly the councillors repaired, determined to set the Regent at defiance. They made every arrangement for rendering their temporary exile as agreeable as possible. The President gave the most elegant suppers, to which he invited all the gayest and wittiest company of Paris. Every night there was a concert and ball for the ladies. The usually grave and solemn judges and councillors joined in cards and other diversions, leading for several weeks a life of the most extravagant pleasure, for no other purpose than to show the Regent of how little consequence they deemed their banishment, and that when they willed it, they could make Pontoise a pleasanter residence than Paris.

Of all the nations in the world the French are the most renowned for singing over their grievances. Of that country it has been remarked with some truth, that its whole history may be traced in its songs. When Law, by the utter failure of his best-laid plans, rendered himself obnoxious, satire of course seized hold upon him, and, while caricatures of his person appeared in all the shops, the streets resounded with songs, in which neither he nor the Regent was spared. Many of these songs were far from decent; and one of them in particular counselled the application of all his notes to the most ignoble use to which paper can be applied. But the following, preserved in the letters of the Duchess of Orleans, was the best and the most popular, and was to be heard for months in all the carrefours of Paris. The application of the chorus is happy enough :--

Aussitot que Lass arriva
Dans notre bonne ville,
Monsieur le Regent publia
Que Lass serait utile
Pour retablir la nation.
La faridondaine! la faridondon.

25

Mais il nous a tous enrich!,
Biribi!
A la facon de Barbari,
Mort ami!

Ce parpaillot, pour attirer
Tout l'argent de la France,
Songea d'abord a s'assurer
De notre confiance.
Il fit son abjuration.
La faridondaine! la faridondon!
Mais le fourbe s'est converti,
Biribi!
A la facon de Barbari,
Mon ami!

Lass, le fils aine de Satan
Nous met tous a l'aumone,
Il nous a pris tout notre argent
Et n'en rend a personne.
Mais le Regent, humain et bon,
La faridondaine! la faridondon!
Nous rendra ce qu'on nous a pris,
Biribi!
A la facon de Barbari,
Mon ami!

The following smart epigram is of the same date:--

Lundi, j'achetai des actions;
Mardi, je gagnai des millions;
Mercredi, j'arrangeai mon menage,
Jeudi, je pris un equipage,
Vendredi, je m'en fus au bal,
Et Samedi, a l'Hopital.

Among the caricatures that were abundantly published, and that showed as plainly as graver matters, that the nation had awakened to a sense of its folly, was one, a fac-simile of which is preserved in the "Memoires de la Regence." It was thus described by its author: "The 'Goddess of Shares,' in her triumphal car, driven by the Goddess of Folly. Those who are drawing the car are impersonations of the Mississippi, with his wooden leg, the South Sea, the Bank of England, the Company of the West of Senegal, and of various assurances. Lest the car should not roll fast enough, the agents of these companies, known by their long fox-tails and their cunning looks, turn round the spokes of the wheels, upon which are marked the names of the several stocks, and their value, sometimes high and sometimes low, according to the turns of the wheel. Upon the ground are the merchandise, day-books and ledgers of legitimate commerce, crushed under the chariot of Folly. Behind is an immense crowd of persons, of all ages, sexes, and conditions, clamoring after Fortune, and fighting with each other to get a portion of the shares which she distributes so bountifully among them. In the clouds sits a demon, blowing bubbles of soap, which are also the objects of the admiration and cupidity of the crowd, who jump upon one another's backs to reach them ere they burst. Right in the pathway of the car, and blocking up the passage, stands a large building, with three doors, through one of which it must pass, if it proceeds further, and all the crowd along with it. Over the first door are the words, "Hopital des Foux," over the second, "Hopital des Malades," and over the third, "Hopital des Gueux." Another caricature represented Law sitting in a large cauldron, boiling over the flames of popular madness, surrounded by an impetuous multitude, who were pouring all their gold and silver into it, and receiving gladly in exchange the bits of paper which he distributed among them by handsfull.

While this excitement lasted, Law took good care not to expose himself unguarded in the streets. Shut up in the apartments of the Regent, he was secure from all attack, and, whenever he ventured abroad, it was either incognito, or in one of the Royal carriages, with a powerful escort. An amusing anecdote is recorded of the detestation in which he was held by the people, and the ill treatment he would have met, had he fallen into their hands. A gentleman, of the name of Boursel, was passing in his carriage down the Rue St. Antoine, when his further progress was stayed by a hackneycoach that had blocked up the road. M. Boursel's servant called impatiently to the hackneycoachman to get out of the way, and, on his refusal, struck him a blow on the face. A crowd was soon drawn together by the disturbance, and M. Boursel got out of the carriage to restore order. The hackney-coachman, imagining that he had now another assailant, bethought him of an expedient to rid himself of both, and called out as loudly as he was able, "Help! help! murder! murder! Here are Law and his servant going to kill me! Help! help!" At this cry, the people came out of their shops, armed with sticks and other weapons, while the mob gathered stones to inflict summary vengeance upon the supposed financier. Happily for M. Boursel and his servant, the door of the church of the Jesuits stood wide open, and, seeing the fearful odds against them, they rushed towards it with all speed. They reached the altar, pursued by the people, and would have been ill treated even there, if, finding the door open leading to the sacristy, they had not sprang through, and closed it after them. The mob were then persuaded to leave the church by the alarmed and indignant priests; and, finding M. Boursel's carriage still in the streets, they vented their ill-will against it, and did it considerable damage.

The twenty-five millions secured on the municipal revenues of the city of Paris, bearing so low an interest as two and a half per cent., were not very popular among the large holders of Mississippi stock. The conversion of the securities was, therefore, a work of considerable difficulty; for many preferred to retain the falling paper of Law's Company, in the hope that a favourable turn might take place. On the 15th of August, with a view to hasten the conversion, an edict was passed, declaring that all notes for sums between one thousand and ten thousand livres; should not pass current, except for the purchase of annuities and bank accounts, or for the payment of instalments still due on the shares of the company.

In October following another edict was passed, depriving these notes of all value whatever after the month of November next ensuing. The management of the mint, the farming of the revenue, and all the other advantages and privileges of the India, or Mississippi Company, were taken from them, and they were reduced to a mere private company. This was the deathblow to the whole system, which had now got into the hands of its enemies. Law had lost all influence in the Council of Finance, and the company, being despoiled of its immunities, could no longer hold out the shadow of a prospect of being able to fulfil its engagements. All those suspected of illegal profits at the time the public delusion was at its height, were sought out and amerced in heavy fines. It was previously ordered that a list of the original proprietors should be made out, and that such persons as still retained their shares should place them in deposit with the company, and that those who had neglected to complete the shares for which they had put down their names, should now purchase them of the company, at the rate of 13,500 livres for each share of 500 livres. Rather than submit to pay this enormous sum for stock which was actually at a discount, the shareholders packed up all their portable effects, and endeavoured to find a refuge in foreign countries. Orders were immediately issued to the authorities at the ports and frontiers, to apprehend all travellers who sought to leave the kingdom, and keep them in custody, until it was ascertained whether they had any plate or jewellery with them, or were concerned in the late stock-jobbing. Against such few as escaped, the punishment of death was recorded, while the most arbitrary proceedings were instituted against those who remained.

Law himself, in a moment of despair, determined to leave a country where his life was no longer secure. He at first only demanded permission to retire from Paris to one of his country-seats; a permission which the Regent cheerfully granted. The latter was much affected at the unhappy turn affairs had taken, but his faith continued unmoved in the truth and efficacy of Law's financial system. His eyes were opened to his own errors, and during the few remaining years of his life, he constantly longed for an opportunity of again establishing the system upon a securer basis. At Law's last interview with the Prince, he is reported to have said--" I confess that I have committed many faults; I committed them because I am a man, and all men are liable to error; but I declare to you most solemnly that none of them proceeded from wicked or dishonest motives, and that nothing of the kind will be found in the whole course of my conduct."

Two or three days after his departure the Regent sent him a very kind letter, permitting him to leave the kingdom whenever he pleased, and stating that he had ordered his passports to be made ready. He at the same time offered him any sum of money he might require. Law respectfully declined the money, and set out for Brussels in a postchaise belonging to Madame de Prie, the mistress of the Duke of Bourbon, escorted by six horse-guards. From thence he proceeded to Venice, where he remained for some months, the object of the greatest curiosity to the people, who believed him to be the possessor of enormous wealth. No opinion, however, could be more erroneous. With more generosity than could have been expected from a man who during the greatest part of his life had been a professed gambler, he had refused to enrich himself at the expense of a ruined nation. During the height of the popular frenzy for Mississippi stock, he had never doubted of the final success of his projects, in making France the richest and most powerful nation of Europe. He invested all his gains in the purchase of landed property in France - a sure proof of his own belief in the stability of his schemes. He had hoarded no plate or jewellery, and sent no money, like the dishonest jobbers, to foreign countries. His all, with the exception of one diamond, worth about five or six thousand pounds sterling, was invested in the French soil; and when he left that country, he left it almost a beggar. This fact alone ought to rescue his memory from the charge of knavery, so often and so unjustly brought against him.

As soon as his departure was known, all his estates and his valuable library were confiscated. Among the rest, an annuity of 200,000 livres, (8000 pounds sterling,) on the lives of his wife and children, which had been purchased for five millions of livres, was forfeited, notwithstanding that a special edict, drawn up for the purpose in the days of his prosperity, had expressly declared that it should never be confiscated for any cause whatever. Great discontent existed among the people that Law had been suffered to escape. The mob and the Parliament would have been pleased to have seen him hanged. The few who had not suffered by the commercial revolution, rejoiced that the quack had left the country; but all those (and they were by far the most numerous class) whose fortunes were implicated, regretted that his intimate knowledge of the distress of the country, and of the causes that had led to it, had not been rendered more available in discovering a remedy.

At a meeting of the Council of Finance, and the general council of the Regency, documents were laid upon the table, from which it appeared that the amount of notes in circulation was 2700 millions. The

Regent was called upon to explain how it happened that there was a discrepancy between the dates at which these issues were made, and those of the edicts by which they were authorised. He might have safely taken the whole blame upon himself, but he preferred that an absent man should bear a share of it, and he therefore stated that Law, upon his own authority, had issued 1200 millions of notes at different times, and that he (the Regent) seeing that the thing had been irrevocably done, had screened Law, by antedating the decrees of the council, which authorised the augmentation. It would have been more to his credit if he had told the whole truth while he was about it, and acknowledged that it was mainly through his extravagance and impatience that Law had been induced to overstep the bounds of safe speculation. It was also ascertained that the national debt, on the 1st of January, 1721, amounted to upwards of $100 millions of livres, or more than 124,000,000 pounds sterling, the interest upon which was 3,196,000 pounds. A commission, or visa, was forthwith appointed to examine into all the securities of the state creditors, who were to be divided into five classes, the first four comprising those who had purchased their securities with real effects, and the latter comprising those who could give no proofs that the transactions they had entered into were real and bona fide. The securities of the latter were ordered to be destroyed, while those of the first four classes were subjected to a most rigid and jealous scrutiny. The result of the labours of the visa was a report, in which they counselled the reduction of the interest upon these securities to fifty-six millions of livres. They justified this advice by a statement of the various acts of peculation and extortion which they had discovered, and an edict to that effect was accordingly published and duly registered by the parliaments of the kingdom.

Another tribunal was afterwards established, under the title of the Chambre de l'Arsenal, which took cognizance of all the malversations committed in the financial departments of the government during the late unhappy period. A Master of Requests, named Falhonet, together with the Abbe Clement, and two clerks in their employ, had been concerned in divers acts of peculation, to the amount of upwards of a million of livres. The first two were sentenced to be beheaded, and the latter to be hanged; but their punishment was afterwards commuted into imprisonment for life in the Bastile. Numerous other acts of dishonesty were discovered, and punished by fine and imprisonment.

D'Argenson shared with Law and the Regent the unpopularity which had alighted upon all those concerned in the Mississippi madness. He was dismissed from his post of Chancellor, to make room for D'Aguesseau; but he retained the title of Keeper of the Seals, and was allowed to attend the councils whenever he pleased. He thought it better, however, to withdraw from Paris, and live for a time a life of seclusion at his country-seat. But he was not formed for retirement, and becoming moody and discontented, he aggravated a disease under which he had long laboured, and died in less than a twelvemonth. The populace of of Paris so detested him, that they carried their hatred even to his grave. As his funeral procession passed to the church of St. Nicholas du Chardonneret, the burying-place of his family, it was beset by a riotous mob, and his two sons, who were following as chief-mourners, were obliged to drive as fast as they were able down a by-street to escape personal violence.

As regards Law, he for some time entertained a hope that he should be recalled to France, to aid in establishing its credit upon a firmer basis. The death of the Regent, in 1723, who expired suddenly, as he was sitting by the fireside conversing with his mistress, the Duchess de Phalaris, deprived him of that hope, and he was reduced to lead his former life of gambling. He was more than once obliged to pawn his diamond, the sole remnant of his vast wealth, but successful play generally enabled him to redeem it. Being persecuted by his creditors at Rome, he proceeded to Copenhagen, where he received permission from the English ministry to reside in his native country, his pardon for the murder of Mr. Wilson having been sent over to him in 1719. He was brought over in the admiral's ship, a circumstance which gave occasion for a short debate in the House of Lords. Earl Coningsby complained that a man, who had renounced both his country and his religion, should have been treated with such honour, and expressed his belief that his presence in England, at a time when the people were so bewildered by the nefarious practices of the South Sea directors, would be attended with no little danger. He gave notice of a motion on the subject; but it was allowed to drop, no other member of the House having the slightest participation in his lordship's fears. Law remained for about four years in England, and then proceeded to Venice, where he died in 1729, in very embarrassed circumstances. The following epitaph was written at the time :--

"Ci git cet Ecossais celebre,
Ce calculateur sans egal,
Qui, par les regles de l'algebre,
A mis la France a l'Hopital."

His brother, William Law, who had been concerned with him in the administration both of the Bank and the Louisiana Company, was imprisoned in the Bastile for alleged malversation, but no guilt was ever proved against him. He was liberated after fifteen months, and became the founder of a family, which is still known in France under the title of Marquises of Lauriston.

In the next chapter will be found an account of the madness which infected the people of England at the same time, and under very similar circumstances, but which, thanks to the energies and good sense of a constitutional government, was attended with results far less disastrous than those which were seen in France.

The South Sea Bubble

At length corruption, like a general flood,
Did deluge all, and avarice creeping on,
Spread, like a low-born mist, and hid the sun.
Statesmen and patriots plied alike the stocks,
Peeress and butler shared alike the box;
And judges jobbed, and bishops bit the town,
And mighty dukes packed cards for half-a-crown:
Britain was sunk in lucre's sordid charms. --*Pope*.

The South Sea Company was originated by the celebrated Harley, Earl of Oxford, in the year 1711, with the view of restoring public credit, which had suffered by the dismissal of the Whig ministry, and of providing for the discharge of the army and navy debentures, and other parts of the floating debt, amounting to nearly ten millions sterling. A company of merchants, at that time without a name, took this debt upon themselves, and the government agreed to secure them, for a certain period, the interest of six per cent. To provide for this interest, amounting to 600,000 pounds per annum, the duties upon wines, vinegar, India goods, wrought silks, tobacco, whale-fins, and some other articles, were rendered permanent. The monopoly of the trade to the South Seas was granted, and the company, being incorporated by Act of Parliament, assumed the title by which it has ever since been known. The minister took great credit to himself for his share in this transaction, and the scheme was always called by his flatterers "the Earl of Oxford's masterpiece."

Even at this early period of its history, the most visionary ideas were formed by the company and the public of the immense riches of the eastern coast of South America. Everybody had heard of the gold and silver mines of Peru and Mexico; every one believed them to be inexhaustible, and that it was only necessary to send the manufactures of England to the coast, to be repaid a hundredfold in gold and silver ingots by the natives. A report, industriously spread, that Spain was willing to concede four ports, on the coasts of Chili and Peru, for the purposes of traffic, increased the general confidence; and for many years the South Sea Company's stock was in high favour.

Philip V of Spain, however, never had any intention of admitting the English to a free trade in the ports of Spanish America. Negotiations were set on foot, but their only result was the assiento contract, or the privilege of supplying the colonies with negroes for thirty years, and of sending once a year a vessel, limited both as to tonnage and value of cargo, to trade with Mexico, Peru, or Chili. The latter permission was only granted upon the hard condition, that the King of Spain should enjoy one-fourth of the profits, and a tax of five per cent. on the remainder. This was a great disappointment to the Earl of Oxford and his party, who were reminded much oftener than they found agreeable of the

"Parturiunt montes, nascitur ridiculus mus,"

But the public confidence in the South Sea Company was not shaken. The Earl of Oxford declared, that Spain would permit two ships, in addition to the annual ship, to carry out merchandise during the first year; and a list was published, in which all the ports and harbours of these coasts were pompously set forth as open to the trade of Great Britain. The first voyage of the annual ship was not made till the year 1717, and in the following year the trade was suppressed by the rupture with Spain.

The King's speech, at the opening of the session of 1717, made pointed allusion to the state of public credit, and recommended that proper measures should be taken to reduce the national debt. The two great monetary corporations, the South Sea Company and the Bank of England, made proposals to Parliament on the 20th of May ensuing. The South Sea Company prayed that their capital stock of ten millions might be increased to twelve, by subscription or otherwise, and offered to accept five per cent. instead of six upon the whole amount. The Bank made proposals equally advantageous. The House debated for some time, and finally three acts were passed, called the South Sea Act, the Bank Act, and the General Fund Act. By the first, the proposals of the South Sea Company were accepted, and that body held itself ready to advance the sum of two millions towards discharging the principal and interest of the debt due by the state for the four lottery funds of the ninth and tenth years of Queen Anne. By the second act, the Bank received a lower rate of interest for the sum of 1,775,027 pounds 15 shillings due to it by the state, and agreed to deliver up to be cancelled as many Exchequer bills as amounted to two millions sterling, and to accept of an annuity of one hundred thousand pounds, being after the rate of five per cent, the whole redeemable at one year's notice. They were further required to be ready to advance, in case of need, a sum not exceeding 2,500,000 pounds upon the same terms of five per cent interest, redeemable by Parliament. The General Fund Act recited the various deficiencies, which were to be made good by the aids derived from the foregoing sources.

The name of the South Sea Company was thus continually before the public. Though their trade with the South American States produced little or no augmentation of their revenues, they continued to flourish as a monetary corporation. Their stock was in high request, and the directors, buoyed up with success, began to think of new means for extending their influence. The Mississippi scheme of John Law, which so dazzled and captivated the French people, inspired them with an idea that they could carry on the same game in England. The anticipated failure of his plans did not divert them from their intention. Wise in their own conceit, they imagined they could avoid his faults, carry on their schemes for ever, and stretch the cord of credit to its extremest tension, without causing it to snap asunder.

It was while Law's plan was at its greatest height of popularity, while people were crowding in thousands to the Rue Quincampoix, and ruining themselves with frantic eagerness, that the South Sea directors laid before Parliament their famous plan for paying off the national debt. Visions of boundless wealth floated before the fascinated eyes of the people in the two most celebrated countries of Europe. The English commenced their career of extravagance somewhat later than the French; but as soon as the delirium seized them, they were determined not to be outdone. Upon the 22nd of January 1720, the House of Commons resolved itself into a Committee of the whole House, to take into consideration that part of the King's speech at the opening of the session which related to the public debts, and the proposal of the South Sea Company towards the redemption and sinking of the same. The proposal set forth at great length, and under several heads, the debts of the state, amounting to 30,981,712 pounds, which the Company were anxious to take upon themselves, upon consideration of five per cent. per annum, secured to them until Midsummer 1727; after which time, the whole was to become redeemable at the pleasure of the legislature, and the interest to be reduced to four per cent. The proposal was received with great favour; but the Bank of England had many friends in the House of Commons, who were desirous that that body should share in the advantages that were likely to accrue. On behalf of this corporation it was represented, that they had performed great and eminent services to the state, in the most difficult times, and deserved, at least, that if any advantage was to be made by public bargains of this nature, they should be preferred before a company that had never done any thing for the nation. The further consideration of the matter was accordingly postponed for five days. In the mean time, a plan was drawn up by the Governors of the Bank. The South Sea Company, afraid that the Bank might offer still more advantageous terms to the government than themselves, reconsidered their former proposal, and made some alterations in it, which they hoped would render it more acceptable. The principal change was a stipulation that the government might redeem these debts at the expiration of four years, instead of seven, as at first suggested. The Bank resolved not to be outbidden in this singular auction, and the Governors also reconsidered their first proposal, and sent in a new one.

Thus, each corporation having made two proposals, the House began to deliberate. Mr. Robert Walpole was the chief speaker in favour of the Bank, and Mr. Aislabie, the Chancellor of the Exchequer, the principal advocate on behalf of the South Sea Company. It was resolved, on the 2nd of February, that the proposals of the latter were most advantageous to the country. They were accordingly received, and leave was given to bring in a bill to that effect.

Exchange Alley was in a fever of excitement. The Company's stock, which had been at a hundred and thirty the previous day, gradually rose to three hundred, and continued to rise with the most astonishing rapidity during the whole time that the bill in its several stages was under discussion. Mr. Walpole was almost the only statesman in the House who spoke out boldly against it. He warned them, in eloquent and solemn language, of the evils that would ensue. It countenanced, he said, "the dangerous practice of stockjobbing, and would divert the genius of the nation from trade and industry. It would hold out a dangerous lure to decoy the unwary to their ruin, by making them part with the earnings of their labour for a prospect of imaginary wealth. The great principle of the project was an evil of first-rate magnitude; it was to raise artificially the value of the stock, by exciting and keeping up a general infatuation, and by promising dividends out of funds which could never be adequate to the purpose." In a prophetic spirit he added, that if the plan succeeded, the directors would become masters of the government, form a new and absolute aristocracy in the kingdom, and control the resolutions of the legislature. If it failed, which he was convinced it would, the result would bring general discontent and ruin upon the country. Such would be the delusion, that when the evil day came, as come it would, the people would start up, as from a dream, and ask themselves if these things could have been true. All his eloquence was in vain. He was looked upon as a false prophet, or compared to the hoarse raven, croaking omens of evil. His friends, however, compared him to Cassandra, predicting evils which would only be believed when they came home to men's hearths, and stared them in the face at their own boards. Although, in former times, the House had listened with the utmost attention to every word that fell from his lips, the benches became deserted when it was known that he would speak on the South Sea question.

The bill was two months in its progress through the House of Commons. During this time every exertion was made by the directors and their friends, and more especially by the Chairman, the noted Sir John Blunt, to raise the price of the stock. The most extravagant rumours were in circulation. Treaties between England and Spain were spoken of, whereby the latter was to grant a free trade to all her colonies; and the rich produce of the mines of Potosi-la-Paz was to be brought to England until silver should become almost as plentiful as iron. For cotton and woollen goods, with which we could supply them in abundance, the dwellers in Mexico were to empty their golden mines. The company of merchants trading to the South Seas would be the richest the world ever saw, and every hundred pounds invested in it would produce hundreds per annum to the stockholder. At last the stock was raised by these means to near four hundred; but, after fluctuating a good deal, settled at three hundred and thirty, at which price it remained when the bill passed the Commons by a majority of 172 against 55.

In the House of Lords the bill was hurried through all its stages with unexampled rapidity. On the 4th of April it was read a first time; on the 5th, it was read a second time; on the 6th, it was committed; and on the 7th, was read a third time, and passed.

Several peers spoke warmly against the scheme; but their warnings fell upon dull, cold ears. A speculating frenzy had seized them as well as the plebeians. Lord North and Grey said the bill was unjust in its nature, and might prove fatal in its consequences, being calculated to enrich the few and impoverish the many. The Duke of Wharton followed; but, as he only retailed at second-hand the arguments so eloquently stated by Walpole in the Lower House, he was not listened to with even the same attention that had been bestowed upon Lord North and Grey. Earl Cowper followed on the same side, and compared the bill to the famous horse of the siege of Troy. Like that, it was ushered in and received with great pomp and acclamations of joy, but bore within it treachery and destruction. The Earl of Sunderland endeavoured to answer all objections; and, on the question being put, there appeared only seventeen peers against, and eighty-three in favour of the project. The very same day on which it passed the Lords, it received the Royal assent, and became the law of the land.

It seemed at that time as if the whole nation had turned stockjobbers. Exchange Alley was every day blocked up by crowds, and Cornhill was impassable for the number of carriages. Everybody came to purchase stock. "Every fool aspired to be a knave." In the words of a ballad, published at the time, and sung about the streets, ["A South Sea Ballad; or, Merry Remarks upon Exchange Alley Bubbles. To a new tune, called ' The Grand Elixir; or, the Philosopher's Stone Discovered.'"]

Then stars and garters did appear
Among the meaner rabble;
To buy and sell, to see and hear,
The Jews and Gentiles squabble.

The greatest ladies thither came,
And plied in chariots daily,
Or pawned their jewels for a sum
To venture in the Alley.

The inordinate thirst of gain that had afflicted all ranks of society, was not to be slaked even in the South Sea. Other schemes, of the most extravagant kind, were started. The share-lists were speedily filled up, and an enormous traffic carried on in shares, while, of course, every means were resorted to, to raise them to an artificial value in the market.

Contrary to all expectation, South Sea stock fell when the bill received the Royal assent. On the 7th of April the shares were quoted at three hundred and ten, and. on the following day, at two hundred and ninety. Already the directors had tasted the profits of their scheme, and it was not likely that they should quietly allow the stock to find its natural level, without an effort to raise it. Immediately their busy emissaries were set to work. Every person interested in the success of the project endeavoured to draw a knot of listeners around him, to whom he expatiated on the treasures of the South American seas. Exchange Alley was crowded with attentive groups. One rumour alone, asserted with the utmost confidence, had an immediate effect upon the stock. It was said, that Earl Stanhope had received overtures in France from the Spanish Government to exchange Gibraltar and Port Mahon for some places on the coast of Peru, for the security and enlargement of the trade in the South Seas. Instead of one annual ship trading to those ports, and allowing the King of Spain twenty-five per cent. out of the profits, the Company might build and charter as many ships as they pleased, and pay no per centage whatever to any foreign potentate.

"Visions of ingots danced before their eyes,"

and stock rose rapidly. On the 12th of April, five days after the bill had become law, the directors opened their books for a subscription of a million, at the rate of 300 pounds for every 100 pounds capital. Such was the concourse of persons, of all ranks, that this first subscription was found to amount to above two millions of original stock. It was to be paid at five payments, of 60 pounds each for every 100 pounds. In a few days the stock advanced to three hundred and forty, and the subscriptions were sold for double the price of the first payment. To raise the stock still higher, it was declared, in a general court of directors, on the 21st of April, that the midsummer dividend should be ten per cent., and that all subscriptions should be entitled to the same. These resolutions answering the end designed, the directors, to improve the infatuation of the monied men, opened their books for a second subscription of a million, at four hundred per cent. Such was the frantic eagerness of people of every class to speculate in these funds, that in the course of a few hours no less than a million and a half was subscribed at that rate.

In the mean time, innumerable joint-stock companies started up everywhere. They soon received the name of Bubbles, the most appropriate that imagination could devise. The populace are often most happy in the nicknames they employ. None could be more apt than that of Bubbles. Some of them lasted for a week, or a fortnight, and were no more heard of, while others could not even live out that short span of existence. Every evening produced new schemes, and every morning new projects. The highest of the aristocracy were as eager in this hot pursuit of gain as the most plodding jobber in Cornhill. The Prince of Wales became governor of one company, and is said to have cleared 40,000 pounds by his speculations. [Coxe's Walpole, Correspondence between Mr. Secretary Craggs and Earl Stanhope.] The Duke of Bridgewater started a scheme for the improvement of London and Westminster, and the Duke of Chandos another. There were nearly a hundred different projects, each more extravagant and deceptive than the other. To use the words of the "Political State," they were "set on foot and promoted by crafty knaves, then pursued by multitudes of covetous fools, and at last appeared to be, in effect, what their vulgar appellation denoted them to be -- bubbles and mere cheats." It was computed that near one million and a half sterling was won and lost by these unwarrantable practices, to the impoverishment of many a fool, and the enriching of many a rogue.

Some of these schemes were plausible enough, and, had they been undertaken at a time when the public mind was unexcited, might have been pursued with advantage to all concerned. But they were established merely with the view of raising the shares in the market. The projectors took the first opportunity of a rise to sell out, and next morning the scheme was at an end. Maitland, in his History of London, gravely informs us, that one of the projects which received great encouragement, was for the establishment of a company "to make deal-boards out of saw-dust." This is, no doubt, intended as a joke; but there is abundance of evidence to show that dozens of schemes hardly a whir more reasonable, lived their little day, ruining hundreds ere they fell. One of them was for a wheel for perpetual motion -- capital, one million; another was "for encouraging the breed of horses in England, and improving of glebe and church lands, and repairing and rebuilding parsonage and vicarage houses." Why the clergy, who were so mainly interested in the latter clause, should have taken so much interest in the first, is only to be explained on the supposition that the scheme was projected by a knot of the foxhunting parsons, once so common in England. The shares of this company were rapidly subscribed for. But the most absurd and preposterous of all, and which showed, more completely than any other, the utter madness of the people, was one, started by an unknown adventurer, entitled "company for carrying on an undertaking of great advantage, but nobody to know what it is." Were not the fact stated by scores of credible witnesses, it would be impossible to believe that any person could have been duped by such a project. The man of genius who essayed this bold and successful inroad upon public credulity, merely stated in his prospectus that the required capital was half a million, in five thousand shares of 100 pounds each, deposit 2 pounds per share. Each subscriber, paying his deposit, would be entitled to 100 pounds per annum per share. How this immense profit was to be obtained, he did not condescend to inform them at that time, but promised, that in a month full particulars should be duly announced, and a call made for the remaining 98 pounds of the subscription. Next morning, at nine o'clock, this great man opened an office in Cornhill. Crowds of people beset his door, and when he shut up at three o'clock, he found that no less than one thousand shares had been subscribed for, and the deposits paid. He was thus, in five hours, the winner of 2,000 pounds. He was philosopher enough to be contented with his venture, and set off the same evening for the Continent. He was never heard of again.

Well might Swift exclaim, comparing Change Alley to a gulf in the South Sea,--

Subscribers here by thousands float,
And jostle one another down,
Each paddling in his leaky boat,
And here they fish for gold, and drown.

Now buried in the depths below,
Now mounted up to heaven again,
They reel and stagger to and fro,
At their wit's end, like drunken men

Meantime, secure on Garraway cliffs,
A savage race, by shipwrecks fed,
Lie waiting for the foundered skiffs,
And strip the bodies of the dead.

Another fraud that was very successful, was that of the "Globe Permits," as they were called. They were nothing more than square pieces of playing cards, on which was the impression of a seal, in wax, bearing the sign of the Globe Tavern, in the neighbourhood of Exchange Alley, with the inscription of "Sail Cloth Permits." The possessors enjoyed no other advantage from them than permission to subscribe, at some future time, to a new sail-cloth manufactory, projected by one who was then known to be a man of fortune, but who was afterwards involved in the peculation and punishment of the South Sea directors. These permits sold for as much as sixty guineas in the Alley.

Persons of distinction, of both sexes, were deeply engaged in all these bubbles, those of the male sex going to taverns and coffee-houses to meet their brokers, and the ladies resorting for the same purpose to the shops of milliners and haberdashers. But it did not follow that all these people believed in the feasibility of the schemes to which they subscribed; it was enough for their purpose that their shares would, by stock-jobbing arts, be soon raised to a premium, when they got rid of them with all expedition to the really credulous. So great was the confusion of the crowd in the alley, that shares in the same bubble were known to have been sold at the same instant ten per cent. higher at one end of the alley than at the other. Sensible men beheld the extraordinary infatuation of the people with sorrow and alarm. There were some, both in and out of Parliament, who foresaw clearly the ruin that was impending. Mr. Walpole did not cease his gloomy forebodings. His fears were shared by all the thinking few, and impressed most forcibly upon the government. On the 11th of June, the day the Parliament rose, the

King published a proclamation, declaring that all these unlawful projects should be deemed public nuisances, and prosecuted accordingly, and forbidding any broker, under a penalty of five hundred pounds, from buying or selling any shares in them. Notwithstanding this proclamation, roguish speculators still carried them on, and the deluded people still encouraged them. On the 12th of July, an order of the Lords Justices assembled in privy council was published, dismissing all the petitions that had been presented for patents and charters, and dissolving all the bubble companies. The following copy of their lordships' order, containing a list of all these nefarious projects, will not be deemed uninteresting at the present day, when there is but too much tendency in the public mind to indulge in similar practices :-

"At the Council Chamber, Whitehall, the 12th day of July, 1720. Present, their Excellencies the Lords Justices in Council.

"Their Excellencies, the Lords Justices in council, taking into consideration the many inconveniences arising to the public from several projects set on foot for raising of joint stock for various purposes, and that a great many of his Majesty's subjects have been drawn in to part with their money on pretence of assurances that their petitions for patents and charters, to enable them to carry on the same, would be granted: to prevent such impositions, their Excellencies, this day, ordered the said several petitions, together with such reports from the Board of Trade, and from his Majesty's Attorney and Solicitor General, as had been obtained thereon, to be laid before them, and after mature consideration thereof, were pleased, by advice of his Majesty's Privy Council, to order that the said petitions be dismissed, which are as follow :--

"1. Petition of several persons, praying letters patent for carrying on a fishing trade, by the name of the Grand Fishery of Great Britain.

"2. Petition of the Company of the Royal Fishery of England, praying letters patent for such further powers as will effectually contribute to carry on the said fishery.

"3. Petition of George James, on behalf of himself and divers persons of distinction concerned in a national fishery; praying letters patent of incorporation to enable them to carry on the same.

"4. Petition of several merchants, traders, and others, whose names are thereunto subscribed, praying to be incorporated for reviving and carrying on a whale fishery to Greenland and elsewhere.

"5. Petition of Sir John Lambert, and others thereto subscribing, on behalf of themselves and a great number of merchants, praying to be incorporated for carrying on a Greenland trade, and particularly a whale fishery in Davis's Straits.

"6. Another petition for a Greenland trade.

"7. Petition of several merchants, gentlemen, and citizens, praying to be incorporated. for buying and building of ships to let or freight.

"8. Petition of Samuel Antrim and others, praying for letters patent for sowing hemp and flax.

"9. Petition of several merchants, masters of ships, sail-makers, and manufacturers of sail-cloth, praying a charter of incorporation, to enable them to carry on and promote the said manufactory by a joint stock.

"10. Petition of Thomas Boyd, and several hundred merchants, owners and masters of ships, sailmakers, weavers, and other traders, praying a charter of incorporation, empowering them to borrow money for purchasing lands, in order to the manufacturing sail-cloth and fine Holland.

"11. Petition on behalf of several persons interested in a patent granted by the late King William and Queen Mary, for the making of linen and sail-cloth, praying that no charter may be granted to any persons whatsoever for making sail-cloth, but that the privilege now enjoyed by them may be confirmed, and likewise an additional power to carry on the cotton and cotton-silk manufactures.

"12. Petition of several citizens, merchants, and traders in London, and others, subscribers to a British stock, for a general insurance from fire in any part of England, praying to be incorporated for carrying on the said undertaking.

"13. Petition of several of his Majesty's loyal snbjects of the city of London, and other parts of Great Britain, praying to be incorporated, for carrying on a general insurance from losses by fire within the kingdom of England.

"14. Petition of Thomas Burges, and others his Majesty's subjects thereto subscribing, in behalf of themselves and others, subscribers to a fund of 1,200,000 pounds, for carrying on a trade to his Majesty's German dominions, praying to be incorporated, by the name of the Harburg Company.

"15. Petition of Edward Jones, a dealer in timber, on behalf of himself and others, praying to be incorporated for the importation of timber from Germany.

"16. Petition of several merchants of London, praying a charter of incorporation for carrying on a salt-work.

"17. Petition of Captain Macphedris, of London, merchant, on behalf of himself and several merchants, clothiers, hatters, dyers, and other traders, praying a charter of incorporation, empowering them to raise a sufficient sum of money to purchase lands for planting and rearing a wood called madder, for the use of dyers.

"18. Petition of Joseph Galendo, of London, snuff-maker, praying a patent for his invention to prepare and cure Virginia tobacco for snuff in Virginia, and making it into the same in all his Majesty's dominions."

LIST OF BUBBLES.

The following Bubble Companies were by the same order declared to be illegal, and abolished accordingly :--

1. For the importation of Swedish iron.

2. For supplying London with sea-coal. Capital, three millions.

3. For building and rebuilding houses throughout all England. Capital, three millions.

4. For making of muslin.

5. For carrying on and improving the British alum works.

6. For effectually settling the island of Blanco and Sal Tartagus.

7. For supplying the town of Deal with fresh water.

8. For the importation of Flanders lace.

9. For improvement of lands in Great Britain. Capital, four millions.

10. For encouraging the breed of horses in England, and improving of glebe and church lands, and for repairing and rebuilding parsonage and vicarage houses.

11. For making of iron and steel in Great Britain.

12. For improving the land in the county of Flint. Capital, one million.

13. For purchasing lands to build on. Capital, two millions.

14. For trading in hair.

15. For erecting salt-works in Holy Island. Capital, two millions.

16. For buying and selling estates, and lending money on mortgage.

17. For carrying on an undertaking of great advantage, but nobody to know what it is.

18. For paving the streets of London. Capital, two millions.

19. For furnishing funerals to any part of Great Britain.

20. For buying and selling lands and lending money at interest. Capital, five millions.

21. For carrying on the Royal Fishery of Great Britain. Capital, ten millions.

22. For assuring of seamen's wages.

23. For erecting loan-offices for the assistance and encouragement of the industrious. Capital, two millions.

24. For purchasing and improving leasable lands. Capital, four millions.

25. For importing pitch and tar, and other naval stores, from North Britain and America.

26. For the clothing, felt, and pantile trade.

27. For purchasing and improving a manor and royalty in Essex.

28. For insuring of horses. Capital, two millions.

29. For exporting the woollen manufacture, and importing copper, brass, and iron. Capital, four millions.

30. For a grand dispensary. Capital, three millions.

31. For erecting mills and purchasing lead mines. Capital, two millions.

32. For improving the art of making soap.

33. For a settlement on the island of Santa Cruz.

34. For sinking pits and smelting lead ore in Derbyshire.

35. For making glass bottles and other glass.

36. For a wheel for perpetual motion. Capital, one million.

37. For improving of gardens.

38. For insuring and increasing children's fortunes.

39. For entering and loading goods at the custom-house, and for negotiating business for merchants.

40. For carrying on a woollen manufacture in the north of England.

41. For importing walnut-trees from Virginia. Capital, two millions.

42. For making Manchester stuffs of thread and cotton.

43. For making Joppa and Castile soap.

44. For improving the wrought-iron and steel manufactures of this kingdom. Capital, four millions.

45. For dealing in lace, Hollands, cambrics, lawns, &c. Capital, two millions.

46. For trading in and improving certain commodities of the produce of this kingdom, &c. Capital, three millions.

47. For supplying the London markets with cattle.

48. For making looking-glasses, coach glasses, &c. Capital, two millions.

49. For working the tin and lead mines in Cornwall and Derbyshire.

50. For making rape-oil.

51. For importing beaver fur. Capital, two millions.

52. For making pasteboard and packing-paper.

53. For importing of oils and other materials used in the woollen manufacture.

54. For improving and increasing the silk manufactures.

55. For lending money on stock, annuities, tallies, &c.

56. For paying pensions to widows and others, at a small discount. Capital, two millions.

57. For improving malt liquors. Capital, four millions.

58. For a grand American fishery.

59. For purchasing and improving the fenny lands in Lincolnshire. Capital, two millions.

60. For improving the paper manufacture of Great Britain.

61. The Bottomry Company.

62. For drying malt by hot air.

63. For carrying on a trade in the river Oronooko.

64. For the more effectual making of baize, in Colchester and other parts of Great Britain.

65. For buying of naval stores, supplying the victualling, and paying the wages of the workmen.

66. For employing poor artificers, and furnishing merchants and others with watches.

67. For improvement of tillage and the breed of cattle.

68. Another for the improvement of our breed of horses.

69. Another for a horse-insurance.

70. For carrying on the corn trade of Great Britain.

71. For insuring to all masters and mistresses the losses they may sustain by servants. Capital, three millions.

72. For erecting houses or hospitals, for taking in and maintaining illegitimate children. Capital, two millions.

73. For bleaching coarse sugars, without the use of fire or loss of substance.

74. For building turnpikes and wharfs in Great Britain.

75. For insuring from thefts and robberies.

76. For extracting silver from lead.

77. For making China and Delft ware. Capital, one million.

78. For importing tobacco, and exporting it again to Sweden and the north of Europe. Capital, four millions.

79. For making iron with pit coal.

80. For furnishing the cities of London and Westminster with hay and straw. Capital, three millions.

81. For a sail and packing cloth manufactory in Ireland.

82. For taking up ballast.

83. For buying and fitting out ships to suppress pirates.

84. For the importation of timber from Wales. Capital, two millions.

85. For rock-salt.

86. For the transmutation of quicksilver into a malleable fine metal.

Besides these bubbles, many others sprang up daily, in spite of the condemnation of the Government and the ridicule of the still sane portion of the public. The print-shops teemed with caricatures, and the newspapers with epigrams and satires, upon the prevalent folly. An ingenious card-maker published a pack of South Sea playing-cards, which are now extremely rare, each card containing, besides the usual figures, of a very small size, in one corner, a caricature of a bubble company, with appropriate verses underneath. One of the most famous bubbles was "Puckle's Machine Company," for discharging round and square cannon-balls and bullets, and making a total revolution in the art of war. Its pretensions to public favour were thus summed up, on the eight of spades :--

A rare invention to destroy the crowd
Of fools at home, instead of fools abroad.
Fear not, my friends, this terrible machine,
They're only wounded who have shares therein.

The nine of hearts was a caricature of the English Copper and Brass Company, with the following epigram :--

The headlong fool that wants to be a swopper
Of gold and silver coin for English copper,
May, in Change Alley, prove himself an ass,
And give rich metal for adulterate brass.

The eight of diamonds celebrated the Company for the Colonization of Acadia, with this doggrel :--

He that is rich and wants to fool away
A good round sum in North America,
Let him subscribe himself a headlong sharer,
And asses' ears shall honour him or bearer.

And in a similar style every card of the pack exposed some knavish scheme, and ridiculed the persons who were its dupes. It was computed that the total amount of the sums proposed for carrying on these projects was upwards of three hundred millions sterling, a sum so immense that it exceeded the value of all the lands in England at twenty years' purchase.

44

It is time, however, to return to the great South Sea gulf, that swallowed the fortunes of so many thousands of the avaricious and the credulous. On the 29th of May, the stock had risen as high as five hundred, and about two-thirds of the government annuitants had exchanged the securities of the state for those of the South Sea Company. During the whole of the month of May the stock continued to rise, and on the 28th it was quoted at five hundred and fifty. In four days after this it took a prodigious leap, rising suddenly from five hundred and fifty to eight hundred and ninety. It was now the general opinion that the stock could rise no higher, and many persons took that opportunity of selling out, with a view of realising their profits. Many noblemen and persons in the train of the King, and about to accompany him to Hanover, were also anxious to sell out. So many sellers, and so few buyers, appeared in the Alley on the 3rd of June, that the stock fell at once from eight hundred and ninety to six hundred and forty. The directors were alarmed, and gave their agents orders to buy. Their efforts succeeded. Towards evening confidence was restored, and the stock advanced to seven hundred and fifty. It continued at this price, with some slight fluctuation, until the company closed their books on the 22nd of June.

It would be needless and uninteresting to detail the various arts employed by the directors to keep up the price of stock. It will be sufficient to state that it finally rose to one thousand per cent. It was quoted at this price in the commencement of August. The bubble was then full-blown, and began to quiver and shake, preparatory to its bursting.

Many of the government annuitants expressed dissatisfaction against the directors. They accused them of partiality in making out the lists for shares in each subscription. Further uneasiness was occasioned by its being generally known that Sir John Blunt, the chairman, and some others, had sold out. During the whole of the month of August the stock fell, and on the 2nd of September it was quoted at seven hundred only.

The state of things now became alarming. To prevent, if possible, the utter extinction of public confidence in their proceedings, the directors summoned a general court of the whole corporation, to meet in Merchant Tailors' Hall, on the 8th of September. By nine o'clock in the morning, the room was filled to suffocation; Cheapside was blocked up by a crowd unable to gain admittance, and the greatest excitement prevailed. The directors and their friends mustered in great. numbers. Sir John Fellowes, the sub-governor, was called to the chair. He acquainted the assembly with the cause of their meeting, read to them the several resolutions of the court of directors, and gave them an account of their proceedings; of the taking in the redeemable and unredeemable funds, and of the subscriptions in money. Mr. Secretary Craggs then made a short speech, wherein he commended the conduct of the directors, and urged that nothing could more effectually contribute to the bringing this scheme to perfection than union among themselves. He concluded with a motion for thanking the court of directors for their prudent and skilful management, and for desiring them to proceed in such manner as they should think most proper for the interest and advantage of the corporation. Mr. Hungerford, who had rendered himself very conspicuous in the House of Commons for his zeal in behalf of the South Sea Company, and who was shrewdly suspected to have been a considerable gainer by knowing the right time to sell out, was very magniloquent on this occasion. He said that he had seen the rise and fall, the decay and resurrection of many communities of this nature, but that, in his opinion, none had ever performed such wonderful things in so short a time as the South Sea Company. They had done more than the crown, the pulpit, or the bench could do. They had reconciled all parties in one common interest; they had laid asleep, if not wholly extinguished, all the domestic jars and animosities of the nation. By the rise of their stock, monied men had vastly increased their fortunes; country-gentlemen had seen the value of their lands doubled and trebled in their hands. They had at the same time done good to the Church, not a few of the reverend clergy having got great sums by the project. In short, they had enriched the whole nation, and he hoped they had not forgotten themselves. There was some hissing at the latter part of this speech, which for the extravagance of its eulogy was not far removed from satire; but the directors and their friends, and all the winners in the room, applauded vehemently. The Duke of Portland spoke in a similar strain, and expressed his great wonder why anybody should be dissatisfied: of course, he was a winner by his speculations, and in a condition similar to that of the fat alderman in Joe Miller's Jests, who, whenever he had eaten a good dinner, folded his hands upon his paunch, and expressed his doubts whether there could be a hungry man in the world.

Several resolutions were passed at this meeting, but they had no effect upon the public. Upon the very same evening the stock fell to six hundred and forty, and on the morrow to five hundred and forty. Day after day it continued to fall, until it was as low as four hundred. In a letter dated September 13th, from Mr. Broderick, M.P. to Lord Chancellor Middleton, and published in Coxo's Walpole, the former says,--"Various are the conjectures why the South Sea directors have suffered the cloud to break so early. I made no doubt but they would do so when they found it to their advantage. They have stretched credit so far beyond what it would bear, that specie proves insufficient to support it. Their most considerable men have drawn out, securing themselves by the losses of the deluded, thoughtless numbers, whose understandings have been overruled by avarice and the hope of making mountains out of mole-hills. Thousands of families will be reduced to beggary. The consternation is inexpressible-- the rage beyond description, and the case altogether so desperate that I do not see any plan or scheme so much as thought of for averting the blow, so that I cannot pretend to guess what is next to be done." Ten days afterwards, the stock still falling, he writes,--" The Company have yet come to no determination, for they are in such a wood that they know not which way to turn. By several gentlemen lately come to town, I perceive the very name of a South-Sea-man grows abominable in every country. A great many goldsmiths are already run off, and more will daily. I question whether one-third, nay, one-fourth, of them can stand it. From the very beginning, I founded my judgment of the whole affair upon the unquestionable maxim, that ten millions (which is more than our running cash) could not circulate two hundred millions, beyond which our paper credit extended. That, therefore, whenever that should become doubtful, be the cause what it would, our noble state machine must inevitably fall to the ground."

On the 12th of September, at the earnest solicitation of Mr. Secretary Craggs, several conferences were held between the directors of the South Sea and the directors of the Bank. A report which was circulated, that the latter had agreed to circulate six millions of the South Sea Company's bonds, caused the stock to rise to six hundred and seventy; but in the afternoon, as soon as the report was known to be groundless, the stock fell again to five hundred and eighty; the next day to five hundred and seventy, and so gradually to four hundred. [Gay (the poet), in that disastrous year, had a present from young Craggs of some South Sea stock, and once supposed himself to be master of twenty thousand pounds. His friends persuaded him to sell his share, but he dreamed of dignity and splendour, and could not bear to obstruct his own fortune. He was then importuned to sell as much as would purchase a hundred a year for life, "which," says Fenton, "will make you sure of a clean shirt and a shoulder of mutton every day." This counsel was rejected; the profit and principal were lost, and Gay sunk under the calamity so low that his life became in danger.--Johnson's Lives of the Poets.]

The ministry were seriously alarmed at the aspect of affairs. The directors could not appear in the streets without being insulted; dangerous riots were every moment apprehended. Despatches were sent off to the King at Hanover, praying his immediate return. Mr. Walpole, who was staying at his country-seat, was sent for, that he might employ his known influence with the directors of the Bank of England to induce them to accept the proposal made by the South Sea Company for circulating a number of their bonds.

The Bank was very unwilling to mix itself up with the affairs of the Company; it dreaded being involved in calamities which it could not relieve, and received all overtures with visible reluctance. But the universal voice of the nation called upon it to come to the rescue. Every person of note in commercial politics was called in to advise in the emergency. A rough draft of a contract drawn up by Mr. Walpole was ultimately adopted as the basis of further negotiations, and the public alarm abated a little.

On the following day, the 20th of September, a general court of the South Sea Company was held at Merchant Tailors' Hall, in which resolutions were carried, empowering the directors to agree with the Bank of England, or any other persons, to circulate the Company's bonds, or make any other agreement with the Bank which they should think proper. One of the speakers, a Mr. Pulteney, said it was most surprising to see the extraordinary panic which had seized upon the people. Men were running to and fro in alarm and terror, their imaginations filled with some great calamity, the form and dimensions of which nobody knew.

"Black it stood as night--
Fierce as ten furies--terrible as hell."

At a general court of the Bank of England held two days afterwards, the governor informed them of the several meetings that had been held on the affairs of the South Sea Company, adding that the directors had not yet thought fit to come to any decision upon the matter. A resolution was then proposed, and carried without a dissentient voice, empowering the directors to agree with those of the South Sea to circulate their bonds, to what sum, and upon what terms, and for what time, they might think proper.

Thus both parties were at liberty to act as they might judge best for the public interest. Books were opened at the Bank for a subscription of three millions for the support of public credit, on the usual terms of 15 pounds per cent. deposit, per cent. premium, and 5 pounds. per cent. interest. So great was the concourse of people in the early part of the morning, all eagerly bringing their money, that it was thought the subscription would be filled that day; but before noon, the tide turned. In spite of all that could be done to prevent it, the South Sea Company's stock fell rapidly. Their bonds were in such discredit, that a run commenced upon the most eminent goldsmiths and bankers, some of whom having lent out great sums upon South Sea stock were obliged to shut up their shops and abscond. The Sword-blade Company, who had hitherto been the chief cashiers of the South Sea Company, stopped payment. This being looked upon as but the beginning of evil, occasioned a great run upon the Bank, who were now obliged to pay out money much faster than they had received it upon the subscription in the morning. The day succeeding was a holiday (the 29th of September), and the Bank had a little breathing time. They bore up against the storm; but their former rivals, the South Sea Company, were wrecked upon it. Their stock fell to one hundred and fifty, and gradually, after various fluctuations, to one hundred and thirty-five.

The Bank, finding they were not able to restore public confidence, and stem the tide of ruin, without running the risk of being swept away with those they intended to save, declined to carry out the agreement into which they had partially entered. They were under no obligation whatever to continue; for the so called Bank contract was nothing more than the rough draught of an agreement, in which blanks had been left for several important particulars, and which contained no penalty for their secession. "And thus," to use the words of the Parliamentary History, "were seen, in the space of eight months, the rise, progress, and fall of that mighty fabric, which, being wound up by mysterious springs to a wonderful height, had fixed the eyes and expectations of all Europe, but whose foundation, being fraud, illusion, credulity, and infatuation, fell to the ground as soon as the artful management of its directors was discovered."

In the hey-day of its blood, during the progress of this dangerous delusion, the manners of the nation became sensibly corrupted. The Parliamentary inquiry, set on foot to discover the delinquents, disclosed scenes of infamy, disgraceful alike to the morals of the offenders and the intellects of the people among whom they had arisen. It is a deeply interesting study to investigate all the evils that were the result. Nations, like individuals, cannot become desperate gamblers with impunity. Punishment is sure to overtake them sooner or later. A celebrated writer [Smollett.] is quite wrong, when he says, "that such an era as this is the most unfavourable for a historian; that no reader of sentiment and imagination can be entertained or interested by a detail of transactions such as these, which admit of no warmth, no colouring, no embellishment; a detail of which only serves to exhibit an inanimate picture of tasteless vice and mean degeneracy." On the contrary, and Smollett might have discovered it, if he had been in the humour--the subject is capable of inspiring as much interest as even a novelist can desire. Is there no warmth in the despair of a plundered people?--no life and animation in the picture which might be drawn of the woes of hundreds of impoverished and ruined families? of the wealthy of yesterday become the beggars of to-day? of the powerful and influential changed into exiles and outcasts, and the voice of self-reproach and imprecation resounding from every corner of the land? Is it a dull or uninstructive picture to see a whole people shaking suddenly off the trammels of reason, and running wild after a golden vision, refusing obstinately to believe that it is not real, till, like a deluded hind running after an ignis fatuus, they are plunged into a quagmire ? But in this false spirit has history too often been written. The intrigues of unworthy courtiers to gain the favour of still more unworthy kings; or the records of murderous battles and sieges have been dilated on, and told over and over again, with all the eloquence of style and all the charms of fancy; while the circumstances which have most deeply affected the morals and welfare of the people, have been passed over with but slight notice as dry and dull, and capable of neither warmth nor colouring.

During the progress of this famous bubble, England presented a singular spectacle. The public mind was in a state of unwholesome fermentation. Men were no longer satisfied with the slow but sure profits of cautious industry. The hope of boundless wealth for the morrow made them heedless and extravagant for to-day. A luxury, till then unheard-of, was introduced, bringing in its train a corresponding laxity of morals. The overbearing insolence of ignorant men, who had arisen to sudden wealth by successful gambling, made men of true gentility of mind and manners, blush that gold should have power to raise the unworthy in the scale of society. The haughtiness of some of these "cyphering cits," as they were termed by Sir Richard Steele, was remembered against them in the day of their adversity. In the Parliamentary inquiry, many of the directors suffered more for their insolence than for their peculation. One of them, who, in the full-blown pride of an ignorant rich man, had said that he would feed his horse upon gold, was reduced almost to bread and water for himself; every haughty look, every overbearing speech, was set down, and repaid them a hundredfold in poverty and humiliation.

The state of matters all over the country was so alarming, that George I shortened his intended stay in Hanover, and returned in all haste to England. He arrived on the 11th of November, and Parliament was summoned to meet on the 8th of December. In the mean time, public meetings were held in every considerable town of the empire, at which petitions were adopted, praying the vengeance of the Legislature upon the South Sea directors, who, by their fraudulent practices, had brought the nation to the brink of ruin. Nobody seemed to imagine that the nation itself was as culpable as the South Sea Company. Nobody blamed the credulity and avarice of the people,--the degrading lust of gain, which had swallowed up every nobler quality in the national character, or the infatuation which had made the multitude run their heads with such frantic eagerness into the net held out for them by scheming projectors. These things were never mentioned. The people were a simple, honest, hard-working people, ruined by a gang of robbers, who were to be hanged, drawn, and quartered without mercy.

This was the almost unanimous feeling of the country. The two Houses of Parliament were not more reasonable. Before the guilt of the South Sea directors was known, punishment was the only cry. The King, in his speech from the throne, expressed his hope that they would remember that all their prudence, temper, and resolution were necessary to find out and apply the proper remedy for their misfortunes. In the debate on the answer to the address, several speakers indulged in the most violent invectives against the directors of the South Sea project. The Lord Molesworth was particularly vehement. "It had been said by some, that there was no law to punish the directors of the South Sea Company, who were justly looked upon as the authors of the present misfortunes of the state. In his opinion they ought, upon this occasion, to follow the example of the ancient Romans, who, having no law against parricide, because their legislators supposed no son could be so unnaturally wicked as to embrue his hands in his father's blood, made a law to punish this heinous crime as soon as it was committed. They adjudged the guilty wretch to be sown in a sack, and thrown alive into the Tyber. He looked upon the contrivers and executors of the villanous South Sea scheme as the parricides of their country, and should be satisfied to see them tied in like manner in sacks, and thrown into the Thames." Other members spoke with as much want of temper and discretion. Mr. Walpole was more moderate. He recommended that their first care should be to restore public credit. "If the city of London were on fire, all wise men would aid in extinguishing the flames, and preventing the spread of the conflagration before they inquired after the incendiaries. Public credit had received a dangerous wound, and lay bleeding, and they ought to apply a speedy remedy to it. It was time enough to punish the assassin afterwards." On the 9th of December an address, in answer to his Majesty's speech, was agreed upon, after an amendment, which was carried without a division, that words should be added expressive of the determination of the House not only to seek a remedy for the national distresses, but to punish the authors of them.

The inquiry proceeded rapidly. The directors were ordered to lay before the House a full account of all their proceedings. Resolutions were passed to the effect that the calamity was mainly owing to the vile arts of stockjobbers, and that nothing could tend more to the re-establishment of public credit than a law to prevent this infamous practice. Mr. Walpole then rose, and said, that "as he had previously hinted, he had spent some time upon a scheme for restoring public credit, but that, the execution of it depending upon a position which had been laid down as fundamental, he thought it proper, before he opened out his scheme, to be informed whether he might rely upon that foundation. It was, whether the subscription of public debts and encumbrances, money subscriptions, and other contracts, made with the South Sea Company should remain in the present state?" This question occasioned an animated debate. It was finally agreed, by a majority of 259 against 117, that all these contracts should remain in their present state, unless altered for the relief of the proprietors by a general court of the South Sea Company, or set aside by due course of law. On the following day Mr. Walpole laid before a committee of the whole House his scheme for the restoration of public credit, which was, in substance, to ingraft nine millions of South Sea stock into the Bank of England, and the same sum into the East India Company, upon certain conditions. The plan was favourably received by the House. After some few objections, it was ordered that proposals should be received from the two great corporations. They were both unwilling to lend their aid, and the plan met with a warm but fruitless opposition at the general courts summoned for the purpose of deliberating upon it. They, however, ultimately agreed upon the terms on which they would consent to circulate the South Sea bonds, and their report, being presented to the committee, a bill was brought in, under the superintendence of Mr. Walpole, and safely carried through both Houses of Parliament.

A bill was at the same time brought in, for restraining the South Sea directors, governor, sub-governor, treasurer, cashier, and clerks from leaving the kingdom for a twelvemonth, and for discovering their estates and effects, and preventing them from transporting or alienating the same. All the most influential members of the House supported the bill. Mr. Shippen, seeing Mr. Secretary Craggs in his place, and believing the injurious rumours that were afloat of that minister's conduct in the South Sea business, determined to touch him to the quick. He said, he was glad to see a British House of Commons resuming its pristine vigour and spirit, and acting with so much unanimity for the public good. It was necessary to secure the persons and estates of the South Sea directors and their officers; "but," he added, looking fixedly at Mr. Craggs as he spoke, "there were other men in high station, whom, in time, he would not be afraid to name, who were no less guilty than the directors." Mr. Craggs arose in great wrath, and said, that if the innuendo were directed against him, he was ready to give satisfaction to any man who questioned him, either in the House or out of it. Loud cries of order immediately arose on every side. In the midst of the uproar Lord Molesworth got up, and expressed his wonder at the boldness of Mr. Craggs in challenging the whole House of Commons. He, Lord Molesworth, though somewhat old, past sixty, would answer Mr. Craggs whatever he had to say in the House, and he trusted there were plenty of young men beside him, who would not be afraid to look Mr. Craggs in the face, out of the House. The cries of order again resounded from every side; the members arose simultaneously; everybody seemed to be vociferating at once. The Speaker in vain called order. The confusion lasted several minutes, during which Lord Molesworth and Mr. Craggs were almost the only members who kept their seats. At last the call for Mr. Craggs became so violent that he thought proper to submit to the universal feeling of the House, and explain his unparliamentary expression. He said, that by giving satisfaction to the impugners of his conduct in that House, he did not mean that he would fight, but that he would explain his conduct. Here the matter ended, and the House proceeded to debate in what manner they should conduct their inquiry into the affairs of the South Sea Company, whether in a grand or a select committee. Ultimately, a Secret Committee of thirteen was appointed, with power to send for persons, papers, and records.

The Lords were as zealous and as hasty as the Commons. The Bishop of Rochester said the scheme had been like a pestilence. The Duke of Wharton said the House ought to show no respect of persons; that, for his part, he would give up the dearest friend he had, if he had been engaged in the project. The nation had been plundered in a most shameful and flagrant manner, and he would go as far as anybody in the punishment of the offenders. Lord Stanhope said, that every farthing possessed by the criminals, whether directors or not directors, ought to be confiscated, to make good the public losses.

During all this time the public excitement was extreme. We learn, from Coxe's *Walpole*, that the very name of a South Sea director was thought to be synonymous. with every species of fraud and villany. Petitions from counties, cities, and boroughs, in all parts of the kingdom, were presented, crying for the justice due to an injured nation and the punishment of the villanous peculators. Those moderate men, who would not go to extreme lengths, even in the punishment of the guilty, were accused of being accomplices, were exposed to repeated insults and virulent invectives, and devoted, both in anonymous letters and public writings, to the speedy vengeance of an injured people. The accusations against Mr. Aislabie, Chancellor of the Exchequer, and Mr. Craggs, another member of the ministry, were so loud, that the House of Lords resolved to proceed at once into the investigation concerning them. It was ordered, on the 21st of January, that all brokers concerned in the South Sea scheme should lay before the House an account of the stock or subscriptions bought or sold by them for any of the officers of the Treasury or Exchequer, or in trust for any of them, since Michaelmas 1719. When this account was delivered, it appeared that large quantities of stock had been transferred to the use of Mr. Aislabie. Five of the South Sea directors, including Mr. Edward Gibbon, the grandfather of the celebrated historian, were ordered into the custody of the black rod. Upon a motion made by Earl Stanhope, it was unanimously resolved, that the taking in or giving credit for stock without a valuable consideration actually paid or sufficiently secured; or the purchasing stock by any director or agent of the South Sea Company, for the use or benefit of any member of the administration, or any member of either House of Parliament, during such time as the South Sea Bill was yet pending in Parliament, was a notorious and dangerous corruption. Another resolution was passed a few days afterwards, to the effect that several of the directors and officers of the Company having, in a clandestine manner, sold their own stock to the Company, had been guilty of a notorious fraud and breach of trust, and had thereby mainly caused the unhappy turn of affairs that had so much affected public credit. Mr. Aislabie resigned his office as Chancellor of the Exchequer, and absented himself from Parliament until the formal inquiry into his individual guilt was brought under the consideration of the Legislature.

In the mean time, Knight, the treasurer of the Company, and who was entrusted with all the dangerous secrets of the dishonest directors, packed up his books and documents, and made his escape from the country. He embarked in disguise, in a small boat on the river, and proceeding to a vessel hired for the purpose, was safely conveyed to Calais. The Committee of Secrecy informed the House of the circumstance, when it was resolved unanimously that two addresses should be presented to the King; the first praying that he would issue a proclamation, offering a reward for the apprehension of Knight; and the second, that he would give immediate orders to stop the ports, and to take effectual care of the coasts, to prevent the said Knight, or any other officers of the South Sea Company, from escaping out of the kingdom. The ink was hardly dry upon these addresses before they were carried to the King by Mr. Methuen, deputed by the House for that purpose. The same evening a royal proclamation was issued, offering a reward of two thousand pounds for the apprehension of Knight. The Commons ordered the doors of the House to be locked, and the keys to be placed upon the table. General Ross, one of the members of the Committee of Secrecy, acquainted them that they had already discovered a train of the deepest villany and fraud that Hell had ever contrived to ruin a nation, which in due time they would lay before the House. In the mean time, in order to a further discovery, the Committee thought it highly necessary to secure the persons of some of the directors and principal South Sea officers, and to seize their papers. A motion to this effect having been made, was carried unanimously. Sir Robert Chaplin, Sir Theodore Janssen, Mr. Sawbridge, and Mr. F. Eyles, members of the House, and directors of the South Sea Company, were summoned to appear in their places, and answer for their corrupt practices. Sir Theodore Janssen and Mr. Sawbridge answered to their names, and endeavoured to exculpate themselves. The House heard them patiently, and then ordered them to withdraw. A motion was then made, and carried nemine contradicente, that they had been guilty of a notorious breach of trust--had occasioned much loss to great numbers of his Majesty's subjects, and had highly prejudiced the public credit. It was then ordered that, for their offence, they should be expelled the House, and taken into the custody of the sergeant-at-arms. Sir Robert Chaplin and Mr. Eyles, attending in their places four days afterwards, were also expelled the House. It was resolved at the same time to address the King, to give directions to his ministers at foreign courts to make application for Knight, that he might be delivered up to the English authorities, in ease he took refuge in any of their dominions. The King at once agreed, and messengers were despatched to all parts of the Continent the same night.

Among the directors taken into custody, was Sir John Blunt, the man whom popular opinion has generally accused of having been the original author and father of the scheme. This man, we are informed by Pope, in his epistle to Allen, Lord Bathurst, was a dissenter, of a most religious deportment, and professed to be a great believer. He constantly declaimed against the luxury and corruption of the age, the partiality of parliaments, and the misery of party spirit. He was particularly eloquent against avarice in great and noble persons. He was originally a scrivener, and afterwards became, not only a director, but the most active manager of the South Sea Company. Whether it was during his career in this capacity that he first began to declaim against the avarice of the great, we are not informed. He certainly must have seen enough of it to justify his severest anathema; but if the preacher had himself been free from the vice he condemned, his declamations would have had a better effect. He was brought

51

up in custody to the bar of the House of Lords, and underwent a long examination. He refused to answer several important questions. He said he had been examined already by a committee of the House of Commons, and as he did not remember his answers, and might contradict himself, he refused to answer before another tribunal. This declaration, in itself an indirect proof of guilt, occasioned some commotion in the House. He was again asked peremptorily whether he had ever sold any portion of the stock to any member of the administration, or any member of either House of Parliament, to facilitate the passing of the bill. He again declined to answer. He was anxious, he said, to treat the House with all possible respect, but he thought it hard to be compelled to accuse himself. After several ineffectual attempts to refresh his memory, he was directed to withdraw. A violent discussion ensued between the friends and opponents of the ministry. It was asserted that the administration were no strangers to the convenient taciturnity of Sir John Blunt. The Duke of Wharton made a reflection upon the Earl Stanhope, which the latter warmly resented. He spoke under great excitement, and with such vehemence as to cause a sudden determination of blood to the head. He felt himself so ill that he was obliged to leave the House and retire to his chamber. He was cupped immediately, and also let blood on the following morning, but with slight relief. The fatal result was not anticipated. Towards evening he became drowsy, and turning himself on his face, expired. The sudden death of this statesman caused great grief to the nation. George I was exceedingly affected, and shut himself up for some hours in his closet, inconsolable for his loss.

Knight, the treasurer of the company, was apprehended at Tirlemont, near Liege, by one of the secretaries of Mr. Leathes, the British resident at Brussels, and lodged in the citadel of Antwerp. Repeated applications were made to the court of Austria to deliver him up, but in vain. Knight threw himself upon the protection of the states of Brabant, and demanded to be tried in that country. It was a privilege granted to the states of Brabant by one of the articles of the Joyeuse Entree, that every criminal apprehended in that country should be tried in that country. The states insisted on their privilege, and refused to deliver Knight to the British authorities. The latter did not cease their solicitations; but in the mean time, Knight escaped from the citadel.

On the 16th of February the Committee of Secrecy made their first report to the House. They stated that their inquiry had been attended with numerous difficulties and embarrassments; every one they had examined had endeavoured, as far as in him lay, to defeat the ends of justice. In some of the books produced before them, false and fictitious entries had been made; in others, there were entries of money, with blanks for the name of the stockholders. There were frequent erasures and alterations, and in some of the books leaves were torn out. They also found that some books of great importance had been destroyed altogether, and that some had been taken away or secreted. At the very entrance into their inquiry, they had observed that the matters referred to them were of great variety and extent. Many persons had been intrusted with various parts in the execution of the law, and under colour thereof had acted in an unwarrantable manner, in disposing of the properties of many thousands of persons, amounting to many millions of money. They discovered that, before the South Sea Act was passed, there was an entry in the Company's books of the sum of 1,259,325 pounds, upon account of stock stated to have been sold to the amount of 574,500 pounds. This stock was all fictitious, and had been disposed of with a view to promote the passing of the bill. It was noted as sold at various days, and at various prices, from 150 to 325 per cent. Being surprised to see so large an account disposed of, at a time when the Company were not empowered to increase their capital, the committee determined to investigate most carefully the whole transaction. The governor, sub-governor, and several directors were brought before them, and examined rigidly. They found that, at the time these entries were made, the Company was not in possession of such a quantity of stock, having in their own right only a small quantity, not exceeding thirty thousand pounds at the utmost. Pursuing the inquiry, they found that this amount of stock, was to be esteemed as taken in or holden by the Company, for the benefit of the pretended purchasers, although no mutual agreement was made for its delivery or acceptance at any certain time. No money was paid down, nor any deposit or security whatever given to the Company by the supposed purchasers; so that if the stock had fallen, as might have been expected, had the act not passed, they would have sustained no loss. If, on the contrary, the price of stock advanced (as it actually did by the success of the scheme), the difference by the advanced price was to be made good to them. Accordingly, after the passing of the act, the account of stock was made up and adjusted with Mr. Knight, and the pretended purchasers were paid the difference out of the Company's cash. This fictitious stock, which had been chiefly at the disposal of Sir John Blunt, Mr. Gibbon, and Mr. Knight, was distributed among several members of the government and their connexions, by way of bribe, to facilitate the passing of the bill. To the Earl of Sunderland was assigned 50,000 pounds of this stock; to the Duchess of Kendal 10,000 pounds; to the Countess of Platen 10,000 pounds; to her two nieces 10,000 pounds; to Mr. Secretary Craggs 30,000 pounds; to Mr. Charles Stanhope (one of the Secretaries of the Treasury) 10,000 pounds; to the Swordblade Company 50,000 pounds. It also appeared that Mr. Stanhope had received the enormous sum of 250,000 pounds as the difference in the price of some stock, through the hands of Turner, Caswall, and Co., but that his name had been partly erased from their books, and altered to Stangape. Aislabie, the Chancellor of the Exchequer, had made profits still more abominable. He had an account with the same firm, who were also South Sea directors, to the amount of 794,451 pounds. He had, besides, advised the Company to make their second subscription one million and a half, instead of a million, by their own authority, and without any warrant. The third subscription had been conducted in a manner as disgraceful. Mr. Aislabie's name was down for 70,000 pounds; Mr. Craggs, senior, for 659,000 pounds; the Earl of Sunderland's for 160,000 pounds; and Mr. Stanhope for 47,000 pounds. This report was succeeded by six others, less important. At the end of the last, the committee declared that the absence of Knight, who had been principally intrusted, prevented them from carrying on their inquiries.

The first report was ordered to be printed, and taken into consideration on the next day but one succeeding. After a very angry and animated debate, a series of resolutions were agreed to, condemnatory of the conduct of the directors, of the members of the Parliament and of the administration concerned with them; and declaring that they ought, each and all, to make satisfaction out of their own estates for the injury they had done the public. Their practices were declared to be corrupt, infamous, and dangerous; and a bill was ordered to be brought in for the relief of the unhappy sufferers.

Mr. Charles Stanhope was the first person brought to account for his share in these transactions. He urged in his defence that, for some years past, he had lodged all the money he was possessed of in Mr. Knight's hands, and whatever stock Mr. Knight had taken in for him, he had paid a valuable consideration for it. As to the stock that had been bought for him by Turner, Caswall, and Co. he knew nothing about it. Whatever had been done in that matter was done without his authority, and he could not be responsible for it. Turner and Co. took the latter charge upon themselves, but it was notorious to every unbiassed and unprejudiced person that Mr. Stanhope was a gainer of the 250,000 pounds which lay in the hands of that firm to his credit. He was, however, acquitted by a majority of three only. The greatest exertions were made to screen him. Lord Stanhope, the son of the Earl of Chesterfield, went round to the wavering members, using all the eloquence he was possessed of to induce them either to vote for the acquittal or to absent themselves from the house. Many weak-headed country-gentlemen were led astray by his persuasions, and the result was as already stated. The acquittal caused the greatest discontent throughout the country. Mobs of a menacing character assembled in different parts of London; fears of riots were generally entertained, especially as the examination of a still greater delinquent was expected by many to have a similar termination. Mr. Aislabie, whose high office and deep responsibilities should have kept him honest, even had native principle been insufficient, was very justly regarded as perhaps the greatest criminal of all. His case was entered into on the day succeeding the acquittal of Mr. Starthope. Great excitement prevailed, and the lobbies and avenues of the house were beset by crowds, impatient to know the result. The debate lasted the whole day. Mr. Aislabie found few friends: his guilt was so apparent and so heinous that nobody had courage to stand up in his favour. It was finally resolved, without a dissentient voice, that Mr. Aislabie had encouraged and promoted the destructive execution of the South Sea scheme with a view to his own exorbitant profit, and had combined with the directors in their pernicious practices to the ruin of the public trade and credit of the kingdom: that he should for his offences be ignominiously expelled from the House of Commons, and committed a close prisoner to the Tower of London; that he should be restrained from going out of the kingdom for a whole year, or till the end of the next session of Parliament; and that he should make out a correct account of all his estate, in order that it might be applied to the relief of those who had suffered by his malpractices.

This verdict caused the greatest joy. Though it was delivered at half-past twelve at night, it soon spread over the city. Several persons illuminated their houses in token of their joy. On the following day, when Mr. Aislabie was conveyed to the Tower, the mob assembled on Tower-hill with the intention of hooting and pelting him. Not succeeding in this, they kindled a large bonfire, and danced around it in the exuberance of their delight. Several bonfires were made in other places; London presented the appearance of a holiday, and people congratulated one another as if they had just escaped from some great calamity. The rage upon the acquittal of Mr. Stanhope had grown to such a height that none could tell where it would have ended, had Mr. Aislabie met with the like indulgence.

To increase the public satisfaction, Sir George Caswall, of the firm of Turner, Caswall, & Co. was expelled the House on the following day, and ordered to refund the sum of 250,000 pounds.

That part of the report of the Committee of Secrecy which related to the Earl of Sunderland was next taken into consideration. Every effort was made to clear his Lordship from the imputation. As the case against him rested chiefly on the evidence extorted from Sir John Blunt, great pains were taken to make it appear that Sir John's word was not to be believed, especially in a matter affecting the honour of a peer and privy councillor. All the friends of the ministry rallied around the Earl, it being generally reported that a verdict of guilty against him would bring a Tory ministry into power. He was eventually acquitted, by a majority of 233 against 172; but the country was convinced of his guilt. The greatest indignation was everywhere expressed, and menacing mobs again assembled in London. Happily no disturbances took place.

This was the day on which Mr. Craggs, the elder, expired. The morrow had been appointed for the consideration of his case. It was very generally believed that he had poisoned himself. It appeared, however, that grief for the loss of his son, one of the Secretaries of the Treasury, who had died five weeks previously of the small-pox, preyed much on his mind. For this son, dearly beloved, he had been amassing vast heaps of riches: he had been getting money, but not honestly; and he for whose sake he had bartered his honour and sullied his fame, was now no more. The dread of further exposure increased his trouble of mind, and ultimately brought on an apoplectic fit, in which he expired. He left a fortune of a million and a half, which was afterwards confiscated for the benefit of the sufferers by the unhappy delusion he had been so mainly instrumental in raising.

One by one the case of every director of the Company was taken into consideration. A sum amounting to two millions and fourteen thousand pounds was confiscated from their estates towards repairing the mischief they had done, each man being allowed a certain residue, in proportion to his conduct and circumstances, with which he might begin the world anew. Sir John Blunt was only allowed 5,000 pounds out of his fortune of upwards of 183,000 pounds; Sir John Fellows was allowed 10,000 pounds out of 243,000 pounds; Sir Theodore Janssen, 50,000 pounds out of 243,000 pounds; Mr. Edward Gibbon, 10,000 pounds out of 106,000 pounds.; Sir John Lambert, 5000 pounds out of 72,000 pounds.

Others, less deeply involved, were treated with greater liberality. Gibbon, the historian, whose grandfather was the Mr. Edward Gibbon so severely mulcted, has given, in the Memoirs of his Life and Writings, an interesting account of the proceedings in Parliament at this time. He owns that he is not an unprejudiced witness; but, as all the writers from which it is possible to extract any notice of the proceedings of these disastrous years, were prejudiced on the other side, the statements of the great historian become of additional value. If only on the principle of audi alteram partem, his opinion is entitled to consideration. "In the year 1716," he says, "my grandfather was elected one of the directors of the South Sea Company, and his books exhibited the proof that before his acceptance of that fatal office, he had acquired an independent fortune of 60,000 pounds. But his fortune was overwhelmed in the shipwreck of the year twenty, and the labours of thirty years were blasted in a single day. Of the use or abuse of the South Sea scheme, of the guilt or innocence of my grandfather and his brother directors, I am neither a competent nor a disinterested judge. Yet the equity of modern times must condemn the violent and arbitrary proceedings, which would have disgraced the cause of justice, and rendered injustice still more odious. No sooner had the nation awakened from its golden dream, than a popular, and even a Parliamentary clamour, demanded its victims; but it was acknowledged on all sides, that the directors, however guilty, could not be touched by any known laws of the land. The intemperate notions of Lord Molesworth were not literally acted on; but a bill of pains and penalties was introduced -- a retro-active statute, to punish the offences which did not exist at the time they were committed. The Legislature restrained the persons of the directors, imposed an exorbitant security for their appearance, and marked their character with a previous note of ignominy. They were compelled to deliver, upon oath, the strict value of their estates, and were disabled from making any transfer or alienation of any part of their property. Against a bill of pains and penalties, it is the common right of every subject to be heard by his counsel at the bar. They prayed to be heard. Their prayer was refused, and their oppressors, who required no evidence, would listen to no defence. It had been at first proposed, that one eighth of their respective estates should be allowed for the future support of the directors; but it was speciously urged, that in the various shades of opulence and guilt, such a proportion would be too light for many, and for some might possibly be too heavy. The character and conduct of each man were separately weighed; but, instead of the calm solemnity of a judicial inquiry, the fortune and honour of thirty-three Englishmen were made the topics of hasty conversation, the sport of a lawless majority; and the basest member of the committee, by a malicious word, or a silent vote, might indulge his general spleen or personal animosity. Injury was aggravated by insult, and insult was embittered by pleasantry. Allowances of 20 pounds or 1 shilling were facetiously moved. A vague report that a director had formerly been concerned in another project, by which some unknown persons had lost their money, was admitted as a proof of his actual guilt. One man was ruined because he had dropped a foolish speech, that his horses should feed upon gold; another, because he was grown so proud, that one day, at the Treasury, he had refused a civil answer to persons much above him. All were condemned, absent and unheard, in arbitrary fines and forfeitures, which swept away the greatest part of their substance. Such bold oppression can scarcely be shielded by the omnipotence of Parliament. My grandfather could not expect to be treated with more lenity than his companions. His Tory principles and connexions rendered him obnoxious to the ruling powers. His name was reported in a suspicious secret. His well-known abilities could not plead the excuse of ignorance or error. In the first proceedings against the South Sea directors, Mr. Gibbon was one of the first taken into custody, and in the final sentence the measure of his fine proclaimed him eminently guilty. The total estimate, which he delivered on oath to the House of Commons, amounted to 106,543 pounds 5 shillings 6 pence, exclusive of antecedent settlements. Two different allowances of 15,000 pounds and of 10,000 pounds were moved for Mr. Gibbon; but, on the question being put, it was carried without a division for the smaller sum. On these ruins, with the skill and credit of which Parliament had not been able to despoil him, my grandfather, at a mature age, erected the edifice of a new fortune. The labours of sixteen years were amply rewarded; and I have reason to believe that the second structure was not much inferior to the first."

The next consideration of the Legislature, after the punishment of the directors, was to restore public credit. The scheme of Walpole had been found insufficient, and had fallen into disrepute. A computation was made of the whole capital stock of the South Sea Company at the end of the year 1720. It was found to amount to thirty-seven millions eight hundred thousand pounds, of which the stock allotted to all the proprietors only amounted to twenty-four millions five hundred thousand pounds. The remainder of thirteen millions three hundred thousand pounds belonged to the Company in their corporate capacity, and was the profit they had made by the national delusion. Upwards of eight millions of this were taken from the Company, and divided among the proprietors and subscribers generally, making a dividend of about 33 pounds 6 shillings 8 pence per cent. This was a great relief. It was further ordered, that such persons as had borrowed money from the South Sea Company upon stock actually transferred and pledged at the time of borrowing to or for the use of the Company, should be free from all demands, upon payment of ten per cent. of the sums so borrowed. They had lent about eleven millions in this manner, at a time when prices were unnaturally raised; and they now received back one million one hundred thousand, when prices had sunk to their ordinary level.

But it was a long time before public credit was thoroughly restored. Enterprise, like Icarus, had soared too high, and melted the wax of her wings; like Icarus, she had fallen into a sea, and learned, while floundering in its waves, that her proper element was the solid ground. She has never since attempted so high a flight.

In times of great commercial prosperity there has been a tendency to over-speculation on several occasions since then. The success of one project generally produces others of a similar kind. Popular imitativeness will always, in a trading nation, seize hold of such successes, and drag a community too anxious for profits into an abyss from which extrication is difficult. Bubble companies, of a kind similar to those engendered by the South Sea project, lived their little day in the famous year of the panic, 1825. On that occasion, as in 1720, knavery gathered a rich harvest from cupidity, but both suffered when the day of reckoning came. The schemes of the year 1836 threatened, at one time, results as disastrous; but they were happily averted before it was too late. The South Sea project thus remains, and, it is to be hoped, always will remain, the greatest example in British history, of the infatuation of the people for commercial gambling. From the bitter experience of that period, posterity may learn how dangerous it is to let speculation riot unrestrained, and to hope for enormous profits from inadequate causes. Degrading as were the circumstances, there is wisdom to be gained from the lesson which they teach.

The Tulipomania

Quis furor o cives! -- *Lucan.*

The tulip,--so named, it is said, from a Turkish word, signifying a turban,-- was introduced into western Europe about the middle of the sixteenth century. Conrad Gesner, who claims the merit of having brought it into repute,--little dreaming of the extraordinary commotion it was to make in the world,--says that he first saw it in the year 1559, in a garden at Augsburg, belonging to the learned Counsellor Herwart, a man very famous in his day for his collection of rare exotics. The bulbs were sent to this gentleman by a friend at Constantinople, where the flower had long been a favourite. In the course of ten or eleven years after this period, tulips were much sought after by the wealthy, especially in Holland and Germany. Rich people at Amsterdam sent for the bulbs direct to Constantinople, and paid the most extravagant prices for them. The first roots planted in England were brought from Vienna in 1600. Until the year 1634 the tulip annually increased in reputation, until it was deemed a proof of bad taste in any man of fortune to be without a collection of them. Many learned men, including Pompeius de Angelis and the celebrated Lipsius of Leyden, the author of the treatise "De Constantia," were passionately fond of tulips. The rage for possessing them soon caught the middle classes of society, and merchants and shopkeepers, even of moderate means, began to vie with each other in the rarity of these flowers and the preposterous prices .they paid for them. A trader at Harlaem was known to pay one-half of his fortune for a single root--not with the design of selling it again at a profit, but to keep in his own conservatory for the admiration of his acquaintance.

One would suppose that there must have been some great virtue in this flower to have made it so valuable in the eyes of so prudent a people as the Dutch; but it has neither the beauty nor the perfume of the rose--hardly the beauty of the "sweet, sweet-pea;" neither is it as enduring as either. Cowley, it is true, is loud in its praise. He says--

"The tulip next appeared, all over gay,
But wanton, full of pride, and full of play;
The world can't show a dye but here has place;
Nay, by new mixtures, she can change her face;
Purple and gold are both beneath her care-
The richest needlework she loves to wear;
Her only study is to please the eye,
And to outshine the rest in finery."

This, though not very poetical, is the description of a poet. Beckmann, in his History of Inventions, paints it with more fidelity, and in prose more pleasing than Cowley's poetry. He says, "There are few plants which acquire, through accident, weakness, or disease, so many variegations as the tulip. When uncultivated, and in its natural state, it is almost of one colour, has large leaves, and an extraordinarily long stem. When it has been weakened by cultivation, it becomes more agreeable in the eyes of the florist. The petals are then paler, smaller, and more diversified in hue; and the leaves acquire a softer green colour. Thus this masterpiece of culture, the more beautiful it turns, grows so much the weaker, so that, with the greatest skill and most careful attention, it can scarcely be transplanted, or even kept alive."

Many persons grow insensibly attached to that which gives them a great deal of trouble, as a mother often loves her sick and ever-ailing child better than her more healthy offspring. Upon the same principle we must account for the unmerited encomia lavished upon these fragile blossoms. In 1634, the rage among the Dutch to possess them was so great that the ordinary industry of the country was neglected, and the population, even to its lowest dregs, embarked in the tulip trade. As the mania increased, prices augmented, until, in the year 1635, many persons were known to invest a fortune of 100,000 florins in the purchase of forty roots. It then became necessary to sell them by their weight in perits, a small weight less than a grain. A tulip of the species called Admiral Liefken, weighing 400 perits, was worth 4400 florins; an Admiral Von der Eyk, weighing 446 perits, was worth 1260 florins; a shilder of 106 perits was worth 1615 florins; a viceroy of 400 perits, 3000 florins, and, most precious of all, a Semper Augustus, weighing 200 perits, was thought to be very cheap at 5500 florins. The latter was much sought after, and even an inferior bulb might command a price of 2000 florins. It is related that, at one time, early in 1636, there were only two roots of this description to be had in all Holland, and those not of the best. One was in the possession of a dealer in Amsterdam, and the other in Harlaem. So anxious were the speculators to obtain them that one person offered the fee-simple of twelve acres of building ground for the Harlaem tulip. That of Amsterdam was bought for 4600 florins, a new carriage, two grey horses, and a complete suit of harness. Munting, an industrious author of that day, who wrote a folio volume of one thousand pages upon the tulipomania, has preserved the following list of the various articles, and their value, which were delivered for one single root of the rare species called the viceroy :--

	florins.
Two lasts of wheat...............	448
Four lasts of rye...............	558
Four fat oxen...................	480
Eight fat swine.................	240
Twelve fat sheep................	120
Two hogsheads of wine...........	70
Four tuns of beer..............	32
Two tons of butter.............	192
One thousand lbs. of cheese.....	120
A complete bed..................	100
A suit of clothes..............	80
A silver drinking cup..........	60

	2500

People who had been absent from Holland, and whose chance it was to return when this folly was at its maximum, were sometimes led into awkward dilemmas by their ignorance. There is an amusing instance of the kind related in Blainville's Travels. A wealthy merchant, who prided himself not a little on his rare tulips, received upon one occasion a very valuable consignment of merchandise from the Levant. Intelligence of its arrival was brought him by a sailor, who presented himself for that purpose at the counting-house, among bales of goods of every description. The merchant, to reward him for his news, munificently made him a present of a fine red herring for his breakfast. The sailor had, it appears, a great partiality for onions, and seeing a bulb very like an onion lying upon the counter of this liberal trader, and thinking it, no doubt, very much out of its place among silks and velvets, he slily seized an opportunity and slipped it into his pocket, as a relish for his herring. He got clear off with his prize, and proceeded to the quay to eat his breakfast. Hardly was his back turned when the merchant missed his valuable Semper Augustus, worth three thousand florins, or about 280 pounds sterling. The whole establishment was instantly in an uproar; search was everywhere made for the precious root, but it was not to be found. Great was the merchant's distress of mind. The search was renewed, but again without success. At last some one thought of the sailor.

The unhappy merchant sprang into the street at the bare suggestion. His alarmed household followed him. The sailor, simple soul! had not thought of concealment. He was found quietly sitting on a coil of ropes, masticating the last morsel of his "onion." Little did he dream that he had been eating a breakfast whose cost might have regaled a whole ship's crew for a twelvemonth; or, as the plundered merchant himself expressed it, "might have sumptuously feasted the Prince of Orange and the whole court of the Stadtholder." Anthony caused pearls to be dissolved in wine to drink the health of Cleopatra; Sir Richard Whittington was as foolishly magnificent in an entertainment to King Henry V; and Sir Thomas Gresham drank a diamond, dissolved in wine, to the health of Queen Elizabeth, when she opened the Royal Exchange: but the breakfast of this roguish Dutchman was as splendid as either. He had an advantage, too, over his wasteful predecessors: their gems did not improve the taste or the wholesomeness of their wine, while his tulip was quite delicious with his red herring. The most unfortunate part of the business for him was, that he remained in prison for some months, on a charge of felony, preferred against him by the merchant.

Another story is told of an English traveller, which is scarcely less ludicrous. This gentleman, an amateur botanist, happened to see a tulip-root lying in the conservatory of a wealthy Dutchman. Being ignorant of its quality, he took out his penknife, and peeled off its coats, with the view of making experiments upon it. When it was by this means reduced to half its original size, he cut it into two equal sections, making all the time many learned remarks on the singular appearances of the unknown bulb. Suddenly the owner pounced upon him, and, with fury in his eyes, asked him if he knew what he had been doing? "Peeling a most extraordinary onion," replied the philosopher. "Hundert tausend duyvel," said the Dutchman; "it's an Admiral Van der Eyck." "Thank you," replied the traveller, taking out his note-book to make a memorandum of the same; "are these admirals common in your country?" "Death and the devil," said the Dutchman, seizing the astonished man of science by the collar; "come before the syndic, and you shall see." In spite of his remonstrances, the traveller was led through the streets, followed by a mob of persons. When brought into the presence of the magistrate, he learned, to his consternation, that the root upon which he had been experimentalizing was worth four thousand florins; and, notwithstanding all he could urge in extenuation, he was lodged in prison until he found securities for the payment of this sum.

The demand for tulips of a rare species increased so much in the year 1636, that regular marts for their sale were established on the Stock Exchange of Amsterdam, in Rotterdam, Harlaem, Leyden, Alkmar, Hoorn, and other towns. Symptoms of gambling now became, for the first time, apparent. The stockjobbers, ever on the alert for a new speculation, dealt largely in tulips, making use of all the means they so well knew how to employ, to cause fluctuations in prices. At first, as in all these gambling mania, confidence was at its height, and everybody gained. The tulip-jobbers speculated in the rise and fall of the tulip stocks, and made large profits by buying when prices fell, and selling out when they rose. Many individuals grew suddenly rich. A golden bait hung temptingly out before the people, and, one after the other, they rushed to the tulip marts, like flies around a honeypot. Every one imagined that the passion for tulips would last for ever, and that the wealthy from every part of the world would send to Holland, and pay whatever prices were asked for them. The riches of Europe would be concentrated on the shores of the Zuyder Zee, and poverty banished from the favoured clime of Holland. Nobles, citizens, farmers, mechanics, seamen, footmen, maidservants, even chimney-sweeps and old clotheswomen, dabbled in tulips. People of all grades converted their property into cash, and invested it in flowers. Houses and lands were offered for sale at ruinously low prices, or assigned in payment of bargains made at the tulip-mart. Foreigners became smitten with the same frenzy, and money poured into Holland from all directions. The prices of the necessaries of life rose again by degrees; houses and lands, horses and carriages, and luxuries of every sort, rose in value with them, and for some months Holland seemed the very antechamber of Plutus. The operations of the trade became so extensive and so intricate, that it was found necessary to draw up a code of laws for the guidance of the dealers. Notaries and clerks were also appointed, who devoted themselves exclusively to the interests of the trade. The designation of public notary was hardly known in some towns, that of tulip notary usurping its place. In the smaller towns, where there was no exchange, the principal tavern was usually selected as the "showplace," where high and low traded in tulips, and confirmed their bargains over sumptuous entertainments. These dinners were sometimes attended by two or three hundred persons, and large vases of tulips, in full bloom, were placed at regular intervals upon the tables and sideboards, for their gratification during the repast.

At last, however, the more prudent began to see that this folly could not last for ever. Rich people no longer bought the flowers to keep them in their gardens, but to sell them again at cent. per cent. profit. It was seen that somebody must lose fearfully in the end. As this conviction spread, prices fell, and never rose again. Confidence was destroyed, and a universal panic seized upon the dealers. A had agreed to purchase ten Sempers Augustines from B, at four thousand florins each, at six weeks after the signing of the contract. B was ready with the flowers at the appointed time; but the price had fallen to three or four hundred florins, and A refused either to pay the difference or receive the tulips. Defaulters were announced day after day in all the towns of Holland. Hundreds who, a few months previously, had begun to doubt that there was such a thing as poverty in the land, suddenly found themselves the possessors of a few bulbs, which nobody would buy, even though they offered them at one quarter of the sums they had paid for them. The cry of distress resounded everywhere, and each man accused his neighbour. The few who had contrived to enrich themselves hid their wealth from the knowledge of their fellow-citizens, and invested it in the English or other funds. Many who, for a brief season, had emerged from the humbler walks of life, were cast back into their original obscurity. Substantial merchants were reduced almost to beggary, and many a representative of a noble line saw the fortunes of his house ruined beyond redemption.

When the first alarm subsided, the tulip-holders in the several towns held public meetings to devise what measures were best to be taken to restore public credit. It was generally agreed, that deputies should be sent from all parts to Amsterdam, to consult with the government upon some remedy for the evil. The Government at first refused to interfere, but advised the tulip-holders to agree to some plan among themselves. Several meetings were held for this purpose; but no measure could be devised likely to give satisfaction to the deluded people, or repair even a slight portion of the mischief that had been done. The language of complaint and reproach was in everybody's mouth, and all the meetings were of the most stormy character. At last, however, after much bickering and ill-will, it was agreed, at Amsterdam, by the assembled deputies, that all contracts made in the height of the mania, or prior to the month of November 1636, should be declared null and void, and that, in those made after that date, purchasers should be freed from their engagements, on paying ten per cent. to the vendor. This decision gave no satisfaction. The vendors who had their tulips on hand were, of course, discontented, and those who had pledged themselves to purchase, thought themselves hardly treated. Tulips which had, at one time, been worth six thousand florins, were now to be procured for five hundred; so that the composition of ten per cent. was one hundred florins more than the actual value. Actions for breach of contract were threatened in all the courts of the country; but the latter refused to take cognizance of gambling transactions.

The matter was finally referred to the Provincial Council at the Hague, and it was confidently expected that the wisdom of this body would invent some measure by which credit should be restored. Expectation was on the stretch for its decision, but it never came. The members continued to deliberate week after week, and at last, after thinking about it for three months, declared that they could offer no final decision until they had more information. They advised, however, that, in the mean time, every vendor should, in the presence of witnesses, offer the tulips in natura to the purchaser for the sums agreed upon. If the latter refused to take them, they might be put up for sale by public auction, and the original contractor held responsible for the difference between the actual and the stipulated price. This was exactly the plan recommended by the deputies, and which was already shown to be of no avail. There was no court in Holland which would enforce payment. The question was raised in Amsterdam, but the judges unanimously refused to interfere, on the ground that debts contracted in gambling were no debts in law.

Thus the matter rested. To find a remedy was beyond the power of the government. Those who were unlucky enough to have had stores of tulips on hand at the time of the sudden reaction were left to bear their ruin as philosophically as they could; those who had made profits were allowed to keep them; but the commerce of the country suffered a severe shock, from which it was many years ere it recovered.

The example of the Dutch was imitated to some extent in England. In the year 1636 tulips were publicly sold in the Exchange of London, and the jobbers exerted themselves to the utmost to raise them to the fictitious value they had acquired in Amsterdam. In Paris also the jobbers strove to create a tulipomania. In both cities they only partially succeeded. However, the force of example brought the flowers into great favour, and amongst a certain class of people tulips have ever since been prized more highly than any other flowers of the field. The Dutch are still notorious for their partiality to them, and continue to pay higher prices for them than any other people. As the rich Englishman boasts of his fine race-horses or his old pictures, so does the wealthy Dutchman vaunt him of his tulips.

In England, in our day, strange as it may appear, a tulip will produce more money than an oak. If one could be found, rara in tetris, and black as the black swan alluded to by Juvenal, its price would equal that of a dozen acres of standing corn. In Scotland, towards the close of the seventeenth century, the highest price for tulips, according to the authority of a writer in the supplement to the third edition of the "Encyclopedia Britannica," was ten guineas. Their value appears to have diminished from that time till the year 1769, when the two most valuable species in England were the Don Quevedo and the Valentinier, the former of which was worth two guineas and the latter two guineas and a half. These prices appear to have been the minimum. In the year 1800, a common price was fifteen guineas for a single bulb. In 1835, so foolish were the fanciers, that a bulb of the species called the Miss Fanny Kemble was sold by public auction in London for seventy-five pounds. Still more astonishing was the price of a tulip in the possession of a gardener in the King's Road, Chelsea. In his catalogues, it was labelled at two hundred guineas! Thus a flower, which for beauty and perfume was surpassed by the abundant roses of the garden,--a nosegay of which might be purchased for a penny,--was priced at a sum which would have provided an industrious labourer and his family with food, and clothes, and lodging for six years! Should chickweed and groundsel ever come into fashion, the wealthy would, no doubt, vie with each other in adorning their gardens with them, and paying the most extravagant prices for them. In so doing, they would hardly be more foolish than the admirers of tulips. The common prices for these flowers at the present time vary from five to fifteen guineas, according to the rarity of the species.

Relics

A fouth o' auld knick-knackets,
Rusty airn caps and jinglin' jackets,
Wad haud the Lothians three, in tackets,
A towmond guid;
An' parritch pats, and auld saut backets,
Afore the flood. -- *Burns*.

The love for relics is one which will never be eradicated as long as feeling and affection are denizens of the heart. It is a love which is most easily excited in the best and kindliest natures, and which few are callous enough to scoff at. Who would not treasure the lock of hair that once adorned the brow of the faithful wife, now cold in death, or that hung down the neck of a beloved infant, now sleeping under the sward? Not one. They are home-relics, whose sacred worth is intelligible to all; spoils rescued from the devouring grave, which, to the affectionate, are beyond all price. How dear to a forlorn survivor the book over whose pages he has pored with one departed! How much greater its value, if that hand, now cold, had written a thought, an opinion, or a name, upon the leaf! Besides these sweet, domestic relics, there are others, which no one can condemn; relics sanctified by that admiration of greatness and goodness which is akin to love; such as the copy of Montaigne's Florio, with the name of Shakspeare upon the leaf, written by the poet of all time himself; the chair preserved at Antwerp, in which Rubens sat when he painted the immortal "Descent from the Cross;" or the telescope, preserved in the Museum of Florence, which aided Galileo in his sublime discoveries. Who would not look with veneration upon the undoubted arrow of William Tell--the swords of Wallace or of Hampden--or the Bible whose leaves were turned by some stern old father of the faith?

Thus the principle of reliquism is hallowed and enshrined by love. But from this germ of purity how numerous the progeny of errors and superstitions! Men, in their admiration of the great, and of all that appertained to them, have forgotten that goodness is a component part of true greatness, and have made fools of themselves for the jaw-bone of a saint, the toe-nail of an apostle, the handkerchief a king blew his nose in, or the rope that hanged a criminal. Desiring to rescue some slight token from the graves of their predecessors, they have confounded the famous and the infamous, the renowned and the notorious. Great saints, great sinners; great philosophers, great quacks; great conquerors, great murderers; great ministers, great thieves; each and all have had their admirers, ready to ransack earth, from the equator to either pole, to find a relic of them.

The reliquism of modern times dates its origin from the centuries immediately preceding the Crusades. The first pilgrims to the Holy Land brought back to Europe thousands of apocryphal relics, in the purchase of which they had expended all their store. The greatest favourite was the wood of the true cross, which, like the oil of the widow, never diminished. It is generally asserted, in the traditions of the Romish Church, that the Empress Helen, the mother of Constantine the Great, first discovered the veritable "true cross" in her pilgrimage to Jerusalem. The Emperor Theodosius made a present of the greater part of it to St. Ambrose, Bishop of Milan, by whom it was studded with precious stones, and deposited in the principal church of that city. It was carried away by the Huns, by whom it was burnt, after they had extracted the valuable jewels it contained. Fragments, purporting to have been cut from it were, in the eleventh and twelfth centuries, to be found in almost every church in Europe, and would, if collected together in one place, have been almost sufficient to have built a cathedral. Happy was the sinner who could get a sight of one of them; happier he who possessed one! To obtain them the greatest dangers were cheerfully braved. They were thought to preserve from all evils, and to cure the most inveterate diseases. Annual pilgrimages were made to the shrines that contained them, and considerable revenues collected from the devotees.

Next in renown were those precious relics, the tears of the Saviour. By whom and in what manner they were preserved, the pilgrims did not often inquire. Their genuineness was vouched by the Christians of the Holy Land, and that was sufficient. Tears of the Virgin Mary, and tears of St. Peter, were also to be had, carefully enclosed in little caskets, which the pious might wear in their bosoms. After the tears the next most precious relics were drops of the blood of Jesus and the martyrs. Hair and toe-nails were also in great repute, and were sold at extravagant prices. Thousands of pilgrims annually visited Palestine in the eleventh and twelfth centuries, to purchase pretended relics for the home market. The majority of them had no other means of subsistence than the profits thus obtained. Many a nail, cut from the filthy foot of some unscrupulous ecclesiastic, was sold at a diamond's price, within six months after its severance from its parent toe, upon the supposition that it had once belonged to a saint. Peter's toes were uncommonly prolific, for there were nails enough in Europe, at the time of the Council of Clermont, to have filled a sack, all of which were devoutly believed to have grown on the sacred feet of that great apostle. Some of them are still shown in the cathedral of Aix-la-Chapelle. The pious come from a distance of a hundred German miles to feast their eyes upon them.

At Port Royal, in Paris, is kept with great care a thorn, which the priests of that seminary assert to be one of the identical thorns that bound the holy head of the Son of God. How it came there, and by whom it was preserved, has never been explained. This is the famous thorn, celebrated in the long dissensions of the Jansenists and the Molenists, and which worked the miraculous cure upon Mademoiselle Perrier: by merely kissing it, she was cured of a disease of the eyes of long standing. [Voltaire, Siecle de Louis XIV.]

What traveller is unacquainted with the Santa Scala, or Holy Stairs, at Rome? They were brought from Jerusalem along with the true cross, by the Empress Helen, and were taken from the house which, according to popular tradition, was inhabited by Pontius Pilate. They are said to be the steps which Jesus ascended and descended when brought into the presence of the Roman governor. They are held in the greatest veneration at Rome: it is sacrilegious to walk upon them. The knees of the faithful must alone touch them in ascending or descending, and that only after they have reverentially kissed them.

Europe still swarms with these religious relics. There is hardly a Roman Catholic church in Spain, Portugal, Italy, France, or Belgium, without one or more of them. Even the poorly endowed churches of the villages boast the possession of miraculous thigh-bones of the innumerable saints of the Romish calendar. Aix-la-Chapelle is proud of the veritable chasse, or thigh-bone of Charlemagne, which cures lameness. Halle has a thighbone of the Virgin Mary; Spain has seven or eight, all said to be undoubted relics. Brussels at one time preserved, and perhaps does now, the teeth of St. Gudule. The faithful, who suffered from the tooth-ache, had only to pray, look at them, and be cured. Some of these holy bones have been buried in different parts of the Continent. After a certain lapse of time, water is said to ooze from them, which soon forms a spring, and cures all the diseases of the faithful. At a church in Halle, there is a famous thigh-bone, which cures barrenness in women. Of this bone, which is under the special superintendence of the Virgin, a pleasant story is related by the incredulous. There resided at Ghent a couple who were blessed with all the riches of this world, but whose happiness was sore troubled by the want of children. Great was the grief of the lady, who was both beautiful and loving, and many her lamentations to her husband. The latter, annoyed by her unceasing sorrow, advised her to make a pilgrimage to the celebrated chasse of the Virgin. She went, was absent a week, and returned with a face all radiant with joy and pleasure. Her lamentations ceased, and, in nine months afterwards, she brought forth a son. But, oh! the instability of human joys! The babe, so long desired and so greatly beloved, survived but a few months. Two years passed over the heads of the disconsolate couple, and no second child appeared to cheer their fire-side. A third year passed away with the same result, and the lady once more began to weep. "Cheer up, my love," said her husband, "and go to the holy chasse, at Halle; perhaps the Virgin will again listen to your prayers." The lady took courage at the thought, wiped away her tears, and proceeded on the morrow towards Halle. She was absent only three days, and returned home sad, weeping, and sorrow-stricken. "What is the matter?" said her husband; "is the Virgin unwilling to listen to your prayers ?" "The Virgin is willing enough," said the disconsolate wife, "and will do what she can for me; but I shall never have any more children! The priest! the priest!--He is gone from Halle, and nobody knows where to find him!"

It is curious to remark the avidity manifested in all ages, and in all countries, to obtain possession of some relic of any persons who have been much spoken of, even for their crimes. When William Longbeard, leader of the populace of London, in the reign of Richard I, was hanged at Smithfield, the utmost eagerness was shown to obtain a hair from his head, or a shred from his garments. Women came from Essex, Kent, Suffolk, Sussex, and all the surrounding counties, to collect the mould at the foot of his gallows. A hair of his beard was believed to preserve from evil spirits, and a piece of his clothes from aches and pains.

In more modern days, a similar avidity was shown to obtain a relic of the luckless Masaniello, the fisherman of Naples. After he had been raised by mob favour to a height of power more despotic than monarch ever wielded, he was shot by the same populace in the streets, as if he had been a mad dog. His headless trunk was dragged through the mire for several hours, and cast at night-fall into the city ditch. On the morrow the tide of popular feeling turned once more in his favour. His corpse was sought, arrayed in royal robes, and buried magnificently by torch-light in the cathedral, ten thousand armed men, and as many mourners, attending at the ceremony. The fisherman's dress which he had worn was rent into shreds by the crowd, to be preserved as relics; the door of his hut was pulled off its hinges by a mob of women, and eagerly cut up into small pieces, to be made into images, caskets, and other mementos. The scanty furniture of his poor abode became of more value than the adornments of a palace; the ground he had walked upon was considered sacred, and, being collected in small phials, was sold at its weight in gold, and worn in the bosom as an amulet.

Almost as extraordinary was the frenzy manifested by the populace of Paris on the execution of the atrocious Marchioness de Brinvilliers. There were grounds for the popular wonder in the case of Masaniello, who was unstained with personal crimes. But the career of Madame de Brinvilliers was of a nature to excite no other feelings than disgust and abhorrence. She was convicted of poisoning several persons, and sentenced to be burned in the Place de Greve, and to have her ashes scattered to the winds. On the day of her execution, the populace, struck by her gracefulness and beauty, inveighed against the severity of her sentence. Their pity soon increased to admiration, and, ere evening, she was considered a saint. Her ashes were industriously collected, even the charred wood, which had aided to consume her, was eagerly purchased by the populace. Her ashes were thought to preserve from witchcraft.

In England many persons have a singular love for the relics of thieves and murderers, or other great criminals. The ropes with which they have been hanged are very often bought by collectors at a guinea per foot. Great sums were paid for the rope which hanged Dr. Dodd, and for those more recently which did justice upon Mr. Fauntleroy for forgery, and on Thurtell for the murder of Mr. Weare. The murder of

Maria Marten, by Corder, in the year 1828, excited the greatest interest all over the country. People came from Wales and Scotland, and even from Ireland, to visit the barn where the body of the murdered woman was buried. Every one of them was anxious to carry away some memorial of his visit. Pieces of the barn-door, tiles from the roof, and, above all, the clothes of the poor victim, were eagerly sought after. A lock of her hair was sold for two guineas, and the purchaser thought himself fortunate in getting it so cheaply.

So great was the concourse of people to visit the house in Camberwell Lane, where Greenacre murdered Hannah Brown, in 1837, that it was found necessary to station a strong detachment of police on the spot. The crowd was so eager to obtain a relic of the house of this atrocious criminal, that the police were obliged to employ force to prevent the tables and chairs, and even the doors, from being carried away.

In earlier times, a singular superstition was attached to the hand of a criminal who had suffered execution. It was thought that by merely rubbing the dead hand on the body, the patient afflicted with the king's evil would be instantly cured. The executioner at Newgate, sixty or seventy years ago, derived no inconsiderable revenue from this foolish practice. The possession of the hand was thought to be of still greater efficacy in the cure of diseases and the prevention of misfortunes. In the time of Charles II as much as ten guineas was thought a small price for one of these disgusting relics.

When the maniac, Thom, or Courtenay, was shot, in the spring of 1838, the relic-hunters were immediately in motion to obtain a memento of so extraordinary an individual. His long, black beard and hair, which were cut off by the surgeons, fell into the hands of his disciples, by whom they are treasured with the utmost reverence. A lock of his hair commands a great price, not only amongst his followers, but among the more wealthy inhabitants of Canterbury and its neighbourhood. The tree against which he fell when he was shot, has already been stripped of all its bark by the curious, and bids fair to be entirely demolished within a twelvemonth. A letter, with his signature to it, is paid for in gold coins; and his favourite horse promises to become as celebrated as his master. Parties of ladies and gentlemen have come to Boughton from a distance of a hundred and fifty miles, to visit the scene of that fatal affray, and stroke on the back the horse of the "mad Knight of Malta." If a strict watch had not been kept over his grave for months, the body would have been disinterred, and the bones carried away as memorials.

Among the Chinese no relics are more valued than the boots which have been worn by an upright magistrate. In Davis's interesting Description of the Empire of China, we are informed, that whenever a judge of unusual integrity resigns his situation, the people all congregate to do him honour. If he leaves the city where he has presided, the crowd accompany him from his residence to the gates, where his boots are drawn off with great ceremony, to be preserved in the hall of justice. Their place is immediately supplied by a new pair, which, in their turn, are drawn off to make room for others before he has worn them five minutes, it being considered sufficient to consecrate them that he should have merely drawn them on.

Among the most favourite relics of modern times, in Europe, are Shakspeare's mulberry-tree, Napoleon's willow, and the table at Waterloo, on which the Emperor wrote his despatches. Snuffboxes of Shakspeare's mulberry-tree, are comparatively rare, though there are doubtless more of them in the market than were ever made of the wood planted by the great bard. Many a piece of alien wood passes under this name. The same may be said of Napoleon's table at Waterloo. The original has long since been destroyed, and a round dozen of counterfeits along with it. Many preserve the simple stick of wood; others have them cut into brooches and every variety of ornament; but by far the greater number prefer them as snuff-boxes. In France they are made into bonbonnieres, and are much esteemed by the many thousands whose cheeks still glow, and whose eyes still sparkle at the name of Napoleon.

Bullets from the field of Waterloo, and buttons from the coats of the soldiers who fell in the fight, are still favourite relics in Europe. But the same ingenuity which found new tables after the old one was destroyed, has cast new bullets for the curious. Many a one who thinks himself the possessor of a bullet which aided in giving peace to the world on that memorable day, is the owner of a dump, first extracted from the ore a dozen years afterwards. Let all lovers of genuine relics look well to their money before they part with it to the ciceroni that swarm in the village of Waterloo.

Few travellers stop at the lonely isle of St. Helena, without cutting a twig from the willow that droops over the grave of Napoleon. Many of them have since been planted in different parts of Europe, and have grown into trees as large as their parent. Relic-hunters, who are unable to procure a twig of the original, are content with one from these. Several of them are growing in the neighbourhood of London, more prized by their cultivators than any other tree in their gardens. But in relics, as in everything else, there is the use and the abuse. The undoubted relics of great men, or great events, will always possess attractions for the thinking and refined. There are few who would not join with Cowley in the extravagant wish introduced in his lines "written while sitting in a chair made of the remains of the ship in which Sir Francis Drake sailed round the world:"--

"And I myself, who now love quiet too,
Almost as much as any chair can do,
Would yet a journey take
An old wheel of that chariot to see,
Which Phaeton so rashly brake."

Modern Prophecies

As epidemic terror of the end of the world has several times spread over the nations. The most remarkable was that which seized Christendom about the middle of the tenth century. Numbers of fanatics appeared in France, Germany, and Italy at that time, preaching that the thousand years prophesied in the Apocalypse as the term of the world's duration, were about to expire, and that the Son of Man would appear in the clouds to judge the godly and the ungodly. The delusion appears to have been discouraged by the church, but it nevertheless spread rapidly among the people. [See Gibbon and Voltaire for further notice of this subject.]

The scene of the last judgment was expected to be at Jerusalem. In the year 999, the number of pilgrims proceeding eastward, to await the coming of the Lord in that city, was so great that they were compared to a desolating army. Most of them sold their goods and possessions before they quitted Europe, and lived upon the proceeds in the Holy Land. Buildings of every sort were suffered to fall into ruins. It was thought useless to repair them, when the end of the world was so near. Many noble edifices were deliberately pulled down. Even churches, usually so well maintained, shared the general neglect. Knights, citizens, and serfs, travelled eastwards in company, taking with them their wives and children, singing psalms as they went, and looking with fearful eyes upon the sky, which they expected each minute to open, to let the Son of God descend in his glory.

During the thousandth year the number of pilgrims increased. Most of them were smitten with terror as with a plague. Every phenomenon of nature filled them with alarm. A thunder-storm sent them all upon their knees in mid-march. It was the opinion that thunder was the voice of God, announcing the day of judgment. Numbers expected the earth to open, and give up its dead at the sound. Every meteor in the sky seen at Jerusalem brought the whole Christian population into the streets to weep and pray. The pilgrims on the road were in the same alarm :--

"Lorsque, pendant la nuit, un globe de lumiere
S'echappa quelquefois de la voute des cieux,
Et traca dans sa chute un long sillon de feux,
La troupe suspendit sa marche solitaire."
[*Charlemagne: Poeme epique*, par Lucien Buonaparte.]

Fanatic preachers kept up the flame of terror. Every shooting star furnished occasion for a sermon, in which the sublimity of the approaching judgment was the principal topic.

The appearance of comets has been often thought to foretell the speedy dissolution of this world. Part of this belief still exists; but the comet is no longer looked upon as the sign, but the agent of destruction. So lately as in the year 1832 the greatest alarm spread over the Continent of Europe, especially in Germany, lest the comet, whose appearance was then foretold by astronomers, should destroy the earth. The danger of our globe was gravely discussed. Many persons refrained from undertaking or concluding any business during that year, in consequence solely of their apprehension that this terrible comet would dash us and our world to atoms.

During seasons of great pestilence men have often believed the prophecies of crazed fanatics, that the end of the world was come. Credulity is always greatest in times of calamity. Prophecies of all sorts are rife on such occasions, and are readily believed, whether for good or evil. During the great plague, which ravaged all Europe, between the years 1345 and 1350, it was generally considered that the end of the world was at hand. Pretended prophets were to be found in all the principal cities of Germany, France, and Italy, predicting that within ten years the trump of the Archangel would sound, and the Saviour appear in the clouds to call the earth to judgment.

No little consternation was created in London in 1736 by the prophecy of the famous Whiston, that the world would be destroyed in that year, on the 13th of October. Crowds of people went out on the appointed day to Islington, Hampstead, and the fields intervening, to see the destruction of London, which was to be the "beginning of the end." A satirical account of this folly is given in Swift's Miscellanies, vol. iii. entitled, "A True and Faithful Narrative of what passed in London on a Rumour of the Day of Judgment." An authentic narrative of this delusion would be interesting; but this solemn witticism of Pope and Gay is not to be depended upon.

In the year 1761 the citizens of London were again frightened out of their wits by two shocks of an earthquake, and the prophecy of a third, which was to destroy them altogether. The first shock was felt on the 8th of February, and threw down several chimneys in the neighbourhood of Limehouse and Poplar; the second happened on the 8th of March, and was chiefly felt in the north of London, and towards Hampstead and Highgate. It soon became the subject of general remark, that there was exactly an interval of a month between the shocks; and a crack-brained fellow, named Bell, a soldier in the Life Guards, was so impressed with the idea that there would be a third in another month, that he lost his senses altogether, and ran about the streets predicting the destruction of London on the 5th of April. Most people thought that the first would have been a more appropriate day; but there were not wanting thousands who confidently believed the prediction, and took measures to transport themselves and families from the scene of the impending calamity. As the awful day approached, the excitement became intense, and great numbers of credulous people resorted to all the villages within a circuit of twenty miles, awaiting the doom of London. Islington, Highgate, Hampstead, Harrow, and Blackheath, were crowded with panic-stricken fugitives, who paid exorbitant prices for accommodation to the housekeepers of these secure retreats. Such as could not afford to pay for lodgings at any of those places, remained in London until two or three days before the time, and then encamped in the surrounding fields, awaiting the tremendous shock which was to lay their high city all level with the dust. As happened during a similar panic in the time of Henry VIII, the fear became contagious, and hundreds who had laughed at the prediction a week before, packed up their goods, when they saw others doing so, and hastened away. The river was thought to be a place of great security, and all the merchant vessels in the port were filled with people, who passed the night between the 4th and 5th on board, expecting every instant to see St. Paul's totter, and the towers of Westminster Abbey rock in the wind and fall amid a cloud of dust. The greater part of the fugitives returned on the following day, convinced that the prophet was a false one; but many judged it more prudent to allow a week to elapse before they trusted their dear limbs in London. Bell lost all credit in a short time, and was looked upon even by the most credulous as a mere madman. He tried some other prophecies, but nobody was deceived by them; and, in a few months afterwards, he was confined in a lunatic asylum.

A panic terror of the end of the world seized the good people of Leeds and its neighbourhood in the year 1806. It arose from the following circumstances. A hen, in a village close by, laid eggs, on which were inscribed, in legible characters, the words "Christ is coming." Great numbers visited the spot, and examined these wondrous eggs, convinced that the day of judgment was near at hand. Like sailors in a storm, expecting every instant to go to the bottom, the believers suddenly became religious, prayed violently, and flattered themselves that they repented them of their evil courses. But a plain tale soon put them down, and quenched their religion entirely. Some gentlemen, hearing of the matter, went one fine morning, and caught the poor hen in the act of laying one of her miraculous eggs. They soon ascertained beyond doubt that the egg had been inscribed with some corrosive ink, and cruelly forced up again into the bird's body. At this explanation, those who had prayed, now laughed, and the world wagged as merrily as of yore.

At the time of the plague in Milan, in 1630, of which so affecting a description has been left us by Ripamonte, in his interesting work "De Peste Mediolani", the people, in their distress, listened with avidity to the predictions of astrologers and other impostors. It is singular enough that the plague was foretold a year before it broke out. A large comet appearing in 1628, the opinions of astrologers were divided with regard to it. Some insisted that it was a forerunner of a bloody war; others maintained that it predicted a great famine; but the greater number, founding their judgment upon its pale colour, thought it portended a pestilence. The fulfilment of their prediction brought them into great repute while the plague was raging.

Other prophecies were current, which were asserted to have been delivered hundreds of years previously. They had a most pernicious effect upon the mind of the vulgar, as they induced a belief in fatalism. By taking away the hope of recovery - that greatest balm in every malady - they increased threefold the ravages of the disease. One singular prediction almost drove the unhappy people mad. An ancient couplet, preserved for ages by tradition, foretold, that in the year 1630 the devil would poison all Milan. Early one morning in April, and before the pestilence had reached its height, the passengers were surprised to see that all the doors in the principal streets of the city were marked with a curious daub, or spot, as if a sponge, filled with the purulent matter of the plague-sores, had been pressed against them. The whole population were speedily in movement to remark the strange appearance, and the greatest alarm spread rapidly. Every means was taken to discover the perpetrators, but in vain. At last the ancient prophecy was remembered, and prayers were offered up in all the churches that the machinations of the Evil One might be defeated. Many persons were of opinion that the emissaries of foreign powers were employed to spread infectious poison over the city; but by far the greater number were convinced that the powers of hell had conspired against them, and that the infection was spread by supernatural agencies. In the mean time the plague increased fearfully. Distrust and alarm took possession of every mind. Everything was believed to have been poisoned by the devil; the waters of the wells, the standing corn in the fields, and the fruit upon the trees. It was believed that all objects of touch were poisoned; the walls of the houses, the pavement of the streets, and the very handles of the doors. The populace were raised to a pitch of ungovernable fury. A strict watch was kept for the devil's emissaries, and any man who wanted to be rid of an enemy, had only to say that he had seen him besmearing a door with ointment; his fate was certain death at the hands of the mob. An old man, upwards of eighty years of age, a daily frequenter of the church of St. Antonio, was seen, on rising from his knees, to wipe with the skirt of his cloak the stool on which he was about to sit down. A cry was raised immediately that he was besmearing the seat with poison. A mob of women, by whom the church was crowded, seized hold of the feeble old man, and dragged him out by the hair of his head, with horrid oaths and imprecations. He was trailed in this manner through the mire to the house of the municipal judge, that he might be put to the rack, and forced to discover his accomplices; but he expired on the way. Many other victims were sacrificed to the popular fury. One Mora, who appears to have been half a chemist and half a barber, was accused of being in league with the devil to poison Milan. His house was surrounded, and a number of chemical preparations were found. The poor man asserted, that they were intended as preservatives against infection; but some physicians, to whom they were submitted, declared they were poison. Mora was put to the rack, where he for a long time asserted his innocence. He confessed at last, when his courage was worn down by torture, that he was in league with the devil and foreign powers to poison the whole city; that he had anointed the doors, and infected the fountains of water. He named several persons as his accomplices, who were apprehended and put to a similar torture. They were all found guilty, and executed. Mora's house was rased to the ground, and a column erected on the spot, with an inscription to commemorate his guilt.

While the public mind was filled with these marvellous occurrences, the plague continued to increase. The crowds that were brought together to witness the executions, spread the infection among one another. But the fury of their passions, and the extent of their credulity, kept pace with the violence of the plague; every wonderful and preposterous story was believed. One, in particular, occupied them to the exclusion, for a long time, of every other. The Devil himself had been seen. He had taken a house in Milan, in which he prepared his poisonous unguents, and furnished them to his emissaries for distribution. One man had brooded over such tales till he became firmly convinced that the wild flights of his own fancy were realities. He stationed himself in the market-place of Milan, and related the following story to the crowds that gathered round him. He was standing, he said, at the door of the cathedral, late in the evening, and when there was nobody nigh, he saw a dark-coloured chariot, drawn by six milk-white horses, stop close beside him. The chariot was followed by a numerous train of domestics in dark liveries, mounted on dark-coloured steeds. In the chariot there sat a tall stranger of a majestic aspect; his long black hair floated in the wind--fire flashed from his large black eyes, and a curl of ineffable scorn dwelt upon his lips. The look of the stranger was so sublime that he was awed, and trembled with fear when he gazed upon him. His complexion was much darker than that of any man he had ever seen, and the atmosphere around him was hot and suffocating. He perceived immediately that he was a being of another world. The stranger, seeing his trepidation, asked him blandly, yet majestically, to mount beside him. He had no power to refuse, and before he was well aware that he had moved, he found himself in the chariot. Onwards they went, with the rapidity of the wind, the stranger speaking no word, until they stopped before a door in the high-street of Milan. There was a crowd of people in the street, but, to his great surprise, no one seemed to notice the extraordinary equipage and its numerous train. From this he concluded that they were invisible. The house at which they stopped appeared to be a shop, but the interior was like a vast half-ruined palace. He went with his mysterious guide through several large and dimly-lighted rooms. In one of them, surrounded by huge pillars of marble, a senate of ghosts was assembled, debating on the progress of the plague. Other parts of the building were enveloped in the thickest darkness, illumined at intervals by flashes of lightning, which allowed him to distinguish a number of gibing and chattering skeletons, running about and pursuing each other, or playing at leap-frog over one another's backs. At the rear of the mansion was a wild, uncultivated plot of ground, in the midst of which arose a black rock. Down its sides rushed with fearful noise a torrent of poisonous water, which, insinuating itself through the soil, penetrated to all the springs of the city, and rendered them unfit for use. After he had been shown all this, the stranger led him into another large chamber, filled with gold and precious stones, all of which he offered him if he would kneel down and worship him, and consent to smear the doors and houses of Milan with a pestiferous salve which he held out to him. tie now knew him to be the Devil, and in that moment of temptation, prayed to God to give him strength to resist. His prayer was heard - he refused the bribe. The stranger scowled horribly upon him - a loud clap of thunder burst over his head - the vivid lightning flashed in his eyes, and the next moment he found himself standing alone at the porch of the cathedral. He repeated this strange tale day after day, without any variation, and all the populace were firm believers in its truth. Repeated search was made to discover the mysterious house, but all in vain. The man pointed out several as resembling it, which were searched by the police; but the Demon of the Pestilence was not to be found, nor the hall of ghosts, nor the poisonous fountain. But the minds of the people were so impressed with the idea that scores of witnesses, half crazed by disease, came forward to swear that they also had seen the diabolical stranger, and had heard his chariot, drawn by the milk-white steeds, rumbling over the streets at midnight with a sound louder than thunder.

The number of persons who confessed that they were employed by the Devil to distribute poison is almost incredible. An epidemic frenzy was abroad, which seemed to be as contagious as the plague. Imagination was as disordered as the body, and day after day persons came voluntarily forward to accuse themselves. They generally had the marks of disease upon them, and some died in the act of confession.

During the great plague of London, in 1665, the people listened with similar avidity to the predictions of quacks and fanatics. Defoe says, that at that time the people were more addicted to prophecies and astronomical conjurations, dreams, and old wives' tales than ever they were before or since. Almanacs, and their predictions, frightened them terribly. Even the year before the plague broke out, they were greatly alarmed by the comet which then appeared, and anticipated that famine, pestilence, or fire would follow. Enthusiasts, while yet the disease had made but little progress, ran about the streets, predicting that in a few days London would be destroyed.

A still more singular instance of the faith in predictions occurred in London in the year 1524. The city swarmed at that time with fortune-tellers and astrologers, who were consulted daily by people of every class in society on the secrets of futurity. As early as the month of June 1523, several of them concurred in predicting that, on the 1st day of February, 1524, the waters of the Thames would swell to such a height as to overflow the whole city of London, and wash away ten thousand houses. The prophecy met implicit belief. It was reiterated with the utmost confidence month after month, until so much alarm was excited that many families packed up their goods, and removed into Kent and Essex. As the time drew nigh, the number of these emigrants increased. In January, droves of workmen might be seen, followed by their wives and children, trudging on foot to the villages within fifteen or twenty miles, to await the catastrophe. People of a higher class were also to be seen, in waggons and other vehicles, bound on a similar errand. By the middle of January, at least twenty thousand persons had quitted the doomed city, leaving nothing but the bare walls of their homes to be swept away by the impending floods. Many of the richer sort took up their abode on the heights of Highgate, Hampstead, and Blackheath; and some erected tents as far away as Waltham Abbey, on the north, and Croydon, on the south of the Thames. Bolton, the prior of St. Bartholomew's, was so alarmed that he erected, at very great expense, a sort of fortress at Harrow-on-the-Hill, which he stocked with provisions for two months. On the 24th of January, a week before the awful day which was to see the destruction of London, he removed thither, with the brethren and officers of the priory and all his household. A number of boats were conveyed in waggons to his fortress, furnished abundantly with expert rowers, in case the flood, reaching so high as Harrow, should force them to go further for a resting-place. Many wealthy citizens prayed to share his retreat, but the Prior, with a prudent forethought, admitted only his personal friends, and those who brought stores of eatables for the blockade.

At last the morn, big with the fate of London, appeared in the east. The wondering crowds were astir at an early hour to watch the rising of the waters. The inundation, it was predicted, would be gradual, not sudden; so that they expected to have plenty of time to escape, as soon as they saw the bosom of old Thames heave beyond the usual mark. But the majority were too much alarmed to trust to this, and thought themselves safer ten or twenty miles off. The Thames, unmindful of the foolish crowds upon its banks, flowed on quietly as of yore. The tide ebbed at its usual hour, flowed to its usual height, and then ebbed again, just as if twenty astrologers had not pledged their words to the contrary. Blank were their faces as evening approached, and as blank grew the faces of the citizens to think that they had made such fools of themselves. At last night set in, and the obstinate river would not lift its waters to sweep away even one house out of the ten thousand. Still, however, the people were afraid to go to sleep. Many hundreds remained up till dawn of the next day, lest the deluge should come upon them like a thief in the night.

On the morrow, it was seriously discussed whether it would not be advisable to duck the false prophets in the river. Luckily for them, they thought of an expedient which allayed the popular fury. They asserted that, by an error (a very slight one) of a little figure, they had fixed the date of this awful inundation a whole century too early. The stars were right after all, and they, erring mortals, were wrong. The present generation of cockneys was safe, and London 'would be washed away, not in 1524, but in 1624. At this announcement, Bolton, the prior, dismantled his fortress, and the weary emigrants came back.

An eye-witness of the great fire of London, in an account preserved among the Harleian MSS. in the British Museum, and recently published in the Transactions of the Royal Society of Antiquaries, relates another instance of the credulity of the Londoners. The writer, who accompanied the Duke of York day by day through the district included between the Fleet-bridge and the Thames, states that, in their efforts to check the progress of the flames, they were much impeded by the superstition of the people. Mother Shipton, in one of her prophecies, had said that London would be reduced to ashes, and they refused to make any efforts to prevent it. [This prophecy seems to have been that set forth at length in the popular *Life of Mother Shipton* :--

"When fate to England shall restore
A king to reign as heretofore,
Great death in London shall be though,
And many houses be laid low."]

A son of the noted Sir Kenelm Digby, who was also a pretender to the gifts of prophecy, persuaded them that no power on earth could prevent the fulfilment of the prediction; for it was written in the great book of fate that London was to be destroyed. Hundreds of persons, who might have rendered valuable assistance, and saved whole parishes from devastation, folded their arms and looked on. As many more gave themselves up, with the less compunction, to plunder a city which they could not save.

The prophecies of Mother Shipton are still believed in many of the rural districts of England. In cottages and servants' halls her reputation is great; and she rules, the most popular of British prophets, among all the uneducated, or half-educated, portions of the community. She is generally supposed to have been born at Knaresborough, in the reign of Henry VII, and to have sold her soul to the Devil for the power of foretelling future events. Though during her lifetime she was looked upon as a witch, she yet escaped the witch's fate, and died peaceably in her bed at an extreme old age, near Clifton in Yorkshire. A stone is said to have been erected to her memory in the church-yard of that place, with the following epitaph :--

"Here lies she who never lied;
Whose skill often has been tried:
Her prophecies shall still survive,
And ever keep her name alive."

"Never a day passed," says her traditionary biography, "wherein she did not relate something remarkable, and that required the most serious consideration. People flocked to her from far and near, her fame was so great. They went to her of all sorts, both old and young, rich and poor, especially young maidens, to be resolved of their doubts relating to things to come; and all returned wonderfully satisfied in the explanations she gave to their questions." Among the rest, went the Abbot of Beverley, to whom she foretold the suppression of the monasteries by Henry VIII; his marriage with Anne Boleyn; the fires for heretics in Smithfield, and the execution of Mary Queen of Scots. She also foretold the accession of James I, adding that, with him,

"From the cold North,
Every evil should come forth."

On a subsequent visit she uttered another prophecy, which, in the opinion of her believers, still remains unfulfilled, but may be expected to be realised during the present century:--

"The time shall come when seas of blood
Shall mingle with a greater flood.
Great noise there shall be heard--great shouts and cries,
And seas shall thunder louder than the skies;
Then shall three lions fight with three, and bring
Joy to a people, honour to a king.
That fiery year as soon as o'er,
Peace shall then be as before;
Plenty shall everywhere be found,
And men with swords shall plough the ground."

But the most famous of all her prophecies is one relating to London. Thousands of persons still shudder to think of the woes that are to burst over this unhappy realm, when London and Highgate are joined by one continuous line of houses. This junction, which, if the rage for building lasts much longer, in the same proportion as heretofore, bids fair to be soon accomplished, was predicted by her shortly before her death. Revolutions -- the fall of mighty monarchs, and the shedding of much blood are to signalise that event. The very angels, afflicted by our woes, are to turn aside their heads, and weep for hapless Britain.

But great as is the fame of Mother Shipton, she ranks but second in the list of British prophets. Merlin, the mighty Merlin, stands alone in his high pre-eminence -- the first and greatest. As old Drayton sings, in his Poly-olbion :--

"Of Merlin and his skill what region doth not hear?
The world shall still be full of Merlin every year.
A thousand lingering years his prophecies have run,
And scarcely shall have end till time itself be done."

Spenser, in his divine poem, has given us a powerfid description of this renowned seer--

".......who had in magic more insight
Than ever him before, or after, living wight.

"For he by words could call out of the sky
Both sun and moon, and make them him obey;

75

The land to sea, and sea to mainland dry,
And darksome night he eke could turn to day--
Huge hosts of men he could, alone, dismay.
And hosts of men and meanest things could frame,
Whenso him list his enemies to fray,
That to this day, for terror of his name,
The fiends do quake, when any him to them does name.

"And soothe men say that he was not the sonne,
Of mortal sire or other living wighte,
But wondrously begotten and begoune
By false illusion of a guileful sprite,
On a faire ladye nun."

In these verses the poet has preserved the popular belief with regard to Merlin, who is generally supposed to have been a contemporary of Vortigern. Opinion is divided as to whether he were a real personage, or a mere impersonation, formed by the poetic fancy of a credulous people. It seems most probable that such a man did exist, and that, possessing knowledge as much above the comprehension of his age, as that possessed by Friar Bacon was beyond the reach of his, he was endowed by the wondering crowd with the supernatural attributes that Spenser has enumerated.

Geoffrey of Monmouth translated Merlin's poetical odes, or prophecies, into Latin prose, and he was much reverenced, not only by Geoffrey, but by most of,the old annalists. In a "Life of Merlin, with his Prophecies and Predictions. interpreted and made good by our English Annals," by Thomas Heywood, published in the reign of Charles I, we find several of these pretended prophecies. They seem, however, to have been all written by Heywood himself. They are in terms too plain and positive to allow any one to doubt for a moment of their having been composed ex post facto. Speaking of Richard I, he says :--

"The Lion's heart will 'gainst the Saracen rise,
And purchase from him many a glorious prize;
The rose and lily shall at first unite,
But, parting of the prey prove opposite. * * *
But while abroad these great acts shall be done;
All things at home shall to disorder run.
Cooped up and caged then shall the Lion be,
But, after sufferance, ransomed and set free."

The simple-minded Thomas Heywood gravely goes on to inform us, that all these things actually came to pass. Upon Richard III he is equally luminous. He says :--

"A hunch-backed monster, who with teeth is born,
The mockery of art and nature's scorn;
Who from the womb preposterously is hurled,
And, with feet forward, thrust into the world,
Shall, from the lower earth on which he stood,
Wade, every step he mounts, knee-deep in blood.
He shall to th' height of all his hopes aspire,

And, clothed in state, his ugly shape admire;
But, when he thinks himself most safe to stand,
From foreign parts a native whelp shall land."

Another of these prophecies after the event tells us that Henry VIII should take the power from Rome, "and bring it home unto his British bower;" that he should "root out from the land all the razored skulls;" and that he should neither spare "man in his rage nor woman in his lust;" and that, in the time of his next successor but one, "there should come in the fagot and the stake." Master Heywood closes Merlin's prophecies at his own day, and does not give even a glimpse of what was to befall England after his decease. Many other prophecies, besides those quoted by him, were, he says, dispersed abroad, in his day, under the name of Merlin; but he gives his readers a taste of one only, and that is the following :--

"When hempe is ripe and ready to pull,
Then Englishman beware thy skull."

This prophecy, which, one would think, ought to have put him in mind of the gallows, the not unusual fate of false prophets, and perchance his own, he explains thus:-- "In this word HEMPE be five letters. Now, by reckoning the five successive princes from Henry VIII, this prophecy is easily explained: H signifieth King Henry before named; E, Edward, his son, the sixth of that name; M, Mary, who succeeded him; P, Philip of Spain, who, by marrying Queen Mary, participated with her in the English diadem; and, lastly, E signifieth Queen Elizabeth, after whose death there was a great feare that some troubles might have arisen about the crown." As this did not happen, Heywood, who was a sly rogue in a small way, gets out of the scrape by saying, "Yet proved this augury true, though not according to the former expectation; for, after the peaceful inauguration of King James, there was great mortality, not in London only, but through the whole kingdom, and from which the nation was not quite clean in seven years after."

This is not unlike the subterfuge of Peter of Pontefract, who had prophesied the death and deposition of King John, and who was hanged by that monarch for his pains. A very graphic and amusing account of this pretended prophet is given by Grafton, in his *Chronicles of England*. There is so much homely vigour about the style of the old annalist, that it would be a pity to give the story in other words than his own. [*Chronicles of England*, by Richard Grafton; London, 1568, p. 106.] "In the meanwhile," says he, "the priestes within England had provided them a false and counterfeated prophet, called Peter Wakefielde, a Yorkshire man, who was an hermite, an idle gadder about, and a pratlyng marchant. Now to bring this Peter in credite, and the kyng out of all credite with his people, diverse vaine persons bruted dayly among the commons of the realme, that Christe had twice appered unto him in the shape of a childe, betwene the prieste's handes, once at Yorke, another tyme at Pomfret; and that he had breathed upon him thrice, saying, 'Peace, peace, peace,' and teachyng many things, which he anon declared to the bishops, and bid the people amend their naughtie living. Being rapt also in spirite, they sayde he behelde the joyes of heaven and sorowes of hell, for scant were there three in the realme, sayde he, that lived Christainly.

"This counterfeated soothsayer prophecied of King John, that he should reigne no longer than the Ascension-day next followyng, which was in the yere of our Lord 1211, and was the thirteenth yere from his coronation; and this, he said, he had by revelation. Then it was of him demanded, whether he should be slaine or be deposed, or should voluntarily give over the crowne? He aunswered, that he could not tell; but of this he was sure (he sayd), that neither he nor any of his stock or lineage should reigne after that day.

"The king hering of this, laughed much at it, and made but a scoff thereat. 'Tush!' saith he, 'it is but an ideot knave, and such an one as lacketh his right wittes.' But when this foolish prophet had so escaped the daunger of the Kinge's displeasure, and that he made no more of it, he gate him abroad, and prated thereof at large, as he was a very idle vagabond, and used to trattle and talke more than ynough, so that they which loved the King caused him anon after to be apprehended as a malefactor, and to be throwen in prison, the King not yet knowing thereof.

"Anone after the fame of this phantasticall prophet went all the realme over, and his name was knowen everywhere, as foolishnesse is much regarded of the people, where wisdome is not in place; specially because he was then imprisoned for the matter, the rumour was the larger, their wonderynges were the wantoner, their practises the foolisher, their busye talkes and other idle doinges the greater. Continually from thence, as the rude manner of people is, olde gossyps tales went abroad, new tales were invented, fables were added to fables, and lyes grew upon lyes. So that every daye newe slanders were laide upon the King, and not one of them true. Rumors arose, blasphemyes were sprede, the enemyes rejoyced, and treasons by the priestes were mainteyned; and what lykewise was surmised, or other subtiltye practised, all was then lathered upon this foolish prophet, as 'thus saith Peter Wakefield;' 'thus hath he prophecied;' ' and thus it shall come to pass;' yea, many times, when he thought nothing lesse. And when the Ascension-day was come, which was prophecyed of before, King John commanded his royal tent to be spread in the open fielde, passing that day with his noble counseyle and men of honour, in the greatest solemnitie that ever he did before; solacing himself with musickale instrumentes and songs, most in sight among his trustie friendes. When that day was paste in all prosperitie and myrth, his enemyes being confused, turned all into an allegorical understanding to make the prophecie good, and sayde, "he is no longer King, for the Pope reigneth, and not he." [King John was labouring under a sentence of excommunication at the time.]

"Then was the King by his council perswaded that this false prophet had troubled the realme, perverted the heartes of the people, and raysed the commons against him; for his wordes went over the sea, by the help of his prelates, and came to the French King's care, and gave to him a great encouragement to invade the lande. He had not else done it so sodeinely. But he was most lowly deceived, as all they are and shall be that put their trust in such dark drowsye dreames of hipocrites. The King therefore commanded that he should be hanged up, and his sonne also with him, lest any more false prophets should arise of that race."

Heywood, who was a great stickler for the truth of all sorts of prophecies, gives a much more favourable account of this Peter of Pomfret, or Pontefract, whose fate he would, in all probability, have shared, if he had had the misfortune to have flourished in the same age. He says, that Peter, who was not only a prophet, but a bard, predicted divers of King John's disasters, which fell out accordingly. On being taxed for a lying prophet in having predicted that the King would be deposed before .he entered into the fifteenth year of his reign, he answered him boldly, that all he had said was justifiable and true; for that, having given up his crown to the Pope, and paying him an annual tribute, the Pope reigned, and not he. Heywood thought this explanation to be perfectly satisfactory, and the prophet's faith for ever established.

But to return to Merlin. Of him even to this day it may be said, in the words which Burns has applied to another notorious personage,

"Great was his power and great his fame;
Far kenned and noted is his name."

His reputation is by no means confined to the land of his birth, but extends through most of the nations of Europe. A very curious volume of his Life, Prophecies, and Miracles, written, it is supposed, by Robert de Bosron, was printed at Paris in 1498, which states, that the Devil himself was his father, and that he spoke the instant he was born, and assured his mother, a very virtuous young woman, that she should not die in child-bed with him, as her ill-natured neighbours had predicted. The judge of the district, hearing of so marvellous an occurrence, summoned both mother and child to appear before him; and they went accordingly the same day. To put the wisdom of the young prophet most effectually to the test, the judge asked him if he knew his own father? To which the infant Merlin replied, in a clear, sonorous voice, "Yes, my father is the Devil; and I have his power, and know all things, past, present, and to come." His worship clapped his hands in astonishment, and took the prudent resolution of not molesting so awful a child, or its mother either.

Early tradition attributes the building of Stonehenge to the power of Merlin. It was believed that those mighty stones were whirled through the air, at his command, from Ireland to Salisbury Plain, and that he arranged them in the form in which they now stand, to commemorate for ever the unhappy fate of three hundred British chiefs, who were massacred on that spot by the Saxons.

At Abergwylly, near Caermarthen, is still shown the cave of the prophet and the scene of his incantations. How beautiful is the description of it given by Spenser in his "Faerie Queene." The lines need no apology for their repetition here, and any sketch of the great prophet of Britain would be incomplete without them :--

"There the wise Merlin, whilom wont (they say),
To make his wonne low underneath the ground,
In a deep delve far from the view of day,
That of no living wight he mote be found,
Whenso he counselled with his sprites encompassed round.

"And if thou ever happen that same way
To travel, go to see that dreadful place;
It is a hideous, hollow cave, they say,
Under a rock that lies a little space
From the swift Barry, tumbling down apace
Amongst the woody hills of Dynevoure;
But dare thou not, I charge, in any case,
To enter into that same baleful bower,
For fear the cruel fiendes should thee unwares devour!

"But, standing high aloft, low lay thine care,
And there such ghastly noise of iron chaines,
And brazen caudrons thou shalt rombling heare,
Which thousand sprites, with long-enduring paines,
Doe tosse, that it will stun thy feeble braines;
And often times great groans and grievous stownds,
When too huge toile and labour them constraines;

And often times loud strokes and ringing sounds
From under that deep rock most horribly rebounds.

"The cause, they say, is this. A little while
Before that Merlin died, he did intend
A brazen wall in compass, to compile
About Cayr Merdin, and did it commend
Unto these sprites to bring to perfect end;
During which work the Lady of the Lake,
Whom long he loved, for him in haste did send,
Who thereby forced his workmen to forsake,
Them bound till his return their labour not to slake.

"In the mean time, through that false ladie's traine,
He was surprised, and buried under biere,
Ne ever to his work returned again;
Natheless these fiendes may not their work forbeare,
So greatly his commandement they fear,
But there doe toile and travaile day and night,
Until that brazen wall they up doe reare."

[Faerie Queene, b. 3. c. 3. s. 6--13.]

Amongst other English prophets, a belief in whose power has not been entirely effaced by the light of advancing knowledge, is Robert Nixon, the Cheshire idiot, a contemporary of Mother Shipton. The popular accounts of this man say, that he was born of poor parents, not far from Vale Royal, on the edge of the forest of Delamere. He was brought up to the plough, but was so ignorant and stupid, that nothing could be made of him. Everybody thought him irretrievably insane, and paid no attention to the strange, unconnected discourses which he held. Many of his prophecies are believed to have been lost in this manner. But they were not always destined to be wasted upon dull and inattentive ears. An incident occurred which brought him into notice, and established his fame as a prophet of the first calibre. He was ploughing in a field when he suddenly stopped from his labour, and, with a wild look and strange gestures, exclaimed, "Now, Dick! now, Harry! O, ill done, Dick! O, well done, Harry! Harry has gained the day!" His fellow labourers in the field did not know what to make of this rhapsody; but the next day cleared up the mystery. News was brought by a messenger, in hot haste, that at the very instant when Nixon had thus ejaculated, Richard III had been slain at the battle of Bosworth, and Henry VII proclaimed King of England.

It was not long before the fame of the new prophet reached the ears of the King, who expressed a wish to see and converse with him. A messenger was accordingly despatched to bring him to court; but long before he reached Cheshire, Nixon knew and dreaded the honours that awaited him. Indeed it was said, that at the very instant the King expressed the wish, Nixon was, by supernatural means, made acquainted with it, and that he ran about the town of Over in great distress of mind, calling out, like a madman, that Henry had sent for him, and that he must go to court, and be clammed; that is, starved to death. These expressions excited no little wonder; but, on the third day, the messenger arrived, and carried him to court, leaving on the minds of the good people of Cheshire an impression that their prophet was one of the greatest ever born. On his arrival King Henry appeared to be troubled exceedingly at the loss of a valuable diamond, and asked Nixon if he could inform him where it was to be found. Henry had hidden the diamond himself, with a view to test the prophet's skill. Great, therefore, was his surprise when

Nixon answered him in the words of the old proverb, "Those who hide can find." From that time forth the King implicitly believed that he had the gift of prophecy, and ordered all his words to be taken down.

During all the time of his residence at court he was in constant fear of being starved to death, and repeatedly told the King that such would be his fate, if he were not allowed to depart, and return into his own country. Henry would not suffer it, but gave strict orders to all his officers and cooks to give him as much to eat as he wanted. He lived so well, that for some time he seemed to be thriving like a nobleman's steward, and growing as fat as an alderman. One day the king went out hunting, when Nixon ran to the palace gate, and entreated on his knees that he might not be left behind to be starved. The King laughed, and, calling an officer, told him to take especial care of the prophet during his absence, and rode away to the forest. After his departure, the servants of the palace began to jeer at and insult Nixon, whom they imagined to be much better treated than he deserved. Nixon complained to the officer, who, to prevent him from being further molested, locked him up in the King's own closet, and brought him regularly his four meals a day. But it so happened that a messenger arrived from the King to this officer, requiring his immediate presence at Winchester, on a matter of life and death. So great was his haste to obey the King's command, that he mounted on the horse behind the messenger, and rode off, without bestowing a thought upon poor Nixon. He did not return till three days afterwards, when, remembering the prophet for the first time, he went to the King's closet, and found him lying upon the floor, starved to death, as he had predicted.

Among the prophecies of his which are believed to have been fulfilled, are the following, which relate to the times of the Pretender :--

"A great man shall come into England,
But the son of a King
Shall take from him the victory."

"Crows shall drink the blood of many nobles,
And the North shall rise against the South."
"The cock of the North shall be made to flee,
And his feather be plucked for his pride,
That he shall almost curse the day that he was born,"

All these, say his admirers, are as clear as the sun at noon-day. The first denotes the defeat of Prince Charles Edward, at the battle of Culloden, by the Duke of Cumberland; the second, the execution of Lords Derwentwater, Balmerino, and Lovat; and the third, the retreat of the Pretender from the shores of Britain. Among the prophecies that still remain to be accomplished, are the following :--

"Between seven, eight, and nine,
In England wonders shall be seen;
Between nine and thirteen
All sorrow shall be done!"

"Through our own money and our men
Shall a dreadful war begin.
Between the sickle and the suck
All England shall have a pluck,"

"Foreign nations shall invade England with snow on their helmets, and shall bring plague, famine, and murder in the skirts of their garments."

"The town of Nantwich shall be swept away by a flood."

Of the two first of these no explanation has yet been attempted; but some event or other will doubtless be twisted into such a shape as will fit them. The third, relative to the invasion of England by a nation with snow on their helmets, is supposed by the old women to foretell most clearly the coming war with Russia. As to the last, there are not a few in the town mentioned who devoutly believe that such will be its fate. Happily for their peace of mind, the prophet said nothing of the year that was to witness the awful calamity; so that they think it as likely to be two centuries hence as now.

The popular biographers of Nixon conclude their account of him by saying, that "his prophecies are by some persons thought fables; yet by what has come to pass, it is now thought, and very plainly appears, that most of them have proved, or will prove, true; for which we, on all occasions, ought not only to exert our utmost might to repel by force our enemies, but to refrain from our abandoned and wicked course of life, and to make our continual prayer to God for protection and safety." To this, though a non sequitur, every one will cry Amen!

Besides the prophets, there have been the almanack makers, Lilly, Poor Robin, Partridge, and Francis Moore, physician, in England, and Matthew Laensbergh, in France and Belgium. But great as were their pretensions, they were modesty itself in comparison with Merlin, Shipton, and Nixon, who fixed their minds upon higher things than the weather, and who were not so restrained in their flights of fancy as to prophesy for only one year at a time. After such prophets as they, the almanack makers hardly deserve to be mentioned; no, not even the renowned Partridge, whose wonderful prognostications set all England agog in 1708, and whose death, at a time when he was still alive and kicking, was so pleasantly and satisfactorily proved by Isaac Bickerstaff. The anti-climax would be too palpable, and they and their doings must be left uncommemorated.

Popular Admiration for Great Thieves

Jack. Where shall we find such another set of practical philosophers who, to a man, are above the fear of death?
Wat. Sound men and true!
Robin. Of tried courage and indefatigable industry!
Ned. Who is there here that would not die for his friend?
Harry. Who is there here that would betray him for his interest?
Mat. Show me a gang of courtiers that could say as much!
Dialogue of thieves in the Beggars' Opera.

Whether it be that the multitude, feeling the pangs of poverty, sympathise with the daring and ingenious depredators who take away the rich man's superfluity, or whether it be the interest that mankind in general feel for the records of perilous adventures, it is certain that the populace of all countries look with admiration upon great and successful thieves. Perhaps both these causes combine to invest their career with charms in the popular eye. Almost every country in Europe has its traditional thief, whose exploits are recorded with all the graces of poetry, and whose trespasses --

"-- are cited up in rhymes, And sung by children in succeeding times."

[Shakspeare's Rape of Lucretia.]

Those travellers who have made national manners and characteristics their peculiar study, have often observed and remarked upon this feeling. The learned Abbe le Blanc, who resided for some time in England at the commencement of the eighteenth century, says, in his amusing letters on the English and French nations, that he continually met with Englishmen who were not less vain in boasting of the success of their highwaymen than of the bravery of their troops. Tales of their address, their cunning, or their generosity, were in the mouths of everybody, and a noted thief was a kind of hero in high repute. He adds that the mob, in all countries, being easily moved, look in general with concern upon criminals going to the gallows; but an English mob looked upon such scenes with 'extraordinary interest: they delighted to see them go through their last trials with resolution, and applauded those who were insensible enough to die as they had lived, braving the justice both of God and men: such, he might have added, as the noted robber Macpherson, of whom the old ballad says--

"Sae rantingly, sae wantonly,
Sae dauntingly gaed he:
He played a spring, and danced it round
Beneath the gallows tree."

Among these traditional thieves the most noted in England, or perhaps in any country, is Robin Hood, a name which popular affection has encircled with a peculiar halo. "He robbed the rich to give to the poor;" and his reward has been an immortality of fame, a tithe of which would be thought more than sufficient to recompense a benefactor of his species. Romance and poetry have been emulous to make him all their own; and the forest of Sherwood, in which he roamed with his merry men, armed with their long bows, and clad in Lincoln green, has become the resort of pilgrims, and a classic spot sacred to his memory. The few virtues he had, which would have ensured him no praise if he had been an honest man, have been blazoned forth by popular renown during seven successive centuries, and will never be forgotten while the English tongue endures. His charity to the poor, and his gallantry and respect for women, have made him the pre-eminent thief of all the world.

Among English thieves of a later date, who has not heard of Claude Duval, Dick Turpin, Jonathan Wild, and Jack Sheppard, those knights of the road and of the town, whose peculiar chivalry formed at once the dread and the delight of England during the eighteenth century ? Turpin's fame is unknown to no portion of the male population of England after they have attained the age of ten. His wondrous ride from London to York has endeared him to the imagination of millions; his cruelty in placing an old woman upon a fire, to force her to tell him where she had hidden her money, is regarded as a good joke; and his proud bearing upon the scaffold is looked upon as a virtuous action. The Abbe le Blanc, writing in 1737, says he was continually entertained with stories of Turpin -- how, when he robbed gentlemen, he would generously leave them enough to continue their journey, and exact a pledge from them never to inform against him, and how scrupulous such gentlemen were in keeping their word. He was one day told a story with which the relator was he the highest degree delighted. Turpin, or some other noted robber, stopped a man whom he knew to be very rich, with the usual salutation --" Your money or your life!" but not finding more than five or six guineas about him, he took the liberty of entreating him, in the most affable manner, never to come out so ill provided; adding that, if he fell in with him, and he had no more than such a paltry sum, he would give him a good licking. Another story, told by one of Turpin's admirers, was of a robbery he had committed upon a Mr. C. near Cambridge. He took from this gentleman his watch, his snuff-box, and all his money but two shillings, and, before he left him, required his word of honour that he would not cause him to be pursued or brought before a justice. The promise being given, they both parted very courteously. They afterwards met at Newmarket, and renewed their acquaintance. Mr. C. kept his word religiously; he not only refrained from giving Turpin into custody, but made a boast that he had fairly won some of his money back again in an honest way. Turpin offered to bet with him on some favourite horse, and Mr. C. accepted the wager with as good a grace as he could have done from the best gentleman in England. Turpin lost his bet and paid it immediately, and was so smitten with the generous behaviour of Mr. C. that he told him how deeply he regretted that the trifling affair which had happened between them did not permit them to drink together. The narrator of this anecdote was quite proud that England was the birthplace of such a highwayman.

[The Abbe, in the second volume, in the letter No. 79, dressed to Monsieur de Buffon, gives the following curious particulars of the robbers of 1757, which are not without interest at this day, if it were only to show the vast improvement which has taken place since that period :-- "It is usual, in travelling, to put ten or a dozen guineas in a separate pocket, as a tribute to the first that comes to demand them: the right of passport, which custom has established here in favour of the robbers, who are almost the only highway surveyors in England, has made this necessary; and accordingly the English call these fellows the 'Gentlemen of the Road,' the government letting them exercise their jurisdiction upon travellers without giving them any great molestation. To say the truth, they content themselves with only taking the money of those who obey without disputing; but notwithstanding their boasted humanity, the lives of those who endeavour to get away are not always safe. They are very strict and severe in levying their impost; and if a man has not wherewithal to pay them, he may run the chance of getting himself knocked on the head for his poverty.

"About fifteen years ago, these robbers, with the view of maintaining their rights, fixed up papers at the doors of rich people about London, expressly forbidding all persons, of whatsoever quality or condition, from going out of town without ten guineas and a watch about them, on pain of death. In bad times, when there is little or nothing to be got on the roads, these fellows assemble in gangs, to raise contributions even in London itself; and the watchmen seldom trouble themselves to interfere with them in their vocation."]

Not less familiar to the people of England is the career of Jack Sheppard, as brutal a ruffian as ever disgraced his country, but who has claims upon the popular admiration which are very generally acknowledged. He did not, like Robin Hood, plunder the rich to relieve the poor, nor rob with an uncouth sort of courtesy, like Turpin; but he escaped from Newgate with the fetters on his limbs. This achievement, more than once repeated, has encircled his felon brow with the wreath of immortality, and made him quite a pattern thief among the populace. He was no more than twenty-three years of age at the time of his execution, and he died much pitied by the crowd. His adventures were the sole topics of conversation for months; the print-shops were filled with his effigies, and a fine painting of him was made by Sir Richard Thornhill. The following complimentary verses to the artist appeared in the "British Journal" of November 28th, 1724.

"Thornhill! 'tis thine to gild with fame
Th' obscure, and raise the humble name;
To make the form elude the grave,
And Sheppard from oblivion save!

Apelles Alexander drew--
Cesar is to Aurelius due;
Cromwell in Lilly's works doth shine,
And Sheppard, Thornhill, lives in thine!"

So high was Jack's fame that a pantomime entertainment, called "Harlequin Jack Sheppard," was devised by one Thurmond, and brought out with great success at Drury Lane Theatre. All the scenes were painted from nature, including the public-house that the robber frequented in Claremarket, and the condemned cell from which he had made his escape in Newgate.

The Rev. Mr. Villette, the editor of the "Annals of Newgate," published in 1754, relates a curious sermon which, he says, a friend of his heard delivered by a street-preacher about the time of Jack's execution. The orator, after animadverting on the great care men took of their bodies, and the little care they bestowed upon their souls, continued as follows, by way of exemplifying the position:-- "We have a remarkable instance of this in a notorious malefactor, well known by the name of Jack Sheppard. What amazing difficulties has he overcome! what astonishing things has he performed! and all for the sake of a stinking, miserable carcass; hardly worth the hanging! How dexterously did he pick the chain of his padlock with a crooked nail! how manfully he burst his fetters asunder! -- climb up the chimney! -- wrench out an iron bar! -- break his way through a stone wall! -- make the strong door of a dark entry fly before him, till he got upon the leads of the prison! then, fixing a blanket to the wall with a spike, he stole out of the chapel. How intrepidly did he descend to the top of the turner's house! -- how cautiously pass down the stair, and make his escape to the street door!

"Oh! that ye were all like Jack Sheppard! Mistake me not, my brethren; I don't mean in a carnal, but in a spiritual sense, for I propose to spiritualise these things. What a shame it would be if we should not think it worth our while to take as much pains, and employ as many deep thoughts, to save our souls as he has done to preserve his body!

"Let me exhort ye, then, to open the locks of your hearts with the nail of repentance! Burst asunder the fetters of your beloved lusts! -- mount the chimney of hope! -- take from thence the bar of good resolution! -- break through the stone wall of despair, and all the strongholds in the dark entry of the valley of the shadow of death! Raise yourselves to the leads of divine meditation! -- fix the blanket of faith with the spike of the church! let yourselves down to the turner's house of re signation, and descend the stairs of humility! So shall you come to the door of deliverance from the prison of iniquity, and escape the clutches of that old executioner the Devil!"

But popular as the name of Jack Sheppard was immediately after he had suffered the last penalty of his crimes, it was as nothing compared to the vast renown which he has acquired in these latter days, after the lapse of a century and a quarter. Poets too often, are not fully appreciated till they have been dead a hundred years, and thieves, it would appear, share the disadvantage. But posterity is grateful if our contemporaries are not; and Jack Sheppard, faintly praised in his own day, shines out in ours the hero of heroes, preeminent above all his fellows. Thornhill made but one picture of the illustrious robber, but Cruikshank has made dozens, and the art of the engraver has multiplied them into thousands and tens of thousands, until the populace of England have become as familiar with Jack's features as they are with their own. Jack, the romantic, is the hero of three goodly volumes, and the delight of the circulating libraries; and the theatres have been smitten with the universal enthusiasm. Managers have set their playmongers at work, and Jack's story has been reproduced in the shape of drama, melodrama, and farce, at half a dozen places of entertainment at once. Never was such a display of popular regard for a hero as was exhibited in London in 1840 for the renowned Jack Sheppard: robbery acquired additional lustre in the popular eye, and not only Englishmen, but foreigners, caught the contagion; and one of the latter, fired by the example, robbed and murdered a venerable, unoffending, and too confiding nobleman, whom it was his especial duty to have obeyed and protected. But he was a coward and a wretch; -- it was a solitary crime -- he had not made a daring escape from dungeon walls, or ridden from London to York, and he died amid the execrations of the people, affording a melancholy exemplification of the trite remark, that every man is not great who is desirous of being so.

Jonathan Wild, whose name has been immortalised by Fielding, was no favourite with the people. He had none of the virtues which, combined with crimes, make up the character of the great thief. He was a pitiful fellow, who informed against his comrades, and was afraid of death. This meanness was not to be forgiven by the crowd, and they pelted him with dirt and stones on his way to Tyburn, and expressed their contempt by every possible means. How different was their conduct to Turpin and Jack Sheppard, who died in their neatest attire, with nosegays in their button-holes, and with the courage that a crowd expects! It was anticipated that the body of Turpin would have been delivered up to the surgeons for dissection, and the people seeing some men very busily employed in removing it, suddenly set upon them, rescued the body, bore it about the town in triumph, and then buried it in a very deep grave, filled with quick-lime, to hasten the progress of decomposition. They would not suffer the corpse of their hero, of the man who had ridden from London to York in four-and-twenty hours to be mangled by the rude hands of unmannerly surgeons.

The death of Claude Duval would appear to have been no less triumphant. Claude was a gentlemanly thief. According to Butler, in the famous ode to his memory, he

"Taught the wild Arabs of the road
To rob in a more gentle mode;
Take prizes more obligingly than those
Who never had breen bred filous;
And how to hang in a more graceful fashion
Than e'er was known before to the dull English nation."

In fact, he was the pink of politeness, and his gallantry to the fair sex was proverbial. When he was caught at last, pent in "stone walls and chains and iron grates," -- their grief was in proportion to his rare merits and his great fame. Butler says, that to his dungeon

"-- came ladies from all parts,
To offer up close prisoners their hearts,
Which he received as tribute due--
* * * *
Never did bold knight, to relieve
Distressed dames, such dreadful feats achieve,
As feeble damsels, for his sake,
Would have been proud to undertake,
And, bravely ambitious to redeem
The world's loss and their own,
Strove who should have the honour to lay down,
And change a life with him."

Among the noted thieves of France, there is none to compare with the famous Aimerigot Tetenoire, who flourished in the reign of Charles VI. This fellow was at the head of four or five hundred men, and possessed two very strong castles in Limousin and Auvergne. There was a good deal of the feudal baron about him, although he possessed no revenues but such as the road afforded him. At his death he left a singular will. "I give and bequeath," said the robber, "one thousand five hundred francs to St. George's Chapel, for such repairs as it may need. To my sweet girl who so tenderly loved me, I give two thousand five hundred; and the surplus I give to my companions. I hope they will all live as brothers, and divide it amicably among them. If they cannot agree, and the devil of contention gets among them, it is no fault of mine; and I advise them to get a good strong, sharp axe, and break open my strong box. Let them scramble for what it contains, and the Devil seize the hindmost." The people of Auvergne still recount with admiration the daring feats of this brigand.

Of later years, the French thieves have been such unmitigated scoundrels as to have left but little room for popular admiration. The famous Cartouche, whose name has become synonymous with ruffian in their language, had none of the generosity, courtesy, and devoted bravery which are so requisite to make a robber-hero. He was born at Paris, towards the end of the seventeenth century, and broken alive on the wheel in November 1727. He was, however, sufficiently popular to have been pitied at his death, and afterwards to have formed the subject of a much admired drama, which bore his name, and was played with great success in all the theatres of France during the years 1734, 5, and 6. In our own day the

French have been more fortunate in a robber; Vidocq bids fair to rival the fame of Turpin and Jack Sheppard. Already he has become the hero of many an apocryphal tale -- already his compatriots boast of his manifold achievements, and express their doubts whether any other country in Europe could produce a thief so clever, so accomplished, so gentlemanly, as Vidocq.

Germany has its Schinderhannes, Hungary its Schubry, and Italy and Spain a whole host of brigands, whose names and exploits are familiar as household words in the mouths of the children and populace of those countries. The Italian banditti are renowned over the world; and many of them are not only very religious (after a fashion), but very charitable. Charity from such a source is so unexpected, that the people dote upon them for it. One of them, when he fell into the hands of the police, exclaimed, as they led him away, "Ho fatto pitt carita!" -- " I have given away more in charity than any three convents in these provinces." And the fellow spoke truth.

In Lombardy, the people cherish the memory of two notorious robbers, who flourished about two centuries ago under the Spanish government. Their story, according to Macfarlane, is contained in a little book well known to all the children of the province, and read by them with much more gusto than their Bibles.

Schinderhannes, the robber of the Rhine, is a great favourite on the banks of the river which he so long kept in awe. Many amusing stories are related by the peasantry of the scurvy tricks he played off upon rich Jews, or too-presuming officers of justice -- of his princely generosity, and undaunted courage. In short, they are proud of him, and would no more consent to have the memory of his achievements dissociated from their river than they would to have the rock of Ehrenbreitstein blown to atoms by gunpowder.

There is another robber-hero, of whose character and exploits the people of Germany speak admiringly. Mausch Nadel was captain of a considerable band that infested the Rhine, Switzerland, Alsatia, and Lorraine during the years 1824, 5, and 6. Like Jack Sheppard, he endeared himself to the populace by his most hazardous escape from prison. Being confined, at Bremen, in a dungeon, on the third story of the prison of that town, he contrived to let himself down without exciting the vigilance of the sentinels, and to swim across the Weser, though heavily laden with irons. When about half way over, he was espied by a sentinel, who fired at him, and shot him in the calf of the leg: but the undaunted robber struck out manfully, reached the shore, and was out of sight before the officers of justice could get ready their boats to follow him. He was captured again in 1826, tried at Mayence, and sentenced to death. He was a tall, strong, handsome man, and his fate, villain as he was, excited much sympathy all over Germany. The ladies especially were loud in their regret that nothing could be done to save a hero so good-looking, and of adventures so romantic, from the knife of the headsman.

Mr. Macfarlane, in speaking of Italian banditti, remarks, that the abuses of the Catholic religion, with its confessions and absolutions, have tended to promote crime of this description. But, he adds, more truly, that priests and monks have not done half the mischief which has been perpetrated by ballad-mongers and story-tellers. If he had said play-wrights also, the list would have been complete. In fact, the theatre, which can only expect to prosper, in a pecuniary sense, by pandering to the tastes of the people, continually recurs to the annals of thieves and banditti for its most favourite heroes. These theatrical robbers; with their picturesque attire, wild haunts, jolly, reckless, devil-may-care manners, take a wonderful hold upon the imagination, and, whatever their advocates may say to the contrary, exercise a very pernicious influence upon public morals. In the Memoirs of the Duke of Guise upon the Revolution of Naples in 1647 and 1648, it is stated, that the manners, dress, and mode of life of the Neapolitan banditti were rendered so captivating upon the stage, that the authorities found it absolutely necessary to forbid the representation of dramas in which they figured, and even to prohibit their costume at the masquerades. So numerous were the banditti at this time, that the Duke found no difficulty in raising an army of. them, to aid him in his endeavours to seize on the throne of Naples. He thus describes them; [See also "Foreign Quarterly Review," vol. iv. p. 398.]

"They were three thousand five hundred men, of whom the oldest came short of five and forty years, and the youngest was above twenty. They were all tall and well made, with long black hair, for the most part curled, coats of black Spanish leather, with sleeves of velvet, or cloth of gold, cloth breeches with gold lace, most of them scarlet; girdles of velvet, laced with gold, with two pistols on each side; a cutlass hanging at a belt, suitably trimmed, three fingers broad and two feet long; a hawking-bag at their girdle, and a powder-flask hung about their neck with a great silk riband. Some of them carried firelocks, and others blunder-busses; they had all good shoes, with silk stockings, and every one a cap of cloth of gold, or cloth of silver, of different colours, on his head, which was very delightful to the eye."

"The Beggars' Opera," in our own country, is another instance of the admiration that thieves excite upon the stage. Of the extraordinary success of this piece, when first produced, the following account is given in the notes to "The Dunciad," and quoted by Johnson in his "Lives of the Poets." "This piece was received with greater applause than was ever known. Besides being acted in London sixty-three days without interruption, and renewed the next season with equal applause, it spread into all the great towns of England; was played in many places to the thirtieth and fortieth time; at Bath and Bristol, &c. fifty. It made its progress into Wales, Scotland, and Ireland, where it was performed twenty-four days successively. The ladies carried about with them the favourite songs of it in fans, and houses were furnished with it in screens. The fame of it was not confined to the author only. The person who acted Polly, till then obscure, became all at once the favourite of the town; [Lavinia Fenton, afterwards Duchess of Bolton.] her pictures were engraved and sold in great numbers; her life written, books of letters and verses to her published, and pamphlets made even of her sayings and jests. Furthermore, it drove out of England, for that season, the Italian Opera, which had carried all before it for ten years." Dr. Johnson, in his Life of the Author, says, that Herring, afterwards Archbishop of Canterbury, censured the opera, as giving encouragement, not only to vice, but to crimes, by making the highwayman the hero, and dismissing him at last unpunished; and adds, that it was even said, that after the exhibition the gangs of robbers were evidently multiplied. The Doctor doubts the assertion, giving as his reason that highwaymen and housebreakers seldom frequent the playhouse, and that it was not possible for any one to imagine that he might rob with safety, because he saw Macheath reprieved upon the stage. But if Johnson had wished to be convinced, he might very easily have discovered that highwaymen and housebreakers did frequent the theatre, and that nothing was more probable than that a laughable representation of successful villany should induce the young and the already vicious to imitate it. Besides, there is the weighty authority of Sir John Fielding, the chief magistrate of Bow Street, who asserted positively, and proved his assertion by the records of his office, that the number of thieves was greatly increased at the time when that opera was so popular.

We have another instance of the same result much nearer our own times. Schiller's "Rauber," that wonderful play, written by a green youth, perverted the taste and imagination of all the young men in Germany. An accomplished critic of our own country (Hazlitt), speaking of this play, says it was the first he ever read, and such was the effect it produced on him, that "it stunned him, like a blow." After the lapse of five-and-twenty years he could not forget it; it was still, to use his own words, "an old dweller in the chambers of his brain," and he had not even then recovered enough from it, to describe how it was. The high-minded, metaphysical thief, its hero, was so warmly admired, that several raw students, longing to imitate a character they thought so noble, actually abandoned their homes and their colleges, and betook themselves to the forests and wilds to levy contributions upon travellers. They thought they would, like Moor, plunder the rich, and deliver eloquent soliloquies to the setting sun or the rising moon; relieve the poor when they met them, and drink flasks of Rhenish with their free companions in rugged mountain passes, or in tents in the thicknesses of the forests. But a little experience wonderfully cooled their courage; they found that real, every-day robbers were very unlike the conventional banditti of the stage, and that three months in prison, with bread and water for their fare, and damp straw to lie upon, was very well to read about by their own fire sides, but not very agreeable to undergo in their own proper persons.

Lord Byron, with his soliloquising, high-souled thieves, has, in a slight degree, perverted the taste of the greenhorns and incipient rhymesters of his country. As yet, however, they have shown more good sense than their fellows of Germany, and have not taken to the woods or the highways. Much as they admire Conrad the Corsair, they will not go to sea, and hoist the black flag in emulation of him. By words only, and not by deeds, they testify their admiration, and deluge the periodicals and music shops of the hand with verses describing pirates' and bandits' brides, and robber adventures of every kind.

But it is the play-wright who does most harm; and Byron has fewer sins of this nature to answer for than Gay or Schiller, and the modern dramatizers of Jack Sheppard. With the aid of scenery, fine dresses, and music, and the very false notions they convey, they vitiate the public taste, not knowing,

"----------- vulgaires rimeurs
Quelle force ont les arts pour demolir les moeurs."

In the penny theatres that abound in the poor and populous districts of London, and which are chiefly frequented by striplings of idle and dissolute habits, tales of thieves and murderers are more admired, and draw more crowded audiences, than any other species of representation. There the footpad, the burglar, and the highwayman are portrayed in unnatural colours, and give pleasant lessons in crime to their delighted listeners. There the deepest tragedy and the broadest farce are represented in the career of the murderer and the thief, and are applauded in proportion to their depth and their breadth. There, whenever a crime of unusual atrocity is committed, it is brought out afresh, with all its disgusting incidents copied from the life, for the amusement of those who will one day become its imitators.

With the mere reader the case is widely different; and most people have a partiality for knowing the adventures of noted rogues. Even in fiction they are delightful: witness the eventful story of Gil Blas de Santillane, and of that great rascal Don Guzman d'Alfarache. Here there is no fear of imitation. Poets, too, without doing mischief, may sing of such heroes when they please, wakening our sympathies for the sad fate of Gilderoy, or Macpherson the Dauntless; or celebrating in undying verse the wrongs and the revenge of the great thief of Scotland, Rob Roy. If, by the music of their sweet rhymes, they can convince the world that such heroes are but mistaken philosophers, born a few ages too late, and having both a theoretical and practical love for

"The good old rule, the simple plan,
That they should take who have the power,
That they should keep who can,"

the world may, perhaps, become wiser, and consent to some better distribution of its good things, by means of which thieves may become reconciled to the age, and the age to them. The probability, however, seems to be, that the charmers will charm in vain, charm they ever so wisely.

Influence of Politics and Religión on the Hair and Beard

Speak with respect and honour
Both of the beard and the beard's owner.
Hudibras.

The famous declaration of St. Paul, "that long hair was a shame unto a man" has been made the pretext for many singular enactments, both of civil and ecclesiastical governments. The fashion of the hair and the cut of the beard were state questions in France and England from the establishment of Christianity until the fifteenth century.

We find, too, that in much earlier times men were not permitted to do as they liked with their own hair. Alexander the Great thought that the beards of his soldiery afforded convenient handles for the enemy to lay hold of, preparatory to cutting off their heads; and, with the view of depriving them of this advantage, he ordered the whole of his army to be closely shaven. His notions of courtesy towards an enemy were quite different from those entertained by the North American Indians, amongst whom it is held a point of honour to allow one "chivalrous lock" to grow, that the foe, in taking the scalp, may have something to catch hold of.

At one time, long hair was the symbol of sovereignty in Europe. We learn from Gregory of Tours that, among the successors of Clovis, it was the exclusive privilege of the royal family to have their hair long, and curled. The nobles, equal to kings in power, would not show any inferiority in this respect, and wore not only their hair, but their beards, of an enormous length. This fashion lasted, with but slight changes, till the time of Louis the Debonnaire, but his successors, up to Hugh Capet, wore their hair short, by way of distinction. Even the serfs had set all regulation at defiance, and allowed their locks and beards to grow.

At the time of the invasion of England by William the Conqueror, the Normans wore their hair very short. Harold, in his progress towards Hastings, sent forward spies to view the strength and number of the enemy. They reported, amongst other things, on their return, that "the host did almost seem to be priests, because they had all their face and both their lips shaven." The fashion among the English at the time was to wear the hair long upon the head and the upper lip, but to shave the chin. When the haughty victors had divided the broad lands of the Saxon thanes and franklins among them, when tyranny of every kind was employed to make the English feel that they were indeed a subdued and broken nation, the latter encouraged the growth of their hair, that they might resemble as little as possible their cropped and shaven masters.

This fashion was exceedingly displeasing to the clergy, and prevailed to a considerable extent in France and Germany. Towards the end of the eleventh century, it was decreed by the Pope, and zealously supported by the ecclesiastical authorities all over Europe, that such persons as wore long hair should be excommunicated while living, and not be prayed for when dead. William of Malmesbury relates, that the famous St. Wulstan, Bishop of Worcester, was peculiarly indignant whenever he saw a man with long

93

hair. He declaimed against the practice as one highly immoral, criminal, and beastly. He continually carried a small knife in his pocket, and whenever anybody, offending in this respect, knelt before him to receive his blessing, he would whip it out slily, and cut off a handful, and then, throwing it in his face, tell him to cut off all the rest, or he would go to hell.

But fashion, which at times it is possible to move with a wisp, stands firm against a lever; and men preferred to run the risk of damnation to parting with the superfluity of their hair. In the time of Henry I, Anselm, Archbishop of Canterbury, found it necessary to republish the famous decree of excommunication and outlawry against the offenders; but, as the court itself had begun to patronize curls, the fulminations of the church were unavailing. Henry I and his nobles wore their hair in long ringlets down their backs and shoulders, and became a scandalum magnatum in the eyes of the godly. One Serlo, the King's chaplain, was so grieved in spirit at the impiety of his master, that he preached a sermon from the well-known text of St. Paul, before the assembled court, in which he drew so dreadful a picture of the torments that awaited them in the other world, that several of them burst into tears, and wrung their hair, as if they would have pulled it out by the roots. Henry himself was observed to weep. The priest, seeing the impression he had made, determined to strike while the iron was hot, and, pulling a pair of scissors from his pocket, cut the king's hair in presence of them all. Several of the principal courtiers consented to do the like, and, for a short time, long hair appeared to be going out of fashion. But the courtiers thought, after the first glow of their penitence had been cooled by reflection, that the clerical Dalilah had shorn them of their strength, and, in less than six months, they were as great sinners as ever.

Anselm, the Archbishop of Canterbury, who had been a monk of Bec, in Normandy, and who had signalized himself at Rouen by his fierce opposition to long hair, was still anxious to work a reformation in this matter. But his pertinacity was far from pleasing to the King, who had finally made up his mind to wear ringlets. There were other disputes, of a more serious nature, between them; so that when the Archbishop died, the King was so glad to be rid of him, that he allowed the see to remain vacant for five years. Still the cause had other advocates, and every pulpit in the land resounded with anathemas against that disobedient and long-haired generation. But all was of no avail. Stowe, in writing of this period, asserts, on the authority of some more ancient chronicler, "that men, forgetting their birth, transformed themselves, by the length of their haires, into the semblance of woman kind;" and that when their hair decayed from age, or other causes, "they knit about their heads certain rolls and braidings of false hair." At last accident turned the tide of fashion. A knight of the court, who was exceedingly proud of his beauteous locks, dreamed one night that, as he lay in bed, the devil sprang upon him, and endeavoured to choke him with his own hair. He started in affright, and actually found that he had a great quantity of hair in his mouth. Sorely stricken in conscience, and looking upon the dream as a warning from Heaven, he set about the work of reformation, and cut off his luxuriant tresses the same night. The story was soon bruited abroad; of course it was made the most of by the clergy, and the knight, being a man of influence and consideration, and the acknowledged leader of the fashion, his example, aided by priestly exhortations, was very generally imitated. Men appeared almost as decent as St. Wulstan himself could have wished, the dream of a dandy having proved more efficacious than the entreaties of a saint. But, as Stowe informs us, "scarcely was one year past, when all that thought themselves courtiers fell into the former vice, and contended with women in their long haires." Henry, the King, appears to have been quite uninfluenced by the dreams of others, for even his own would not induce him a second time to undergo a cropping from priestly shears. It is said, that he was much troubled at this time by disagreeable visions. Having offended the church in this and other respects, he could get no sound refreshing sleep, and used to imagine that he saw all the bishops, abbots, and monks of every degree, standing around his bed-side, and threatening to belabour him with their pastoral staves; which sight, we are told, so frightened him, that he often started naked out of his bed, and attacked the phantoms sword in hand. Grimbalde, his physician, who, like most of his fraternity at that day, was an ecclesiastic, never hinted that his dreams were the result of a bad digestion, but told him to shave his head, be reconciled to the Church, and reform himself with alms and prayer. But he would not take this good advice, and it was not until he had been nearly drowned a year afterwards, in a violent storm at sea, that he repented of his evil ways, cut his hair short, and paid proper deference to the wishes of the clergy.

In France, the thunders of the Vatican with regard to long curly hair were hardly more respected than in England. Louis VII. however, was more obedient than his brother-king, and cropped himself as closely as a monk, to the great sorrow of all the gallants of his court. His Queen, the gay, haughty, and pleasure-seeking Eleanor of Guienne, never admired him in this trim, and continually reproached him with imitating, not only the headdress, but the asceticism of the monks. From this cause, a coldness arose between them. The lady proving at last unfaithful to her shaven and indifferent lord, they were divorced, and the Kings of France lost the rich provinces of Guienne and Poitou, which were her dowry. She soon after bestowed her hand and her possessions upon Henry Duke of Normandy, afterwards Henry II of England, and thus gave the English sovereigns that strong footing in France which was for so many centuries the cause of such long and bloody wars between the nations.

When the Crusades had drawn all the smart young fellows into Palestine, the clergy did not find it so difficult to convince the staid burghers who remained in Europe, of the enormity of long hair. During the absence of Richard Coeur de Lion, his English subjects not only cut their hair close, but shaved their faces. William Fitzosbert, or Long-beard, the great demagogue of that day, reintroduced among the people who claimed to be of Saxon origin the fashion of long hair. He did this with the view of making them as unlike as possible to the citizens and the Normans. He wore his own beard hanging down to his waist, from whence the name by which he is best known to posterity.

The Church never showed itself so great an enemy to the beard as to long hair on the head. It generally allowed fashion to take its own course, both with regard to the chin and the upper lip. This fashion varied continually; for we find that, in little more than a century after the time of Richard I, when beards were short, that they had again become so long as to be mentioned in the famous epigram made by the Scots who visited London in 1327, when David, son of Robert Bruce, was married to Joan, the sister of King Edward. This epigram, which was stuck on the church-door of St. Peter Stangate, ran as follows--

"Long beards heartlesse,
Painted hoods witlesse,
Gray coats gracelesse,
Make England thriftlesse."

When the Emperor Charles V. ascended the throne of Spain, he had no beard. It was not to be expected that the obsequious parasites who always surround a monarch, could presume to look more virile than their master. Immediately all the courtiers appeared beardless, with the exception of such few grave old men as had outgrown the influence of fashion, and who had determined to die bearded as they had lived. Sober people in general saw this revolution with sorrow and alarm, and thought that every manly virtue would be banished with the beard. It became at the time a common saying,--

"Desde que no hay barba, no hay mas alma."
We have no longer souls since we have lost our beards.

95

In France, also, the beard fell into disrepute after the death of Henry IV, from the mere reason that his successor was too young to have one. Some of the more immediate friends of the great Bearnais, and his minister Sully among the rest, refused to part with their beards, notwithstanding the jeers of the new generation.

Who does not remember the division of England into the two great parties of Roundheads and Cavaliers? In those days, every species of vice and iniquity was thought by the Puritans to lurk in the long curly tresses of the Monarchists, while the latter imagined that their opponents were as destitute of wit, of wisdom, and of virtue, as they were of hair. A man's locks were the symbol of his creed, both in politics and religion. The more abundant the hair, the more scant the faith; and the balder the head, the more sincere the piety.

But among all the instances of the interference of governments with men's hair, the most extraordinary, not only for its daring, but for its success is that of Peter the Great, in 1705. By this time, fashion had condemned the beard in every other country in Europe, and with a voice more potent than Popes or Emperors, had banished it from civilized society. But this only made the Russians cling more fondly to their ancient ornament, as a mark to distinguish them from foreigners, whom they hated. Peter, however resolved that they should be shaven. If he had been a man deeply read in history, he might have hesitated before he attempted so despotic an attack upon the time-hallowed customs and prejudices of his countrymen; but he was not. He did not know or consider the danger of the innovation; he only listened to the promptings of his own indomitable will, and his fiat went forth, that not only the army, but all ranks of citizens, from the nobles to the serfs, should shave their beards. A certain time was given, that people might get over the first throes of their repugnance, after which every man who chose to retain his beard was to pay a tax of one hundred roubles. The priests and the serfs were put on a lower footing, and allowed to retain theirs upon payment of a copeck every time they passed the gate of a city. Great discontent existed in consequence, but the dreadful fate of the Strelitzes was too recent to be forgotten, and thousands who had the will had not the courage to revolt. As is well remarked by a writer in the "Encyclopedia Britannica," they thought it wiser to cut off their beards than to run the risk of incensing a man who would make no scruple in cutting off their heads. Wiser, too, than the popes and bishops of a former age, he did not threaten them with eternal damnation, but made them pay in hard cash the penalty of their disobedience. For many years, a very considerable revenue was collected from this source. The collectors gave in receipt for its payment a small copper coin, struck expressly for the purpose, and called the "borodovaia," or "the bearded." On one side it bore the figure of a nose, mouth, and moustachios, with a long bushy beard, surmounted by the words," Deuyee Vyeatee," "money received;" the whole encircled by a wreath, and stamped with the black eagle of Russia. On the reverse, it bore the date of the year. Every man who chose to wear a beard was obliged to produce this receipt on his entry into a town. Those who were refractory, and refused to pay the tax, were thrown into prison.

Since that day, the rulers of modern Europe have endeavoured to persuade, rather than to force, in all matters pertaining to fashion. The Vatican troubles itself no more about beards or ringlets, and men may become hairy as bears, if such is their fancy, without fear of excommunication or deprivation of their political rights. Folly has taken a new start, and cultivates the moustachio.

Even upon this point governments will not let men alone. Religion as yet has not meddled with it; but perhaps it will; and politics already influence it considerably. Before the revolution of 1830, neither the French nor Belgian citizens were remarkable for their moustachios; but, after that event, there was hardly a shopkeeper either in Paris or Brussels whose upper lip did not suddenly become hairy with real or mock moustachios. During a temporary triumph gained by the Dutch soldiers over the citizens of

Louvain, in October 1830, it became a standing joke against the patriots, that they shaved their faces clean immediately; and the wits of the Dutch army asserted, that they had gathered moustachios enough from the denuded lips of the Belgians to stuff mattresses for all the sick and wounded in their hospital.

The last folly of this kind is still more recent. In the German newspapers, of August 1838, appeared an ordonnance, signed by the King of Bavaria, forbidding civilians, on any pretence whatever, to wear moustachios, and commanding the police and other authorities to arrest, and cause to be shaved, the offending parties. "Strange to say," adds "Le Droit," the journal from which this account is taken, "moustachios disappeared immediately, like leaves from the trees in autumn; everybody made haste to obey the royal order, and not one person was arrested.

The King of Bavaria, a rhymester of some celebrity, has taken a good many poetical licences in his time. His licence in this matter appears neither poetical nor reasonable. It is to be hoped that he will not take it into his royal head to make his subjects shave theirs; nothing but that is wanting to complete their degradation.

Duels and Ordeals

There was an ancient sage philosopher,
Who swore the world, as he could prove,
Was mad of fighting. --*Hudibras.*

Most writers, in accounting for the origin of duelling, derive it from the warlike habits of those barbarous nations who overran Europe in the early centuries of the Christian era, and who knew no mode so effectual for settling their differences as the point of the sword. In fact, duelling, taken in its primitive and broadest sense, means nothing more than combatting, and is the universal resort of all wild animals, including man, to gain or defend their possessions, or avenge their insults. Two dogs who tear each other for a bone, or two bantams fighting on a dunghill for the love of some beautiful hen, or two fools on Wimbledon Common, shooting at each other to satisfy the laws of offended honour, stand on the same footing in this respect, and are, each and all, mere duellists. As civilization advanced, the best informed men naturally grew ashamed of such a mode of adjusting disputes, and the promulgation of some sort of laws for obtaining redress for injuries was the consequence. Still there were many cases in which the allegations of an accuser could not be rebutted by any positive proof on the part of the accused; and in all these, which must have been exceedingly numerous in the early stages of European society, the combat was resorted to. From its decision there was no appeal. God was supposed to nerve the arm of the combatant whose cause was just, and to grant him the victory over his opponent. As Montesquieu well remarks, ["Esprit des Loix," liv. xxviii. chap. xvii.] this belief was not unnatural among a people just emerging from barbarism. Their manners being wholly warlike, the man deficient in courage, the prime virtue of his fellows, was not unreasonably suspected of other vices besides cowardice, which is generally found to be co-existent with treachery. He, therefore, who showed himself most valiant in the encounter, was absolved by public opinion from any crime with which he might be charged. As a necessary consequence, society would have been reduced to its original elements, if the men of thought, as distinguished from the men of action, had not devised some means for taming the unruly passions of their fellows. With this view, governments commenced by restricting within the narrowest possible limits the cases in which it was lawful to prove or deny guilt by the single combat. By the law of Gondebaldus, King of the Burgundians, passed in the year 501, the proof by combat was allowed in all legal proceedings, in lieu of swearing. In the time of Charlemagne, the Burgundian practice had spread over the empire of the Francs, and not only the suitors for justice, but the witnesses, and even the judges, were obliged to defend their cause, their evidence, or their decision, at the point of the sword. Louis the Debonnaire, his successor, endeavoured to remedy the growing evil, by permitting the duel only in appeals of felony, in civil cases, or issue joined in a writ of right, and in cases of the court of chivalry, or attacks upon a man's knighthood. None were exempt from these trials, but women, the sick and the maimed, and persons under fifteen or above sixty years of age. Ecclesiastics were allowed to produce champions in their stead. This practice, in the course of time, extended to all trials of civil and criminal cases, which had to be decided by battle.

The clergy, whose dominion was an intellectual one, never approved of a system of jurisprudence which tended so much to bring all things under the rule of the strongest arm. From the first they set their faces against duelling, and endeavoured, as far as the prejudices of their age would allow them, to curb the warlike spirit, so alien from the principles of religion. In the Council of Valentia, and afterwards in the Council of Trent, they excommunicated all persons engaged in duelling, and not only them, but even the assistants and spectators, declaring the custom to be hellish and detestable, and introduced by the Devil for the destruction both of body and soul. They added, also, that princes who connived at duels, should

99

be deprived of all temporal power, jurisdiction, and dominion over the places where they had permitted them to be fought. It will be seen hereafter that this clause only encouraged the practice which it was intended to prevent.

But it was the blasphemous error of these early ages to expect that the Almighty, whenever he was called upon, would work a miracle in favour of a person unjustly accused. The priesthood, in condemning the duel, did not condemn the principle on which it was founded. They still encouraged the popular belief of Divine interference in all the disputes or differences that might arise among nations or individuals. It was the very same principle that regulated the ordeals, which, with all their influence, they supported against the duel. By the former, the power of deciding the guilt or innocence was vested wholly in their hands, while, by the latter, they enjoyed no power or privilege at all. It is not to be wondered at, that for this reason, if for no other, they should have endeavoured to settle all differences by the peaceful mode. While that prevailed, they were as they wished to be, the first party in the state; but while the strong arm of individual prowess was allowed to be the judge in all doubtful cases, their power and influence became secondary to those of nobility.

Thus, it was not the mere hatred of bloodshed which induced them to launch the thunderbolts excommunication against the combatants; it a desire to retain the power, which, to do them justice, they were, in those times, the persons best qualified to wield. The germs of knowledge and civilization lay within the bounds of their order; for they were the representatives of the intellectual, as the nobility were of the physical power of man. To centralize this power in the Church, and make it the judge of the last resort in all appeals, both in civil and criminal cases, they instituted five modes of trial, the management of which lay wholly in their hands. These were the oath upon the Evangelists; the ordeal of the cross, and the fire ordeal, for persons in the higher ranks; the water ordeal, for the humbler classes; and, lastly, the Corsned, or bread and cheese ordeal, for members of their own body.

The oath upon the Evangelists was taken in the following manner: the accused who was received to this proof, says Paul Hay, Count du Chastelet, in his Memoirs of Bertrand du Guesclin, swore upon a copy of the New Testament, and on the relics of the holy martyrs, or on their tombs, that he was innocent of the crime imputed to him. He was also obliged to find twelve persons, of acknowledged probity, who should take oath at the same time, that they believed him innocent. This mode of trial led to very great abuses, especially in cases of disputed inheritance, where the hardest swearer was certain of the victory. This abuse was one of the principal causes which led to the preference given to the trial by battle. It is not all surprising that a feudal baron, or captain of the early ages, should have preferred the chances of a fair fight with his opponent, to a mode by which firm perjury would always be successful.

The trial by, or judgment of, the cross, which Charlemagne begged his sons to have recourse to, in case of disputes arising between them, was performed thus:-- When a person accused of any crime had declared his innocence upon oath, and appealed to the cross for its judgment in his favour, he was brought into the church, before the altar. The priests previously prepared two sticks exactly like one another, upon one of which was carved a figure of the cross. They were both wrapped up with great care and many ceremonies, in a quantity of fine wool, and laid upon the altar, or on the relics of the saints. A solemn prayer was then offered up to God, that he would be pleased to discover, by the judgment of his holy cross, whether the accused person were innocent or guilty. A priest then approached the altar, and took up one of the sticks, and the assistants unswathed it reverently. If it was marked with the cross, the accused person was innocent; if unmarked, he was guilty. It would be unjust to assert, that the judgments thus delivered were, in all cases, erroneous; and it would be absurd to believe that they were left altogether to chance. Many true judgments were doubtless given, and, in all probability, most

100

conscientiously; for we cannot but believe that the priests endeavoured beforehand to convince themselves by secret inquiry and a strict examination of the circumstances, whether the appellant were innocent or guilty, and that they took up the crossed or uncrossed stick accordingly. Although, to all other observers, the sticks, as enfolded in the wool, might appear exactly similar, those who enwrapped them could, without any difficulty, distinguish the one from the other.

By the fire-ordeal the power of deciding was just as unequivocally left in their hands. It was generally believed that fire would not burn the innocent, and the clergy, of course, took care that the innocent, or such as it was their pleasure or interest to declare so, should be so warned before undergoing the ordeal, as to preserve themselves without any difficulty from the fire. One mode of ordeal was to place red-hot ploughshares on the ground at certain distances, and then, blindfolding the accused person, make him walk barefooted over them. If he stepped regularly in the vacant spaces, avoiding the fire, he was adjudged innocent; if he burned himself, he was declared guilty. As none but the clergy interfered with the arrangement of the ploughshares, they could always calculate beforehand the result of the ordeal. To find a person guilty, they had only to place them at irregular distances, and the accused was sure to tread upon one of them. When Emma, the wife of King Ethelred, and mother of Edward the Confessor, was accused of a guilty familiarity with Alwyn, Bishop of Winchester, she cleared her character in this manner. The reputation, not only of their order, but of a queen, being at stake, a verdict of guilty was not to be apprehended from any ploughshares which priests had the heating of. This ordeal was called the Judicium Dei, and sometimes the Vulgaris Purgatio, and might also be tried by several other methods. One was to hold in the hand, unhurt, a piece of red-hot iron, of the weight of one, two, or three pounds. When we read not only that men with hard hands, but women of softer and more delicate skin, could do this with impunity, we must be convinced that the hands were previously rubbed with some preservative, or that the apparently hot iron was merely cold iron painted red. Another mode was to plunge the naked arm into a caldron of boiling water. The priests then enveloped it in several folds of linen and flannel, and kept the patient confined within the church, and under their exclusive care, for three days. If, at the end of that time, the arm appeared without a scar, the innocence of the accused person was firmly established. [Very similar to this is the fire-ordeal of the modern Hindoos,. which is thus described in Forbes's "Oriental Memoirs," vol. i. c. xi.--" When a man, accused of a capital crime, chooses to undergo the ordeal trial, he is closely confined for several days; his right hand and arm are covered with thick wax-cloth, tied up and sealed, in the presence of proper officers, to prevent deceit. In the English districts the covering was always sealed with the Company's arms, and the prisoner placed under an European guard. At the time fixed for the ordeal, a caldron of oil is placed over a fire; when it boils, a piece of money is dropped into the vessel; the prisoner's arm is unsealed, and washed in the presence of his judges and accusers. During this part of the ceremony, the attendant Brahmins supplicate the Deity. On receiving their benediction, the accused plunges his hand into the boiling fluid, and takes out the coin. The arm is afterwards again Sealed up until the time appointed for a re-examination. The seal is then broken: if no blemish appears, the prisoner is declared innocent; if the contrary, he suffers the punishment due to his crime." * * * On this trial the accused thus addresses the element before plunging his hand into the boiling oil:-- "Thou, O fire! pervadest all things. O cause of purity! who givest evidence of virtue and of sin, declare the truth in this my hand!" If no juggling were practised, the decisions by this ordeal would be all the same way; but, as some are by this means declared guilty, and others innocent, it is clear that the Brahmins, like the Christian priests of the middle ages, practise some deception in saving those whom they wish to be thought guiltless.]

As regards the water-ordeal, the same trouble was not taken. It was a trial only for the poor and humble, and, whether they sank or swam, was thought of very little consequence. Like the witches of more modern times, the accused were thrown into a pond or river; if they sank, and were drowned, their surviving friends had the consolation of knowing that they were innocent; if they swam, they were guilty. In either case society was rid of them.

But of all the ordeals, that which the clergy reserved for themselves was the one least likely to cause any member of their corps to be declared guilty. The most culpable monster in existence came off clear when tried by this method. It was called the Corsned, and was thus performed. A piece of barley bread and a piece of cheese were laid upon the altar, and the accused priest, in his full canonicals, and surrounded by all the pompous adjuncts of Roman ceremony, pronounced certain conjurations, and prayed with great fervency for several minutes. The burden of his prayer was, that if he were guilty of the crime laid to his charge, God would send his angel Gabriel to stop his throat, that he might not be able to swallow the bread and cheese. There is no instance upon record of a priest having been choked in this manner. [An ordeal very like this is still practised in India. Consecrated rice is the article chosen, instead of bread and cheese. Instances are not rare in which, through the force of imagination, guilty persons are not able to swallow a single grain. Conscious of their crime, and fearful of the punishment of Heaven, they feel a suffocating sensation in their throat when they attempt it, and they fall on their knees, and confess all that is laid to their charge. The same thing, no doubt, would have happened with the bread and cheese of the Roman church, if it had been applied to any others but ecclesiastics. The latter had too much wisdom to be caught in a trap of their own setting.]

When, under Pope Gregory VII, it was debated whether the Gregorian chant should be introduced into Castile, instead of the Musarabic, given by St. Isidore, of Seville, to the churches of that kingdom, very much ill feeling was excited. The churches refused to receive the novelty, and it was proposed that the affair should be decided by a battle between two champions, one chosen from each side. The clergy would not consent to a mode of settlement which they considered impious, but had no objection to try the merits of each chant by the fire ordeal. A great fire was accordingly made, and a book of the Gregorian and one of the Musarabic chant were thrown into it, that the flames might decide which was most agreeable to God by refusing to burn it. Cardinal Baronius, who says he was an eye-witness of the miracle, relates, that the book of the Gregorian chant was no sooner laid upon the fire, than it leaped out uninjured, visibly, and with a great noise. Every one present thought that the saints had decided in favour of Pope Gregory. After a slight interval, the fire was extinguished; but, wonderful to relate! the other book of St. Isidore was found covered with ashes, but not injured in the slightest degree. The flames had not even warmed it. Upon this it was resolved, that both were alike agreeable to God, and that they should be used by turns in all the churches of Seville? [Histoire de Messire Bertrand du Guesclin, par Paul Hay du Chastelet. Livre i. chap. xix.]

If the ordeals had been confined to questions like this, the laity would have had little or no objection to them; but when they were introduced as decisive in all the disputes that might arise between man and man, the opposition of all those whose prime virtue was personal bravery, was necessarily excited. In fact, the nobility, from a very early period, began to look with jealous eyes upon them. They were not slow to perceive their true purport, which was no other than to make the Church the last court of appeal in all cases, both civil and criminal: and not only did the nobility prefer the ancient mode of single combat from this cause, in itself a sufficient one, but they clung to it because an acquittal gained by those displays of courage and address which the battle afforded, was more creditable in the eyes of their compeers, than one which it required but little or none of either to accomplish. To these causes may be added another, which was, perhaps, more potent than either, in raising the credit of the judicial combat at the expense of the ordeal. The noble institution of chivalry was beginning to take root, and, notwithstanding the clamours of the clergy, war was made the sole business of life, and the only elegant pursuit of the aristocracy. The fine spirit of honour was introduced, any attack upon which was only to be avenged in the lists, within sight of applauding crowds, whose verdict of approbation was far more gratifying than the cold and formal acquittal of the ordeal. Lothaire, the son of Louis I, abolished that by fire and the trial of the cross within his dominions; but in England they were allowed so late as the time of Henry III, in the early part of whose reign they were prohibited by an order of council. In the mean time, the Crusades had brought the institution of chivalry to the full height of perfection. The chivalric spirit soon achieved the downfall of the ordeal system, and established the judicial combat on a basis too firm to be shaken. It is true that with the fall of chivalry, as an institution, fell the tournament, and the encounter in the lists; but the duel, their offspring, has survived to this day, defying the efforts of sages and philosophers to eradicate it. Among all the errors bequeathed to us by a barbarous age, it has proved the most pertinacious. It has put variance between men's reason and their honour; put the man of sense on a level with the fool, and made thousands who condemn it submit to it, or practise it. Those who are curious to see the manner in which these combats were regulated, may consult the learned Montesquieu, where they will find a copious summary of the code of ancient duelling. ["Esprit des Loix," livre xxviii. chap. xxv.] Truly does he remark, in speaking of the clearness and excellence of the arrangements, that, as there were many wise matters which were conducted in a very foolish manner, so there were many foolish matters conducted very wisely. No greater exemplification of it could be given, than the wise and religious rules of the absurd and blasphemous trial by battle.

In the ages that intervened between the Crusades and the new era that was opened out by the invention of gunpowder and printing, a more rational system of legislation took root. The inhabitants of cities, engaged in the pursuits of trade and industry, were content to acquiesce in the decisions of their judges and magistrates whenever any differences arose among them. Unlike the class above them, their habits and manners did not lead them to seek the battle-field on every slight occasion. A dispute as to the price of a sack of corn, a bale of broad-cloth, or a cow, could be more satisfactorily adjusted before the mayor or bailiff of their district. Even the martial knights and nobles, quarrelsome as they were, began to see that the trial by battle would lose its dignity and splendour if too frequently resorted to. Governments also shared this opinion, and on several occasions restricted the cases in which it was legal to proceed to this extremity. In France, before the time of Louis IX, duels were permitted only in cases of Lese Majesty, Rape, Incendiarism, Assassination, and Burglary. Louis IX, by taking off all restriction, made them legal in civil eases. This was not found to work well, and, in 1303, Philip the Fair judged it necessary to confine them, in criminal matters, to state offences, rape, and incendiarism; and in civil cases, to questions of disputed inheritance. Knighthood was allowed to be the best judge of its own honour, and might defend or avenge it as often as occasion arose.

Among the earliest duels upon record, is a very singular one that took place in the reign of Louis II (A.D. 878). Ingelgerius, Count of Gastinois, was one morning discovered by his Countess dead in bed at her side. Gontran, a relation of the Count, accused the Countess of having murdered her husband, to whom, he asserted, she had long been unfaithful, and challenged her to produce a champion to do battle in her behalf, that he might establish her guilt by killing him.[Memoires de Brantome touchant les Duels.] All the friends and relatives of the Countess believed in her innocence; but Gontran was so stout and bold and renowned a warrior, that no one dared to meet him, for which, as Brantome quaintly says, "Mauvais et poltrons parens estaient." The unhappy Countess began to despair, when a champion suddenly appeared in the person of Ingelgerius, Count of Anjou, a boy of sixteen years of age, who had been held by the Countess on the baptismal font, and received her husband's name. He tenderly loved his godmother, and offered to do battle in her cause against any and every opponent. The King endeavoured to persuade the generous boy from his enterprise, urging the great strength, tried skill, and invincible courage of the challenger; but he persisted in his resolution, to the great sorrow of all the court, who said it was a cruel thing to permit so brave and beautiful a child to rush to such butchery and death.

When the lists were prepared, the Countess duly acknowledged her champion, and the combatants commenced the onset. Gontran rode so fiercely at his antagonist, and hit him on the shield with such impetuosity, that he lost his own balance and rolled to the ground. The young Count, as Gontran fell, passed his lance through his body, and then dismounting, cut off his head, which, Brantome says, "he presented to the King, who received it most graciously, and was very joyful, as much so as if any one had made him a present of a city." The innocence of the Countess was then proclaimed with great rejoicings; and she kissed her godson, and wept over his neck with joy, in the presence of all the assembly.

When the Earl of Essex was accused, by Robert de Montfort, before King Henry II, in 1162, of having traitorously suffered the royal standard of England to fall from his hands in a skirmish with the Welsh, at Coleshill, five years previously, the latter offered to prove the truth of the charge by single combat. The Earl of Essex accepted the challenge, and the lists were prepared near Reading. An immense concourse of persons assembled to witness the battle. Essex at first fought stoutly, but, losing his temper and self-command, he gave an advantage to his opponent, which soon decided the struggle. He was unhorsed, and so severely wounded, that all present thought he was dead. At the solicitation of his relatives, the monks of the Abbey of Reading were allowed to remove the body for interment, and Montfort was declared the victor. Essex, however, was not dead, but stunned only, and, under the care of the monks, recovered in a few weeks from his bodily injuries. The wounds of his mind were not so easily healed. Though a loyal and brave subject, the whole realm believed him a traitor and a coward because he had been vanquished. He could not brook to return to the world deprived of the good opinion of his fellows; he, therefore, made himself a monk, and passed the remainder of his days within the walls of the Abbey.

Du Chastelet relates a singular duel that was proposed in Spain.[Histoire de Messire Bertrand du Guesclin, livre i. chap. xix.] A Christian gentleman of Seville sent a challenge to a Moorish cavalier, offering to prove against him, with whatever weapons he might choose, that the religion of Jesus Christ was holy and divine, and that of Mahomet impious and damnable. The Spanish prelates did not choose that Christianity should be com promised within their jurisdiction by the result of any such combat, and they commanded the knight, under pain of excommunication, to withdraw the challenge.

The same author relates, that under Otho I a question arose among jurisconsults, viz. whether grandchildren, who had lost their father, should share equally with their uncles in the property of their grandfather, at the death of the latter. The difficulty of this question was found so insurmountable, that none of the lawyers of that day could resolve it. It was at last decreed, that it should be decided by single combat. Two champions were accordingly chosen; one for, and the other against, the claims of the little ones. After a long struggle, the champion of the uncles was unhorsed and slain; and it was, therefore, decided, that the right of the grandchildren was established, and that they should enjoy the same portion of their grandfather's possessions that their father would have done had he been alive.

Upon pretexts, just as frivolous as these, duels continued to be fought in most of the countries of Europe during the whole of the fourteenth and fifteenth centuries. A memorable instance of the slightness of the pretext on which a man could be forced to fight a duel to the death, occurs in the Memoirs of the brave Constable, Du Guesclin. The advantage he had obtained, in a skirmish before Rennes, against William Brembre, an English captain, so preyed on the spirits of William Troussel, the chosen friend and companion of the latter, that nothing would satisfy him but a mortal combat with the Constable. The Duke of Lancaster, to whom Troussel applied for permission to fight the great Frenchman, forbade the battle, as not warranted by the circumstances. Troussel nevertheless burned with a fierce desire to cross his weapon with Du Guesclin, and sought every occasion to pick a quarrel with him. Having so good a will for it, of course he found a way. A relative of his had been taken prisoner by the Constable, in whose hands he remained till he was able to pay his ransom. Troussel resolved to make a quarrel out of this, and despatched a messenger to Du Guesclin, demanding the release of his prisoner, and offering a bond, at a distant date, for the payment of the ransom. Du Guesclin, who had received intimation of the hostile purposes of the Englishman, sent back word, that he would not accept his bond, neither would he release his prisoner, until the full amount of his ransom was paid. As soon as this answer was received, Troussel sent a challenge to the Constable, demanding reparation for the injury he had done his honour, by refusing his bond, and offering a mortal combat, to be fought three strokes with the lance, three with the sword, and three with the dagger. Du Guesclin, although ill in bed with the ague, accepted the challenge, and gave notice to the Marshal d'Andreghem, the King's Lieutenant-General in Lower Normandy, that he might fix the day and the place of combat. The Marshal made all necessary arrangements, upon condition that he who was beaten should pay a hundred florins of gold to feast the nobles and gentlemen who were witnesses of the encounter.

The Duke of Lancaster was very angry with his captain, and told him, that it would be a shame to his knighthood and his nation, if he forced on a combat with the brave Du Guesclin, at a time when he was enfeebled by disease and stretched on the couch of suffering. Upon these representations, Troussel, ashamed of himself, sent notice to Du Guesclin that he was willing to postpone the duel until such time as he should be perfectly recovered. Du Guesclin replied, that he could not think of postponing the combat, after all the nobility had received notice of it; that he had sufficient strength left, not only to meet, but to conquer such an opponent as he was; and that, if he did not make his appearance in the lists at the time appointed, he would publish him everywhere as a man unworthy to be called a knight, or to wear an honourable sword by his side. Troussel carried this haughty message to the Duke of Lancaster, who immediately gave permission for the battle.

On the day appointed, the two combatants appeared in the lists, in the presence of several thousand spectators. Du Guesclin was attended by the flower of the French nobility, including the Marshal de Beaumanoir, Olivier de Mauny, Bertrand de Saint Pern, and the Viscount de la Belliere, while the Englishman appeared with no more than the customary retinue of two seconds, two squires, two coutilliers, or daggermen, and two trumpeters. The first onset was unfavourable to the Constable: he received so heavy a blow on his shield-arm, that he fell forward to the left, upon his horse's neck, and, being weakened by his fever, was nearly thrown to the ground. All his friends thought he could never recover himself, and began to deplore his ill fortune; but Du Guesclin collected his energies for a decisive effort, and, at the second charge, aimed a blow at the shoulder of his enemy, which felled him to the earth, mortally wounded. He then sprang from his horse, sword in hand, with the intention of cutting off the head of his fallen foe, when the Marshal D'Andreghem threw a golden wand into the arena, as a signal that hostilities should cease. Du Guesclin was proclaimed the victor, amid the joyous acclamations of the crowd, and retiring, left the field to the meaner combatants, who were afterwards to make sport for the people. Four English and as many French squires fought for some time with pointless lances, when the French, gaining the advantage, the sports were declared at an end.

In the time of Charles VI, about the beginning of the fifteenth century, a famous duel was ordered by the Parliament of Paris. The Sieur de Carrouges being absent in the Holy Land, his lady was violated by the Sieur Legris. Carrouges, on his return, challenged Legris to mortal combat, for the twofold crime of violation and slander, inasmuch as he had denied his guilt, by asserting that the lady was a willing party. The lady's asseverations of innocence were held to be no evidence by the Parliament, and the duel was commanded with all the ceremonies. "On the day appointed," says Brantome, [Memoires de Brantome touchant les Duels.] "the lady came to witness the spectacle in her chariot; but the King made her descend, judging her unworthy, because she was criminal in his eyes till her innocence was proved, and caused her to stand upon a scaffold to await the mercy of God and this judgment by the battle. After a short struggle, the Sieur de Carrouges overthrew his enemy, and made him confess both the rape and the slander. He was then taken to the gallows and hanged in the presence of the multitude; while the innocence of the lady was proclaimed by the heralds, and recognized by her husband, the King, and all the spectators."

105

Numerous battles, of a similar description, constantly took place, until the unfortunate issue of one encounter of the kind led the French King, Henry II, to declare solemnly, that he would never again permit any such encounter, whether it related to a civil or criminal case, or the honour of a gentleman.

This memorable combat was fought in the year 1547. Francois de Vivonne, Lord of La Chataigneraie, and Guy de Chabot, Lord of Jarnac, had been friends from their early youth, and were noted at the court of Francis I for the gallantry of their bearing and the magnificence of their retinue. Chataigneraie, who knew that his friend's means were not very ample, asked him one day, in confidence, how it was that he contrived to be so well provided? Jarnac replied, that his father had married a young and beautiful woman, who, loving the son far better than the sire, supplied him with as much money as he desired. La Chataigneraie betrayed the base secret to the Dauphin, the Dauphin to the King, the King to his courtiers, and the courtiers to all their acquaintance. In a short time it reached the ears of the old Lord de Jarnac, who immediately sent for his son, and demanded to know in what manner the report had originated, and whether he had been vile enough not only to carry on such a connexion, but to boast of it? De Jarnac indignantly denied that he had ever said so, or given reason to the world to say so, and requested his father to accompany him to court, and confront him with his accuser, that he might see the manner in which he would confound him. They went accordingly, and the younger De Jarnac, entering a room where the Dauphin, La Chataigneraie, and several courtiers were present, exclaimed aloud, "That whoever had asserted, that he maintained a criminal connexion with his mother-in-law, was a liar and a coward!" Every eye was turned to the Dauphin and La Chataigneraie, when the latter stood forward, and asserted, that De Jarnac had himself avowed that such was the fact, and he would extort from his lips another confession of it. A case like this could not be met or rebutted by any legal proof, and the royal council ordered that it should be decided by single combat. The King, however, set his face against the duel [Although Francis showed himself in this case an enemy to duelling, yet, in his own case, he had not the same objection. Every reader of history must remember his answer to the challenge of the Emperor Charles V. The Emperor wrote that he had failed in his word, and that he would sustain their quarrel single-handed against him. Francis replied, that he lied -- qu'il en avait menti par la gorge, and that he was ready to meet him in single combat whenever and wherever he pleased.] and forbade them both, under pain of his high displeasure, to proceed any further in the matter. But Francis died in the following year, and the Dauphin, now Henry II, who was himself compromised, resolved that the combat should take place. The lists were prepared in the court-yard of the chateau of St. Germain-en-Laye, and the 10th of July 1547 was appointed for the encounter. The cartels of the combatants, which are preserved in the "Memoires de Castelnau," were as follow:--

"Cartel of Francois de Vivonne, Lord of La Chataigneraie.

"Sire,

"Having learned that Guy Chabot de Jarnac, being lately at Compeigne, asserted, that whoever had said that he boasted of having criminal intercourse with his mother-in-law, was wicked and a wretch,-- I, Sire, with your good-will and pleasure, do answer, that he has wickedly lied, and will lie as many times as he denies having said that which I affirm he did say; for I repeat, that he told me several times, and boasted of it, that he had slept with his mother-in-law.

"Francois de Vivonne."

To this cartel De Jarnac replied :--

"Sire,

"With your good will and permission, I say, that Francois de Vivonne has lied in the imputation which he has cast upon me, and of which I spoke to you at Compeigne. I, therefore, entreat you, Sire, most humbly, that you be pleased to grant us a fair field, that we may fight this battle to the death.

"Guy Chabot."

The preparations were conducted on a scale of the greatest magnificence, the King having intimated his intention of being present. La Chataigneraie made sure of the victory, and invited the King and a hundred and fifty of the principal personages of the court to sup with him in the evening, after the battle, in a splendid tent, which he had prepared at the extremity of the lists. De Jarnac was not so confident, though perhaps more desperate. At noon, on the day appointed, the combatants met, and each took the customary oath, that he bore no charms or amulets about him, or made use of any magic, to aid him against his antagonist. They then attacked each other, sword in hand. La Chataigneraie was a strong, robust man, and over confident; De Jarnac was nimble, supple, and prepared for the worst. The combat lasted for some time doubtful, until De Jarnac, overpowered by the heavy blows of his opponent, covered his head with his shield, and, stooping down, endeavoured to make amends by his agility for his deficiency of strength. In this crouching posture he aimed two blows at the left thigh of La Chataigneraie, who had left it uncovered, that the motion of his leg might not be impeded. Each blow was successful, and, amid the astonishment of all the spectators, and to the great regret of the King, La Chataigneraie rolled over upon the sand. He seized his dagger, and made a last effort to strike De Jarnac; but he was unable to support himself, and fell powerless into the arms of the assistants. The officers now interfered, and De Jarnac being declared the victor, fell down upon his knees, uncovered his head, and, clasping his hands together, exclaimed:-- "O Domine, non sum dignus!" La Chataigneraie was so mortified by the result of the encounter, that he resolutely refused to have his wounds dressed. He tore off the bandages which the surgeons applied, and expired two days afterwards. Ever since that time, any sly and unforeseen attack has been called by the French a coup de Jarnac. Henry was so grieved at the loss of his favourite, that he made the solemn oath already alluded to, that he would never again, so long as he lived, permit a due]. Some writers have asserted, and among others, Mezeraie, that he issued a royal edict forbidding them. This has been doubted by others, and, as there appears no registry of the edict in any of the courts, it seems most probable that it was never issued. This opinion is strengthened by the fact, that two years afterwards, the council ordered another duel to be fought, with similar forms, but with less magnificence, on account of the inferior rank of the combatants. It is not anywhere stated, that Henry interfered to prevent it, notwithstanding his solemn oath; but that, on the contrary, he encouraged it, and appointed the Marshal de la Marque to see that it was conducted according to the rules of chivalry. The disputants were Fendille and D'Aguerre, two gentlemen of the household, who, quarrelling in the King's chamber, had proceeded from words to blows. The council, being informed of the matter, decreed that it could only be decided in the lists. Marshal de la Marque, with the King's permission, appointed the city of Sedan as the place of combat. Fendille, who was a bad swordsman, was anxious to avoid an encounter with D'Aguerre, who was one of the most expert men of the age; but the council authoritatively commanded that he should fight, or be degraded from all his honours. D'Aguerre appeared in the field attended by Francois de Vendome, Count de Chartres, while Fendille was accompanied by the Duke de Nevers. Fendille appears to have been not only an inexpert swordsman, but a thorough coward; one who, like Cowley, might have heaped curses on the man,

"-------(Death's factor sure), who brought
Dire swords into this peaceful world."

On the very first encounter he was thrown from his horse, and, confessing on the ground all that his victor required of him, slunk away ignominiously from the arena.

One is tempted to look upon the death of Henry II as a judgment upon him for his perjury in the matter of duelling. In a grand tournament instituted on the occasion of the marriage of his daughter, he broke several lances in encounters with some of the bravest knights of the time. Ambitious of still further renown, he would not rest satisfied until he had also engaged the young Count de Montgomeri. He received a wound in the eye from the lance of this antagonist, and died from its effects shortly afterwards, in the forty-first year of his age.

In the succeeding reigns of Francis II, Charles IX, and Henry III, the practice of duelling increased to an alarming extent. Duels were not rare in the other countries of Europe at the same period; but in France they were so frequent, that historians, in speaking of that age, designate it as "l'epoque de la fureur des duels." The Parliament of Paris endeavoured, as far as in its power lay, to discourage the practice. By a decree dated the 26th of June 1559, it declared all persons who should be present at duels, or aiding and abetting in them, to be rebels to the King, transgressors of the law, and disturbers of the public peace.

When Henry III was assassinated at St. Cloud, in 1589, a young gentleman, named L'isle Marivaut, who had been much beloved by him, took his death so much to heart, that he resolved not to survive him. Not thinking suicide an honourable death, and wishing, as he said, to die gloriously in revenging his King and master, he publicly expressed his readiness to fight anybody to the death who should assert that Henry's assassination was not a great misfortune to the community. Another youth, of a fiery temper and tried courage, named Marolles, took him at his word, and the day and place of the combat were forthwith appointed. When the hour had come, and all were ready, Marolles turned to his second, and asked whether his opponent had a casque or helmet only, or whether he wore a sallade, or headpiece. Being answered a helmet only, he said gaily, "So much the better; for, sir, my second, you shall repute me the wickedest man in all the world, if I do not thrust my lance right through the the middle of his head and kill him." Truth to say, he did so at the very first onset, and the unhappy L'isle Marivaut expired without a groan. Brantome, who relates this story, adds, that the victor might have done as he pleased with the body, cut off the head, dragged it out of the camp, or exposed it upon an ass, but that, being a wise and very courteous gentleman, he left it to the relatives of the deceased to be honourably buried, contenting himself with the glory of his triumph, by which he gained no little renown and honour among the ladies of Paris.

On the accession of Henry IV that monarch pretended to set his face against duelling; but such was the influence of early education and the prejudices of society upon him, that he never could find it in his heart to punish a man for this offence. He thought it tended to foster a warlike spirit among his people. When the chivalrous Crequi demanded his permission to fight Don Philippe de Savoire, he is reported to have said, "Go, and if I were not a King, I would be your second." It is no wonder that when such were known to be the King's disposition, his edicts attracted but small attention. A calculation was made by M. de Lomenie, in the year 1607, that since the accession of Henry, in 1589, no less than four thousand French gentlemen had lost their lives in these conflicts, which, for the eighteen years, would have been at the rate of four or five in a week, or eighteen per month! Sully, who reports this fact in his Memoirs, does not throw the slightest doubt upon its exactness, and adds, that it was chiefly owing to the facility and ill-advised good-nature of his royal master that the bad example had so empoisoned the court, the city, and the whole country. This wise minister devoted much of his time and attention to the subject; for the rage, he says, was such as to cause him a thousand pangs, and the King also. There was hardly a man moving in what was called good society, who had not been engaged in a duel either as principal or second; and if there were such a man, his chief desire was to free himself from the imputation of non-duelling, by picking a quarrel with somebody. Sully constantly wrote letters to the King, in which he prayed him to renew the edicts against this barbarous custom, to aggravate the punishment against offenders, and never, in any instance, to grant a pardon, even to a person who had wounded another in a duel, much less to any one who had taken away life. He also advised, that some sort of tribunal, or court of honour, should be established, to take cognizance of injurious and slanderous language, and of all such matters as usually led to duels; and that the justice to be administered by this court should be sufficiently prompt and severe to appease the complainant, and make the offender repent of his aggression.

Henry, being so warmly pressed by his friend and minister, called together an extraordinary council in the gallery of the palace of Fontainebleau, to take the matter into consideration. When all the members were assembled, his Majesty requested that some person conversant with the subject would make a report to him on the origin, progress, and different forms of the duel. Sully complacently remarks, that none of the counsllors gave the King any great reason to felicitate them on their erudition. In fact, they all remained silent. Sully held his peace with the rest; but he looked so knowing, that the King turned towards him, and said:-- " Great master! by your face I conjecture that you know more of this matter than you would have us believe. I pray you, and indeed I command, that you tell us what you think and what you know." The coy minister refused, as he says, out of mere politeness to his more ignorant colleagues; but, being again pressed by the King, he entered into a history of duelling both in ancient and modern times. He has not preserved this history in his Memoirs; and, as none of the ministers or counsellors present thought proper to do so, the world is deprived of a discourse which was, no doubt, a learned and remarkable one. The result was, that a royal edict was issued, which Sully lost no time in transmitting to the most distant provinces, with a distinct notification to all parties concerned that the King was in earnest, and would exert the full rigour of the law in punishment of the offenders. Sully himself does not inform us what were the provisions of the new law; but Father Matthias has been more explicit, and from him we learn, that the Marshals of France were created judges of a court of chivalry, for the hearing of all causes wherein the honour of a noble or gentleman was concerned, and that such as resorted to duelling should be punished by death and confiscation of property, and that the seconds and assistants should lose their rank, dignity, or offices, and be banished from the court of their sovereign. [Le Pere Matthias, tome ii. livre iv.]

But so strong a hold had the education and prejudice of his age upon the mind of the King, that though his reason condemned, his sympathies approved the duel. Notwithstanding this threatened severity, the number of duels did not diminish, and the wise Sully had still to lament the prevalence of an evil which menaced society with utter disorganization. In the succeeding reign the practice prevailed, if possible, to a still greater extent, until the Cardinal de Richelieu, better able to grapple with it than Sully had been, made some severe examples in the very highest classes. Lord Herbert, the English ambassador at the court of Louis XIII repeats, in his letters, an observation that had been previously made in the reign of Henry IV, that it was rare to find a Frenchman moving in good society who had not killed his man in a duel. The Abbe Millot says of this period, that the duel madness made the most terrible ravages. Men had actually a frenzy for combatting. Caprice and vanity, as well as the excitement of passion, imposed the necessity of fighting. Friends were obliged to enter into the quarrels of their friends, or be themselves called out for their refusal, and revenge became hereditary in many families. It was reckoned that in twenty years eight thousand letters of pardon had been issued to persons who had killed others in single combat. ["Elemens de l'Histoire de France, vol. iii. p. 219.]

Other writers confirm this statement. Amelot de Houssaye, in his Memoirs, says, upon this subject, that duels were so common in the first years of the reign of Louis XIII, that the ordinary conversation of persons when they met in the morning was, "Do you know who fought yesterday?" and after dinner, "Do you know who fought this morning?" The most infamous duellist at that period was De Bouteville. It was not at all necessary to quarrel with this assassin to be forced to fight a duel with him. When he heard that any one was very brave, he would go to him, and say, "People tell me that you are brave; you and I must fight together!" Every morning the most notorious bravos and duellists used to assemble at his house, to take a breakfast of bread and wine, and practise fencing. M. de Valencay, who was afterwards elevated to the rank of a cardinal, ranked very high in the estimation of De Bouteville and his gang. Hardly a day passed but what he was engaged in some duel or other, either as principal or second; and he once challenged De Bouteville himself, his best friend, because De Bouteville had fought a duel without inviting him to become his second. This quarrel was only appeased on the promise of De Bouteville that, in his next encounter, he would not fail to avail himself of his services. For that purpose he went out the same day, and picked a quarrel with the Marquis des Portes. M. de Valencay, according to agreement, had the pleasure of serving as his second, and of running through the body M. de Cavois, the second of the Marquis des Portes, a man who had never done him any injury, and whom he afterwards acknowledged he had never seen before.

Cardinal Richelieu devoted much attention to this lamentable state of public morals, and seems to have concurred with his great predecessor, Sully, that nothing but the most rigorous severity could put a stop to the evil. The subject indeed was painfully forced upon him by his enemies. The Marquis de Themines, to whom Richelieu, then Bishop of Lucon, had given offence by some representations he had made to Mary of Medicis, determined, since he could not challenge an ecclesiastic, to challenge his brother. An opportunity was soon found. Themines, accosting the Marquis de Richelieu, complained, in an insulting tone, that the Bishop of Lucon had broken his faith. The Marquis resented both the manner and matter of his speech, and readily accepted a challenge. They met in the Rue d'Angouleme, and the unfortunate Richelieu was stabbed to the heart, and instantly expired. From that moment the Bishop became the steady foe of the practice of duelling. Reason and the impulse of brotherly love alike combined to make him detest it, and when his power in France was firmly established, he set vigorously about repressing it. In his "Testament Politique," he has collected his thoughts upon the subject, in the chapter entitled "Des moyens d'arreter les Duels." In spite of the edicts that he published, the members of the nobility persisted in fighting upon the most trivial and absurd pretences. At last Richelieu made a terrible example. The infamous De Bouteville challenged and fought the Marquis de Beuoron; and, although the duel itself was not fatal to either, its consequences were fatal to both. High as they were, Richelieu resolved that the law should reach them, and they were both tried, found guilty, and beheaded. Thus did society get rid of one of the most bloodthirsty scoundrels that ever polluted it.

In 1632 two noblemen fought a duel, in which they were both killed. The officers of justice had notice of the breach of the law, and arrived at the scene of combat before the friends of the parties had time to remove the bodies. In conformity with the Cardinal's severe code upon the subject, the bodies were ignominiously stripped, and hanged upon a gallows, with their heads downwards, for several hours, within sight of all the people. [Mercure de France, vol. xiii.] This severity sobered the frenzy of the nation for a time; but it was soon forgotten. Men's minds were too deeply imbued with a false notion of honour to be brought to a right way of thinking: by such examples, however striking, Richelieu was unable to persuade them to walk in the right path, though he could punish them for choosing the wrong one. He had, with all his acuteness, miscalculated the spirit of duelling. It was not death that a duellist feared: it was shame, and the contempt of his fellows. As Addison remarked more than eighty years afterwards, "Death was not sufficient to deter men who made it their glory to despise it; but if every one who fought a duel were to stand in the pillory, it would quickly diminish the number of those imaginary men of honour, and put an end to so absurd a practice." Richelieu never thought of this.

Sully says, that in his time the Germans were also much addicted to duelling. There were three places where it was legal to fight; Witzburg, in Franconia, and Uspach and Halle, in Swabia. Thither, of course, vast numbers repaired, and murdered each other under sanction of the law. At an earlier period, in Germany, it was held highly disgraceful to refuse to fight. Any one who surrendered to his adversary for a simple wound that did not disable him, was reputed infamous, and could neither cut his beard, bear arms, mount on horseback, or hold any Office in the state. He who fell in a duel was buried with great pomp and splendour.

In the year 1652, just after Louis XIV had attained his majority, a desperate duel was fought between the Dukes de Beaufort and De Nemours, each attended by four gentlemen. Although brothers-in-law, they had long been enemies, and their constant dissensions had introduced much disorganization among the troops which they severally commanded. Each had long sought an opportunity for combat, which at last arose on a misunderstanding relative to the places they were to occupy at the council board. They fought with pistols, and, at the first discharge, the Duke de Nemours was shot through the body, and almost instantly expired. Upon this the Marquis de Villars, who seconded Nemours, challenged Hericourt, the second of the Duke de Beaufort, a man whom he had never before seen; and the challenge being accepted, they fought even more desperately than their principals. This combat, being with swords, lasted longer than the first, and was more exciting to the six remaining gentlemen who stayed to witness it. The result was fatal to Hericourt, who fell pierced to the heart by the sword of De Villars. Anything more savage than this can hardly be imagined. Voltaire says such duels were frequent, and the compiler of the "Dictionnaire d'Anecdotes" informs us, that the number of seconds was not fixed. As many as ten, or twelve, or twenty, were not unfrequent, and they often fought together after their principals were disabled. The highest mark of friendship one man could manifest towards another, was to choose him for his second; and many gentlemen were so desirous of serving in this capacity, that they endeavoured to raise every slight misunderstanding into a quarrel, that they might have the pleasure of being engaged in it. The Count de Bussy Rabutin relates an instance of this in his Memoirs. He says, that as he was one evening coming out of the theatre, a gentleman, named Bruc, whom he had not before known, stopped him very politely, and, drawing him aside, asked him if it was true that the Count de Thianges had called him (Bruc) a drunkard? Bussy replied, that he really did not know, for he saw the Count very seldom. "Oh! he is your uncle!" replied Bruc; "and, as I cannot have satisfaction from him, because he lives so far off in the country, I apply to you." "I see what you are at," replied Bussy, "and, since you wish to put me in my uncle's place, I answer, that whoever asserted that he called you a drunkard, told a lie !" "My brother said so," replied Bruc, "and he is a child." "Horsewhip him, then, for his falsehood," returned De Bussy. "I will not have my brother called a liar," returned Bruc, determined to quarrel with him; "so draw, and defend yourself!" They both drew their swords in the public street, but were separated by the spectators. They agreed, however, to fight on a future occasion, and with all regular forms of the duello. A few days afterwards, a gentleman, whom De Bussy had never before seen, and whom he did not know, even by name, called upon him, and asked if he might have the privilege of serving as his second. He added, that he neither knew him nor Bruc, except by reputation, but, having made up his mind to be second to one of them, he had decided upon accompanying De Bussy as the braver man of the two. De Bussy thanked him very sincerely for his politeness, but begged to be excused, as he had already engaged four seconds to accompany him, and he was afraid that if he took any more, the affair would become a battle instead of a duel.

When such quarrels as these were looked upon as mere matters of course, the state of society must have been indeed awful. Louis XIV very early saw the evil, and as early determined to remedy it. It was not, however, till the year 1679, when he instituted the "Chambre Ardente," for the trial of the slow poisoners and pretenders to sorcery, that he published any edict against duelling. In that year his famous edict was promulgated, in which he reiterated and confirmed the severe enactments of his predecessors, Henry IV and Louis XIII, and expressed his determination never to pardon any offender. By this celebrated ordinance a supreme court of honour was established, composed of the Marshals of France. They were bound, on taking the office, to give to every one who brought a well-founded complaint before them, such reparation as would satisfy the justice of the case. Should any gentleman against whom complaint was made refuse to obey the mandate of the court of honour, he might be punished by fine and imprisonment; and when that was not possible, by reason of his absenting himself from the kingdom, his estates might be confiscated till his return.

Every man who sent a challenge, be the cause of offence what it might, was deprived of all redress from the court of honour--suspended three years from the exercise of any office in the state--was further imprisoned for two years, and sentenced to pay a fine of half his yearly income. He who accepted a challenge, was subject to the same punishment. Any servant, or other person, who knowingly became the bearer of a challenge, was, if found guilty, sentenced to stand in the pillory and be publicly whipped for the first offence, and for the second, sent for three years to the galleys.

Any person who actually fought, was to be held guilty of murder, even though death did not ensue, and was to be punished accordingly. Persons in the higher ranks of life were to be beheaded, and those of the middle class hanged upon a gallows, and their bodies refused Christian burial.

At the same time that Louis published this severe edict, he exacted a promise from his principal nobility that they would never engage in a duel on any pretence whatever. He never swerved from his resolution to pursue all duellists with the utmost rigour, and many were executed in various parts of the country. A slight abatement of the evil was the consequence, and in the course of a few years one duel was not fought where twelve had been fought previously. A medal was struck to commemorate the circumstance, by the express command of the King. So much had he this object at heart, that, in his will, he particularly recommended to his successor the care of his edict against duelling, and warned him against any ill-judged lenity to those who disobeyed it. A singular law formerly existed in Malta with regard to duelling. By this law it was permitted, but only upon condition that the parties should fight in one particular street. If they presumed to settle their quarrel elsewhere, they were held guilty of murder, and punished accordingly. What was also very singular, they were bound, under heavy penalties, to put up their swords when requested to do so by a priest, a knight, or a woman. It does not appear, however, that the ladies or the knights exercised this mild and beneficent privilege to any great extent; the former were too often themselves the cause of duels, and the latter sympathised too much in the wounded honour of the combatants to attempt to separate them. The priests alone were the great peacemakers. Brydone says, that a cross was always painted on the wall opposite to the spot where a knight had been killed, and that in the "street of duels" he counted about twenty of them. [Brydone's "Tour in Malta." 1772.]

In England the private duel was also practised to a scandalous extent, towards the end of the sixteenth and beginning of the seventeenth centuries. The judicial combat now began to be more rare, but several instances of it are mentioned in history. One was instituted in the reign of Elizabeth, and another so late as the time of Charles I. Sir Henry Spelman gives an account of that which took place in Elizabeth's reign, which is curious, perhaps the more so when we consider that it was perfectly legal, and that similar combats remained so till the year 1819. A proceeding having been instituted in the Court of Common Pleas for the recovery of certain manorial rights in the county of Kent, the defendant offered to prove by single combat his right to retain possession. The plaintiff accepted the challenge, and the Court having no power to stay the proceedings, agreed to the champions who were to fight in lieu of the principals. The Queen commanded the parties to compromise; but it being represented to Her Majesty that they were justified by law in the course they were pursuing, she allowed them to proceed. On the day appointed, the Justices of the Common Pleas, and all the council engaged in the cause, appeared as umpires of the combat, at a place in Tothill-fields, where the lists had been prepared. The champions were ready for the encounter, and the plaintiff and defendant were publicly called to come forward and acknowledge them. The defendant answered to his name, and recognised his champion with the due formalities, but the plaintiff did not appear. Without his presence and authority the combat could not take place; and his absence being considered an abandonment of his claim, he was declared to be nonsuited, and barred for ever from renewing his suit before any other tribunal whatever.

The Queen appears to have disapproved personally of this mode of settling a disputed claim, but her judges and legal advisers made no attempt to alter the barbarous law. The practice of private duelling excited more indignation, from its being of every-day occurrence. In the time of James I the English were so infected with the French madness, that Bacon, when he was Attorney-general, lent the aid of his powerful eloquence to effect a reformation of the evil. Informations were exhibited in the Star Chamber against two persons, named Priest and Wright, for being engaged, as principal and second, in a duel, on which occasion he delivered a charge that was so highly approved of by the Lords of the Council, that they ordered it to be printed and circulated over the country, as a thing "very meet and worthy to be remembered and made known unto the world." He began by considering the nature and greatness of the mischief of duelling. "It troubleth peace -- it disfurnisheth war -- it bringeth calamity upon private men, peril upon the state, and contempt upon the law. Touching the causes of it," he observed, "that the first motive of it, no doubt, is a false and erroneous imagination of honour and credit; but then, the seed of this mischief being such, it is nourished by vain discourses and green and unripe conceits. Hereunto may be added, that men have almost lost the true notion and understanding of fortitude and valour. For fortitude distinguisheth of the grounds of quarrel whether they be just; and not only so, but whether they be worthy, and setteth a better price upon men's lives than to bestow them idly. Nay, it is weakness and disesteem of a man's self to put a man's life upon such liedger performances. A man's life is not to be trifled with: it is to be offered up and sacrificed to honourable services, public merits, good causes, and noble adventures. It is in expense of blood as it is in expense of money. It is no liberality to make a profusion of money upon every vain occasion, neither is it fortitude to make effusion of blood, except the cause of it be worth." [See "Life and Character of Lord Bacon," by Thomas Martin, Barrister-at-law.]

The most remarkable event connected with duelling in this reign was that between Lord Sanquir, a Scotch nobleman, and one Turner, a fencing-master. In a trial of skill between them, his lordship's eye was accidentally thrust out by the point of Turner's sword. Turner expressed great regret at the circumstance, and Lord Sanquir bore his loss with as much philosophy as he was master of, and forgave his antagonist. Three years afterwards, Lord Sanquir was at Paris, where he was a constant visitor at the court of Henry IV. One day, in the course of conversation, the affable monarch inquired how he had lost his eye. Sanquir, who prided himself on being the most expert swordsman of the age, blushed as he replied that it was inflicted by the sword of a fencing-master. Henry, forgetting his assumed character of an antiduellist, carelessly, and as a mere matter of course, inquired whether the man lived? Nothing more was said, but the query sank deep into the proud heart of the Scotch baron, who returned shortly afterwards to England, burning for revenge. His first intent was to challenge the fencing-master to single combat, but, on further consideration, he deemed it inconsistent with his dignity to meet him as an equal in fair and open fight. He therefore hired two bravos, who set upon the fencing-master, and murdered him in his own house at Whitefriars. The assassins were taken and executed, and a reward of one thousand pounds offered for the apprehension of their employer. Lord Sanquir concealed himself for several days, and then surrendered to take his trial, in the hope (happily false) that Justice would belie her name, and be lenient to a murderer because he was a nobleman, who, on a false point of honour, had thought fit to take revenge into his own hands. The most powerful intercessions were employed in his favour, but James, to his credit, was deaf to them all. Bacon, in his character of Attorney-general, prosecuted the prisoner to conviction; and he died the felon's death, on the 29th of June, 1612, on a gibbet erected in front of the gate of Westminster Hall.

With regard to the public duel, or trial by battle, demanded under the sanction of the law, to terminate a quarrel which the ordinary course of justice could with difficulty decide, Bacon was equally opposed to it, and thought that in no case should it be granted. He suggested that there should be declared a constant and settled resolution in the state to abolish it altogether; that care should be taken that the evil be no more cockered, nor the humour of it fed, but that all persons found guilty should be rigorously punished by the Star Chamber, and these of eminent quality banished from the court.

In the succeeding reign, when Donald Mackay, the first Lord Reay, accused David Ramsay of treason, in being concerned with the Marquis of Hamilton in a design upon the crown of Scotland, he was challenged by the latter to make good his assertion by single combat. [See "History of the House and Clan of Mackay."] It had been at first the intention of the government to try the case by the common law, but Ramsay thought he would stand a better chance of escape by recurring to the old and almost exploded custom, but which was still the right of every man in appeals of treason. Lord Reay readily accepted the challenge, and both were confined in the Tower until they found security that they would appear on a certain day, appointed by the court, to determine the question. The management of the affair was delegated to the Marischal Court of Westminster, and the Earl of Lindsay was created Lord Constable of England for the purpose. Shortly before the day appointed, Ramsay confessed in substance all that Lord Reay had laid to his charge, upon which Charles I put a stop to the proceedings.

But in England, about this period, sterner disputes arose among men than those mere individual matters which generate duels. The men of the Commonwealth encouraged no practice of the kind, and the subdued aristocracy carried their habits and prejudices elsewhere, and fought their duels at foreign courts. Cromwell's Parliament, however, -- although the evil at that time was not so crying, -- published an order, in 1654, for the prevention of duels, and the punishment of all con cerned in them. Charles II, on his restoration, also issued a proclamation upon the subject. In his reign an infamous duel was fought -- infamous, not only from its own circumstances, but from the lenity that was shown to the principal offenders.

The worthless Duke of Buckingham, having debauched the Countess of Shrewsbury, was challenged by her husband to mortal combat, in January 1668. Charles II endeavoured to prevent the duel, not from any regard to public morality, but from fear for the life of his favourite. He gave commands to the Duke of Albemarle to confine Buckingham to his house, or take some other measures to prevent him flora fighting. Albemarle neglected the order, thinking that the King himself might prevent the combat by some surer means. The meeting took place at Barn Elms, the injured Shrewsbury being attended by Sir John Talbot, his relative, and Lord Bernard Howard, son of the Earl of Arundel. Buckingham was accompanied by two of his dependants, Captain Holmes and Sir John Jenkins. According to the barbarous custom of the age, not only the principals, but the seconds, engaged each other. Jenkins was pierced to the heart, and left dead upon the field, and Sir John Talbot severely wounded in both arms. Buckingham himself escaping with slight wounds, ran his unfortunate antagonist through the body, and then left the field with the wretched woman, the cause of all the mischief, who, in the dress of a page, awaited the issue of the conflict in a neighbouring wood, holding her paramour's horse to avoid suspicion. Great influence was exerted to save the guilty parties from punishment, and the master, as base as the favourite, made little difficulty in granting a free pardon to all concerned. In a royal proclamation issued shortly afterwards, Charles II formally pardoned the murderers, but declared his intention never to extend, in future, any mercy to such offenders. It would be hard after this to say who was the most infamous, the King, the favourite, or the courtezan.

In the reign of Queen Anne, repeated complaints were made of the prevalence of duelling. Addison,

Swift, Steele, and other writers, employed their powerful pens in reprobation of it. Steele especially, in the "Tatler" and "Guardian," exposed its impiety and absurdity, and endeavoured, both by argument and by ridicule, to bring his countrymen to a right way of thinking. [See "Spectator," Nos. 84. 97, and 99; and "Tatler," Nos. 25, 26, 29, 31, 38, and 39; and "Guardian," No. 20.] His comedy of "The Conscious Lovers" contains an admirable exposure of the abuse of the word honour, which led men into an error so lamentable. Swift, writing upon the subject, remarked that he could see no harm in rogues and fools shooting each other. Addison and Steele took higher ground, and the latter, in the "Guardian," summed up nearly all that could be said upon the subject in the following impressive words: -- "A Christian and a gentleman are made inconsistent appellations of the same person. You are not to expect eternal life if you do not forgive injuries, and your mortal life is rendered uncomfortable if you are not ready to commit a murder in resentment of an affront; for good sense, as well as religion, is so utterly banished the world that men glory in their very passions, and pursue trifles with the utmost vengeance, so little do they know that to forgive is the most arduous pitch human nature can arrive at. A coward has often fought -- a coward has often conquered, but a coward never forgave." Steele also published a pamphlet, in which he gave a detailed account of the edict of Louis XIV, and the measures taken by that monarch to cure his subjects of their murderous folly.

On the 8th of May, 1711, Sir Cholmely Deering, M.P. for the county of Kent, was slain in a duel by Mr. Richard Thornhill, also a member of the House of Commons. Three days afterwards, Sir Peter King brought the subject under the notice of the Legislature, and after dwelling at considerable length on the alarming increase of the practice, obtained leave to bring in a bill for the prevention and punishment of duelling. It was read a first time that day, and ordered for a second reading in the ensuing week.

About the same time the attention of the Upper House of Parliament was also drawn to the subject in the most painful manner. Two of its most noted members would have fought, had it not been that Queen Anne received notice of their intention, and exacted a pledge that they would desist; while a few months afterwards, two other of its members lost their lives in one of the most remarkable duels upon record. The first affair, which happily terminated without a meeting, was between the Duke of Marlborough and the Earl Pawlet. The latter, and fatal encounter, was between the Duke of Hamilton and Lord Mohun.

The first arose out of a debate in the Lords upon the conduct of the Duke of Ormond, in refusing to hazard a general engagement with the enemy, in which Earl Pawlet remarked that nobody could doubt the courage of the Duke of Ormond. "He was not like a certain general, who led troops to the slaughter, to cause great numbers of officers to be knocked on the head in a battle, or against stone walls, in order to fill his pockets by disposing of their commissions." Every one felt that the remark was aimed at the Duke of Marlborough, but he remained silent, though evidently suffering in mind. Soon after the House broke up, the Earl Pawlet received a visit from Lord Mohun, who told him that the Duke of Marlborough was anxious to come to an explanation with him relative to some expressions he had made use of in that day's debate, and therefore prayed him to "go and take a little air in the country." Earl Pawlet did not affect to misunderstand the hint, but asked him in plain terms whether he brought a challenge from the Duke. Lord Mohun said his message needed no explanation, and that he (Lord Mohun) would accompany the Duke of Marlborough. He then took his leave, and Earl Pawlet returned home and told his lady that he was going out to fight a duel with the Duke of Marlborough. His lady, alarmed for her lord's safety, gave notice of his intention to the Earl of Dartmouth, who immediately, in the Queen's name, sent to the Duke of Marlborough, and commanded him not to stir abroad. He also caused Earl Pawlet's house to be guarded by two sentinels; and having taken these precautions, informed the Queen of the whole affair. Her Majesty sent at once for the Duke, expressed her abhorrence of the custom of duelling, and required his word of honour that he would proceed no further. The Duke pledged his word accordingly, and the affair terminated.

The lamentable duel between the Duke of Hamilton and Lord Mohun took place in November 1712, and sprang from the following circumstances. A lawsuit had been pending for eleven years between these two noblemen, and they looked upon each other in consequence with a certain degree of coldness. They met together on the 13th of November in the chambers of Mr. Orlebar, a Master in Chancery, when, in the course of conversation, the Duke of Hamilton reflected upon the conduct of one of the witnesses in the cause, saying that he was a person who had neither truth nor justice in him. Lord Mohun, somewhat nettled at this remark, applied to a witness favourable to his side, made answer hastily, that Mr. Whiteworth, the person alluded to, had quite as much truth and justice in him as the Duke of Hamilton. The Duke made no reply, and no one present imagined that he took offence at what was said; and when he went out, of the room, he made a low and courteous salute to the Lord Mohun. In the evening, General Macartney called twice upon the Duke with a challenge from Lord Mohun, and failing in seeing him, sought him a third time at a tavern, where he found him, and delivered his message. The Duke accepted the challenge, and the day after the morrow, which was Sunday, the 15th of November, at seven in the morning, was appointed for the meeting.

At that hour they assembled in Hyde Park, the Duke being attended by his relative, Colonel Hamilton, and the Lord Mohun by General Macartney. They jumped over a ditch into a place called the Nursery, and prepared for the combat. The Duke of Hamilton, turning to General Macartney, said, "Sir, you are the cause of this, let the event be what it will." Lord Mohun did not wish that the seconds should engage, but the Duke insisted that "Macartney should have a share in the dance." All being ready, the two principals took up their positions, and fought with swords so desperately that, after a short time, they both fell down, mortally wounded. The Lord Mohun expired upon the spot, and the Duke of Hamilton in the arms of his servants as they were carrying him to his coach.

This unhappy termination caused the greatest excitement, not only in the metropolis, but all over the country. The Tories, grieved at the loss of the Duke of Hamilton, charged the fatal combat on the Whig party, whose leader, the Duke of Marlborough, had so recently set the example of political duels. They. called Lord Mohun the bully of the Whig faction, (he had already killed three men in duels, and been twice tried for murder), and asserted openly, that the quarrel was concocted between him and General Macartney to rob the country of the services of the Duke of Hamilton by murdering him. It was also asserted, that the wound of which the Duke died was not inflicted by Lord Mohun, but by Macartney; and every means was used to propagate this belief. Colonel Hamilton, against whom and Macartney the coroner's jury had returned a verdict of wilful murder, surrendered a few days afterwards, and was examined before a privy council sitting at the house of Lord Dartmouth. He then deposed, that seeing Lord Mohun fall, and the Duke upon him, he ran to the Duke's assistance, and that he might with the more ease help him, he flung down both their swords, and, as he was raising the Duke up, he saw Macartney, make a push at him. Upon this deposition a royal proclamation was immediately issued, offering a reward of 500 pounds for the apprehension of Macartney, to which the Duchess of Hamilton afterwards added a reward of 300 pounds.

Upon the further examination of Colonel Hamilton, it was found that reliance could not be placed on all his statements, and that he contradicted himself in several important particulars. He was arraigned at the Old Bailey for the murder of Lord Mohun, the whole political circles of London being in a fever of excitement for the result. All the Tory party prayed for his acquittal, and a Tory mob surrounded the doors and all the avenues leading to the court of justice for many hours before the trial began. The examination of witnesses lasted seven hours. The criminal still persisted in accusing General Macartney of the murder of the Duke of Hamilton, but, in other respects, say the newspapers of the day, prevaricated foully. He was found guilty of manslaughter. This favourable verdict was received with universal applause, "not only from the court and all the gentlemen present, but the common people showed a mighty satisfaction, which they testified by loud and repeated huzzas." ["Post Boy," December l3th, 1712.]

As the popular delirium subsided, and men began to reason coolly upon the subject, they disbelieved the assertions of Colonel Hamilton, that Macartney had stabbed the Duke, although it was universally admitted that he had been much too busy and presuming. Hamilton was shunned by all his former companions, and his life rendered so irksome to him, that he sold out of the Guards, and retired to private life, in which he died heart-broken four years afterwards.

General Macartney surrendered about the same time, and was tried for murder in the Court of King's Bench. He was, however, found guilty of manslaughter only.

At the opening of the session of Parliament of 1713, the Queen made pointed allusion in her speech to the frequency of duelling, and recommended to the Legislature to devise some speedy and effectual remedy for it. A bill to that effect was brought forward, but thrown out on the second reading, to the very great regret of all the sensible portion of the community.

A famous duel was fought in 1765 between Lord Byron and Mr. Chaworth. The dispute arose at a club-dinner, and was relative to which of the two had the largest quantity of game on his estates. Infuriated by wine and passion, they retired instantly into an adjoining room, and fought with swords across a table, by the feeble glimmer of a tallow-candle. Mr. Chaworth, who was the more expert swordsman of the two, received a mortal wound, and shortly afterwards expired. Lord Byron was brought to trial for the murder before the House of Lords; and it appearing clearly, that the duel was not premeditated, but fought at once, and in the heat of passion, he was found guilty of manslaughter only, and ordered to be discharged upon payment of his fees. This was a very bad example for the country, and duelling of course fell into no disrepute after such a verdict.

In France, more severity was exercised. In the year 1769, the Parliament of Grenoble took cognizance of the delinquency of the Sieur Duchelas, one of its members, who challenged and killed in a duel a captain of the Flemish legion. The servant of Duchelas officiated as second, and was arraigned with his master for the murder of the captain. They were both found guilty. Duchelas was broken alive on the wheel, and the servant condemned to the galleys for life.

A barbarous and fiercely-contested duel was fought in November 1778, between two foreign adventurers, at Bath, named Count Rice and the Vicomte du Barri. Some dispute arose relative to a gambling transaction, in the course of which Du Barri contradicted an assertion of the other, by saying, "That is not true!" Count Rice immediately asked him if he knew the very disagreeable meaning of the words he had employed. Du Barri said he was perfectly well aware of their meaning, and that Rice might interpret them just as he pleased. A challenge was immediately given and accepted. Seconds were sent for, who, arriving with but little delay, the whole party, though it was not long after midnight, proceeded to a place called Claverton Down, where they remained with a surgeon until daylight. They then prepared for the encounter, each being armed with two pistols and a sword. The ground having been marked out by the seconds, Du Barri fired first, and wounded his opponent in the thigh. Count Rice then levelled his pistol, and shot Du Barri mortally in the breast. So angry were the combatants, that they refused to desist; both stepped back a few paces, and then rushing forward, discharged their second pistols at each other. Neither shot took effect, and both throwing away their pistols, prepared to finish the sanguinary struggle by the sword. They took their places, and were advancing towards each other, when the Vicomte du Barri suddenly staggered, grew pale, and, falling to the ground, exclaimed, "Je vous demande ma vie." His opponent had but just time to answer, that he granted it, when the unfortunate Du Barri turned upon the grass, and expired with a heavy groan. The survivor of this savage conflict was then removed to his lodgings, where he lay for some weeks in a dangerous state. The coroner's jury, in the mean while, sat upon the body of Du Barri, and disgraced themselves by returning a verdict of manslaughter only. Count Rice, upon his recovery, was indicted for the murder notwithstanding this verdict. On his trial he entered into a long defence of his conduct, pleading the fairness of the duel, and its unpremeditated nature; and, at the same time, expressing his deep regret for the unfortunate death of Du Barri, with whom for many years he had been bound in ties of the strictest friendship. These considerations appear to have weighed with the jury, and this fierce duellist was again found guilty of manslaughter only, and escaped with a merely nominal punishment.

A duel, less remarkable from its circumstances, but more so from the rank of the parties, took place in 1789. The combatants on this occasion were the Duke of York and Colonel Lenox, the nephew and heir of the Duke of Richmond. The cause of offence was given by the Duke of York, who had said, in presence of several officers of the Guards, that words had been used to Colonel Lenox at Daubigny's to which no gentleman ought to have submitted. Colonel Lenox went up to the Duke on parade, and asked him publicly whether he had made such an assertion. The Duke of York, without answering his question, coldly ordered him to his post. When parade was over, he took an opportunity of saying publicly in the orderly room before Colonel Lenox, that he desired no protection from his rank as a prince and his station as commanding officer; adding that, when he was off duty, he wore a plain brown coat like a private gentleman, and was ready as such to give satisfaction. Colonel Lenox desired nothing better than satisfaction; that is to say, to run the chance of shooting the Duke through the body, or being himself shot. He accordingly challenged his Royal Highness, and they met on Wimbledon Common. Colonel Lenox fired first, and the ball whizzed past the head of his opponent, so near to it as to graze his projecting curl. The Duke refused to return the fire, and the seconds interfering, the affair terminated.

Colonel Lenox was very shortly afterwards engaged in another duel arising out of this. A Mr. Swift wrote a pamphlet in reference to the dispute between him and the Duke of York, at some expressions in which he took so much offence, as to imagine that nothing but a shot at the writer could atone for them. They met on the Uxbridge Road, but no damage was done to either party.

The Irish were for a long time renowned for their love of duelling. The slightest offence which it is possible to imagine that one man could offer to another, was sufficient to provoke a challenge. Sir Jonah Barrington relates, in his Memoirs, that, previous to the Union, during the time of a disputed election in Dublin, it was no unusual thing for three-and-twenty duels to be fought in a day. Even in times of less excitement, they were so common as to be deemed unworthy of note by the regular chroniclers of events, except in cases where one or both of the combatants were killed.

In those days, in Ireland, it was not only the man of the military, but of every profession, who had to work his way to eminence with the sword or the pistol. Each political party had its regular corps of bullies, or fire-eaters, as they were called, who qualified themselves for being the pests of society by spending all their spare time in firing at targets. They boasted that they could hit an opponent in any part of his body they pleased, and made up their minds before the encounter began whether they should kill him, disable, or disfigure him for life -- lay him on a bed of suffering for a twelve-month, or merely graze a limb.

The evil had reached an alarming height, when, in the year 1808, an opportunity was afforded to King George III of showing in a striking manner his detestation of the practice, and of setting an example to the Irish that such murders were not to be committed with impunity. A dispute arose, in the month of June 1807, between Major Campbell and Captain Boyd, officers of the 21st regiment, stationed in Ireland, about the proper manner of giving the word of command on parade. Hot words ensued on this slight occasion, and the result was a challenge from Campbell to Boyd. They retired into the mess-room shortly afterwards, and each stationed himself at a corner, the distance obliquely being but seven paces. Here, without friends or seconds being present, they fired at each other, and Captain Boyd fell mortally wounded between the fourth and fifth ribs. A surgeon who came in shortly, found him sitting in a chair, vomiting and suffering great agony. He was led into another room, Major Campbell following, in great distress and perturbation of mind. Boyd survived but eighteen hours; and just before his death, said, in reply to a question from his opponent, that the duel was not fair, and added, "You hurried me, Campbell -- you're a bad man." --- "Good God!" replied Campbell, "will you mention before these gentlemen, was not everything fair? Did you not say that you were ready?" Boyd answered faintly, "Oh, no! you know I wanted you to wait and have friends." On being again asked whether all was fair, the dying man faintly murmured "Yes:" but in a minute after, he said, "You're a bad man!" Campbell was now in great agitation, and wringing his hands convulsively, he exclaimed, "Oh, Boyd! you are the happiest man of the two! Do you forgive me?" Boyd replied, "I forgive you -- I feel for you, as I know you do for me." He shortly afterwards expired, and Major Campbell made his escape from Ireland, and lived for some months with his family under an assumed name, in the neighbourhood of Chelsea. He was, however, apprehended, and brought to trial at Armagh, in August 1808. He said while in prison, that, if found guilty of murder, he should suffer as an example to duellists in Ireland; but he endeavoured to buoy himself up, with the hope that the jury would only convict him of manslaughter. It was proved in evidence upon the trial, that the duel was not fought immediately after the offence was given, but that Major Campbell went home and drank tea with his family, before he sought Boyd for the fatal encounter. The jury returned a verdict of wilful murder against him, but recommended him to mercy on the ground that the duel had been a fair one. He was condemned to die on the Monday following, but was afterwards respited for a few days longer. In the mean time the greatest exertions were made in his behalf. His unfortunate wife went upon her knees before the Prince of Wales, to move him to use his influence with the King, in favour of her unhappy husband. Everything a fond wife and a courageous woman could do, she tried, to gain the royal clemency; but George III was inflexible, in consequence of the representations of the Irish Viceroy that an example was necessary. The law was therefore allowed to take its course, and the victim of a false spirit of honour died the death of a felon.

The most inveterate duellists of the present day are the students in the Universities of Germany. They fight on the most frivolous pretences, and settle with swords and pistols the schoolboy disputes which in other countries are arranged by the more harmless medium of the fisticuffs. It was at one time the custom among these savage youths to prefer the sword combat, for the facility it gave them of cutting off the noses of their opponents. To disfigure them in this manner was an object of ambition, and the German duellists reckoned the number of these disgusting trophies which they had borne away, with as much satisfaction as a successful general the provinces he had reduced or the cities he had taken.

But it would be wearisome to enter into the minute detail of all the duels of modern times. If an examination were made into the general causes which produced them, it would be found that in every case they had been either of the most trivial or the most unworthy nature. Parliamentary duels were at one time very common, and amongst the names of those who have soiled a great reputation by conforming to the practice, may be mentioned those of Warren Hastings, Sir Philip Francis, Wilkes, Pitt, Fox, Grattan, Curran, Tierney, and Canning. So difficult is it even for the superior mind to free itself from the trammels with which foolish opinion has enswathed it -- not one of these celebrated persons who did not in his secret soul condemn the folly to which he lent himself. The bonds of reason, though iron-strong, are easily burst through; but those of folly, though lithe and frail as the rushes by a stream, defy the stoutest heart to snap them asunder. Colonel Thomas, an officer of the Guards, who was killed in a duel, added the following clause to his will the night before he died: -- "In the first place, I commit my soul to Almighty God, in hope of his mercy and pardon for the irreligious step I now (in compliance with the unwarrantable customs of this wicked world) put myself under the necessity of taking." How many have been in the same state of mind as this wise, foolish man! He knew his error, and abhorred it, but could not resist it, for fear of the opinion of the prejudiced and unthinking. No other could have blamed him for refusing to fight a duel.

The list of duels that have sprung from the most degrading causes might be stretched out to an almost indefinite extent. Sterne's father fought a duel about a goose; and the great Raleigh about a tavern bill. [Raleigh, at one period of his life, appeared to be an inveterate duellist, and it was said of him that he had been engaged in more encounters of the kind than any man of note among his contemporaries. More than one fellow-creature he had deprived of life; but he lived long enough to be convinced of the sinfulness of his conduct, and made a solemn vow never to fight another duel. The following anecdote of his forbearance is well known, but it will bear repetition :--

A dispute arose in a coffee-house between him and a young man on some trivial point, and the latter, losing his temper, impertinently spat in the face of the veteran. Sir Walter, instead of running him through the body, as many would have done, or challenging him to mortal combat, coolly took out his handkerchief, wiped his face, and said, "Young man, if I could as easily wipe from my conscience the stain of killing you, as I can this spittle from my face, you should not live another minute." The young man immediately begged his pardon.] Scores of duels (many of them fatal) have been fought from disputes at cards, or a place at a theatre, while hundreds of challenges, given and accepted over-night, in a fit of drunkenness, have been fought out the next morning to the death of one or both of the antagonists.

Two of the most notorious duels of modern times had their origin in causes no more worthy than the quarrel of a dog and the favour of a prostitute: that between Macnamara and Montgomery arising from the former; and that between Best and Lord Camelford, from the latter. The dog of Montgomery attacked a dog belonging to Macnamara, and each master interfering in behalf of his own animal, high words ensued. The result was the giving and accepting a challenge to mortal combat. The parties met on the following day, when Montgomery was shot dead, and his antagonist severely wounded. This affair created a great sensation at the time, and Heaviside, the surgeon who attended at the fatal field to render his assistance, if necessary, was arrested as an accessory to the murder, and committed to Newgate.

In the duel between Best and Lord Camelford, two pistols were used which were considered to be the best in England. One of them was thought slightly superior to the other, and it was agreed that the belligerents should toss up a piece of money to decide the choice of weapons. Best gained it, and, at the first discharge, Lord Camelford fell, mortally wounded. But little sympathy was expressed for his fate; he was a confirmed duellist, had been engaged in many meetings of the kind, and the blood of more than one fellow-creature lay at his door. As he had sowed, so did he reap; and the violent man met an appropriate death.

It now only remains to notice the means that have been taken to stay the prevalence of this madness of false honour in the various countries of the civilized world. The efforts of the governments of France and England have already been mentioned, and their want of success is but too well known. The same efforts have been attended with the same results elsewhere. In despotic countries, where the will of the monarch has been strongly expressed and vigorously supported, a diminution of the evil has for a while resulted, but only to be increased again, when death relaxed the iron grasp, and a successor appeared of less decided opinions upon the subject. This was the case in Prussia under the great Frederick, of whose aversion to duelling a popular anecdote is recorded. It is stated of him that he permitted duelling in his army, but only upon the condition that the combatants should fight in presence of a whole battalion of infantry, drawn up on purpose, to see fair play. The latter received strict orders, when one of the belligerents fell, to shoot the other immediately. It is added, that the known determination of the King effectually put a stop to the practice.

The Emperor Joseph II of Austria was as firm as Frederick, although the measures he adopted were not so singular. The following letter explains his views on the subject:--

"To GENERAL * * * * *

"MY GENERAL,

"You will immediately arrest the Count of K. and Captain W. The Count is young, passionate, and influenced by wrong notions of birth and a false spirit of honour. Captain W. is an old soldier, who will adjust every dispute with the sword and pistol, and who has received the challenge of the young Count with unbecoming warmth.

"I will suffer no duelling in my army. I despise the principles of those who attempt to justify the practice, and who would run each other through the body in cold blood.

"When I have officers who bravely expose themselves to every danger in facing the enemy -- who at all times exhibit courage, valour, and resolution in attack and defence, I esteem them highly. The coolness with which they meet death on such occasions is serviceable to their country, and at the same time redounds to their own honour; but should there be men amongst them who are ready to sacrifice everything to their vengeance and hatred, I despise them. I consider such a man as no better than a Roman gladiator.

"Order a court-martial to try the two officers. Investigate the subject of their dispute with that impartiality which I demand from every judge; and he that is guilty, let him be a sacrifice to his fate and the laws.

"Such a barbarous custom, which suits the age of the Tamerlanes and Bajazets, and which has often had such melancholy effects on single families, I will have suppressed and punished, even if it should deprive me of one half of my officers. There are still men who know how to unite the character of a hero with that of a good subject; and he only can be so who respects the laws.

" JOSEPH."

"August 1771."

[Vide the Letters of Joseph II to distinguished Princes and Statesmen, published for the first time in England in "The Pamphleteer" for 1821. They were originally published in Germany a few years previously, and throw a great light upon the character of that monarch and the events of his reign.]

In the United States of America the code varies considerably. In one or two of the still wild and simple States of the Far West, where no duel has yet been fought, there is no specific law upon the subject beyond that in the Decalogue, which says, "Thou shalt do no murder." But duelling everywhere follows the steps of modern civilization, and by the time the backwoodsman is transformed into the citizen, he has imbibed the false notions of honour which are prevalent in Europe, and around him, and is ready, like his progenitors, to settle his differences with the pistol. In the majority of the States the punishment for challenging, fighting, or acting as second, is solitary imprisonment and hard labour for any period less than a year, and disqualification for serving any public office for twenty years. In Vermont the punishment is total disqualification for office, deprivation of the rights of citizenship, and a fine; in fatal cases, the same punishment as that of murderers. In Rhode Island, the combatant, though death does not ensue, is liable to be carted to the gallows, with a rope about his neck, and to sit in this trim for an hour, exposed to the peltings of the mob. He may be further imprisoned for a year, at the option of the magistrate. In Connecticut the punishment is total disqualification for office or employ, and a fine, varying from one hundred to a thousand dollars. The laws of Illinois require certain officers of the state to make oath, previous to their instalment, that they have never been, nor ever will be, concerned in a duel. ["Encyclopedia Americana," art. Duelling.]

Amongst the edicts against duelling promulgated at various times in Europe, may be mentioned that of Augustus King of Poland, in 1712, which decreed the punishment of death against principals and seconds, and minor punishments against the bearers of a challenge. An edict was also published at Munich, in 1773, according to which both principals and seconds, even in duels where no one was either killed or wounded, should be hanged, and their bodies buried at the foot of the gallows. The King of Naples issued an ordinance against duelling in 1838, in which the punishment of death is decreed against all concerned in a fatal duel. The bodies of those killed, and of those who may be executed in consequence, are to be buried in unconsecrated ground, and without any religious ceremony; nor is any monument to be erected on the spot. The punishment for duels in which either, or both, are wounded, and for those in which no damage whatever is done, varies according to the case, and consists of fine, imprisonment, loss of rank and honours, and incapacity for filling any public situation. Bearers of challenges may also be punished with fine and imprisonment.

It might be imagined that enactments so severe all over the civilized world would finally eradicate a custom, the prevalence of which every wise and good man must deplore. But the frowns of the law never yet have taught, and never will teach, men to desist from this practice, as long as it is felt that the lawgiver sympathises with it in his heart. The stern judge upon the bench may say to the unfortunate wight who has been called a liar by some unmannerly opponent, "If you challenge him, you meditate murder, and are guilty of murder !" but the same judge, divested of his robes of state, and mixing in the world with other men, would say, "If you do not challenge him, if you do not run the risk of making yourself a murderer, you will be looked upon as a mean-spirited wretch, unfit to associate with your fellows, and deserving nothing but their scorn and their contempt!" It is society, and not the duellist, who is to blame. Female influence, too, which is so powerful in leading men either to good or to evil, takes, in this case, the evil part. Mere animal bravery has, unfortunately, such charms in the female eye, that a successful duellist is but too often regarded as a sort of hero; and the man who refuses to fight, though of truer courage, is thought a poltroon, who may be trampled on. Mr. Graves, a member of the American Legislature, who, early in 1838, killed a Mr. Cilley in a duel, truly and eloquently said, on the floor of the House of Representatives, when lamenting the unfortunate issue of that encounter, that society was more to blame than he was. "Public opinion," said the repentant orator, "is practically the paramount law of the land. Every other law, both human and divine, ceases to be observed; yea, withers and perishes in contact with it. It was this paramount law of this nation, and of this House, that forced me, under the penalty of dishonour, to subject myself to the code, which impelled me unwillingly into this tragical affair. Upon the heads of this nation, and at the doors of this House, rests the blood with which my unfortunate hands have been stained!"

As long as society is in this mood; as long as it thinks that the man who refuses to resent an insult, deserved that insult, and should be scouted accordingly, so long, it is to be feared, will duelling exist, however severe the laws may be. Men must have redress for injuries inflicted, and when those injuries are of such a nature that no tribunal will take cognizance of them, the injured will take the law into their own hands, and right themselves in the opinion of their fellows, at the hazard of their lives. Much as the sage may affect to despise the opinion of the world, there are few who would not rather expose their lives a hundred times than be condemned to live on, in society, but not of it -- a by-word of reproach to all who know their history, and a mark for scorn to point his finger at.

The only practicable means for diminishing the force of a custom which is the disgrace of civilization, seems to be the establishment of a court of honour, which should take cognizance of all those delicate and almost intangible offences which yet wound so deeply. The court established by Louis XIV might be taken as a model. No man now fights a duel when a fit apology has been offered, and it should be the duty of this court to weigh dispassionately the complaint of every man injured in his honour, either by word or deed, and to force the offender to make a public apology. If he refused the apology, he would be the breaker of a second law; an offender against a high court, as well as against the man he had injured, and might be punished with fine and imprisonment, the latter to last until he saw the error of his conduct, and made the concession which the court demanded.

If, after the establishment of this tribunal, men should be found of a nature so bloodthirsty as not to be satisfied with its peaceful decisions, and should resort to the old and barbarous mode of an appeal to the pistol, some means might be found of dealing with them. To hang them as murderers would be of no avail; for to such men death would have few terrors. Shame alone would bring them to reason. The following code, it is humbly suggested to all future legislators upon the subject, would, in conjunction with the establishment of a court of honour, do much towards eradicating this blot from society. Every man who fought a duel, even though he did not wound his opponent, should be tried, and, upon proof of the fact, be sentenced to have his right hand cut off. The world would then know his true character as long as he lived. If his habits of duelling were so inveterate, and he should learn to fire a pistol with his left hand, he should, upon conviction of a second offence, lose that hand also. This law, which should allow no commutation of the punishment, under any circumstances, would lend strength and authority to the court of honour. In the course of a few years duelling would be ranked amongst exploded follies, and men would begin to wonder that a custom so barbarous and so impious had ever existed amongst them.

The Love of the Marvelous and the Disbelief of the True

"Well, son John," said the old woman, "and what wonderful things did you meet with all the time you were at sea?" - " Oh! mother," replied John, "I saw many strange things." -- " Tell us all about them," replied his mother, "for I long to hear your adventures." -- " Well, then," said John, "as we were sailing over the Line, what do you think we saw?" - "I can't imagine," replied his mother. -- " Well, we saw a fish rise out of the sea, and fly over our ship!" "Oh! John! John! what a liar you are!" said his mother, shaking her head, and smiling incredulously. "True as death? said John; "and we saw still more wonderful things than that." -- " Let us hear them," said his mother, shaking her head again; "and tell the truth, John, if you can." -- " Believe it, or believe it not, as you please," replied her son; "but as we were sailing up the Red Sea, our captain thought he should like some fish for dinner; so he told us to throw our nets, and catch some." -- " Well," inquired his mother, seeing that he paused in his story. "Well," rejoined her son, "we did throw them, and, at the very first haul, we brought up a chariot-wheel, made all of gold, and inlaid with diamonds!" "Lord bless us!" said his mother, "and what did the captain say ?" -- " Why, he said it was one of the wheels of Pharaoh's chariot, that had lain in the Red Sea ever since that wicked King was drowned, with all his host, while pursuing the Israelites." -- " Well, well," said his mother, lifting up her hands in admiration; "now, that's very possible, and I think the captain was a very sensible man. Tell me such stories as that, and I'll believe you; but never talk to me of such things as flying fish! No, no, John, such stories won't go down with me, I can assure you!"

Such old women as the sailor's mother, in the above well-known anecdote, are by no means rare in the world. Every age and country has produced them. They have been found in high places, and have sat down among the learned of the earth. Instances must be familiar to every reader in which the same person was willing, with greedy credulity, to swallow the most extravagant fiction, and yet refuse credence to a philosophical fact. The same Greeks who believed readily that Jupiter wooed Leda in the form of a swan, denied stoutly that there were any physical causes for storms and thunder, and treated as impious those who attempted to account for them on true philosophical principles.

The reasons that thus lead mankind to believe the marvellously false, and to disbelieve the marvellously true, may be easily gathered. Of all the offspring of Time, Error is the most ancient, and is so old and familiar an acquaintance, that Truth, when discovered, comes upon most of us like an intruder, and meets the intruder's welcome. We all pay an involuntary homage to antiquity -- a "blind homage," as Bacon calls it in his "Novum Organum," which tends greatly to the obstruction of truth. To the great majority of mortal eyes, Time sanctifies everything that he does not destroy. The mere fact of anything being spared by the great foe makes it a favourite with us, who are sure to fall his victims. To call a prejudice "time-hallowed," is to open a way for it into hearts where it never before penetrated. Some peculiar custom may disgrace the people amongst whom it flourishes; yet men of a little wisdom refuse to aid in its extirpation, merely because it is old. Thus it is with human belief, and thus it is we bring shame upon our own intellect.

To this cause may be added another, also mentioned by Lord Bacon -- a misdirected zeal in matters of religion, which induces so many to decry a newly-discovered truth, because the Divine records contain no allusion to it, or because, at first sight, it appears to militate, not against religion, but against some obscure passage which has never been fairly interpreted. The old woman in the story could not believe

125

that there was such a creature as a flying-fish, because her Bible did not tell her so, but she believed that her son had drawn up the golden and bejewelled wheel from the Red Sea, because her Bible informed her that Pharaoh was drowned there.

Upon a similar principle the monks of the inquisition believed that the devil appeared visibly among men, that St. Anthony pulled his nose with a pair of red-hot pincers, and that the relics of the saints worked miracles; yet they would not believe Galileo, when he proved that the earth turned round the sun.

Keppler, when he asserted the same fact, could gain no bread, and little credence; but when he pretended to tell fortunes and cast nativities, the whole town flocked to him, and paid him enormous fees for his falsehood.

When Roger Bacon invented the telescope and the magic-lantern, no one believed that the unaided ingenuity of man could have done it; but when some wiseacres asserted that the devil had appeared to him, and given him the knowledge which he turned to such account, no one was bold enough to assert that it was improbable. His hint that saltpetre, sulphur, and charcoal, mixed in certain proportions, would produce effects similar to thunder and lightning, was disregarded or disbelieved; but the legend of the brazen head which delivered oracles, was credited for many ages.

[Godwin, in his "Lives of the Necromancers," gives the following version of this legend. Friar Bacon and Friar Bungay entertained the project of enclosing England with a wall, so as to render it inaccessible to any invader. They accordingly raised the devil, as the person best able to inform them how this was to be done. The devil advised them to make a brazen head, with all the internal structure and organs of a human head. The construction would cost them much time, and they must wait with patience till the faculty of speech descended upon it. Finally, however, it would become an oracle, and, if the question were propounded to it, would teach them the solution of their problem. The friars spent seven years in bringing the subject to perfection, and waited day after day in expectation that it would utter articulate sounds. At length nature became exhausted in them, and they lay down to sleep, having first given it strictly in charge to a servant of theirs, clownish in nature, but of strict fidelity, that he should awaken them the moment the image began to speak. That period arrived. The head uttered sounds, but such as the clown judged unworthy of notice. "Time is!" it said. No notice was taken, and a long pause ensued. "Time was!" -- a similar pause, and no notice. "Time is passed!" The moment these words were uttered, a tremendous storm ensued, with thunder and lightning, and the head was shivered into a thousand pieces. Thus the experiment of Friar Bacon and Friar Bungay came to nothing.]

Solomon De Cans, who, in the time of Cardinal Richelieu, conceived the idea of a steam-engine, was shut up in the Bastille as a madman, because the idea of such an extraordinary instrument was too preposterous for the wise age that believed in all the absurdities of witchcraft.

When Harvey first proved the circulation of the blood, every tongue was let loose against him. The thing was too obviously an imposition, and an attempt to deceive that public who believed that a king's touch had power to cure the scrofula. That a dead criminal's hand, rubbed against a wen, would cure it, was reasonable enough; but that the blood flowed through the veins was beyond all probability.

In our own day, a similar fate awaited the beneficent discovery of Dr. Jenner. That vaccination could abate the virulence of, or preserve from, the smallpox, was quite incredible; none but a cheat and a quack could assert it: but that the introduction of the vaccine matter into the human frame could endow men with the qualities of a cow, was quite probable. Many of the poorer people actually dreaded that their children would grow hairy and horned as cattle, if they suffered them to be vaccinated.

The Jesuit, Father Labat, the shrewd and learned traveller in South America, relates an experiment which he made upon the credulity of some native Peruvians. Holding a powerful lens in his hand, and concentrating the rays of the sun upon the naked arm of an admiring savage, he soon made him roar with pain. All the tribe looked on, first with wonder, and then with indignation and wonder both combined. In vain the philosopher attempted to explain the cause of the phenomenon - in vain he offered to convince them that there was nothing devilish in the experiment - he was thought to be in league with the infernal gods to draw down the fire from Heaven, and was looked upon, himself, as an awful and supernatural being. Many attempts were made to gain possession of the lens, with the view of destroying it, and thereby robbing the Western stranger of the means of bringing upon them the vengeance of his deities.

Very similar was the conduct of that inquiring Brahmin, which is related by Forbes in his Oriental Memoirs. The Brahmin had a mind better cultivated than his fellows; he was smitten with a love for the knowledge of Europe -- read English books -- pored over the pages of the Encyclopedia, and profited by various philosophical instruments; but on religious questions the Brahmin was firm to the faith of his caste and the doctrine of the Metempsychosis. Lest he might sacrilegiously devour his progenitors, he abstained from all animal food; and thinking that he ate nothing which enjoyed life, he supported himself, like his brethren, upon fruits and vegetables. All the knowledge that did not run counter to this belief, he sought after with avidity, and bade fair to become the wisest of his race. In an evil hour, his English friend and instructor exhibited a very powerful solar microscope, by means of which he showed him that every drop of water that he drank teemed with life -- that every fruit was like a world, covered with innumerable animalculae, each of which was fitted by its organization for the sphere in which it moved, and had its wants, and the capability of supplying them as completely as visible animals millions of times its bulk. The English philosopher expected that his Hindoo friend would be enraptured at the vast field of knowledge thus suddenly opened out to him, but he was deceived. The Brahmin from that time became an altered man -- thoughtful, gloomy, reserved, and discontented. He applied repeatedly to his friend that he would make him a present of the microscope; but as it was the only one of its kind in India, and the owner set a value upon it for other reasons, he constantly refused the request, but offered him the loan of it for any period he might require. But nothing short of an unconditional gift of the instrument would satisfy the Brahmin, who became at last so importunate that the patience of the Englishman was exhausted, and he gave it him. A gleam of joy shot across the care-worn features of the Hindoo as he clutched it, and bounding with an exulting leap into the garden, he seized a large stone, and dashed the instrument into a thousand pieces. When called upon to explain his extraordinary conduct, he said to his friend, "Oh that I had remained in that happy state of ignorance wherein you first found me! Yet will I confess that, as my knowledge increased, so did my pleasure, until I beheld the last wonders of the microscope; from that moment I have been tormented by doubt and perplexed by mystery: my mind, overwhelmed by chaotic confusion, knows not where to rest, nor how to extricate itself from such a maze. I am miserable, and must continue to be so, until I enter on another stage of existence. I am a solitary individual among fifty millions of people, all educated in the same belief with myself -- all happy in their ignorance! So may they ever remain! I shall keep the secret within my own bosom, where it will corrode my peace and break my rest. But I shall have some satisfaction in knowing that I alone feel those pangs which, had I not destroyed the instrument, might have been extensively communicated, and rendered thousands miserable! Forgive me, my valuable friend! and oh, convey no more implements of knowledge and destruction!"

Many a learned man may smile at the ignorance of the Peruvian and the Hindoo, unconscious that he himself is just as ignorant and as prejudiced. Who does not remember the outcry against the science of geology, which has hardly yet subsided? Its professors were impiously and absurdly accused of designing to "hurl the Creator from his throne." They were charged with sapping the foundations of religion, and of propping atheism by the aid of a pretended science.

The very same principle which leads to the rejection of the true, leads to the encouragement of the false. Thus we may account for the success which has attended great impostors, at times when the truth, though not half so wondrous as their impositions, has been disregarded. as extravagant and preposterous. The man who wishes to cheat the people, must needs found his operations upon some prejudice or belief that already exists. Thus the philosophic pretenders who told fortunes by the stars cured all diseases by one nostrum, and preserved from evil by charms and amulets, ran with the current of popular belief. Errors that were consecrated by time and long familiarity, they heightened and embellished, and succeeded to their hearts' content; but the preacher of truth had a foundation to make as well as a superstructure, a difficulty which did not exist for the preacher of error. Columbus preached a new world, but was met with distrust and incredulity; had he preached with as much zeal and earnestness the discovery of some valley in the old one, where diamonds hung upon the trees, or a herb grew that cured all the ills incidental to humanity, he would have found a warm and hearty welcome -- might have sold dried cabbage leaves for his wonderful herb, and made his fortune.

In fact, it will be found in the history of every generation and race of men, that whenever a choice of belief between the "Wondrously False" and the "Wondrously True" is given to ignorance or prejudice, that their choice will be fixed upon the first, for the reason that it is most akin to their own nature. The great majority of mankind, and even of the wisest among us, are still in the condition of the sailor's mother -- believing and disbelieving on the same grounds that she did -- protesting against the flying fish, but cherishing the golden wheels. Thousands there are amongst us, who, rather than pin their faith in the one fish, would believe not only in the wheel of gold, but the chariot - not only in the chariot, but in the horses and the driver.

Popular Follies of Great Cities

La faridondaine -- la faridondon,
Vive la faridondaine!--*Beranger.*

The popular humours of a great city are a never-failing source of amusement to the man whose sympathies are hospitable enough to embrace all his kind, and who, refined though he may be himself, will not sneer at the humble wit or grotesque peculiarities of the boozing mechanic, the squalid beggar, the vicious urchin, and all the motley group of the idle, the reckless, and the imitative that swarm in the alleys and broadways of a metropolis. He who walks through a great city to find subjects for weeping, may, God knows, find plenty at every corner to wring his heart; but let such a man walk on his course, and enjoy his grief alone -- we are not of those who would accompany him. The miseries of us poor earthdwellers gain no alleviation from the sympathy of those who merely hunt them out to be pathetic over them. The weeping philosopher too often impairs his eyesight by his woe, and becomes unable from his tears to see the remedies for the evils which he deplores. Thus it will often be found that the man of no tears is the truest philanthropist, as he is the best physician who wears a cheerful face, even in the worst of cases.

So many pens have been employed to point out the miseries, and so many to condemn the crimes and vices, and more serious follies of the multitude, that our's shall not increase the number, at least in this chapter. Our present task shall be less ungracious, and wandering through the busy haunts of great cities, we shall seek only for amusement, and note as we pass a few of the harmless follies and whimsies of the poor.

And, first of all, walk where we will, we cannot help hearing from every side a phrase repeated with delight, and received with laughter, by men with hard hands and dirty faces -- by saucy butcher lads and errand-boys -- by loose women -- by hackney coachmen, cabriolet drivers, and idle fellows who loiter at the corners of streets. Not one utters this phrase without producing a laugh from all within hearing. It seems applicable to every circumstance, and is the universal answer to every question; in short, it is the favourite slang phrase of the day, a phrase that, while its brief season of popularity lasts, throws a dash of fun and frolicsomeness over the existence of squalid poverty and ill-requited labour, and gives them reason to laugh as well as their more fortunate fellows in a higher stage of society.

London is peculiarly fertile in this sort of phrases, which spring up suddenly, no one knows exactly in what spot, and pervade the whole population in a few hours, no one knows how. Many years ago the favourite phrase (for, though but a monosyllable, it was a phrase in itself) was Quoz. This odd word took the fancy of the multitude in an extraordinary degree, and very soon acquired an almost boundless meaning. When vulgar wit wished to mark its incredulity and raise a laugh at the same time, there was no resource so sure as this popular piece of slang. When a man was asked a favour which he did not choose to grant, he marked his sense of the suitor's unparalleled presumption by exclaiming Quoz! When a mischievous urchin wished to annoy a passenger, and create mirth for his chums, he looked him in the face, and cried out Quoz! and the exclamation never failed in its object. When a disputant was desirous of throwing a doubt upon the veracity of his opponent, and getting summarily rid of an argument which he could not overturn, he uttered the word Quoz, with a contemptuous curl of his lip and an impatient shrug of his shoulders. The universal monosyllable conveyed all his meaning, and not

129

only told his opponent that he lied, but that he erred egregiously if he thought that any one was such a nincompoop as to believe him. Every alehouse resounded with Quoz; every street corner was noisy with it, and every wall for miles around was chalked with it.

But, like all other earthly things, Quoz had its season, and passed away as suddenly as it arose, never again to be the pet and the idol of the populace. A new claimant drove it from its place, and held undisputed sway till, in its turn, it was hurled from its pre-eminence, and a successor appointed in its stead.

"What a shocking bad hat!" was the phrase that was next in vogue. No sooner had it become universal, than thousands of idle but sharp eyes were on the watch for the passenger whose hat showed any signs, however slight, of ancient service. Immediately the cry arose, and, like the what-whoop of the Indians, was repeated by a hundred discordant throats. He was a wise man who, finding himself under these circumstances "the observed of all observers," bore his honours meekly. He who showed symptoms of ill-feeling at the imputations cast upon his hat, only brought upon himself redoubled notice. The mob soon perceive whether a man is irritable, and, if of their own class, they love to make sport of him. When such a man, and with such a hat, passed in those days through a crowded neighbourhood, he might think himself fortunate if his annoyances were confined to the shouts and cries of the populace. The obnoxious hat was often snatched from his head, and thrown into the gutter by some practical joker, and then raised, covered with mud, upon the end of a stick, for the admiration of the spectators, who held their sides with laughter, and exclaimed in the pauses of their mirth, "Oh! what a shocking bad hat! .... What a shocking bad hat!" Many a nervous, poor man, whose purse could but ill spare the outlay, doubtless purchased a new hat before the time, in order to avoid exposure in this manner.

The origin of this singular saying, which made fun for the metropolis for months, is not involved in the same obscurity as that which shrouds the origin of Quoz and some others. There had been a hotly-contested election for the borough of Southwark, and one of the candidates was an eminent hatter. This gentleman, in canvassing the electors, adopted a somewhat professional mode of conciliating their good-will, and of bribing them without letting them perceive that they were bribed. Whenever he called upon or met a voter whose hat was not of the best material, or, being so, had seen its best days, he invariably said, "What a shocking bad hat you have got; call at my warehouse, and you shall have a new one!" Upon the day of election this circumstance was remembered, and his opponents made the most of it, by inciting the crowd to keep up an incessant cry of "What a shocking bad hat!" all the time the honourable candidate was addressing them. From Southwark the phrase spread over all London, and reigned, for a time, the supreme slang of the season.

Hookey Walker, derived from the chorus of a popular ballad, was also high in favour at one time, and served, like its predecessor, Quoz, to answer all questions. In the course of time the latter word alone became the favourite, and was uttered with a peculiar drawl upon the first syllable, and a sharp turn upon the last. If a lively servant girl was importuned for a kiss by a fellow she did not care about, she cocked her little nose, and cried "Walker!" If a dustman asked his friend for the loan of a shilling, and his friend was either unable or unwilling to accommodate him, the probable answer he would receive was "Walker!" If a drunken man was reeling along the streets, and a boy pulled his coat-tails, or a man knocked his hat over his eyes to make fun of him, the joke was always accompanied by the same exclamation. This lasted for two or three months, and "Walker!" walked off the stage, never more to be revived for the entertainment of that or any future generation.

The next phrase was a most preposterous one. Who invented it, how it arose, or where it was first heard, are alike unknown. Nothing about it is certain, but that for months it was the slang par excellence of the Londoners, and afforded them a vast gratification. "There he goes with his eye out!" or "There she goes with her eye out!" as the sex of the party alluded to might be, was in the mouth of everybody who knew the town. The sober part of the community were as much puzzled by this unaccountable saying as the vulgar were delighted with it. The wise thought it very foolish, but the many thought it very funny, and the idle amused themselves by chalking it upon walls, or scribbling it upon monuments. But, "all that's bright must fade," even in slang. The people grew tired of their hobby, and "There he goes with his eye out!" was heard no more in its accustomed haunts.

Another very odd phrase came into repute in a brief space afterwards, in the form of the impertinent and not universally apposite query, "Has your mother sold her mangle?" But its popularity was not of that boisterous and cordial kind which ensures a long continuance of favour. What tended to impede its progress was, that it could not be well applied to the older portions of society. It consequently ran but a brief career, and then sank into oblivion. Its successor enjoyed a more extended fame, and laid its foundations so deep, that years and changing fashions have not sufficed to eradicate it. This phrase was "Flare up!" and it is, even now, a colloquialism in common use. It took its rise in the time of the Reform riots, when Bristol was nearly half burned by the infuriated populace. The flames were said to have flared up in the devoted city. Whether there was anything peculiarly captivating in the sound, or in the idea of these words, is hard to say; but whatever was the reason, it tickled the mob-fancy mightily, and drove all other slang out of the field before it. Nothing was to be heard all over London but "flare up!" It answered all questions, settled all disputes, was applied to all persons, all things, and all circumstances, and became suddenly the most comprehensive phrase in the English language. The man who had overstepped the bounds of decorum in his speech was said to have flared up; he who had paid visits too repeated to the gin-shop, and got damaged in consequence, had flared up. To put one's-self into a passion; to stroll out on a nocturnal frolic, and alarm a neighbourhood, or to create a disturbance in any shape, was to flare up. A lovers' quarrel was a fare up; so was a boxing-match between two blackguards in the streets, and the preachers of sedition and revolution recommended the English nation to flare up, like the French. So great a favourite was the word, that people loved to repeat it for its very sound. They delighted apparently in hearing their own organs articulate it; and labouring men, when none who could respond to the call were within hearing, would often startle the aristocratic echoes of the West by the well-known slang phrase of the East. Even in the dead hours of the night, the ears of those who watched late, or who could not sleep, were saluted with the same sound. The drunkard reeling home showed that he was still a man and a citizen, by calling "flare up" in the pauses of his hiccough. Drink had deprived him of the power of arranging all other ideas; his intellect was sunk to the level of the brute's; but he clung to humanity by the one last link of the popular cry. While he could vociferate that sound, he had rights as an Englishman, and would not sleep in a gutter, like a dog! Onwards he went, disturbing quiet streets and comfortable people by his whoop, till exhausted nature could support him no more, and he rolled powerless into the road. When, in due time afterwards, the policeman stumbled upon him as he lay, that guardian of the peace turned the full light of his lantern on his face, and exclaimed, "Here's a poor devil who's been flaring up!" Then came the stretcher, on which the victim of deep potations was carried to the watchhouse, and pitched into a dirty cell, among a score of wretches about as far gone as himself, who saluted their new comrade by a loud, long shout of flare up!

So universal was this phrase, and so enduring seemed its popularity, that a speculator, who knew not the evanescence of slang, established a weekly newspaper under its name. But he was like the man who built his house upon the sand; his foundation gave way under him, and the phrase and the newspaper were washed into the mighty sea of the things that were. The people grew at last weary of the monotony, and "flare up" became vulgar even among them. Gradually it was left to little boys who did not know the world, and in process of time sank altogether into neglect. It is now heard no more as a piece of popular slang; but the words are still used to signify any sudden outburst either of fire, disturbance, or ill-nature.

The next phrase that enjoyed the favour of the million was less concise, and seems to have been originally aimed against precocious youths who gave themselves the airs of manhood before their time. "Does your mother know you're out?" was the provoking query addressed to young men of more than reasonable swagger, who smoked cigars in the streets, and wore false whiskers to look irresistible. We have seen many a conceited fellow who could not suffer a woman to pass him without staring her out of countenance, reduced at once into his natural insignificance by the mere utterance of this phrase. Apprentice lads and shopmen in their Sunday clothes held the words in abhorrence, and looked fierce when they were applied to them. Altogether the phrase had a very salutary effect, and in a thousand instances showed young Vanity, that it was not half so pretty and engaging as it thought itself. What rendered it so provoking was the doubt it implied as to the capability of self-guidance possessed by the individual to whom it was addressed. "Does your mother know you're out?" was a query of mock concern and solicitude, implying regret and concern that one so young and inexperienced in the ways of a great city should be allowed to wander abroad without the guidance of a parent. Hence the great wrath of those who verged on manhood, but had not reached it, whenever they were made the subject of it. Even older heads did not like it; and the heir of a ducal house, and inheritor of a warrior's name, to whom they were applied by a cabriolet driver, who was ignorant of his rank, was so indignant at the affront, that he summoned the offender before the magisterial bench. The fellow had wished to impose upon his Lordship by asking double the fare he was entitled to, and when his Lordship resisted the demand, he was insultingly asked "if his mother knew he was out?" All the drivers on the stand joined in the query, and his Lordship was fain to escape their laughter by walking away with as much haste as his dignity would allow. The man pleaded ignorance that his customer was a Lord, but offended justice fined him for his mistake.

When this phrase had numbered its appointed days, it died away, like its predecessors, and "Who are you?" reigned in its stead. This new favourite, like a mushroom, seems to have sprung up in a night, or, like a frog in Cheapside, to have come down in a sudden shower. One day it was unheard, unknown, uninvented; the next it pervaded London; every alley resounded with it; every highway was musical with it,

"And street to street, and lane to lane flung back
The one unvarying cry."

The phrase was uttered quickly, and with a sharp sound upon the first and last words, leaving the middle one little more than an aspiration. Like all its compeers which had been extensively popular, it was applicable to almost every variety of circumstance. The lovers of a plain answer to a plain question did not like it at all. Insolence made use of it to give offence; ignorance, to avoid exposing itself; and waggery, to create laughter. Every new comer into an alehouse tap-room was asked unceremoniously, "Who are you?" and if he looked foolish, scratched his head, and did not know what to reply, shouts of boisterous merriment resounded on every side. An authoritative disputant was not unfrequently put down, and presumption of every kind checked by the same query. When its popularity was at its height, a gentleman, feeling the hand of a thief in his pocket, turned suddenly round, and caught him in the act, exclaiming, "Who are you?" The mob which gathered round applauded to the very echo, and thought it the most capital joke they had ever heard -- the very acme of wit -- the very essence of humour. Another circumstance, of a similar kind, gave an additional fillip to the phrase, and infused new life and vigour into it, just as it was dying away. The scene occurred in the chief criminal court of the kingdom. A prisoner stood at the bar; the offence with which he had been charged was clearly proved against him;

his counsel had been heard, not in his defence, but in extenuation, insisting upon his previous good life and character, as reasons for the lenity of the court. "And where are your witnesses?" inquired the learned judge who presided. "Please you, my Lord, I knows the prisoner at the bar, and a more honester feller never breathed," said a rough voice in the gallery. The officers of the court looked aghast, and the strangers tittered with ill-suppressed laughter. "Who are you?" said the Judge, looking suddenly up, but with imperturbable gravity. The court was convulsed; the titter broke out into a laugh, and it was several minutes before silence and decorum could be restored. When the Ushers recovered their self-possession, they made diligent search for the profane transgressor; but he was not to be found. Nobody knew him; nobody had seen him. After a while the business of the court again proceeded. The next prisoner brought up for trial augured favourably of his prospects when he learned that the solemn lips of the representative of justice had uttered the popular phrase as if he felt and appreciated it. There was no fear that such a judge would use undue severity; his heart was with the people; he understood their language and their manners, and would make allowances for the temptations which drove them into crime. So thought many of the prisoners, if we may infer it from the fact, that the learned judge suddenly acquired an immense increase of popularity. The praise of his wit was in every mouth, and "Who are you?" renewed its lease, and remained in possession of public favour for another term in consequence.

But it must not be supposed that there were no interregni between the dominion of one slang phrase and another. They did not arise in one long line of unbroken succession, but shared with song the possession of popular favour. Thus, when the people were in the mood for music, slang advanced its claims to no purpose, and, when they were inclined for slang, the sweet voice of music wooed them in vain. About twenty years ago London resounded with one chorus, with the love of which everybody seemed to be smitten. Girls and boys, young men and old, maidens and wives, and widows, were all alike musical. There was an absolute mania for singing, and the worst of it was, that, like good Father Philip, in the romance of "The Monastery," they seemed utterly unable to change their tune. "Cherry ripe!" "Cherry ripe!" was the universal cry of all the idle in the town. Every unmelodious voice gave utterance to it; every crazy fiddle, every cracked flute, every wheezy pipe, every street organ was heard in the same strain, until studious and quiet men stopped their ears in desperation, or fled miles away into the fields or woodlands, to be at peace. This plague lasted for a twelvemonth, until the very name of cherries became an abomination in the land. At last the excitement wore itself away, and the tide of favour set in a new direction. Whether it was another song or a slang phrase, is difficult to determine at this distance of time; but certain it is, that very shortly afterwards, people went mad upon a dramatic subject, and nothing was to be heard of but "Tom and Jerry." Verbal wit had amused the multitude long enough, and they became more practical in their recreation. Every youth on the town was seized with the fierce desire of distinguishing himself, by knocking down the "charlies," being locked up all night in a watchhouse, or kicking up a row among loose women and blackguard men in the low dens of St. Giles's. Imitative boys vied with their elders in similar exploits, until this unworthy passion, for such it was, had lasted, like other follies, its appointed time, and the town became merry after another fashion. It was next thought the height of vulgar wit to answer all questions by placing the point of the thumb upon the tip of the nose, and twirling the fingers in the air. If one man wished to insult or annoy another, he had only to make use of this cabalistic sign in his face, and his object was accomplished. At every street corner where a group was assem- bled, the spectator who was curious enough to observe their movements, would be sure to see the fingers of some of them at their noses, either as a mark of incredulity, surprise, refusal, or mockery, before he had watched two minutes. There is some remnant of this absurd custom to be seen to this day; but it is thought low, even among the vulgar.

About six years ago, London became again most preposterously musical. The vox populi wore itself hoarse by singing the praises of "The Sea, the Sea!" If a stranger (and a philosopher) had walked through London, and listened to the universal chorus, he might have constructed a very pretty theory upon the love of the English for the sea-service, and our acknowledged superiority over all other nations upon that element. "No wonder," he might have said, "that this people is invincible upon the ocean. The love of it mixes with their daily thoughts: they celebrate it even in the market-place: their street-minstrels excite charity by it; and high and low, young and old, male and female, chant Io paeans in its praise. Love is not honoured in the national songs of this warlike race -- Bacchus is no god to them; they are men of sterner mould, and think only of 'the Sea, the Sea!' and the means of conquering upon it."

Such would, doubtless, have been his impression if he had taken the evidence only of his ears. Alas! in those days for the refined ears that were musical! great was their torture when discord, with its thousand diversities of tone, struck up this appalling anthem -- there was no escape from it. The migratory minstrels of Savoy caught the strain, and pealed it down the long vistas of quiet streets, till their innermost and snuggest apartments re-echoed with the sound. Men were obliged to endure this crying evil for full six months, wearied to desperation, and made sea-sick on the dry land.

Several other songs sprang up in due succession afterwards, but none of them, with the exception of one, entitled "All round my Hat," enjoyed any extraordinary share of favour, until an American actor introduced a vile song called "Jim Crow." The singer sang his verses in appropriate costume, with grotesque gesticulations, and a sudden whirl of his body at the close of each verse. It took the taste of the town immediately, and for months the ears of orderly people were stunned by the senseless chorus-

"Turn about and wheel about,
And do just so--
Turn about and wheel about,
And jump, Jim Crow!"

Street-minstrels blackened their faces in order to give proper effect to the verses; and fatherless urchins, who had to choose between thieving and singing for their livelihood, took the latter course, as likely to be the more profitable, as long as the public taste remained in that direction. The uncouth dance, its accompaniment, might be seen in its full perfection on market nights in any great thoroughfare; and the words of the song might be heard, piercing above all the din and buzz of the ever-moving multitude. He, the calm observer, who during the hey-day popularity of this doggrel,

"Sate beside the public way,
Thick strewn with summer dust, and saw the stream
Of people there was hurrying to and fro,
Numerous as gnats upon the evening gleam,"

might have exclaimed with Shelley, whose fine lines we quote, that

"The million, with fierce song and maniac dance,
Did rage around."

The philosophic theorist we have already supposed soliloquising upon the English character, and forming his opinion of it from their exceeding love for a sea-song, might, if he had again dropped suddenly into London, have formed another very plausible theory to account for our unremitting efforts for the abolition of the Slave Trade. "Benevolent people!" he might have said, "how unbounded are your sympathies! Your unhappy brethren of Africa, differing from you only in the colour of their skins, are so dear to you, and you begrudge so little the twenty millions you have paid on their behalf, that you love to have a memento of them continually in your sight. Jim Crow is the representative of that injured race, and as such is the idol of your populace! See how they all sing his praises! -- how they imitate his peculiarities! -- how they repeat his name in their moments of leisure and relaxation! They even carve images of him to adorn their hearths, that his cause and his sufferings may never be forgotten ! Oh, philanthropic England! -- oh, vanguard of civilization!"

Such are a few of the peculiarities of the London multitude, when no riot, no execution, no murder, no balloon, disturbs the even current of their thoughts. These are the whimseys of the mass - the harmless follies by which they unconsciously endeavour to lighten the load of care which presses upon their existence. The wise man, even though he smile at them, will not altogether withhold his sympathy, and will say, "Let them enjoy their slang phrases and their choruses if they will; and if they cannot be happy, at least let them be merry." To the Englishman, as well as to the Frenchman of whom Beranger sings, there may be some comfort in so small a thing as a song, and we may, own with him that

"Au peuple attriste
Ce qui rendra la gaite,
C'est la GAUDRIOLE!
O gue!
C'est la GAUDRIOLE!"

The O. P. Mania

And these things bred a great combustion in the town.
Wagstaffe's "Apparition of Mother Haggis."

The acrimonious warfare carried on for a length of time by the playgoers of London against the proprietors of Covent-Garden Theatre, is one of the most singular instances upon record of the small folly which will sometimes pervade a multitude of intelligent men. Carried on at first from mere obstinacy by a few, and afterwards for mingled obstinacy and frolic by a greater number, it increased at last to such a height, that the sober dwellers in the provinces held up their hands in astonishment, and wondered that the people of London should be such fools. As much firmness and perseverance displayed in a better cause, might have achieved important triumphs; and we cannot but feel regret, in recording this matter, that so much good and wholesome energy should have been thrown away on so unworthy an object. But we will begin with the beginning, and trace the O. P. mania from its source.

On the night of the 20th of September, 1808, the old theatre of Covent-Garden was totally destroyed by fire. Preparations were immediately made for the erection of a more splendid edifice, and the managers, Harris and the celebrated John Philip Kemble, announced that the new theatre should be without a rival in Europe. In less than three months, the rubbish of the old building was cleared away, and the foundation-stone of the new one laid with all due ceremony by the Duke of Sussex. With so much celerity were the works carried on that, in nine months more, the edifice was completed, both without and within. The opening night was announced for the 18th of September 1809, within two days of a twelvemonth since the destruction of the original building.

But the undertaking had proved more expensive than the Committee anticipated. To render the pit entrance more commodious, it had been deemed advisable to remove a low public-house that stood in the way. This turned out a matter of no little difficulty, for the proprietor was a man well skilled in driving a hard bargain. The more eager the Committee showed themselves to come to terms with him for his miserable pot-house, the more grasping he became in his demands for compensation. They were ultimately obliged to pay him an exorbitant sum. Added to this, the interior decorations were on the most costly scale; and Mrs. Siddons, and other members of the Kemble family, together with the celebrated Italian singer, Madame Catalani, had been engaged at very high salaries. As the night of opening drew near, the Committee found that they had gone a little beyond their means; and they issued a notice, stating that, in consequence of the great expense they had been at in building the theatre, and the large salaries they had agreed to pay, to secure the services of the most eminent actors, they were under the necessity of fixing the prices of admission at seven shillings to the boxes and four shillings to the pit, instead of six shillings and three and sixpence, as heretofore.

This announcement created the greatest dissatisfaction. The boxes might have borne the oppression, but the dignity of the pit was wounded. A war-cry was raised immediately. For some weeks previous to the opening, a continual clatter was kept up in clubs and coffee-rooms, against what was considered a most unconstitutional aggression on the rights of play-going man. The newspapers assiduously kept up the excitement, and represented, day after day, to the managers the impolicy of the proposed advance. The bitter politics of the time were disregarded, and Kemble and Covent-Garden became as great sources of interest as Napoleon and France. Public attention was the more fixed upon the proceedings at Covent-

Garden, since it was the only patent theatre then in existence, Drury-Lane theatre having also been destroyed by fire in the month of February previous. But great as was the indignation of the lovers of the drama at that time, no one could have anticipated the extraordinary lengths to which opposition would be carried.

First Night, September 20th. -- The performances announced were the tragedy of "Macbeth" and the afterpiece of "The Quaker." The house was excessively crowded (the pit especially) with persons who had gone for no other purpose than to make a disturbance. They soon discovered another grievance to add to the list. The whole of the lower, and three-fourths of the upper tier of boxes, were let out for the season; so that those who had paid at the door for a seat in the boxes, were obliged to mount to a level with the gallery. Here they were stowed into boxes which, from their size and shape, received the contemptuous, and not inappropriate designation of pigeon-holes. This was considered in the light of a new aggression upon established rights; and long before the curtain drew up, the managers might have heard in their green-room the indignant shouts of "Down with the pigeon-holes!" -- " Old prices for ever!" Amid this din the curtain rose, and Mr. Kemble stood forward to deliver a poetical address in honour of the occasion. The riot now began in earnest; not a word of the address was audible, from the stamping and groaning of the people in the pit. This continued, almost without intermission, through the five acts of the tragedy. Now and then, the sublime acting of Mrs. Siddons, as "the awful woman," hushed the noisy multitude into silence, in spite of themselves: but it was only for a moment; the recollection of their fancied wrongs made them ashamed of their admiration, and they shouted and hooted again more vigorously than before. The comedy of Munden in the afterpiece met with no better reception; not a word was listened to, and the curtain fell amid still increasing uproar and shouts of "Old prices!" Some magistrates, who happened to be present, zealously came to the rescue, and appeared on the stage with copies of the Riot Act. This ill-judged proceeding made the matter worse. The men of the pit were exasperated by the indignity, and strained their lungs to express how deeply they felt it. Thus remained the war till long after midnight, when the belligerents withdrew from sheer exhaustion.

Second Night. -- The crowd was not so great; all those who had gone on the previous evening to listen to the performances, now stayed away, and the rioters had it nearly all to themselves. With the latter, "the play was not the thing," and Macheath and Polly sang in "The Beggar's Opera" in vain. The actors and the public appeared to have changed sides -- the audience acted, and the actors listened. A new feature of this night's proceedings was the introduction of placards. Several were displayed from the pit and boxes, inscribed in large letters with the words, "Old prices." With a view of striking terror, the constables who had been plentifully introduced into the house, attacked the placard-bearers, and succeeded, after several severe battles, in dragging off a few of them to the neighbouring watch-house, in Bow Street. Confusion now became worse and worse confounded. The pitites screamed themselves hoarse; while, to increase the uproar, some mischievous frequenters of the upper regions squeaked through dozens of cat-calls, till the combined noise was enough to blister every tympanum in the house.

Third Night.--The appearance of several gentlemen in the morning at the bar of the Bow Street police office, to answer for their riotous conduct, had been indignantly commented upon during the day. All augured ill for the quiet of the night. The performances announced were "Richard the Third" and "The Poor Soldier," but the popularity of the tragedy could not obtain it a hearing. The pitites seemed to be drawn into closer union by the attacks made upon them, and to act more in concert than on the previous nights. The placards were, also, more numerous; not only the pit, but the boxes and galleries exhibited them. Among the most conspicuous, was one inscribed, "John Bull against John Kemble. -- Who'll win?" Another bore "King George for ever! but no King Kemble." A third was levelled against Madame Catalani, whose large salary was supposed to be one of the causes of the increased prices, and was inscribed "No foreigners to tax us -- we're taxed enough already." This last was a double-barrelled one, expressing both dramatic and political discontent, and was received with loud cheers by the pitites.

The tragedy and afterpiece were concluded full two hours before their regular time; and the cries for Mr. Kemble became so loud, that the manager thought proper to obey the summons. Amid all these scenes of uproar he preserved his equanimity, and was never once betrayed into any expression of petulance or anger. With some difficulty he obtained a hearing. He entered into a detail of the affairs of the theatre, assuring the audience at the same time of the solicitude of the proprietors to accommodate themselves to the public wish. This was received with some applause, as it was thought at first to manifest a willingness to come back to the old prices, and the pit eagerly waited for the next sentence, that was to confirm their hopes. That sentence was never uttered, for Mr. Kemble, folding his arms majestically, added, in his deep tragic voice, "Ladies and Gentlemen, I wait here to know what you want!" Immediately the uproar was renewed, and became so tremendous and so deafening, that the manager, seeing the uselessness of further parley, made his bow and retired.

A gentleman then rose in the boxes and requested a hearing. He obtained it without difficulty. He began by inveighing in severe terms against the pretended ignorance of Mr. Kemble, in asking them so offensively what they wanted, and concluded by exhorting the people never to cease their opposition until they brought down the prices to their old level. The speaker, whose name was understood to be Leigh, then requested a cheer for the actors, to show that no disrespect was intended them. The cheer was given immediately.

A barrister of the name of Smythe then rose to crave another hearing for Mr. Kemble. The manager stood forth again, calm, unmoved, and severe. "Ladies and gentlemen," said he, "I wait here to know your wishes." Mr. Leigh, who took upon himself, "for that night only," the character of popular leader, said, the only reply he could give was one in three words, "the old prices." Hereat the shouts of applause again rose, till the building rang. Still serene amid the storm, the manager endeavoured to enter into explanations. The men of the pit would hear nothing of the sort. They wanted entire and absolute acquiescence. Less would not satisfy them; and, as Mr. Kemble only wished to explain, they would not hear a word. He finally withdrew amid a noise to which Babel must have been comparatively silent.

Fourth night. -- The rioters were more obstinate than ever. The noises were increased by the addition of whistles, bugle-horns, and watchmen's rattles, sniffling, snorting, and clattering from all parts of the house. Human lungs were taxed to the uttermost, and the stamping on the floor raised such a dust as to render all objects but dimly visible. In placards, too, there was greater variety. The loose wits of the town had all day been straining their ingenuity to invent new ones. Among them were, "Come forth, O Kemble! come forth and tremble!" "Foolish John Kemble, we'll make you tremble!" and "No cats! no Catalani! English actors for ever!"

Those who wish to oppose a mob successfully, should never lose their temper. It is a proof of weakness which masses of people at once perceive, and never fail to take advantage of. Thus, when the managers unwisely resolved to fight the mob with their own weapons, it only increased the opposition it was intended to allay. A dozen pugilists, commanded by a notorious boxer of the day, were introduced into the pit, to use the argumentum ad hominem to the rioters. Continual scuffles ensued: but the invincible resolution of the playgoers would not allow them to quail; it rather aroused them to renewed opposition, and a determination never to submit or yield. It also strengthened their cause, by affording them further ground of complaint against the managers.

139

The performances announced on the bills were the opera of "Love in a Village," and "Who wins?" but the bills had it all to themselves, for neither actors nor public were much burthened with them. The latter, indeed, afforded some sport. The title was too apt to the occasion to escape notice, and shouts of "Who wins? who wins?" displaced for a time the accustomed cry of old prices.

After the fall of the curtain, Mr. Leigh, with another gentleman, again spoke, complaining bitterly of the introduction of the prize-fighters, and exhorting the public never to give in. Mr. Kemble was again called forward; but when he came, the full tide of discord ran so strongly against him that, being totally unable to stem it, he withdrew. Each man seemed to shout as if he had been a Stentor; and when his lungs were wearied, took to his feet and stamped, till all the black coats in his vicinity became grey with dust. At last the audience were tired out, and the theatre was closed before eleven o'clock.

Fifth night. -- The play was Coleman's amusing comedy of "John Bull." There was no diminution of the uproar. Every note on the diapason of discord was run through. The prize-fighters, or hitites as they were called, mustered in considerable numbers, and the battles between them and the pitites were fierce and many. It was now, for the first time, that the letters O.P. came into general use as an abbreviation of the accustomed watchword of old prices. Several placards were thus inscribed; and, as brevity is so desirable in shouting, the mob adopted the emendation. As usual, the manager was called for. After some delay he came forward, and was listened to with considerable patience. He repeated, in respectful terms, the great loss that would be occasioned to the proprietors by a return to the old prices, and offered to submit a statement of their accounts to the eminent lawyers, Sir Vicary Gibbs and Sir Thomas Plumer; the eminent merchants, Sir Francis Baring and Mr. Angerstein; and Mr. Whitmore, the Governor of the Bank of England. By their decision as to the possibility of carrying on the theatre at the old prices, he would consent to be governed, and he hoped the public would do the same. This reasonable proposition was scouted immediately. Not even the high and reputable names he had mentioned were thought to afford any guarantee for impartiality. The pitites were too wrong-headed to abate one iota of their pretensions; and they had been too much insulted by the prize-fighters in the manager's pay, to show any consideration for him, or agree to any terms he might propose. They wanted full acquiescence, and nothing less. Thus the conference broke off, and the manager retired amid a storm of hisses.

An Irish gentleman, named O'Reilly, then stood up in one of the boxes. With true Irish gallantry, he came to the rescue of an ill-used lady. He said he was disgusted at the attacks made upon Madame Catalani, the finest singer in the world, and a lady inestimable in private life. It was unjust, unmanly, and un-English to make the innocent suffer for the guilty; and he hoped this blot would be no longer allowed to stain a fair cause. As to the quarrel with the manager, he recommended them to persevere. They were not only wronged by his increased prices, but insulted by his boxers, and he hoped, that before they had done with him, they would teach him a lesson he would not soon forget. The gallant Hibernian soon became a favourite, and sat down amid loud cheers.

Sixth night. - No signs of a cessation of hostilities on the one side, or of a return to the old prices on the other. The playgoers seemed to grow more united as the managers grew more obstinate. The actors had by far the best time of it; for they were spared nearly all the labour of their parts, and merely strutted on the stage to see how matters went on, and then strutted off again. Notwithstanding the remonstrance of Mr. O'Reilly on the previous night, numerous placards reflecting upon Madame Catalani were exhibited. One was inscribed with the following doggrel :-

"Seventeen thousand a-year goes pat,

To Kemble, his sister, and Madame Cat."

On another was displayed, in large letters, "No compromise, old prices, and native talent!" Some of these were stuck against the front of the boxes, and others were hoisted from the pit on long poles. The following specimens will suffice to show the spirit of them; wit they had none, or humour either, although when they were successively exhibited, they elicited roars of laughter:--

"John Kemble alone is the cause of this riot;
When he lowers his prices, John Bull will be quiet."

"John Kemble be damn'd,
We will not be cramm'd."
"Squire Kemble
Begins to tremble."

The curtain fell as early as nine o'clock, when there being loud calls for Mr. Kemble, he stood forward. He announced that Madame Catalani, against whom so unjustifiable a prejudice had been excited, had thrown up her engagement rather than stand in the way of any accommodation of existing differences. This announcement was received with great applause. Mr. Kemble then went on to vindicate himself and co-proprietors from the charge of despising public opinion. No assertion, he assured them, could be more unjust. They were sincerely anxious to bring these unhappy differences to a close, and he thought he had acted in the most fair and reasonable manner in offering to submit the accounts to an impartial committee, whose decision, and the grounds for it, should be fully promulgated. This speech was received with cheering, but interrupted at the close by some individuals, who objected to any committee of the manager's nomination. This led to a renewal of the uproar, and it was some time before silence could be obtained. When, at last, he was able to make himself heard, he gave notice, that until the decision of the committee had been drawn up, the theatre should remain closed. Immediately every person in the pit stood up, and a long shout of triumph resounded through the house, which was heard at the extremity of Bow Street. As if this result had been anticipated, a placard was at the same moment hoisted, inscribed, "Here lies the body of NEW PRICE, an ugly brat and base born, who expired on the 23rd of September 1809, aged six days. -- Requiescat in pace!"

Mr. Kemble then retired, and the pitites flung up their hats in the air, or sprang over the benches, shouting and hallooing in the exuberance of their joy; and thus ended the first act of this popular farce.

The committee ultimately chosen differed from that first named, Alderman Sir Charles Price, Bart. and Mr. Silvester, the Recorder of London, being substituted for Sir Francis Baring and Sir Vicary Gibbs. In a few days they had examined the multitudinous documents of the theatre, and agreed to a report which was published in all the newspapers, and otherwise distributed. They stated the average profits of the six preceding years at 6 and 3/8 per cent, being only 1 and 3/8 per cent. beyond the legal interest of money, to recompense the proprietors for all their care and enterprise. Under the new prices they would receive 3 and 1/2 per cent. profit; but if they returned to the old prices, they would suffer a loss of fifteen shillings per cent. upon their capital. Under these circumstances, they could do no other than recommend the proprietors to continue the new prices.

This report gave no satisfaction. It certainly convinced the reasonable, but they, unfortunately, were in a minority of one to ten. The managers, disregarding the outcry that it excited, advertised the recommencement of the performances for Wednesday the 4th of October following. They endeavoured to pack the house with their friends, but the sturdy O.P. men were on the alert, and congregated in the pit in great numbers. The play was "The Beggar's Opera," but, as on former occasions, it was wholly inaudible. The noises were systematically arranged, and the actors, seeing how useless it was to struggle against the popular feeling, hurried over their parts as quickly as they could, and the curtain fell shortly after nine o'clock. Once more the manager essayed the difficult task of convincing madness by appealing to reason. As soon as the din of the rattles and post-horns would permit him to speak, he said, he would throw himself on the fairness of the most enlightened metropolis in the world. He was sure, however strongly they might feel upon the subject, they would not be accessory to the ruin of the theatre, by insisting upon a return to the former prices. Notwithstanding the little sop he had thrown out to feed the vanity of this roaring Cerberus, the only answer he received was a renewal of the noise, intermingled with shouts of "Hoax! hoax! imposition!" Mr. O'Reilly, the gallant friend of Madame Catalani, afterwards addressed the pit, and said no reliance could be placed on the report of the committee. The profits of the theatre were evidently great: they had saved the heavy salary of Madame Catalani; and by shutting out the public from all the boxes but the pigeon-holes, they made large sums. The first and second tiers were let at high rents to notorious courtesans, several of whom he then saw in the house; and it was clear that the managers preferred a large revenue from this impure source to the reasonable profits they would receive from respectable people. Loud cheers greeted this speech; every eye was turned towards the boxes, and the few ladies in them immediately withdrew. At the same moment, some inveterate pitite hoisted a large placard, on which was inscribed,

"We lads of the pit
Will never submit."

Several others were introduced. One of them was a caricature likeness of Mr. Kemble, asking, "What do you want?" with a pitite replying, "The old prices, and no pigeon-holes!" Others merely bore the drawing of a large key, in allusion to a notorious house in the neighbourhood, the denizens of which were said to be great frequenters of the private boxes. These appeared to give the managers more annoyance than all the rest, and the prize-fighters made vigorous attacks upon the holders of them. Several persons were, on this night, and indeed nearly every night, taken into custody, and locked up in the watchhouse. On their appearance the following morning, they were generally held to bail in considerable sums to keep the peace. This proceeding greatly augmented the animosity of the pit.

It would be useless to detail the scenes of confusion which followed night after night. For about three weeks the war continued with unabated fury. Its characteristics were nearly always the same. Invention was racked to discover new noises, and it was thought a happy idea when one fellow got into the gallery with a dustman's bell, and rang it furiously. Dogs were also brought into the boxes, to add their sweet voices to the general uproar. The animals seemed to join in it con amore, and one night a large mastiff growled and barked so loudly, as to draw down upon his exertions three cheers from the gratified pitites.

So strong did the popular enthusiasm run in favour of the row, that well-dressed ladies appeared in the boxes with the letters O. P. on their bonnets. O. P. hats for the gentlemen were still more common, and some were so zealous in the cause, as to sport waistcoats with an O embroidered upon one flap and a P on the other. O.P. toothpicks were also in fashion; and gentlemen and ladies carried O.P. handkerchiefs, which they waved triumphantly whenever the row was unusually deafening. The latter suggested the idea of O. P. flags, which were occasionally unfurled from the gallery to the length of a dozen feet. Sometimes the first part of the night's performances were listened to with comparative patience, a majority of the manager's friends being in possession of the house. But as soon as the half-price commenced, the row began again in all its pristine glory. At the fall of the curtain it soon became customary to sing "God save the King," the whole of the O.P.'s joining in loyal chorus. Sometimes this was followed by "Rule Britannia;" and, on two or three occasions, by a parody of the national anthem, which excited great laughter. A verse may not be uninteresting as a specimen.

"O Johnny Bull, be true,
Confound the prices new,
And make them fall!
Curse Kemble's politics,
Frustrate his knavish tricks,
On thee our hopes we fix,
T' upset them all !"

This done, they scrambled over the benches, got up sham fights in the pit, or danced the famous O.P. dance. The latter may as well be described here: half a dozen, or a dozen fellows formed in a ring, and stamped alternately with the right and left foot, calling out at regular intervals, O. P. - O. P. with a drawling and monotonous sound. This uniformly lasted till the lights were put out, when the rioters withdrew, generally in gangs of ten or twenty, to defend themselves from sudden attacks on the part of the constables.

An idea seemed about this time to break in upon them, that notwithstanding the annoyance they caused the manager, they were aiding to fill his coffers. This was hinted at in some of the newspapers, and the consequence was, that many stayed away to punish him, if possible, under the silent system. But this did not last long. The love of mischief was as great an incentive to many of them as enmity to the new prices. Accidental circumstances also contributed to disturb the temporary calm. At the Westminster quarter-sessions, on the 27th of October, bills of indictment were preferred against forty-one persons for creating a disturbance and interrupting the performances of the theatre. The grand jury ignored twenty-seven of the bills, left two undecided, and found true bills against twelve. The latter exercised their right of traverse till the ensuing sessions. The preferment of these bills had the effect of re-awakening the subsiding excitement. Another circumstance about the same time gave a still greater impetus to it, and furnished the rioters with a chief, round whom they were eager to rally. Mr. Clifford, a barrister, appeared in the pit on the night of the 31st of October, with the letters O. P. on his hat. Being a man of some note, he was pounced upon by the constables, and led off to Bow Street police office, where Brandon, the box-keeper, charged him with riotous and disorderly conduct. This was exactly what Clifford wanted. He told the presiding magistrate, a Mr. Read, that he had purposely displayed the letters on his hat, in order that the question of right might be determined before a competent tribunal. He denied that he had committed any offence, and seemed to manifest so intimate an acquaintance with the law upon the subject, that the magistrate, convinced by his reasoning, ordered his immediate dismissal, and stated that he had been taken into custody without the slightest grounds. The result was made known in the theatre a few minutes afterwards, where Mr. Clifford, on his appearance victorious, was received with reiterated huzzas. On his leaving the house, he was greeted by a mob of five or six hundred persons, who had congregated outside to do him honour as he passed. From that night the riots may be said to have recommenced, and "Clifford and O. P." became the rallying cry of the party. The officious box-keeper became at the same time the object of the popular dislike, and the contempt with which the genius and fine qualities of Mr. Kemble would not permit them to regard him, was fastened upon his underling. So much ill-feeling was directed towards the latter, that at this time a return to the old prices, unaccompanied by his dismissal, would not have made the manager's peace with the pitites.

In the course of the few succeeding weeks, during which the riots continued with undiminished fury, O. P. medals were struck, and worn in great numbers in the theatre. A few of the ultra-zealous even wore them in the streets. A new fashion also came into favour for hats, waistcoats, and handkerchiefs, on which the mark, instead of the separate letters O and P, was a large O, with a small P in the middle of it: thus,

```
XXXXXXXX
X          X
X    XXX   X
X    X X   X
X    XXX   X
X    X     X
X    X     X
X          X
XXXXXXXX
```

The managers, seeing that Mr. Clifford was so identified with the rioters, determined to make him responsible. An action was accordingly brought against him and other defendants in the Court of King's Bench. On the 20th of November, the Attorney-general moved, before Lord Ellenborough, for a rule to show cause why a criminal information should not be filed against Clifford for unlawfully conspiring with certain others to intimidate the proprietors of Covent-Garden Theatre, and force them, to their loss and detriment, to lower their prices of admission. The rule was granted, and an early day fixed for the trial. In the mean time, these proceedings kept up the acerbity of the O. P.s, and every night at the fall of the curtain, three groans were given for John Kemble and three cheers for John Bull.

It was during this year that the national Jubilee was celebrated, in honour of tile fiftieth year of the reign of George III. When the riots had reached their fiftieth night, the O. P.s also determined to have a jubilee. All their previous efforts in the way of roaring, great as they were, were this night outdone, and would have continued long after "the wee short hour," had not the managers wisely put the extinguisher upon them and the lights about eleven o'clock.

Pending the criminal prosecution against himself, Mr. Clifford brought an action for false imprisonment against Brandon. The cause was fixed for trial in the Court of Common Pleas, on the 5th of December, before Lord Chief-Justice Mansfield. From an early hour in the morning all the avenues leading to the court were thronged with an eager multitude; all London was in anxiety for the resuit. So dense was the crowd, that counsel found the greatest difficulty in making their way into court. Mr. Sergeant Best was retained on the part of the plaintiff, and Mr. Sergeant Shepherd for the defence. The defendant put two pleas upon the record; first, that he was not guilty, and secondly, that he was justified. Sergeant Best, in stating the plaintiff's case, blamed the managers for all the disturbances that had taken place, and contended that his client, in affixing the letters O. P. to his hat, was not guilty of any offence. Even if he had joined in the noises, which he had not, his so doing would not subject him to the penalties for rioting. Several witnesses were then called to prove the capture of Mr. Clifford, the hearing of the case before the magistrate at Bow Street, and his ultimate dismissal. Sergeant Shepherd was heard at great length on the other side, and contended that his client was perfectly justified in taking into custody a man who was inciting others to commit a breach of the peace.

The Lord Chief-Justice summed up, with an evident bias in favour of the defendant. He said an undue apprehension of the rights of an audience had got abroad. Even supposing the object of the rioters to be fair and legal, they were not authorized to carry it by unfair means. In order to constitute a riot, it was not necessary that personal violence should be committed, and it seemed to him that the defendant had not acted in an improper manner in giving into custody a person who, by the display of a symbol, was encouraging others to commit a riot.

The jury retired to consider their verdict. The crowd without and within the court awaited the result in feverish suspense. Half an hour elapsed, when the jury returned with a verdict for the plaintiff -- Damages, five pounds. The satisfaction of the spectators was evident upon their countenances, that of the judge expressed the contrary feeling. Turning to the foreman of the jury, his Lordship asked upon which of the two points referred to them, namely, the broad question, whether a riot had been committed, and, if committed, whether the plaintiff had participated in it, they had found their verdict?

The foreman stated, that they were all of opinion generally that the plaintiff had been illegally arrested. This vague answer did not satisfy his Lordship, and he repeated his question. He could not, however, obtain a more satisfactory reply. Evidently vexed at what he deemed the obtuseness or partiality of the jury, he turned to the bar, and said, that a spirit of a mischievous and destructive nature was abroad, which, if not repressed, threatened awful consequences. The country would be lost, he said, and the government overturned, if such a spirit were encouraged; it was impossible it could end in good. Time, the destroyer and fulfiller of predictions, has proved that his Lordship was a false prophet. The harmless O. P. war has been productive of no such dire results.

It was to be expected that after this triumph, the war in the pit would rage with redoubled acrimony. A riot beginning at half-price would not satisfy the excited feelings of the O. P.s on the night of such a victory. Long before the curtain drew up, the house was filled with them, and several placards were exhibited, which the constables and friends of the managers strove, as usual, to tear into shreds. One of them, which met this fate, was inscribed, "Success to O.P.! A British jury for ever!" It was soon replaced by another of a similar purport. It is needless to detail the uproar that ensued; the jumping, the fighting, the roaring, and the howling. For nine nights more the same system was continued; but the end was at hand.

On the 14th a grand dinner was given at the Crown and Anchor tavern, to celebrate the victory of Mr. Clifford. "The reprobators of managerial insolence," as they called themselves, attended in considerable numbers; and Mr. Clifford was voted to the chair. The cloth had been removed, and a few speeches made, when the company were surprised by a message that their arch-enemy himself solicited the honour of an audience. It was some time ere they could believe that Mr. Kemble had ventured to such a place. After some parley the manager was admitted, and a conference was held. A treaty was ultimately signed and sealed, which put an end to the long-contested wars of O.P., and restored peace to the drama.

All this time the disturbance proceeded at the theatre with its usual spirit. It was now the sixty-sixth night of its continuance, and the rioters were still untired -- still determined to resist to the last. In the midst of it a gentleman arrived from the Crown and Anchor, and announced to the pit that Mr. Kemble had attended the dinner, and had yielded at last to the demand of the public. He stated, that it had been agreed upon between him and the Committee for defending the persons under prosecution, that the boxes should remain at the advanced price; that the pit should be reduced to three shillings and sixpence; that the private boxes should be done away with; and that all prosecutions, on both sides, should be immediately stayed. This announcement was received with deafening cheers. As soon as the first burst of enthusiasm was over, the O. P.s became anxious for a confirmation of the intelligence, and commenced a loud call for Mr. Kemble. He had not then returned from the Crown and Anchor; but of this the pitites were not aware, and for nearly half an hour they kept up a most excruciating din. At length the great actor made his appearance, in his walking dress, with his cane in hand, as he had left the tavern. It was a long time before he could obtain silence. He apologized in the most respectful terms for appearing before them in such unbecoming costume, which was caused solely by his ignorance that he should have to appear before them that night. After announcing, as well as occasional interruptions would allow, the terms that had been agreed upon, he added, "In order that no trace or recollection of the past differences, which had unhappily prevailed so long, should remain, he was instructed by the proprietors to say, that they most sincerely lamented the course that had been pursued, and engaged that, on their parts, all legal proceedings should forthwith be put a stop to." The cheering which greeted this speech was interrupted at the close by loud cries from the pit of "Dismiss Brandon," while one or two exclaimed, "We want old prices generally, -- six shillings for the boxes." After an ineffectual attempt to address them again upon this point, Mr. Kemble made respectful and repeated obeisances, and withdrew. The noises still continued, until Munden stood forward, leading by the hand the humbled box-keeper, contrition in his looks, and in his hands a written apology, which he endeavoured to read. The uproar was increased threefold by his presence, and, amid cries of "We won't hear him!" "Where's his master?" he was obliged to retire. Mr. Harris, the son of Kemble's co-manager, afterwards endeavoured to propitiate the audience in his favour; but it was of no avail; nothing less than his dismissal would satisfy the offended majesty of the pit. Amid this uproar the curtain finally fell, and the O. P. dance was danced for the last time within the walls of Covent Garden.

On the following night it was announced that Brandon had resigned his situation. This turned the tide of popular ill-will. The performances were "The Wheel of Fortune," and an afterpiece. The house was crowded to excess; a desire to be pleased was manifest on every countenance, and when Mr. Kemble, who took his favourite character of Penruddock, appeared upon the stage, he was greeted with the most vehement applause. The noises ceased entirely, and the symbols of opposition disappeared. The audience, hushed into attention, gave vent to no sounds but those of admiration for the genius of the actor. When, in the course of his part, he repeated the words, "So! I am in London again !" the aptness of the expression to the circumstances of the night, was felt by all present, and acknowledged by a round of boisterous and thrice repeated cheering. It was a triumphant scene for Mr. Kemble after his long annoyances. He had achieved a double victory. He had, not only as a manager, soothed the obstinate opposition of the play-goers, but as an actor he had forced from one of the largest audiences he had ever beheld, approbation more cordial and unanimous than he had ever enjoyed before. The popular favour not only turned towards him; it embraced everybody connected with the theatre, except the poor victim, Brandon. Most of the favourite actors were called before the curtain to make their bow, and receive the acclamations of the pit. At the close of the performances, a few individuals, implacable and stubborn, got up a feeble cry of "Old prices for the boxes;" but they were quickly silenced by the reiterated cheers of the majority, or by cries of "Turn them out!" A placard, the last of its race, was at the same time exhibited in the front of the pit, bearing, in large letters, the words "We are satisfied."

Thus ended the famous wars of O. P., which, for a period of nearly three months, had kept the metropolis in an uproar. And after all, what was the grand result? As if the whole proceeding had been a parody upon the more destructive, but scarcely more sensible wars recorded in history, it was commenced in injustice, carried on in bitterness of spirit, and ended, like the labour of the mountain, in a mouse. The abatement of sixpence in the price of admission to the pit, and the dismissal of an unfortunate servant, whose only fault was too much zeal in the service of his employers, -- such were the grand victories of the O. P.'s.

The Thugs, or Phansigars

Orribili favelle -- parole di dolor.--*Dante.*

Among the black deeds which Superstition has imposed as duties upon her wretched votaries, none are more horrible than the practices of the murderers, who, under the name of Thugs, or Phansigars, have so long been the scourge of India. For ages they have pursued their dark and dreadful calling, moulding assassination into a science, or extolling it as a virtue, worthy only to be practised by a race favoured of Heaven. Of late years this atrocious delusion has excited much attention, both in this country and in India; an attention which, it is to be hoped, will speedily lead to the uprooting of a doctrine so revolting and anti-human. Although the British Government has extended over Hindostan for so long a period, it does not appear that Europeans even suspected the existence of this mysterious sect until the commencement of the present century. In the year 1807, a gang of Thugs, laden with the plunder of murdered travellers, was accidentally discovered. The inquiries then set on foot revealed to the astonished Government a system of iniquity unparalleled in the history of man. Subsequent investigation extended the knowledge; and by throwing light upon the peculiar habits of the murderers, explained the reason why their crimes had remained so long undiscovered. In the following pages will be found an epitome of all the information which has reached Europe concerning them, derived principally from Dr. Sherwood's treatise upon the subject, published in 1816, and the still more valuable and more recent work of Mr. Sleeman, entitled the "Ramaseeana; or, Vocabulary of the peculiar Language of the Thugs."

The followers of this sect are called Thugs, or T'hugs, and their profession Thuggee. In the south of India they are called Phansigars: the former word signifying "a deceiver;" and the latter, "a strangler." They are both singularly appropriate. The profession of Thuggee is hereditary, and embraces, it is supposed, in every part of India, a body of at least ten thousand individuals, trained to murder from their childhood; carrying it on in secret and in silence, yet glorying in it, and holding the practice of it higher than any earthly honour. During the winter months, they usually follow some reputable calling, to elude suspicion; and in the summer, they set out in gangs over all the roads of India, to plunder and destroy. These gangs generally contain from ten to forty Thugs, and sometimes as many as two hundred. Each strangler is provided with a noose, to despatch the unfortunate victim, as the Thugs make it a point never to cause death by any other means. When the gangs are very large, they divide into smaller bodies; and each taking a different route, they arrive at the same general place of rendezvous to divide the spoil. They sometimes travel in the disguise of respectable traders; sometimes as sepoys or native soldiers; and at others, as government officers. If they chance to fall in with an unprotected wayfarer, his fate is certain. One Thug approaches him from behind, and throws the end of a sash round his neck; the other end is seized by a second at the same instant, crossed behind the neck, and drawn tightly, while with their other hand the two Thugs thrust his head forward to expedite the strangulation: a third Thug seizes the traveller by the legs at the same moment, and he is thrown to the ground, a corpse before he reaches it.

But solitary travellers are not the prey they are anxious to seek. A wealthy caravan of forty or fifty individuals has not unfrequently been destroyed by them; not one soul being permitted to escape. Indeed, there is hardly an instance upon record of any one's escape from their hands, so surely are their measures taken, and so well do they calculate beforehand all the risks and difficulties of the undertaking. Each individual of the gang has his peculiar duty allotted to him. Upon-approaching a town, or serai, two or three, known as the Soothaes, or "inveiglers," are sent in advance to ascertain if any travellers are there; to learn, if possible, the amount of money or merchandize they carry with them, their hours of starting in the morning, or any other particulars that may be of use. If they can, they enter into conversation with them, pretend to be travelling to the same place, and propose, for mutual security, to travel with them. This intelligence is duly communicated to the remainder of the gang. The place usually chosen for the murder is some lonely part of the road in the vicinity of a jungle, and the time, just before dusk. At given signals, understood only by themselves, the scouts of the party station themselves in the front, in the rear, and on each side, to guard against surprise. A strangler and assistant strangler, called Bhurtote and Shamshea, place themselves, the one on the right, and the other on the left of the victim, without exciting his suspicion. At another signal the noose is twisted, drawn tightly by a strong hand at each extremity, and the traveller, in a few seconds, hurried into eternity. Ten, twelve, twenty, and in some instances, sixty persons have been thus despatched at the same moment. Should any victim, by a rare chance, escape their hands, he falls into those of the scouts who are stationed within hearing, who run upon him and soon overpower him.

Their next care is to dispose of the bodies. So cautious are they to prevent detection, that they usually break all the joints to hasten decomposition. They then cut open the body to prevent it swelling in the grave and causing fissures in the soil above, by which means the jackals might be attracted to the spot, and thereby lead to discovery. When obliged to bury the body in a frequented district, they kindle a fire over the grave to obliterate the traces of the newly turned earth. Sometimes the grave-diggers of the party, whose office, like that of all the rest, is hereditary, are despatched to make the graves in the morning at some distant spot, by which it is known the travellers will pass. The stranglers, in the mean time, journey quietly with their victims, conversing with them in the most friendly manner. Towards nightfall they approach the spot selected for their murder; the signal is given, and they fall into the graves that have been ready for them since day-break. On one occasion, related by Captain Sleeman, a party of fifty-nine people, consisting of fifty-two men and seven women, were thus simultaneously strangled, and thrown into the graves prepared for them in the morning. Some of these travellers were on horseback and well armed, but the Thugs, who appear to have been upwards of two hundred in a gang, had provided against all risk of failure. The only one left alive of all that numerous party, was an infant four years old, who was afterwards initiated into all the mysteries of Thuggee.

If they cannot find a convenient opportunity for disposing of the bodies, they carry them for many miles, until they come to a spot secure from intrusion, and to a soil adapted to receive them. If fear of putrefaction admonishes them to use despatch, they set up a large screen or tent, as other travellers do, and bury the body within the enclosure, pretending, if inquiries are made, that their women are within. But this only happens when they fall in with a victim unexpectedly. In murders which they have planned previously, the finding of a place of sepulture is never left to hazard.

Travellers who have the misfortune to lodge in the same choultry or hostelry, as the Thugs, are often murdered during the night. It is either against their creed to destroy a sleeper, or they find a difficulty in placing the noose round the neck of a person in a recumbent position. When this is the case, the slumberer is suddenly aroused by the alarm of a snake or a scorpion. He starts to his feet, and finds the fatal sash around his neck. -- He never escapes.

In addition to these Thugs who frequent the highways, there are others, who infest the rivers, and are called Pungoos. They do not differ in creed, but only in a few of their customs, from their brethren on shore. They go up and down the rivers in their own boats, pretending to be travellers of consequence, or pilgrims, proceeding to, or returning from Benares, Allahabad, or other sacred places. The boatmen, who are also Thugs, are not different in appearance from the ordinary boatmen on the river. The artifices used to entice victims on board are precisely similar to those employed by the highway Thugs. They send out their "inveiglers" to scrape acquaintance with travellers, and find out the direction in which they are journeying. They always pretend to be bound for the same place, and vaunt the superior accommodation of the boat by which they are going. The travellers fall into the snare, are led to the Thug captain, who very often, to allay suspicion, demurs to take them, but eventually agrees for a moderate sum. The boat strikes off into the middle of the stream; the victims are amused and kept in conversation for hours by their insidious foes, until three taps are given on the deck above. This is a signal from the Thugs on the look-out that the coast is clear. In an instant the fatal noose is ready, and the travellers are no more. The bodies are then thrown, warm and palpitating, into the river, from a hole in the side of the boat, contrived expressly for the purpose.

A river Thug, who was apprehended, turned approver, to save his own life, and gave the following evidence relative to the practices of his fraternity: -- "We embarked at Rajmahul. The travellers sat on one side of the boat, and the Thugs on the other; while we three (himself and two "stranglers,") were placed in the stern, the Thugs on our left, and the travellers on our right. Some of the Thugs, dressed as boatmen, were above deck, and others walking along the bank of the river, and pulling the boat by the joon, or rope, and all, at the same time, on the look-out. We came up with a gentleman's pinnace and two baggage-boats, and were obliged to stop, and let them go on. The travellers seemed anxious; but were quieted by being told that the men at the rope were tired, and must take some refreshment. They pulled out something, and began to eat; and when the pinnace had got on a good way, they resumed their work, and our boat proceeded. It was now afternoon; and, when a signal was given above, that all was clear, the five Thugs who sat opposite the travellers sprang in upon them, and, with the aid of others, strangled them. Having done this, they broke their spinal bones, and then threw them out of a hole made at the side, into the river, and kept on their course; the boat being all this time pulled along by the men on the bank."

That such atrocities as these should have been carried on for nearly two centuries without exciting the attention of the British Government, seems incredible. But our wonder will be diminished when we reflect upon the extreme caution of the Thugs, and the ordinary dangers of travelling in India. The Thugs never murder a man near his own home, and they never dispose of their booty near the scene of the murder. They also pay, in common with other and less atrocious robbers, a portion of their gains to the Polygars, or native authorities of the districts in which they reside, to secure protection. The friends and relatives of the victims, perhaps a thousand miles off, never surmise their fate till a period has elapsed when all inquiry would be fruitless, or, at least, extremely difficult. They have no clue to the assassins, and very often impute to the wild beasts of the jungles the slaughter committed by that wilder beast, man.

There are several gradations through which every member of the fraternity must regularly pass before he arrives at the high office of a Bhurtote, or strangler. He is first employed as a scout -- then as a sexton -- then as a Shumseea, or holder of hands, and lastly as a Bhurtote. When a man who is not of Thug lineage, or who has not been brought up from his infancy among them, wishes to become a strangler, he solicits the oldest, and most pious and experienced Thug, to take him under his protection and make him his disciple; and under his guidance he is regularly initiated. When he has acquired sufficient experience in the lower ranks of the profession, he applies to his Gooroo, or preceptor, to give the finishing grace to his education, and make a strangler of him. An opportunity is found when a solitary traveller is to be murdered; and the tyro, with his preceptor, having seen that the proposed victim is asleep, and in safe keeping till their return, proceed to a neighbouring field and perform several religious ceremonies, accompanied by three or four of the oldest and steadiest members of the gang. The Gooroo first offers up a prayer to the goddess, saying, "Oh, Kalee! Kun-kalee! Bhud-kalee! Oh, Kalee! Maha-kalee!

Calkutta Walee! if it seems fit to thee that the traveller now at our lodging should die by the hands of this thy slave, vouchsafe us thy good omen." They then sit down and watch for the good omen; and if they receive it within half an hour, conclude that their goddess is favourable to the claims of the new candidate for admission. If they have a bad omen, or no omen at all, some other Thug must put the traveller to death, and the aspirant must wait a more favourable opportunity, purifying himself in the mean time by prayer and humiliation for the favour of the goddess. If the good omen has been obtained, they return to their quarters; and the Gooroo takes a handkerchief and, turning his face to the west, ties a knot at one end of it, inserting a rupee, or other piece of silver. This knot is called the goor khat, or holy knot, and no man who has not been properly ordained is allowed to tie it. The aspirant receives it reverently in his right hand from his Gooroo, and stands over the sleeping victim, with a Shumseea, or holder of hands, at his side. The traveller is aroused, the handkerchief is passed around his neck, and, at a signal from the Gooroo, is drawn tight till the victim is strangled; the Shumseea holding his hands to prevent his making any resistance. The work being now completed, the Bhurtote (no longer an aspirant, but an admitted member) bows down reverently in the dust before his Gooroo, and touches his feet with both his hands, and afterwards performs the same respect to his relatives and friends who have assembled to witness the solemn ceremony. He then waits for another favourable omen, when he unties the knot and takes out the rupee, which he gives to his Gooroo, with any other silver which he may have about him. The Gooroo adds some of his own money, with which he purchases what they call goor, or consecrated sugar, when a solemn sacrifice is performed, to which all the gang are invited. The relationship between the Gooroo and his disciple is accounted the most holy that can be formed, and subsists to the latest period of life. A Thug may betray his father, but never his Gooroo.

Dark and forbidding as is the picture already drawn, it will become still darker and more repulsive, when we consider the motives which prompt these men to systematic murder. Horrible as their practices would be, if love of plunder alone incited them, it is infinitely more horrible to reflect that the idea of duty and religion is joined to the hope of gain, in making them the scourges of their fellows. If plunder were their sole object, there would be reason to hope, that when a member of the brotherhood grew rich, he would rest from his infernal toils; but the dismal superstition which he cherishes tells him never to desist. He was sent into the world to be a slayer of men, and he religiously works out his destiny. As religiously he educates his children to pursue the same career, instilling into their minds, at the earliest age, that Thuggee is the noblest profession a man can follow, and that the dark goddess they worship will always provide rich travellers for her zealous devotees.

The following is the wild and startling legend upon which the Thugs found the divine origin of their sect. They believe that, in the earliest ages of the world, a gigantic demon infested the earth, and devoured mankind as soon as they were created. He was of so tall a stature, that when he strode through the most unfathomable depths of the great sea, the waves, even in tempest, could not reach above his middle. His insatiable appetite for human flesh almost unpeopled the world, until Bhawanee, Kalee, or Davee, the goddess of the Thugs, determined to save mankind by the destruction of the monster. Nerving herself for the encounter, she armed herself with an immense sword; and, meeting with the demon, she ran him through the body. His blood flowed in torrents as he fell dead at her feet; but from every drop there sprang up another monster, as rapacious and as terrible as the first. Again the goddess upraised her massive sword, and hewed down the hellish brood by hundreds; but the more she slew, the more numerous they became. Every drop of their blood generated a demon; and, although the goddess endeavoured to lap up the blood ere it sprang into life, they increased upon her so rapidly, that the labour of killing became too great for endurance. The perspiration rolled down her arms in large drops, and she was compelled to think of some other mode of exterminating them. In this emergency, she created two men out of the perspiration of her body, to whom she confided the holy task of delivering the earth from the monsters. To each of the men she gave a handkerchief, and showed them how to kill without shedding blood. From her they learned to tie the fatal noose; and they became, under her tuition, such

150

expert stranglers, that, in a very short space of time, the race of demons became extinct.

When there were no more to slay, the two men sought the great goddess, in order to return the handkerchiefs. The grateful Bhawanee desired that they would retain them, as memorials of their heroic deeds; and in order that they might never lose the dexterity that they had acquired in using them, she commanded that, from thenceforward, they should strangle men. These were the two first Thugs, and from them the whole race have descended. To the early Thugs the goddess was more direct in her favours, than she has been to their successors. At first, she undertook to bury the bodies of all the men they slew and plundered, upon the condition that they should never look back to see what she was doing. The command was religiously observed for many ages, and the Thugs relied with implicit faith upon the promise of Bhawanee; but as men became more corrupt, the ungovernable curiosity of a young Thug offended the goddess, and led to the withdrawal of a portion of her favour. This youth, burning with a desire to see how she made her graves, looked back, and beheld her in the act, not of burying, but of devouring, the body of a man just strangled. Half of the still palpitating remains was dangling over her lips. She was so highly displeased that she condemned the Thugs, from that time forward, to bury their victims themselves. Another account states that the goddess was merely tossing the body in the air; and that, being naked, her anger was aggravated by the gaze of mortal eyes upon her charms. Before taking a final leave of her devotees, she presented them with one of her teeth for a pickaxe, one of her ribs for a knife, and the hem of her garment for a noose. She has not since appeared to human eyes.

The original tooth having been lost in the lapse of ages, new pickaxes have been constructed, with great care and many ceremonies, by each considerable gang of Thugs, to be used in making the graves of strangled travellers. The pickaxe is looked upon with the utmost veneration by the tribe. A short account of the process of making it, and the rites performed, may be interesting, as showing still further their gloomy superstition. In the first place, it is necessary to fix upon a lucky day. The chief Thug then instructs a smith to forge the holy instrument: no other eye is permitted to see the operation. The smith must engage in no other occupation until it is completed, and the chief Thug never quits his side during the process. When the instrument is formed, it becomes necessary to consecrate it to the especial service of Bhawnee. Another lucky day is chosen for this ceremony, care being had in the mean time that the shadow of no earthly thing fall upon the pickaxe, as its efficacy would be for ever destroyed. A learned Thug then sits down; and turning his face to the west, receives the pickaxe in a brass dish. After muttering some incantation, he throws it into a pit already prepared for it, where it is washed in clear water. It is then taken out, and washed again three times; the first time in sugar and water, the second in sour milk, and the third in spirits. It is then dried, and marked from the head to the point with seven red spots. This is the first part of the ceremony: the second consists in its purification by fire. The pickaxe is again placed upon the brass dish, along with a cocoa-nut, some sugar, cloves, white sandal-wood, and other articles. A fire of the mango tree, mixed with dried cow-dung, is then kindled; and the officiating Thug, taking the pickaxe with both hands, passes it seven times through the flames.

It now remains to be ascertained whether the goddess is favourable to her followers. For this purpose, the cocoa-nut is taken from the dish and placed upon the ground. The officiating Thug, turning to the spectators, and holding the axe uplifted, asks, "Shall I strike?" Assent being given, he strikes the nut with the but-end of the axe, exclaiming, "All hail! mighty Davee! great mother of us all!" The spectators respond, "All hail! mighty Davee! and prosper thy children, the Thugs!"

If the nut is severed at the first blow, the goddess is favourable; if not, she is unpropitious: all their labour is thrown away, and the ceremony must be repeated upon some more fitting occasion. But if the sign be favourable, the axe is tied carefully in a white cloth and turned towards the west, all the

151

spectators prostrating themselves before it. It is then buried in the earth, with its point turned in the direction the gang wishes to take on their approaching expedition. If the goddess desires to warn them that they will be unsuccessful, or that they have not chosen the right track, the Thugs believe that the point of the axe will veer round, and point to the better way. During an expedition, it is entrusted to the most prudent and exemplary Thug of the party: it is his care to hold it fast. If by any chance he should let it fall, consternation spreads through the gang: the goddess is thought to be offended; the enterprise is at once abandoned; and the Thugs return home in humiliation and sorrow, to sacrifice to their gloomy deity, and win back her estranged favour. So great is the reverence in which they hold the sacred axe, that a Thug will never break an oath that he has taken upon it. He fears that, should he perjure himself, his neck would be so twisted by the offended Bhawanee as to make his face turn to his back; and that, in the course of a few days, he would expire in the most excruciating agonies.

The Thugs are diligent observers of signs and omens. No expedition is ever undertaken before the auspices are solemnly taken. Upon this subject Captain Sleeman says, "Even the most sensible approvers, who have been with me for many years, as well Hindoos as Mussulmans, believe that their good or ill success depended upon the skill with which the omens were discovered and interpreted, and the strictness with which they were observed and obeyed. One of the old Sindouse stock told me, in presence of twelve others, from Hydrabad, Behar, the Dooah, Oude, Rajpootana, and Bundelcund, that, had they not attended to these omens, they never could have thrived as they did. In ordinary cases of murder, other men seldom escaped punishment, while they and their families had, for ten generations, thrived, although they had murdered hundreds of people. 'This,' said the Thug,' could never have been the case had we not attended to omens, and had not omens been intended for us. There were always signs around us to guide us to rich booty, and warn us of danger, had we been always wise enough to discern them and religious enough to attend to them.' Every Thug present concurred with him from his soul."

A Thug, of polished manners and great eloquence, being asked by a native gentleman, in the presence of Captain Sleeman, whether he never felt compunction in murdering innocent people, replied with a smile that he did not. "Does any man," said he, "feel compunction in following his trade? and are not all our trades assigned us by Providence?" He was then asked how many people he had killed with his own hands in the course of his life? "I have killed none," was the reply. "What! and have you not been describing a number of murders in which you were concerned?" "True; but do you suppose that I committed them? Is any man killed by man's killing? Is it not the hand of God that kills, and are we not the mere instruments in the hands of God?"

Upon another occasion, Sahib, an approver, being asked if he had never felt any pity or compunction at murdering old men or young children, or persons with whom he had sat and conversed, and who had told him, perchance, of their private affairs -- their hopes and their fears, their wives and their little ones? replied unhesi- tatingly that he never did. From the time that the omens were favourable, the Thugs considered all the travellers they met as victims thrown into their hands by their divinity to be killed. The Thugs were the mere instruments in the hands of Bhawanee to destroy them. "If we did not kill them," said Sahib, "the goddess would never again be propitious to us, and we and our families would be involved in misery and want. If we see or hear a bad omen, it is the order of the goddess not to kill the travellers we are in pursuit of, and we dare not disobey."

As soon as an expedition has been planned, the goddess is consulted. On the day chosen for starting, which is never during the unlucky months of July, September, and December, nor on a Wednesday or Thursday; the chief Thug of the party fills a brass jug with water, which he carries in his right hand by his side. With his left, he holds upon his breast the sacred pickaxe, wrapped carefully in a white cloth, along with five knots of turmeric, two copper, and one silver coin. He then moves slowly on, followed by the whole of the gang, to some field or retired place, where halting, with his countenance turned in the direction they wish to pursue, he lifts up his eyes to heaven, saying, "Great goddess! universal mother! if this, our meditated expedition, be fitting in thy sight, vouchsafe to help us, and give us the signs of thy approbation." All the Thugs present solemnly repeat the prayer after their leader, and wait in silence for the omen. If within half an hour they see Pilhaoo, or good omen on the left, it signifies that the goddess has taken them by the left hand to lead them on; if they see the Thibaoo, or omen on the right, it signifies that she has taken them by the right hand also. The leader then places the brazen pitcher on the ground and sits down beside it, with his face turned in the same direction for seven hours, during which time his followers make all the necessary preparations for the journey. If, during this interval, no unfavourable signs are observed, the expedition advances slowly, until it arrives at the bank of the nearest stream, when they all sit down and eat of the goor, or consecrated sugar. Any evil omens that are perceived after this ceremony may be averted by sacrifices; but any evil omens before, would at once put an end to the expedition.

Among the evil omens are the following: -- If the brazen pitcher drops from the hand of the Jemadar or leader, it threatens great evil either to him or to the gang -- sometimes to both. If they meet a funeral procession, a blind man, a lame man, an oil-vender, a carpenter, a potter, or a dancing-master, the expedition will be dangerous. In like manner it is unlucky to sneeze, to meet a woman with an empty pail, a couple of jackals, or a hare. The crossing of their path by the latter is considered peculiarly inauspicious. Its cry at night on the left is sometimes a good omen, but if they hear it on the right it is very bad; a warning sent to them from Bhawanee that there is danger if they kill. Should they disregard this warning, and led on by the hope of gain, strangle any traveller, they would either find no booty on him, or such booty as would eventually lead to the ruin and dispersion of the gang. Bhawanee would be wroth with her children; and causing them to perish in the jungle, would send the hares to drink water out of their skulls.

The good omens are quite as numerous as the evil. It promises a fortunate expedition, if, on the first day, they pass through a village where there is a fair. It is also deemed fortunate, if they hear wailing for the dead in any village but their own. To meet a woman with a pitcher full of water upon her head, bodes a prosperous journey and a safe return. The omen is still more favourable if she be in a state of pregnancy. It is said of the Thugs of the Jumaldehee and Lodaha tribes, that they always make the youngest Thug of the party kick the body of the first person they strangle, five times on the back, thinking that it will bring them good luck. This practice, however, is not general. If they hear an ass bray on the left at the commencement of an expedition, and an another soon afterwards on the right, they believe that they shall be supereminently successful, that they shall strangle a multitude of travellers, and find great booty.

After every murder a solemn sacrifice, called the Tuponee, is performed by all the gang. The goor, or consecrated sugar, is placed upon a large cloth or blanket, which is spread upon the grass. Beside it is deposited the sacred pickaxe, and a piece of silver for an offering. The Jemadar, or chief of the party, together with all the oldest and most prudent Thugs, take their places upon the cloth, and turn their faces to the west. Those inferior Thugs who cannot find room upon the privileged cloth, sit round as close to it as possible. A pit is then dug, into which the Jemadar pours a small quantity of the goor, praying at the same time that the goddess will always reward her followers with abundant spoils. All the Thugs repeat the prayer after him. He then sprinkles water upon the pickaxe, and puts a little of the goor upon the head of every one who has obtained a seat beside him on the cloth. A short pause ensues, when the signal for strangling is given, as if a murder were actually about to be committed, and each Thug eats his goor in solemn silence. So powerful is the impression made upon their imagination by this ceremony, that it almost drives them frantic with enthusiasm. Captain Sleeman relates, that when he reproached a Thug for his share in a murder of great atrocity, and asked him whether he never felt pity; the man replied, "We all feel pity sometimes; but the goor of the Tuponee changes our nature; it would change the nature of a horse. Let any man once taste of that goor, and he will be a Thug, though he know all the trades and have all the wealth in the world. I never was in want of food; my mother's family was opulent, and her relations high in office. I have been high in office myself, and became so great a favourite wherever I went that I was sure of promotion; yet I was always miserable when absent from my gang, and obliged to return to Thuggee. My father made me taste of that fatal goor, when I was yet a mere boy; and if I were to live a thousand years I should never be.able to follow any other trade."

The possession of wealth, station in society, and the esteem of his fellows, could not keep this man from murder. From his extraordinary confession we may judge of the extreme difficulty of exterminating a sect who are impelled to their horrid practises, not only by the motives of self-interest which govern mankind in general, but by a fanaticism which fills up the measure of their whole existence. Even severity seems thrown away upon the followers of this brutalizing creed. To them, punishment is no example; they have no sympathy for a brother Thug who is hung at his own door by the British Government, nor have they any dread of his fate. Their invariable idea is, that their goddess only suffers those Thugs to fall into the hands of the law, who have contravened the peculiar observances of Thuggee, and who have neglected the omens she sent them for their guidance.

To their neglect of the warnings of the goddess they attribute all the reverses which have of late years befallen their sect. It is expressly forbidden, in the creed of the old Thugs, to murder women or cripples. The modern Thugs have become unscrupulous upon this point, murdering women, and even children, with unrelenting barbarity. Captain Sleeman reports several conversations upon this subject, which he held at different times with Thugs, who had been taken prisoners, or who had turned approvers. One of them, named Zolfukar, said, in reply to the Captain, who accused him of murdering women, "Yes, and was not the greater part of Feringeea's and my gang seized, after we had murdered the two women and the little girl, at Manora, in 1830? and were we not ourselves both seized soon after? How could we survive things like that? Our ancestors never did such things." Lalmun, another Thug, in reply to a similar question, said, "Most of our misfortunes have come upon us for the murder of women. We all knew that they would come upon us some day, for this and other great sins. We were often admonished, but we did not take warning; and we deserve our fates." In speaking of the supposed protection which their goddess had extended to them in former times, Zolfukar said: -- "Ah! we had some regard for religion then! We have lost it since. All kinds of men have been made Thugs, and all classes of people murdered, without distinction; and little attention has been paid to omens. How, after this, could we think to escape? * * * * Davee never forsook us till we neglected her!"

It might be imagined that men who spoke in this manner of the anger of the goddess, and who, even in custody, showed so much veneration for their unhappy calling, would hesitate before they turned informers, and laid bare the secrets and exposed the haunts of their fellows: -- among the more civilized ruffians of Europe, we often find the one chivalrous trait of character, which makes them scorn a reward that must be earned by the blood of their accomplices: but in India there is no honour among thieves. When the approvers are asked, if they, who still believe in the power of the terrible goddess Davee, are not afraid to incur her displeasure by informing of their fellows, they reply, that Davee has done her worst in abandoning them. She can inflict no severer punishment, and therefore gives herself no further concern about her degenerate children. This cowardly doctrine is, however, of advantage to the Government that seeks to put an end to the sect, and has thrown a light upon their practices, which could never have been obtained from other sources.

Another branch of the Thug abomination has more recently been discovered by the indefatigable Captain Sleeman. The followers of this sect are called MEGPUNNAS, and they murder travellers, not to rob them of their wealth, but of their children, whom they afterwards sell into slavery. They entertain the same religious opinions as the Thugs, and have carried on their hideous practices, and entertained their dismal superstition, for about a dozen years with impunity. The report of Captain Sleeman states, that the crime prevails almost exclusively in Delhi and the native principalities, or Rajpootana of Ulwar and Bhurtpore; and that it first spread extensively after the siege of Bhurtpore in 1826.

The original Thugs never or rarely travel with their wives; but the Megpunnas invariably take their families with them, the women and children being used to inveigle the victims. Poor travellers are always chosen by the Megpunnas as the objects of their murderous traffic. The females and children are sent on in advance to make acquaintance with emigrants or beggars on the road, travelling with their families, whom they entice to pass the night in some secluded place, where they are afterwards set upon by the men, and strangled. The women take care of the children. Such of them as are beautiful are sold at a high price to the brothels of Delhi, or other large cities; while the boys and ill-favoured girls are sold for servants at a more moderate rate. These murders are perpetrated perhaps five hundred miles from the homes of the unfortunate victims; and the children thus obtained, deprived of all their relatives, are never inquired after. Even should any of their kin be alive, they are too far off and too poor to institute inquiries. One of the members, on being questioned, said the Megpunnas made more money than the other Thugs; it was more profitable to kill poor people for the sake of their children, than rich people for their wealth. Megpunnaism is supposed by its votaries to be, like Thuggee, under the immediate protection of the great goddess Davee, or Kalee, whose favour is to be obtained before the commencement of every expedition, and whose omens, whether of good or evil, are to be diligently sought on all occasions. The first apostle to whom she communicated her commands for the formation of the new sect, and the rules and ordinances by which it was to be guided, was called Kheama Jemadar. He was considered so holy a man, that the Thugs and Megpunnas considered it an extreme felicity to gaze upon and touch him. At the moment of his arrest by the British authorities, a fire was raging in the village, and the inhabitants gathered round him and implored him to intercede with his god, that the flames might be extinguished. The Megpunna, says the tradition, stretched forth his hand to heaven, prayed, and the fire ceased immediately.

There now only remain to be considered the exertions that have been made to remove from the face of India this purulent and disgusting sore. From the year 1807 until 1826, the proceedings against Thuggee were not carried on with any extraordinary degree of vigour; but, in the latter year, the Government seems to have begun to act upon a settled determination to destroy it altogether. From 1826 to 1855, both included, there were committed to prison, in the various Presidencies, 1562 persons accused of this crime. Of these, 328 were hanged; 999 transported; 77 imprisoned for life; 71 imprisoned for shorter periods; 21 held to bail; and only 21 acquitted. Of the remainder, 31 died in prison, before they were brought to trial, 11 escaped, and 49 turned approvers.

One Feringeea, a Thug leader of great notoreity, was delivered up to justice in the year 1830, in consequence of the reward of five hundred rupees offered for his apprehension by the Government. He was brought before Captain Sleeman, at Sangir, in the December of that year, and offered, if his life were spared, to give such information as would lead to the arrest of several extensive gangs which had carried on their murderous practices undetected for several years. He mentioned the place of rendezvous, for the following February, of some well organized gangs, who were to proceed into Guzerat and Candeish. Captain Sleeman appeared to doubt his information; but accompanied the Thug to a mango grove, two stages from Sangir, on the road to Seronage. They reached this place in the evening, and in the morning Feringeea pointed out three places in which he and his gang had, at different intervals, buried the bodies of three parties of travellers whom they had murdered. The sward had grown over all the spots, and not the slightest traces were to be seen that it had ever been disturbed. Under the sod of Captain Sleeman's tent were found the bodies of the first party, consisting of a pundit and his six attendants, murdered in 1818. Another party of five, murdered in 1824, were under the ground at the place where the Captain's horses had been tied up for the night; and four Brahmin carriers of the Ganges water, with a woman, were buried under his sleeping tent. Before the ground was moved, Captain Sleeman expressed some doubts; but Feringeea, after looking at the position of some neighbouring trees, said be would risk his life on the accuracy of his remembrance. The workmen dug five feet without discovering the bodies; but they were at length found a little beyond that depth, exactly as the Thug had described them. With this proof of his knowledge of the haunts of his brethren, Feringeea was promised his liberty and pardon if he would aid in bringing to justice the many large gangs to which he had belonged, and which were still prowling over the country. They were arrested in the February following, at the place of rendezvous pointed out by the approver, and most of them condemned and executed.

So far we learn from Captain Sleeman, who only brought down his tables to the close of the year 1835. A writer in the "Foreign Quarterly Review" furnishes an additional list of 241 persons, committed to prison in 1836, for being concerned in the murder and robbery of 474 individuals. Of these criminals, 91 were sentenced to death, and 22 to imprisonment for life, leaving 306, who were sentenced to transportation for life, or shorter periods of imprisonment, or who turned approvers, or died in gaol. Not one of the whole number was acquitted.

Great as is this amount of criminals who have been brought to justice, it is to be feared that many years must elapse before an evil so deeply rooted can be eradicated. The difficulty is increased by the utter hopelessness of reformation as regards the survivors. Their numbers are still calculated to amount to ten thousand persons, who, taking the average of three murders annually for each, as calculated by Captain Sleeman and other writers, murder every year thirty thousand of their fellow creatures. This average is said to be under the mark; but even if we were to take it at only a third of this calculation, what a frightful list it would be! When religion teaches men to go astray, they go far astray indeed!

The Crusades

They heard, and up they sprung upon the wing
Innumerable. As when the potent rod
Of Amram's son, in Egypt's evil day,
Waved round the coast, up call'd a pitchy cloud
Of locusts, warping on the eastern wind
That o'er the realm of impious Pharaoh hung
Like night, and darken'd all the realm of Nile,
So numberless were they. * * * *
All in a moment through the gloom were seen
Ten thousand banners rise into the air,
With orient colours waving. With them rose
A forest huge of spears; and thronging helms
Appear'd, and serried shields, in thick array,
Of depth immeasurable. *Paradise Lost.*

Every age has its peculiar folly -- some scheme, project, or phantasy into which it plunges, spurred on either by the love of gain, the necessity of excitement, or the mere force of imitation. Failing in these, it has some madness, to which it is goaded by political or religious causes, or both combined. Every one of these causes influenced the Crusades, and conspired to render them the most extraordinary instance upon record of the extent to which popular enthusiasm can be carried. History in her solemn page informs us, that the crusaders were but ignorant and savage men, that their motives were those of bigotry unmitigated, and that their pathway was one of blood and tears. Romance, on the other hand, dilates upon their piety and heroism and pourtrays in her most glowing and impassioned hues their virtue and magnanimity, the imperishable honour they acquired for themselves, and the great services they rendered to Christianity. In the following pages we shall ransack the stores of both, to discover the true spirit that animated the motley multitude who took up arms in the service of the Cross, leaving history to vouch for facts, but not disdaining the aid of contemporary poetry and romance to throw light upon feelings, motives, and opinions.

In order to understand thoroughly the state of public feeling in Europe at the time when Peter the Hermit preached the holy war, it will be necessary to go back for many years anterior to that event. We must make acquaintance with the pilgrims of the eighth, ninth, and tenth centuries, and learn the tales they told of the dangers they had passed, and the wonders they had seen. Pilgrimages to the Holy Land seem at first to have been undertaken by converted Jews, and by Christian devotees of lively imagination, pining with a natural curiosity to visit the scenes which of all others were most interesting in their eyes. The pious and the impious alike flocked to Jerusalem, -- the one class to feast their sight on the scenes hallowed by the life and sufferings of their Lord, and the other, because it soon became a generally received opinion, that such a pilgrimage was sufficient to rub off the long score of sins, however atrocious. Another and very numerous class of pilgrims were the idle and roving, who visited Palestine then as the moderns visit Italy or Switzerland now, because it was the fashion, and because they might please their vanity by retailing, on their return, the adventures they had met with. But the really pious formed the great majority. Every year their numbers increased, until at last they became so numerous as to be called the "armies of the Lord." Full of enthusiasm, they set the danger and difficulty of the way at defiance, and lingered with holy rapture on every scene described in the Evangelists. To them it was bliss indeed to drink the clear waters of the Jordan, or be baptized in the same stream where John had baptized the Saviour. They wandered with awe and pleasure in the purlieus of the Temple, on the solemn Mount of Olives, or the awful Calvary, where a God had bled for sinful men. To these pilgrims every object was precious. Relics were eagerly sought after; flagons of water from Jordan, or paniers of mould from the hill of the Crucifixion, were brought home, and sold at extravagant prices to churches and monasteries. More apocryphical relics, such as the wood of the true cross, the tears of the Virgin Mary, the hems of her garments, the toe-nails and hair of the Apostles -- even the tents that Paul had helped to manufacture -- were exhibited for sale by the knavish in Palestine, and brought back to Europe "with wondrous cost and care." A grove of a hundred oaks would not have furnished all the wood sold in little morsels as remnants of the true cross; and the tears of Mary, if collected together, would have filled a cistern.

For upwards of two hundred years the pilgrims met with no impediment in Palestine. The enlightened Haroun Al Reschid, and his more immediate successors, encouraged the stream which brought so much wealth into Syria, and treated the wayfarers with the utmost courtesy. The race of Fatemite caliphs, -- who, although in other respects as tolerant, were more distressed for money, or more unscrupulous in obtaining it, than their predecessors of the house of Abbas, -- imposed a tax of a bezant for each pilgrim that entered Jerusalem. This was a serious hardship upon the poorer sort, who had begged their weary way across Europe, and arrived at the bourne of all their hopes without a coin. A great outcry was immediately raised, but still the tax was rigorously levied. The pilgrims unable to pay were compelled to remain at the gate of the holy city until some rich devotee arriving with his train, paid the tax and let them in. Robert of Normandy, father of William the Conqueror, who, in common with many other nobles of the highest rank, undertook the pilgrimage, found on his arrival scores of pilgrims at the gate, anxiously expecting his coming to pay the tax for them. Upon no occasion was such a boon refused.

The sums drawn from this source were a mine of wealth to the Moslem governors of Palestine, imposed as the tax had been at a time when pilgrimages had become more numerous than ever. A strange idea had taken possession of the popular mind at the close of the tenth and commencement of the eleventh century. It was universally believed that the end of the world was at hand; that the thousand years of the Apocalypse were near completion, and that Jesus Christ would descend upon Jerusalem to judge mankind. All Christendom was in commotion. A panic terror seized upon the weak, the credulous, and the guilty, who in those days formed more than nineteen twentieths of the population. Forsaking their homes, kindred, and occupation, they crowded to Jerusalem to await the coming of the Lord, lightened, as they imagined, of a load of sin by their weary pilgrimage. To increase the panic, the stars were observed to fall from heaven, earthquakes to shake the land, and violent hurricanes to blow down the forests. All these, and more especially the meteoric phenomena, were looked upon as the forerunners of the approaching judgments. Not a meteor shot athwart the horizon that did not fill a district with alarm, and send away to Jerusalem a score of pilgrims, with staff in hand and wallet on their back, praying as they went for the remission of their sins. Men, women, and even children, trudged in droves to the holy city, in expectation of the day when the heavens would open, and the Son of God descend in his glory. This extraordinary delusion, while it augmented the numbers, increased also the hardships of the pilgrims. Beggars became so numerous on all the highways between the west of Europe and Constantinople that the monks, the great alms-givers upon these occasions, would have brought starvation within sight of their own doors, if they had not economized their resources, and left the devotees to shift for themselves as they could. Hundreds of them were glad to subsist upon the berries that ripened by the road, who, before this great flux, might have shared the bread and flesh of the monasteries.

But this was not the greatest of their difficulties. On their arrival in Jerusalem they found that a sterner race had obtained possession of the Holy Land. The caliphs of Bagdad had been succeeded by the harsh

Turks of the race of Seljook, who looked upon the pilgrims with contempt and aversion. The Turks of the eleventh century were more ferocious and less scrupulous than the Saracens of the tenth. They were annoyed at the immense number of pilgrims who overran the country, and still more so because they showed no intention of quitting it. The hourly expectation of the last judgment kept them waiting; and the Turks, apprehensive of being at last driven from the soil by the swarms that were still arriving, heaped up difficulties in their way. Persecution of every kind awaited them. They were plundered, and beaten with stripes, and kept in suspense for months at the gates of Jerusalem, unable to pay the golden bezant that was to facilitate their entrance.

When the first epidemic terror of the day of judgment began to subside, a few pilgrims ventured to return to Europe, their hearts big with indignation at the insults they had suffered. Everywhere as they passed they related to a sympathizing auditory the wrongs of Christendom. Strange to say, even these recitals increased the mania for pilgrimage. The greater the dangers of the way, the more chance that sins of deep dye would be atoned for. Difficulty and suffering only heightened the merit, and fresh hordes issued from every town and village, to win favour in the sight of Heaven by a visit to the holy sepulchre. Thus did things continue during the whole of the eleventh century.

The train that was to explode so fearfully was now laid, and there wanted but the hand to apply the torch. At last the man appeared upon the scene. Like all who have ever achieved so great an end, Peter the hermit was exactly suited to the age; neither behind it, nor in advance of it; but acute enough to penetrate its mystery ere it was discovered by any other. Enthusiastic, chivalrous, bigoted, and, if not insane, not far removed from insanity, he was the very prototype of the time. True enthusiasm is always persevering and always eloquent, and these two qualities were united in no common degree in the person of this extraordinary preacher. He was a monk of Amiens, and ere he assumed the hood had served as a soldier. He is represented as having been ill favoured and low in stature, but with an eye of surpassing brightness and intelligence. Having been seized with the mania of the age, he visited Jerusalem, and remained there till his blood boiled to see the cruel persecution heaped upon the devotees. On his return home he shook the world by the eloquent story of their wrongs.

Before entering into any further details of the astounding results of his preaching, it will be advisable to cast a glance at the state of the mind of Europe, that we may understand all the better the causes of his success. First of all, there was the priesthood, which, exercising as it did the most conspicuous influence upon the fortunes of society, claims the largest share of attention. Religion was the ruling idea of that day, and the only civiliser capable of taming such wolves as then constituted the flock of the faithful. The clergy were all in all; and though they kept the popular mind in the most slavish subjection with regard to religious matters, they furnished it with the means of defence against all other oppression except their own. In the ecclesiastical ranks were concentrated all the true piety, all the learning, all the wisdom of the time; and, as a natural consequence, a great portion of power, which their very wisdom perpetually incited them to extend. The people knew nothing of kings and nobles, except in the way of injuries inflicted. The first ruled for, or more properly speaking against, the barons, and the barons only existed to brave the power of the kings, or to trample with their iron heels upon the neck of prostrate democracy. The latter had no friend but the clergy, and these, though they necessarily instilled the superstition from which they themselves were not exempt, yet taught the cheering doctrine that all men were equal in the sight of heaven. Thus, while Feudalism told them they had no rights in this world, Religion told them they had every right in the next. With this consolation they were for the time content, for political ideas had as yet taken no root. When the clergy, for other reasons, recommended the Crusade, the people joined in it with enthusiasm. The subject of Palestine filled all minds; the pilgrims' tales of two centuries warmed every imagination; and when their friends, their guides, and their instructors preached a war so much in accordance with their own prejudices and modes of thinking, the enthusiasm rose into a frenzy.

But while religion inspired the masses, another agent was at work upon the nobility. These were fierce and lawless; tainted with every vice, endowed with no virtue, and redeemed by one good quality alone, that of courage. The only religion they felt was the religion of fear. That and their overboiling turbulence alike combined to guide them to the Holy Land. Most of them had sins enough to answer for. They lived with their hand against every man; and with no law but their own passions. They set at defiance the secular power of the clergy, but their hearts quailed at the awful denunciations of the pulpit with regard to the life to come. War was the business and the delight of their existence; and when they were promised remission of all their sins upon the easy condition of following their favourite bent, is it to be wondered at that they rushed with enthusiasm to the onslaught, and became as zealous in the service of the Cross as the great majority of the people, who were swayed by more purely religious motives? Fanaticism and the love of battle alike impelled them to the war, while the kings and princes of Europe had still another motive for encouraging their zeal. Policy opened their eyes to the great advantages which would accrue to themselves, by the absence of so many restless, intriguing, and blood-thirsty men, whose insolence it required more than the small power of royalty to restrain within due bounds. Thus every motive was favourable to the Crusades. Every class of society was alike incited to join or encourage the war; kings and the clergy by policy, the nobles by turbulence and the love of dominion, and the people by religious zeal and the concentrated enthusiasm of two centuries, skilfully directed by their only instructors.

It was in Palestine itself that Peter the Hermit first conceived the grand idea of rousing the powers of Christendom to rescue the Christians of the East from the thraldom of the Mussulmans, and the sepulchre of Jesus from the rude hands of the infidel. The subject engrossed his whole mind. Even in the visions of the night he was full of it. One dream made such an impression upon him, that he devoutly believed the Saviour of the world himself appeared before him, and promised him aid and protection in his holy undertaking. If his zeal had ever wavered before, this was sufficient to fix it for ever.

Peter, after he had performed all the penances and duties of his pilgrimage, demanded an interview with Simeon, the Patriarch of the Greek Church at Jerusalem. Though the latter was a heretic in Peter's eyes, yet he was still a Christian, and felt as acutely as himself for the persecutions heaped by the Turks upon the followers of Jesus. The good prelate entered fully into his views, and, at his suggestion, wrote letters to the Pope, and to the most influential monarchs of Christendom, detailing the sorrows of the faithful, and urging them to take up arms in their defence. Peter was not a laggard in the work. Taking an affectionate farewell of the Patriarch, he returned in all haste to Italy. Pope Urban II. occupied the apostolic chair. It was at that time far from being an easy seat. His predecessor, Gregory, had bequeathed him a host of disputes with the Emperor Henry IV. of Germany, and he had made Philip I. of France his enemy by his strenuous opposition to an adulterous connexion formed by that monarch. So many dangers encompassed him about, that the Vatican was no secure abode, and he had taken refuge in Apulia, under the protection of the renowned Robert Guiscard. Thither Peter appears to have followed him, though in what spot their meeting took place is not stated with any precision by ancient chroniclers or modern historians. Urban received him most kindly; read, with tears in his eyes, the epistle from the Patriarch Simeon, and listened to the eloquent story of the Hermit with an attention which showed how deeply he sympathised with the woes of the Christian church. Enthusiasm is contagious, and the Pope appears to have caught it instantly from one whose zeal was so unbounded. Giving the Hermit full powers, he sent him abroad to preach the holy war to all the nations and potentates of Christendom. The Hermit preached, and countless thousands answered to his call. France, Germany, and Italy started at his voice, and prepared for the deliverance of Zion. One of the early historians of the Crusade, who was himself an eye-witness of the rapture of Europe, [Guibert de Nogent] describes the personal appearance

160

of the Hermit at this time. He says, that there appeared to be something of divine in every thing which he said or did. The people so highly reverenced him, that they plucked hairs from the mane of his mule, that they might keep them as relics. While preaching, he wore in general a woollen tunic, with a dark-coloured mantle, which fell down to his heels. His arms and feet were bare, and he ate neither flesh nor bread, supporting himself chiefly upon fish and wine. "He set out," says the chronicler, "from whence I know not; but we saw him passing through the towns and villages, preaching every where, and the people surrounding him in crowds, loading him with offerings, and celebrating his sanctity with such great praises that I never remember to have seen such honours bestowed upon any one." Thus he went on, untired, inflexible, and full of devotion, communicating his own madness to his hearers, until Europe was stirred from its very depths.

While the Hermit was appealing with such signal success to the people, the Pope appealed with as much success to those who were to become the chiefs and leaders of the expedition. His first step was to call a council at Placentia, in the autumn of the year 1095. Here, in the assembly of the clergy, the Pope debated the grand scheme, and gave audience to emissaries who had been sent from Constantinople by the Emperor of the East to detail the progress made by the Turks in their design of establishing themselves in Europe. The clergy were of course unanimous in support of the Crusade, and the council separated, each individual member of it being empowered to preach it to his people.

But Italy could not be expected to furnish all the aid required; and the Pope crossed the Alps to inspire the fierce and powerful nobility and chivalrous population of Gaul. His boldness in entering the territory, and placing himself in the power of his foe, King Philip of France, is not the least surprising feature of his mission. Some have imagined that cool policy alone actuated him, while others assert, that it was mere zeal, as warm and as blind as that of Peter the Hermit. The latter opinion seems to be the true one. Society did not calculate the consequences of what it was doing. Every man seemed to act from impulse only; and the Pope, in throwing himself into the heart of France, acted as much from impulse as the thousands who responded to his call. A council was eventually summoned to meet him at Clermont, in Auvergne, to consider the state of the church, reform abuses, and, above all, make preparations for the war. It was in the midst of an extremely cold winter, and the ground was covered with snow. During seven days the council sat with closed doors, while immense crowds from all parts of France flocked into the town, in expectation that the Pope himself would address the people. All the towns and villages for miles around were filled with the multitude; even the fields were encumbered with people, who, unable to procure lodging, pitched their tents under the trees and by the way-side. All the neighbourhood presented the appearance of a vast camp.

During the seven days' deliberation, a sentence of excommunication was passed upon King Philip for adultery with Bertrade de Montfort, Countess of Anjou, and for disobedience to the supreme authority of the apostolic see. This bold step impressed the people with reverence for so stern a church, which in the discharge of its duty showed itself no respecter of persons. Their love and their fear were alike increased, and they were prepared to listen with more intense devotion to the preaching of so righteous and inflexible a pastor. The great square before the cathedral church of Clermont became every instant more densely crowded as the hour drew nigh when the Pope was to address the populace. Issuing from the church in his frill canonicals, surrounded by his cardinals and bishops in all the splendour of Romish ecclesiastical costume, the Pope stood before the populace on a high scaffolding erected for the occasion, and covered with scarlet cloth. A brilliant array of bishops and cardinals surrounded him; and among them, humbler in rank, but more important in the world's eye, the Hermit Peter, dressed in his simple and austere habiliments. Historians differ as to whether or not Peter addressed the crowd, but as all agree that he was present, it seems reasonable to suppose that he spoke. But it was the oration of the Pope that was most important. As he lifted up his hands to ensure attention, every voice immediately became still. He began by detailing the miseries endured by their brethren in the Holy Land; how the plains of Palestine were desolated by the outrageous heathen, who with the sword and the firebrand carried wailing into the dwellings and flames into the possessions of the faithful; how Christian wives and daughters were defiled by pagan lust; how the altars of the true God were desecrated, and the relics of the saints trodden under foot. "You," continued the eloquent pontiff, (and Urban the Second was one of the most eloquent men of the day,) "you, who hear me, and who have received the true faith, and been endowed by God with power, and strength, and greatness of soul, -- whose ancestors have been the prop of Christendom, and whose kings have put a barrier against the progress of the infidel, -- I call upon you to wipe off these impurities from the face of the earth, and lift your oppressed fellow-christians from the depths into which they have been trampled. The sepulchre of Christ is possessed by the heathen, the sacred places dishonoured by their vileness. Oh, brave knights and faithful people! offspring of invincible fathers! ye will not degenerate from your ancient renown. Ye will not be restrained from embarking in this great cause by the tender ties of wife or little ones, but will remember the words of the Saviour of the world himself, 'Whosoever loves father and mother more than me is not worthy of me. Whosoever shall abandon for my name's sake his house, or his brethren, or his sisters, or his father, or his mother, or his wife, or his children, or his lands, shall receive a hundredfold, and shall inherit eternal life.'"

The warmth of the pontiff communicated itself to the crowd, and the enthusiasm of the people broke out several times ere he concluded his address. He went on to pourtray, not only the spiritual but the temporal advantages, that should accrue to those who took up arms in the service of the Cross. Palestine was, he said, a land flowing with milk and honey, and precious in the sight of God, as the scene of the grand events which had saved mankind. That land, he promised, should be divided among them. Moreover, they should have full pardon for all their offences, either against God or man. "Go, then," he added, "in expiation of your sins; and go assured, that after this world shall have passed away, imperishable glory shall be yours in the world which is to come." The enthusiasm was no longer to be restrained, and loud shouts interrupted the speaker; the people exclaiming as if with one voice, "Dieu le veult! Dieu le veult!" With great presence of mind Urban took advantage of the outburst, and as soon as silence was obtained, continued: "Dear brethren, to-day is shown forth in you that which the Lord has said by his evangelist, 'When two or three are gathered together in my name, there will I be in the midst of them to bless them.' If the Lord God had not been in your souls, you would not all have pronounced the same words; or rather God himself pronounced them by your lips, for it was He that put them in your hearts. Be they, then, your war-cry in the combat, for those words came forth from God. Let the army of the Lord when it rushes upon His enemies shout but that one cry, 'Dieu le veult! Dieu le veult!' Let whoever is inclined to devote himself to this holy cause make it a solemn engagement, and bear the cross of the Lord either on his breast or his brow till he set out, and let him who is ready to begin his march place the holy emblem on his shoulders, in memory of that precept of our Saviour, 'He who does not take up his cross and follow me is not worthy of me.'"

The news of this council spread to the remotest parts of Europe in an incredibly short space of time. Long before the fleetest horseman could have brought the intelligence it was known by the people in distant provinces, a fact which was considered as nothing less than supernatural. But the subject was in everybody's mouth, and the minds of men were prepared for the result. The enthusiastic only asserted what they wished, and the event tallied with their prediction. This was, however, quite enough in those days for a miracle, and as a miracle every one regarded it.

For several months after the council of Clermont, France and Germany presented a singular spectacle. The pious, the fanatic, the needy, the dissolute, the young and the old, even women and children, and the halt and lame, enrolled themselves by hundreds. In every village the clergy were busied in keeping up the excitement, promising eternal rewards to those who assumed the red cross, and fulminating the most awful denunciations against all the worldly-minded who refused or even hesitated. Every debtor who joined the crusade was freed by the papal edict from the claims of his creditors; outlaws of every grade were made equal with the honest upon the same conditions. The property of those who went was placed under the protection of the church, and St. Paul and St. Peter themselves were believed to descend from their high abode, to watch over the chattels of the absent pilgrims. Signs and portents were seen in the air to increase the fervour of the multitude. An aurora-borealis of unusual brilliancy appeared, and thousands of the crusaders came out to gaze upon it, prostrating themselves upon the earth in adoration. It was thought to be a sure prognostic of the interposition of the Most High; and a representation of his armies fighting with and overthrowing the infidels. Reports of wonders were everywhere rife. A monk had seen two gigantic warriors on horseback, the one representing a Christian and the other a Turk, fighting in the sky with flaming swords, the Christian of course overcoming the Paynim. Myriads of stars were said to have fallen from heaven, each representing the fall of a Pagan foe. It was believed at the same time that the Emperor Charlemagne would rise from the grave, and lead on to victory the embattled armies of the Lord. A singular feature of the popular madness was the enthusiasm of the women. Everywhere they encouraged their lovers and husbands to forsake all things for the holy war. Many of them burned the sign of the cross upon their breasts and arms, and coloured the wound with a red dye, as a lasting memorial of their zeal. Others, still more zealous, impressed the mark by the same means upon the tender limbs of young children and infants at the breast.

Guibert de Nogent tells of a monk who made a large incision upon his forehead in the form of a cross, which he coloured with some powerful ingredient, telling the people that an angel had done it when he was asleep. This monk appears to have been more of a rogue than a fool, for he contrived to fare more sumptuously than any of his brother pilgrims, upon the strength of his sanctity. The crusaders everywhere gave him presents of food and money, and he became quite fat ere he arrived at Jerusalem, notwithstanding the fatigues of the way. If he had acknowledged in the first place that he had made the wound himself, he would not have been thought more holy than his fellows; but the story of the angel was a clincher.

All those who had property of any description rushed to the mart to change it into hard cash. Lands and houses could be had for a quarter of their value, while arms and accoutrements of war rose in the same proportion. Corn, which had been excessively dear in anticipation of a year of scarcity, suddenly became plentiful; and such was the diminution in the value of provisions, that seven sheep were sold for five deniers.[Guibert de Nogent] The nobles mortgaged their estates for mere trifles to Jews and unbelievers, or conferred charters of immunity upon the towns and communes within their fiefs, for sums which, a few years previously, they would have rejected with disdain. The farmer endeavoured to sell his plough, and the artisan his tools, to purchase a sword for the deliverance of Jerusalem. Women disposed of their trinkets for the same purpose. During the spring and summer of this year (1096) the roads teemed with crusaders, all hastening to the towns and villages appointed as the rendezvous of the district. Some were on horseback, some in carts, and some came down the rivers in boats and rafts, bringing their wives and children, all eager to go to Jerusalem. Very few knew where Jerusalem was. Some thought it fifty thousand miles away, while others imagined that it was but a month's journey, while at sight of every town or castle, the children exclaimed, "Is that Jerusalem ? Is that the city ?"[Guibert de Nogent] Parties of knights and nobles might be seen travelling eastward, and amusing themselves as they went with the knightly diversion of hawking to lighten the fatigues of the way.

Guibert de Nogent, who did not write from hearsay, but from actual observation, says, the enthusiasm was so contagious, that when any one heard the orders of the Pontiff, he went instantly to solicit his neighbours and friends to join with him in "the way of God," for so they called the proposed expedition.

The Counts Palatine were full of the desire to undertake the journey, and all the inferior knights were animated with the same zeal. Even the poor caught the flame so ardently, that no one paused to think of the inadequacy of his means, or to consider whether he ought to yield up his house and his vine and his fields. Each one set about selling his property, at as low a price as if he had been held in some horrible captivity, and sought to pay his ransom without loss of time. Those who had not determined upon the journey, joked and laughed at those who were thus disposing of their goods at such ruinous prices, prophesying that the expedition would be miserable and their return worse. But they held this language only for a day. The next, they were suddenly seized with the same frenzy as the rest. Those who had been loudest in their jeers gave up all their property for a few crowns, and set out with those they had so laughed at a few hours before. In most cases the laugh was turned against them, for when it became known that a man was hesitating, his more zealous neighbouts sent him a present of a knitting needle or a distaff, to show their contempt of him. There was no resisting this, so that the fear of ridicule contributed its fair contingent to the armies of the Lord.

Another effect of the crusade was, the religious obedience with which it inspired the people and the nobility for that singular institution "The Truce of God." At the commencement of the eleventh century, the clergy of France, sympathizing for the woes of the people, but unable to diminish them, by repressing the rapacity and insolence of the feudal chiefs, endeavoured to promote universal good-will by the promulgation of the famous "Peace of God." All who conformed to it bound themselves by oath not to take revenge for any injury, not to enjoy the fruits of property usurped from others, nor to use deadly weapons; in reward of which they would receive remission of all their sins. However benevolent the intention of this "Peace," it led to nothing but perjury, and violence reigned as uncontrolled as before. In the year 1041 another attempt was made to soften the angry passions of the semi-barbarous chiefs, and the "Truce of God" was solemnly proclaimed. The truce lasted from the Wednesday evening to the Monday morning of every week, in which interval it was strictly forbidden to recur to violence on any pretext, or to seek revenge for any injury. It was impossible to civilize men by these means; few even promised to become peaceable for so unconscionable a period as five days a week; or, if they did, they made ample amends on the two days left open to them. The truce was afterwards shortened from the Saturday evening to the Monday morning; but little or no diminution of violence and bloodshed was the consequence. At the council of Clermont, Urban II. again solemnly pro- claimed the truce. So strong was the religious feeling, that every one hastened to obey. All minor passions disappeared before the grand passion of crusading; the noble ceased to oppress, the robber to plunder, and the people to complain; but one idea was in all hearts, and there seemed to be no room for any other.

The encampments of these heterogeneous multitudes offered a singular aspect. Those vassals who ranged themselves under the banners of their lord, erected tents around his castle; while those who undertook the war on their own account, constructed booths and huts in the neighbourhood of the towns or villages, preparatory to their joining some popular leader of the expedition. The meadows of France were covered with tents. As the belligerents were to have remission of all their sins on their arrival in Palestine, hundreds of them gave themselves up to the most unbounded licentiousness: the courtezan, with the red cross upon her shoulders, plied her shameless trade with sensual pilgrims, without scruple on either side: the lover of good cheer gave loose rein to his appetite, and drunkenness and debauchery flourished. Their zeal in the service of the Lord was to wipe out all faults and follies, and they had the same surety of salvation as the rigid anchorite. This reasoning had charms for the ignorant, and the sounds of lewd revelry and the voice of prayer rose at the same instant from the camp.

It is now time to speak of the leaders of the expedition. Great multitudes ranged themselves under the command of Peter the Hermit, whom, as the originator, they considered the most appropriate leader of the war. Others joined the banner of a bold adventurer, whom history has dignified with no other name than that of Gautier sans Avoir, or Walter the Pennyless, but who is represented as having been of noble family, and well skilled in the art of war. A third multitude from Germany flocked around the standard of a monk, named Gottschalk, of whom nothing is known, except that he was a fanatic of the deepest dye. All these bands, which together are said to have amounted to three hundred thousand men, women, and children, were composed of the vilest rascality of Europe. Without discipline, principle, or true courage, they rushed through the nations like a pestilence, spreading terror and death wherever they went. The first multitude that set forth was led by Walter the Pennyless early in the spring of 1096, within a very few months after the Council of Clermont. Each man of that irregular host aspired to be his own master: like their nominal leader, each was poor to penury, and trusted for subsistence on his journey to the chances of the road. Rolling through Germany like a tide, they entered Hungary, where, at first, they were received with some degree of kindness by the people. The latter had not yet caught sufficient of the fire of enthusiasm to join the crusade themselves, but were willing enough to forward the cause by aiding those embarked in it. Unfortunately, this good understanding did not last long. The swarm were not contented with food for their necessities, but craved for luxuries also: they attacked and plundered the dwellings of the country people, and thought nothing of murder where resistance was offered. On their arrival before Semlin, the outraged Hungarians collected in large numbers, and, attacking the rear of the crusading host, slew a great many of the stragglers, and, taking away their arms and crosses, affixed them as trophies to the walls of the city. Walter appears to have been in no mood or condition to make reprisals; for his army, destructive as a plague of locusts when plunder urged them on, were useless against any regular attack from a determined enemy. Their rear continued to be thus harassed by the wrathful Hungarians until they were fairly out of their territory. On his entrance into Bulgaria, Walter met with no better fate; the cities and towns refused to let him pass; the villages denied him provisions; and the citizens and country people uniting, slaughtered his followers by hundreds. The progress of the army was more like a retreat than an advance; but as it was impossible to stand still, Walter continued his course till he arrived at Constantinople, with a force which famine and the sword had diminished to one-third of its original number.

The greater multitude, led by the enthusiastic Hermit, followed close upon his heels, with a bulky train of baggage, and women and children, sufficient to form a host of themselves. If it were possible to find a rabble more vile than the army of Walter the Pennyless it was that led by Peter the Hermit. Being better provided with means, they were not reduced to the necessity of pillage in their progress through Hungary; and had they taken any other route than that which led through Semlin, might perhaps have traversed the country without molestation. On their arrival before that city, their fury was raised at seeing the arms and red crosses of their predecessors hanging as trophies over the gates. Their pent-up ferocity exploded at the sight. The city was tumultuously attacked, and the besiegers entering, not by dint of bravery, but of superior numbers, it was given up to all the horrors which follow when Victory, Brutality, and Licentiousness are linked together. Every evil passion was allowed to revel with impunity, and revenge, lust, and avarice, -- each had its hundred victims in unhappy Semlin. Any maniac can kindle a conflagration, but it requires many wise men to put it out. Peter the Hermit had blown the popular fury into a flame, but to cool it again was beyond his power. His followers rioted unrestrained, until the fear of retaliation warned them to desist. When the King of Hungary was informed of the disasters of Semlin, he marched with a sufficient force to chastise the Hermit, who at the news broke up his camp and retreated towards the Morava, a broad and rapid stream that joins the Danube a few miles to the eastward of Belgrade. Here a party of indignant Bulgarians awaited him, and so harassed him as to make the passage of the river a task both of difficulty and danger. Great numbers of his infatuated followers perished in the waters, and many fell under the swords of the Bulgarians. The ancient chronicles do not mention the amount of the Hermit's loss at this passage, but represent it in general terms as very great.

At Nissa the Duke of Bulgaria fortified himself, in fear of an assault; but Peter, having learned a little wisdom from experience, thought it best to avoid hostilities. He passed three nights in quietness under the walls, and the duke, not wishing to exasperate unnecessarily so fierce and rapacious a host, allowed the townspeople to supply them with provisions. Peter took his departure peaceably on the following morning, but some German vagabonds falling behind the main body of the army, set fire to the mills and house of a Bulgarian, with whom, it appears, they had had some dispute on the previous evening. The citizens of Nissa, who had throughout mistrusted the crusaders, and were prepared for the worst, sallied out immediately, and took signal vengeance. The spoilers were cut to pieces, and the townspeople pursuing the Hermit, captured all the women and children who had lagged in the rear, and a great quantity of baggage. Peter hereupon turned round and marched back to Nissa, to demand explanation of the Duke of Bulgaria. The latter fairly stated the provocation given, and the Hermit could urge nothing in palliation of so gross an outrage. A negotiation was entered into which promised to be successful, and the Bulgarians were about to deliver up the women and children when a party of undisciplined crusaders, acting solely upon their own suggestion, endeavoured to scale the walls and seize upon the town. Peter in vain exerted his authority; the confusion became general, and after a short but desperate battle, the crusaders threw down their arms and fled in all directions. Their vast host was completely routed, the slaughter being so great among them as to be counted, not by hundreds, but by thousands.

It is said that the Hermit fled from this fatal field to a forest a few miles from Nissa, abandoned by every human creature. It would be curious to know whether, after so dire a reverse,

. . . . "His enpierced breast
Sharp sorrow did in thousand pieces rive,"

or whether his fiery zeal still rose superior to calamity, and pictured the eventual triumph of his cause. He, so lately the leader of a hundred thousand men, was now a solitary skulker in the forests, liable at every instant to be discovered by some pursuing Bulgarian, and cut off in mid career. Chance at last brought him within sight of an eminence where two or three of his bravest knights had collected five hundred of the stragglers. These gladly received the Hermit, and a consultation having taken place, it was resolved to gather together the scattered remnants of the army. Fires were lighted on the hill, and scouts sent out in all directions for the fugitives. Horns were sounded at intervals to make known that friends were near, and before nightfall the Hermit saw himself at the head of seven thousand men. During the succeeding day he was joined by twenty thousand more, and with this miserable remnant of his force he pursued his route towards Constantinople. The bones of the rest mouldered in the forests of Bulgaria.

On his arrival at Constantinople, where he found Walter the Pennyless awaiting him, he was hospitably received by the Emperor Alexius. It might have been expected that the sad reverses they had undergone would have taught his followers common prudence; but, unhappily for them, their turbulence and love of plunder were not to be restrained. Although they were surrounded by friends, by whom all their wants were liberally supplied, they could not refrain from rapine. In vain the Hermit exhorted them to tranquillity; he possessed no more power over them, in subduing their passions, than the obscurest soldier of the host, They set fire to several public buildings in Constantinople, out of pure mischief, and stripped the lead from the roofs of the churches, which, they afterwards sold for old metal in the purlieus of the city. From this time may be dated the aversion which the Emperor Alexius entertained for the crusaders, and which was afterwards manifested in all his actions, even when he had to deal with the chivalrous and more honourable armies which arrived after the Hermit. He seems to have imagined that the Turks themselves were enemies less formidable to his power than these outpourings of the refuse of Europe: he soon found a pretext to hurry them into Asia Minor. Peter crossed the Bosphorus with

Walter, hut the excesses of his followers were such, that, despairing of accomplishing any good end by remaining at their head, he left them to themselves, and returned to Constantinople, on the pretext of making arrangements with the government of Alexius for a proper supply of provisions. The crusaders, forgetting that they were in the enemy's country, and that union, above all things, was desirable, gave themselves up to dissensions. Violent disputes arose between the Lombards and Normans, commanded by Walter the Pennyless, and the Franks and Germans, led out by Peter. The latter separated themselves from the former, and, choosing for their leader one Reinaldo, or Reinhold, marched forward, and took possession of the fortress of Exorogorgon. The Sultan Solimaun was on the alert, with a superior force. A party of crusaders, which had been detached from the fort, and stationed at a little distance as an ambuscade, were surprised and cut to pieces, and Exorogorgon invested on all sides. The siege was protracted for eight days, during which the Christians suffered the most acute agony from the want of water. It is hard to say how long the hope of succour or the energy of despair would have enabled them to hold out: their treacherous leader cut the matter short by renouncing the Christian faith, and delivering up the fort into the hands of the Sultan. He was followed by two or three of his officers; all the rest, refusing to become Mahometans, were ruthlessly put to the sword. Thus perished the last wretched remnant of the vast multitude which had traversed Europe with Peter the Hermit.

Walter the Pennyless and his multitude met as miserable a fate. On the news of the disasters of Exorogorgon, they demanded to be led instantly against the Turks. Walter, who only wanted good soldiers to have made a good general, was cooler of head, and saw all the dangers of such a step. His force was wholly insufficient to make any decisive movement in a country where the enemy was so much superior, and where, in case of defeat, he had no secure position to fall back upon; and he therefore expressed his opinion against advancing until the arrival of reinforcements. This prudent counsel found no favour: the army loudly expressed their dissatisfaction at their chief, and prepared to march forward without him. Upon this, the brave Walter put himself at their head, and rushed to destruction. Proceeding towards Nice, the modern Isnik, he was intercepted by the army of the Sultan: a fierce battle ensued in which the Turks made fearful havoc; out of twenty-five thousand Christians, twenty-two thousand were slain, and among them Gautier himself, who fell pierced by seven mortal wounds. The remaining three thousand retreated upon Civitot, where they intrenched themselves.

Disgusted as was Peter the Hermit at the excesses of the multitude, who, at his call, had forsaken Europe, his heart was moved with grief and pity at their misfortunes. All his former zeal revived: casting himself at the feet of the Emperor Alexius, he implored him, with tears in his eyes, to send relief to the few survivors at Civitot. The Emperor consented, and a force was sent, which arrived just in time to save them from destruction. The Turks had beleaguered the place, and the crusaders were reduced to the last extremity. Negotiations were entered into, and the last three thousand were conducted in safety to Constantinople. Alexius had suffered too much by their former excesses to be very desirous of retaining them in his capital: he therefore caused them all to be disarmed, and, furnishing each with a sum of money, he sent them back to their own country. While these events were taking place, fresh hordes were issuing from the woods and wilds of Germany, all bent for the Holy Land. They were commanded by a fanatical priest, named Gottschalk, who, like Gautier and Peter the Hermit, took his way through Hungary. History is extremely meagre in her details of the conduct and fate of this host, which amounted to at least one hundred thousand men. Robbery and murder seem to have journeyed with them, and the poor Hungarians were rendered almost desperate by their numbers and rapacity. Karloman, the king of the country, made a bold effort to get rid of them; for the resentment of his people had arrived at such a height, that nothing short of the total extermination of the crusaders would satisfy them. Gottschalk had to pay the penalty, not only for the ravages of his own bands, but for those of the swarms that had come before him. He and his army were induced, by some means or other, to lay down their arms: the savage Hungarians, seeing them thus defenceless, set upon them, and slaughtered them in great numbers. How many escaped their arrows, we are not informed; but not one of them reached Palestine.

Other swarms, under nameless leaders, issued from Germany and France, more brutal and more frantic than any that had preceded them. Their fanaticism surpassed by far the wildest freaks of the followers of the Hermit. In bands, varying in numbers from one to five thousand, they traversed the country in all directions, bent upon plunder and massacre. They wore the symbol of the crusade upon their shoulders, but inveighed against the folly of proceeding to the Holy Land to destroy the Turks, while they left behind them so many Jews, the still more inveterate enemies of Christ. They swore fierce vengeance against this unhappy race, and murdered all the Hebrews they could lay their hands on, first subjecting them to the most horrible mutilation. According to the testimony of Albert Aquensis, they lived among each other in the most shameless profligacy, and their vice was only exceeded by their superstition. Whenever they were in search of Jews, they were preceded by a goose and goat, which they believed to be holy, and animated with divine power to discover the retreats of the unbelievers. In Germany alone they slaughtered more than a thousand Jews, notwithstanding all the efforts of the clergy to save them. So dreadful was the cruelty of their tormentors, that great numbers of Jews committed self-destruction to avoid falling into their hands.

Again it fell to the lot of the Hungarians to deliver Europe from these pests. When there were no more Jews to murder, the bands collected in one body, and took the old route to the Holy Land, a route stained with the blood of three hundred thousand who had gone before, and destined also to receive theirs. The number of these swarms has never been stated; but so many of them perished in Hungary, that contemporary writers, despairing of giving any adequate idea of their multitudes, state that the fields were actually heaped with their corpses, and that for miles in its course the waters of the Danube were dyed with their blood. It was at Mersburg, on the Danube, that the greatest slaughter took place, -- a slaughter so great as to amount almost to extermination. The Hungarians for a while disputed the passage of the river, but the crusaders forced their way across, and attacking the city with the blind courage of madness, succeeded in making a breach in the walls. At this moment of victory an unaccountable fear came over them. Throwing down their arms they fled panic-stricken, no one knew why, and no one knew whither. The Hungarians followed, sword in hand, and cut them down without remorse, and in such numbers, that the stream of the Danube is said to have been choked up by their unburied bodies.

This was the worst paroxysm of the madness of Europe; and this passed, her chivalry stepped upon the scene. Men of cool heads, mature plans, and invincible courage stood forward to lead and direct the grand movement of Europe upon Asia. It is upon these men that romance has lavished her most admiring epithets, leaving to the condemnation of history the vileness and brutality of those who went before. Of these leaders the most distinguished were Godfrey of Bouillon Duke of Lorraine, and Raymond Count of Toulouse. Four other chiefs of the royal blood of Europe also assumed the Cross, and led each his army to the Holy Land: Hugh, Count of Vermandois, brother of the King of France; Robert, Duke of Normandy, the elder brother of William Rufus; Robert Count of Flanders, and Boemund Prince of Tarentum, eldest son of the celebrated Robert Guiscard. These men were all tinged with the fanaticism of the age, but none of them acted entirely from religious motives. They were neither utterly reckless like Gautier sans Avoir, crazy like Peter the Hermit, nor brutal like Gottschalk the Monk, but possessed each of these qualities in a milder form; their valour being tempered by caution, their religious zeal by worldly views, and their ferocity by the spirit of chivalry. They saw whither led the torrent of the public will; and it being neither their wish nor their interest to stem it, they allowed themselves to be carried with it, in the hope that it would lead them at last to a haven of aggrandizement. Around them congregated many minor chiefs, the flower of the nobility of France and Italy, with some few from Germany, England, and Spain. It was wisely conjectured that armies so numerous would find a difficulty in procuring provisions if they all journeyed by the same road. They, therefore, resolved to separate, Godfrey de Bouillon proceeding through Hungary and Bulgaria, the Count of Toulouse through Lombardy and Dalmatia, and the other leaders through Apulia to Constantinople, where the several divisions were to reunite. The forces under these leaders have been variously estimated. The Princess Anna Comnena talks of them as having been as numerous as the sands on the sea-shore, or the stars in the firmament. Fulcher of Chartres is more satisfactory, and exaggerates less magnificently, when he states, that all the divisions, when they had sat down before Nice in Bithynia, amounted to one hundred thousand horsemen, and six hundred thousand men on foot, exclusive of the priests, women and children. Gibbon is of opinion that this amount is exaggerated; but thinks the actual numbers did not fall very far short of the calculation. The Princess Anna afterwards gives the number of those under Godfrey of Bouillon as eighty thousand foot and horse; and supposing that each of the other chiefs led an army as numerous, the total would be near half a million. This must be over rather than under the mark, as the army of Godfrey of Bouillon was confessedly the largest when it set out, and suffered less by the way than any other.

The Count of Vermandois was the first who set foot on the Grecian territory. On his arrival at Durazzo he was received with every mark of respect and courtesy by the agents of the Emperor, and his followers were abundantly supplied with provisions. Suddenly however, and without cause assigned, the Count was arrested by order of the Emperor Alexius, and conveyed a close prisoner to Constantinople. Various motives have been assigned by different authors as having induced the Emperor to this treacherous and imprudent proceeding. By every writer he has been condemned for so flagrant a breach of hospitality and justice. The most probable reason for his conduct appears to be that suggested by Guibert of Nogent, who states that Alexius, fearful of the designs of the crusaders upon his throne, resorted to this extremity in order afterwards to force the Count to take the oath of allegiance to him, as the price of his liberation. The example of a prince so eminent as the brother of the King of France, would, he thought, be readily followed by the other chiefs of the Crusade. In the result he was wofully disappointed, as every man deserves to be who commits positive evil that doubtful good may ensue. But this line of policy accorded well enough with the narrowmindedness of the Emperor, who, in the enervating atmosphere of his highly civilized and luxurious court, dreaded the influx of the hardy and ambitious warriors of the West, and strove to nibble away by unworthy means, the power which he had not energy enough to confront. If danger to himself had existed from the residence of the chiefs in his dominions, he might easily have averted it, by the simple means of placing himself at the head of the European movement, and directing its energies to their avowed object, the conquest of the Holy Land. But the Emperor, instead of being, as he might have been, the lord and leader of the Crusades, which he had himself aided in no inconsiderable degree to suscitate by his embassies to the Pope, became the slave of men who hated and despised him. No doubt the barbarous excesses of the followers of Gautier and Peter the Hermit made him look upon the whole body of them with disgust, but it was the disgust of a little mind, which is glad of any excuse to palliate or justify its own irresolution and love of ease.

Godfrey of Bouillon traversed Hungary in the most quiet and orderly manner. On his arrival at Mersburg he found the country strewed with the mangled corpses of the Jew-killers, and demanded of the King of Hungary for what reason his people had set upon them. The latter detailed the atrocities they had committed, and made it so evident to Godfrey that the Hungarians had only acted in self-defence, that the high-minded leader declared himself satisfied and passed on, without giving or receiving molestation. On his arrival at Philippopoli, he was informed for the first time of the imprisonment of the Count of Vermandois. He immediately sent messengers to the Emperor, demanding the Count's release, and threatening, in case of refusal, to lay waste the country with fire and sword. After waiting a day at Philippopoli he marched on to Adrianople, where he was met by his messengers returning with the Emperor's refusal. Godfrey, the bravest and most determined of the leaders of the Crusade, was not a man to swerve from his word, and the country was given up to pillage. Alexius here committed another blunder. No sooner did he learn from dire experience that the crusader was not an utterer of idle threats, than he consented to the release of the prisoner. As he had been unjust in the first instance, he became cowardly in the second, and taught his enemies (for so the crusaders were forced to consider themselves) a lesson which they took care to remember to his cost, that they could hope nothing from his sense of justice, but every thing from his fears. Godfrey remained encamped for several weeks in the neighbourhood of Constantinople, to the great annoyance of Alexius, who sought by every means to extort from him the homage he had extorted from Vermandois. Sometimes he acted as if at open and declared war with the crusaders, and sent his troops against them. Sometimes he refused to supply them with food, and ordered the markets to be shut against them, while at other times he was all for peace and goodwill, and sent costly presents to Godfrey. The honest, straightforward crusader was at last so wearied by his false kindness, and so pestered by his attacks, that, allowing his indignation to get the better of his judgment, he gave up the country around Constantinople to be plundered by his soldiers. For six days the flames of the farm-houses around struck terror into the heart of Alexius, but as Godfrey anticipated they convinced him of his error. Fearing that Constantinople itself would be the next object of attack, he sent messengers to demand an interview with Godfrey, offering at the same time to leave his son as a hostage for his good faith. Godfrey agreed to meet him, and, whether to put an end to these useless dissensions, or for some other unexplained reason, he rendered homage to Alexius as his liege lord. He was thereupon loaded with honours, and, according to a singular custom of that age, underwent the ceremony of the "adoption of honour," as son to the Emperor. Godfrey, and his brother Baudouin de Bouillon, conducted themselves with proper courtesy on this occasion, but were not able to restrain the insolence of their followers, who did not conceive themselves bound to keep any terms with a man so insincere as he had shown himself. One barbarous chieftain, Count Robert of Paris, carried his insolence so far as to seat himself upon the throne, an insult which Alexius merely resented with a sneer, but which did not induce him to look with less mistrust upon the hordes that were still advancing.

It is impossible, notwithstanding his treachery, to avoid feeling some compassion for the Emperor, whose life at this time was rendered one long scene of misery by the presumption of the crusaders, and his not altogether groundless fears of the evil they might inflict upon him, should any untoward circumstance force the current of their ambition to the conquest of his empire. His daughter, Anna Comnena, feelingly deplores his state of life at this time, and a learned German, [M. Wilken's Geschichte der Kreuzzuge.] in a recent work, describes it, on the authority of the Princess, in the following manner:--

"To avoid all occasion of offence to the Crusaders, Alexius complied with all their whims, and their (on many occasions) unreasonable demands, even at the expense of great bodily exertion, at a time when he was suffering severely under the gout, which eventually brought him to his grave. No crusader who desired an interview with him was refused access: he listened with the utmost patience to the long-winded harangues which their loquacity or zeal continually wearied him with: he endured, without expressing any impatience, the unbecoming and haughty language which they permitted themselves to employ towards him, and severely reprimanded his officers when they undertook to defend the dignity of the Imperial station from these rude assaults; for he trembled with apprehension at the slightest disputes, lest they might become the occasion of greater evil. Though the Counts often appeared before him with trains altogether unsuitable to their dignity and to his -- sometimes with an entire troop, which completely filled the Royal apartment -- the Emperor held his peace. He listened to them at all hours; he often seated himself on his throne at day-break to attend to their wishes and requests, and the evening twilight saw him still in the same place. Very frequently he could not snatch time to refresh himself with meat and drink. During many nights he could not obtain any repose, and was obliged to indulge in an unrefreshing sleep upon his throne, with his head resting on his hands. Even this slumber was continually disturbed by the appearance and harangues of some newly-arrived rude knights. When all the courtiers, wearied out by the efforts of the day and by night-watching, could no longer keep themselves on their feet, and sank down exhausted -- some upon benches and others on the floor -- Alexius still rallied his strength to listen with seeming attention to the wearisome chatter of the Latins, that they might have no occasion or pretext for discontent. In such a state of fear and anxiety, how could

Alexius comport himself with dignity and like an Emperor ?"

Alexius, however, had himself to blame, in a great measure, for the indignities he suffered: owing to his insincerity, the crusaders mistrusted him so much, that it became at last a common saying, that the Turks and Saracens were not such inveterate foes to the Western or Latin Christians as the Emperor Alexius and the Greeks.[Wilken] It would be needless in this sketch, which does not profess to be so much a history of the Crusades as of the madness of Europe, from which they sprang, to detail the various acts of bribery and intimidation, cajolery and hostility, by which Alexius contrived to make each of the leaders in succession, as they arrived, take the oath of allegiance to him as their Suzerain. One way or another he exacted from each the barren homage on which he had set his heart, and they were then allowed to proceed into Asia Minor. One only, Raymond de St. Gilles, Count of Toulouse, obstinately refused the homage.

Their residence in Constantinople was productive of no good to the armies of the Cross. Bickerings and contentions on the one hand, and the influence of a depraved and luxurious court on the other, destroyed the elasticity of their spirits, and cooled the first ardour of their enthusiasm. At one time the army of the Count of Toulouse was on the point of disbanding itself; and, had not their leader energetically removed them across the Bosphorus, this would have been the result. Once in Asia, their spirits in some degree revived, and the presence of danger and difficulty nerved them to the work they had undertaken. The first operation of the war was the siege of Nice, to gain possession of which all their efforts were directed.

Godfrey of Bouillon and the Count of Vermandois were joined under its walls by each host in succession, as it left Constantinople. Among the celebrated crusaders who fought at this siege, we find, besides the leaders already mentioned, the brave and generous Tancred, whose name and fame have been immortalized in the Gerusalemme Liberata, the valorous Bishop of Puy, Baldwin, afterwards King of Jerusalem, and Peter the Hermit, now an almost solitary soldier, shorn of all the power and influence he had formerly possessed. Kilij Aslaun, the Sultan of Roum, and chief of the Seljukian Turks, whose deeds, surrounded by the false halo of romance, are familiar to the readers of Tasso, under the name of Soliman, marched to defend this city, but was defeated after several obstinate engagements, in which the Christians showed a degree of heroism that quite astonished him. The Turkish chief had expected to find a wild undisciplined multitude, like that under Peter the Hermit, without leaders capable of enforcing obedience; instead of which he found the most experienced leaders of the age at the head of armies that had just fanaticism enough to be ferocious, but not enough to render them ungovernable. In these engagements, many hundreds fell on both sides; and on both sides the most revolting barbarity was practised: the crusaders cut off the heads of the fallen Mussulmans, and sent them in paniers to Constantinople, as trophies of their victory. After the temporary defeat of Kilij Aslaun, the siege of Nice was carried on with redoubled vigour. The Turks defended themselves with the greatest obstinacy, and discharged showers of poisoned arrows upon the crusaders. When any unfortunate wretch was killed under the walls, they let down iron hooks from above, and drew the body up, which, after stripping and mutilating, they threw back again at the besiegers. The latter were well supplied with provisions, and for six-and-thirty days the siege continued without any relaxation of the efforts on either side. Many tales are told of the almost superhuman heroism of the Christian leaders -- how one man put a thousand to flight; and how the arrows of the faithful never missed their mark. One anecdote of Godfrey of Bouillon, related by Albert of Aix, is worth recording, not only as showing the high opinion entertained of his valour, but as showing the contagious credulity of the armies -- a credulity which as often led them to the very verge of defeat, as it incited them to victory. One Turk, of gigantic stature, took his station day by day on the battlements of Nice, and, bearing an enormous bow, committed great havoc among the Christian host. Not a shaft he sped, but bore death upon its point; and, although the Crusaders aimed

171

repeatedly at his breast, and he stood in the most exposed position, their arrows fell harmless at his feet. He seemed to be invulnerable to attack; and a report was soon spread abroad, that he was no other than the Arch Fiend himself, and that mortal hand could not prevail against him. Godfrey of Bouillon, who had no faith in the supernatural character of the Mussulman, determined, if possible, to put an end to the dismay which was rapidly paralyzing the exertions of his best soldiers. Taking a huge cross-bow, he stood forward in front of the army, to try the steadiness of his hand against the much-dreaded archer: the shaft was aimed directly at his heart, and took fatal effect. The Moslem fell amid the groans of the besieged, and the shouts of Deus adjuva! Deus adjuva! the war-cry of the besiegers.

At last the crusaders imagined that they had overcome all obstacles, and were preparing to take possession of the city, when to their great astonishment they saw the flag of the Emperor Alexius flying from the battlements. An emissary of the Emperor, named Faticius or Tatin, had contrived to gain admission with a body of Greek troops at a point which the crusaders had left unprotected, and had persuaded the Turks to surrender to him rather than to the crusading forces. The greatest indignation prevailed in the army when this stratagem was discovered, and the soldiers were, with the utmost difficulty, prevented from renewing the attack and besieging the Greek emissary.

The army, however, continued its march, and by some means or other was broken into two divisions; some historians say accidentally, [Fulcher of Chartres. -- Guibert de Nogent. -- Vital.] while others affirm by mutual consent, and for the convenience of obtaining provisions on the way. [William of Tyre. -- Mills. -- Wilken, &c.] The one division was composed of the forces under Bohemund, Tancred, and the Duke of Normandy; while the other, which took a route at some distance on the right, was commanded by Godfrey of Bouillon and the other chiefs. The Sultan of Roum, who, after his losses at Nice, had been silently making great efforts to crush the crusaders at one blow, collected in a very short time all the multitudinous tribes that owed him allegiance, and with an army which, according to a moderate calculation, amounted to two hundred thousand men, chiefly cavalry, he fell upon the first division of the Christian host in the valley of Dorylaeum. It was early in the morning of the 1st of July 1097, when the crusaders saw the first companies of the Turkish horsemen pouring down upon them from the hills. Bohemund had hardly time to set himself in order, and transport his sick and helpless to the rear, when the overwhelming force of the Orientals was upon him. The Christian army, composed principally of men on foot, gave way on all sides, and the hoofs of the Turkish steeds, and the poisoned arrows of their bowmen, mowed them down by hundreds. After having lost the flower of their chivalry, the Christians retreated upon their baggage, when a dreadful slaughter took place. Neither women nor children, nor the sick, were spared. Just as they were reduced to the last extremity, Godfrey of Bouillon and the Count of Toulouse made their appearance on the field, and turned the tide of battle. After an obstinate engagement the Turks fled, and their rich camp fell into the bands of the enemy. The loss of the crusaders amounted to about four thousand men, with several chiefs of renown, among whom were Count Robert of Paris and William the brother of Tancred. The loss of the Turks, which did not exceed this number, taught them to pursue a different mode of warfare. The Sultan was far from being defeated. With his still gigantic army, he laid waste all the country on either side of the crusaders. The latter, who were unaware of the tactics of the enemy, found plenty of provisions in the Turkish camp; but so far from economizing these resources, they gave themselves up for several days to the most unbounded extravagance. They soon paid dearly for their heedlessness. In the ravaged country of Phrygia, through which they advanced towards Antiochetta, they suffered dreadfully for want of food for themselves and pasture for their cattle. Above them was a scorching sun, almost sufficient of itself to dry up the freshness of the land, a task which the firebrands of the Sultan had but too surely effected, and water was not to be had after the first day of their march. The pilgrims died at the rate of five hundred a-day. The horses of the knights perished on the road, and the baggage which they had aided to transport, was either placed upon dogs, sheep, and swine, or abandoned altogether. In some of the calamities that afterwards befell them, the Christians gave themselves up to the most reckless profligacy; but upon this occasion, the dissensions which prosperity had engendered, were all forgotten. Religion, often disregarded, arose in the stern presence of misfortune, and cheered them as they died by the promises of eternal felicity.

At length they reached Antiochetta, where they found water in abundance, and pastures for their expiring cattle. Plenty once more surrounded them, and here they pitched their tents. Untaught by the bitter experience of famine, they again gave themselves up to luxury and waste.

On the 18th of October they sat down before the strong city of Antioch, the siege of which, and the events to which it gave rise, are among the most extraordinary incidents of the Crusade. The city, which is situated on an eminence, and washed by the river Orontes, is naturally a very strong position, and the Turkish garrison were well supplied with provisions to endure a long siege. In this respect the Christians were also fortunate, but, unluckily for themselves, unwise. Their force amounted to three hundred thousand fighting men; and we are informed by Raymond d'Argilles, that they had so much provision, that they threw away the greater part of every animal they killed, being so dainty, that they would only eat particular parts of the beast. So insane was their extravagance, that in less than ten days famine began to stare them in the face. After making a fruitless attempt to gain possession of the city by a coup de main, they, starving themselves, sat down to starve out the enemy. But with want came a cooling of enthusiasm. The chiefs began to grow weary of the expedition. Baldwin had previously detached himself from the main body of the army, and, proceeding to Edessa, had intrigued himself into the supreme power in that little principality. The other leaders were animated with less zeal than heretofore. Stephen of Chartres and Hugh of Vermandois began to waver, unable to endure the privations which their own folly and profusion had brought upon them. Even Peter the Hermit became sick at heart ere all was over. When the famine had become so urgent that they were reduced to eat human flesh in the extremity of their hunger, Bohemund and Robert of Flanders set forth on an expedition to procure a supply. They were in a slight degree successful; but the relief they brought was not economized, and in two days they were as destitute as before. Faticius, the Greek commander and representative of Alexius, deserted with his division under pretence of seeking for food, and his example was followed by various bodies of crusaders.

Misery was rife among those who remained, and they strove to alleviate it by a diligent attention to signs and omens. These, with extraordinary visions seen by the enthusiastic, alternately cheered and depressed them according as they foretold the triumph or pictured the reverses of the Cross. At one time a violent hurricane arose, levelling great trees with the ground, and blowing down the tents of the Christian leaders. At another time an earthquake shook the camp, and was thought to prognosticate some great impending evil to the cause of Christendom. But a comet which appeared shortly afterwards, raised them from the despondency into which they had fallen; their lively imaginations making it assume the form of a flaming cross leading them on to victory. Famine was not the least of the evils they endured. Unwholesome food, and the impure air from the neighbouring marshes, engendered pestilential diseases, which carried them off more rapidly than the arrows of the enemy. A thousand of them died in a day, and it became at last a matter of extreme difficulty to afford them burial. To add to their misery, each man grew suspicious of his neighbour; for the camp was infested by Turkish spies, who conveyed daily to the besieged intelligence of the movements and distresses of the enemy. With a ferocity, engendered by despair, Bohemund caused two spies, whom he had detected, to be roasted alive in presence of the army, and within sight of the battlements of Antioch. But even this example failed to reduce their numbers, and the Turks continued to be as well informed as the Christians themselves of all that was passing in the camp.

The news of the arrival of a reinforcement of soldiers from Europe, with an abundant stock of

173

provisions, came to cheer them when reduced to the last extremity. The welcome succour landed at St. Simeon, the port of Antioch, and about six miles from that city. Thitherwards the famishing crusaders proceeded in tumultuous bands, followed by Bohemund and the Count of Toulouse, with strong detachments of their retainers and vassals, to escort the supplies in safety to the camp. The garrison of Antioch, forewarned of this arrival, was on the alert, and a corps of Turkish archers was despatched to lie in ambuscade among the mountains and intercept their return. Bohemund, laden with provisions, was encountered in the rocky passes by the Turkish host. Great numbers of his followers were slain, and he himself had just time to escape to the camp with the news of his defeat. Godfrey of Bouillon, the Duke of Normandy, and the other leaders had heard the rumour of this battle, and were at that instant preparing for the rescue. The army was immediately in motion, animated both by zeal and by hunger, and marched so rapidly as to intercept the victorious Turks before they had time to reach Antioch with their spoil. A fierce battle ensued, which lasted from noon till the going down of the sun. The Christians gained and maintained the advantage, each man fighting as if upon himself alone had depended the fortune of the day. Hundreds of Turks perished in the Orontes, and more than two thousand were left dead upon the field of battle. All the provision was recaptured and brought in safety to the camp, whither the crusaders returned singing Allelulia! or shouting Deus adjuva! Deus adjuva!

This relief lasted for some days, and, had it been duly economized, would have lasted much longer; but the chiefs had no authority, and were unable to exercise any control over its distribution. Famine again approached with rapid strides, and Stephen Count of Blois, not liking the prospect, withdrew from the camp, with four thousand of his retainers, and established himself at Alexandretta. The moral influence of this desertion was highly prejudicial upon those who remained; and Bohemund, the most impatient and ambitious of the chiefs, foresaw that, unless speedily checked, it would lead to the utter failure of the expedition. It was necessary to act decisively; the army murmured at the length of the siege, and the Sultan was collecting his forces to crush them. Against the efforts of the crusaders Antioch might have held out for months; but treason within effected that, which courage without might have striven for in vain.

Baghasihan, the Turkish Prince or Emir of Antioch, had under his command an Armenian of the name of Phirouz, whom he had intrusted with the defence of a tower on that part of the city wall which overlooked the passes of the mountains. Bohemund, by means of a spy who had embraced the Christian religion, and to whom he had given his own name at baptism, kept up a daily communication with this captain, and made him the most magnificent promises of reward, if he would deliver up his post to the Christian knights. Whether the proposal was first made by Bohemund or by the Armenian is uncertain, but that a good understanding soon existed between them, is undoubted; and a night was fixed for the execution of the project. Bohemund communicated the scheme to Godfrey and the Count of Toulouse, with the stipulation that, if the city were won, he, as the soul of the enterprise, should enjoy the dignity of Prince of Antioch. The other leaders hesitated: ambition and jealousy prompted them to refuse their aid in furthering the views of the intriguer. More mature consideration decided them to acquiesce, and seven hundred of the bravest knights were chosen for the expedition, the real object of which, for fear of spies, was kept a profound secret from the rest of the army. When all was ready, a report was promulgated, that the seven hundred were intended to form an ambuscade for a division of the Sultan's army, which was stated to be approaching.

Everything favoured the treacherous project of the Armenian captain, who, on his solitary watchtower, received due intimation of the approach of the crusaders. The night was dark and stormy; not a star was visible above, and the wind howled so furiously as to overpower all other sounds: the rain fell in torrents, and the watchers on the towers adjoining to that of Phirouz could not hear the tramp of the armed knights for the wind, nor see them for the obscurity of the night and the dismalness of the weather. When within shot of the walls, Bohemund sent forward an interpreter to confer with the Armenian. The latter urged them to make haste, and seize the favourable interval, as armed men, with lighted torches, patrolled the battlements every half hour, and at that instant they had just passed. The chiefs were instantly at the foot of the wall: Phirouz let down a rope; Bohemund attached it to the end of a ladder of hides, which was then raised by the Armenian, and held while the knights mounted. A momentary fear came over the spirits of the adventurers, and every one hesitated. At last Bohemund, [Vide William of Tyre.] encouraged by Phirouz from above, ascended a few steps on the ladder, and was followed by Godfrey, Count Robert of Flanders, and a number of other knights. As they advanced, others pressed forward, until their weight became too great for the ladder, which, breaking, precipitated about a dozen of them to the ground, where they fell one upon the other, making a great clatter with their heavy coats of mail. For a moment they thought that all was lost; but the wind made so loud a howling as it swept in fierce gusts through the mountain gorges -- and the Orontes, swollen by the rain, rushed so noisily along -- that the guards heard nothing. The ladder was easily repaired, and the knights ascended two at a time, and reached the platform in safety, When sixty of them had thus ascended, the torch of the coming patrol was seen to gleam at the angle of the wall. Hiding themselves behind a buttress, they awaited his coming in breathless silence. As soon as he arrived at arm's length, he was suddenly seized, and, before he could open his lips to raise an alarm, the silence of death closed them up for ever. They next descended rapidly the spiral staircase of the tower, and, opening the portal, admitted the whole of their companions. Raymond of Toulouse, who, cognizant of the whole plan, had been left behind with the main body of the army, heard at this instant the signal horn, which announced that an entry had been effected, and, leading on his legions, the town was attacked from within and without.

Imagination cannot conceive a scene more dreadful than that presented by the devoted city of Antioch on that night of horror. The crusaders fought with a blind fury, which fanaticism and suffering alike incited. Men, women, and children were indiscriminately slaughtered till the streets ran in gore. Darkness increased the destruction, for when morning dawned the crusaders found themselves with their swords at the breasts of their fellow-soldiers, whom they had mistaken for foes. The Turkish commander fled, first to the citadel, and that becoming insecure, to the mountains, whither he was pursued and slain, his grey head brought back to Antioch as a trophy. At daylight the massacre ceased, and the crusaders gave themselves up to plunder. They found gold, and jewels, and silks, and velvets in abundance, but, of provisions, which were of more importance to them, they found but little of any kind. Corn was excessively scarce, and they discovered to their sorrow that in this respect the besieged had been but little better off than the besiegers.

Before they had time to instal themselves in their new position, and take the necessary measures for procuring a supply, the city was invested by the Turks. The Sultan of Persia had raised an immense army, which he intrusted to the command of Kerbogha, the Emir of Mosul, with instructions to sweep the Christian locusts from the face of the land. The Emir effected junction with Kilij Aslaun, and the two armies surrounded the city. Discouragement took complete possession of the Christian host, and numbers of them contrived to elude the vigilance of the besiegers, and escape to Count Stephen of Blots at Alexandretta, to whom they related the most exaggerated tales of the misery they had endured, and the utter hopelessness of continuing the war. Stephen forthwith broke up his camp and retreated towards Constantinople. On his way he was met by the Emperor Alexius, at the head of a considerable force, hastening to take possession of the conquests made by the Christians in Asia. As soon as he heard of their woeful plight, he turned back, and proceeded with the Count of Blots to Constantinople, leaving the remnant of the crusaders to shift for themselves.

The news of this defection increased the discouragement at Antioch. All the useless horses of the army had been slain and eaten, and dogs, cats, and rats were sold at enormous prices. Even vermin were becoming scarce. With increasing famine came a pestilence, so that in a short time but sixty thousand remained of the three hundred thousand that had originally invested Antioch. But this bitter extremity, while it annihilated the energy of the host, only served to knit the leaders more firmly together; and Bohemund, Godfrey, and Tancred swore never to desert the cause as long as life lasted. The former strove in vain to reanimate the courage of his followers. They were weary and sick at heart, and his menaces and promises were alike thrown away. Some of them had shut themselves up in the houses, and refused to come forth. Bohemund, to drive them to their duty, set fire to the whole quarter, and many of them perished in the flames, while the rest of the army looked on with the utmost indifference. Bohemund, animated himself by a worldly spirit, did not know the true character of the crusaders, nor understand the religious madness which had brought them in such shoals from Europe. A priest, more clear-sighted, devised a scheme which restored all their confidence, and inspired them with a courage so wonderful as to make the poor sixty thousand emaciated, sick, and starving zealots, put to flight the well-fed and six times as numerous legions of the Sultan of Persia.

This priest, a native of Provence, was named Peter Barthelemy, and whether he were a knave or an enthusiast, or both; a principal, or a tool in the hands of others, will ever remain a matter of doubt. Certain it is, however, that he was the means of raising the siege of Antioch, and causing the eventual triumph of the armies of the Cross. When the strength of the crusaders was completely broken by their sufferings, and hope had fled from every bosom, Peter came to Count Raymond of Toulouse, and demanded an interview on matters of serious moment. He was immediately admitted. He said that, some weeks previously, at the time the Christians were besieging Antioch, he was reposing alone in his tent, when he was startled by the shock of the earthquake, which had so alarmed the whole host. Through violent terror of the shock he could only ejaculate, God help me! when turning round he saw two men standing before him, whom he at once recognized by the halo of glory around them as beings of another world. One of them appeared to be an aged man, with reddish hair sprinkled with grey, black eyes, and a long flowing grey beard. The other was younger, larger, and handsomer, and had something more divine in his aspect. The elderly man alone spoke, and informed him that he was the Holy Apostle St. Andrew, and desired him to seek out the Count Raymond, the Bishop of Puy, and Raymond of Altopulto, and ask them why the Bishop did not exhort the people, and sign them with the cross which he bore. The Apostle then took him, naked in his shirt as he was, and transported him through the air into the heart of the city of Antioch, where he led him into the church of St. Peter, at that time a Saracen mosque. The Apostle made him stop by the pillar close to the steps by which they ascend on the south side to the altar, where hung two lamps, which gave out a light brighter than that of the noonday sun; the younger man, whom he did not at that time know, standing afar off, near the steps of the altar. The Apostle then descended into the ground and brought up a lance, which he gave into his hand, telling him that it was the very lance that had opened the side whence had flowed the salvation of the world. With tears of joy he held the holy lance, and implored the Apostle to allow him to take it away and deliver it into the hands of Count Raymond. The Apostle refused, and buried the lance again in the ground, commanding him, when the city was won from the infidels, to go with twelve chosen men, and dig it up again in the same place. The Apostle then transported him back to his tent, and the two vanished from his sight. He had neglected, he said, to deliver this message, afraid that his wonderful tale would not obtain credence from men of such high rank. After some days he again saw the holy vision, as he was gone out of the camp to look for food. This time the divine eyes of the younger looked reproachfully upon him. He implored the Apostle to choose some one else more fitted for the mission, but the Apostle refused, and smote him with a disorder of the eyes, as a punishment for his disobedience. With an obstinacy unaccountable even to himself, he had still delayed. A third time the Apostle and his companion had appeared to him, as he was in a tent with his master William at St. Simeon. On that occasion St. Andrew told him to bear his command to the Count of Toulouse not to bathe in the waters of the Jordan when he came to it, but to cross over in a boat, clad in a shirt and breeches of linen, which he should sprinkle with the sacred waters of the river. These clothes he was afterwards to preserve along with the holy lance. His master William, although he could not see the saint, distinctly heard the voice giving orders to that effect. Again he neglected to execute the commission, and again the saints appeared to him, when he was at the port of Mamistra, about to sail for Cyprus, and St. Andrew threatened him with eternal perdition if he refused longer. Upon this he made up his mind to divulge all that had been revealed to him.

The Count of Toulouse, who, in all probability, concocted this precious tale with the priest, appeared struck with the recital, and sent immediately for the Bishop of Puy and Raymond of Altapulto. The Bishop at once expressed his disbelief of the whole story, and refused to have anything to do in the matter. The Count of Toulouse, on the contrary, saw abundant motives, if not for believing, for pretending to believe; and, in the end, he so impressed upon the mind of the Bishop the advantage that might be derived from it, in working up the popular mind to its former excitement, that the latter reluctantly agreed to make search in due form for the holy weapon. The day after the morrow was fixed upon for the ceremony, and, in the mean time, Peter was consigned to the care of Raymond, the Count's chaplain, in order that no profane curiosity might have an opportunity of cross-examining him, and putting him to a nonplus.

Twelve devout men were forthwith chosen for the undertaking, among whom were the Count of Toulouse and his chaplain. They began digging at sunrise, and continued unwearied till near sunset, without finding the lance; -- they might have dug till this day with no better success, had not Peter himself sprung into the pit, praying to God to bring the lance to light, for the strengthening and victory of his people. Those who hide know where to find; and so it was with Peter, for both he and the lance found their way into the hole at the same time. On a sudden, he and Raymond, the chaplain, beheld its point in the earth, and Raymond, drawing it forth, kissed it with tears of joy, in sight of the multitude which had assembled in the church. It was immediately enveloped in a rich purple cloth, already prepared to receive it, and exhibited in this state to the faithful, who made the building resound with their shouts of gladness.

Peter had another vision the same night, and became from that day forth "dreamer of dreams," in general, to the army. He stated on the following day, that the Apostle Andrew and "the youth with the divine aspect" appeared to him again, and directed that the Count of Toulouse, as a reward for his persevering piety, should carry the Holy Lance at the head of the army, and that the day on which it was found should be observed as a solemn festival throughout Christendom. St. Andrew showed him, at the same time, the holes in the feet and hands of his benign companion; and he became convinced that he stood in the awful presence of THE REDEEMER.

Peter gained so much credit by his visions that dreaming became contagious. Other monks beside himself were visited by the saints, who promised victory to the host if it would valiantly hold out to the last, and crowns of eternal glory to those who fell in the fight. Two deserters, wearied of the fatigues and privations of the war, who had stealthily left the camp, suddenly returned, and seeking Bohemund, told him that they had been met by two apparitions, who, with great anger, had commanded them to return. The one of them said, that he recognized his brother, who had been killed in battle some months before, and that he had a halo of glory around his head. The other, still more hardy, asserted that the apparition which had spoken to him was the Saviour himself, who had promised eternal happiness as his reward if he returned to his duty, but the pains of eternal fire if he rejected the cross. No one thought of disbelieving these men. The courage of the army immediately revived; despondency gave way to hope; every arm grew strong again, and the pangs of hunger were for a time disregarded. The enthusiasm which had led them from Europe burned forth once more as brightly as ever, and they demanded, with loud cries, to be led against the enemy. The leaders were not unwilling. In a battle lay their only chance of salvation; and although Godfrey, Bohemund, and Tancred received the story of the lance with much suspicion, they were too wise to throw discredit upon an imposture which bade fair to open the gates of victory.

Peter the Hermit was previously sent to the camp of Kerbogha to propose that the quarrel between the two religions should be decided by a chosen number of the bravest soldiers of each army. Kerbogha turned from him with a look of contempt, and said he could agree to no proposals from a set of such miserable beggars and robbers. With this uncourteous answer Peter returned to Antioch. Preparations were immediately commenced for an attack upon the enemy: the latter continued to be perfectly well informed of all the proceedings of the Christian camp. The citadel of Antioch, which remained in their possession, overlooked the town, and the commander of the fortress could distinctly see all that was passing within. On the morning of the 28th of June 1098 a black flag, hoisted from its highest tower, announced to the besieging army that the Christians were about to sally forth.

The Moslem leaders knew the sad inroads that famine and disease had made upon the numbers of the foe: they knew that not above two hundred of the knights had horses to ride upon, and that the foot soldiers were sick and emaciated; but they did not know the almost incredible valour which superstition had infused into their hearts. The story of the lance they treated with the most supreme contempt, and, secure of an easy victory, they gave themselves no trouble in preparing for the onslaught. It is related that Kerbogha was playing a game at chess, when the black flag on the citadel gave warning of the enemy's approach, and that, with true oriental coolness, he insisted upon finishing the game ere he bestowed any of his attention upon a foe so unworthy. The defeat of his advanced post of two thousand men aroused him from his apathy.

The crusaders, after this first victory, advanced joyfully towards the mountains, hoping to draw the Turks to a place where their cavalry would be unable to manoeuvre. Their spirits were light and their courage high, as led on by the Duke of Normandy, Count Robert of Flanders, and Hugh of Vermandois, they came within sight of the splendid camp of the enemy. Godfrey of Bouillon and Adhemar, Bishop of Puy, followed immediately after these leaders, the latter clad in complete armour, and bearing the Holy Lance within sight of the whole army: Bohemund and Tancred brought up the rear.

Kerbogha, aware at last that his enemy was not so despicable, took vigorous measures to remedy his mistake, and, preparing himself to meet the Christians in front, he despatched the Sultan Soliman, of Roum, to attack them in the rear. To conceal this movement, he set fire to the dried weeds and grass with which the ground was covered, and Soliman, taking a wide circuit with his cavalry, succeeded, under cover of the smoke, in making good his position in the rear. The battle raged furiously in front; the arrows of the Turks fell thick as hail, and their well-trained squadrons trod the crusaders under their hoofs like stubble. Still the affray was doubtful; for the Christians had the advantage of the ground, and were rapidly gaining upon the enemy, when the overwhelming forces of Soliman arrived in the rear. Godfrey and Tancred flew to the rescue of Bohemund, spreading dismay in the Turkish ranks by their fierce impetuosity. The Bishop of Puy was left almost alone with the Provencals to oppose the legions commanded by Kerbogha in person; but the presence of the Holy Lance made a hero of the meanest soldier in his train. Still, however, the numbers of the enemy seemed interminable. The Christians, attacked on every side, began at last to give way, and the Turks made sure of victory.

At this moment a cry was raised in the Christian host that the saints were fighting on their side. The battle-field was clear of the smoke from the burning weeds, which had curled away, and hung in white clouds of fantastic shape on the brow of the distant mountains. Some imaginative zealot, seeing this dimly through the dust of the battle, called out to his fellows, to look at the army of saints, clothed in white, and riding upon white horses, that were pouring over the hills to the rescue. All eyes were immediately turned to the distant smoke; faith was in every heart; and the old battle-cry, God wills it! God wills it! resounded through the field, as every soldier, believing that God was visibly sending His armies to his aid, fought with an energy unfelt before. A panic seized the Persian and Turkish hosts, and they gave way in all directions. In vain Kerbogha tried to rally them. Fear is more contagious than enthusiasm, and they fled over the mountains like deer pursued by the hounds. The two leaders, seeing the uselessness of further efforts, fled with the rest; and that immense army was scattered over Palestine, leaving nearly seventy thousand of its dead upon the field of battle.

Their magnificent camp fell into the hands of the enemy, with its rich stores of corn, and its droves of sheep and oxen. Jewels, gold, and rich velvets in abundance were distributed among the army. Tancred followed the fugitives over the hills, and reaped as much plunder as those who had remained in the camp. The way, as they fled, was covered with valuables, and horses of the finest breed of Arabia became so plentiful, that every knight of the Christians was provided with a steed. The crusaders, in this battle, acknowledge to have lost nearly ten thousand men.

Their return to Antioch was one of joy indeed: the citadel was surrendered at once, and many of the Turkish garrison embraced the Christian faith, and the rest were suffered to depart. A solemn thanksgiving was offered up by the Bishop of Puy, in which the whole army joined, and the Holy Lance was visited by every soldier.

The enthusiasm lasted for some days, and the army loudly demanded to be led forward to Jerusalem, the grand goal of all their wishes: but none of their leaders was anxious to move; -- the more prudent among them, such as Godfrey and Tancred, for reasons of expediency; and the more ambitious, such as the Count of Toulouse and Bohemund, for reasons of self-interest. Violent dissensions sprang up again between all the chiefs. Raymond of Toulouse, who was left at Antioch to guard the town, had summoned the citadel to surrender, as soon as he saw that there was no fear of any attack upon the part of the Persians; and the other chiefs found, upon their return, his banner waving on its walls. This had given great offence to Bohemund, who had stipulated the principality of Antioch as his reward for winning the town in the first instance. Godfrey and Tancred supported his claim, and, after a great deal of bickering, the flag of Raymond was lowered from the tower, and that of Bohemund hoisted in its stead, who assumed from that time the title of Prince of Antioch. Raymond, however, persisted in retaining possession of one of the city gates and its adjacent towers, which he held for several months, to the great annoyance of Bohemund and the scandal of the army. The Count became in consequence extremely unpopular, although his ambition was not a whit more unreasonable than that of Bohemund himself, nor of Baldwin, who had taken up his quarters at Edessa, where he exercised the functions of a petty sovereign.

The fate of Peter Barthelemy deserves to be recorded. Honours and consideration had come thick upon him after the affair of the lance, and he consequently felt bound in conscience to continue the dreams which had made him a personage of so much importance. The mischief of it was, that like many other liars he had a very bad memory, and he contrived to make his dreams contradict each other in the most palpable manner. St. John one night appeared to him, and told one tale, while, a week after, St. Paul told a totally different story, and held out hopes quite incompatible with those of his apostolic brother. The credulity of that age had a wide maw, and Peter's visions must have been absurd and outrageous indeed, when the very men who had believed in the lance refused to swallow any more of his wonders. Bohemund at last, for the purpose of annoying the Count of Toulouse, challenged poor Peter to prove the truth of his story of the lance by the fiery ordeal. Peter could not refuse a trial so common in that age, and being besides encouraged by the Count and his chaplain, Raymond, an early day was appointed for the ceremony. The previous night was spent in prayer and fasting, according to custom, and Peter came forth in the morning bearing the lance in his hand, and walked boldly up to the fire. The whole army gathered round, impatient for the result, many thousands still believing that the lance was genuine and Peter a holy man. Prayers having been said by Raymond d'Agilles, Peter walked into the flames, and had got nearly through, when pain caused him to lose his presence of mind: the heat too affected his eyes, and, in his anguish, he turned round unwittingly, and passed through the fire again, instead of stepping out of it, as he should have done. The result was, that he was burned so severely, that he never recovered, and, after lingering for some days, he expired in great agony.

Most of the soldiers were suffering either from wounds, disease, or weariness, and it was resolved by Godfrey, -- the tacitly acknowledged chief of the enterprize, -- that the army should have time to refresh itself ere they advanced upon Jerusalem. It was now July, and he proposed that they should pass the hot months of August and September within the walls of Antioch, and march forward in October with renewed vigour, and numbers increased by fresh arrivals from Europe. This advice was finally adopted, although the enthusiasts of the army continued to murmur at the delay. In the mean time the Count of Vermandois was sent upon an embassy to the Emperor Alexius at Constantinople, to reproach him for his base desertion of the cause, and urge him to send the reinforcements he had promised. The Count faithfully executed his mission, (of which, by the way, Alexius took no notice whatever,) and remained for some time at Constantinople, till his zeal, never very violent, totally evaporated. He then returned to France, sick of the Crusade, and determined to intermeddle with it no more.

The chiefs, though they had determined to stay at Antioch for two months, could not remain quiet for so long a time. They would, in all probability, have fallen upon each other, had there been no Turks in Palestine upon whom they might vent their impetuosity. Godfrey proceeded to Edessa, to aid his brother Baldwin in expelling the Saracens from his principality, and the other leaders carried on separate hostilities against them as caprice or ambition dictated. At length the impatience of the army to be led against Jerusalem became so great that the chiefs could no longer delay, and Raymond, Tancred, and Robert of Normandy marched forward with their divisions, and laid siege to the small but strong town of Marah. With their usual improvidence, they had not food enough to last a beleaguering army for a week. They suffered great privations in consequence, till Bohemund came to their aid and took the town by storm. In connexion with this siege, the chronicler, Raymond d'Agilles, (the same Raymond, the chaplain, who figured in the affair of the Holy Lance,) relates a legend, in the truth of which he devoutly believed, and upon which Tasso has founded one of the most beautiful passages of his poem. It is worth preserving, as showing the spirit of the age and the source of the extraordinary courage manifested by the crusaders on occasions of extreme difficulty. "One day," says Raymond, "Anselme de Ribeaumont beheld young Engelram, the son of the Count de St. Paul, who had been killed at Marsh, enter his tent. 'How is it,' said Anselme to him, 'that you, whom I saw lying dead on the field of battle, are full of life ?' -- 'You must know,' replied Engelram, 'that those who fight for Jesus Christ never die.' -- ' But whence,' resumed Anselme, 'comes that strange brightness that surrounds you ?' Upon this Engelram pointed to the sky, where Anselme saw a palace of diamond and crystal. 'It is thence,' said he, 'that I derive the beauty which surprises you. My dwelling is there; a still finer one is prepared for you, and you shall soon come to inhabit it. Farewell! we shall meet again to-morrow.' With these words Engelram returned to heaven. Anselme, struck by the vision, sent the next morning for the priests, received the sacrament; and although full of health, took a last farewell of all his friends, telling them that he was about to leave this world. A few hours afterwards, the enemy having made a sortie, Anselme went out against them sword in hand, and was struck on the forehead by a stone from a Turkish sling, which sent him to heaven, to the beautiful palace that was prepared for him."

New disputes arose between the Prince of Antioch and the Count of Toulouse with regard to the capture of this town, which were with the utmost difficulty appeased by the other chiefs. Delays also took place in the progress of the army, especially before Arches, and the soldiery were so exasperated that they were on the point of choosing new leaders to conduct them to Jerusalem. Godfrey, upon this, set fire to his camp at Arches, and marched forward. He was immediately joined by hundreds of the Provencals of the Count of Toulouse. The latter, seeing the turn affairs were taking, hastened after them, and the whole host proceeded towards the holy city, so long desired amid sorrow, and suffering, and danger. At Emmaus they were met by a deputation from the Christians of Bethlehem, praying for immediate aid against the oppression of the infidels. The very name of Bethlehem, the birthplace of the Saviour, was music to their ears, and many of them wept with joy to think they were approaching a spot so hallowed. Albert of Aix informs us that their hearts were so touched that sleep was banished from the camp, and that, instead of waiting till the morning's dawn to recommence their march, they set out shortly after midnight, full of hope and enthusiasm. For upwards of four hours the mail-clad legions tramped steadfastly forward in the dark, and when the sun arose in unclouded splendour, the towers and pinnacles of Jerusalem gleamed upon their sight. All the tender feelings of their nature were touched; no longer brutal fanatics, but meek and humble pilgrims, they knelt down upon the sod, and with tears in their eyes, exclaimed to one another, "Jerusalem ! Jerusalem!" Some of them kissed the holy ground, others stretched themselves at full length upon it, in order that their bodies might come in contact with the greatest possible extent of it, and others prayed aloud. The women and children who had followed the camp from Europe, and shared in all its dangers, fatigues, and privations, were more boisterous in their joy; the former from long-nourished enthusiasm, and the latter from mere imitation, [Guibert de Nogent relates a curious instance of the imitativeness of these juvenile crusaders. He says that, during the siege of Antioch, the Christian and Saracen boys used to issue forth every evening from the town and camp in great numbers under the command of captains chosen from among themselves. Armed with sticks instead of swords, and stones instead of arrows, they ranged themselves in battle order, and shouting each the war-cry of their country, fought with the utmost desperation. Some of them lost their eyes, and many became cripples for life from the injuries they received on these occasions.] and prayed, and wept, and laughed till they almost put the more sober to the blush.

The first ebullition of their gladness having subsided, the army marched forward, and invested the city on all sides. The assault was almost immediately begun; but after the Christians had lost some of their bravest knights, that mode of attack was abandoned, and the army commenced its preparations for a regular siege. Mangonels, moveable towers, and battering rams, together with a machine called a sow, made of wood, and covered with raw hides, inside of which miners worked to undermine the walls, were forthwith constructed; and to restore the courage and discipline of the army, which had suffered from the unworthy dissensions of the chiefs, the latter held out the hand of friendship to each other, and Tancred and the Count of Toulouse embraced in sight of the whole camp. The clergy aided the cause with their powerful voice, and preached union and goodwill to the highest and the lowest. A solemn procession was also ordered round the city, in which the entire army joined, prayers being offered up at every spot which gospel records had taught them to consider as peculiarly sacred.

The Saracens upon the ramparts beheld all these manifestations without alarm. To incense the Christians, whom they despised, they constructed rude crosses, and fixed them upon the walls, and spat upon and pelted them with dirt and stones. This insult to the symbol of their faith raised the wrath of the crusaders to that height that bravery became ferocity and enthusiasm madness. When all the engines of war were completed the attack was recommenced, and every soldier of the Christian army fought with a vigour which the sense of private wrong invariably inspires. Every man had been personally outraged, and the knights worked at the battering-rams with as much readiness as the meanest soldiers. The Saracen arrows and balls of fire fell thick and fast among them, but the tremendous rams still heaved against the walls, while the best marksmen of the host were busily employed in the several floors of the moveable towers in dealing death among the Turks upon the battlements. Godfrey, Raymond, Tancred, and Robert of Normandy, each upon his tower, fought for hours with unwearied energy, often repulsed, but ever ready to renew the struggle. The Turks, no longer despising the enemy, defended themselves with the utmost skill and bravery till darkness brought a cessation of hostilities. Short was the sleep that night in the. Christian camp. The priests offered up solemn prayers in the midst of the attentive soldiery for the triumph of the Cross in this last great struggle, and as soon as morning dawned every one was in readiness for the affray. The women and children lent their aid, the latter running unconcerned to and fro while the arrows fell fast around them, bearing water to the thirsty combatants. The saints were believed to be aiding their efforts, and the army, impressed with this idea, surmounted difficulties under which a force thrice as numerous, but without their faith, would have quailed and been defeated. Raymond of Toulouse at last forced his way into the city by escalade, while at the very same moment Tancred and Robert of Normandy succeeded in bursting open one of the gates. The Turks flew to repair the mischief, and Godfrey of Bouillon, seeing the battlements comparatively deserted, let down the drawbridge of his moveable tower, and sprang forward, followed by all the knights of his train. In an instant after, the banner of the Cross floated upon the walls of Jerusalem. The crusaders, raising once more their redoubtable war-cry, rushed on from every side, and the city was taken. The battle raged in the streets for several hours, and the Christians, remembering their insulted faith, gave no quarter to young or old, male or female, sick or strong. Not one of the leaders thought himself at liberty to issue orders for staying the carnage, and if he had, he would not have been obeyed. The Saracens fled in great numbers to the mosque of Soliman, but they had not time to fortify themselves within it ere the Christians were upon them. Ten thousand persons are said to have perished in that building alone.

Peter the Hermit, who had remained so long under the veil of neglect, was repaid that day for all his zeal and all his sufferings. As soon as the battle was over, the Christians of Jerusalem issued forth from their hiding-places to welcome their deliverers. They instantly recognized the Hermit as the pilgrim who, years before, had spoken to them so eloquently of the wrongs and insults they had endured, and promised to stir up the princes and people of Europe in their behalf. They clung to the skirts of his garments in the fervour of their gratitude, and vowed to remember him for ever in their prayers. Many of them shed tears about his neck, and attributed the deliverance of Jerusalem solely to his courage and perseverance. Peter afterwards held some ecclesiastical office in the Holy City, but what it was, or what was his ultimate fate, history has forgotten to inform us. Some say that he returned to France and founded a monastery, but the story does not rest upon sufficient authority.

The grand object for which the popular swarms of Europe had forsaken their homes was now accomplished. The Moslem mosques of Jerusalem were converted into churches for a purer faith, and the mount of Calvary and the sepulchre of Christ were profaned no longer by the presence or the power of the infidel. Popular frenzy had fulfilled its mission, and, as a natural consequence, it began to subside from that time forth. The news of the capture of Jerusalem brought numbers of pilgrims from Europe, and, among others, Stephen Count of Chartres and Hugh of Vermandois, to atone for their desertion; but nothing like the former enthusiasm existed among the nations.

Thus then ends the history of the first Crusade. For the better understanding of the second, it will be necessary to describe the interval between them, and to enter into a slight sketch of the history of Jerusalem under its Latin kings, the long and fruitless wars they continued to wage with the unvanquished Saracens, and the poor and miserable results which sprang from so vast an expenditure of zeal, and so deplorable a waste of human life.

The necessity of having some recognized chief was soon felt by the crusaders, and Godfrey de Bouillon, less ambitious than Bohemund, or Raymond of Toulouse, gave his cold consent to wield a sceptre which the latter chiefs would have clutched with eagerness. He was hardly invested with the royal mantle before the Saracens menaced his capital. With much vigour and judgment he exerted himself to follow up the advantages he had gained, and marching out to meet the enemy before they had time to besiege him in Jerusalem, he gave them battle at Ascalon, and defeated them with great loss. He did not, however, live long to enjoy his new dignity, being seized with a fatal illness when he had only reigned nine months. To him succeeded his brother, Baldwin of Edessa. The latter monarch did much to improve the condition of Jerusalem and to extend its territory, but was not able to make a firm footing for his successors. For fifty years, in which the history of Jerusalem is full of interest to the historical student, the crusaders were exposed to fierce and constant hostilities, often gaining battles and territory, and as often losing them, but becoming every day weaker and more divided, while the Saracens became stronger and more united to harass and root them out. The battles of this period were of the most chivalrous character, and deeds of heroism were done by the handful of brave knights that remained in Syria, which have hardly their parallel in the annals of war. In the course of time, however, the Christians could not avoid feeling some respect for the courage, and admiration for the polished manners and advanced civilization of the Saracens, so much superior to the rudeness and semi-barbarism of Europe at that day. Difference of faith did not prevent them from forming alliances with the dark-eyed maidens of the East. One of the first to set the example of taking a Paynim spouse was King Baldwin himself, and these connexions in time became, not only frequent, but almost universal, among such of the knights as had resolved to spend their lives in Palestine. These Eastern ladies were obliged, however, to submit to the ceremony of baptism before they could be received to the arms of a Christian lord. These, and their offspring, naturally looked upon the Saracens with less hatred than did the zealots who conquered Jerusalem, and who thought it a sin deserving the wrath of God to spare an unbeliever. We find, in consequence, that the most obstinate battles waged during the reigns of the later Kings of Jerusalem were fought by the new and raw levies who from time to time arrived from Europe, lured by the hope of glory, or spurred by fanaticism. The latter broke without scruple the truces established between the original settlers and the Saracens, and drew down severe retaliation upon many thousands of their brethren in the faith, whose prudence was stronger than their zeal, and whose chief desire was to live in peace.

Things remained in this unsatisfactory state till the close of the year 1145, when Edessa, the strong frontier town of the Christian kingdom, fell into the bauds of the Saracens. The latter were commanded by Zenghi, a powerful and enterprising monarch, and, after his death, by his son Nourheddin, as powerful and enterprising as his father. An unsuccessful attempt was made by the Count of Edessa to regain the fortress, but Nourheddin, with a large army, came to the rescue, and after defeating the Count with great slaughter, marched into Edessa and caused its fortifications to be rased to the ground, that the town might never more be a bulwark of defence for the kingdom of Jerusalem. The road to the capital was now open, and consternation seized the hearts of the Christians. Nourheddin, it was known, was only waiting for a favourable opportunity to advance upon Jerusalem, and the armies of the Cross, weakened and divided, were not in a condition to make any available resistance. The clergy were filled with grief and alarm, and wrote repeated letters to the Pope and the sovereigns of Europe, urging the expediency of a new Crusade for the relief of Jerusalem. By far the greater number of the priests of Palestine were natives of France, and these naturally looked first to their own country. The solicitations they sent to Louis the Seventh were urgent and oft repeated, and the chivalry of France began to talk once more of arming in the defence of the birthplace of Jesus. The kings of Europe, whose interest it had not been to take any part in the first Crusade, began to bestir themselves in this; and a man appeared, eloquent as Peter the Hermit, to arouse the people as he had done.

We find, however, that the enthusiasm of the second did not equal that of the first Crusade: in fact, the mania had reached its climax in the time of Peter the Hermit, and decreased regularly from that period.

The third Crusade was less general than the second, and the fourth than the third, and so on, until the public enthusiasm was quite extinct, and Jerusalem returned at last to the dominion of its old masters without a convulsion in Christendom. Various reasons have been assigned for this; and one very generally put forward is, that Europe was wearied with continued struggles, and had become sick of "precipitating itself upon Asia." M. Guizot, in his admirable lectures upon European civilization, successfully combats this opinion, and offers one of his own, which is far more satisfactory. He says, in his eighth lecture, "It has been often repeated, that Europe was tired of continually invading Asia. This expression appears to me exceedingly incorrect. It is not possible that human beings can be wearied with what they have not done -- that the labours of their forefathers can fatigue them. Weariness is a personal, not an inherited feeling. The men of the thirteenth century were not fatigued by the Crusades of the twelfth. They were influenced by another cause. A great change had taken place in ideas, sentiments, and social conditions. The same desires and the same wants were no longer felt. The same things were no longer believed. The people refused to believe what their ancestors were persuaded of."

This is, in fact, the secret of the change; and its truth becomes more apparent as we advance in the history of the Crusades, and compare the state of the public mind at the different periods when Godfrey of Bouillon, Louis VII. and Richard I. were chiefs and leaders of the movement. The Crusades themselves were the means of operating a great change in national ideas, and advancing the civilization of Europe. In the time of Godfrey, the nobles were all-powerful and all-oppressive, and equally obnoxious to kings and people. During their absence along with that portion of the community the deepest sunk in ignorance and superstition, both kings and people fortified themselves against the renewal of aristocratic tyranny, and in proportion as they became free, became civliized. It was during this period that in France, the grand centre of the crusading madness, the communes began to acquire strength, and the monarch to possess a tangible and not a merely theoretic authority. Order and comfort began to take root, and, when the second Crusade was preached, men were in consequence much less willing to abandon their homes than they had been during the first. Such pilgrims as had returned from the Holy Land came back with minds more liberal and expanded than when they set out. They had come in contact with a people more civilized than themselves; they had seen something more of the world, and had lost some portion, however small, of the prejudice and bigotry of ignorance. The institution of chivalry had also exercised its humanizing influence, and coming bright and fresh through the ordeal of the Crusades, had softened the character and improved the hearts of the aristocratic order. The Trouveres and Troubadours, singing of love and war in strains pleasing to every class of society, helped to root out the gloomy superstitions which, at the first Crusade, filled the minds of all those who were able to think. Men became in consequence less exclusively under the mental thraldom of the priesthood, and lost much of the credulity which formerly distinguished them. The Crusades appear never to have excited so much attention in England as on the continent of Europe; not because the people were less fanatical than their neighbours, but because they were occupied in matters of graver interest. The English were suffering too severely from the recent successful invasion of their soil, to have much sympathy to bestow upon the distresses of people so far away as the Christians of Palestine; and we find that they took no part in the first Crusade, and very little in the second. Even then those who engaged in it were chiefly Norman knights and their vassals, and not the Saxon franklins and population, who no doubt thought, in their sorrow, as many wise men have thought since, that charity should begin at home.

Germany was productive of more zeal in the cause, and her raw, uncivilized hordes continued to issue forth under the banners of the Cross in numbers apparently undiminished, when the enthusiasm had long been on the wane in other countries. They were sunk at that time in a deeper slough of barbarism than the livelier nations around them, and took, in consequence, a longer period to free themselves from their prejudices. In fact, the second Crusade drew its chief supplies of men from that quarter, where alone the expedition can be said to have retained any portion of popularity.

Such was the state of the mind of Europe when Pope Eugenius, moved by the reiterated entreaties of the Christians of Syria, commissioned St. Bernard to preach a new crusade. St. Bernard was a man eminently qualified for the mission. He was endowed with an eloquence of the highest order, could move an auditory to tears, or laughter, or fury, as it pleased him, and had led a life of such rigid and self-denying virtue, that not even calumny could lift her finger and point it at him. He had renounced high prospects in the church, and contented himself with the simple abbacy of Clairvaux, in order that he might have the leisure he desired, to raise his powerful voice against abuses wherever he found them. Vice met in him an austere and uncompromising reprover; no man was too high for his reproach, and none too low for his sympathy. He was just as well suited for his age as Peter the Hermit had been for the age preceding. He appealed more to the reason, his predecessor to the passions; Peter the Hermit collected a mob, while St. Bernard collected an army. Both were endowed with equal zeal and perseverance, springing, in the one, from impulse, and in the other from conviction, and a desire to increase the influence of the church, that great body of which he was a pillar and an ornament.

One of the first converts he made was in himself a host. Louis VII. was both superstitious and tyrannical, and, in a fit of remorse for the infamous slaughter he had authorised at the sacking of Vitry, he made a vow to undertake the journey to the Holy Land. [The sacking of Vitry reflects indelible disgrace upon Louis VII. His predecessors had been long engaged in resistance to the outrageous powers assumed by the Popes, and Louis continued the same policy. The ecclesiastical chapter of Bourges, having elected an Archbishop without his consent, he proclaimed the election to be invalid, and took severe and prompt measures against the refractory clergy. Thibault, Count de Champagne, took up arms in defence of the Papal authority, and intrenched himself in the town of Vitry. Louis was immediately in the field to chastise the rebel, and he besieged the town with so much vigour, that the Count was forced to surrender. Upwards of thirteen hundred of the inhabitants, fully one half of whom were women and children, took refuge in the church; and, when the gates of the city were opened, and all resistance had ceased, Louis inhumanly gave orders to set fire to the church, and a thousand persons perished in the flames.] He was in this disposition when St. Bernard began to preach, and wanted but little persuasion to embark in the cause. His example had great influence upon the nobility, who, impoverished as many of them were by the sacrifices made by their fathers in the holy wars, were anxious to repair their ruined fortunes by conquests on a foreign shore. These took the field with such vassals as they could command, and, in a very short time, an army was raised amounting to two hundred thousand men. At Vezelai the monarch received the cross from the hands of St. Bernard, on a platform elevated in sight of all the people. Several nobles, three bishops, and his Queen, Eleanor of Aquitaine, were present at this ceremony, and enrolled themselves under the banners of the Cross, St. Bernard cutting up his red sacerdotal vestments, and making crosses of them, to be sewn on the shoulders of the people. An exhortation from the Pope was read to the multitude, granting remission of their sins to all who should join the Crusade, and directing that no man on that holy pilgrimage should encumber himself with heavy baggage and vain superfluities, and that the nobles should not travel with dogs or falcons, to lead them from the direct road, as had happened to so many during the first Crusade.

The command of the army was offered to St. Bernard; but he wisely refused to accept a station for which his habits had unqualified him. After consecrating Louis with great solemnity, at St. Denis, as chief of the expedition, he continued his course through the country, stirring up the people wherever he went. So high an opinion was entertained of his sanctity, that he was thought to be animated by the spirit of prophecy, and to be gifted with the power of working miracles. Many women, excited by his eloquence, and encouraged by his predictions, forsook their husbands and children, and, clothing themselves in male attire, hastened to the war. St. Bernard himself wrote a letter to the Pope, detailing his success, and stating, that in several towns there did not remain a single male inhabitant capable of bearing arms, and that everywhere castles and towns were to be seen filled with women weeping for their absent husbands. But in spite of this apparent enthusiasm, the numbers who really took up arms were inconsiderable, and not to be compared to the swarms of the first Crusade. A levy of no more than two hundred thousand men, which was the utmost the number amounted to, could hardly have depopulated a country like France to the extent mentioned by St. Bernard. His description of the state of the country appears, therefore, to have been much more poetical than true.

Suger, the able minister of Louis, endeavoured to dissuade him from undertaking so long a journey at a time when his own dominions so much needed his presence. But the king was pricked in his conscience by the cruelties of Vitry, and was anxious to make the only reparation which the religion of that day considered sufficient. He was desirous moreover of testifying to the world, that though he could brave the temporal power of the church when it encroached upon his prerogatives, he could render all due obedience to its spiritual decrees whenever it suited his interest or tallied with his prejudices to so do. Suger, therefore, implored in vain, and Louis received the pilgrim's staff at St. Denis, and made all preparations for his pilgrimage.

In the mean time St. Bernard passed into Germany, where similar success attended his preaching. The renown of his sanctity had gone before him, and he found everywhere an admiring audience. Thousands of people, who could not understand a word he said, flocked around him to catch a glimpse of so holy a man; and the knights enrolled themselves in great numbers in the service of the Cross, each receiving from his hands the symbol of the cause. But the people were not led away as in the days of Gottschalk. We do not find that they rose in such tremendous masses of two and three hundred thousand men, swarming over the country like a plague of locusts. Still the enthusiasm was very great. The extraordinary tales that were told and believed of the miracles worked by the preacher brought the country people from far and near. Devils were said to vanish at his sight, and diseases of the most malignant nature to be cured by his touch. [Philip, Archdeacon of the cathedral of Liege, wrote a detailed account of all the miracles performed by St. Bernard during thirty-four days of his mission. They averaged about ten per day. The disciples of St. Bernard complained bitterly that the people flocked around their master in such numbers, that they could not see half the miracles he performed. But they willingly trusted the eyes of others, as far as faith in the miracles went, and seemed to vie with each other whose credulity should be greatest.] The Emperor Conrad caught at last the contagion from his subjects, and declared his intention to follow the Cross.

The preparations were carried on so vigorously under the orders of Conrad, that in less than three months he found himself at the head of an army containing at least one hundred and fifty thousand effective men, besides a great number of women who followed their husbands and lovers to the war. One troop of them rode in the attitude and armour of men: their chief wore gilt spurs and buskins, and thence acquired the epithet of the golden-footed lady. Conrad was ready to set out long before the French Monarch, and in the month of June 1147, he arrived before Constantinople, having passed through Hungary and Bulgaria without offence to the inhabitants.

Manuel Comnenus, the Greek Emperor, successor not only to the throne, but to the policy of Alexius, looked with alarm upon the new levies who had come to eat up his capital and imperil its tranquillity. Too weak to refuse them a passage through his dominions, too distrustful of them to make them welcome when they came, and too little assured of the advantages likely to result to himself from the war, to feign a friendship which he did not feel, the Greek Emperor gave offence at the very outset. His subjects, in the pride of superior civilization, called the Germans barbarians, while the latter, who, if semi-barbarous, were at least honest and straight-forward, retorted upon the Greeks by calling them double-faced knaves and traitors. Disputes continually arose between them, and Conrad, who had preserved so much good order among his followers during their passage, was unable to restrain their indignation when they arrived at Constantinople. For some offence or other which the Greeks had given them, but which is rather hinted at than stated by the scanty historians of the day, the Germans broke into the magnificent pleasure garden of the Emperor, where he had a valuable collection of tame animals, for which the grounds had been laid out in woods, caverns, groves, and streams, that each might follow in captivity his natural habits. The enraged Germans, meriting the name of barbarians that had been bestowed upon them, laid waste this pleasant retreat, and killed or let loose the valuable animals it contained. Manuel, who is said to have beheld the devastation from his palace windows without power or courage to prevent it, was completely disgusted with his guests, and resolved, like his predecessor Alexius, to get rid of them on the first opportunity. He sent a message to Conrad respectfully desiring an interview, but the German refused to trust himself within the walls of Constantinople. The Greek Emperor, on his part, thought it compatible neither with his dignity nor his safety to seek the German, and several days were spent in insincere negotiations. Manuel at length agreed to furnish the crusading army with guides to conduct it through Asia Minor; and Conrad passed over the Hellespont with his forces, the advanced guard being commanded by himself, and the rear by the warlike Bishop of Freysinghen.

Historians are almost unanimous in their belief that the wily Greek gave instructions to his guides to lead the army of the German Emperor into dangers and difficulties. It is certain, that instead of guiding them through such districts of Asia Minor as afforded water and provisions, they led them into the wilds of Cappadocia, where neither was to be procured, and where they were suddenly attacked by the Sultaun of the Seljukian Turks, at the head of an immense force. The guides, whose treachery is apparent from this fact alone, fled at the first sight of the Turkish army, and the Christians were left to wage unequal warfare with their enemy, entangled and bewildered in desert wilds. Toiling in their heavy mail, the Germans could make but little effective resistance to the attacks of the Turkish light horse, who were down upon them one instant, and out of sight the next. Now in the front and now in the rear, the agile foe showered his arrows upon them, enticing them into swamps and hollows, from which they could only extricate themselves after long struggles and great losses. The Germans, confounded by this mode of warfare, lost all conception of the direction they were pursuing, and went back instead of forward. Suffering at the same time for want of provisions, they fell an easy prey to their pursuers. Count Bernhard, one of the bravest leaders of the German expedition, was surrounded, with his whole division, not one of whom escaped the Turkish arrows. The Emperor himself had nearly fallen a victim, and was twice severely wounded. So persevering was the enemy, and so little able were the Germans to make even a show of resistance, that when Conrad at last reached the city of Nice, he found that, instead of being at the head of an imposing force of one hundred thousand foot and seventy thousand horse, he had but fifty or sixty thousand men, and these in the most worn and wearied condition.

Totally ignorant of the treachery of the Greek Emperor, although he had been warned to beware of it, Louis VII. proceeded, at the head of his army, through Worms and Ratisbon, towards Constantinople. At Ratisbon he was met by a deputation from Manuel, bearing letters so full of hyperbole and flattery, that Louis is reported to have blushed when they were read to him by the Bishop of Langres. The object of the deputation was to obtain from the French King a promise to pass through the Grecian territories in a peaceable and friendly manner, and to yield to the Greek Emperor any conquest he might make in Asia Minor. The first part of the proposition was immediately acceded to, but no notice was taken of the second and more unreasonable. Louis marched on, and, passing through Hungary, pitched his tents in the outskirts of Constantinople.

On his arrival, Manuel sent him a friendly invitation to enter the city, at the head of a small train. Louis at once accepted it, and was met by the Emperor at the porch of his palace. The fairest promises were made; every art that flattery could suggest was resorted to, and every argument employed, to induce him to yield his future conquests to the Greek. Louis obstinately refused to pledge himself, and returned to his army, convinced that the Emperor was a man not to be trusted. Negotiations were, however, continued for several days, to the great dissatisfaction of the French army. The news that arrived of a treaty entered into between Manuel and the Turkish Sultan changed their dissatisfaction into fury, and the leaders demanded to be led against Constantinople, swearing that they would raze the treacherous city to the ground. Louis did not feel inclined to accede to this proposal, and, breaking up his camp, he crossed over into Asia.

Here he heard, for the first time, of the mishaps of the German Emperor, whom he found in a woeful plight under the walls of Nice. The two monarchs united their forces, and marched together along the sea-coast to Ephesus; but Conrad, jealous, it would appear, of the superior numbers of the French, and not liking to sink into a vassal, for the time being, of his rival, withdrew abruptly with the remnant of his legions, and returned to Constantinople. Manuel was all smiles and courtesy. He condoled with the German so feelingly upon his losses, and cursed the stupidity or treachery of the guides with such apparent heartiness, that Conrad was half inclined to believe in his sincerity.

Louis, marching onward in the direction of Jerusalem, came up with the enemy on the banks of the Meander. The Turks contested the passage of the river, but the French bribed a peasant to point out a ford lower down: crossing the river without difficulty, they attacked the Turks with much vigour, and put them to flight. Whether the Turks were really defeated, or merely pretended to be so, is doubtful; but the latter supposition seems to be the true one. It is probable that it was part of a concerted plan to draw the invaders onwards to more unfavourable ground, where their destruction might be more certain. If such were the scheme, it succeeded to the heart's wish of its projectors. The crusaders, on the third day after their victory, arrived at a steep mountain-pass, on the summit of which the Turkish host lay concealed so artfully, that not the slightest vestige of their presence could be perceived. "With labouring steps and slow," they toiled up the steep ascent, when suddenly a tremendous fragment of rock came bounding down the precipices with an awful crash, bearing dismay and death before it. At the same instant the Turkish archers started from their hiding-places, and discharged a shower of arrows upon the foot soldiers, who fell by hundreds at a time. The arrows rebounded harmlessly against the iron mail of the knights, which the Turks observing, took aim at their steeds, and horse and rider fell down the steep into the rapid torrent which rushed below. Louis, who commanded the rear-guard, received the first intimation of the onslaught from the sight of his wounded and flying soldiers, and, not knowing the numbers of the enemy, he pushed vigorously forward to stay, by his presence, the panic which had taken possession of his army. All his efforts were in vain. Immense stones continued to be hurled upon them as they advanced, bearing men and horse before them; and those who succeeded in forcing their way to the top, were met hand-to-hand by the Turks, and cast down headlong upon their companions. Louis himself fought with the energy of desperation, but had great difficulty to avoid falling into the enemy's hands. He escaped at last under cover of the night, with the remnant of his forces, and took up his position before Attalia. Here he restored the discipline and the courage of his disorganized and disheartened followers, and debated with his captains the plan that was to be pursued. After suffering severely both from disease and famine, it was resolved that they should march to Antioch, which still remained an independent principality under the successors of Bohemund of Tarentum. At this time the sovereignty was vested in the person of Raymond, the uncle of Eleanor of Aquitaine. This Prince, presuming upon his relationship to the French Queen, endeavoured to withdraw Louis from the grand object of the Crusade -- the defence of the kingdom of Jerusalem, and secure his co-operation in extending the limits and the power of his principality of Antioch. The Prince of Tripoli formed a similar design, but Louis rejected the offers of both, and marched after a short delay to Jerusalem. The Emperor Conrad was there before him, having left Constantinople with promises of assistance from Manuel Comnenus; assistance which never arrived, and was never intended.

A great council of the Christian princes of Palestine and the leaders of the Crusade was then summoned, to discuss the future operations of the war. It was ultimately determined that it would further the cause of the Cross in a greater degree if the united armies, instead of proceeding to Edessa, laid siege to the city of Damascus, and drove the Saracens from that strong position. This was a bold scheme, and, had it been boldly followed out, would have insured, in all probability, the success of the war. But the Christian leaders never learned from experience the necessity of union, that very soul of great enterprises. Though they all agreed upon the policy of the plan, yet every one had his own notions as to the means of executing it. The Princes of Antioch and Tripoli were jealous of each other, and of the King of Jerusalem. The Emperor Conrad was jealous of the King of France, and the King of France was disgusted with them all. But he had come out to Palestine in accordance with a solemn vow; his religion, though it may be called bigotry, was sincere; and he determined to remain to the very last moment that a chance was left, of effecting any good for the cause he had set his heart on.

The siege of Damascus was accordingly commenced, and with so much ability and vigour that the Christians gained a considerable advantage at the very outset. For weeks the siege was pressed, till the shattered fortifications and diminishing resistance of the besieged gave evidence that the city could not hold out much longer. At that moment the insane jealousy of the leaders led to dissensions that soon caused the utter failure, not only of the siege, but of the Crusade. A modern cookery-book, in giving a recipe for cooking a hare, says, "first catch your hare, and then kill it;" a maxim of indisputable wisdom. The Christian chiefs on this occasion had not so much sagacity, for they began a violent dispute among themselves for the possession of a city which was still unconquered. There being already a Prince of Antioch and a Prince of Tripoli, twenty claimants started for the principality of Damascus, and a grand council of the leaders was held to determine the individual on whom the honour should devolve. Many valuable days were wasted in this discussion, the enemy in the mean while gaining strength from their inactivity. It was at length, after a stormy deliberation, agreed that Count Robert of Flanders, who had twice visited the Holy Land, should be invested with the dignity. The other claimants refused to recognise him, or to co-operate in the siege, until a more equitable arrangement had been made. Suspicion filled the camp; the most sinister rumours of intrigues and treachery were set afloat; and the discontented candidates withdrew at last to the other side of the city, and commenced operations on their own account, without a probability of success. They were soon joined by the rest of the army. The consequence was that the weakest side of the city, and that on which they had already made considerable progress in the work of demolition, was left uncovered. The enemy was prompt to profit by the mistake, and received an abundant supply of provisions, and refortified the walls, before the crusaders came to their senses again. When this desirable event happened, it was too late. Saph Eddin, the powerful Emir of Mousoul, was in the neighbourhood, at the head of a large army, advancing by forced marches to the relief of the city. The siege was abruptly abandoned, and the foolish crusaders returned to Jerusalem, having done nothing to weaken the enemy, but every thing to weaken themselves.

The freshness of enthusiasm had now completely subsided; -- even the meanest soldiers were sick at heart. Conrad, from whose fierce zeal at the outset so much might have been expected, was wearied with reverses, and returned to Europe with the poor remnant of his host. Louis lingered a short time longer, for very shame, but the pressing solicitations of his minister Suger induced him to return to France. Thus ended the second Crusade. Its history is but a chronicle of defeats. It left the kingdom of Jerusalem in a worse state than when it quitted Europe, and gained nothing but disgrace for its leaders and discouragement for all concerned.

St. Bernard, who had prophesied a result so different, fell after this into some disrepute, and experienced, like many other prophets, the fate of being without honour in his own country. What made the matter worse, he could not obtain it in any other. Still, however, there were not wanting zealous advocates to stand forward in his behalf, and stem the tide of incredulity, which, unopposed, would have carried away his reputation. The Bishop of Freysinghen declared that prophets were not always able to prophesy, and that the vices of the crusaders drew down the wrath of Heaven upon them. But the most ingenious excuse ever made for St. Bernard is to be found in his life by Geoffroi de Clairvaux, where he pertinaciously insists that the Crusade was not unfortunate. St. Bernard, he says, had prophesied a happy result, and that result could not be considered other than happy which had peopled heaven with so glorious an army of martyrs. Geoffroi was a cunning pleader, and, no doubt, convinced a few of the zealous; but plain people, who were not wanting even in those days, retained their own opinion, or, what amounts to the same thing, "were convinced against their will."

We now come to the consideration of the third Crusade, and of the causes which rendered it necessary. The epidemic frenzy, which had been cooling ever since the issue of the first expedition, was now extinct, or very nearly so, and the nations of Europe looked with cold indifference upon the armaments of their princes. But chivalry had flourished in its natural element of war, and was now in all its glory. It continued to supply armies for the Holy Land when the popular ranks refused to deliver up their able-bodied swarms. Poetry, which, more than religion, inspired the third Crusade, was then but "caviare to the million," who had other matters, of sterner import, to claim all their attention. But the knights and their retainers listened with delight to the martial and amatory strains of the minstrels, minnesangers, trouveres, and troubadours, and burned to win favour in ladies' eyes by showing prowess in Holy Land. The third was truly the romantic era of the Crusades. Men fought then, not so much for the sepulchre of Jesus, and the maintenance of a Christian kingdom in the East, as to gain glory for themselves in the best, and almost only field, where glory could be obtained. They fought, not as zealots, but as soldiers; not for religion, but for honour; not for the crown of martyrdom, but for the favour of the lovely.

It is not necessary to enter into a detail of the events by which Saladin attained the sovereignty of the East, or how, after a succession of engagements, he planted the Moslem banner once more upon the battlements of Jerusalem. The Christian knights and population, including the grand orders of St. John, the Hospitallers, and the Templars, were sunk in an abyss of vice, and torn by unworthy jealousies and dissensions, were unable to resist the well-trained armies which the wise and mighty Saladin brought forward to crush them. But the news of their fall created a painful sensation among the chivalry of Europe, whose noblest members were linked to the dwellers in Palestine by many ties, both of blood and friendship. The news of the great battle of Tiberias, in which Saladin defeated the Christian host with terrible slaughter, arrived first in Europe, and was followed in quick succession by that of the capture of Jerusalem, Antioch, Tripoli, and other cities. Dismay seized upon the clergy. The Pope (Urban III.) was so affected by the news that he pined away for grief, and was scarcely seen to smile again, until he sank into the sleep of death. [James of Vitry -- William de Nangis.] His successor, Gregory VIII. felt the loss as acutely, but had better strength to bear it, and instructed all the clergy of the Christian world to stir up the people to arms for the recovery of the Holy Sepulchre. William, Archbishop of Tyre, a humble follower in the path of Peter the Hermit, left Palestine to preach to the Kings of Europe the miseries he had witnessed, and to incite them to the rescue. The renowned Frederick Barbarossa, the Emperor of Germany, speedily collected an army, and passing over into Syria with less delay than had ever before awaited a crusading force, defeated the Saracens, and took possession of the city of Iconium. He was unfortunately cut off in the middle of his successful career, by imprudently bathing in the Cydnus [The desire of comparing two great men has tempted many writers to drown Frederick in the river Cydnus, in which Alexander so imprudently bathed (Q. Curt. lib. iii. c. 4, 5.): but, from the march of the Emperor, I rather judge that his Saleph is the Calycadnus, a stream of less fame, but of a longer course. -- Gibbon] while he was overheated, and the Duke of Suabia took the command of the expedition. The latter did not prove so able a general, and met with nothing but reverses, although he was enabled to maintain a footing at Antioch until assistance arrived from Europe.

Henry II. of England and Philip Augustus of France, at the head of their chivalry, supported the Crusade with all their influence, until wars and dissensions nearer home estranged them from it for a time. The two kings met at Gisors in Normandy in the month of January 1188, accompanied by a brilliant train of knights and warriors. William of Tyre was present, and expounded the cause of the Cross with considerable eloquence, and the whole assembly bound themselves by oath to proceed to Jerusalem. It was agreed at the same time that a tax, called Saladin's tithe, and consisting of the tenth part of all possessions, whether landed or personal, should be enforced over Christendom, upon every one who was either unable or unwilling to assume the Cross. The lord of every feof, whether lay or ecclesiastical, was charged to raise the tithe within his own jurisdiction; and any one who refused to pay his quota, became by that act the bondsman and absolute property of his lord. At the same time the greatest indulgence was shown to those who assumed the Cross; no man was at liberty to stay them by process of any kind, whether for debt, or robbery, or murder. The King of France, at the breaking up of the conference, summoned a parliament at Paris, where these resolutions were solemnly confirmed, while Henry II. did the same for his Norman possessions at Rouen, and for England at Geddington, in Northamptonshire. To use the words of an ancient chronicler, [Stowe.] "he held a parliament about the voyage into the Holy Land, and troubled the whole land with the paying of tithes towards it."

But it was not England only that was "troubled" by the tax. The people of France also looked upon it with no pleasant feelings, and appear from that time forth to have changed their indifference for the Crusade into aversion. Even the clergy, who were exceedingly willing that other people should contribute half, or even all their goods in furtherance of their favourite scheme, were not at all anxious to contribute a single sous themselves. Millot ["Elemens de l'Histoire de France."] relates that several of them cried out against the impost. Among the rest the clergy of Rheims were called upon to pay their quota, but sent a deputation to the King, begging him to be contented with the aid of their prayers, as they were too poor to contribute in any other shape. Philip Augustus knew better, and by way of giving them a lesson, employed three nobles of the vicinity to lay waste the church lands. The clergy, informed of the outrage, applied to the King for redress. "I will aid you with my prayers," said the Monarch condescendingly," and will intreat those gentlemen to let the church alone." He did as he had promised, but in such a manner, that the nobles, who appreciated the joke, continued their devastations as before. Again the clergy applied to the King. "What would you have of me?" he replied, in answer to their remonstrances: "You gave me your prayers in my necessity, and I have given you mine in yours." The clergy understood the argument, and thought it the wiser course to pay their quota of Saladin's tithe without further parley.

This anecdote shows the unpopularity of the Crusade. If the clergy disliked to contribute, it is no wonder that the people felt still greater antipathy. But the chivalry of Europe was eager for the affray: the tithe was rigorously collected, and armies from England, France, Burgundy, Italy, Flanders, and Germany, were soon in the field; The two kings who were to have led it, were, however, drawn into broils by an aggression of Richard; Duke of Guienne, better known as Richard Coeur de Lion, upon the territory of the Count of Toulouse, and the proposed journey to Palestine was delayed. War continued to rage between France and England, and with so little probability of a speedy termination, that many of the nobles, bound to the Crusade, left the two Monarchs to settle their differences at their leisure, and proceeded to Palestine without them.

Death at last stepped in and removed Henry II. from the hostility of his foes, and the treachery and ingratitude of his children. His son Richard immediately concluded an alliance with Philip Augustus, and the two young, valiant, and impetuous Monarchs, united all their energies to forward the Crusade. They met with a numerous and brilliant retinue at Nonancourt in Normandy, where, in sight of their assembled chivalry, they embraced as brothers, and swore to live as friends and true allies, until a period of forty days after their return from the Holy Land. With a view of purging their camp from the follies and vices which had proved so ruinous to preceding expeditions, they drew up a code of laws for the government of the army. Gambling had been carried to a great extent, and had proved the fruitful source of quarrels and bloodshed, and one of their laws prohibited any person in the army, beneath the degree of a knight, from playing at any game for money. [Strutt's "Sports and Pastimes."] Knights and clergymen might play for money, but no one was permitted to lose or gain more than twenty shillings in a day, under a penalty of one hundred shillings. The personal attendants of the Monarchs were also allowed to play to the same extent. The penalty in their case for infraction was that they should be whipped naked through the army for the space of three days. Any crusader, who struck another and drew blood, was ordered to have his hand cut off; and whoever slew a brother crusader was condemned to be tied alive to the corpse of his victim and buried with him. No young women were allowed to follow the army, to the great sorrow of many vicious and of many virtuous dames, who had not courage to elude the decree by dressing in male attire. But many high-minded and affectionate maidens and matrons, bearing the sword or the spear, followed their husbands and lovers to the war in spite of King Richard, and in defiance of danger. The only women allowed to accompany the army in their own habiliments, were washerwomen, of fifty years complete, and any others of the fair sex who had reached the same age.

These rules having been promulgated, the two monarchs marched together to Lyons, where they separated, agreeing to meet again at Messina. Philip proceeded across the Alps to Genoa, where he took ship, and was conveyed in safety to the place of rendezvous. Richard turned in the direction of Marseilles, where he also took ship for Messina. His impetuous disposition hurried him into many squabbles by the way, and his knights and followers, for the most part as brave and as foolish as himself, imitated him very zealously in this particular. At Messina the Sicilians charged the most exorbitant prices for every necessary of life. Richard's army in vain remonstrated. From words they came to blows, and, as a last resource, plundered the Sicilians, since they could not trade with them. Continual battles were the consequence, in one of which Lebrun, the favourite attendant of Richard, lost his life. The peasantry from far and near came flocking to the aid of the townspeople, and the battle soon became general. Richard, irritated at the loss of his favourite, and incited by a report that Tancred, the King of Sicily, was fighting at the head of his own people, joined the melee with his boldest knights, and, beating back the Sicilians, attacked the city, sword in hand, stormed the battlements, tore down the flag of Sicily, and planted his own in its stead. This collision gave great offence to the King of France, who became from that time jealous of Richard, and apprehensive that his design was not so much to re-establish the Christian Kingdom of Jerusalem, as to make conquests for himself. He, however, exerted his influence to restore peace between the English and Sicilians, and shortly afterwards set sail for Acre, with distrust of his ally germinating in his heart.

Richard remained behind for some weeks, in a state of inactivity quite unaccountable in one of his temperament. He appears to have had no more squabbles with the Sicilians, but to have lived an easy luxurious life, forgetting, in the lap of pleasure, the objects for which he had quitted his own dominions and the dangerous laxity he was introducing into his army. The superstition of his soldiers recalled him at length to a sense of his duty: a comet was seen for several successive nights, which was thought to menace them with the vengeance of Heaven for their delay. Shooting stars gave them similar warning; and a fanatic, of the name of Joachim, with his drawn sword in his hand, and his long hair streaming wildly over his shoulders, went through the camp, howling all night long, and predicting plague, famine, and every other calamity, if they did not set out immediately. Richard did not deem it prudent to neglect the intimations; and, after doing humble penance for his remissness, he set sail for Acre.

A violent storm dispersed his fleet, but he arrived safely at Rhodes with the principal part of the armament. Here he learned that three of his ships had been stranded on the rocky coasts of Cyprus, and that the ruler of the island, Isaac Comnenus, had permitted his people to pillage the unfortunate crews, and had refused shelter to his betrothed bride, the Princess Berengaria, and his sister, who, in one of the vessels, had been driven by stress of weather into the port of Limisso. The fiery monarch swore to be revenged, and, collecting all his vessels, sailed back to Limisso. Isaac Comnenus refused to apologize or explain, and Richard, in no mood to be trifled with, landed on the island, routed with great loss the forces sent to oppose him, and laid the whole country under contribution.

On his arrival at Acre, he found the whole of the chivalry of Europe there before him. Guy of Lusignan, the King of Jerusalem, had long before collected the bold Knights of the Temple, the Hospital, and St. John, and had laid siege to Acre, which was resolutely defended by the Sultan Saladin, with an army magnificent both for its numbers and its discipline. For nearly two years the crusaders had pushed the siege, and made efforts almost superhuman to dislodge the enemy. Various battles had taken place in the open fields with no decisive advantage to either party, and Guy of Lusignan had begun to despair of taking that strong position without aid from Europe. His joy was extreme on the arrival of Philip with all his chivalry, and he only awaited the coming of Coeur de Lion to make one last decisive attack upon the town. When the fleet of England was first seen approaching the shores of Syria, a universal shout arose from the Christian camp; and when Richard landed with his train, one louder still pierced to the very mountains of the south, where Saladin lay with all his army.

It may be remarked as characteristic of this Crusade, that the Christians and the Moslems no longer looked upon each other as barbarians, to whom mercy was a crime. Each host entertained the highest admiration for the bravery and magnanimity of the other, and in their occasional truces met upon the most friendly terms. The Moslem warriors were full of courtesy to the Christian knights, and had no other regret than to think that such fine fellows were not Mahomedans. The Christians, with a feeling precisely similar, extolled to the skies the nobleness of the Saracens, and sighed to think that such generosity and valour should be sullied by disbelief in the Gospel of Jesus. But when the strife began, all these feelings disappeared, and the struggle became mortal.

The jealousy excited in the mind of Philip by the events of Messina still rankled, and the two monarchs refused to act in concert. Instead of making a joint attack upon the town, the French monarch assailed it alone, and was repulsed. Richard did the same, and with the same result. Philip tried to seduce the soldiers of Richard from their allegiance by the offer of three gold pieces per month to every knight who would forsake the banners of England for those of France. Richard met the bribe by another, and promised four pieces to every French knight who should join the Lion of England. In this unworthy rivalry their time was wasted, to the great detriment of the discipline and efficiency of their followers. Some good was nevertheless effected; for the mere presence of two such armies prevented the besieged city from receiving supplies, and the inhabitants were reduced by famine to the most woeful straits. Saladin did not deem it prudent to risk a general engagement by coming to their relief, but preferred to wait till dissension had weakened his enemy, and made him an easy prey. Perhaps if he had been aware of the real extent of the extremity in Acre, he would have changed his plan; but, cut off from the town, he did not know their misery till it was too late. After a short truce the city capitulated upon terms so severe that Saladin afterwards refused to ratify them. The chief conditions were, that the precious wood of the true cross, captured by the Moslems in Jerusalem, should be restored; that a sum of two hundred thousand gold pieces should be paid; and that all the Christian prisoners in Acre should be released, together with two hundred knights and a thousand soldiers, detained in captivity by Saladin. The eastern monarch, as may be well conceived, did not set much store on the wood of the cross, but was nevertheless anxious to keep it, as he knew its possession by the Christians would do more than a victory to restore their courage. He refused, therefore, to deliver it up, or to accede to any of the conditions; and

Richard, as he had previously threatened, barbarously ordered all the Saracen prisoners in his power to be put to death.

The possession of the city only caused new and unhappy dissensions between the Christian leaders. The Archduke of Austria unjustifiably hoisted his flag on one of the towers of Acre, which Richard no sooner saw than he tore it down with his own hands, and trampled it under his feet. Philip, though he did not sympathise with the Archduke, was piqued at the assumption of Richard, and the breach between the two monarchs became wider than ever. A foolish dispute arose at the same time between Guy of Lusignan and Conrad of Montferrat for the crown of Jerusalem. The inferior knights were not slow to imitate the pernicious example, and jealousy, distrust, and ill-will reigned in the Christian camp. In the midst of this confusion the King of France suddenly announced his intention to return to his own country. Richard was filled with indignation, and exclaimed, "Eternal shame light on him, and on all France, if, for any cause, he leave this work unfinished!" But Philip was not to be stayed. His health had suffered by his residence in the East, and, ambitious of playing a first part, he preferred to play none at all, than to play second to King Richard. Leaving a small detachment of Burgundians behind, he returned to France with the remainder of his army; and Coeur de Lion, without feeling, in the multitude of his rivals, that he had lost the greatest, became painfully convinced that the right arm of the enterprize was lopped off.

After his departure, Richard re-fortified Acre, restored the Christian worship in the churches, and, leaving a Christian garrison to protect it, marched along the sea-coast towards Ascalon. Saladin was on the alert, and sent his light horse to attack the rear of the Christian army, while he himself, miscalculating their weakness since the defection of Philip, endeavoured to force them to a general engagement. The rival armies met near Azotus. A fierce battle ensued, in which Saladin was defeated and put to flight, and the road to Jerusalem left free for the crusaders.

Again discord exerted its baleful influence, and prevented Richard from following up his victory. His opinion was constantly opposed by the other leaders, all jealous of his bravery and influence; and the army, instead of marching to Jerusalem, or even to Ascalon, as was first intended, proceeded to Jaffa, and remained in idleness until Saladin was again in a condition to wage war against them.

Many months were spent in fruitless hostilities and as fruitless negotiations. Richard's wish was to recapture Jerusalem; but there were difficulties in the way, which even his bold spirit could not conquer. His own intolerable pride was not the least cause of the evil; for it estranged many a generous spirit, who would have been willing to co-operate with him in all cordiality. At length it was agreed to march to the Holy City; but the progress made was so slow and painful, that the soldiers murmured, and the leaders meditated retreat. The weather was hot and dry, and there was little water to be procured. Saladin had choked up the wells and cisterns on the route, and the army had not zeal enough to push forward amid such privation. At Bethlehem a council was held, to debate whether they should retreat or advance. Retreat was decided upon, and immediately commenced. It is said, that Richard was first led to a hill, whence he could obtain a sight of the towers of Jerusalem, and that he was so affected at being so near it, and so unable to relieve it, that he hid his face behind his shield, and sobbed aloud.

The army separated into two divisions, the smaller falling back upon Jaffa, and the larger, commanded by Richard and the Duke of Burgundy, returning to Acre. Before the English monarch had made all his preparations for his return to Europe, a messenger reached Acre with the intelligence that Jaffa was besieged by Saladin, and that, unless relieved immediately, the city would be taken. The French, under the Duke of Burgundy, were so wearied with the war, that they refused to aid their brethren in Jaffa. Richard, blushing with shame at their pusillanimity, called his English to the rescue, and arrived just in time to save the city. His very name put the Saracens to flight, so great was their dread of his prowess. Saladin regarded him with the warmest admiration, and when Richard, after his victory, demanded peace, willingly acceded. A truce was concluded for three years and eight months, during which Christian pilgrims were to enjoy the liberty of visiting Jerusalem without hindrance or payment of any tax. The crusaders were allowed to retain the cities of Tyre and Jaffa, with the country intervening. Saladin, with a princely generosity, invited many of the Christians to visit Jerusalem; and several of the leaders took advantage of his offer to feast their eyes upon a spot which all considered so sacred. Many of them were entertained for days in the Sultan's own palace, from which they returned with their tongues laden with the praises of the noble infidel. Richard and Saladin never met, though the impression that they did will remain on many minds, who have been dazzled by the glorious fiction of Sir Walter Scott. But each admired the prowess and nobleness of soul of his rival, and agreed to terms far less onerous than either would have accepted, had this mutual admiration not existed.[Richard left a high reputation in Palestine. So much terror did his name occasion, that the women of Syria used it to frighten their children for ages afterwards. Every disobedient brat became still when told that King Richard was coming. Even men shared the panic that his name created; and a hundred years afterwards, whenever a horse shied at any object in the way, his rider would exclaim, "What! dost thou think King Richard is in the bush?"]

The King of England no longer delayed his departure, for messengers from his own country brought imperative news that his presence was required to defeat the intrigues that were fomenting against his crown. His long imprisonment in the Austrian dominions and final ransom are too well known to be dwelt upon. And thus ended the third Crusade, less destructive of human life than the two first, but quite as useless.

The flame of popular enthusiasm now burned pale indeed, and all the efforts of popes and potentates were insufficient to rekindle it. At last, after flickering unsteadily, like a lamp expiring in the socket, it burned up brightly for one final instant, and was extinguished for ever.

The fourth Crusade, as connected with popular feeling, requires little or no notice. At the death of Saladin, which happened a year after the conclusion of his truce with Richard of England, his vast empire fell to pieces. His brother Saif Eddin, or Saphaddin, seized upon Syria, in the possession of which he was troubled by the sons of Saladin. When this intelligence reached Europe, the Pope, Celestine III. judged the moment favourable for preaching a new Crusade. But every nation in Europe was unwilling and cold towards it. The people had no ardour, and Kings were occupied with more weighty matters at home. The only Monarch of Europe who encouraged it was the Emperor Henry of Germany, under whose auspices the Dukes of Saxony and Bavaria took the field at the head of a considerable force. They landed in Palestine, and found anything but a welcome from the Christian inhabitants. Under the mild sway of Saladin, they had enjoyed repose and toleration, and both were endangered by the arrival of the Germans. They looked upon them in consequence as over-officious intruders, and gave them no encouragement in the warfare against Saphaddin. The result of this Crusade was even more disastrous than the last -- for the Germans contrived not only to embitter the Saracens against the Christians of Judea, but to lose the strong city of Jaffa, and cause the destruction of nine-tenths of the army with which they had quitted Europe. And so ended the fourth Crusade.

The fifth was more important, and had a result which its projectors never dreamed of -- no less than the sacking of Constantinople, and the placing of a French dynasty upon the imperial throne of the eastern

Caesars. Each succeeding Pope, however much he may have differed from his predecessors on other points, zealously agreed in one, that of maintaining by every possible means the papal ascendancy. No scheme was so likely to aid in this endeavour as the Crusades. As long as they could persuade the kings and nobles of Europe to fight and die in Syria, their own sway was secured over the minds of men at home. Such being their object, they never inquired whether a Crusade was or was not likely to be successful, whether the time were well or ill chosen, or whether men and money could be procured in sufficient abundance. Pope Innocent III. would have been proud if he could have bent the refractory Monarchs of England and France into so much submission. But John and Philip Augustus were both engaged. Both had deeply offended the church, and had been laid under her ban, and both were occupied in important reforms at home; Philip in bestowing immunities upon his subjects, and John in having them forced from him. The emissaries of the Pope therefore plied them in vain; -- but as in the first and second Crusades, the eloquence of a powerful preacher incited the nobility, and through them a certain portion of the people, Foulque, Bishop of Neuilly, an ambitious and enterprizing prelate, entered fully into the views of the Court of Rome, and preached the Crusade wherever he could find an audience. Chance favoured him to a degree he did not himself expect, for he had in general found but few proselytes, and those few but cold in the cause. Theobald, Count of Champagne, had instituted a grand tournament, to which he had invited all the nobles from far and near. Upwards of two thousand knights were present with their retainers, besides a vast concourse of people to witness the sports. In the midst of the festivities Foulque arrived upon the spot, and conceiving the opportunity to be a favourable one, he addressed the multitude in eloquent language, and passionately called upon them to enrol themselves for the new Crusade. The Count de Champagne, young, ardent, and easily excited, received the cross at his hands. The enthusiasm spread rapidly. Charles Count of Blois followed the example, and of the two thousand knights present, scarcely one hundred and fifty refused. The popular phrensy seemed on the point of breaking out as in the days of yore. The Count of Flanders, the Count of Bar, the Duke of Burgundy, and the Marquis of Montferrat, brought all their vassals to swell the train, and in a very short space of time an effective army was on foot and ready to march to Palestine.

The dangers of an overland journey were too well understood, and the crusaders endeavoured to make a contract with some of the Italian states to convey them over in their vessels. Dandolo, the aged Doge of Venice, offered them the galleys of the Republic; but the crusaders, on their arrival in that city, found themselves too poor to pay even half the sum demanded. Every means was tried to raise money; the crusaders melted down their plate, and ladies gave up their trinkets. Contributions were solicited from the faithful, but came in so slowly, as to make it evident to all concerned, that the faithful of Europe were outnumbered by the prudent. As a last resource, Dandolo offered to convey them to Palestine at the expense of the Republic, if they would previously aid in the recapture of the city of Zara, which had been seized from the Venetians a short time previously by the King of Hungary. The crusaders consented, much to the displeasure of the Pope, who threatened excommunication upon all who should be turned aside from the voyage to Jerusalem. But notwithstanding the fulminations of the church, the expedition never reached Palestine. The siege of Zara was speedily undertaken. After a long and brave defence, the city surrendered at discretion, and the crusaders were free, if they had so chosen it, to use their swords against the Saracens. But the ambition of the chiefs had been directed, by unforeseen circumstances, elsewhere.

After the death of Manuel Comnenus, the Greek empire had fallen a prey to intestine divisions. His son Alexius II. had succeeded him, but was murdered after a very short reign by his uncle Andronicus, who seized upon the throne. His reign also was but of short duration. Isaac Angelus, a member of the same family, took up arms against the usurper, and having defeated and captured him in a pitched battle, had him put to death. He also mounted the throne only to be cast down from it. His brother Alexius deposed him, and to incapacitate him from reigning, put out his eyes, and shut him up in a dungeon. Neither was Alexius III. allowed to remain in peaceable possession of the throne; the son of the unhappy Isaac, whose name also was Alexius, fled from Constantinople, and hearing that the crusaders had undertaken the siege of Zara, made them the most magnificent offers if they would afterwards aid him in deposing his uncle. His offers were, that if by their means he was re-established in his father's dominions, he would place the Greek church under the authority of the Pope of Rome, lend the whole force of the Greek Empire to the conquest of Palestine, and distribute two hundred thousand marks of silver among the crusading army. The offer was accepted, with a proviso on the part of some of the leaders, that they should be free to abandon the design, if it met with the disapproval of the Pope. But this was not to be feared. The submission of the schismatic Greeks to the See of Rome was a greater bribe to the Pontiff, than the utter annihilation of the Saracen power in Palestine would have been.

The crusaders were soon in movement for the imperial city. Their operations were skilfully and courageously directed, and spread such dismay as to paralyse the efforts of the usurper to retain possession of his throne. After a vain resistance, he abandoned the city to its fate, and fled no one knew whither. The aged and blind Isaac was taken from his dungeon by his subjects, and placed upon the throne ere the crusaders were apprized of the flight of his rival. His son Alexius IV. was afterwards associated with him in the sovereignty.

But the conditions of the treaty gave offence to the Grecian people, whose prelates refused to place themselves under the dominion of the See of Rome. Alexius at first endeavoured to persuade his subjects to submission, and prayed the crusaders to remain in Constantinople until they had fortified him in the possession of a throne which was yet far from secure. He soon became unpopular with his subjects; and breaking faith with regard to the subsidies, he offended the crusaders. War was at length declared upon him by both parties; by his people for his tyranny, and by his former friends for his treachery. He was seized in his palace by his own guards and thrown into prison, while the crusaders were making ready to besiege his capital. The Greeks immediately proceeded to the election of a new Monarch; and looking about for a man with courage, energy, and perseverance, they fixed upon Alexius Ducas, who, with almost every bad quality, was possessed of the virtues they needed. He ascended the throne under the name of Murzuphlis. One of his first acts was to rid himself of his youngest predecessor -- a broken heart had already removed the blind old Isaac -- no longer a stumbling block in his way -- and the young Alexius was soon after put to death in his prison.

War to the knife was now declared between the Greeks and the Franks, and early in the spring of the year 1204, preparations were commenced for an assault upon Constantinople. The French and Venetians entered into a treaty for the division of the spoils among their soldiery, for so confident were they of success, that failure never once entered into their calculations. This confidence led them on to victory, while the Greeks, cowardly as treacherous people always are, were paralysed by a foreboding of evil. It has been a matter of astonishment to all historians, that Murzuphlis, with the reputation for courage which he had acquired, and the immense resources at his disposal, took no better measures to repel the onset of the crusaders. Their numbers were as a mere handful in comparison with those which he could have brought against them; and if they had the hopes of plunder to lead them on, the Greeks had their homes to fight for, and their very existence as a nation to protect. After an impetuous assault, repulsed for one day, but renewed with double impetuosity on another, the crusaders lashed their vessels against the walls, slew every man who opposed them, and, with little loss to themselves, entered the city. Murzuphlis fled, and Constantinople was given over to be pillaged by the victors. The wealth they found was enormous. In money alone there was sufficient to distribute twenty marks of silver to each knight, ten to each squire or servant at arms, and five to each archer. Jewels, velvets, silks, and every luxury of attire, with rare wines and fruits, and valuable merchandise of every description, also fell into their hands, and were bought by the trading Venetians, and the proceeds distributed among the army. Two thousand persons were put to the sword; but had there been less plunder to take up the attention of the victors, the slaughter would in all probability have been much greater.

In many of the bloody wars which defile the page of history, we find that soldiers, utterly reckless of the works of God, will destroy his masterpiece, man, with unsparing brutality, but linger with respect around the beautiful works of art. They will slaughter women and children, but spare a picture; will hew down the sick, the helpless, and the hoary-headed, but refrain from injuring a fine piece of sculpture. The Latins, on their entrance into Constantinople, respected neither the works of God nor man, but vented their brutal ferocity upon the one and satisfied their avarice upon the other. Many beautiful bronze statues, above all price as works of art, were broken into pieces to be sold as old metal. The finely-chiselled marble, which could be put to no such vile uses, was also destroyed, with a recklessness; if possible, still more atrocious. [The following is a list of some of the works of art thus destroyed, from Nicetas, a contemporary Greek author: -- 1st. A colossal Juno, from the forum of Constantine, the head of which was so large that four horses could scarcely draw it from the place where it stood to the palace. 2d. The statue of Paris presenting the apple to Venus. 3d. An immense bronze pyramid, crowned by a female figure, which turned with the wind. 4th. The colossal statue of Bellerophon, in bronze, which was broken down and cast into the furnace. Under the inner nail of the horse's hind foot on the left side, was found a seal wrapped in a woollen cloth. 5th. A figure of Hercules, by Lysimachus, of such vast dimensions that the thumb was equal in circumference to the waist of a man. 6th. The Ass and his driver, cast by order of Augustus after the battle of Actium, in commemoration of his having discovered the position of Antony through the means of an ass-driver. 7th. The Wolf suckling the twins of Rome. 8th. The Gladiator in combat with a lion. 9th. The Hippopotamus. 10th. The Sphinxes. 11th. An eagle fighting with a serpent. 12th. A beautiful statue of Helen. 13th. A group, with a monster somewhat resembling a bull, engaged in deadly conflict with a serpent; and many other works of art, too numerous to mention.]

The carnage being over, and the spoil distributed, six persons were chosen from among the Franks and six from among the Venetians, who were to meet and elect an Emperor, previously binding themselves by oath to select the individual best qualified among the candidates. The choice wavered between Baldwin, Count of Flanders, and Boniface, Marquis of Montferrat, but fell eventually upon the former. He was straightway robed in the imperial purple, and became the founder of a new dynasty. He did not live long to enjoy his power, or to consolidate it for his successors, who, in their turn, were soon swept away. In less than sixty years the rule of the Franks at Constantinople was brought to as sudden and disastrous a termination as the reign of Murzuphlis: and this was the grand result of the fifth Crusade.

Pope Innocent III, although he had looked with no very unfavourable eye upon these proceedings, regretted that nothing had been done for the relief of the Holy Land; still, upon every convenient occasion, he enforced the necessity of a new Crusade. Until the year 1213, his exhortations had no other effect than to keep the subject in the mind of Europe. Every spring and summer, detachments of pilgrims continued to set out for Palestine to the aid of their brethren, but not in sufficient numbers to be of much service. These periodical passages were called the passagiuum Martii, or the passage of March, and the passagium Johannis, or the passage of the festival of St. John. These did not consist entirely of soldiers, armed against the Saracen, but of pilgrims led by devotion, and in performance of their vows, bearing nothing with them but their staff and their wallet. Early in the spring of 1213 a more extraordinary body of crusaders was raised in France and Germany. An immense number of boys and girls, amounting, according to some accounts, to thirty thousand, were incited by the persuasion of two monks to undertake the journey to Palestine. They were, no doubt, composed of the idle and deserted children who generally swarm in great cities, nurtured in vice and daring, and ready for anything. The object of the monks seems to have been the atrocious one of inveigling them into slave ships, on pretence of sending them to Syria, and selling them for slaves on the coast of Africa. [See Jacob de Voragine and Albericus.]

Great numbers of these poor victims were shipped at Marseilles; but the vessels, with the exception of two or three, were wrecked on the shores of Italy, and every soul perished. The remainder arrived safely in Africa, and were bought up as slaves, and sent off into the interior of the country. Another detachment arrived at Genoa; but the accomplices in this horrid plot having taken no measures at that port, expecting them all at Marseilles, they were induced to return to their homes by the Genoese.

Fuller, in his quaint history of the "Holy Warre," says that this Crusade was done by the instinct of the devil; and he adds a reason, which may provoke mirth now, but which was put forth by the worthy historian in all soberness and sincerity. He says, "the devil, being cloyed with the murdering of men, desired a cordial of children's blood to comfort his weak stomach;" as epicures, when tired of mutton, resort to lamb for a change.

It appears from other authors that the preaching of the vile monks had such an effect upon these deluded children that they ran about the country, exclaiming, "O, Lord Jesus, restore thy cross to us!" and that neither bolts nor bars, the fear of fathers, nor the love of mothers, was sufficient to restrain them from journeying to Jerusalem.

The details of these strange proceedings are exceedingly meagre and confused, and none of the contemporary writers who mention the subject have thought it worth while to state the names of the monks who originated the scheme, or the fate they met for their wickedness. Two merchants of Marseilles, who were to have shared in the profits, were, it is said, brought to justice for some other crime, and suffered death; but we are not informed whether they divulged any circumstances relating to this matter.

Pope Innocent III does not seem to have been aware that the causes of this juvenile Crusade were such as have been stated, for, upon being informed that numbers of them had taken the Cross, and were marching to the Holy Land, he exclaimed, "These children are awake, while we sleep!" He imagined, apparently, that the mind of Europe was still bent on the recovery of Palestine, and that the zeal of these children implied a sort of reproach upon his own lukewarmness. Very soon afterwards, he bestirred himself with more activity, and sent an encyclical letter to the clergy of Christendom, urging them to preach a new Crusade. As usual, a number of adventurous nobles, who had nothing else to do, enrolled themselves with their retainers. At a council of Lateran, which was held while these bands were collecting, Innocent announced that he himself would take the Cross, and lead the armies of Christ to the defence of his sepulchre. In all probability he would have done so, for he was zealous enough; but death stepped in, and destroyed his project ere it was ripe. His successor encouraged the Crusade, though he refused to accompany it; and the armament continued in France, England, and Germany. No leaders of any importance joined it from the former countries. Andrew, King of Hungary, was the only monarch who had leisure or inclination to leave his dominions. The Dukes of Austria and Bavaria joined him with a considerable army of Germans, and marching to Spalatro, took ship for Cyprus, and from thence to Acre.

The whole conduct of the King of Hungary was marked by pusillanimity and irresolution. He found himself in the Holy Land at the head of a very efficient army; the Saracens were taken by surprise, and were for some weeks unprepared to offer any resistance to his arms. He defeated the first body sent to oppose him, and marched towards Mount Tabor, with the intention of seizing upon an important fortress which the Saracens had recently constructed. He arrived without impediment at the Mount, and might have easily taken it; but a sudden fit of cowardice came over him, and he returned to Acre without striking a blow. He very soon afterwards abandoned the enterprise altogether, and returned to his own country.

Tardy reinforcements arrived at intervals from Europe; and the Duke of Austria, now the chief leader of the expedition, had still sufficient forces at his command to trouble the Saracens very seriously. It was resolved by him, in council with the other chiefs, that the whole energy of the Crusade should be directed upon Egypt, the seat of the Saracen power in its relationship to Palestine, and from whence were drawn the continual levies that were brought against them by the Sultan. Damietta, which commanded the river Nile, and was one of the most important cities of Egypt, was chosen as the first point of attack. The siege was forthwith commenced, and carried on with considerable energy, until the crusaders gained possession of a tower, which projected into the middle of the stream, and was looked upon as the very key of the city.

While congratulating themselves upon this success, and wasting in revelry the time which should have been employed in pushing the advantage, they received the news of the death of the wise Sultan Saphaddin. His two sons, Camhel and Cohreddin, divided his empire between them. Syria and Palestine fell to the share of Cohreddin, while Egypt was consigned to the other brother, who had for some time exercised the functions of Lieutenant of that country. Being unpopular among the Egyptians, they revolted against him, giving the crusaders a finer opportunity for making a conquest than they had ever enjoyed before. But, quarrelsome and licentious as they had been from time immemorial, they did not see that the favourable moment had come; or, seeing, could not profit by it. While they were revelling or fighting among themselves, under the walls of Damietta, the revolt was put down, and Camhel firmly established on the throne of Egypt. In conjunction with his brother, Cohreddin, his next care was to drive the Christians from Damietta, and, for upwards of three months, they bent all their efforts to throw in supplies to the besieged, or draw on the besiegers to a general engagement. In neither were they successful; and the famine in Damietta became so dreadful, that vermin of every description were thought luxuries, and sold for exorbitant prices. A dead dog became more valuable than a live ox in time of prosperity. Unwholesome food brought on disease, and the city could hold out no longer, for absolute want of men to defend the walls.

Cohreddin and Camhel were alike interested in the preservation of so important a position, and, convinced of the certain fate of the city, they opened a conference with the crusading chiefs, offering to yield the whole of Palestine to the Christians, upon the sole condition of the evacuation of Egypt. With a blindness and wrong-headedness almost incredible, these advantageous terms were refused, chiefly through the persuasion of Cardinal Pelagius, an ignorant and obstinate fanatic, who urged upon the Duke of Austria and the French and English leaders, that infidels never kept their word; that their offers were deceptive, and merely intended to betray. The conferences were brought to an abrupt termination by the crusaders, and a last attack made upon the walls of Damietta. The besieged made but slight resistance, for they had no hope, and the Christians entered the city, and found, out of seventy thousand people, but three thousand remaining: so fearful had been the ravages of the twin fiends, plague and famine.

Several months were spent in Damietta. The climate either weakened the frames or obscured the understandings of the Christians; for, after their conquest, they lost all energy, and abandoned themselves more unscrupulously than ever to riot and debauchery. John of Brienne, who, by right of his wife, was the nominal sovereign of Jerusalem, was so disgusted with the pusillanimity, arrogance, and dissensions of the chiefs, that he withdrew entirely from them, and retired to Acre. Large bodies also returned to Europe, and Cardinal Pelagius was left at liberty to blast the whole enterprise whenever it pleased him. He managed to conciliate John of Brienne, and marched forward with these combined forces to attack Cairo. It was only when he had approached within a few hours' march of that city, that he discovered the inadequacy of his army. He turned back immediately, but the Nile had risen since his departure; the sluices were opened, and there was no means of reaching Damietta. In this strait, he sued for the peace he had formerly spurned, and, happily for himself, found the generous brothers, Camhel and Cohreddin, still willing to grant it. Damietta was soon afterwards given up, and the Cardinal returned to Europe. John of Brienne retired to Acre, to mourn the loss of his kingdom, embittered against the folly of his pretended friends, who had ruined where they should have aided him. And thus ended the sixth Crusade.

The seventh was more successful. Frederic II, Emperor of Germany, had often vowed to lead his armies to the defence of Palestine, but was as often deterred from the journey by matters of more pressing importance. Cohreddin was a mild and enlightened monarch, and the Christians of Syria enjoyed repose and toleration under his rule: but John of Brienne was not willing to lose his kingdom without an effort; and the Popes in Europe were ever willing to embroil the nations for the sake of extending their own power. No monarch of that age was capable of rendering more effective assistance than Frederic of Germany. To inspire him with more zeal, it was proposed that he should wed the young Princess, Violante, daughter of John of Brienne, and heiress of the kingdom of Jerusalem. Frederic consented with joy and eagerness. The Princess was brought from Acre to Rome without delay, and her marriage celebrated on a scale of great magnificence. Her father, John of Brienne, abdicated all his rights in favour of his son-in-law, and Jerusalem had once more a king, who had not only the will, but the power, to enforce his claims. Preparations for the new crusade were immediately commenced, and in the course of six months the Emperor was at the head of a well-disciplined army of sixty thousand men. Matthew Paris informs us, that an army of the same amount was gathered in England; and most of the writers upon the Crusades adopt his statement. When John of Brienne was in England, before his daughter's marriage with the Emperor was thought of, praying for the aid of Henry III. and his nobles to recover his lost kingdom, he did not meet with much encouragement. Grafton, in his Chronicle, says, "he departed again without any great comfort." But when a man of more influence in European politics appeared upon the scene, the English nobles were as ready to sacrifice themselves in the cause as they had been in the time of Coeur de Lion.

The army of Frederic encamped at Brundusium; but a pestilential disease having made its appearance among them, their departure was delayed for several months. In the mean time the Empress Violante died in child-bed. John of Brienne, who had already repented of his abdication, and was besides incensed against Frederic for many acts of neglect and insult, no sooner saw the only tie which bound them, severed by the death of his daughter, than he began to bestir himself, and make interest with the Pope to undo what he had done, and regain the honorary crown he had renounced. Pope Gregory the Ninth, a man of a proud, unconciliating, and revengeful character, owed the Emperor a grudge for many an act of disobedience to his authority, and encouraged the overtures of John of Brienne more than he should have done. Frederic, however, despised them both, and, as soon as his army was convalescent, set sail for Acre. He had not been many days at sea, when he was himself attacked with the malady, and obliged to return to Otranto, the nearest port. Gregory, who had by this time decided in the interest of John of Brienne, excommunicated the Emperor for returning from so holy an expedition on any pretext whatever. Frederic at first treated the excommunication with supreme contempt; but when he got well, he gave his Holiness to understand that he was not to be outraged with impunity, and sent some of his troops to ravage the Papal territories. This, however, only made the matter worse, and Gregory despatched messengers to Palestine, forbidding the faithful, under severe pains and penalties, to hold any intercourse with the excommunicated Emperor. Thus between them both, the scheme which they had so much at heart bade fair to be as effectually ruined as even the Saracens could have wished. Frederic still continued his zeal in the Crusade, for he was now King of Jerusalem, and fought for himself, and not for Christendom, or its representative, Pope Gregory. Hearing that John of Brienne was preparing to leave

Europe, he lost no time in taking his own departure, and arrived safely at Acre. It was here that he first experienced the evil effects of excommunication. The Christians of Palestine refused to aid him in any way, and looked with distrust, if not with abhorrence, upon him. The Templars, Hospitallers, and other knights, shared at first the general feeling; but they were not men to yield a blind obedience to a distant potentate, especially when it compromised their own interests. When, therefore, Frederic prepared to march upon Jerusalem without them, they joined his banners to a man.

It is said, that previous to quitting Europe, the German Emperor had commenced a negotiation with the Sultan Camhel for the restoration of the Holy Land, and that Camhel, who was jealous of the ambition of his brother Cohreddin, was willing to stipulate to that effect, on condition of being secured by Frederic in the possession of the more important territory of Egypt. But before the crusaders reached Palestine, Camhel was relieved from all fears by the death of his brother. He nevertheless did not think it worth while to contest with the crusaders the barren corner of the earth which had already been dyed with so much Christian and Saracen blood, and proposed a truce of three years, only stipulating, in addition, that the Moslems should be allowed to worship freely in the Temple of Jerusalem. This happy termination did not satisfy the bigoted Christians of Palestine. The tolerance they fought for themselves, they were not willing to extend to others, and they complained bitterly of the privilege of free worship allowed to their opponents. Unmerited good fortune had made them insolent, and they contested the right of the Emperor to become a party to any treaty, as long as he remained under the ecclesiastical ban. Frederic was disgusted with his new subjects; but, as the Templars and Hospitallers remained true to him, he marched to Jerusalem to be crowned. All the churches were shut against him, and he could not even find a priest to officiate at his coronation. He had despised the Papal authority too long to quail at it now, when it was so unjustifiably exerted, and, as there was nobody to crown him, he very wisely crowned himself. He took the royal diadem from the altar with his own hands, and boldly and proudly placed it on his brow. No shouts of an applauding populace made the welkin ring, no hymns of praise and triumph resounded from the ministers of religion; but a thousand swords started from their scabbards, to testify that their owners would defend the new monarch to the death.

It was hardly to be expected that he would renounce for any long period the dominion of his native land for the uneasy crown and barren soil of Palestine. He had seen quite enough of his new subjects before he was six months among them, and more important interests called him home. John of Brienne, openly leagued with Pope Gregory against him, was actually employed in ravaging his territories at the head of a papal army. This intelligence decided his return. As a preliminary step, he made those who had contemned his authority feel, to their sorrow, that he was their master. He then set sail, loaded with the curses of Palestine. And thus ended the seventh Crusade, which, in spite of every obstacle and disadvantage, had been productive of more real service to the Holy Land than any that had gone before; a result solely attributable to the bravery of Frederic and the generosity of the Sultan Camhel.

Soon after the Emperor's departure a new claimant started for the throne of Jerusalem, in the person of Alice, Queen of Cyprus, and half-sister of the Mary who, by her marriage, had transferred her right to John of Brienne. The grand military orders, however, clung to Frederic, and Alice was obliged to withdraw.

So peaceful a termination to the Crusade did not give unmixed pleasure in Europe. The chivalry of France and England were unable to rest, and long before the conclusion of the truce, were collecting their armies for an eighth expedition. In Palestine, also, the contentment was far from universal. Many petty Mahomedan states in the immediate vicinity were not parties to the truce, and harassed the frontier towns incessantly. The Templars, ever turbulent, waged bitter war with the Sultan of Aleppo, and in the end were almost exterminated. So great was the slaughter among them that Europe resounded with the sad story of their fate, and many a noble knight took arms to prevent the total destruction of an order associated with so many high and inspiring remembrances. Camhel, seeing the preparations that were making, thought that his generosity had been sufficiently shown, and the very day the truce was at an end assumed the offensive, and marching forward to Jerusalem took possession of it, after routing the scanty forces of the Christians. Before this intelligence reached Europe a large body of crusaders was on the march, headed by the King of Navarre, the Duke of Burgundy, the Count de Bretagne, and other leaders. On their arrival, they learned that Jerusalem had been taken, but that the Sultan was dead, and his kingdom torn by rival claimants to the supreme power. The dissensions of their foes ought to have made them united, but, as in all previous Crusades, each feudal chief was master of his own host, and acted upon his own responsibility, and without reference to any general plan. The consequence was that nothing could be done. A temporary advantage was gained by one leader, who had no means of improving it, while another was defeated, without means of retrieving himself. Thus the war lingered till the battle of Gaza, when the King of Navarre was defeated with great loss, and compelled to save himself from total destruction by entering into a hard and oppressive treaty with the Emir of Karac.

At this crisis aid arrived from England, commanded by Richard Earl of Cornwall, the namesake of Coeur de Lion, and inheritor of his valour. His army was strong, and full of hope. They had confidence in themselves and in their leader, and looked like men accustomed to victory. Their coming changed the aspect of affairs. The new Sultan of Egypt was at war with the Sultan of Damascus, and had not forces to oppose two enemies so powerful. He therefore sent messengers to meet the English Earl, offering an exchange of prisoners and the complete cession of the Holy Land. Richard, who had not come to fight for the mere sake of fighting, agreed at once to terms so advantageous, and became the deliverer of Palestine without striking a blow. The Sultan of Egypt then turned his whole force against his Moslem enemies, and the Earl of Cornwall returned to Europe. Thus ended the eighth Crusade, the most beneficial of all. Christendom had no further pretence for sending her fierce levies to the East. To all appearance, the holy wars were at an end: the Christians had entire possession of Jerusalem, Tripoli, Antioch, Edessa, Acre, Jaffa, and, in fact, of nearly all Judea; and, could they have been at peace among themselves, they might have overcome, without great difficulty, the jealousy and hostility of their neighhours. A circumstance, as unforeseen as it was disastrous, blasted this fair prospect, and reillumed, for the last time, the fervour and fury of the Crusades.

Gengis Khan and his successors had swept over Asia like a tropical storm, overturning in their progress the landmarks of ages. Kingdom after kingdom was cast down as they issued, innumerable, from the far recesses of the North and East, and, among others, the empire of Korasmin was overrun by these all-conquering hordes. The Korasmins, a fierce, uncivilized race, thus driven from their homes, spread themselves, in their turn, over the south of Asia with fire and sword, in search of a resting place. In their impetuous course they directed themselves towards Egypt, whose Sultan, unable to withstand the swarm that had cast their longing eyes on the fertile valleys of the Nile, endeavoured to turn them from their course. For this purpose, he sent emissaries to Barbaquan, their leader, inviting them to settle in Palestine; and the offer being accepted by the wild horde, they entered the country before the Christians received the slightest intimation of their coming. It was as sudden as it was overwhelming. Onwards, like the simoom, they came, burning and slaying, and were at the walls of Jerusalem before the inhabitants had time to look round them. They spared neither life nor property; they slew women and children, and priests at the altar, and profaned even the graves of those who had slept for ages. They tore down every vestige of the Christian faith, and committed horrors unparalleled in the history of warfare. About seven thousand of the inhabitants of Jerusalem sought safety in retreat; but before they were out of sight, the banner of the Cross was hoisted upon the walls by the savage foe to decoy them back. The artifice was but too successful. The poor fugitives imagined that help had arrived from another direction, and turned back to regain their homes. Nearly the whole of them were massacred, and the streets of

Jerusalem ran with blood.

The Templars, Hospitallers, and Teutonic knights forgot their long and bitter animosities, and joined hand in hand to rout out this desolating foe. They intrenched themselves in Jaffa with all the chivalry of Palestine that yet remained, and endeavoured to engage the Sultans of Emissa and Damascus to assist them against the common enemy. The aid obtained from the Moslems amounted at first to only four thousand men, but with these reinforcements Walter of Brienne, the Lord of Jaffa, resolved to give battle to the Korasrains. The conflict was as deadly as despair on the one side, and unmitigated ferocity on the other, could make it. It lasted with varying fortune for two days, when the Sultan of Emissa fled to his fortifications, and Walter of Brienne fell into the enemy's hands. The brave knight was suspended by the arms to a cross in sight of the walls of Jaffa, and the Korasminian leader declared that he should remain in that position until the city surrendered. Walter raised his feeble voice, not to advise surrender, but to command his soldiers to hold out to the last. But his gallantry was unavailing. So great had been the slaughter, that out of the grand array of knights, there now remained but sixteen Hospitallers, thirty-three Templars, and three Teutonic cavaliers. These with the sad remnant of the army fled to Acre, and the Korasmins were masters of Palestine.

The Sultans of Syria preferred the Christians to this fierce horde for their neighbours. Even the Sultan of Egypt began to regret the aid he had given to such barbarous foes, and united with those of Emissa and Damascus to root them from the land. The Korasmins amounted to but twenty thousand men, and were unable to resist the determined hostility which encompassed them on every side. The Sultans defeated them in several engagements, and the peasantry rose up in masses to take vengeance upon them. Gradually their numbers were diminished. No mercy was shown them in defeat. Barbaquan, their leader, was slain, and after five years of desperate struggles they were finally extirpated, and Palestine became once more the territory of the Mussulmans.

A short time previous to this devastating irruption, Louis IX. fell sick in Paris, and dreamed in the delirium of his fever that he saw the Christian and Moslem hosts fighting before Jerusalem, and the Christians defeated with great slaughter. The dream made a great impression on his superstitious mind, and he made a solemn vow that if ever he recovered his health, he would take a pilgrimage to the Holy Land. When the news of the misfortunes of Palestine, and the awful massacres at Jerusalem and Jaffa, arrived in Europe, St. Louis remembered him of his dream. More persuaded than ever, that it was an intimation direct from Heaven, he prepared to take the Cross at the head of his armies, and march to the deliverance of the Holy Sepulchre. From that moment he doffed the royal mantle of purple and ermine, and dressed in the sober serge becoming a pilgrim. All his thoughts were directed to the fulfilment of his design, and although his kingdom could but ill spare him, he made every preparation to leave it. Pope Innocent IV. applauded his zeal and afforded him every assistance. He wrote to Henry III. of England to forward the cause in his dominions, and called upon the clergy and laity all over Europe to contribute towards it. William Longsword, the celebrated Earl of Salisbury, took the Cross at the head of a great number of valiant knights and soldiers. But the fanaticism of the people was not to be awakened either in France or England. Great armies were raised, but the masses no longer sympathized. Taxation had been the great cooler of zeal. It was no longer a disgrace even to a knight if he refused to take the Cross. Rutebeuf, a French minstrel, who flourished about this time (1250), composed a dialogue between a crusader and a non-crusader, which the reader will find translated in "Way's Fabliaux." The crusader uses every argument to persuade the non-crusader to take up arms, and forsake every thing, in the holy cause; but it is evident from the greater force of the arguments used by the noncrusader, that he was the favourite of the minstrel. To a most urgent solicitation of his friend, the crusader, he replies,

"I read thee right, thou boldest good
To this same land I straight should hie,
And win it back with mickle blood,
Nor gaine one foot of soil thereby.
While here dejected and forlorn,
My wife and babes are left to mourn;
My goodly mansion rudely marred,
All trusted to my dogs to guard.
But I, fair comrade, well I wot
An ancient saw, of pregnant wit,
Doth bid us keep what we have got,
And troth I mean to follow it."

This being the general feeling, it is not to be wondered at that Louis IX. was occupied fully three years in organizing his forces, and in making the necessary preparations for his departure. When all was ready he set sail for Cyprus, accompanied by his Queen, his two brothers, the Counts d'Anjou and d'Artois, and a long train of the noblest chivalry of France. His third brother, the Count de Poitiers, remained behind to collect another corps of crusaders, and followed him in a few months afterwards. The army united at Cyprus, and amounted to fifty thousand men, exclusive of the English crusaders under William Longsword. Again, a pestilential disease made its appearance, to which many hundreds fell victims. It was in consequence found necessary to remain in Cyprus until the spring. Louis then embarked for Egypt with his whole host; but a violent tempest separated his fleet, and he arrived before Damietta with only a few thousand men. They were, however, impetuous and full of hope; and although the Sultan Melick Shah was drawn up on the shore with a force infinitely superior, it was resolved to attempt a landing without waiting the arrival of the rest of the army. Louis himself in wild impatience sprang from his boat, and waded on shore; while his army, inspired by his enthusiastic bravery, followed, shouting the old war-cry of the first crusaders, Dieu le veut! Dieu le veut! A panic seized the Turks. A body of their cavalry attempted to bear down upon the crusaders, but the knights fixed their large shields deep in the sands of the shore. and rested their lances upon them, so that they projected above, and formed a barrier so imposing, that the Turks, afraid to breast it, turned round and fairly took to flight. At the moment of this panic, a false report was spread in the Saracen host, that the Sultan had been slain. The confusion immediately became general -- the deroute was complete: Damietta itself was abandoned, and the same night the victorious crusaders fixed their headquarters in that city. The soldiers who had been separated from their chief by the tempest, arrived shortly afterwards; and Louis was in a position to justify the hope, not only of the conquest of Palestine, but of Egypt itself.

But too much confidence proved the bane of his army. They thought, as they had accomplished so much, that nothing more remained to be done, and gave themselves up to ease and luxury. When, by the command of Louis, they marched towards Cairo, they were no longer the same men; success, instead of inspiring, had unnerved them; debauchery had brought on disease, and disease was aggravated by the heat of a climate to which none of them were accustomed. Their progress towards Massoura, on the road to Cairo, was checked by the Thanisian canal, on the banks of which the Saracens were drawn up to dispute the passage. Louis gave orders that a bridge should be thrown across; and the operations commenced under cover of two cat-castles, or high moveable towers. The Saracens soon destroyed them by throwing quantities of Greek fire, the artillery of that day, upon them, and Louis was forced to think of some other means of effecting his design. A peasant agreed, for a considerable bribe, to point out a ford where the army might wade across, and the Count d'Artois was despatched with fourteen hundred men to attempt it, while Louis remained to face the Saracens with the main body of the army. The Count d'Artois got safely over, and defeated the detachment that had been sent to oppose his landing. Flushed with the victory, the brave Count forgot the inferiority of his numbers, and pursued the panic-stricken enemy into Massoura. He was now completely cut off from the aid of his brother-crusaders, which the Moslems perceiving, took courage and returned upon him, with a force swollen by the garrison of Massoura, and by reinforcements from the surrounding districts. The battle now became hand to hand. The Christians fought with the energy of desperate men, but the continually increasing numbers of the foe surrounded them completely, and cut off all hope, either of victory or escape. The Count d'Artois was among the foremost of the slain, and when Louis arrived to the rescue, the brave advance-guard was nearly cut to pieces. Of the fourteen hundred but three hundred remained. The fury of the battle was now increased threefold. The French King and his troops performed prodigies of valour, and the Saracens, under the command of the Emir Ceccidun, fought as if they were determined to exterminate, in one last decisive effort, the new European swarm that had settled upon their coast. At the fall of the evening dews the Christians were masters of the field of Massoura, and flattered themselves that they were the victors. Self-love would not suffer them to confess that the Saracens had withdrawn, and not retreated; but their leaders were too wofully convinced that that fatal field had completed the disorganization of the Christian army, and that all hopes of future conquest were at an end.

Impressed with this truth, the crusaders sued for peace. The Sultan insisted upon the immediate evacuation of Damietta, and that Louis himself should be delivered as hostage for the fulfilment of the condition. His army at once refused, and the negotiations were broken off. It was now resolved to attempt a retreat; but the agile Saracens, now in the front and now in the rear, rendered it a matter of extreme difficulty, and cut off the stragglers in great numbers. Hundreds of them were drowned in the Nile; and sickness and famine worked sad ravage upon those who escaped all other casualties. Louis himself was so weakened by disease, fatigue, and discouragement that he was hardly able to sit upon his horse. In the confusion of the flight he was separated from his attendants, and left a total stranger upon the sands of Egypt, sick, weary, and almost friendless. One knight, Geffry de Sergines, alone attended him, and led him to a miserable hut in a small village, where for several days he lay in the hourly expectation of death. He was at last discovered and taken prisoner by the Saracens, who treated him with all the honour due to his rank and all the pity due to his misfortunes. Under their care his health rapidly improved, and the next consideration was that of his ransom.

The Saracens demanded, besides money, the cession of Acre, Tripoli, and other cities of Palestine. Louis unhesitatingly refused, and conducted himself with so much pride and courage that the Sultan declared he was the proudest infidel he had ever beheld. After a good deal of haggling, the Sultan agreed to waive these conditions, and a treaty was finally concluded. The city of Damietta was restored; a truce of ten years agreed upon, and ten thousand golden bezants paid for the release of Louis and the liberation of all the captives. Louis then withdrew to Jaffa, and spent two years in putting that city, and Cesarea, with the other possessions of the Christians in Palestine, into a proper state of defence. He then returned to his own country, with great reputation as a saint, but very little as a soldier.

Matthew Paris informs us that, in the year 1250, while Louis was in Egypt, "thousands of the English were resolved to go to the holy war, had not the King strictly guarded his ports and kept his people from running out of doors." When the news arrived of the reverses and captivity of the French King, their ardour cooled; and the Crusade was sung of only, but not spoken of.

In France, a very different feeling was the result. The news of the King's capture spread consternation through the country. A fanatic monk of Citeaux suddenly appeared in the villages, preaching to the people, and announcing that the Holy Virgin, accompanied by a whole army of saints and martyrs, had appeared to him, and commanded him to stir up the shepherds and farm labourers to the defence of the Cross. To them only was his discourse addressed, and his eloquence was such that thousands flocked around him, ready to follow wherever he should lead. The pastures and the corn-fields were deserted, and the shepherds, or pastoureaux, as they were termed, became at last so numerous as to amount to upwards of fifty thousand, -- Millot says one hundred thousand men. [Elemens de l'Histoire de France.] The Queen Blanche, who governed as Regent during the absence of the King, encouraged at first the armies of the pastoureaux; but they soon gave way to such vile excesses that the peaceably disposed were driven to resistance. Robbery, murder, and violation marked their path; and all good men, assisted by the government, united in putting them down. They were finally dispersed, but not before three thousand of them had been massacred. Many authors say that the slaughter was still greater.

The ten years' truce concluded in 1264, and St. Louis was urged by two powerful motives to undertake a second expedition for the relief of Palestine. These were fanaticism on the one hand, and a desire of retrieving his military fame on the other, which had suffered more than his parasites liked to remind him of. The Pope, of course, encouraged his design, and once more the chivalry of Europe began to bestir themselves. In 1268, Edward, the heir of the English monarchy, announced his determination to join the Crusade; and the Pope (Clement IV.) wrote to the prelates and clergy to aid the cause by their persuasions and their revenues. In England, they agreed to contribute a tenth of their possessions; and by a parliamentary order, a twentieth was taken from the corn and moveables of all the laity at Michaelmas.

In spite of the remonstrances of the few clearheaded statesmen who surrounded him, urging the ruin that might in consequence fall upon his then prosperous kingdom, Louis made every preparation for his departure. The warlike nobility were nothing loth, and in the spring of 1270, the King set sail with an army of sixty thousand men. He was driven by stress of weather into Sardinia, and while there, a change in his plans took place. Instead of proceeding to Acre, as he originally intended, he shaped his course for Tunis, on the African coast. The King of Tunis had some time previously expressed himself favourably disposed towards the Christians and their religion, and Louis, it appears, had hopes of converting him, and securing his aid against the Sultan of Egypt. "What honour would be mine," he used to say, "if I could become godfather to this Mussulman King." Filled with this idea he landed in Africa, near the site of the city of Carthage, but found that he had reckoned without his host. The King of Tunis had no thoughts of renouncing his religion, nor intention of aiding the Crusaders in any way. On the contrary, he opposed their landing with all the forces that could be collected on so sudden an emergency. The French, however, made good their first position, and defeated the Moslems with considerable loss. They also gained some advantage over the reinforcements that were sent to oppose them; but an infectious flux appeared in the army, and put a stop to all future victories. The soldiers died at the rate of a hundred in a day. The enemy, at the same time, made as great havoc as the plague. St. Louis himself was one of the first attacked by the disease. His constitution had been weakened by fatigues, and even before he left France he was unable to bear the full weight of his armour. It was soon evident to his sorrowing soldiers that their beloved monarch could not long survive. He lingered for some days, and died in Carthage, in the fifty-sixth year of his age, deeply regretted by his army and his subjects, and leaving behind him one of the most singular reputations in history. He is the model-king of ecclesiastical writers, in whose eyes his very defects became virtues, because they were manifested in furtherance of their cause. More unprejudiced historians, while they condemn his fanaticism, admit that he was endowed with many high and rare qualities; that he was in no one point behind his age, and, in many, in advance of it.

His brother, Charles of Anjou, in consequence of a revolution in Sicily, had become King of that country. Before he heard of the death of Louis, he had sailed from Messina with large reinforcements. On his landing near Carthage, he advanced at the head of his army, amid the martial music of drums and trumpets. He was soon informed how inopportune was his rejoicing, and shed tears before his whole army, such as no warrior would have been ashamed to shed. A peace was speedily agreed upon with the King of Tunis, and the armies of France and Sicily returned to their homes.

So little favour had the Crusade found in England, that even the exertions of the heir to the throne had only collected a small force of fifteen hundred men. With these few Prince Edward sailed from Dover to Bourdeaux, in the expectation that he would find the French King in that city. St. Louis, however, had left a few weeks previously; upon which Edward followed him to Sardinia, and afterwards to Tunis. Before his arrival in Africa, St. Louis was no more, and peace had been concluded between France and Tunis. He determined, however, not to relinquish the Crusade. Returning to Sicily, he passed the winter in that country, and endeavoured to augment his little army. In the spring he set sail for Palestine, and arrived in safety at Acre. The Christians were torn, as usual, by mutual jealousies and animosities. The two great military orders were as virulent and as intractable as ever; opposed to each other, and to all the world. The arrival of Edward had the effect of causing them to lay aside their unworthy contention, and of uniting heart to heart, in one last effort for the deliverance of their adopted country. A force of six thousand effective warriors was soon formed to join those of the English prince, and preparations were made for the renewal of hostilities. The Sultan, Bibars or Bendocdar, [Mills, in his history, gives the name of this chief as Al Malek al Dhaker Rokneddin Abulfeth Bibars al Ali al Bundokdari al Salehi."] a fierce Mamluke, who had been placed on the throne by a bloody revolution, was at war with all his neighbours, and unable, for that reason, to concentrate his whole strength against them. Edward took advantage of this; and marching boldly forward to Nazareth, defeated the Turks and gained possession of that city. This was the whole amount of his successes. The hot weather engendered disease among his troops, and he himself, the life and soul of the expedition, fell sick among the first. He had been ill for some time, and was slowly recovering, when a messenger desired to speak with him on important matters, and to deliver some despatches into his own hand. While the Prince was occupied in examining them, the traitorous messenger drew a dagger from his belt, and stabbed him in the breast. The wound fortunately was not deep, and Edward had gained a portion of his strength. He struggled with the assassin, and put him to death with his own dagger, at the same time calling loudly for assistance. [The reader will recognise the incident which Sir Walter Scott has introduced into his beautiful romance, "The Talisman," and which, with the licence claimed by poets and romancers, he represents as having befallen King Richard I.] His attendants came at his call, and found him bleeding profusely, and ascertained on inspection that the dagger was poisoned. Means were instantly taken to purify the wound; and an antidote was sent by the Grand Master of the Templars which removed all danger from the effects of the poison. Camden, in his history, has adopted the more popular, and certainly more beautiful, version of this story, which says that the Princess Eleonora, in her love for her gallant husband, sucked the poison from his wound at the risk of her own life: to use the words of old Fuller, "It is a pity so pretty a story should not be true; and that so sovereign a remedy as a woman's tongue, anointed with the virtue of loving affection," should not have performed the good deed.

Edward suspected, and doubtless not without reason, that the assassin was employed by the Sultan of Egypt. But it amounted to suspicion only; and by the sudden death of the assassin, the principal clue to the discovery of the truth was lost for ever. Edward, on his recovery, prepared to resume the offensive; but the Sultan, embarrassed by the defence of interests which, for the time being, he considered of more importance, made offers of peace to the crusaders. This proof of weakness on the part of the enemy was calculated to render a man of Edward's temperament more anxious to prosecute the war; but he had also other interests to defend. News arrived in Palestine of the death of his father, King Henry III; and his presence being necessary in England, he agreed to the terms of the Sultan. These were, that the Christians should be allowed to retain their possessions in the Holy Land, and that a truce of ten years should be proclaimed. Edward then set sail for England; and thus ended the last Crusade.

The after-fate of the Holy Land may be told in a few words. The Christians, unmindful of their past sufferings and of the jealous neighbours they had to deal with, first broke the truce by plundering some Egyptian traders near Margat. The Sultan immediately revenged the outrage by taking possession of Margat, and war once more raged between the nations. Margat made a gallant defence, but no reinforcements arrived from Europe to prevent its fall. Tripoli was the next, and other cities in succession, until at last Acre was the only city of Palestine that remained in possession of the Christians.

The Grand Master of the Templars collected together his small and devoted band; and with the trifling aid afforded by the King of Cyprus, prepared to defend to the death the last possession of his order. Europe was deaf to his cry for aid, the numbers of the foe were overwhelming, and devoted bravery was of no avail. In that disastrous siege the Christians were all but exterminated. The King of Cyprus fled when he saw that resistance was vain, and the Grand Master fell at the head of his knights, pierced with a hundred wounds. Seven Templars, and as many Hospitallets, alone escaped from the dreadful carnage. The victorious Moslems then set fire to the city, and the rule of the Christians in Palestine was brought to a close for ever.

This intelligence spread alarm and sorrow among the clergy of Europe, who endeavoured to rouse once more the energy and enthusiasm of the nations, in the cause of the Holy Land: but the popular mania had run its career; the spark of zeal had burned its appointed time, and was never again to be re-illumined. Here and there a solitary knight announced his determination to take up arms, and now and then a king gave cold encouragement to the scheme; but it dropped almost as soon as spoken of, to be renewed again, still more feebly, at some longer interval.

Now what was the grand result of all these struggles? Europe expended millions of her treasures, and the blood of two millions of her children; and a handful of quarrelsome knights retained possession of Palestine for about one hundred years! Even had Christendom retained it to this day, the advantage, if confined to that, would have been too dearly purchased. But notwithstanding the fanaticism that originated, and the folly that conducted them, the Crusades were not productive of unmitigated evil. The feudal chiefs became better members of society, by coming in contact, in Asia, with a civilization superior to their own; the people secured some small instalments of their rights; kings, no longer at war with their nobility, had time to pass some good laws; the human mind learned some little wisdom from hard experience, and, casting off the slough of superstition in which the Roman clergy had so long enveloped it, became prepared to receive the seeds of the approaching Reformation. Thus did the all-wise Disposer of events bring good out of evil, and advance the civilization and ultimate happiness of the nations of the West, by means of the very fanaticism that had led them against the East. But the whole subject is one of absorbing interest; and if carried fully out in all its bearings, would consume more space than the plan of this work will allow. The philosophic student will draw his own conclusions; and he can have no better field for the exercise of his powers than this European madness; its advantages and disadvantages; its causes and results.

The Witch Mania

What wrath of gods, or wicked influence
Of tears, conspiring wretched men t' afflict,
Hath pour'd on earth this noyous pestilence,
That mortal minds doth inwardly infect
With love of blindness and of ignorance?

Spencer's Tears of the Muses.

Countrymen: "Hang her! beat her! kill her!"
Justice: "How now? Forbear this violence!"
Mother Sawyer: "A crew of villains -- a knot of bloody hangmen! set to torment me! I know not why."
Justice: "Alas! neighbour Banks, are you a ringleader in mischief? Fie! to abuse an aged woman!"
Banks: "Woman! -- a she hell-cat, a witch! To prove her one, we no sooner set fire on the thatch of her house, but in she came running, as if the Devil had sent her in a barrel of gunpowder."

Ford's Witch of Edmonton.

The belief that disembodied spirits may be permitted to revisit this world, has its foundation upon that sublime hope of immortality, which is at once the chief solace and greatest triumph of our reason. Even if revelation did not teach us, we feel that we have that within us which shall never die; and all our experience of this life but makes us cling the more fondly to that one repaying hope. But in the early days of "little knowledge," this grand belief became the source of a whole train of superstitions, which, in their turn, became the fount from whence flowed a deluge of blood and horror. Europe, for a period of two centuries and a half, brooded upon the idea, not only that parted spirits walked the earth to meddle in the affairs of men, but that men had power to summon evil spirits to their aid to work woe upon their fellows. An epidemic terror seized upon the nations; no man thought himself secure, either in his person or possessions, from the machinations of the devil and his agents. Every calamity that befell him, he attributed to a witch. If a storm arose and blew down his barn, it was witchcraft; if his cattle died of a murrain-if disease fastened upon his limbs, or death entered suddenly, and snatched a beloved face from his hearth -- they were not visitations of Providence, but the works of some neighbouring hag, whose wretchedness or insanity caused the ignorant to raise their finger, and point at her as a witch. The word was upon everybody's tongue -- France, ItaLy, Germany, England, Scotland, and the far North, successively ran mad upon this subject, and for a long series of years, furnished their tribunals with so many trials for witchcraft that other crimes were seldom or never spoken of. Thousands upon thousands of unhappy persons fell victims to this cruel and absurd delusion. In many cities of Germany, as will be shown more fully in its due place hereafter, the average number of executions for this pretended crime, was six hundred annually, or two every day, if we leave out the Sundays, when, it is to be supposed, that even this madness refrained from its work.

A misunderstanding of the famous text of the Mosaic law, "Thou shalt not suffer a witch to live," no doubt led many conscientious men astray, whose superstition, warm enough before, wanted but a little corroboration to blaze out with desolating fury. In all ages of the world men have tried to hold converse with superior beings; and to pierce, by their means, the secrets of futurity. In the time of Moses, it is evident that there were impostors, who trafficked upon the credulity of mankind, and insulted the supreme majesty of the true God by pretending to the power of divination. Hence the law which Moses, by Divine command, promulgated against these criminals; but it did not follow, as the superstitious monomaniacs of the middle ages imagined, that the Bible established the existence of the power of divination by its edicts against those who pretended to it. From the best authorities, it appears that the Hebrew word, which has been rendered, venefica, and witch, means a poisoner and divineress -- a dabbler in spells, or fortune-teller. The modern witch was a very different character, and joined to her pretended power of foretelling future events that of working evil upon the life, limbs, and possessions of mankind. This power was only to be acquired by an express compact, signed in blood, with the devil himself, by which the wizard or witch renounced baptism, and sold his or her immortal soul to the evil one, without any saving clause of redemption.

There are so many wondrous appearances in nature, for which science and philosophy cannot, even now, account, that it is not surprising that, when natural laws were still less understood, men should have attributed to supernatural agency every appearance which they could not otherwise explain. The merest tyro now understands various phenomena which the wisest of old could not fathom. The schoolboy knows why, upon high mountains, there should, on certain occasions, appear three or four suns in the firmament at once; and why the figure of a traveller upon one eminence should be reproduced, inverted, and of a gigantic stature, upon another. We all know the strange pranks which imagination can play in certain diseases -- that the hypochondriac can see visions and spectres, and that there have been cases in which men were perfectly persuaded that they were teapots. Science has lifted up the veil, and rolled away all the fantastic horrors in which our forefathers shrouded these and similar cases. The man who now imagines himself a wolf, is sent to the hospital, instead of to the stake, as in the days of the witch mania; and earth, air, and sea are unpeopled of the grotesque spirits that were once believed to haunt them.

Before entering further into the history of Witchcraft, it may be as well if we consider the absurd impersonation of the evil principle formed by the monks in their legends. We must make acquaintance with the primum mobile, and understand what sort of a personage it was, who gave the witches, in exchange for their souls, the power to torment their fellow-creatures. The popular notion of the devil was, that he was a large, ill-formed, hairy sprite, with horns, a long tail, cloven feet, and dragon's wings. In this shape he was constantly brought on the stage by the monks in their early "miracles" and "mysteries." In these representations he was an important personage, and answered the purpose of the clown in the modern pantomime. The great fun for the people was to see him well belaboured by the saints with clubs or cudgels, and to hear him howl with pain as he limped off, maimed by the blow of some vigorous anchorite. St. Dunstan generally served him the glorious trick for which he is renowned -- catching hold of his nose with a pair of red-hot pincers, till

"Rocks and distant dells resounded with his cries."

Some of the saints spat in his face, to his very great annoyance; and others chopped pieces off his tail, which, however, always grew on again. This was paying him in his own coin, and amused the populace mightily; for they all remembered the scurvy tricks he had played them and their forefathers. It was believed that he endeavoured to trip people up, by laying his long invisible tail in their way, and giving it a sudden whisk when their legs were over it; -- that he used to get drunk, and swear like a trooper, and be so mischievous in his cups as to raise tempests and earthquakes, to destroy the fruits of the earth and the barns and homesteads of true believers; -- that he used to run invisible spits into people by way of amusing himself in the long winter evenings, and to proceed to taverns and regale himself with the best, offering in payment pieces of gold which, on the dawn of the following morning, invariably turned into slates. Sometimes, disguised as a large drake, he used to lurk among the bulrushes, and frighten the weary traveller out of his wits by his awful quack. The reader will remember the lines of Burns in his address to the "De'il," which so well express the popular notion on this point --

"Ae dreary, windy, winter night,
The stars shot down wi' sklentin light,
Wi' you, mysel, I got a fright
Ayont the lough;
Ye, like a rash-bush, stood in sight
Wi' waving sough.

"The cudgel in my nieve did shake,
Each bristled hair stood like a stake,
When wi' an eldritch stour, 'quaick! quaick!'
Among the springs
Awa ye squatter'd, like a drake,
On whistling wings."

In all the stories circulated and believed about him, he was represented as an ugly, petty, mischievous spirit, who rejoiced in playing off all manner of fantastic tricks upon poor humanity. Milton seems to have been the first who succeeded in giving any but a ludicrous description of him. The sublime pride which is the quintessence of evil, was unconceived before his time. All other limners made him merely grotesque, but Milton made him awful. In this the monks showed themselves but miserable romancers; for their object undoubtedly was to represent the fiend as terrible as possible: but there was nothing grand about their Satan; on the contrary, he was a low mean devil, whom it was easy to circumvent and fine fun to play tricks with. But, as is well and eloquently remarked by a modern writer, [See article on Demonology, in the sixth volume of the "Foreign Quarterly Review."] the subject has also its serious side. An Indian deity, with its wild distorted shape and grotesque attitude, appears merely ridiculous when separated from its accessories and viewed by daylight in a museum; but restore it to the darkness of its own hideous temple, bring back to our recollection the victims that have bled upon its altar, or been crushed beneath its ear, and our sense of the ridiculous subsides into aversion and horror. So, while the superstitious dreams of former times are regarded as mere speculative insanities, we may be for a moment amused with the wild incoherences of the patients; but, when we reflect, that out of these hideous misconceptions of the principle of evil arose the belief in witchcraft -- that this was no dead faith, but one operating on the whole being of society, urging on the wisest and the mildest to deeds of murder, or cruelties scarcely less than murder -- that the learned and the beautiful, young and old, male and female, were devoted by its influence to the stake and the scaffold -- every feeling disappears, except that of astonishment that such things could be, and humiliation at the thought that the delusion was as lasting as it was universal.

Besides this chief personage, there was an infinite number of inferior demons, who played conspicuous parts in the creed of witchcraft. The pages of Bekker, Leloyer, Bodin, Delrio, and De Lancre abound with descriptions of the qualities of these imps and the functions which were assigned them. From these authors, three of whom were commissioners for the trial of witches, and who wrote from the confessions made by the supposed criminals and the evidence delivered against them, and from the more recent work of M. Jules Garinet, the following summary of the creed has been, with great pains, extracted. The student who is desirous of knowing more, is referred to the works in question; he will find enough in

213

every leaf to make his blood curdle with shame and horror: but the purity of these pages shall not be soiled by anything so ineffably humiliating and disgusting as a complete exposition of them; what is here culled will be a sufficient sample of the popular belief, and the reader would but lose time who should seek in the writings of the Demonologists for more ample details. He will gain nothing by lifting the veil which covers their unutterable obscenities, unless, like Sterne, he wishes to gather fresh evidence of "what a beast man is." In that case, he will find plenty there to convince him that the beast would be libelled by the comparison.

It was thought that the earth swarmed with millions of demons of both sexes, many of whom, like the human race, traced their lineage up to Adam, who, after the fall, was led astray by devils, assuming the forms of beautiful women to deceive him. These demons "increased and multiplied," among themselves, with the most extraordinary rapidity. Their bodies were of the thin air, and they could pass though the hardest substances with the greatest ease. They had no fixed residence or abiding place, but were tossed to and fro in the immensity of space. When thrown together in great multitudes, they excited whirlwinds in the air and tempests in the waters, and took delight in destroying the beauty of nature and the monuments of the industry of man. Although they increased among themselves like ordinary creatures, their numbers were daily augmented by the souls of wicked men -- of children still-born -- of women who died in childbed, and of persons killed in duels. The whole air was supposed to be full of them, and many unfortunate men and women drew them by thousands into their mouths and nostrils at every inspiration; and the demons, lodging in their bowels or other parts of their bodies, tormented them with pains and diseases of every kind, and sent them frightful dreams. St. Gregory of Nice relates a story of a nun who forgot to say her benedicite, and make the sign of the cross, before she sat down to supper, and who, in consequence, swallowed a demon concealed among the leaves of a lettuce. Most persons said the number of these demons was so great that they could not be counted, but Wierus asserted that they amounted to no more than seven millions, four hundred and five thousand, nine hundred, and twenty-six; and that they were divided into seventy-two companies or battalions, to each of which there was a prince or captain. They could assume any shape they pleased. When they were male, they were called incubi; and when female, succubi. They sometimes made themselves hideous; and at other times, they assumed shapes of such transcendant loveliness, that mortal eyes never saw beauty to compete with theirs.

Although the devil and his legions could appear to mankind at any time, it was generally understood that he preferred the night between Friday and Saturday. If Satan himself appeared in human shape, he was never perfectly, and in all respects, like a man. He was either too black or too white -- too large or too small, or some of his limbs were out of proportion to the rest of his body. Most commonly his feet were deformed; and he was obliged to curl up and conceal his tall in some part of his habiliments; for, take what shape he would, he could not get rid of that encumbrance. He sometimes changed himself into a tree or a river; and upon one occasion he transformed himself into a barrister, as we learn from Wierus, book iv, chapter ix. In the reign of Philippe le Bel, he appeared to a monk in the shape of a dark man, riding a tall black horse -- then as a friar -- afterwards as an ass, and finally as a coach-wheel. Instances are not rare in which both he and his inferior demons have taken the form of handsome young men; and, successfully concealing their tails, have married beautiful young women, who have had children by them. Such children were easily recognizable by their continual shrieking -- by their requiring five nurses to suckle them, and by their never growing fat.

All these demons were at the command of any individual, who would give up his immortal soul to the prince of evil for the privilege of enjoying their services for a stated period. The wizard or witch could send them to execute the most difficult missions: whatever the witch commanded was performed, except it was a good action, in which case the order was disobeyed, and evil worked upon herself instead.

At intervals, according to the pleasure of Satan, there was a general meeting of the demons and all the witches. This meeting was called the Sabbath, from its taking place on the Saturday or immediately after midnight on Fridays. These Sabbaths were sometimes held for one district, sometimes for another, and once at least, every year, it was held on the Brocken, or among other high mountains, as a general sabbath of the fiends for the whole of Christendom.

The devil generally chose a place where four roads met, as the scene of this assembly, or if that was not convenient, the neighbourhood of a lake. Upon this spot nothing would ever afterwards grow, as the hot feet of the demons and witches burnt the principle of fecundity from the earth, and rendered it barren for ever. When orders had been once issued for the meeting of the Sabbath, all the wizards and witches who failed to attend it were lashed by demons with a rod made of serpents or scorpions, as a punishment for their inattention or want of punctuality.

In France and England, the witches were supposed to ride uniformly upon broomsticks; but in Italy and Spain, the devil himself, in the shape of a goat, used to transport them on his back, which lengthened or shortened according to the number of witches he was desirous of accommodating. No witch, when proceeding to the Sabbath, could get out by a door or window, were she to try ever so much. Their general mode of ingress was by the keyhole, and of egress, by the chimney, up which they flew, broom and all, with the greatest ease. To prevent the absence of the witches from being noticed by their neighbours, some inferior demon was commanded to assume their shapes and lie in their beds, feigning illness, until the Sabbath was over.

When all the wizards and witches had arrived at the place of rendezvous, the infernal ceremonies of the Sabbath began. Satan, having assumed his favourite shape of a large he-goat, with a face in front and another in his haunches, took his seat upon a throne; and all present, in succession, paid their respects to him, and kissed him in his face behind. This done, he appointed a master of the ceremonies, in company with whom he made a personal examination of all the wizards and witches, to see whether they had the secret mark about them by which they were stamped as the devil's own. This mark was always insensible to pain. Those who had not yet been marked, received the mark from the master of the ceremonies; the devil at the same time bestowing nicknames upon them. This done, they all began to sing and. dance in the most furious manner, until some one arrived who was anxious to be admitted into their society. They were then silent for a while, until the new-comer had denied his salvation, kissed the devil, spat upon the Bible, and sworn obedience to him in all things. They then began dancing again with all their might, and singing these words,

"Alegremos, Alegremos!
Que gente va tenemos!"

In the course of an hour or two, they generally became wearied of this violent exercise, and then they all sat down and recounted the evil deeds they had done since their last meeting. Those who had not been malicious and mischievous enough towards their fellow-creatures, received personal chastisement from Satan himself, who flogged them with thorns or scorpions till they were covered with blood, and unable to sit or stand.

When this ceremony was concluded, they were all amused by a dance of toads. Thousands of these creatures sprang out of the earth; and standing on their hind-legs, danced, while the devil played the

215

bagpipes or the trumpet. These toads were all endowed with the faculty of speech, and entreated the witches to reward them with the flesh of unbaptized babes for their exertions to give them pleasure. The witches promised compliance. The devil bade them remember to keep their word; and then stamping his foot, caused all the toads to sink into the earth in an instant. The place being thus cleared, preparation was made for the banquet, where all manner of disgusting things were served up and greedily devoured by the demons and witches; although the latter were sometimes regaled with choice meats and expensive wines from golden plates and crystal goblets; but they were never thus favoured unless they had done an extraordinary number of evil deeds since the last period of meeting.

After the feast, they began dancing again; but such as had no relish for any more exercise in that way, amused themselves by mocking the holy sacrament of baptism. For this purpose, the toads were again called up, and sprinkled with filthy water; the devil making the sign of the cross, and all the witches calling out, "In nomine Patrica, Aragueaco Petrica, agora! agora! Valentia, jouando goure gaits goustia!" which meant, "In the name of Patrick, Petrick of Aragon, -- now, now, all our ills are over!"

When the devil wished to be particularly amused, he made the witches strip off their clothes and dance before him, each with a cat tied round her neck, and another dangling from her body in form of a tail. When the cock crew, they all disappeared, and the Sabbath was ended.

This is a summary of the belief which prevailed for many centuries nearly all over Europe, and which is far from eradicated even at this day. It was varied in some respects in several countries, but the main points were the same in France, Germany, Great Britain, Italy, Spain, and the far North of Europe.

The early annals of France abound with stories of supposed sorcery, but it was not until the time of Charlemagne that the crime acquired any great importance. "This monarch," says M. Jules Garinet, ["Histoire de la Magie en France. Rois de la seconde race," page 29.] "had several times given orders that all necromancers, astrologers, and witches should be driven from his states; but as the number of criminals augmented daily, he found it necessary at last to resort to severer measures. In consequence, he published several edicts, which may be found at length in the 'Capitulaire de Baluse.' By these, every sort of magic, enchantment, and witchcraft was forbidden; and the punishment of death decreed against those who in any way evoked the devil -- compounded love-philters -- afflicted either man or woman with barrenness -- troubled the atmosphere -- excited tempests -- destroyed the fruits of the earth -- dried up the milk of cows, or tormented their fellow-creatures with sores and diseases. All persons found guilty of exercising these execrable arts, were to be executed immediately upon conviction, that the earth might be rid of the burthen and curse of their presence; and those even who consulted them might also be punished with death. [M. Michaud, in his "History of the Crusades," M. Guinguene, in his "Literary History of Italy," and some other critics, have objected to Tasso's poem, that he has attributed to the Crusaders a belief in magic, which did not exist at that time. If these critics had referred to the Edicts of Charlemagne, they would have seen that Tasso was right, and that a disposition too eager to spy out imperfections in a great work was leading themselves into error.]

After this time, prosecutions for witchcraft are continually mentioned, especially by the French historians. It was a crime imputed with so much ease, and repelled with so much difficulty, that the powerful, whenever they wanted to ruin the weak, and could fix no other imputation upon them, had only to accuse them of witchcraft to ensure their destruction. Instances, in which this crime was made the pretext for the most violent persecution, both of individuals and of communities, whose real offences were purely political or religious, must be familiar to every reader. The extermination of the Stedinger, in 1234; of the Templars, from 1307 to 1313; the execution of Joan of Arc, in 1429; and the unhappy scenes of Arras, in 1459; are the most prominent. The first of these is perhaps the least known, but is not among the least remarkable. The following account, from Dr. Kortum's interesting history ["Entstehungsgeschichte der freistadlischen Bunde im Mittelalter, von Dr. F. Kortum." 1827.] of the republican confederacies of the Middle Ages, will show the horrible convenience of imputations of witchcraft, when royal or priestly wolves wanted a pretext for a quarrel with the sheep.

The Frieslanders, inhabiting the district from the Weser to the Zuydersee, had long been celebrated for their attachment to freedom, and their successful struggles in its defence. As early as the eleventh century, they had formed a general confederacy against the encroachments of the Normans and the Saxons, which was divided into seven seelands, holding annually a diet under a large oaktree at Aurich, near the Upstalboom. Here they managed their own affairs, without the control of the clergy and ambitious nobles who surrounded them, to the great scandal of the latter. They already had true notions of a representative government. The deputies of the people levied the necessary taxes, deliberated on the affairs of the community, and performed, in their simple and patriarchal manner; nearly all the functions of the representative assemblies of the present day. Finally, the Archbishop of Bremen, together with the Count of Oldenburg and other neighbouring potentates, formed a league against that section of the Frieslanders, known by the name of the Stedinger, and succeeded, after harassing them, and sowing dissensions among them for many years, in bringing them under the yoke. But the Stedinger, devotedly attached to their ancient laws, by which they had attained a degree of civil and religious liberty very uncommon in that age, did not submit without a violent struggle. They arose in insurrection, in the year 1204, in defence of the ancient customs of their country -- refused to pay taxes to the feudal chiefs, or tithes to the clergy, who had forced themselves into their peaceful retreats, and drove out many of their oppressors. For a period of eight-and-twenty years the brave Stedinger continued the struggle single-handed against the forces of the Archbishops of Bremen and the Counts of Oldenburg, and destroyed, in the year 1232, the strong castle of Slutterberg, near Delmenhorst, built by the latter nobleman as a position from which he could send out his marauders to plunder and destroy the possessions of the peasantry.

The invincible courage of these poor people proving too strong for their oppressors to cope with by the ordinary means of warfare, the Archbishop of Bremen applied to Pope Gregory IX. for his spiritual aid against them. That prelate entered cordially into the cause, and launching forth his anathema against the Stedinger as heretics and witches, encouraged all true believers to assist in their extermination. A large body of thieves and fanatics broke into their country in the year 1233, killing and burning wherever they went, and not sparing either women or children, the sick or the aged, in their rage. The Stedinger, however, rallied in great force, routed their invaders, and killed in battle their leader, Count Burckhardt of Oldenburg, with many inferior chieftains.

Again the pope was applied to, and a crusade against the Stedinger was preached in all that part of Germany. The pope wrote to all the bishops and leaders of the faithful an exhortation to arm, to root out from the land those abominable witches and wizards. "The Stedinger," said his Holiness, "seduced by the devil, have abjured all the laws of God and man; slandered the Church -- insulted the holy sacraments -- consulted witches to raise evil spirits -- shed blood like water -- taken the lives of priests, and concocted an infernal scheme to propagate the worship of the devil, whom they adore under the name of Asmodi. The devil appears to them in different shapes; sometimes as a goose or a duck, and at others in the figure of a pale, black-eyed youth, with a melancholy aspect, whose embrace fills their hearts with eternal hatred against the holy church of Christ. This devil presides at their Sabbaths, when they all kiss him and dance around him. He then envelopes them in total darkness, and they all, male and female, give themselves up to the grossest and most disgusting debauchery."

217

In consequence of these letters of the pope, the Emperor of Germany, Frederic II, also pronounced his ban against them. The Bishops of Ratzebourg, Lubeck, Osnabruek, Munster, and Minden took up arms to exterminate them, aided by the Duke of Brabant, the Counts of Holland, of Cloves, of the Mark, of Oldenburg, of Egmond, of Diest, and many other powerful nobles. An army of forty thousand men was soon collected, which marched, under the command of the Duke of Brabant, into the country of the Stedinger. The latter mustered vigorously in defence of their lives and liberties, but could raise no greater force, including every man capable of bearing arms, than eleven thousand men to cope against the overwhelming numbers of their foe. They fought with the energy of despair, but all in vain. Eight thousand of them were slain on the field of battle; the whole race was exterminated; and the enraged conquerors scoured the country in all directions -- slew the women and children and old men -- drove away the cattle -- fired the woods and cottages, and made a total waste of the land.

Just as absurd and effectual was the charge brought against the Templars in 1307, when they had rendered themselves obnoxious to the potentates and prelacy of Christendom. Their wealth, their power, their pride, and their insolence had raised up enemies on every side; and every sort of accusation was made against them, but failed to work their overthrow, until the terrible cry of witchcraft was let loose upon them. This effected its object, and the Templars were extirpated. They were accused of having sold their souls to the devil, and of celebrating all the infernal mysteries of the witches' Sabbath. It was pretended that, when they admitted a novice into their order, they forced him to renounce his salvation and curse Jesus Christ; that they then made him submit to many unholy and disgusting ceremonies, and forced him to kiss the Superior on the cheek, the navel, and the breech; and spit three times upon a crucifix. That all the members were forbidden to have connexion with women, but might give themselves up without restraint to every species of unmentionable debauchery. That when, by any mischance, a Templar infringed this order, and a child was born, the whole order met, and tossed it about like a shuttlecock from one to the other until it expired; that they then roasted it by a slow fire, and with the fat which trickled from it anointed the hair and beard of a large image of the devil. It was also said that, when one of the knights died, his body was burnt into a powder, and then mixed with wine and drunk by every member of the order. Philip IV, who, to exercise his own implacable hatred, invented, in all probability, the greater part of these charges, issued orders for the immediate arrest of all the Templars in his dominions. The pope afterwards took up the cause with almost as much fervour as the King of France; and in every part of Europe, the Templars were thrown into prison and their goods and estates confiscated. Hundreds of them, when put to the rack, confessed even the most preposterous of the charges against them, and by so doing, increased the popular clamour and the hopes of their enemies. It is true that, when removed from the rack, they denied all they had previously confessed; but this circumstance only increased the outcry, and was numbered as an additional crime against them. They were considered in a worse light than before, and condemned forthwith to the flames, as relapsed heretics. Fifty-nine of these unfortunate victims were all burned together by a slow fire in a field in the suburbs of Paris, protesting to the very last moment of their lives, their innocence of the crimes imputed to them, and refusing to accept of pardon upon condition of acknowledging themselves guilty. Similar scenes were enacted in the provinces; and for four years, hardly a month passed without witnessing the execution of one or more of these unhappy men. Finally, in 1313, the last scene of this tragedy closed by the burning of the Grand-Master, Jacques de Molay, and his companion, Guy, the Commander of Normandy. Anything more atrocious it is impossible to conceive; disgraceful alike to the monarch who originated, the pope who supported, and the age which tolerated the monstrous iniquity. That the malice of a few could invent such a charge, is a humiliating thought for the lover of his species; but that millions of mankind should credit it, is still more so.

The execution of Joan of Arc is the next most notorious example which history affords us, of the imputation of witchcraft against a political enemy. Instances of similar persecution, in which this crime was made the pretext for the gratification of political or religious hatred, might be multiplied to a great extent. But it is better to proceed at once to the consideration of the bull of Pope Innocent, the torch that set fire to the longlaid train, and caused so fearful an explosion over the Christian world. It will be necessary, however, to go back for some years anterior to that event, the better to understand the motives that influenced the Church in the promulgation of that fearful document.

Towards the close of the fourteenth and beginning of the fifteenth century, many witches were burned in different parts of Europe. As a natural consequence of the severe persecution, the crime, or the pretenders to it, increased. Those who found themselves accused and threatened with the penalties, if they happened to be persons of a bad and malicious disposition, wished they had the power imputed to them, that they might be revenged upon their persecutors. Numerous instances are upon record of half-crazed persons being found muttering the spells which were supposed to raise the evil one. When religion and law alike recognized the crime, it is no wonder that the weak in reason and the strong in imagination, especially when they were of a nervous temperament, fancied themselves endued with the terrible powers of which all the world was speaking. The belief of their neighbours did not lag behind their own, and execution was the speedy consequence.

As the fear of witchcraft increased, the Catholic clergy strove to fix the imputation of it upon those religious sects, the pioneers of the Reformation, who began about this time to be formidable to the Church of Rome. If a charge of heresy could not ensure their destruction, that of sorcery and witchcraft never failed. In the year 1459, a devoted congregation of the Waldenses, at Arras, who used to repair at night to worship God in their own manner in solitary places, fell victims to an accusation of sorcery. It was rumored in Arras that in the desert places to which they retired, the devil appeared before them in human form, and read from a large book his laws and ordinances, to which they all promised obedience; that he then distributed money and food among them, to bind them to his service, which done, they gave themselves up to every species of lewdness and debauchery. Upon these rumours, several creditable persons in Arras were seized and imprisoned, together with a number of decrepit and idiotic old women. The rack, that convenient instrument for making the accused confess anything, was of course put in requisition. Monstrelet, in his Chronicle, says that they were tortured until some of them admitted the truth of the whole accusations, and said besides, that they had seen and recognized, in their nocturnal assemblies, many persons of rank; many prelates, seigneurs, governors of bailliages, and mayors of cities, being such names as the examiners had themselves suggested to the victims. Several who had been thus informed against, were thrown into prison, and so horribly tortured, that reason fled, and, in their ravings of pain, they also confessed their midnight meetings with the devil, and the oaths they had taken to serve him. Upon these confessions judgment was pronounced: the poor old women, as usual in such cases, were hanged and burned in the market-place; the more wealthy delinquents were allowed to escape, upon payment of large sums. It was soon after universally recognized that these trials had been conducted in the most odious manner, and that the judges had motives of private vengeance against many of the more influential persons who had been implicated. The Parliament of Paris afterwards declared the sentence illegal, and the judges iniquitous; but its arret was too late to be of service even to those who had paid the fine, or to punish the authorities who had misconducted themselves; for it was not delivered until thirty-two years after the executions had taken place.

In the mean time, accusations of witchcraft spread rapidly in France, Italy, and Germany. Strange to say, that although in the first instance chiefly directed against heretics, the latter were as firm believers in the crime as even the Catholics themselves. In after times we also find that the Lutherans and Calvinists became greater witchburners than ever the Romanists had been: so deeply was the prejudice rooted. Every other point of belief was in dispute, but that was considered by every sect to be as well established as the authenticity of the Scriptures, or the existence of a God.

But at this early period of the epidemic the persecutions were directed by the heads of the Catholic Church. The spread of heresy betokened, it was thought, the coming of Antichrist. Florimond, in his work concerning the Antichrist, lets us fully into the secret of these prosecutions. He says, "All who have afforded us some signs of the approach of Antichrist agree that the increase of sorcery and witchcraft is to distinguish the melancholy period of his advent; and was ever age so afflicted as ours? The seats destined for criminals in our courts of justice are blackened with persons accused of this guilt. There are not judges enough to try them. Our dungeons are gorged with them. No day passes that we do not render our tribunals bloody by the dooms which we pronounce, or in which we do not return to our homes, discountenanced and terrified at the horrible confessions which we have heard. And the devil is accounted so good a master, that we cannot commit so great a number of his slaves to the flames, but what there shall arise from their ashes a sufficient number to supply their place."

Florimond here spoke the general opinion of the Church of Rome; but it never suggested itself to the mind of any person engaged in these trials, that if it were indeed a devil, who raised up so many new witches to fill the places of those consumed, it was no other than one in their own employ -- the devil of persecution. But so it was. The more they burned, the more they found to burn; until it became a common prayer with women in the humbler walks of life, that they might never live to grow old. It was sufficient to be aged, poor, and ill-tempered, to ensure death at the stake or the scaffold.

In the year 1487 there was a severe storm in Switzerland, which laid waste the country for four miles around Constance. Two wretched old women, whom the popular voice had long accused of witchcraft, were arrested on the preposterous charge of having raised the tempest. The rack was displayed, and the two poor creatures extended upon it. In reply to various leading questions from their tormentors, they owned, in their agony, that they were in the constant habit of meeting the devil, that they had sold their souls to him, and that at their command he had raised the tempest. Upon this insane and blasphemous charge they were condemned to die. In the criminal registers of Constance there stands against the name of each the simple but significant phrase, "convicta et combusta."

This case and hundreds of others were duly reported to the ecclesiastical powers. There happened at that time to be a Pontiff at the head of the Church who had given much of his attention to the subject of witchcraft, and who, with the intent of rooting out the crime, did more to increase it than any other man that ever lived. John Baptist Cibo, elected to the Papacy in 1485, under the designation of Innocent VIII, was sincerely alarmed at the number of witches, and launched forth his terrible manifesto against them. In his celebrated bull of 1488, he called the nations of Europe to the rescue of the church of Christ upon earth, emperilled by the arts of Satan, and set forth the horrors that had reached his ears; how that numbers of both sexes had intercourse with the infernal fiends; how by their sorceries they afflicted both man and beast; how they blighted the marriage bed, destroyed the births of women and the increase of cattle; and how they blasted the corn on the ground, the grapes of the vineyard, the fruits of the trees, and the herbs of the field. In order that criminals so atrocious might no longer pollute the earth, he appointed inquisitors in every country, armed with the apostolic power to convict and punish.

It was now that the Witch Mania, properly so called, may be said to have fairly commenced. Immediately a class of men sprang up in Europe, who made it the sole business of their lives to discover and burn the witches. Sprenger, in Germany, was the most celebrated of these national scourges. In his notorious work, the "Malleus Maleficarum," he laid down a regular form of trial, and appointed a course of examination by which the inquisitors in other countries might best discover the guilty. The questions, which were always enforced by torture, were of the most absurd and disgusting nature. The inquisitors were required to ask the suspected whether they had midnight meetings with the devil? whether they attended the witch's sabbath on the Brocken? whether they had their familiar spirits? whether they could raise whirlwinds and call down the lightning? and whether they had sexual intercourse with Satan?

Straightway the inquisitors set to work; Cumarius, in Italy, burned forty-one poor women in one province alone, and Sprenger, in Germany, burned a number which can never be ascertained correctly, but which, it is agreed on all hands, amounted to more than five hundred in a year. The great resemblance between the confessions of the unhappy victims was regarded as a new proof of the existence of the crime. But this is not astonishing. The same questions from the "Malleus Maleficarum," were put to them all, and torture never failed to educe the answer required by the inquisitor. Numbers of people whose imaginations were filled with these horrors, went further in the way of confession than even their tormenters anticipated, in the hope that they would thereby be saved from the rack, and put out of their misery at once. Some confessed that they had had children by the devil; but no one, who had ever been a mother, gave utterance to such a frantic imagining, even in the extremity of her anguish. The childless only confessed it, and were burned instanter as unworthy to live.

For fear the zeal of the enemies of Satan should cool, successive Popes appointed new commissions. One was appointed by Alexander VI, in 1494; another by Leo X, in 1521, and a third by Adrian VI, in 1522. They were all armed with the same powers to hunt out and destroy, and executed their fearful functions but too rigidly. In Geneva alone five hundred persons were burned in the years 1515 and 1516, under the title of Protestant witches. It would appear that their chief crime was heresy, and their witchcraft merely an aggravation. Bartolomeo de Spina has a list still more fearful. He informs us that, in the year 1524, no less than a thousand persons suffered death for witchcraft in the district of Como, and that for several years afterwards the average number of victims exceeded a hundred annually. One inquisitor, Remigius, took great credit to himself for having, during fifteen years, convicted and burned nine hundred.

In France, about the year 1520, fires for the execution of witches blazed in almost every town. Danaeus, in his "Dialogues of Witches," says they were so numerous that it would he next to impossible to tell the number of them. So deep was the thraldom of the human mind, that the friends and relatives of the accused parties looked on and approved. The wife or sister of a murderer might sympathise in his fate, but the wives and husbands of sorcerers and witches had no pity. The truth is that pity was dangerous, for it was thought no one could have compassion on the sufferings of a witch who was not a dabbler in the art: to have wept for a witch would have insured the stake. In some districts, however, the exasperation of the people broke out, in spite of superstition. The inquisitor of a rural township in Piedmont burned the victims so plentifully, and so fast, that there was not a family in the place which did not lose a member. The people at last arose, and the inquisitor was but too happy to escape from the country with whole limbs. The Archbishop of the diocese proceeded afterwards to the trial of such as the inquisitor had left in prison.

Some of the charges were so utterly preposterous that the poor wretches were at once liberated; others met a harder, but the usual fate. Some of them were accused of having joined the witches' dance at midnight under a blasted oak, where they had been seen by creditable people. The husbands of several of these women (two of whom were young and beautiful) swore positively that at the time stated their wives were comfortably asleep in their arms; but it was all in vain. Their word was taken, but the Archbishop told them they had been deceived by the devil and their own senses. It was true they might have had the semblance of their wives in their beds, but the originals were far away, at the devil's dance under the oak. The honest fellows were confounded, and their wives burned forthwith.

221

In the year 1561, five poor women of Verneuil were accused of transforming themselves into cats, and in that shape attending the sabbath of the fiends -- prowling around Satan, who presided over them in the form of a goat, and dancing, to amuse him, upon his back. They were found guilty, and burned. [Bodin, page 95. Garinet, page 125. "Anti-demon de Serclier," page 346.]

In 1564, three wizards and a witch appeared before the Presidents Salvert and D'Avanton: they confessed, when extended on the rack, that they anointed the sheep-pens with infernal unguents to kill the sheep -- that they attended the sabbath, where they saw a great black goat, which spoke to them, and made them kiss him, each holding a lighted candle in his hand while he performed the ceremony. They were all executed at Poitiers.

In 1571, the celebrated sorcerer, Trois Echelles, was burned in the Place de Greve, in Paris. He confessed, in the presence of Charles IX, and of the Marshals de Montmorency, De Retz, and the Sieur du Mazille, physician to the King, that he could perform the most wonderful things by the aid of a devil to whom he had sold himself. He described at great length the saturnalia of the fiends -- the sacrifices which they offered up -- the debaucheries they committed with the young and handsome witches, and the various modes of preparing the infernal unguent for blighting cattle. He said he had upwards of twelve hundred accomplices in the crime of witchcraft in various parts of France, whom he named to the King, and many of whom were afterwards arrested and suffered execution.

At Dole, two years afterwards, Gilles Garnier, a native of Lyons, was indicted for being a loupgarou, or man-wolf, and for prowling in that shape about the country at night to devour little children. The indictment against him, as read by Henri Camus, doctor of laws and counsellor of the King, was to the effect that he, Gilles Garnier, had seized upon a little girl, twelve years of age, whom he drew into a vineyard and there killed, partly with his teeth and partly with his hands, seeming like wolf's paws -- that from thence he trailed her bleeding body along the ground with his teeth into the wood of La Serre, where he ate the greatest portion of her at one meal, and carried the remainder home to his wife; that, upon another occasion, eight days before the festival of All Saints, he was seen to seize another child in his teeth, and would have devoured her had she not been rescued by the country-people -- and that the said child died a few days afterwards of the injuries he had inflicted; that fifteen days after the same festival of All Saints, being again in the shape of a wolf, he devoured a boy thirteen years of age, having previously torn off his leg and thigh with his teeth, and hid them away for his breakfast on the morrow. He was, furthermore, indicted for giving way to the same diabolical and unnatural propensities even in his shape of a man, and that he had strangled a boy in a wood with the intention of eating him, which crime he would have effected if he had not been seen by the neighhours and prevented.

Gilles Garnier was put to the rack, after fifty witnesses had deposed against him: he confessed everything that was laid to his charge. He was, thereupon, brought back into the presence of his judges, when Dr. Camus, in the name of the Parliament of Dole, pronounced the following sentence:--

"Seeing that Gilles Garnier has, by the testimony of credible witnesses, and by his own spontaneous confession, been proved guilty of the abominable crimes of lycanthropy and witchcraft, this court condemns him, the said Gilles, to be this day taken in a cart from this spot to the place of execution, accompanied by the executioner (maitre executeur de la haute justice), where he, by the said executioner, shall be tied to a stake and burned alive, and that his ashes be then scattered to the winds. The Court further condemns him, the said Gilles, to the costs of this prosecution."

"Given at Dole, this 18th day of January, 1573."

In 1578, the Parliament of Paris was occupied for several days with the trial of a man, named Jacques Roller. He, also, was found guilty of being a loup-garou, and in that shape devouring a little boy. He was burnt alive in the Place de Greve.

In 1579, so much alarm was excited in the neighbourhood of Melun by the increase of witches and loup-garous, that a council was held to devise some measures to stay the evil. A decree was passed, that all witches, and consulters with witches, should be punished with death; and not only those, but fortune-tellers and conjurors of every kind. The Parliament of Rouen took up the same question in the following year, and decreed that the possession of a grimoire, or book of spells, was sufficient evidence of witchcraft; and that all persons on whom such books were found should be burned alive. Three councils were held in different parts of France in the year 1583, all in relation to the same subject. The Parliament of Bourdeaux issued strict injunctions to all curates and clergy whatever, to use redoubled efforts to root out the crime of witchcraft. The Parliament of Tours was equally peremptory, and feared the judgments of an offended God, if all these dealers with the devil were not swept from the face of the land. The Parliament of Rheims was particularly severe against the noueurs d'aiguillette, or "tyers of the knot;" people of both sexes, who took pleasure in preventing the consummation of marriage, that they might counteract the command of God to our first parents, to increase and multiply. This Parliament held it to be sinful to wear amulets to preserve from witchcraft; and that this practice might not be continued within its jurisdiction, drew up a form of exorcism, which would more effectually defeat the agents of the devil, and put them to flight.

A case of witchcraft, which created a great sensation in its day, occurred in 1588, at a village in the mountains of Auvergne, about two leagues from Apchon. A gentleman of that place being at his window, there passed a friend of his who had been out hunting, and who was then returning to his own house. The gentleman asked his friend what sport he had had; upon which the latter informed him that he had been attacked in the plain by a large and savage wolf, which he had shot at, without wounding; and that he had then drawn out his hunting-knife and cut off the animal's fore-paw, as it sprang upon his neck to devour him. The huntsman, upon this, put his hand into his bag to pull out the paw, but was shocked to find that it was a woman's hand, with a wedding-ring on the finger. The gentleman immediately recognized his wife's ring, "which," says the indictment against her, "made him begin to suspect some evil of her." He immediately went in search of her, and found her sitting by the fire in the kitchen, with her arm hidden underneath her apron. He tore off her apron with great vehemence, and found that she had no hand, and that the stump was even then bleeding. She was given into custody, and burned at Riom in presence of some thousands of spectators. [Tablier. See also Boguet, "Discours sur les Sorciers;" and M. Jules Garinet, "Histoire de la Magie," page 150.]

In the midst of these executions, rare were the gleams of mercy; few instances are upon record of any acquittal taking place when the charge was witchcraft. The discharge of fourteen persons by the Parliament of Paris, in the year 1589, is almost a solitary example of a return to reason. Fourteen persons, condemned to death for witchcraft, appealed against the judgment to the Parliament of Paris, which for political reasons had been exiled to Tours. The Parliament named four commissioners, Pierre Pigray, the King's surgeon, and Messieurs Leroi, Renard, and Falaiseau, the King's physicians, to visit and examine these witches, and see whether they had the mark of the devil upon them. Pigray, who relates the circumstance in his work on Surgery, book vii, chapter the tenth, says the visit was made in presence of two counsellors of the court. The witches were all stripped naked, and the physicians examined their bodies very diligently, pricking them in all the marks they could find, to see whether they were insensible to pain, which was always considered a certain proof of guilt. They were, however, very sensible of the pricking, and some of them called out very lustily when the pins were driven into them. "We found them," continues Pierre Pigray, "to be very poor, stupid people, and some of them insane; many of them were quite indifferent about life, and one or two of them desired death as a relief for their sufferings. Our opinion was, that they stood more in need of medicine than of punishment, and so we reported to the Parliament. Their case was, thereupon, taken into further consideration, and the Parliament, after mature counsel amongst all the members, ordered the poor creatures to be sent to their homes, without inflicting any punishment upon them."

Such was the dreadful state of Italy, Germany, and France, during the sixteenth century, which was far from being the worst crisis of the popular madness with regard to witchcraft. Let us see what was the state of England during the same period. The Reformation, which in its progress had rooted out so many errors, stopped short at this, the greatest error of all. Luther and Calvin were as firm believers in witchcraft as Pope Innocent himself, and their followers showed themselves more zealous persecutors than the Romanists. Dr. Hutchinson, in his work on Witchcraft, asserts that the mania manifested itself later in England, and raged with less virulence than on the Continent. The first assertion only is true; but though the persecution began later both in England and Scotland, its progress was as fearful as elsewhere.

It was not until more than fifty years after the issuing of the Bull of Innocent VIII. that the Legislature of England thought fit to make any more severe enactments against sorcery than those already in operation. The statute of 1541 was the first that specified the particular crime of witchcraft. At a much earlier period, many persons had suffered death for sorcery in addition to other offences; but no executions took place for attending the witches' sabbath, raising tempests, afflicting cattle with barrenness, and all the fantastic trumpery of the Continent. Two statutes were passed in 1551; the first, relating to false prophecies, caused mainly, no doubt, by the impositions of Elizabeth Barton, the Holy Maid of Kent, in 1534, and the second against conjuration, witchcraft, and sorcery. But even this enactment did not consider witchcraft as penal in itself, and only condemned to death those who by means of spells, incantations, or contracts with the devil, attempted the lives of their neighbours. The statute of Elizabeth, in 1562, at last recognized witchcraft as a crime of the highest magnitude, whether exerted or not to the injury of the lives, limbs, and possessions of the community. From that date, the persecution may be fairly said to have commenced in England. It reached its climax in the early part of the seventeenth century, which was the hottest period of the mania all over Europe.

A few cases of witch persecution in the sixteenth century will enable the reader to form a more accurate idea of the progress of this great error than if he plunged at once into that busy period of its history when Matthew Hopkins and his coadjutors exercised their infernal calling. Several instances occur in England during the latter years of the reign of Elizabeth. At this time the public mind had become pretty familiar with the details of the crime. Bishop Jewell, in his sermons before Her Majesty, used constantly to conclude them by a fervent prayer that she might be preserved from witches. Upon one occasion, in 1598, his words were, "It may please your Grace to understand that witches and sorcerers, within these last four years, are marvellously increased within this your Grace's realm. Your Grace's subjects pine away even unto the death; their colour fadeth -- their flesh rotteth -- their speech is benumbed-- their senses are bereft! I pray God they may never practise further than upon the subject!"

By degrees, an epidemic terror of witchcraft spread into the villages. In proportion as the doctrines of the Puritans took root this dread increased, and, of course, brought persecution in its train. The Church of England has claimed, and is entitled to the merit, of having been less influenced in these matters than any other sect of Christians; but still they were tainted with the superstition of the age. One of the most flagrant instances of cruelty and delusion upon record was consummated under the authority of the Church, and commemorated till a very late period by an annual lecture at the University of Cambridge.

This is the celebrated case of the Witches of Warbois, who were executed about thirty-two years after the passing of the statute of Elizabeth. Although in the interval but few trials are recorded, there is, unfortunately, but too much evidence to show the extreme length to which the popular prejudice was carried. Many women lost their lives in every part of England without being brought to trial at all, from the injuries received at the hands of the people. The number of these can never be ascertained.

The case of the Witches of Warbois merits to be detailed at length, not only from the importance attached to it for so many years by the learned of the University, but from the singular absurdity of the evidence upon which men, sensible in all other respects, could condemn their fellow-creatures to the scaffold.

The principal actors in this strange drama were the families of Sir Samuel Cromwell and a Mr. Throgmorton, both gentlemen of landed property near Warbois, in the county of Huntingdon. Mr. Throgmorton had several daughters, the eldest of whom, Mistress Joan, was an imaginative and melancholy girl, whose head was filled with stories of ghosts and witches. Upon one occasion she chanced to pass the cottage of one Mrs. or, as she was called, Mother Samuel, a very aged, a very poor, and a very ugly woman. Mother Samuel was sitting at her door knitting, with a black cap upon her head, when this silly young lady passed, and taking her eyes from her work she looked steadfastly at her. Mistress Joan immediately fancied that she felt sudden pains in all her limbs, and from that day forth, never ceased to tell her sisters, and everybody about her, that Mother Samuel had bewitched her. The other children took up the cry, and actually frightened themselves into fits whenever they passed within sight of this terrible old woman.

Mr. and Mrs. Throgmorton, not a whit wiser than their children, believed all the absurd tales they had been told; and Lady Cromwell, a gossip of Mrs. Throgmorton, made herself very active in the business, and determined to bring the witch to the ordeal. The sapient Sir Samuel joined in the scheme; and the children thus encouraged gave loose reins to their imaginations, which seem to have been of the liveliest. They soon invented a whole host of evil spirits, and names for them besides, which, they said, were sent by Mother Samuel to torment them continually. Seven spirits especially, they said, were raised from hell by this wicked woman to throw them into fits; and as the children were actually subject to fits, their mother and her commeres gave the more credit to the story. The names of these spirits were, "First Smack," "Second Smack," "Third Smack," "Blue," "Catch," "Hardname," and "Pluck."

Throgmorton, the father, was so pestered by these idle fancies, and yet so well inclined to believe them, that he marched valiantly forth to the hut where Mother Samuel resided with her husband and daughter, and dragged her forcibly into his own grounds. Lady Cromwell, Mrs. Throgmorton, and the girls were in waiting, armed with long pins to prick the witch, and see if they could draw blood from her. Lady Cromwell, who seems to have been the most violent of the party, tore the old woman's cap off her head, and plucking out a handful of her grey hair, gave it to Mrs. Throgmorton to burn, as a charm which would preserve them all from her future machinations. It was no wonder that the poor creature, subjected to this rough usage, should give vent to an involuntary curse upon her tormentors. She did so, and her curse was never forgotten. Her hair, however, was supposed to be a grand specific, and she was allowed to depart, half dead with terror and ill usage. For more than a year, the families of Cromwell and

Throgmorton continued to persecute her, and to assert that her imps afflicted them with pains and fits, turned the milk sour in their pans, and prevented their cows and ewes from bearing. In the midst of these fooleries, Lady Cromwell was taken ill and died. It was then remembered that her death had taken place exactly a year and a quarter since she was cursed by Mother Samuel, and that on several occasions she had dreamed of the witch and a black cat, the latter being of course the arch-enemy of mankind himself.

Sir Samuel Cromwell now conceived himself bound to take more energetic measures against the sorceress, since he had lost his wife by her means. The year and a quarter and the black cat were proofs positive. All the neighbours had taken up the cry of witchcraft against Mother Samuel; and her personal appearance, unfortunately for her, the very ideal of what a witch ought to be, increased the popular suspicion. It would appear that at last the poor woman believed, even to her own disadvantage, that she was what everybody represented her to be. Being forcibly brought into Mr. Throgmorton's house, when his daughter Joan was in one of her customary fits, she was commanded by him and Sir Samuel Cromwell to expel the devil from the young lady. She was told to repeat her exorcism, and to add, "as I am a witch, and the causer of Lady Cromwell's death, I charge thee, fiend, to come out of her!" She did as was required of her, and moreover confessed that her husband and daughter were leagued with her in witchcraft, and had, like her, sold their souls to the devil. The whole family were immediately arrested, and sent to Huntingdon to prison.

The trial was instituted shortly afterwards before Mr. Justice Fenner, when all the crazy girls of Mr. Throgmorton's family gave evidence against Mother Samuel and her family. They were all three put to the torture. The old woman confessed in her anguish that she was a witch -- that she had cast her spells upon the young ladies, and that she had caused the death of Lady Cromwell. The father and daughter, stronger in mind than their unfortunate wife and parent, refused to confess anything, and asserted their innocence to the last. They were all three condemned to be hanged, and their bodies burned. The daughter, who was young and good-looking, excited the pity of many persons, and she was advised to plead pregnancy, that she might gain at least a respite from death. The poor girl refused proudly, on the ground that she would not be accounted both a witch and a strumpet. Her half-witted old mother caught at the idea of a few weeks' longer life, and asserted that she was pregnant. The court was convulsed with laughter, in which the wretched victim herself joined, and this was accounted an additional proof that she was a witch. The whole family were executed on the 7th of April, 1593.

Sir Samuel Cromwell, as lord of the manor, received the sum of 40 pounds out of the confiscated property of the Samuels, which he turned into a rent-charge of 40 shillings yearly, for the endowment of an annual sermon or lecture upon the enormity of witchcraft, and this case in particular, to be preached by a doctor or bachelor of divinity of Queen's College, Cambridge. I have not been able to ascertain the exact date at which this annual lecture was discontinued, but it appears to have been preached so late as 1718, when Dr. Hutchinson published his work upon witchcraft.

To carry on in proper chronological order the history of the witch delusion in the British isles, it will be necessary to examine into what was taking place in Scotland during all that part of the sixteenth century anterior to the accession of James VI. to the crown of England. We naturally expect that the Scotch, -- a people renowned from the earliest times for their powers of imagination, -- should be more deeply imbued with this gloomy superstition than their neighhours of the South. The nature of their soil and climate tended to encourage the dreams of early ignorance. Ghosts, goblins, wraiths, kelpies, and a whole host of spiritual beings, were familiar to the dwellers by the misty glens of the Highlands and the romantic streams of the Lowlands. Their deeds, whether of good or ill, were enshrined in song, and took a greater hold upon the imagination because "verse had sanctified them." But it was not till the religious reformers began the practice of straining Scripture to the severest extremes, that the arm of the law was called upon to punish witchcraft as a crime per se. What Pope Innocent VIII. had done for Germany and France, the preachers of the Reformation did for the Scottish people. Witchcraft, instead of being a mere article of faith, became enrolled in the statute book; and all good subjects and true Christians were called upon to take arms against it. The ninth Parliament of Queen Mary passed an act in 1563, which decreed the punishment of death against witches and consulters with witches, and immediately the whole bulk of the people were smitten with an epidemic fear of the devil and his mortal agents. Persons in the highest ranks of life shared and encouraged the delusion of the vulgar. Many were themselves accused of witchcraft; and noble ladies were shown to have dabbled in mystic arts, and proved to the world that, if they were not witches, it was not for want of the will.

Among the dames who became notorious for endeavouring to effect their wicked ends by the devil's aid, may be mentioned the celebrated Lady Buccleugh, of Branxholme, familiar to all the readers of Sir Walter Scott; the Countess of Lothian, the Countess of Angus, the Countess of Athol, Lady Kerr, the Countess of Huntley, Euphemia Macalzean (the daughter of Lord Cliftonhall), and Lady Fowlis. Among the celebrated of the other sex who were accused of wizzardism was Sir Lewis Ballantyne, the Lord Justice Clerk for Scotland, who, if we may believe Scot of Scotstarvet, "dealt by curiosity with a warlock called Richard Grahame," and prayed him to raise the devil. The warlock consented, and raised him in propria persona, in the yard of his house in the Canongate, "at sight of whom the Lord Justice Clerk was so terrified that he took sickness and thereof died." By such idle reports as these did the envious ruin the reputation of those they hated, though it would appear in this case that Sir Lewis had been fool enough to make the attempt of which he was accused, and that the success of the experiment was the only apocryphal part of the story.

The enemies of John Knox invented a similar tale, which found ready credence among the Roman Catholics; glad to attach any stigma to that grand scourge of the vices of their church. It was reported that he and his secretary went into the churchyard of St. Andrew's with the intent to raise "some sanctes;" but that, by a mistake in their conjurations, they raised the great fiend himself, instead of the saints they wished to consult. The popular rumour added that Knox's secretary was so frightened at the great horns, goggle eyes, and long tail of Satan, that he went mad, and shortly afterwards died. Knox himself was built of sterner stuff, and was not to be frightened.

The first name that occurs in the records of the High Court of Justiciary of persons tried or executed for witchcraft is that of Janet Bowman, in 1572, nine years after the passing of the act of Mary. No particulars of her crimes are given, and against her name there only stand the words, "convict and brynt." It is not, however, to be inferred that, in this interval, no trials or executions took place; for it appears on the authority of documents of unquestioned authenticity in the Advocates' Library at Edinburgh, [Foreign Quarterly Review, vol. vi. page 41.] that the Privy Council made a practice of granting commissions to resident gentlemen and ministers, in every part of Scotland, to examine, try, and execute witches within their own parishes. No records of those who suffered from the sentence of these tribunals have been preserved; but if popular tradition may be believed, even to the amount of one-fourth of its assertions, their number was fearful. After the year 1572, the entries of executions for witchcraft in the records of the High Court become more frequent, but do not average more than one per annum; another proof that trials for this offence were in general entrusted to the local magistracy. The latter appear to have ordered witches to the stake with as little compunction, and after as summary a mode, as modern justices of the peace order a poacher to the stocks.

As James VI. advanced in manhood, he took great interest in the witch trials. One of them especially, that of Gellie Duncan, Dr. Fian, and their accomplices, in the year 1591, engrossed his whole attention, and no doubt suggested in some degree, the famous work on Demonology which he wrote shortly afterwards. As these witches had made an attempt upon his own life, it is not surprising, with his habits, that he should have watched the case closely, or become strengthened in his prejudice and superstition by its singular details. No other trial that could be selected would give so fair an idea of the delusions of the Scottish people as this. Whether we consider the number of victims, the absurdity of the evidence, and the real villany of some of the persons implicated, it is equally extraordinary.

Gellie Duncan, the prime witch in these proceedings, was servant to the Deputy Bailiff of Tranent, a small town in Hadingtonshire, about ten miles from Edinburgh. Though neither old nor ugly (as witches usually were), but young and good-looking, her neighbours, from some suspicious parts of her behaviour, had long considered her a witch. She had, it appears, some pretensions to the healing art. Some cures which she effected were so sudden, that the worthy Bailiff, her master, who, like his neighbours, mistrusted her, considered them no less than miraculous. In order to discover the truth, he put her to the torture; but she obstinately refused to confess that she had dealings with the devil. It was the popular belief that no witch would confess as long as the mark which Satan had put upon her remained undiscovered upon her body. Somebody present reminded the torturing Bailie of this fact, and on examination, the devil's mark was found upon the throat of poor Gellie. She was put to the torture again, and her fortitude giving way under the extremity of her anguish, she confessed that she was indeed a witch -- that she had sold her soul to the devil, and effected all her cures by his aid. This was something new in the witch creed, according to which, the devil delighted more in laying diseases on, than in taking them off; but Gellie Duncan fared no better on that account. The torture was still applied, until she had named all her accomplices, among whom were one Cunningham, a reputed wizard, known by the name of Dr. Fian, a grave and matron-like witch, named Agnes Sampson, Euphemia Macalzean, the daughter of Lord Cliftonhall, already mentioned, and nearly forty other persons, some of whom were the wives of respectable individuals in the city of Edinburgh. Every one of these persons was arrested, and the whole realm of Scotland thrown into commotion by the extraordinary nature of the disclosures which were anticipated.

About two years previous to this time, James had suddenly left his kingdom, and proceeded gallantly to Denmark, to fetch over his bride, the Princess of Denmark, who had been detained by contrary weather in the harbour of Upslo. After remaining for some months in Copenhagen, he set sail with his young bride, and arrived safely in Leith, on the 1st of May 1590, having experienced a most boisterous passage, and been nearly wrecked. As soon as the arrest of Gellie Duncan and Fian became known in Scotland, it was reported by everybody who pretended to be well-informed that these witches and their associates had, by the devil's means, raised the storms which had endangered the lives of the King and Queen. Gellie, in her torture, had confessed that such was the fact, and the whole kingdom waited aghast and open-mouthed for the corroboration about to be furnished by the trial.

Agnes Sampson, the "grave and matron-like" witch implicated by Gellie Duncan, was put to the horrible torture of the pilliewinkis. She laid bare all the secrets of the sisterhood before she had suffered an hour, and confessed that Gellie Duncan, Dr. Fian, Marion Lineup, Euphemia Macalzean, herself, and upwards of two hundred witches and warlocks, used to assemble at midnight in the kirk of North Berwick, where they met the devil; that they had plotted there to attempt the King's life; that they were incited to this by the old fiend himself, who had asserted with a thundering oath that James was the greatest enemy he ever had, and that there would be no peace for the devil's children upon earth until he were got rid of; that the devil upon these occasions always liked to have a little music, and that Gellie Duncan used to play a reel before him on a trump or Jew's harp, to which all the witches danced.

James was highly flattered at the idea that the devil should have said that he was the greatest enemy he ever had. He sent for Gellie Duncan to the palace, and made her play before him the same reel which she had played at the witches' dance in the kirk.

Dr. Fian, or rather Cunningham, a petty schoolmaster at Tranent, was put to the torture among the rest. He was a man who had led an infamous life, was a compounder of and dealer in poisons, and a pretender to magic. Though not guilty of the preposterous crimes laid to his charge, there is no doubt that he was a sorcerer in will, though not in deed, and that he deserved all the misery he endured. When put on the rack, he would confess nothing, and held out so long unmoved, that the severe torture of the boots was resolved upon. He endured this till exhausted nature could bear no longer, when Insensibility kindly stepped in to his aid. When it was seen that he was utterly powerless, and that his tongue cleaved to the roof of his mouth, he was released. Restoratives were administered; and during the first faint gleam of returning consciousness, he was prevailed upon to sign, ere he well knew what he was about, a full confession, in strict accordance with those of Gellie Duncan and Agnes Sampson. He was then remanded to his prison, from which, after two days, he managed, somehow or other, to escape. He was soon recaptured, and brought before the Court of Justiciary, James himself being present. Fian now denied all the circumstances of the written confession which he had signed; whereupon the King, enraged at his "stubborn wilfulness," ordered him once more to the torture. His finger nails were riven out with pincers, and long needles thrust up to the eye into the quick; but still he did not wince. He was then consigned again to the boots, in which, to quote a pamphlet published at the time, [News from Scotland, declaring the damnable life of Dr. Fian.] he continued "so long, and abode so many blows in them, that his legs were crushed and beaten together as small as might be, and the bones and flesh so bruised, that the blood and marrow spouted forth in great abundance, whereby they were made unserviceable for ever."

The astonishing similarity of the confessions of all the persons implicated in these proceedings has often been remarked. It would appear that they actually endeavoured to cause the King's death by their spells and sorceries. Fian, who was acquainted with all the usual tricks of his profession, deceived them with pretended apparitions, so that many of them were really convinced that they had seen the devil. The sum of their confessions was to the following effect:-

Satan, who was, of course, a great foe of the reformed religion, was alarmed that King James should marry a Protestant princess. To avert the consequences to the realms of evil, he had determined to put an end to the King and his bride by raising a storm on their voyage home. Satan, first of all, sent a thick mist over the waters, in the hope that the King's vessel might be stranded on the coast amid the darkness. This failing, Dr. Fian, who, from his superior scholarship, was advanced to the dignity of the devil's secretary, was commanded to summon all the witches to meet their master, each one sailing on a sieve on the high seas.

On All-hallowmas Eve, they assembled to the number of upwards of two hundred, including Gellie Duncan, Agnes Sampson, Euphemia Macalzean, one Barbara Napier, and several warlocks; and each embarking in a riddle, or sieve, they sailed "over the ocean very substantially." After cruising about for some time, they met with the fiend, bearing in his claws a cat, which had been previously drawn nine times through the fire. This he delivered to one of the warlocks, telling him to cast it into the sea, and cry "Hola!" This was done with all solemnity, and immediately the ocean became convulsed -- the waters hissed loudly, and the waves rose mountains high,

"Twisting their arms to the dun-coloured heaven."

The witches sailed gallantly through the tempest they had raised, and landing on the coast of Scotland, took their sieves in their hands, and marched on in procession to the haunted kirk of North Berwick, where the devil had resolved to hold a preaching. Gellie Duncan, the musician of the party, tripped on before, playing on her Jew's harp, and singing,

"Cummer, go ye before, Cummer, go ye;
Gif ye will not go before, Cummer, let me!"

Arrived at the kirk, they paced around it withershins, that is, in reverse of the apparent motion of the sun. Dr. Fian then blew into the key-hole of the door, which opened immediately, and all the witches entered. As it was pitch dark, Fian blew with his mouth upon the candles, which immediately lighted, and the devil was seen occupying the pulpit. He was attired in a black gown and hat, and the witches saluted him, by crying, "All hail, master!" His body was hard, like iron; his face terrible; his nose, like the beak of an eagle; he had great burning eyes; his hands and legs were hairy; and he had long claws upon his hands and feet, and spake with an exceedingly gruff voice. Before commencing his sermon, he called over the names of his congregation, demanding whether they had been good servants, and what success had attended their operations against the life of the King and his bride.

Gray Meill, a crazy old warlock, who acted as beadle or doorkeeper, was silly enough to answer, "that nothing ailed the King yet, God be thanked;" upon which the devil, in a rage, stepped down from the pulpit, and boxed his ears for him. He then remounted, and commenced the preaching, commanding them to be dutiful servants to him, and do all the evil they could. Euphemia Macalzean and Agnes Sampson, bolder than the rest, asked him whether he had brought the image or picture of King James, that they might, by pricking it, cause pains and diseases to fall upon him. "The father of lies" spoke truth for once, and confessed that he had forgotten it; upon which Euphemia Macalzean upbraided him loudly for his carelessness. The devil, however, took it all in good part, although Agnes Sampson and several other women let loose their tongues at him immediately. When they had done scolding, he invited them all to a grand entertainment. A newly buried corpse was dug up, and divided among them, which was all they had in the way of edibles. He was more liberal in the matter of drink, and gave them so much excellent wine that they soon became jolly. Gellie Duncan then played the old tune upon her trump, and the devil himself led off the dance with Euphemia Mac alzean. Thus they kept up the sport till the cock crew.

Agnes Sampson, the wise woman of Keith, as she was called, added some other particulars in her confession. She stated, that on a previous occasion, she had raised an awful tempest in the sea, by throwing a cat into it, with four joints of men tied to its feet. She said also, that on their grand attempt to drown King James, they did not meet with the devil after cruising about, but that he had accompanied them from the first, and that she had seen him dimly in the distance, rolling himself before them over the great waves, in shape and size not unlike a huge haystack. They met with a foreign ship richly laden with wines and other good things, which they boarded, and sunk after they had drunk all the wine, and made themselves quite merry.

Some of these disclosures were too much even for the abundant faith of King James, and he more than once exclaimed, that the witches were like their master, "extreme lyars." But they confessed many other things of a less preposterous nature, and of which they were, no doubt, really guilty. Agnes Sampson said she was to have taken the King's life by anointing his linen with a strong poison. Gellie Duncan used to threaten her neighbours by saying she would send the devil after them; and many persons of weaker minds than usual were frightened into fits by her, and rendered subject to them for the remainder of their lives. Dr. Finn also made no scruple in aiding and abetting murder, and would rid any person of an enemy by means of poison, who could pay him his fee for it. Euphemia Macalzean also was far from being pure. There is no doubt that she meditated the King's death, and used such means to compass it as the superstition of the age directed. She was a devoted partizan of Bothwell, who was accused by many of the witches as having consulted them on the period of the King's death. They were all found guilty, and sentenced to be hanged and burned. Barbara Napier, though found guilty upon other counts, was acquitted upon the charge of having been present at the great witch-meeting in Berwick kirk. The King was highly displeased, and threatened to have the jury indicted for a wilful error upon an assize. They accordingly reconsidered their verdict, and threw themselves upon the King's mercy for the fault they had committed. James was satisfied, and Barbara Napier was hanged along with Gellie Duncan, Agnes Sampson, Dr. Fian, and five-and-twenty others. Euphemia Macalzean met a harder fate. Her connexion with the bold and obnoxious Bothwell, and her share in poisoning one or two individuals who had stood in her way, were thought deserving of the severest punishment the law could inflict. Instead of the ordinary sentence, directing the criminal to be first strangled and then burned, the wretched woman was doomed "to be bound to a stake, and burned in ashes, quick to the death." This cruel sentence was executed on the 25th of June 1591.

These trials had the most pernicious consequences all over Scotland. The lairds and ministers in their districts, armed with due power from the privy council, tried and condemned old women after the most summary fashion. Those who still clung to the ancient faith of Rome were the severest sufferers, as it was thought, after the disclosures of the fierce enmity borne by the devil towards a Protestant King and his Protestant wife, that all the Catholics were leagued with the powers of evil to work woe on the realm of Scotland. Upon a very moderate calculation, it is presumed that from the passing of the act of Queen Mary till the accession of James to the throne of England, a period of thirty-nine years, the average number of executions for witchcraft in Scotland was two hundred annually, or upwards of seventeen thousand altogether. For the first nine years the number was not one quarter so great; but towards the years 1590 to 1593, the number must have been more than four hundred. The case last cited was one of an extraordinary character. The general aspect of the trials will be better seen from that of Isabel Gowdie, which, as it would be both wearisome and disgusting to go through them all, is cited as a fair specimen, although it took place at a date somewhat later than the reign of James. This woman, wearied of her life by the persecutions of her neighbours, voluntarily gave herself up to justice, and made a confession, embodying the whole witch-creed of the period. She was undoubtedly a monomaniac of the most extraordinary kind. She said that she deserved to be stretched upon an iron rack, and that her crimes could never be atoned for, even if she were to be drawn asunder by wild horses. She named a long list of her associates, including nearly fifty women and a few warlocks. They dug up the graves of unchristened infants, whose limbs were serviceable in their enchantments. When they wanted to destroy the crops of an enemy, they yoked toads to his plough, and on the following night Satan himself ploughed the land with his team, and blasted it for the season. The witches had power to assume almost any shape; but they generally chose either that of a cat or a hare, oftenest the latter. Isabel said, that on one occasion, when she was in this disguise, she was sore pressed by a pack of hounds, and had a very narrow escape with her life. She reached her own door at last, feeling the hot breath of the pursuing dogs at her haunches. She managed, however, to hide herself behind a chest, and got time to pronounce the magic words that could alone restore her to her proper shape. They were :--

"Hare! hare!
God send thee care!

I am in a hare's likeness now;
But I shall be a woman e'en now!
Hare! hare!
God send thee care!"

If witches, when in this shape, were bitten by the dogs, they always retained the marks in their human form; but she had never heard that any witch had been bitten to death. When the devil appointed any general meeting of the witches, the custom was that they should proceed through the air mounted on broomsticks, or on corn or bean-straws, pronouncing as they went:--

"Horse and partook, horse and go,
Horse and pellats, ho! ho! ho!"

They generally left behind them a broom, or a three-legged stool, which, when placed in their beds and duly charmed, assumed the human shape till their return. This was done that the neighhours might not know when they were absent.

She added, that the devil furnished his favourite witches with servant imps to attend upon them. These imps were called "The Roaring Lion," "Thief of Hell," "Wait-upon-Herself," "Ranting Roarer," "Care-for-Naught," &c. and were known by their liveries, which were generally yellow, sad-dun, sea-green, pea-green, or grass-green. Satan never called the witches by the names they had received at baptism; neither were they allowed, in his presence, so to designate each other. Such a breach of the infernal etiquette assuredly drew down his most severe displeasure. But as some designation was necessary, he re-baptized them in their own blood by the names of "Able-and-Stout," "Over-the-dike-with-it," "Raise-the-wind," "Pickle-nearest-the-wind," "Batter-them-down-Maggy," "Blow-Kale," and such like. The devil himself was not very particular what name they called him so that it was not "Black John." If any witch was unthinking enough to utter these words, he would rush out upon her, and beat and buffet her unmercifully, or tear her flesh with a wool-card. Other names he did not care about; and once gave instructions to a noted warlock that whenever he wanted his aid, he was to strike the ground three times and exclaim, "Rise up, foul thief!"

Upon this confession many persons were executed. So strong was the popular feeling, that no one once accused of witchcraft was acquitted; at least, acquittals did not average one in a hundred trials. Witch-finding, or witch-pricking became a trade, and a set of mercenary vagabonds roamed about the country, provided with long pins to run into the flesh of supposed criminals. It was no unusual thing then, nor is it now, that in aged persons there should be some spot on the body totally devoid of feeling. It was the object of the witchpricker to discover this spot, and the unhappy wight who did not bleed when pricked upon it, was doomed to the death. If not immediately cast into prison, her life was rendered miserable by the persecution of her neighbours. It is recorded of many poor women, that the annoyances they endured in this way were so excessive, that they preferred death. Sir George Mackenzie, the Lord Advocate, at the time when witch-trials were so frequent, and himself a devout believer in the crime, relates, in his "Criminal Law," first published in 1678, some remarkable instances of it. He says, "I went, when I was a justice-depute, to examine some women who had confessed judicially: and one of them, who was a silly creature, told me, under secrecy, that she had not confessed because she was guilty, but being a poor creature who wrought for her meat, and being defamed for a witch, she knew she should starve; for no person thereafter would either give her meat or lodging, and that all men would beat her and set dogs at her; and that, therefore, she desired to be out of the world; whereupon she wept most bitterly, and upon her knees called God to witness to what she said." Sir George, though not wholly elevated above the prejudices of his age upon this subject, was clearsighted enough to see the danger to society of the undue encouragement given to the witch-prosecutions. He was convinced that three-fourths of them were unjust and unfounded. He says, in the work already quoted, that the persons who were in general accused of this crime, were poor ignorant men and women, who did not understand the nature of the accusation, and who mistook their own superstitious fears for witchcraft. One poor wretch, a weaver, confessed that he was a warlock, and, being asked why, he replied, because "he had seen the devil dancing, like a fly, about the candle!" A simple woman, who, because she was called a witch, believed that she was, asked the judge upon the bench, whether a person might be a witch and not know it? Sir George adds, that all the supposed criminals were subjected to severe torture in prison from their gaolers, who thought they did God good service by vexing and tormenting them; "and I know," says this humane and enlightened magistrate, "that this usage was the ground of all their confession; and albeit, the poor miscreants cannot prove this usage, the actors in it being the only witnesses, yet the judge should be jealous of it, as that which did at first elicit the confession, and for fear of which they dare not retract it." Another author, ["Satan's Invisible World discovered," by the Rev. G. Sinclair.] also a firm believer in witchcraft, gives a still more lamentable instance of a woman who preferred execution as a witch to live on under the imputation. This woman, who knew that three others were to be strangled and burned on an early day, sent for the minister of the parish, and confessed that she had sold her soul to Satan. "Whereupon being called before the judges, she was condemned to die with the rest. Being carried forth to the place of execution, she remained silent during the first, second, and third prayer, and then, perceiving that there remained no more but to rise and go to the stake, she lifted up her body, and, with a loud voice, cried out, "Now all you that see me this day, know that I am now to die as a witch, by my own confession, and I free all men, especially the ministers and magistrates, of the guilt of my blood. I take it wholly upon myself. My blood be upon my own head. And, as I must make answer to the God of heaven presently, I declare I am as free of witchcraft as any child. But, being delated by a malicious woman, and put in prison under the name of a witch, disowned by my husband and friends, and seeing no ground of hope of ever coming out again, I made up that confession to destroy my own life, being weary of it, and choosing rather to die than to live." As a proof of the singular obstinacy and blindness of the believers in witches, it may be stated, that the minister who relates this story only saw in the dying speech of the unhappy woman an additional proof that she was a witch. True indeed is it, that "none are so blind as those who will not see."

It is time, however, to return to James VI, who is fairly entitled to share with Pope Innocent, Sprenger, Bodinus, and Matthew Hopkins the glory or the odium of being at the same time a chief enemy and chief encourager of witchcraft. Towards the close of the sixteenth century, many learned men, both on the Continent and in the isles of Britain, had endeavoured to disabuse the public mind on this subject. The most celebrated were Wierus in Germany, Pietro d'Apone in Italy, and Reginald Scot in England. Their works excited the attention of the zealous James, who, mindful of the involuntary compliment which his merits had extorted from the devil, was ambitious to deserve it by still continuing "his greatest enemie." In the year 1597 he published, in Edinburgh, his famous treatise on Demonology. Its design may be gathered from the following passage in the introduction. "The fearful abounding," says the King, "at this time, and in this country, of these detestable slaves of the devil, the witches, or enchanters, hath moved me, beloved reader, to despatch in post this following treatise of mine, not in any wise, as I protest, to serve for a show of mine own learning and ingene (ingenuity), but only (moved of conscience) to press thereby, so far as I can, to resolve the doubting hearts of many; both that such assaults of Satan are most certainly practised, and that the instrument thereof merits most severely to be punished, against the damnable opinions of two, principally in our age, whereof the one, called Scot, an Englishman, is not ashamed, in public print, to deny that there can be such thing as witchcraft, and so maintains the old error of the Sadducees, in denying of spirits. The other, called Wierus, a German physician, sets out a public apology for all these crafts-folks, whereby procuring for them impunity, he plainly betrays himself to have been one of that profession." In other parts of this treatise, which the author had put into the form of a dialogue to "make it more pleasant and facile," he says, "Witches ought to be put to death, according to the law of God, the civil and imperial law, and the municipal law of all Christian nations: yea, to spare the life, and not strike whom God bids strike, and so severely punish in so odious a treason against God, is not only unlawful, but doubtless as great a sin in the magistrate, as was Saul's sparing Agag." He says also, that the crime is so abominable, that it may be proved by evidence which would not be received against any other offenders, -- young children, who knew not the nature of an oath, and persons of an infamous character, being sufficient witnesses against them; but lest the innocent should be accused of a crime so difficult to be acquitted of, he recommends that in all cases the ordeal should be resorted to. He says, "Two good helps may be used: the one is, the finding of their mark, and the trying the insensibleness thereof; the other is their floating on the water; for, as in a secret murther, if the dead carcass be at any time thereafter handled by the murtherer, it will gush out of blood, as if the blood were crying to Heaven for revenge of the murtherer, (God having appointed that secret supernatural sign for trial of that secret unnatural crime); so that it appears that God hath appointed (for a supernatural sign of the monstrous impiety of witches) that the water shall refuse to receive them in her bosom, that have shaken off them the sacred water of baptism, and wilfully refused the benefit thereof; no, not so much as their eyes are able to shed tears (threaten and torture them as you please), while first they repent (God not permitting them to dissemble their obstinacy in so horrible a crime). Albeit, the womenkind especially, be able otherwise to shed tears at every light occasion, when they will; yea, although it were dissembling, like the crocodiles."

When such doctrines as these were openly promulgated by the highest authority in the realm, and who, in promulgating them, flattered, but did not force the public opinion, it is not surprising that the sad delusion should have increased and multiplied, until the race of wizards and witches replenished the earth. The reputation which he lost by being afraid of a naked sword, he more than regained by his courage in combating the devil. The Kirk showed itself a most zealous coadjutor, especially during those halcyon days when it was not at issue with the King upon other matters of doctrine and prerogative.

On his accession to the throne of England, in 1603, James came amongst a people who had heard with admiration of his glorious deeds against the witches. He himself left no part of his ancient prejudices behind him, and his advent was the signal for the persecution to burst forth in England with a fury equal to that in Scotland. It had languished a little during the latter years of the reign of Elizabeth; but the very first Parliament of King James brought forward the subject. James was flattered by their promptitude, and the act passed in 1604. On the second reading in the House of Lords, the bill passed into a committee, in which were twelve bishops. By it was enacted, "That if any person shall use, practise, or exercise any conjuration of any wicked or evil spirit, or shall consult, covenant with, or feed any such spirit, the first offence to be imprisonment for a year and standing in the pillory once a quarter; the second offence to be death."

The minor punishment seems but rarely to have been inflicted. Every record that has been preserved, mentions that the witches were hanged and burned, or burned without the previous strangling, "alive and quick." During the whole of James's reign, amid the civil wars of his successor, the sway of the Long Parliament, the usurpation of Cromwell, and the reign of Charles II, there was no abatement of the persecution. If at any time it raged with less virulence, it was when Cromwell and the Independents were masters. Dr. Zachary Grey, the editor of an edition of "Hudibras," informs us, in a note to that work, that he himself perused a list of three thousand witches who were executed in the time of the Long Parliament alone. During the first eighty years of the seventeenth century, the number executed has been estimated at five hundred annually, making the frightful total of forty thousand. Some of these cases deserve to be cited. The great majority resemble closely those already mentioned, but two or three of them let in a new light upon the popular superstition.

Every one has heard of the "Lancashire witches," a phrase now used to compliment the ladies of that county for their bewitching beauty; but it is not every one who has heard the story in which it originated. A villainous boy, named Robinson, was the chief actor in the tragedy. He confessed, many years afterwards, that he had been suborned by his father and other persons to give false evidence against the unhappy witches whom he brought to the stake. The time of this famous trial was about the year 1634. This boy Robinson, whose father was a wood-cutter, residing on the borders of Pendle Forest, in Lancashire, spread abroad many rumours against one Mother Dickenson, whom he accused of being a witch. These rumours coming to the ears of the local magistracy, the boy was sent for, and strictly examined. He told the following extraordinary story, without hesitation or prevarication, and apparently in so open and honest a manner, that no one who heard him doubted the truth of it: -- He said, that as he was roaming about in one of the glades of the forest, amusing himself by gathering blackberries, he saw two greyhounds before him, which he thought at the time belonged to some gentleman of the neighbourhood. Being fond of sport, he proposed to have a course, and a hare being started, he incited the hounds to run. Neither of them would stir. Angry at the beasts, he seized hold of a switch, with which he was about to punish them, when one of them suddenly started up in the form of a woman, and the other, of a little boy. He at once recognised the woman to be the witch Mother Dickenson. She offered him some money to induce him to sell his soul to the devil; but he refused. Upon this she took a bridle out of her pocket, and, shaking it over the head of the other little boy, he was instantly turned into a horse. Mother Dickenson then seized him in her arms, sprang upon the horse; and, placing him before her, rode with the swiftness of the wind over forests, fields, bogs, and rivers, until they came to a large barn. The witch alighted at the door; and taking him by the hand, led him inside. There he saw seven old women, pulling at seven halters which hung from the roof. As they pulled, large pieces of meat, lumps of butter, loaves of bread, basins of milk, hot puddings, black puddings, and other rural dainties, fell from the halters on to the floor. While engaged in this charm they made such ugly faces, and looked so fiendish, that he was quite frightened. After they had pulled, in this manner enough for an ample feast, they set-to, and showed, whatever might be said of the way in which their supper was procured, that their epicurism was a little more refined than that of the Scottish witches, who, according to Gellie Duncan's confession, feasted upon dead men's flesh in the old kirk of Berwick. The boy added, that as soon as supper was ready, many other witches came to partake of it, several of whom he named. In consequence of this story, many persons were arrested, and the boy Robinson was led about from church to church, in order that he might point out to the officers, by whom he was accompanied, the hags he had seen in the barn. Altogether about twenty persons were thrown into prison; eight of them were condemned to die, including Mother Dickenson, upon this evidence alone, and executed accordingly. Among the wretches who concocted this notable story, not one was ever brought to justice for his perjury; and Robinson, the father, gained considerable sums by threatening persons who were rich enough to buy off exposure.

Among the ill weeds which flourished amid the long dissensions of the civil war, Matthew Hopkins, the witch-finder, stands eminent in his sphere. This vulgar fellow resided, in the year 1644, at the town of Manningtree, in Essex, and made himself very conspicuous in discovering the devil's marks upon several unhappy witches. The credit he gained by his skill in this instance seems to have inspired him to renewed exertions. In the course of a very short time, whenever a witch was spoken of in Essex, Matthew Hopkins was sure to be present, aiding the judges with his knowledge of "such cattle," as he called them. As his reputation increased, he assumed the title of "Witchfinder General," and travelled through the counties of Norfolk, Essex, Huntingdon, and Sussex, for the sole purpose of finding out witches. In one year he brought sixty poor creatures to the stake. The test he commonly adopted was that of swimming, so highly recommended by King James in his "Demonologie." The hands and feet of the suspected persons were tied together crosswise, the thumb of the right hand to the toe of the left foot, and vice versa. They were then wrapped up in a large sheet or blanket, and laid upon their backs in a pond or river. If they sank, their friends and relatives had the poor consolation of knowing they were innocent, but there was an end of them: if they floated, which, when laid carefully on the water was generally the case, there was also an end of them; for they were deemed guilty of witchcraft, and burned accordingly.

Another test was to make them repeat the Lord's prayer and creed. It was affirmed that no witch could do so correctly. If she missed a word, or even pronounced one incoherently, which in her trepidation, it was most probable she would, she was accounted guilty. It was thought that witches could not weep more than three tears, and those only from the left eye. Thus the conscious innocence of many persons, which gave them fortitude to bear unmerited torture without flinching, was construed by their unmerciful tormentors into proofs of guilt. In some districts the test resorted to was to weigh the culprit against the church Bible. If the suspected witch proved heavier than the Bible, she was set at liberty. This mode was far too humane for the witch-finders by profession. Hopkins always maintained that the most legitimate modes were pricking and swimming.

Hopkins used to travel through his counties like a man of consideration, attended by his two assistants, always putting up at the chief inn of the place, and always at the cost of the authorities. His charges were twenty shillings a town, his expenses of living while there, and his carriage thither and back. This he claimed whether he found witches or not. If he found any, he claimed twenty shillings a head in addition when they were brought to execution. For about three years he carried on this infamous trade, success making him so insolent and rapacious, that high and low became his enemies. The Rev. Mr. Gaul, a clergyman of Houghton, in Huntingdonshire, wrote a pamphlet impugning his pretensions, and accusing him of being a common nuisance. Hopkins replied in an angry letter to the functionaries of Houghton, stating his intention to visit their town; but desiring to know whether it afforded many such sticklers for witchcraft as Mr. Gaul, and whether they were willing to receive and entertain him with the customary hospitality, if he so far honoured them. He added, by way of threat, that in case he did not receive a satisfactory reply, "He would waive their shire altogether, and betake himself to such places where he might do and punish, not only without control, but with thanks and recompence." The authorities of Houghton were not much alarmed at his awful threat of letting them alone. They very wisely took no notice either of him or his letter.

Mr. Gaul describes in his pamphlet one of the modes employed by Hopkins, which was sure to swell his revenues very considerably. It was a proof even more atrocious than the swimming. He says, that the "Witch-finder General" used to take the suspected witch and place her in the middle of a room, upon a stool or table, cross-legged, or in some other uneasy posture. If she refused to sit in this manner, she was bound with strong cords. Hopkins then placed persons to watch her for four-and-twenty hours, during which time she was to be kept without meat or drink. It was supposed that one of her imps would come during that interval, and suck her blood. As the imp might come in the shape of a wasp, a moth, a fly, or other insect, a hole was made in the door or window to let it enter. The watchers were ordered to keep a sharp look-out, and endeavour to kill any insect that appeared in the room. If any fly escaped, and they could not kill it, the woman was guilty; the fly was her imp, and she was sentenced to be burned, and twenty shillings went into the pockets of Master Hopkins. In this manner he made one old woman confess, because four flies had appeared in the room, that she was attended by four imps, named "Ilemazar," "Pye-wackett," "Peck-in-the-crown," and "Grizel-Greedigut."

It is consoling to think that this impostor perished in his own snare. Mr. Gaul's exposure and his own rapacity weakened his influence among the magistrates; and the populace, who began to find that not even the most virtuous and innocent were secure from his persecution, looked upon him with undisguised aversion. He was beset by a mob, at a village in Suffolk, and accused of being himself a wizard. An old reproach was brought against him, that he had, by means of sorcery, cheated the devil out of a certain memorandum-book, in which he, Satan, had entered the names of all the witches in England. "Thus," said the populace, "you find out witches, not by God's aid, but by the devil's." In vain he denied his guilt. The populace longed to put him to his own test. He was speedily stripped, and his thumbs and toes tied together. He was then placed in a blanket, and cast into a pond. Some say that he floated; and that he was taken out, tried, and executed upon no other proof of his guilt. Others assert that he was drowned. This much is positive, that there was an end of him. As no judicial entry of his trial and execution is to be found in any register, it appears most probable that he expired by the hands of the mob. Butler has immortalized this scamp in the following lines of his "Hudibras:"--

"Hath not this present Parliament
A lieger to the devil sent,
Fully empower'd to treat about
Finding revolted witches out?
And has he not within a year
Hang'd threescore of them in one shire?
Some only for not being drown'd,
And some for sitting above ground
Whole days and nights upon their breeches,
And feeling pain, were hang'd for witches;
And some for putting knavish tricks
Upon green geese or turkey chicks;
Or pigs that suddenly deceased
Of griefs unnatural, as he guess'd;
Who proved himself at length a witch,
And made a rod for his own breech."

In Scotland also witch-finding became a trade. They were known under the designation of "common prickers," and, like Hopkins, received a fee for each witch they discovered. At the trial of Janet Peaston, in 1646, the magistrates of Dalkeith "caused John Kincaid, of Tranent, the common pricker, to exercise his craft upon her. He found two marks of the devil's making; for she could not feel the pin when it was put into either of the said marks, nor did the marks bleed when the pin was taken out again. When she was asked where she thought the pins were put in her, she pointed to a part of her body distant from the real place. They were pins of three inches in length." [Pitcairn's "Records of Justiciary."]

These common prickers became at last so numerous, that they were considered nuisances. The judges refused to take their evidence, and in 1678 the privy council of Scotland condescended to hear the complaint of an honest woman, who had been indecently exposed by one of them, and expressed their opinion that common prickers were common cheats.

But such an opinion was not formed in high places before hundreds of innocent persons had fallen victims. The Parliaments had encouraged the delusion both in England and Scotland; and, by arming these fellows with a sort of authority, had in a manner forced the magistrates and ministers to receive their evidence. The fate of one poor old gentleman, who fell a victim to the arts of Hopkins in 1646, deserves to be recorded. Mr. Louis, a venerable clergyman, upwards of seventy years of age, and who had been rector of Framlingham, in Suffolk, for fifty years, excited suspicion that he was a wizard. Being a violent royalist, he was likely to meet with no sympathy at that time; and even his own parishioners, whom he had served so long and so faithfully, turned their backs upon him as soon as he was accused. Placed under the hands of Hopkins, who knew so well how to bring the refractory to confession, the old man, the light of whose intellect had become somewhat dimmed from age, confessed that he was a wizard. He said he had two imps, that continually excited him to do evil; and that one day, when he was walking on the sea-coast, one of them prompted him to express a wish that a ship, whose sails were just visible in the distance, might sink. He consented, and saw the vessel sink before his eyes. He was, upon this confession, tried and condemned. On his trial the flame of reason burned up as brightly as ever. He denied all that had been alleged against him, and cross-examined Hopkins with great tact and severity. After his condemnation, he begged that the funeral service of the church might be read for him. The request was refused, and he repeated it for himself from memory, as he was led to the scaffold.

A poor woman in Scotland was executed upon evidence even less strong than this. John Bain, a common pricker, swore that, as he passed her door, he heard her talking to the devil. She said in defence, that it was a foolish practice she had of talking to herself, and several of her neighbours corroborated her statement; but the evidence of the pricker was received. He swore that none ever talked to themselves who were not witches. The devil's mark being found upon her, the additional testimony of her guilt was deemed conclusive, and she was "convict and brynt."

From the year 1652 to 1682, these trials diminished annually in number, and acquittals were by no means so rare as they had been. To doubt in witchcraft was no longer dangerous. Before country justices, condemnations on the most absurd evidence still continued, but when the judges of the land had to charge the jury, they took a more humane and philosophical view. By degrees, the educated classes (comprised, in those days, within very narrow limits), openly expressed their unbelief of modern witchcraft, although they were not bold enough to deny its existence altogether. Between them and the believers in the old doctrine fierce arguments ensued, and the sceptics were designated Sadducees. To convince them, the learned and Reverend Joseph Glanvil wrote his well-known work, "Sadducismus Triumphatus," and "The Collection of Relations;" the first part intended as a philosophical inquiry into witchcraft, and the power of the devil "to assume a mortal shape;" the latter containing what he considered a multitude of well-authenticated modern instances.

But though progress was made, it was slow. In 1664, the venerable Sir Matthew Hale condemned two women, named Amy Duny and Rose Cullender, to the stake at St. Edmondsbury, upon evidence the most ridiculous. These two old women, whose ugliness gave their neighbours the first idea that they were witches, went to a shop to purchase herrings, and were refused. Indignant at the prejudice against them, they were not sparing of their abuse. Shortly afterward, the daughter of the herring-dealer fell sick, and a cry was raised that she was bewitched by the old women who had been refused the herrings. This girl was subject to epileptic fits. To discover the guilt of Amy Duny and Rose Cullender, the girl's eyes were blinded closely with a shawl, and the witches were commanded to touch her. They did so, and she was immediately seized with a fit. Upon this evidence they were sent to prison. The girl was afterwards touched by an indifferent person, and the force of her imagination was so great, that, thinking it was again the witches, she fell down in a violent fit as before. This, however, was not received in favour of the accused.

The following extract, from the published reports of the trial, will show the sort of evidence which was received:--

"Samuel Pacey, of Leystoff, (a good, sober man,) being sworn, said that, on Thursday the 10th of October last, his younger daughter, Deborah, about nine years old, was suddenly taken so lame that she could not stand on her legs, and so continued till the 17th of the same month, when the child desired to be carried to a bank on the east side of the house, looking towards the sea; and, while she was sitting there, Amy Duny came to this examinant's house to buy some herrings, but was denied. Then she came twice more, but, being as often denied, she went away discontented and grumbling. At this instant of time, the child was taken with terrible fits, complaining of a pain in her stomach, as if she was pricked with pins, shrieking out with a voice like a whelp, and thus continued till the 30th of the same month. This examinant further saith, that Amy Duny, having long had the reputation of a witch, and his child having, in the intervals of her fits, constantly cried out on her, as the cause of her disorder, saying, that the said Amy did appear to her and fright her, he himself did suspect the said Amy to be a witch, and charged her with being the cause of his child's illness, and set her in the stocks. Two days after, his daughter Elizabeth was taken with such strange fits, that they could not force open her mouth without a tap; and the younger child being in the same condition, they used to her the same remedy. Both children grievously complained that Amy Duny and another woman, whose habit and looks they described, did appear to them, and torment them, and would cry out, 'There stands Amy Duny! There stands Rose Cullender!' the other person who afflicted them. Their fits were not alike. Sometimes they were lame on the right side; sometimes on the left; and sometimes so sore, that they could not bear to be touched. Sometimes they were perfectly well in other respects, but they could not hear; at other times, they could not see. Sometimes they lost their speech for one, two, and once for eight, days together. At times they had swooning fits, and, when they could speak, were taken with a fit of coughing, and vomited phlegm and crooked pins; and once a great twopenny nail, with above forty pins; which nail he, the examinant, saw vomited up, with many of the pins. The nail and pins were produced in the court. Thus the children continued for two months, during which time the examinant often made them read in the New Testament, and observed, when they came to the words Lord Jesus, or Christ, they could not pronounce them, but fell into a fit. When they came to the word Satan, or devil, they would point, and say, 'This bites, but makes me speak right well.' Finding his children thus tormented without hopes of recovery, he sent them to his sister, Margaret Arnold, at Yarmouth, being willing to try whether change of air would help them.

"Margaret Arnold was the next witness. Being sworn, she said, that about the 30th of November, Elizabeth and Deborah Pacey came to her house, with her brother, who told her what had happened, and that he thought his children bewitched. She, this examinant, did not much regard it, supposing the children had played tricks, and put the pins into their mouths themselves. She, therefore, took all the pins from their clothes, sewing them with thread instead of pinning them. But, notwithstanding, they raised, at times, at least thirty pins, in her presence, and had terrible fits; in which fits they would cry out upon Amy Duny and Rose Cullender, saying, that they saw them and heard them threatening, as before; that they saw things, like mice, running about the house; and one of them catched one, and threw it into the fire, which made a noise, like a rat. Another time the younger child, being out of doors, a thing like a bee would have forced itself into her mouth, at which the child ran screaming into the house, and before this examinant could come at her, fell into a fit, and vomited a twopenny nail, with a broad head. After that, this examinant asked the child how she came by this nail, when she answered, 'The bee brought the nail, and forced it into my mouth.' At other times, the eldest child told this examinant that she saw flies bring her crooked pins. She would then fall into a fit, and vomit such pins. One time the said child said she saw a mouse, and crept under the table to look for it; and afterwards, the child seemed to put something into her apron, saying, 'She had caught it.' She then ran to the fire, and threw it in, on which there did appear to this examinant something like a flash of gunpowder, although she does own she saw nothing in the child's hand. Once the child, being speechless, but otherwise very sensible, ran up and down the house, crying, 'Hush! hush!' as if she had seen poultry; but this examinant saw nothing. At last the child catched at something, and threw it into the fire. Afterwards, when the child could speak, this examinant asked her what she saw at the time? She answered, that she saw a duck. Another time the youngest child said, after a fit, that Amy Duny had been with her, and tempted her to drown herself, or cut her throat, or otherwise destroy herself. Another time they both cried out upon Amy Duny and Rose Cullender, saying, 'Why don't you come yourselves? Why do you send your imps to torment us?'"

The celebrated Sir Thomas Brown, the author of "Vulgar Errors," was also examined as a witness upon the trial. Being desired to give his opinion of the three persons in court, he said, he was clearly of opinion that they were bewitched. He said, there had lately been a discovery of witches in Denmark, who used the same way of tormenting persons, by conveying crooked pins, needles, and nails into their bodies. That he thought, in such cases, the devil acted upon human bodies by natural means, namely, by exciting and stirring up the superabundant humours, he did afflict them in a more surprising manner by the same diseases their bodies were usually subject to; that these fits might be natural, only raised to a great degree by the subtlety of the devil, co-operating with the malice of these witches.

The evidence being concluded, Sir Matthew Hale addressed the jury. He said, he would waive repeating the evidence, to prevent any mistake, and told the jury, there were two things they had to inquire into. First, Whether or not these children were bewitched; secondly, Whether these women did bewitch them. He said, he did not in the least doubt there were witches; first, Because the Scriptures affirmed it; secondly, Because the wisdom of all nations, particularly our own, had provided laws against witchcraft, which implied their belief of such a crime. He desired them strictly to observe the evidence, and begged of God to direct their hearts in the weighty concern they had in hand, since, to condemn the innocent and let the guilty go free, are both an abomination to the Lord.

The jury then retired, and, in about half an hour, returned a verdict of guilty upon all the indictments, being thirteen in number. The next morning the children came with their father to the lodgings of Sir Matthew Hale, very well, and quite restored to their usual health. Mr. Pacey, being asked at what time their health began to improve, replied, that they were quite well in half an hour after the conviction of the prisoners.

Many attempts were made to induce the unfortunate women to confess their guilt; but in vain, and they were both hanged.

Eleven trials were instituted before Chief-Justice Holt for witchcraft between the years 1694 and 1701. The evidence was of the usual character; but Holt appealed so successfully in each case to the common sense of the jury, that they were every one acquitted. A general feeling seemed to pervade the country that blood enough had been shed upon these absurd charges. Now and then, the flame of persecution burnt up in a remote district; but these instances were no longer looked upon as mere matters of course. They appear, on the contrary, to have excited much attention; a sure proof, if no other were to be obtained, that they were becoming unfrequent.

A case of witchcraft was tried in 1711, before Lord Chief Justice Powell; in which, however, the jury persisted in a verdict of guilty, though the evidence was of the usual absurd and contradictory character, and the enlightened judge did all in his power to bring them to a right conclusion. The accused person was one Jane Wenham, better known as the Witch of Walkerne; and the persons who were alleged to have suffered from her witchcraft were two young women, named Thorne and Street. A witness, named Mr. Arthur Chauncy, deposed, that he had seen Ann Thorne in several of her fits, and that she always recovered upon prayers being said, or if Jane Wenham came to her. He related, that he had pricked the prisoner several times in the arms, but could never fetch any blood from her; that he had seen her vomit pins, when there were none in her clothes or within her reach; and that he had preserved several of them, which he was ready to produce. The judge, however, told him that was needless, as he supposed they were crooked pins.

Mr. Francis Bragge, another witness, deposed, that strange "cakes" of bewitched feathers having been taken from Ann Thorne's pillow, he was anxious to see them. He went into a room where some of these feathers were, and took two of the cakes, and compared them together. They were both of a circular figure, something larger than a crown piece; and he observed that the small feathers were placed in a nice and curious order, at equal distances from each other, making so many radii of the circle, in the centre of which the quill ends of the feathers met. He counted the number of these feathers, and found them to be exactly thirty-two in each cake. He afterwards endeavoured to pull off two or three of them, and observed that they were all fastened together by a sort of viscous matter, which would stretch seven or eight times in a thread before it broke. Having taken off several of these feathers, he removed the viscous matter with his fingers, and found under it, in the centre, some short hairs, black and grey, matted together, which he verily believed to be cat's hair. He also said, that Jane Wenham confessed to him that she had bewitched the pillow, and had practised witchcraft for sixteen years.

The judge interrupted the witness at this stage, and said, he should very much like to see an enchanted feather, and seemed to wonder when he was told that none of these strange cakes had been preserved. His Lordship asked the witness why he did not keep one or two of them, and was informed that they had all been burnt, in order to relieve the bewitched person of the pains she suffered, which could not be so well effected by any other means.

A man, named Thomas Ireland, deposed, that hearing several times a great noise of cats crying and screaming about his house, he went out and frightened them away, and they all ran towards the cottage of Jane Wenham. One of them he swore positively had a face very like Jane Wenham's. Another man, named Burville, gave similar evidence, and swore that he had often seen a cat with Jane Wenham's face. Upon one occasion he was in Ann Thorne's chamber, when several cats came in, and among them the cat above stated. This witness would have favoured the court with a much longer statement, but was stopped by the judge, who said he had heard quite enough.

The prisoner, in her defence, said nothing, but that "she was a clear woman." The learned judge then summed up, leaving it to the jury to determine whether such evidence as they had heard was sufficient to take away the prisoner's life upon the indictment. After a long deliberation they brought in their verdict, that she was guilty upon the evidence. The Judge then asked them whether they found her guilty upon the indictment of conversing with the devil in the shape of a cat? The sapient foreman very gravely answered, "We find her guilty of that." The learned judge then very reluctantly proceeded to pass sentence of death; but, by his persevering exertions, a pardon was at last obtained, and the wretched old woman was set at liberty. In the year 1716, a woman and her daughter, - the latter only nine years of age, -- were hanged at Huntingdon for selling their souls to the devil, and raising a storm by pulling off their stockings and making a lather of soap. This appears to have been the last judicial execution in England. From that time to the year 1736, the populace raised at intervals the old cry, and more than once endangered the lives of poor women by dragging them through ponds on suspicion; but the philosophy of those who, from their position, sooner or later give the tone to the opinions and morals of the poor, was silently working a cure for the evil. The fear of witches ceased to be epidemic, and became individual, lingering only in minds lettered by inveterate prejudice or brutalizing superstition. In the year 1736, the penal statute of James I. was finally blotted from the statutebook, and suffered no longer to disgrace the advancing intelligence of the country. Pretenders to witchcraft, fortune-tellers, conjurors, and all their train, were liable only to the common punishment of rogues and impostors -- imprisonment and the pillory.

In Scotland, the delusion also assumed the same phases, and was gradually extinguished in the light of civilization. As in England the progress of improvement was slow. Up to the year 1665, little or no diminution of the mania was perceptible. In 1643, the General Assembly recommended that the Privy Council should institute a standing commission, composed of any "understanding gentlemen or magistrates," to try the witches, who were stated to have increased enormously of late years. In 1649, an act was passed, confirmatory of the original statute of Queen Mary, explaining some points of the latter which were doubtful, and enacting severe penalties, not only against witches themselves, but against all who covenanted with them, or sought by their means to pry into the secrets of futurity, or cause any evil to the life, lands, or limbs of their neighbours. For the next ten years, the popular madness upon this subject was perhaps more furious than ever; upwards of four thousand persons suffered for the crime during that interval. This was the consequence of the act of parliament and the unparalleled severity of the magistrates; the latter frequently complained that for two witches they burned one day, there were ten to burn the next: they never thought that they themselves were the cause of the increase. In a single circuit, held at Glasgow, Ayr, and Stirling, in 1659, seventeen unhappy creatures were burned by judicial sentence for trafficking with Satan. In one day, (November 7, 1661,) the Privy Council issued no less than fourteen commissions for trials in the provinces. Next year, the violence of the persecution seems to have abated. From 1662 to 1668, although "the understanding gentlemen and magistrates" already mentioned, continued to try and condemn, the High Court of Justiciary had but one offender of this class to deal with, and she was acquitted. James Welsh, a common pricker, was ordered to be publicly whipped through the streets of Edinburgh for falsely accusing a woman of witchcraft; a fact which alone proves that the superior court sifted the evidence in these cases with much more care and severity than it had done a few years previously. The enlightened Sir George Mackenzie, styled by Dryden "the noble wit of Scotland," laboured hard to introduce this rule into court -- that the confessions of the witches should be held of little worth, and that the evidence of the prickers and other interested persons should be received with distrust and jealousy. This was reversing the old practice, and saved many innocent lives. Though a firm believer both in ancient and modern witchcraft, he could not shut his eyes to the atrocities daily committed under the name of justice. In his work on the Criminal Law of Scotland, published in 1678, he says, "From the horridness of this crime, I do conclude that, of all others, it requires the clearest relevancy and most convincing probature; and I condemn, next to the wretches themselves, those cruel and too forward judges who burn persons by thousands as guilty of this crime." In the same year, Sir John Clerk plumply refused to serve as a commissioner on trials for witchcraft, alleging, by way of excuse, "that he was not himself good conjuror enough to be duly qualified." The views entertained by Sir George Mackenzie were so favourably received by the Lords of Session that he was deputed, in 1680, to report to them on the cases of a number of poor women who were then in prison awaiting their trial. Sir George stated that there was no evidence against them whatever but their own confessions, which were absurd and contradictory, and drawn from them by severe torture. They were immediately discharged.

For the next sixteen years, the Lords of Session were unoccupied with trials for witchcraft; not one is entered upon the record: but in 1697, a case occurred, which equalled in absurdity any of those that signalized the dark reign of King James. A girl, named Christiana Shaw, eleven years of age, the daughter of John Shaw of Bargarran, was subject to fits, and being of a spiteful temper, she accused her maid-servant, with whom she had frequent quarrels, of bewitching her. Her story, unfortunately, was believed. Encouraged to tell all the persecutions of the devil which the maid had sent to torment her, she in the end concocted a romance that involved twenty-one persons. There was no other evidence against them but the fancies of this lying child, and the confessions which pain had extorted from them; but upon this no less than five women were condemned, before Lord Blantyre and the rest of the Commissioners, appointed specially by the Privy Council to try this case. They were burned on the

Green at Paisley. The warlock of the party, one John Reed, who was also condemned, hanged himself in prison. It was the general belief in Paisley that the devil had strangled him, lest he should have revealed in his last moments too many of the unholy secrets of witchcraft. This trial excited considerable disgust in Scotland. The Rev. Mr. Bell, a contemporary writer, observed that, in this business, "persons of more goodness and esteem than most of their calumniators were defamed for witches." He adds, that the persons chiefly to blame were "certain ministers of too much forwardness and absurd credulity, and some topping professors in and about Glasgow." [Preface to "Law's Memorials," edited by Sharpe.]

After this trial, there again occurs a lapse of seven years, when the subject was painfully forced upon public attention by the brutal cruelty of the mob at Pittenween. Two women were accused of having bewitched a strolling beggar, who was subject to fits, or who pretended to be so, for the purpose of exciting commiseration. They were cast into prison, and tortured until they confessed. One of them, named Janet Cornfoot, contrived to escape, but was brought back to Pittenween next day by a party of soldiers. On her approach to the town, she was, unfortunately, met by a furious mob, composed principally of fishermen and their wives, who seized upon her with the intention of swimming her. They forced her away to the sea shore, and tying a rope around her body, secured the end of it to the mast of a fishing-boat lying alongside. In this manner they ducked her several times. When she was half dead, a sailor in the boat cut away the rope, and the mob dragged her through the sea to the beach. Here, as she lay quite insensible, a brawny ruffian took down the door of his hut, close by, and placed it on her back. The mob gathered large stones from the beach, and piled them upon her till the wretched woman was pressed to death. No magistrate made the slightest attempt to interfere, and the soldiers looked on, delighted spectators. A great outcry was raised against this culpable remissness, but no judicial inquiry was set on foot. This happened in 1704.

The next case we hear of is that of Elspeth Rule, found guilty of witchcraft before Lord Anstruther at the Dumfries circuit, in 1708. She was sentenced to be marked in the cheek with a redhot iron, and banished the realm of Scotland for life.

Again there is a long interval. In 1718, the remote county of Caithness, where the delusion remained in all its pristine vigour for years after it had ceased elsewhere, was startled from its propriety by the cry of witchcraft. A silly fellow, named William Montgomery, a carpenter, had a mortal antipathy to cats, and, somehow or other, these animals generally chose his back-yard as the scene of their catterwaulings. He puzzled his brains for a long time to know why he, above all his neighbours, should be so pestered; at last he came to the sage conclusion that his tormentors were no cats, but witches. In this opinion he was supported by his maid-servant, who swore a round oath that she had often heard the aforesaid cats talking together in human voices. The next time the unlucky tabbies assembled in his back-yard, the valiant carpenter was on the alert. Arming himself with an axe, a dirk, and a broadsword, he rushed out among them: one of them he wounded in the back, a second in the hip, and the leg of a third he maimed with his axe; but he could not capture any of them. A few days afterwards, two old women of the parish died, and it was said that, when their bodies were laid out, there appeared upon the back of one the mark as of a recent wound, and a similar scar upon the hip of the other. The carpenter and his maid were convinced that they were the very cats, and the whole county repeated the same story. Every one was upon the look-out for proofs corroborative: a very remarkable one was soon discovered. Nanny Gilbert, a wretched old creature of upwards of seventy years of age, was found in bed with her leg broken; as she was ugly enough for a witch, it was asserted that she, also, was one of the cats that had fared so ill at the hands of the carpenter. The latter, when informed of the popular suspicion, asserted that he distinctly remembered to have struck one of the cats a blow with the back of his broadsword, which ought to have broken her leg. Nanny was immediately dragged from her bed, and thrown into prison. Before she was put to the torture, she explained, in a very natural and intelligible manner, how she had broken her limb;

243

but this account did not give satisfaction: the professional persuasions of the torturer made her tell a different tale, and she confessed that she was indeed a witch, and had been wounded by Montgomery on the night stated - that the two old women recently deceased were witches also, besides about a score of others whom she named. The poor creature suffered so much by the removal from her own home, and the tortures inflicted upon her, that she died the next day in prison. Happily for the persons she had named in her confession, Dundas of Arniston, at that time the King's Advocate-general, wrote to the Sheriff-depute, one Captain Ross of Littledean, cautioning him not to proceed to trial, the "thing being of too great difficulty, and beyond the jurisdiction of an inferior court." Dundas himself examined the precognition with great care, and was so convinced of the utter folly of the whole case that he quashed all further proceedings.

We find this same Sheriff-depute of Caithness very active four years afterwards in another trial for witchcraft. In spite of the warning he had received, that all such cases were to be tried in future by the superior courts, he condemned to death an old woman at Dornoch, upon the charge of bewitching the cows and pigs of her neighbours. This poor creature was insane, and actually laughed and clapped her hands at sight of "the bonnie fire" that was to consume her. She had a daughter, who was lame both of her hands and feet, and one of the charges brought against her was, that she had used this daughter as a pony in her excursions to join the devil's sabbath, and that the devil himself had shod her, and produced lameness.

This was the last execution that took place in Scotland for witchcraft. The penal statutes were repealed in 1756, and, as in England, whipping, the pillory, or imprisonment, were declared the future punishments of all pretenders to magic or witchcraft.

Still, for many years after this, the superstition lingered both in England and Scotland, and in some districts is far from being extinct even at this day. But before we proceed to trace it any further than to its legal extinction, we have yet to see the frightful havoc it made in continental Europe from the commencement of the seventeenth to the middle of the eighteenth century. France, Germany, and Switzerland were the countries which suffered most from the epidemic. The number of victims in these countries during the sixteenth century has already been mentioned; but, at the early part of the seventeenth, the numbers are so great, especially in Germany, that were they not to be found in the official records of the tribunals, it would be almost impossible to believe that mankind could ever have been so maddened and deluded. To use the words of the learned and indefatigable Horst, [Zauber Bibliothek. Theil 5.] "the world seemed to be like a large madhouse for witches and devils to play their antics in." Satan was believed to be at everybody's call, to raise the whirlwind, draw down the lightning, blight the productions of the earth, or destroy the health and paralyse the limbs of man. This belief, so insulting to the majesty and beneficence of the Creator, was shared by the most pious ministers of religion. Those who in their morning and evening prayers acknowledged the one true God, and praised him for the blessings of the seed time and the harvest, were convinced that frail humanity could enter into a compact with the spirits of hell to subvert his laws and thwart all his merciful intentions. Successive popes, from Innocent VIII. downwards, promulgated this degrading doctrine, which spread so rapidly that society seemed to be divided into two great factions, the bewitching and the bewitched.

The commissioners named by Innocent VIII. to prosecute the witch-trials in Germany, were Jacob Sprenger, so notorious for his work on demonology, entitled the "Malleus Maleficarum," or "Hammer to knock down Witches," Henry Institor a learned jurisconsult, and the Bishop of Strasburgh. Barnberg, Treves, Cologne, Paderborn, and Wurzburg, were the chief seats of the commissioners, who, during their lives alone, condemned to the stake, on a very moderate calculation, upwards of three thousand victims.

The number of witches so increased, that new commissioners were continually appointed in Germany, France, and Switzerland. In Spain and Portugal the Inquisition alone took cognizance of the crime. It is impossible to search the records of those dark, but now happily nonexisting tribunals; but the mind recoils with affright even to form a guess of the multitudes who perished.

The mode of trial in the other countries is more easily ascertained. Sprenger, in Germany, and Bodinus and Delrio, in France, have left but too ample a record of the atrocities committed in the much-abused names of justice and religion. Bodinus, of great repute and authority in the seventeenth century, says, "The trial of this offence must not be conducted like other crimes. Whoever adheres to the ordinary course of justice perverts the spirit of the law, both Divine and human. He who is accused of sorcery should never be acquitted unless the malice of the prosecutor be clearer than the sun; for it is so difficult to bring full proof of this secret crime, that out of a million of witches not one would be convicted if the usual course were followed!" Henri Boguet, a witch-finder, who styled himself "The Grand Judge of Witches for the Territory of St. Claude," drew up a code for the guidance of all persons engaged in the witch-trials, consisting of seventy articles, quite as cruel as the code of Bodinus. In this document he affirms, that a mere suspicion of witchcraft justifies the immediate arrest and torture of the suspected person. If the prisoner muttered, looked on the ground, and did not shed any tears, all these were proofs positive of guilt! In all cases of witchcraft, the evidence of the child ought to be taken against its parent; and persons of notoriously bad character, although not to be believed upon their oaths on the ordinary occasions of dispute that might arise between man and man, were to be believed, if they swore that any person had bewitched them! Who, when he hears that this diabolical doctrine was the universally received opinion of the ecclesiastical and civil authorities, can wonder that thousands upon thousands of unhappy persons should be brought to the stake? that Cologne should for many years burn its three hundred witches annually? the district of Barnberg its four hundred? Nuremberg, Geneva, Paris, Toulouse, Lyons, and other cities, their two hundred?

A few of these trials may be cited, taking them in the order of priority, as they occurred in different parts of the Continent. In 1595 an old woman residing in a village near Constance, angry at not being invited to share the sports of the country people on a day of public rejoicing, was heard to mutter something to herself, and was afterwards seen to proceed through the fields towards a hill, where she was lost sight of. A violent thunderstorm arose about two hours afterwards, which wet the dancers to the skin, and did considerable damage to the plantations. This woman, suspected before of witchcraft, was seized and imprisoned, and accused of having raised the storm, by filling a hole with wine, and stirring it about with a stick. She was tortured till she confessed, and was burned alive the next evening.

About the same time two sorcerers in Toulouse were accused of having dragged a crucifix about the streets at midnight, stopping at times to spit upon and kick it, and uttering at intervals an exorcism to raise the devil. The next day a hail-storm did considerable damage to the crops, and a girl, the daughter of a shoemaker in the town, remembered to have heard in the night the execrations of the wizards. Her story led to their arrest. The usual means to produce confession were resorted to. The wizards owned that they could raise tempests whenever they pleased, and named several persons who possessed similar powers. They were hanged, and then burned in the market-place, and seven of the persons they had mentioned shared the same fate.

Hoppo and Stadlin, two noted wizards of Germany, were executed in 1599. They implicated twenty or thirty witches, who went about causing women to miscarry, bringing down the lightning of heaven, and making maidens bring forth toads. To this latter fact several girls were found to swear most positively! Stadlin confessed that he had killed seven infants in the womb of one woman.

245

Bodinus highly praises the exertions of a witchfinder, named Nider, in France, who prosecuted so many that he could not calculate them. Some of these witches could, by a single word, cause people to fall down dead; others made women go with child three years instead of nine months; while others, by certain invocations and ceremonies, could turn the faces of their enemies upside down, or twist them round to their backs. Although no witness was ever procured who saw persons in this horrible state, the witches confessed that they had the power, and exercised it. Nothing more was wanting to insure the stake.

At Amsterdam a crazy girl confessed that she could cause sterility in cattle, and bewitch pigs and poultry by merely repeating the magic words Turius und Shurius Inturius! She was hanged and burned. Another woman in the same city, named Kornelis Van Purmerund, was arrested in consequence of some disclosures the former had made. A witness came forward and swore that she one day looked through the window of her hut, and saw Kornelis sitting before a fire muttering something to the devil. She was sure it was to the devil, because she heard him answer her. Shortly afterwards twelve black cats ascended out of the floor, and danced on their hind legs around the witch for the space of about half an hour. They then vanished with a horrid noise, and leaving a disagreeable smell behind them. She also was hanged and burned.

At Bamberg, in Bavaria, the executions from the year 1610 to 1640 were at the rate of about a hundred annually. One woman, suspected of witchcraft, was seized because, having immoderately praised the beauty of a child, it had shortly afterwards fallen ill and died. She confessed upon the rack that the devil had given her the power to work evil upon those she hated, by speaking words in their praise. If she said with unwonted fervour, "What a strong man!" "What a lovely woman!" "What a sweet child!" the devil understood her, and afflicted them with diseases immediately. It is quite unnecessary to state the end of this poor creature. Many women were executed for causing strange substances to lodge in the bodies of those who offended them. Bits of wood, nails, hair, eggshells, bits of glass, shreds of linen and woollen cloth, pebbles, and even hot cinders and knives, were the articles generally chosen. These were believed to remain in the body till the witches confessed or were executed, when they were voided from the bowels, or by the mouth, nostrils, or ears. Modern physicians have often had cases of a similar description under their care, where girls have swallowed needles, which have been voided on the arms, legs, and other parts of the body. But the science of that day could not account for these phenomena otherwise than by the power of the devil; and every needle swallowed by a servant maid cost an old woman her life. Nay, if no more than one suffered in consequence, the district might think itself fortunate. The commissioners seldom stopped short at one victim. The revelations of the rack in most cases implicated half a score.

Of all the records of the witch-trials preserved for the wonder of succeeding ages, that of Wurzburg, from 1627 to 1629, is the most frightful. Hauber, who has preserved this list in his "Acta et Scripta Magica," says, in a note at the end, that it is far from complete, and that there were a great many other burnings too numerous to specify. This record, which relates to the city only, and not to the province of Wurzburg, contains the names of one hundred and fifty-seven persons, who were burned in two years in twenty-nine burnings, averaging from five to six at a time. The list comprises three play-actors, four innkeepers, three common councilmen of Wurzburg, fourteen vicars of the cathedral, the burgomaster's lady, an apothecary's wife and daughter, two choristers of the cathedral, Gobel Babelin the prettiest girl in the town, and the wife, the two little sons, and the daughter of the councillor Stolzenberg. Rich and poor, young and old, suffered alike. At the seventh of these recorded burnings, the victims are described as a wandering boy, twelve years of age, and four strange men and women, found sleeping in the market-place. Thirty-two of the whole number appear to have been vagrants, of both sexes, who, failing to give a satisfactory account of themselves, were accused and found guilty of witchcraft. The number of children on the list is horrible to think upon. The thirteenth and fourteenth burnings comprised four persons, who are stated to have been a little maiden nine years of age, a maiden still less, her sister, their mother, and their aunt, a pretty young woman of twenty-four. At the eighteenth burning the victims were two boys of twelve, and a girl of fifteen; at the nineteenth, the young heir of the noble house of Rotenhahn, aged nine, and two other boys, one aged ten, and the other twelve. Among other entries appear the names of Baunach, the fattest, and Steinacher, the richest burgher in Wurzburg. What tended to keep up the delusion in this unhappy city, and indeed all over Europe, was the number of hypochondriac and diseased persons who came voluntarily forward, and made confession of witchcraft. Several of the victims in the foregoing list, had only themselves to blame for their fate. Many again, including the apothecary's wife and daughter already mentioned, pretended to sorcery, and sold poisons, or attempted by means of charms and incantations to raise the devil. But throughout all this fearful period the delusion of the criminals was as great as that of the judges. Depraved persons who, in ordinary times, would have been thieves or murderers, added the desire of sorcery to their depravity, sometimes with the hope of acquiring power over their fellows, and sometimes with the hope of securing impunity in this world by the protection of Satan. One of the persons executed at the first burning, a prostitute, was heard repeating the exorcism, which was supposed to have the power of raising the arch enemy in the form of a goat. This precious specimen of human folly has been preserved by Horst, in his "Zauberbibliothek." It ran as follows, and was to be repeated slowly, with many ceremonies and waivings of the hand:--

"Lalle, Bachera, Magotte, Baphia, Dajam,
Vagoth Heneche Ammi Nagaz, Adomator
Raphael Immanuel Christus, Tetragrammaton
Agra Jod Loi. Konig! Konig!"

The two last words were uttered quickly, and with a sort of scream, and were supposed to be highly agreeable to Satan, who loved to be called a king. If he did not appear immediately, it was necessary to repeat a further exorcism. The one in greatest repute was as follows, and was to be read backwards, with the exception of the last two words

"Anion, Lalle, Sabolos, Sado, Pater, Aziel
Adonai Sado Vagoth Agra, Jod,
Baphra! Komm! Komm!"

When the witch wanted to get rid of the devil, who was sometimes in the habit of prolonging his visits to an unconscionable length, she had only to repeat the following, also backwards, when he generally disappeared, leaving behind him a suffocating smell: --

"Zellianelle Heotti Bonus Vagotha
Plisos sother osech unicus Beelzebub
Dax! Komm! Komm!"

This nonsensical jargon soon became known to all the idle and foolish boys of Germany. Many an unhappy urchin, who in a youthful frolic had repeated it, paid for his folly the penalty of his life. Three, whose ages varied from ten to fifteen, were burned alive at Wurzburg for no other offence. Of course every other boy in the city became still more convinced of the power of the charm. One boy confessed that he would willingly have sold himself to the devil, if he could have raised him, for a good dinner and cakes every day of his life, and a pony to ride upon. This luxurious youngster, instead of being horsewhipped for his folly, was hanged and burned.

The small district of Lindheim was, if possible, even more notorious than Wurzburg for the number of its witch-burnings. In the year 1633 a famous witch, named Pomp Anna, who could cause her foes to fall sick by merely looking at them, was discovered and burned, along with three of her companions. Every year in this parish, consisting at most of a thousand persons, the average number of executions was five. Between the years 1660 and 1664, the number consumed was thirty. If the executions all over Germany had been in this frightful proportion, hardly a family could have escaped losing one of its members.

In 1627 a ballad entitled the "Druten Zeitung," or the "Witches Gazette," was very popular in Germany. It detailed, according to the titlepage of a copy printed at Smalcald in 1627, "an account of the remarkable events which took place in Franconia, Bamberg, and Wurzburg, with those wretches who from avarice or ambition have sold themselves to the devil, and how they had their reward at last: set to music, and to be sung to the tune of Dorothea." The sufferings of the witches at the stake are explained in it with great minuteness, the poet waxing extremely witty when he describes the horrible contortions of pain upon their countenances, and the shrieks that rent the air when any one of more than common guilt was burned alive. A trick resorted to in order to force one witch to confess, is told in this doggrel as an excellent joke. As she obstinately refused to own that she was in league with the powers of evil, the commissioners suggested that the hangman should dress himself in a bear's skin, with the horns, tail, and all the et ceteras, and in this form penetrate into her dungeon. The woman, in the darkness of her cell, could not detect the imposture, aided as it was by her own superstitious fears. She thought she was actually in the presence of the prince of hell; and when she was told to keep up her courage, and that she should be relieved from the power of her enemies, she fell on her knees before the supposed devil, and swore to dedicate herself hereafter body and soul to his service. Germany is, perhaps, the only country in Europe where the delusion was so great as to have made such detestable verses as these the favourites of the people:--

"Man shickt ein Henkersknecht
Zu ihr in Gefangniss n'unter,
Den man hat kleidet recht,
Mir einer Barnhaute,
Als wenns der Teufel war;
Als ihm die Drut anschaute
Meints ihr Buhl kam daher.

"Sie sprach zu ihm behende,
Wie lasst du mich so lang
In der Obrigkeit Hande?
Hilf mir aus ihren Zwang,
Wie du mir hast verheissen,
Ich bin ja eben dein,
Thu mich aus der Angst entreissen
O liebster Buhle mein ?

[They sent a hangman's assistant down to her in her prison; they clothed him properly in a bear's skin, as if he were the devil. Him, when the witch saw, she thought he was her familiar. She said to him quickly,

"Why hast thou left me so long in the magistrate's hands? Help me out of their power, as thou hast promised, and I will be thine alone. Help me from this anguish, O thou dearest devil (or lover), mine?]

This rare poet adds, that in making such an appeal to the hangman, the witch never imagined the roast that was to be made of her, and puts in, by way of parenthesis, "was not that fine fun!" "Was das war fur ein Spiel!" As feathers thrown into the air show how the wind blows, so this trumpery ballad serves to show the current of popular feeling at the time of its composition.

All readers of history are familiar with the celebrated trial of the Marechale d'Ancre, who was executed in Paris in the year 1617. Although witchcraft was one of the accusations brought against her, the real crime for which she suffered was her ascendency over the mind of Mary of Medicis, and the consequent influence she exercised indirectly over the unworthy King, Louis XIII. Her coachman gave evidence that she had sacrificed a cock at midnight, in one of the churches, and others swore they had seen her go secretly into the house of a noted witch, named Isabella. When asked by what means she had acquired so extraordinary an influence over the mind of the Queen Mother, she replied boldly, that she exercised no other power over her, than that which a strong mind can always exercise over the weak. She died with great firmness.

In two years afterwards scenes far more horrible than any that had yet taken place in France were enacted at Labourt, at the foot of the Pyrenees. The Parliament of Bourdeaux, scandalised at the number of witches who were said to infest Labourt and its neighbourhood, deputed one of its own members, the noted Pierre de l'Ancre, and its President, Espaignel, to inquire into the matter, with full powers to punish the offenders. They arrived at Labourt in May 1619. De l'Ancre wrote a book, setting forth all his great deeds, in this battle against the powers of evil. It is full of obscenity and absurdity; but the facts may be relied on as far as they relate to the number of trials and executions, and the strange confessions which torture forced from the unhappy criminals.

De l'Ancre states as a reason why so many witches were to be found at Labourt, that the country was mountainous and sterile! He discovered many of them from their partiality to smoking tobacco. It may be inferred from this, that he was of the opinion of King James, that tobacco was the "devil's weed." When the commission first sat, the number of persons brought to trial was about forty a day. The acquittals did not average so many as five per cent. All the witches confessed that they had been present at the great Domdaniel, or Sabbath. At these saturnalia the devil sat upon a large gilded throne, sometimes in the form of a goat; sometimes as a gentleman, dressed all in black, with boots, spurs, and sword; and very often as a shapeless mass, resembling the trunk of a blasted tree, seen indistinctly amid the darkness. They generally proceeded to the Domdaniel, riding on spits, pitchforks, or broomsticks, and, on their arrival, indulged with the fiends in every species of debauchery. Upon one occasion they had had the audacity to celebrate this festival in the very heart of the city of Bourdeaux. The throne of the arch fiend was placed in the middle of the Place de Gallienne, and the whole space was covered with the multitude of witches and wizards, who flocked to it from far and near; some arriving even from distant Scotland.

After two hundred poor wretches had been hanged and burned, there seemed no diminution in the number of criminals to be tried. Many of the latter were asked upon the rack what Satan had said, when he found that the commissioners were proceeding with such severity? The general reply was, that he did not seem to care much about it. Some of them asserted, that they had boldly reproached him for suffering the execution of their friends, saying, "Out upon thee, false fiend! thy promise was, that they

249

should not die! Look! how thou hast kept thy word! They have been burned, and are a heap of ashes!" Upon these occasions he was never offended. He would give orders that the sports of the Domdaniel should cease, and producing illusory fires that did not burn, he encouraged them to walk through, assuring them that the fires lighted by the executioner gave no more pain than those. They would then ask him, where their friends were, since they had not suffered; to which the "Father of Lies" invariably replied, that they were happy in a far country, and could see and hear all that was then passing; and that, if they called by name those they wished to converse with, they might hear their voices in reply. Satan then imitated the voices of the defunct witches so successfully, that they were all deceived. Having answered all objections, the orgies recommenced, and lasted till the cock crew.

De l'Ancre was also very zealous in the trial of unhappy monomaniacs for the crime of lycanthropy. Several who were arrested confessed, without being tortured, that they were weir-wolves, and that, at night, they rushed out among the flocks and herds, killing and devouring. One young man at Besancon, with the full consciousness of the awful fate that awaited him, voluntarily gave himself up to the commissioner Espaignel, and confessed that he was the servant of a strong fiend, who was known by the name of "Lord of the Forests." By his power, he was transformed into the likeness of a wolf. The "Lord of the Forests" assumed the same shape, but was much larger, fiercer, and stronger. They prowled about the pastures together at midnight, strangling the watch-dogs that defended the folds, and killing more sheep than they could devour. He felt, he said, a fierce pleasure in these excursions, and howled in excess of joy as he tore with his fangs the warm flesh of the sheep asunder. This youth was not alone in this horrid confession; many others voluntarily owned that they were weir-wolves, and many more were forced by torture to make the same avowal. Such criminals were thought to be too atrocious to be hanged first, and then burned: they were generally sentenced to be burned alive, and their ashes to be scattered to the winds. Grave and learned doctors of divinity openly sustained the possibility of these transformations, relying mainly upon the history of Nebuchadnezzar. They could not imagine why, if he had been an ox, modern men could not become wolves, by Divine permission and the power of the devil. They also contended that, if men should confess, it was evidence enough, if there had been no other. Delrio mentions that one gentleman accused of lycanthropy was put to the torture no less than twenty times, but still he would not confess. An intoxicating draught was then given him, and under its influence he confessed that he was a weir-wolf. Delrio cites this to show the extreme equity of the commissioners. They never burned anybody till he confessed; and if one course of torture would not suffice, their patience was not exhausted, and they tried him again and again, even to the twentieth time! Well may we exclaim, when such atrocities have been committed in the name of religion,

"Quel lion, quel tigre egale en cruaute,
Une injuste fureur qu'arme la piete?"

The trial of the unhappy Urbain Grandier, the curate of Loudun, for bewitching a number of girls in the convent of the Ursulines in that town, was, like that of the Marechale d'Ancre, an accusation resorted to by his enemies to ruin one against whom no other charge could be brought so readily. This noted affair, which kept France in commotion for months, and the true character of which was known even at that time, merits no more than a passing notice in this place. It did not spring from the epidemic dread of sorcery then so prevalent, but was carried on by wretched intriguers, who had sworn to have the life of their foe. Such a charge could not be refuted in 1634: the accused could not, as Bodinus expresses it, "make the malice of the prosecutors more clear than the sun;" and his own denial, however intelligible, honest, and straightforward, was held as nothing in refutation of the testimony of the crazy women who imagined themselves bewitched. The more absurd and contradictory their assertions, the stronger the argument employed by his enemies that the devil was in them. He was burned alive, under circumstances of great cruelty. [A very graphic account of the execution of this unfortunate gentleman is to be found in the excellent romance of M. Alfred de Vigny, entitled "Cinq Mars ;" but if the reader wishes for a full and accurate detail of all the circumstances of one of the most extraordinary trials upon record, he is referred to a work published anonymously, at Amsterdam, in 1693, entitled "Histoire des Diables de Loudun, ou de la Possession des Religieuses Ursulines, et de la Condemnation et du Supplice d'Urbain Grandier."]

A singular instance of the epidemic fear of witchcraft occurred at Lille, in 1639. A pious, but not very sane lady, named Antoinette Bourignon, founded a school, or hospice, in that city. One day, on entering the school-room, she imagined that she saw a great number of little black angels flying about the heads of the children. In great alarm, she told her pupils of what she had seen, warning them to beware of the devil, whose imps were hovering about them. The foolish woman continued daily to repeat the same story, and Satan and his power became the only subject of conversation, not only between the girls themselves, but between them and their instructors. One of them at this time ran away from the school. On being brought back and interrogated, she said she had not run away, but had been carried away by the devil -- she was a witch, and had been one since the age of seven. Some other little girls in the school went into fits at this announcement, and, on their recovery, confessed that they also were witches. At last, the whole of them, to the number of fifty, worked upon each other's imaginations to such a degree that they also confessed that they were witches -- that they attended the Domdaniel, or meeting of the fiends -- that they could ride through the air on broom-sticks, feast on infants' flesh, or creep through a key-hole.

The citizens of Lille were astounded at these disclosures. The clergy hastened to investigate the matter; many of them, to their credit, openly expressed their opinion that the whole affair was an imposture: not so the majority -- they strenuously insisted that the confessions of the children were valid, and that it was necessary to make an example by burning them all for witches. The poor parents, alarmed for their offspring, implored the examining Capuchins with tears in their eyes to save their young lives, insisting that they were bewitched, and not bewitching. This opinion also gained ground in the town. Antoinette Bourignon, who had put these absurd notions into the heads of the children, was accused of witchcraft, and examined before the council. The circumstances of the case seemed so unfavourable towards her that she would not stay for a second examination. Disguising herself as she best could, she hastened out of Lille and escaped pursuit. If she had remained four hours longer, she would have been burned by judicial sentence, as a witch and a heretic. It is to be hoped that, wherever she went, she learned the danger of tampering with youthful minds, and was never again entrusted with the management of children.

The Duke of Brunswick and the Elector of Menz were struck with the great cruelty exercised in the torture of suspected persons, and convinced at the same time that no righteous judge would consider a confession extorted by pain, and contradictory in itself, as sufficient evidence to justify the execution of any accused person. It is related of the Duke of Brunswick that he invited two learned Jesuits to his house, who were known to entertain strong opinions upon the subject of witchcraft, with a view of showing them the cruelty and absurdity of such practises. A woman lay in the dungeon of the city accused of witchcraft, and the Duke, having given previous instructions to the officiating torturers, went with the two Jesuits to hear her confession. By a series of artful leading questions, the poor creature, in the extremity of her anguish, was induced to confess that she had often attended the sabbath of the fiends upon the Brocken -- that she had seen two Jesuits there, who had made themselves notorious, even among witches, for their abominations -- that she had seen them assume the form of goats, wolves, and other animals; and that many noted witches had borne them five, six, and seven children at a birth, who had heads like toads and legs like spiders. Being asked if the Jesuits were far from her, she replied that they were in the room beside her. The Duke of Brunswick led his astounded friends away, and explained the stratagem. This was convincing proof to both of them that thousands of persons had suffered unjustly; they knew their own innocence, and shuddered to think what their fate might have been, if an enemy, instead of a friend, had put such a confession into the mouth of a criminal. One of these Jesuits was Frederick Spee, the author of the "Cautio Criminalis," published in 1631. This work, exposing the horrors of the witch trials, had a most salutary effect in Germany: Schonbrunn, Archbishop and Elector of Menz, abolished the torture entirely within his dominions, and his example was imitated by the Duke of Brunswick and other potentates. The number of supposed witches immediately diminished, and the violence of the mania began to subside. The Elector of Brandenburg issued a rescript, in 1654, with respect to the case of Anna of Ellerbrock, a supposed witch, forbidding the use of torture, and stigmatizing the swimming of witches as an unjust, cruel, and deceitful test.

This was the beginning of the dawn after the long-protracted darkness. The tribunals no longer condemned witches to execution by hundreds in a year. Wurzburg, the grand theatre of the burnings, burned but one, where, forty years previously, it had burned three score. From 1660 to 1670, the electoral chambers in all parts of Germany constantly commuted the sentence of death passed by the provincial tribunals into imprisonment for life, or burning on the cheek.

A truer philosophy had gradually disabused the public mind. Learned men freed themselves from the trammels of a debasing superstition, and governments, both civil and ecclesiastical, repressed the popular delusion they had so long encouraged. The Parliament of Normandy condemned a number of women to death, in the year 1670, on the old charge of riding on broomsticks to the Domdaniel; but Louis XIV. commuted the sentence into banishment for life. The Parliament remonstrated, and sent the King the following remarkable request. The reader will, perhaps, be glad to see this document at length. It is of importance, as the last effort of a legislative assembly to uphold this great error; and the arguments they used, and the instances they quoted, are in the highest degree curious. It reflects honour upon the memory of Louis XIV. that he was not swayed by it.

"REQUEST OF THE PARLIAMENT OF ROUEN TO THE KING, IN 1670.

"SIRE,

"EMBOLDENED by the authority which your Majesty has committed into our hands in the province of Normandy, to try and punish offences, and more particularly those offences of the nature of witchcraft, which tend to the destruction of religion and the ruin of nations, we, your Parliament, remonstrate humbly with your Majesty upon certain cases of this kind which have been lately brought before us. We cannot permit the letter addressed by your Majesty's command to the Attorney-General of this district, for the reprieve of certain persons condemned to death for witchcraft, and for the staying of proceedings in several other cases, to remain unnoticed, and without remarking upon the consequences which may ensue. There is also a letter from your Secretary of State, declaring your Majesty's intention to commute the punishment of these criminals into one of perpetual banishment, and to submit to the opinion of the Procureur-General, and of the most learned members of the Parliament of Paris, whether, in the matter of witchcraft, the jurisprudence of the Parliament of Rouen is to be followed in preference to that of the Parliament of Paris, and of the other parliaments of the kingdom which judge differently.

"Although by the ordinances of the Kings your predecessors, Parliaments have been forbidden to pay any attention to lettres de cachet; we, nevertheless, from the knowledge which we have, in common with the whole kingdom, of the care bestowed by your Majesty for the good of your subjects, and from the submission and obedience to your commandments which we have always manifested, have stayed all proceedings, in conformity to your orders; hoping that your Majesty, considering the importance of the crime of witchcraft, and the consequences likely to ensue from its impunity, will be graciously pleased to grant us once more your permission to continue the trials, and execute judgment upon those found guilty. And as, since we received the letter of your Secretary of State, we have also been made acquainted with the determination of your Majesty, not only to commute the sentence of death passed upon these witches into one of perpetual banishment from the province, but to re-establish them in the possession of their goods and chattels, and of their good fame and character, your Parliament have thought it their duty, on occasion of these crimes, the greatest which men can commit, to make you acquainted with the general and uniform feelings of the people of this province with regard to them; it being, moreover, a question in which are concerned the glory of God and the relief of your suffering subjects, who groan under their fears from the threats and menaces of this sort of persons, and who feel the effects of them every day in the mortal and extraordinary maladies which attack them, and the surprising damage and loss of their possessions.

"Your Majesty knows well that there is no crime so opposed to the commands of God as witchcraft, which destroys the very foundation of religion, and draws strange abominations after it. It is for this reason, Sire, that the Scriptures pronounce the punishment of death against offenders, and that the church and the holy fathers have fulminated their anathemas, and that canonical decisions have one and all decreed the most severe punishments, to deter from this crime; and that the Church of France, animated by the piety of the Kings your predecessors, has expressed so great a horror at it, that, not judging the punishment of perpetual imprisonment, the highest it has the power to inflict, sufficiently severe, it has left such criminals to be dealt with by the secular power.

"It has been the general feeling of all nations that such criminals ought to be condemned to death, and all the ancients were of the same opinion. The law of the "Twelve Tables," which was the principal of the Roman laws, ordains the same punishment. All jurisconsults agreed in it, as well as the constitutions of the Emperors, and more especially those of Constantine and Theodosius, who, enlightened by the Gospel, not only renewed the same punishment, but also deprived, expressly, all persons found guilty of witchcraft of the right of appeal, and declared them to be unworthy of a prince's mercy. And Charles VIII, Sire, inspired by the same sentiments, passed that beautiful and severe ordinance (cette belle et severe ordonnance), which enjoined the judges to punish witches according to the exigencies of the case, under a penalty of being themselves fined or imprisoned, or dismissed from their office; and decreed, at the same time, that all persons who refused to denounce a witch, should be punished as accomplices; and that all, on the contrary, who gave evidence against one, should be rewarded.

"From these considerations, Sire, and in the execution of so holy an ordinance, your parliaments, by their decrees, proportion their punishments to the guilt of the offenders: and your Parliament of Normandy has never, until the present time, found that its practice was different from that of other courts; for all the books which treat upon this matter cite an infinite number of decrees condemning witches to be burnt, or broken on the wheel, or to other punishments. The following are examples: -- In the time of Chilperic, as may be seen in Gregory of Tours, b. vi, c. 35 of his History of France: all the decrees of the Parliament of Paris passed according to, and in conformity with, this ancient jurisprudence of the kingdom, cited by Imbert, in his "Judicial Practice;" all those cited by Monstrelet, in 1459, against the witches of Artois; the decrees of the same Parliament, of the 13th of October 1573, against Mary Le Fief, native of Saumur; of the 21st of October 1596, against the Sieur de Beaumont, who pleaded, in his defence, that he had only sought the aid of the devil for the purpose of unbewitching the afflicted and of curing diseases; of the 4th of July 1606, against Francis du Bose; of the 20th of July

1582, against Abel de la Rue, native of Coulommiers; of the 2nd of October 1593, against Rousseau and his daughter; of 1608, against another Rousseau and one Peley, for witchcraft and adoration of the devil at the Sabbath, under the figure of a he-goat, as confessed by them; the decree of 4th of February 1615, against Leclerc, who appealed from the sentence of the Parliament of Orleans, and who was condemned for having attended the Sabbath, and confessed, as well as two of his accomplices, who died in prison, that he had adored the devil, renounced his baptism and his faith in God, danced the witches' dance, and offered up unholy sacrifices; the decrees of the 6th of May 1616, against a man named Leger, on a similar accusation; the pardon granted by Charles IX to Trois Echelles, upon condition of revealing his accomplices, but afterwards revoked for renewed sorcery on his part; the decree of the Parliament of Paris, cited by Mornac in 1595; the judgments passed in consequence of the commission given by Henry IV to the Sieur de Lancre, councillor of the Parliament of Bourdeaux; of the 20th of March 1619, against Etienne Audibert; those passed by the Chamber of Nerac, on the 26th of June 1620, against several witches; those passed by the Parliament of Toulouse in 1577, as cited by Gregory Tolosanus, against four hundred persons accused of this crime, and who were all marked with the sign of the devil. Besides all these, we might recall to your Majesty's recollection the various decrees of the Parliament of Provence, especially in the case of Gaufredy in 1611; the decrees of the Parliament of Dijon, and those of the Parliament of Rennes, following the example of the condemnation of the Marshal de Rays, who was burned in 1441, for the crime of witchcraft, in presence of the Duke of Brittany; -- all these examples, Sire, prove that the accusation of witchcraft has always been punished with death by the Parliaments of your kingdom, and justify the uniformity of their practice.

"These, Sire, are the motives upon which your Parliament of Normandy has acted in decreeing the punishment of death against the persons lately brought before it for this crime. If it has happened that, on any occasion, these parliaments, and the Parliament of Normandy among the rest, have condemned the guilty to a less punishment than that of death, it was for the reason that their guilt was not of the deepest dye; your Majesty, and the Kings your predecessors, having left full liberty to the various tribunals to whom they delegated the administration of justice, to decree such punishment as was warranted by the evidence brought before them.

"After so many authorities, and punishments ordained by human and divine laws, we humbly supplicate your Majesty to reflect once more upon the extraordinary results which proceed from the malevolence of this sort of people -- on the deaths from unknown diseases, which are often the consequences of their menaces -- on the loss of the goods and chattels of your subjects -- on the proofs of guilt continually afforded by the insensibility of the marks upon the accused -- on the sudden transportation of bodies from one place to another -- on the sacrifices and nocturnal assemblies, and other facts, corroborated by the testimony of ancient and modern authors, and verified by so many eye-witnesses, composed partly of accomplices, and partly of people who had no interest in the trials beyond the love of truth, and confirmed, moreover, by the confessions of the accused parties themselves; and that, Sire, with so much agreement and conformity between the different cases, that the most ignorant persons convicted of this crime have spoken to the same circumstances, and in nearly the same words, as the most celebrated authors who have written about it, all of which may be easily proved to your Majesty's satisfaction by the records of various trials before your parliaments.

"These, Sire, are truths so intimately bound up with the principles of our religion, that, extraordinary although they be, no person has been able to this time to call them in question. If some have cited, in opposition to these truths, the pretended canon of the Council of Ancyre, and a passage from St. Augustin, in a treatise upon the 'Spirit and the Soul', it has been without foundation; and it would be easy to convince your Majesty that neither the one nor the other ought to be accounted of any authority; and, besides that, the canon, in this sense, would be contrary to the opinion of all succeeding councils of the church, Cardinal Baronius, and all learned commentators, agree that it is not to be found in any old edition. In effect, in those editions wherein it is found, it is in another language, and is in direct contradiction to the twenty-third canon of the same council, which condemns sorcery, according to all preceding constitutions. Even supposing that this canon was really promulgated by the Council of Ancyre, we must observe that it was issued in the second century, when the principal attention of the Church was directed to the destruction of paganism. For this reason, it condemns that class of women who said they could pass through the air, and over immense regions, with Diana and Herodias, and enjoins all preachers to teach the falsehood of such an opinion, in order to deter people from the worship of these false divinities; but it does not question the power of the devil over the human body, which is, in fact, proved by the Holy Gospel of Jesus Christ himself. And with regard, Sire, to the pretended passage of St. Augustin, everybody knows that it was not written by him, because the writer, whoever he was, cites Boetius, who died more than eighty years after the time of St. Augustin. Besides, there is still more convincing proof in the fact, that the same father establishes the truth of witchcraft in all his writings, and more particularly in his 'City of God;' and in his first volume, question the 25th, wherein he states that sorcery is a communion between man and the devil, which all good Christians ought to look upon with horror.

"Taking all these things into consideration, Sire, the officers of your Parliament hope, from the justice of your Majesty, that you will be graciously pleased to receive the humble remonstrances they have taken the liberty to make. They are compelled, for the acquittal of their own consciences and in discharge of their duty, to make known to your Majesty, that the decrees they passed against the sorcerers and witches brought before them, were passed after a mature deliberation on the part of all the judges present, and that nothing has been done therein which is not conformable to the universal jurisprudence of the kingdom, and for the general welfare of your Majesty's subjects, of whom there is not one who can say that he is secure from the malevolence of such criminals. We therefore supplicate your Majesty to suffer us to carry into effect the sentences we passed, and to proceed with the trial of the other persons accused of the same crime; and that the piety of your Majesty will not suffer to be introduced during your reign an opinion contrary to the principles of that holy religion for which you have always employed so gloriously both your cares and your arms."

Louis, as we have already mentioned, paid no attention to this appeal. The lives of the old women were spared, and prosecutions for mere witchcraft, unconnected with other offences, were discontinued throughout France. In 1680 an act was passed for the punishment, not of witches, but of pretenders to witchcraft, fortune-tellers, divineresses, and poisoners.

Thus the light broke in upon Germany, France, England, and Scotland about the same time, gradually growing clearer and clearer till the middle of the eighteenth century, when witchcraft was finally reckoned amongst exploded doctrines, and the belief in it confined to the uttermost vulgar. Twice, however, did the madness burst forth again as furious, while it lasted, as ever it had been. The first time in Sweden, in 1669, and the second in Germany, so late as 1749. Both these instances merit particular mention. The first is one of the most extraordinary upon record, and for atrocity and absurdity is unsurpassed in the annals of any nation.

It having been reported to the King of Sweden that the little village of Mohra, in the province of Dalecarlia, was troubled exceedingly with witches, he appointed a commission of clergy and laymen to trace the rumour to its source, with full powers to punish the guilty. On the 12th of August 1669, the commissioners arrived in the bewitched village, to the great joy of the credulous inhabitants. On the following day the whole population, amounting to three thousand persons, assembled in the church. A sermon was preached, "declaring the miserable case of those people that suffered themselves to be deluded by the devil," and fervent prayer was offered up that God would remove the scourge from among them.

The whole assembly then adjourned to the rector's house, filling all the street before it, when the King's commission was read, charging every person who knew anything of the witchery, to come forward and declare the truth. A passion of tears seized upon the multitude; men, women, and children began to weep and sob, and all promised to divulge what they had heard or knew. In this frame of mind they were dismissed to their homes. On the following day they were again called together, when the depositions of several persons were taken publicly before them all. The result was that seventy persons, including fifteen children, were taken into custody. Numbers also were arrested in the neighbouring district of Elfdale. Being put to the torture, they all confessed their guilt. They said they used to go to a gravel-pit that lay hard by the cross-way, where they put a vest upon their heads, and danced "round and round and round about." They then went to the cross-way, and called three times upon the devil; the first time in a low still voice; the second, somewhat louder; and the third, very loudly, with these words, "Antecessor, come, and carry us to Blockula!" This invocation never failed to bring him to their view. He generally appeared as a little old man, in a grey coat, with red and blue stockings, with exceedingly long garters. He had besides a very high-crowned hat, with bands of many-coloured linen enfolded about it, and a long red beard, that hung down to his middle.

The first question he put to them was, whether they would serve him soul and body? On their answering in the affirmative, he told them to make ready for the journey to Blockula. It was necessary to procure, in the first place, "some scrapings of altars and filings of church clocks." Antecessor then gave them a horn, with some salve in it, wherewith they anointed themselves. These preparations ended, he brought beasts for them to ride upon, horses, asses, goats, and monkeys; and, giving them a saddle, a hammer, and a nail, uttered the word of command, and away they went. Nothing stopped them. They flew over churches, high walls, rocks, and mountains, until they came to the green meadow where Blockula was situated. Upon these occasions they carried as many children with them as they could; for the devil, they said, "did plague and whip them if they did not procure him children, insomuch that they had no peace or quiet for him."

Many parents corroborated a part of this evidence, stating that their children had repeatedly told them that they had been carried away in the night to Blockula, where the devil had beaten them black and blue. They had seen the marks in the morning, but they soon disappeared. One little girl was examined, who swore positively that she was carried through the air by the witches, and when at a great height she uttered the holy name of Jesus. She immediately fell to the ground, and made a great hole in her side. "The devil, however, picked her up, healed her side, and carried her away to Blockula." She added, and her mother confirmed her statement, that she had till that day "an exceeding great pain in her side." This was a clencher, and the nail of conviction was driven home to the hearts of the judges.

The place called Blockula, whither they were carried, was a large house, with a gate to it, "in a delicate meadow, whereof they could see no end." There was a very long table in it, at which the witches sat down; and in other rooms "there were very lovely and delicate beds for them to sleep upon."

After a number of ceremonies had been performed, by which they bound themselves, body and soul, to the service of Antecessor, they sat down to a feast, composed of broth, made of colworts and bacon, oatmeal, bread and butter, milk and cheese. The devil always took the chair, and sometimes played to

256

them on the harp or the fiddle, while they were eating. After dinner they danced in a ring, sometimes naked, and sometimes in their clothes, cursing and swearing all the time. Some of the women added particulars too horrible and too obscene for repetition.

Once the devil pretended to be dead, that he might see whether his people regretted him. They instantly set up a loud wail, and wept three tears each for him, at which he was so pleased, that he jumped up among them, and hugged in his arms those who had been most obstreperous in their sorrow.

Such were the principal details given by the children, and corroborated by the confessions of the full-grown witches. Anything more absurd was never before stated in a court of justice. Many of the accused contradicted themselves most palpably; but the commissioners gave no heed to discrepancies. One of them, the parson of the district, stated, in the course of the inquiry, that on a particular night, which he mentioned, he had been afflicted with a headach so agonizing, that he could not account for it otherwise than by supposing he was bewitched. In fact, he thought a score of witches must have been dancing on the crown of his head. This announcement excited great horror among the pious dames of the auditory, who loudly expressed their wonder that the devil should have power to hurt so good a man. One poor witch, who lay in the very jaws of death, confessed that she knew too well the cause of the minister's headach. The devil had sent her with a sledge hammer and a large nail, to drive into the good man's skull. She had hammered at it for some time, but the skull was so enormously thick, that she made no impression upon it. Every hand was held up in astonishment. The pious minister blessed God that his skull was so solid, and he became renowned for his thick head all the days of his life. Whether the witch intended a joke does not appear, but she was looked upon as a criminal more than usually atrocious. Seventy persons were condemned to death on these so awful yet so ridiculous confessions. Twenty-three of them were burned together, in one fire, in the village of Mohra, in the presence of thousands of delighted spectators. On the following day fifteen children were murdered in the same manner; offered up in sacrifice to the bloody Moloch of superstition. The remaining thirty-two were executed at the neighbouring town of Fahluna. Besides these, fifty-six children were found guilty of witchcraft in a minor degree, and sentenced to various punishments, such as running the gauntlet, imprisonment, and public whipping once a week for a twelvemonth.

Long after the occurrence of this case, it was cited as one of the most convincing proofs upon record of the prevalence of witchcraft. When men wish to construct or support a theory, how they torture facts into their service! The lying whimsies of a few sick children, encouraged by foolish parents, and drawn out by superstitious neighbours, were sufficient to set a country in a flame. If, instead of commissioners as deeply sunk in the slough of ignorance as the people they were sent amongst, there had been deputed a few men firm in courage and clear in understanding, how different would have been the result! Some of the poor children who were burned would have been sent to an infirmary; others would have been well flogged; the credulity of the parents would have been laughed at, and the lives of seventy persons spared. The belief in witchcraft remains in Sweden to this day; but, happily, the annals of that country present no more such instances of lamentable aberration of intellect as the one just cited.

In New England, about the same time, the colonists were scared by similar stories of the antics of the devil. All at once a fear seized upon the multitude, and supposed criminals were arrested day after day in such numbers, that the prisons were found too small to contain them. A girl, named Goodwin, the daughter of a mason, who was hypochondriac and subject to fits, imagined that an old Irishwoman, named Glover, had bewitched her. Her two brothers, in whose constitutions there was apparently a predisposition to similar fits, went off in the same way, crying out that the devil and Dame Glover were tormenting them. At times their joints were so stiff that they could not be moved, while at others, said the neighbours, they were so flexible, that the bones appeared softened into sinews. The supposed witch was seized, and, as she could not repeat the Lord's Prayer without making a mistake in it, she was condemned and executed.

But the popular excitement was not allayed. One victim was not enough: the people waited agape for new disclosures. Suddenly two hysteric girls in another family fell into fits daily, and the cry of witchcraft resounded from one end of the colony to the other. The feeling of suffocation in the throat, so common in cases of hysteria, was said by the patients to be caused by the devil himself, who had stuck balls in the windpipe to choke them. They felt the pricking of thorns in every part of the body, and one of them vomited needles. The case of these girls, who were the daughter and niece of a Mr. Parris, the minister of a Calvinist chapel, excited so much attention, that all the weak women in the colony began to fancy themselves similarly afflicted. The more they brooded on it, the more convinced they became. The contagion of this mental disease was as great as if it had been a pestilence. One after the other the women fainted away, asserting, on their recovery, that they had seen the spectres of witches. Where there were three or four girls in a family, they so worked, each upon the diseased imagination of the other, that they fell into fits five or six times in a day. Some related that the devil himself appeared to them, bearing in his hand a parchment roll, and promising that if they would sign an agreement transferring to him their immortal souls, they should be immediately relieved from fits and all the ills of the flesh. Others asserted that they saw witches only, who made them similar promises, threatening that they should never be free from aches and pains till they had agreed to become the devil's. When they refused, the witches pinched, or bit, or pricked them with long pins and needles. More than two hundred persons named by these mischievous visionaries, were thrown into prison. They were of all ages and conditions of life, and many of them of exemplary character. No less than nineteen were condemned and executed before reason returned to the minds of the colonists. The most horrible part of this lamentable history is, that among the victims there was a little child only five years old. Some women swore that they had seen it repeatedly in company with the devil, and that it had bitten them often with its little teeth, for refusing to sign a compact with the Evil One. It can hardly increase our feelings of disgust and abhorrence when we learn that this insane community actually tried and executed a dog for the same offence!

One man, named Cory, stoutly refused to plead to the preposterous indictment against him. As was the practice in such eases, he was pressed to death. It is told of the Sheriff of New England, who superintended the execution, that when this unhappy man thrust out his tongue in his mortal agony, he seized hold of a cane, and crammed it back again into the mouth. If ever there were a fiend in human form, it was this Sheriff; a man, who, if the truth were known, perhaps plumed himself upon his piety -- thought he was doing God good service, and

"Hoped to merit heaven by making earth a hell!"

Arguing still in the firm belief of witchcraft, the bereaved people began to inquire, when they saw their dearest friends snatched away from them by these wide-spreading accusations, whether the whole proceedings were not carried on by the agency of the devil. Might not the great enemy have put false testimony into the mouths of the witnesses, or might not the witnesses be witches themselves? Every man who was in danger of losing his wife, his child, or his sister, embraced this doctrine with avidity. The revulsion was as sudden as the first frenzy. All at once, the colonists were convinced of their error. The judges put a stop to the prosecutions, even of those who had confessed their guilt. The latter were no sooner at liberty than they retracted all they had said, and the greater number hardly remembered the avowals which agony had extorted from them. Eight persons, who had been tried and condemned, were set free; and gradually girls ceased to have fits and to talk of the persecutions of the devil. The judge who had condemned the first criminal executed on this charge, was so smitten with sorrow and humiliation at his folly, that he set apart the anniversary of that day as one of solemn penitence and fasting. He still clung to the belief in witchcraft; no new light had broken in upon him on that subject, but, happily for the community, the delusion had taken a merciful turn. The whole colony shared the feeling; the jurors on the different trials openly expressed their penitence in the churches; and those who had suffered were regarded as the victims, and not the accomplices of Satan.

It is related that the Indian tribes in New England were sorely puzzled at the infatuation of the settlers, and thought them either a race inferior to, or more sinful than the French colonists in the vicinity, amongst whom, as they remarked, "the Great Spirit sent no witches."

Returning again to the continent of Europe, we find that, after the year 1680, men became still wiser upon this subject. For twenty years the populace were left to their belief, but governments in general gave it no aliment in the shape of executions. The edict of Louis XIV. gave a blow to the superstition, from which it never recovered. The last execution in the Protestant cantons of Switzerland was at Geneva, in 1652. The various potentates of Germany, although they could not stay the trials, invariably commuted the sentence into imprisonment, in all cases where the pretended witch was accused of pure witchcraft, unconnected with any other crime. In the year 1701, Thomasius, the learned professor at the University of Halle, delivered his inaugural thesis, "De Crimine Magiae," which struck another blow at the falling monster of popular error. But a faith so strong as that in witchcraft was not to be eradicated at once: the arguments of learned men did not penetrate to the villages and hamlets, but still they achieved great things; they rendered the belief an unworking faith, and prevented the supply of victims, on which for so many ages it had battened and grown strong.

Once more the delusion broke out; like a wild beast wounded to the death, it collected all its remaining energies for the final convulsion, which was to show how mighty it had once been. Germany, which had nursed the frightful error in its cradle, tended it on its death-bed, and Wurzburg, the scene of so many murders on the same pretext, was destined to be the scene of the last. That it might lose no portion of its bad renown, the last murder was as atrocious as the first. This case offers a great resemblance to that of the witches of Mohra and New England, except in the number of its victims. It happened so late as the year 1749, to the astonishment and disgust of the rest of Europe.

A number of young women in a convent at Wurzburg fancied themselves bewitched; they felt, like all hysteric subjects, a sense of suffocation in the throat. They went into fits repeatedly; and one of them, who had swallowed needles, evacuated them at abscesses, which formed in different parts of the body. The cry of sorcery was raised, and a young woman, named Maria Renata Sanger, was arrested on the charge of having leagued with the devil, to bewitch five of the young ladies. It was sworn on the trial that Maria had been frequently seen to clamber over the convent walls in the shape of a pig -- that, proceeding to the cellar, she used to drink the best wine till she was intoxicated; and then start suddenly up in her own form. Other girls asserted that she used to prowl about the roof like a cat, and often penetrate into their chamber, and frighten them by her dreadful howlings. It was also said that she had been seen in the shape of a hare, milking the cows dry in the meadows belonging to the convent; that she used to perform as an actress on the boards of Drury Lane theatre in London, and, on the very same night, return upon a broomstick to Wurzburg, and afflict the young ladies with pains in all their limbs. Upon this evidence she was condemned, and burned alive in the market-place of Wurzburg.

Here ends this frightful catalogue of murder and superstition. Since that day, the belief in witchcraft has fled from the populous abodes of men, and taken refuge in remote villages and districts too wild, rugged, and inhospitable to afford a resting-place for the foot of civilization. Rude fishers and uneducated labourers still attribute every phenomenon of nature which they cannot account for, to the devil and witches. Catalepsy, that wondrous disease, is still thought by ignorant gossips to be the work of Satan; and hypochondriacs, uninformed by science of the nature of their malady, devoutly believe in the reality of their visions. The reader would hardly credit the extent of the delusion upon this subject in the very heart of England at this day. Many an old woman leads a life of misery from the unfeeling insults of her neighbours, who raise the scornful finger and hooting voice at her, because in her decrepitude she is ugly, spiteful, perhaps insane, and realizes in her personal appearance the description preserved by tradition of the witches of yore. Even in the neighbourhood of great towns the taint remains of this once widely-spread contagion. If no victims fall beneath it, the enlightenment of the law is all that prevents a recurrence of scenes as horrid as those of the seventeeth century. Hundreds upon hundreds of witnesses could be found to swear to absurdities as great as those asserted by the infamous Matthew Hopkins.

In the Annual Register for 1760, an instance of the belief in witchcraft is related, which shows how superstition lingers. A dispute arose in the little village of Glen, in Leicestershire, between two old women, each of whom vehemently accused the other of witchcraft. The quarrel at last ran so high that a challenge ensued, and they both agreed to be tried by the ordeal of swimming. They accordingly stripped to their shifts -- procured some men, who tied their thumbs and great toes together, cross-wise, and then, with a cart-rope about their middle, suffered themselves to be thrown into a pool of water. One of them sank immediately, but the other continued struggling a short time upon the surface of the water, which the mob deeming an infallible sign of her guilt, pulled her out, and insisted that she should immediately impeach all her accomplices in the craft. She accordingly told them that, in the neighbouring village of Burton, there were several old women as "much witches as she was." Happily for her, this negative information was deemed sufficient, and a student in astrology, or "white-witch," coming up at the time, the mob, by his direction, proceeded forthwith to Burton in search of all the delinquents. After a little consultation on their arrival, they went to the old woman's house on whom they had fixed the strongest suspicion. The poor old creature on their approach locked the outer door, and from the window of an upstairs room asked what they wanted. They informed her that she was charged with being guilty of witchcraft, and that they were come to duck her; remonstrating with her at the same time upon the necessity of submission to the ordeal, that, if she were innocent, all the world might know it. Upon her persisting in a positive refusal to come down, they broke open the door and carried her out by force, to a deep gravel-pit full of water. They tied her thumbs and toes together and threw her into the water, where they kept her for several minutes, drawing her out and in two or three times by the rope round her middle. Not being able to satisfy themselves whether she were a witch or no, they at last let her go, or, more properly speaking, they left her on the bank to walk home by herself, if she ever recovered. Next day, they tried the same experiment upon another woman, and afterwards upon a third; but, fortunately, neither of the victims lost her life from this brutality. Many of the ringleaders in the outrage were apprehended during the week, and tried before the justices at quarter-sessions. Two of them were sentenced to stand in the pillory and to be imprisoned for a month; and as many as twenty more were fined in small sums for the assault, and bound over to keep the peace for a twelvemonth.

"So late as the year 1785," says Arnot, in his collection and abridgment of Criminal Trials in Scotland, "it was the custom among the sect of Seceders to read from the pulpit an annual confession of sins, national and personal; amongst the former of which was particularly mentioned the 'Repeal by Parliament of the penal statute against witches, contrary to the express laws of God.'"

Many houses are still to be found in England with the horse-shoe (the grand preservative against witchcraft) nailed against the threshold. If any over-wise philosopher should attempt to remove them, the chances are that he would have more broken bones than thanks for his interference. Let any man walk into Cross-street, Hatton-Garden, and from thence into Bleeding-heart Yard, and learn the tales still told and believed of one house in that neighbourhood, and he will ask himself in astonishment if such things can be in the nineteenth century. The witchcraft of Lady Hatton, the wife of the famous Sir Christopher, so renowned for his elegant dancing in the days of Elizabeth, is as devoutly believed as the Gospels. The room is to be seen where the devil seized her after the expiration of the contract he had made with her, and bore her away bodily to the pit of Tophet: the pump against which he dashed her is still pointed out, and the spot where her heart was found, after he had torn it out of her bosom with his iron claws, has received the name of Bleeding-heart Yard, in confirmation of the story. Whether the horse-shoe still remains upon the door of the haunted house, to keep away other witches, is uncertain; but there it was, twelve or thirteen years ago. The writer resided at that time in the house alluded to, and well remembers that more than one old woman begged for admittance repeatedly, to satisfy themselves that it was in its proper place. One poor creature, apparently insane, and clothed in rags, came to the door with a tremendous double-knock, as loud as that of a fashionable footman, and walked straight along the passage to the horse-shoe. Great was the wonderment of the inmates, especially when the woman spat upon the horse-shoe, and expressed her sorrow that she could do no harm while it remained there. After spitting upon, and kicking it again and again, she coolly turned round and left the house, without saying a word to anybody. This poor creature perhaps intended a joke, but the probability is that she imagined herself a witch. In Saffron Hill, where she resided, her ignorant neighbours gave her that character, and looked upon her with no little fear and aversion.

More than one example of the popular belief in witchcraft occurred in the neighbourhood of Hastings so lately as the year 1830. An aged woman, who resided in the Rope-walk of that town, was so repulsive in her appearance, that she was invariably accused of being a witch by all the ignorant people who knew her. She was bent completely double; and though very old, her eye was unusually bright and malignant. She wore a red cloak, and supported herself on a crutch: she was, to all outward appearance, the very beau ideal of a witch. So dear is power to the human heart, that this old woman actually encouraged the popular superstition: she took no pains to remove the ill impression, but seemed to delight that she, old and miserable as she was, could keep in awe so many happier and stronger fellow-creatures. Timid girls crouched with fear when they met her, and many would go a mile out of their way to avoid her. Like the witches of the olden time, she was not sparing of her curses against those who offended her. The child of a woman who resided within two doors of her, was afflicted with lameness, and the mother constantly asserted that the old woman had bewitched her. All the neighbours credited the tale. It was believed, too, that she could assume the form of a cat. Many a harmless puss has been hunted almost to the death by mobs of men and boys, upon the supposition that the animal would start up before them in the true shape of Mother * * * * *.

In the same town there resided a fisherman, -- who is, probably, still alive, and whose name, for that reason, we forbear to mention, -- who was the object of unceasing persecution, because it was said that he had sold himself to the devil. It was currently reported that he could creep through a keyhole, and that he had made a witch of his daughter, in order that he might have the more power over his fellows. It was also believed that he could sit on the points of pins and needles, and feel no pain. His brother-fishermen put him to this test whenever they had an opportunity. In the alehouses which he frequented, they often placed long needles in the cushions of the chairs, in such a manner that he could not fail to pierce himself when he sat down. The result of these experiments tended to confirm their faith in his supernatural powers. It was asserted that he never flinched. Such was the popular feeling in the fashionable town of Hastings only seven years ago; very probably it is the same now.

In the north of England, the superstition lingers to an almost inconceivable extent. Lancashire abounds with witch-doctors, a set of quacks, who pretend to cure diseases inflicted by the devil. The practices of these worthies may be judged of by the following case, reported in the "Hertford Reformer," of the 23rd of June, 1838. The witch-doctor alluded to is better known by the name of the cunning man, and has a large practice in the counties of Lincoln and Nottingham. According to the writer in "The Reformer," the dupe, whose name is not mentioned, had been for about two years afflicted with a painful abscess, and had been prescribed for without relief by more than one medical gentleman. He was urged by some of his friends, not only in his own village, but in neighbouring ones, to consult the witch-doctor, as they were convinced he was under some evil influence. He agreed, and sent his wife to the cunning man, who lived in New Saint Swithin's, in Lincoln. She was informed by this ignorant impostor that her husband's disorder was an infliction of the devil, occasioned by his next-door neighbours, who had made use of certain charms for that purpose. From the description he gave of the process, it appears to be the same as that employed by Dr. Fian and Gellie Duncan, to work woe upon King James. He stated that the neighbours, instigated by a witch, whom he pointed out, took some wax, and moulded it before the fire into the form of her husband, as near as they could represent him; they then pierced the image with pins on all sides -- repeated the Lord's Prayer backwards, and offered prayers to the devil that he would fix his stings into the person whom that figure represented, in like manner as they pierced it with pins. To counteract the effects of this diabolical process, the witch-doctor prescribed a certain medicine, and a charm to be worn next the body, on that part where the disease principally lay. The patient was to repeat the 109th and 119th Psalms every day, or the cure would not be effectual. The fee which he claimed for this advice was a guinea.

So efficacious is faith in the cure of any malady, that the patient actually felt much better after a three weeks' course of this prescription. The notable charm which the quack had given was afterwards opened, and found to be a piece of parchment, covered with some cabalistic characters and signs of the planets.

The next-door neighbours were in great alarm that the witch-doctor would, on the solicitation of the recovering patient, employ some means to punish them for their pretended witchcraft. To escape the infliction, they feed another cunning man, in Nottinghamshire, who told them of a similar charm, which would preserve them from all the malice of their enemies. The writer concludes by saying that, "the doctor, not long after he had been thus consulted, wrote to say that he had discovered that his patient was not afflicted by Satan, as he had imagined, but by God, and would continue, more or less, in the same state till his life's end."

An impostor carried on a similar trade in the neighbourhood of Tunbridge Wells, about the year 1830. He had been in practice for several years, and charged enormous fees for his advice. This fellow pretended to be the seventh son of a seventh son, and to be endowed in consequence with miraculous powers for the cure of all diseases, but especially of those resulting from witchcraft. It was not only the poor who employed him, but ladies who rode in their carriages. He was often sent for from a distance of sixty or seventy miles by these people, who paid all his expenses to and fro, besides rewarding him handsomely. He was about eighty years of age, and his extremely venerable appearance aided his imposition in no slight degree. His name was Okey, or Oakley.

In France, the superstition at this day is even more prevalent than it is in England. Garinet, in his history of Magic and Sorcery in that country, cites upwards of twenty instances which occurred between the years 1805 and 1818. In the latter year, no less than three tribunals were occupied with trials originating in this humiliating belief: we shall cite only one of them. Julian Desbourdes, aged fifty-three, a mason, and inhabitant of the village of Thilouze, near Bordeaux, was taken suddenly ill, in the month of January

1818. As he did not know how to account for his malady, he suspected at last that he was bewitched. He communicated this suspicion to his son-in-law, Bridier, and they both went to consult a sort of idiot, named Baudouin, who passed for a conjuror, or white-witch. This man told them that Desbourdes was certainly bewitched, and offered to accompany them to the house of an old man, named Renard, who, he said, was undoubtedly the criminal. On the night of the 23rd of January all three proceeded stealthily to the dwelling of Renard, and accused him of afflicting persons with diseases, by the aid of the devil. Desbourdes fell on his knees, and earnestly entreated to be restored to his former health, promising that he would take no measures against him for the evil he had done. The old man denied in the strongest terms that he was a wizard; and when Desbourdes still pressed him to remove the spell from him, he said he knew nothing about the spell, and refused to remove it. The idiot Baudouin, the white-witch, now interfered, and told his companions that no relief for the malady could ever be procured until the old man confessed his guilt. To force him to confession they lighted some sticks of sulphur, which they had brought with them for the purpose, and placed them under the old man's nose. In a few moments, he fell down suffocated and apparently lifeless. They were all greatly alarmed; and thinking that they had killed the. man, they carried him out and threw him into a neighbouring pond, hoping to make it appear that he had fallen in accidentally. The pond, however, was not very deep, and the coolness of the water reviving the old man, he opened his eyes and sat up. Desbourdes and Bridier, who were still waiting on the bank, were now more alarmed than before, lest he should recover and inform against them. They, therefore, waded into the pond -- seized their victim by the hair of the head -- beat him severely, and then held him under water till he was drowned.

They were all three apprehended on the charge of murder a few days afterwards. Desbourdes and Bridier were found guilty of aggravated manslaughter only, and sentenced to be burnt on the back, and to work in the galleys for life. The white-witch Baudouin was acquitted, on the ground of insanity.

M. Garinet further informs us that France, at the time he wrote (1818), was overrun by a race of fellows, who made a trade of casting out devils and finding out witches. He adds, also, that many of the priests in the rural districts encouraged the superstition of their parishioners, by resorting frequently to exorcisms, whenever any foolish persons took it into their heads that a spell had been thrown over them. He recommended, as a remedy for the evil, that all these exorcists, whether lay or clerical, should be sent to the galleys, and that the number of witches would then very sensibly diminish.

Many other instances of this lingering belief might be cited both in France and Great Britain, and indeed in every other country in Europe. So deeply rooted are some errors that ages cannot remove them. The poisonous tree that once overshadowed the land, may be cut down by the sturdy efforts of sages and philosophers -- the sun may shine clearly upon spots where venemous things once nestled in security and shade; but still the entangled roots are stretched beneath the surface, and may be found by those who dig. Another king, like James I, might make them vegetate again; and, more mischievous still, another pope, like Innocent VIII, might raise the decaying roots to strength and verdure. Still, it is consoling to think, that the delirium has passed away; that the raging madness has given place to a milder folly; and that we may now count by units the votaries of a superstition which, in former ages, numbered its victims by tens of thousands, and its votaries by millions.

The Slow Poisoners

Pescara. -- The like was never read of.
Stephano. -- In my judgment,
To all that shall but hear it, 't will appear
A most impossible fable.
Pescara. -- Troth, I'll tell you,
And briefly as I can, by what degrees
They fell into this madness. --*Duke of Milan.*

The atrocious system of poisoning, by poisons so slow in their operation, as to make the victim appear, to ordinary observers, as if dying from a gradual decay of nature, has been practised in all ages. Those who are curious in the matter may refer to Beckmann on Secret Poisons, in his "History of Inventions," in which he has collected several instances of it from the Greek and Roman writers. Early in the sixteenth century the crime seems to have gradually increased, till, in the seventeenth, it spread over Europe like a pestilence. It was often exercised by pretended witches and sorcerers, and finally became a branch of education amongst all who laid any claim to magical and supernatural arts. In the twenty-first year of Henry VIII. an act was passed, rendering it high-treason: those found guilty of it, were to be boiled to death.

One of the first in point of date, and hardly second to any in point of atrocity, is the murder by this means of Sir Thomas Overbury, which disgraced the court of James I, in the year 1613. A slight sketch of it will be a fitting introduction to the history of the poisoning mania, which was so prevalent in France and Italy fifty years later.

Robert Kerr, a Scottish youth, was early taken notice of by James I, and loaded with honours, for no other reason that the world could ever discover than the beauty of his person. James, even in his own day, was suspected of being addicted to the most abominable of all offences, and the more we examine his history now, the stronger the suspicion becomes. However that may be, the handsome Kerr, lending his smooth cheek, even in public, to the disgusting kisses of his royal master, rose rapidly in favour. In the year 1613, he was made Lord High Treasurer of Scotland, and created an English peer, by the style and title of Viscount Rochester. Still further honours were in store for him.

In this rapid promotion he had not been without a friend. Sir Thomas Overbury, the King's secretary-who appears, from some threats in his own letters, to have been no better than a pander to the vices of the King, and privy to his dangerous secrets -- exerted all his backstair influence to forward the promotion of Kerr, by whom he was, doubtless, repaid in some way or other. Overbury did not confine his friendship to this, if friendship ever could exist between two such men, but acted the part of an entremetteur, and assisted Rochester to carry on an adulterous intrigue with the Lady Frances Howard, the wife of the Earl of Essex. This woman was a person of violent passions, and lost to all sense of shame. Her husband was in her way, and to be freed from him, she instituted proceedings for a divorce, on grounds which a woman of any modesty or delicacy of feeling would die rather than avow. Her scandalous suit was successful, and was no sooner decided than preparations, on a scale of the greatest magnificence, were made for her marriage with Lord Rochester.

Sir Thomas Overbury, who had willingly assisted his patron to intrigue with the Countess of Essex, seems to have imagined that his marriage with so vile a woman might retard his advancement; he accordingly employed all his influence to dissuade him from it. But Rochester was bent on the match, and his passions were as violent as those of the Countess. On one occasion, when Overbury and the Viscount were walking in the gallery of Whitehall, Overbury was overheard to say, "Well, my Lord, if you do marry that base woman, you will utterly ruin your honour and yourself. You shall never do it with my advice or consent; and, if you do, you had best look to stand fast." Rochester flung from him in a rage, exclaiming with an oath, "I will be even with you for this." These words were the death-warrant of the unfortunate Overbury. He had mortally wounded the pride of Rochester in insinuating that by his (Overbury's) means he might be lowered in the King's favour; and he had endeavoured to curb the burning passions of a heartless, dissolute, and reckless man.

Overbury's imprudent remonstrances were reported to the Countess; and from that moment, she also vowed the most deadly vengeance against him. With a fiendish hypocrisy, however, they both concealed their intentions, and Overbury, at the solicitation of Rochester, was appointed ambassador to the court of Russia. This apparent favour was but the first step in a deep and deadly plot. Rochester, pretending to be warmly attached to the interests of Overbury, advised him to refuse the embassy, which, he said, was but a trick to get him out of the way. He promised, at the same time, to stand between him and any evil consequences which might result from his refusal. Overbury fell into the snare, and declined the embassy. James, offended, immediately ordered his committal to the Tower.

He was now in safe custody, and his enemies had opportunity to commence the work of vengeance. The first thing Rochester did was to procure, by his influence at court, the dismissal of the Lieutenant of the Tower, and the appointment of Sir Jervis Elwes, one of his creatures, to the vacant post. This man was but one instrument, and another being necessary, was found in Richard Weston, a fellow who had formerly been shopman to a druggist. He was installed in the office of under-keeper, and as such had the direct custody of Overbury. So far, all was favourable to the designs of the conspirators.

In the mean time, the insidious Rochester wrote the most friendly letters to Overbury, requesting him to bear his ill-fortune patiently, and promising that his imprisonment should not be of long duration; for that his friends were exerting themselves to soften the King's displeasure. Still pretending the extreme of sympathy for him, he followed up the letters by presents of pastry and other delicacies, which could not be procured in the Tower. These articles were all poisoned. Occasionally, presents of a similar description were sent to Sir Jervis Elwes, with the understanding that these articles were not poisoned, when they were unaccompanied by letters: of these the unfortunate prisoner never tasted. A woman, named Turner, who had formerly kept a house of ill fame, and who had more than once lent it to further the guilty intercourse of Rochester and Lady Essex, was the agent employed to procure the poisons. They were prepared by Dr. Forman, a pretended fortune-teller of Lambeth, assisted by an apothecary named Franklin. Both these persons knew for what purposes the poisons were needed, and employed their skill in mixing them in the pastry and other edibles, in such small quantities as gradually to wear out the constitution of their victim. Mrs. Turner regularly furnished the poisoned articles to the under-keeper, who placed them before Overbury. Not only his food, but his drink was poisoned. Arsenic was mixed with the salt he ate, and cantharides with the pepper. All this time, his health declined sensibly. Every day he grew weaker and weaker; and with a sickly appetite, craved for sweets and jellies. Rochester continued to condole with him, and anticipated all his wants in this respect, sending him abundance of pastry, and occasionally partridges and other game, and young pigs. With the sauce for the game, Mrs. Turner mixed a quantity of cantharides, and poisoned the pork with lunar-caustic. As stated on the trial, Overbury took in this manner poison enough to have poisoned twenty men; but his constitution was strong, and he still lingered. Frank]in, the apothecary, confessed that he prepared with

Dr. Forman seven different sorts of poisons; viz. aquafortis, arsenic, mercury, powder of diamonds, lunar-caustic, great spiders, and cantharides. Overbury held out so long that Rochester became impatient, and in a letter to Lady Essex, expressed his wonder that things were not sooner despatched. Orders were immediately sent by Lady Essex to the keeper to finish with the victim at once. Overbury had not been all this time without suspicion of treachery, although he appears to have had no idea of poison. He merely suspected that it was intended to confine him for life, and to set the King still more bitterly against him. In one of his letters, he threatened Rochester that, unless he were speedily liberated, he would expose his villany to the world. He says, "You and I, ere it be long, will come to a public trial of another nature." * * * "Drive me not to extremities, lest I should say something that both you and I should repent." * * * "Whether I live or die, your shame shall never die, but ever remain to the world, to make you the most odious man living." * * * "I wonder much you should neglect him to whom such secrets of all kinds have passed." * * * "Be these the fruits of common secrets, common dangers?"

All these remonstrances, and hints as to the dangerous secrets in his keeping, were ill-calculated to serve him with a man so reckless as Lord Rochester: they were more likely to cause him to be sacrificed than to be saved. Rochester appears to have acted as if he thought so. He doubtless employed the murderer's reasoning that "dead men tell no tales," when, after receiving letters of this description, he complained to his paramour of the delay. Weston was spurred on to consummate the atrocity; and the patience of all parties being exhausted, a dose of corrosive sublimate was administered to him, in October 1613, which put an end to his sufferings, after he had been for six months in their hands. On the very day of his death, and before his body was cold, he was wrapped up carelessly in a sheet, and buried without any funeral ceremony in a pit within the precincts of the Tower.

Sir Anthony Weldon, in his "Court and Character of James I," gives a somewhat different account of the closing scene of this tragedy. He says, "Franklin and Weston came into Overbury's chamber, and found him in infinite torment, with contention between the strength of nature and the working of the poison; and it being very like that nature had gotten the better in this contention, by the thrusting out of boils, blotches, and blains, they, fearing it might come to light by the judgment of physicians, the foul play that had been offered him, consented to stifle him with the bedclothes, which accordingly was performed; and so ended his miserable life, with the assurance of the conspirators that he died by the poison; none thinking otherwise than these two murderers."

The sudden death -- the indecent haste of the funeral, and the non-holding of an inquest upon the body, strengthened the suspicions that were afloat. Rumour, instead of whispering, began to speak out; and the relatives of the deceased openly expressed their belief that their kinsman had been murdered. But Rochester was still all powerful at court, and no one dared to utter a word to his discredit. Shortly afterwards, his marriage with the Countess of Essex was celebrated with the utmost splendour, the King himself being present at the ceremony.

It would seem that Overbury's knowledge of James's character was deeper than Rochester had given him credit for, and that he had been a true prophet when he predicted that his marriage would eventually estrange James from his minion. At this time, however, Rochester stood higher than ever in the royal favour; but it did not last long - conscience, that busy monitor, was at work. The tongue of rumour was never still; and Rochester, who had long been a guilty, became at last a wretched man. His cheeks lost their colour -- his eyes grew dim; and he became moody, careless, and melancholy. The King seeing him thus, took at length no pleasure in his society, and began to look about for another favourite. George Villiers, Duke of Buckingham, was the man to his mind; quick-witted, handsome, and unscrupulous. The two latter qualities alone were sufficient to recommend him to James I. In proportion as the influence of Rochester declined, that of Buckingham increased. A falling favourite has no friends; and Rumour wagged her tongue against Rochester louder and more pertinaciously than ever. A new favourite, too, generally endeavours to hasten by a kick the fall of the old one; and Buckingham, anxious to work the complete ruin of his forerunner in the King's good graces, encouraged the relatives of Sir Thomas Overbury to prosecute their inquiries into the strange death of their kinsman.

James was rigorous enough in the punishment of offences when he was not himself involved. He piqued himself, moreover, on his dexterity in unravelling mysteries. The affair of Sir Thomas Overbury found him congenial occupation. He set to work by ordering the arrest of Sir Jervis Elwes. James, at this early stage of the proceedings, does not seem to have been aware that Rochester was so deeply implicated. Struck with horror at the atrocious system of slow poisoning, the King sent for all the Judges. According to Sir Anthony Weldon, he knelt down in the midst of them, and said, "My Lords the Judges, it is lately come to my hearing that you have now in examination a business of poisoning. Lord! in what a miserable condition shall this kingdom be (the only famous nation for hospitality in the world) if our tables should become such a snare, as that none could eat without danger of life, and that Italian custom should be introduced among us! Therefore, my Lords, I charge you, as you will answer it at that great and dreadful day of judgment, that you examine it strictly, without layout, affection, or partiality. And if you shall spare any guilty of this crime, God's curse light on you and your posterity! and if I spare any that are guilty, God's curse light on me and my posterity for ever!"

The imprecation fell but too surely upon the devoted house of Stuart. The solemn oath was broken, and God's curse did light upon him and his posterity!

The next person arrested after Sir Jervis Elwes, was Weston, the under-keeper; then Franklin and Mrs. Turner; and, lastly, the Earl and Countess of Somerset, to which dignity Rochester had been advanced since the death of Overbury.

Weston was first brought to trial. Public curiosity was on the stretch. Nothing else was talked of, and the court on the day of trial was crowded to suffocation. The "State Trials" report, that Lord Chief Justice Coke "laid open to the jury the baseness and cowardliness of poisoners, who attempt that secretly against which there is no means of preservation or defence for a man's life; and how rare it was to hear of any poisoning in England, so detestable it was to our nation. But the devil had taught divers to be cunning in it, so that they can poison in what distance of space they please, by consuming the nativum calidum, or humidum radicale, in one month, two or three, or more, as they list, which they four manner of ways do execute; viz. haustu, gustu, odore, and contactu."

When the indictment was read over, Weston made no other reply than, "Lord have mercy upon me! Lord have mercy upon me!" On being asked how he would be tried, he refused to throw himself upon a jury of his country, and declared, that he would be tried by God alone. In this he persisted for some time. The fear of the dreadful punishment for contumacy induced him, at length, to plead "Not guilty," and take his trial in due course of law.

[The punishment for the contumacious was expressed by the words onere, frigore, et fame. By the first was meant that the culprit should be extended on his back on the ground, and weights placed over his body, gradually increased, until he expired. Sometimes the punishment was not extended to this length, and the victim, being allowed to recover, underwent the second portion, the frigore, which consisted in his standing naked in the open air, for a certain space, in the sight of all the people. The third, or fame, was more dreadful, the statute saying, "That he was to be preserved with the coarsest bread that could be got, and water out of the next sink or puddle, to the place of execution; and that day he had water he should have no bread, and that day he had bread, he should have no water;" and in this torment he was to linger as long as nature would hold out.]

All the circumstances against him were fully proved, and he was found guilty and executed at Tyburn. Mrs. Turner, Franklin, and Sir Jervis Elwes were also brought to trial, found guilty, and executed between the 19th of October and the 4th of December 1615; but the grand trial of the Earl and Countess of Somerset did not take place till the month of May following.

On the trial of Sir Jervis Elwes, circumstances had transpired, showing a guilty knowledge of the poisoning on the part of the Earl of Northampton the uncle of Lady Somerset, and the chief falconer Sir Thomas Monson. The former was dead; but Sir Thomas Monson was arrested, and brought to trial. It appeared, however, that he was too dangerous a man to be brought to the scaffold. He knew too many of the odious secrets of James I, and his dying speech might contain disclosures which would compromise the King. To conceal old guilt it was necessary to incur new: the trial of Sir Thomas Monson was brought to an abrupt conclusion, and himself set at liberty!

Already James had broken his oath. He now began to fear that he had been rash in engaging so zealously to bring the poisoners to punishment. That Somerset would be declared guilty there was no doubt, and that he looked for pardon and impunity was equally evident to the King. Somerset, while in the Tower, asserted confidently, that James would not dare to bring him to trial. In this he was mistaken; but James was in an agony. What the secret was between them will now never be known with certainty; but it may be surmised. Some have imagined it to be the vice to which the King was addicted; while others have asserted, that it related to the death of Prince Henry, a virtuous young man, who had held Somerset in especial abhorrence. The Prince died early, unlamented by his father, and, as public opinion whispered at the time, poisoned by Somerset. Probably, some crime or other lay heavy upon the soul of the King; and Somerset, his accomplice, could not be brought to public execution with safety. Hence the dreadful tortures of James, when he discovered that his favourite was so deeply implicated in the murder of Overbury. Every means was taken by the agonized King to bring the prisoner into what was called a safe frame of mind. He was secretly advised to plead guilty, and trust to the clemency of the King. The same advice was conveyed to the Countess. Bacon was instructed by the King to draw up a paper of all the points of "mercy and favour" to Somerset which might result from the evidence; and Somerset was again recommended to plead guilty, and promised that no evil should ensue to him.

The Countess was first tried. She trembled and shed tears during the reading of the indictment, and, in a low voice, pleaded guilty. On being asked why sentence of death should not be passed against her, she replied meekly, "I can much aggravate, but nothing extenuate my fault. I desire mercy, and that the lords will intercede for me with the King." Sentence of death was passed upon her.

Next day the Earl was brought to trial. He appears to have mistrusted the promises of James, and he pleaded not guilty. With a self-possession and confidence, which he felt, probably, from his knowledge of the King's character, he rigorously cross-examined the witnesses, and made a stubborn defence. After a trial which lasted eleven hours, he was found guilty, and condemned to the felon's death.

Whatever may have been the secrets between the criminal and the King, the latter, notwithstanding his terrific oath, was afraid to sign the death-warrant. It might, perchance, have been his own. The Earl and Countess were committed to the Tower, where they remained for nearly five years. At the end of this period, to the surprise and scandal of the community, and the disgrace of its chief magistrate, they both received the royal pardon, but were ordered to reside at a distance from the court. Having been found guilty of felony, the estates of the Earl had become forfeited; but James granted him out of their revenues an income of 4,000 pounds per annum! Shamelessness could go no further.

Of the after life of these criminals nothing is known, except that the love they had formerly borne each other was changed into aversion, and that they lived under the same roof for months together without the interchange of a word.

The exposure of their atrocities did not put a stop to the practice of poisoning. On the contrary, as we shall see hereafter, it engendered that insane imitation which is so strange a feature of the human character. James himself is supposed, with great probability, to have fallen a victim to it. In the notes to "Harris's Life and Writings of James I," there is a good deal of information on the subject. The guilt of Buckingham, although not fully established, rests upon circumstances of suspicion stronger than have been sufficient to lead hundreds to the scaffold. His motives for committing the crime are stated to have been a desire of revenge for the coldness with which the King, in the latter years of his reign, began to regard him; his fear that James intended to degrade him; and his hope that the great influence he possessed over the mind of the heir-apparent would last through a new reign, if the old one were brought to a close.

In the second volume of the "Harleian Miscellany," there is a tract, entitled the "Forerunner of Revenge," written by George Eglisham, doctor of medicine, and one of the physicians to King James. Harris, in quoting it, says that it is full of rancour and prejudice. It is evidently exaggerated; but forms, nevertheless, a link in the chain of evidence. Eglisham says: -- "The King being sick of an ague, the Duke took this opportunity, when all the King's doctors of physic were at dinner, and offered to him a white powder to take, the which he a long time refused; but, overcome with his flattering importunity, he took it in wine, and immediately became worse and worse, falling into many swoonings and pains, and violent fluxes of the belly, so tormented, that his Majesty cried out aloud of this white powder, 'Would to God I had never taken it?" He then tells us "Of the Countess of Buckingham (the Duke's mother) applying the plaister to the King's heart and breast, whereupon he grew faint and short-breathed, and in agony. That the physicians exclaimed, that the King was poisoned; that Buckingham commanded them out of the room, and committed one of them close prisoner to his own chamber, and another to be removed from court; and that, after his Majesty's death, his body and head swelled above measure; his hair, with the skin of his head, stuck to his pillow, and his nails became loose on his fingers and toes." Clarendon, who, by the way, was a partisan of the Duke's, gives a totally different account of James's death. He says, "It was occasioned by an ague (after a short indisposition by the gout)which, meeting many humours in a fat unwieldy body of fifty-eight years old, in four or five fits carried him out of the world. After whose death many scandalous and libellous discourses were raised, without the least colour or ground; as appeared upon the strictest and most malicious examination that could be made, long after, in a time of licence, when nobody was afraid of offending majesty, and when prosecuting the highest reproaches and contumelies against the royal family was held very meritorious." Notwithstanding this confident declaration, the world will hardly be persuaded that there was not some truth in the rumours that were abroad. The inquiries which were instituted were not strict, as he asserts, and all the unconstitutional influence of the powerful favourite was exerted to defeat them. In the celebrated accusations brought against Buckingham by the Earl of Bristol, the poisoning of King James was placed last on the list, and the pages of history bear evidence of the summary mode in which they were, for the time, got rid of.

The man from whom Buckingham is said to have procured his poisons was one Dr. Lamb, a conjuror and empiric, who, besides dealing in poisons, pretended to be a fortune-teller. The popular fury, which broke with comparative harmlessness against his patron, was directed against this man, until he could not appear with safety in the streets of London. His fate was melancholy. Walking one day in Cheapside, disguised, as he thought, from all observers, he was recognized by some idle boys, who began to hoot and pelt him with rubbish, calling out, "The poisoner! the poisoner! Down with the wizard! down with him!" A mob very soon collected, and the Doctor took to his heels and ran for his life. He was pursued and seized in Wood Street, and from thence dragged by the hair through the mire to St. Paul's Cross; the mob beating him with sticks and stones, and calling out, "Kill the wizard! kill the poisoner!"

Charles I, on hearing of the riot, rode from Whitehall to quell it; but he arrived too late to save the victim. Every bone in his body was broken, and he was quite dead. Charles was excessively indignant, and fined the city six hundred pounds for its inability to deliver up the ringleaders to justice.

But it was in Italy that poisoning was most prevalent. From a very early period, it seems to have been looked upon in that country as a perfectly justifiable means of getting rid of an enemy. The Italians of the sixteenth and seventeenth centuries poisoned their opponents with as little compunction as an Englishman of the present day brings an action at law against any one who has done him an injury. The writings of contemporary authors inform us that, when La Spara and La Tophania carried on their infernal trade, ladies put poisonbottles on their dressing-tables as openly, and used them with as little scruple upon others, as modern dames use Eau de Cologne or lavender-water upon themselves. So powerful is the influence of fashion, it can even cause murder to be regarded as a venial peccadillo.

In the memoirs of the last Duke of Guise, who made a Quixotic attempt, in 1648, to seize upon the government of Naples, we find some curious particulars relative to the popular feeling with regard to poisoning. A man, named Gennaro Annese, who, after the short and extraordinary career of Masaniello the fisherman, had established himself as a sort of captain-general of the populace, rendered himself so obnoxious to the Duke of Guise that the adherents of the latter determined to murder him. The captain of the guard, as the Duke himself very coolly informs us, was requested to undertake this office. It was suggested to him that the poniard would be the most effectual instrument, but the man turned up his eyes with pious horror at the proposition. He was ready to poison Gennaro Annese whenever he might be called upon to do so; but to poniard him, he said, would be disgraceful, and unbecoming an officer of the guards! At last poison was agreed upon, and Augustino Molla, an attorney in the Duke's confidence, brought the bottle containing the liquid to show it to his master. The following is the Duke's own account:--

"Augustino came to me at night, and told me: 'I have brought you something which will free you from Gennaro. He deserves death, and it is no great matter after what fashion justice is done upon him. Look at this vial, full of clear and beautiful water: in four days' time, it will punish all his treasons. The captain of the guard has undertaken to give it him; and as it has no taste at all, Gennaro will suspect nothing.'"

The Duke further informs us that the dose was duly administered; but that Gennaro, fortunately for himself, ate nothing for dinner that day but cabbage dressed with oil, which acting as an antidote, caused him to vomit profusely, and saved his life. He was exceedingly ill for five days, but never suspected that he had been poisoned.

In process of time, poison vending became a profitable trade. Eleven years after this period, it was carried on at Rome to such an extent that the sluggish government was roused to interference. Beckmann, in his "History of Inventions," and Lebret, in his "Magazin zum Gebrauche der Staaten Kirche Geschichte," or Magazine of Materials for a History of a State Church, relates that, in the year 1659, it was made known to Pope Alexander VII. that great numbers of young women had avowed in the confessional that they had poisoned their husbands with slow poisons. The Catholic clergy, who in general hold the secrets of the confessional so sacred, were shocked and alarmed at the extraordinary prevalence of the crime. Although they refrained from revealing the names of the penitents, they conceived themselves bound to apprise the head of the church of the enormities that were practised. It was also the subject of general conversation in Rome that young widows were unusually abundant. It was remarked, too, that if any couple lived unhappily together, the husband soon took ill and died. The papal authorities, when once they began to inquire, soon learned that a society of young wives had been formed, and met nightly, for some mysterious purpose, at the house of an old woman named Hieronyma Spara. This hag was a reputed witch and fortune-teller, and acted as president of the young viragos, several of whom, it was afterwards ascertained, belonged to the first families of Rome.

In order to have positive evidence of the practices of this female conclave, a lady was employed by the Government to seek an interview with them. She dressed herself out in the most magnificent style; and having been amply provided with money, she found but little difficulty, when she had stated her object, of procuring an audience of La Spara and her sisterhood. She pretended to be in extreme distress of mind on account of the infidelities and ill-treatment of her husband, and implored La Spara to furnish her with a few drops of the wonderful elixir, the efficacy of which in sending cruel husbands to "their last long sleep" was so much vaunted by the ladies of Rome. La Spara fell into the snare, and sold her some of her "drops," at a price commensurate with the supposed wealth of the purchaser.

The liquor thus obtained was subjected to an analysis, and found to be, as was suspected, a slow poison - clear, tasteless, and limpid, like that spoken of by the Duke of Guise. Upon this evidence the house was surrounded by the police, and La Spara and her companions taken into custody. La Spara, who is described as having been a little, ugly, old woman, was put to the torture, but obstinately refused to confess her guilt. Another of the women, named La Gratiosa, had less firmness, and laid bare all the secrets of the infernal sisterhood. Taking a confession, extorted by anguish on the rack, at its true value (nothing at all), there is still sufficient evidence to warrant posterity in the belief of their guilt. They were found guilty, and condemned, according to their degrees of culpability, to various punishments. La Spara, Gratiosa, and three young women, who had poisoned their husbands, were hanged together at Rome. Upwards of thirty women were whipped publicly through the streets; and several, whose high rank screened them from more degrading punishment, were banished from the country, and mulcted in heavy fines. In a few months afterwards, nine women more were hanged for poisoning; and another bevy, including many young and beautiful girls, were whipped half naked through the streets of Rome.

This severity did not put a stop to the practice, and jealous women and avaricious men, anxious to step into the inheritance of fathers, uncles, or brothers, resorted to poison. As it was quite free from taste, colour, and smell, it was administered without exciting suspicion. The skilful vendors compounded it of different degrees of strength, so that the poisoners had only to say whether they wanted their victims to die in a week, a month, or six months, and they were suited with corresponding doses. The vendors were chiefly women, of whom the most celebrated was a hag, named Tophania, who was in this way accessory to the death of upwards of six hundred persons. This woman appears to have been a dealer in poisons from her girlhood, and resided first at Palermo and then at Naples. That entertaining traveller, Father Lebat, has given, in his Letters from Italy, many curious particulars relating to her. When he was at Civita Vecchia, in 1719, the Viceroy of Naples discovered that poison was extensively sold in the latter city, and that it went by the name of aqueta, or little-water. On making further inquiry, he ascertained that Tophania (who was by this time near seventy years of age, and who seems to have begun her evil courses very soon after the execution of La Spara) sent large quantities of it to all parts of Italy in small vials, with the inscription "Manna of St. Nicholas of Barri."

The tomb of St. Nicholas of Barri was celebrated throughout Italy. A miraculous oil was said to ooze from it, which cured nearly all the maladies that flesh is heir to, provided the recipient made use of it with the due degree of faith. La Tophania artfully gave this name to her poison to elude the vigilance of the custom-house officers, who, in common with everybody else, had a pious respect for St. Nicholas de Barri and his wonderful oil.

The poison was similar to that manufactured by La Spara. Hahnemann the physician, and father of the homoepathic doctrine, writing upon this subject, says it was compounded of arsenical neutral salts, occasioning in the victim a gradual loss of appetite, faintness, gnawing pains in the stomach, loss of strength, and wasting of the lungs. The Abbe Gagliardi says that a few drops of it were generally poured into tea, chocolate, or soup, and its effects were slow, and almost imperceptible. Garelli, physician to the Emperor of Austria, in a letter to Hoffmann, says it was crystallized arsenic, dissolved in a large quantity of water by decoction, with the addition (for some unexplained purpose) of the herb cymbalaria. The Neapolitans called it Aqua Toffnina; and it became notorious all over Europe under the name of Aqua Tophania.

Although this woman carried on her infamous traffic so extensively, it was extremely difficult to meet with her. She lived in continual dread of discovery. She constantly changed her name and residence; and pretending to be a person of great godliness, resided in monasteries for months together. Whenever she was more than usually apprehensive of detection, she sought ecclesiastical protection. She was soon apprised of the search made for her by the Viceroy of Naples, and, according to her practice, took refuge in a monastery. Either the search after her was not very rigid, or her measures were exceedingly well taken; for she contrived to elude the vigilance of the authorities for several years. What is still more extraordinary, as showing the ramifications of her system, her trade was still carried on to as great an extent as before. Lebat informs us that she had so great a sympathy for poor wives who hated their husbands and wanted to get rid of them, but could not afford to buy her wonderful aqua, that she made them presents of it.

She was not allowed, however, to play at this game for ever; she was at length discovered in a nunnery, and her retreat cut off. The Viceroy made several representations to the superior to deliver her up, but without effect. The abbess, supported by the archbishop of the diocese, constantly refused. The public curiosity was in consequence so much excited at the additional importance thus thrust upon the criminal, that thousands of persons visited the nunnery in order to catch a glimpse of her.

The patience of the Viceroy appears to have been exhausted by these delays. Being a man of sense, and not a very zealous Catholic, he determined that even the Church should not shield a criminal so atrocious. Setting the privileges of the nunnery at defiance, he sent a troop of soldiers, who broke over the walls and carried her away vi et armis. The Archbishop, Cardinal Pignatelli, was highly indignant, and threatened to excommunicate and lay the whole city under interdict. All the inferior clergy, animated by the esprit du corps, took up the question, and so worked upon the superstitious and bigoted people, that they were ready to rise in a mass to storm the palace of the Viceroy and rescue the prisoner.

These were serious difficulties; but the Viceroy was not a man to be daunted. Indeed, he seems to have acted throughout with a rare union of astuteness, coolness, and energy. To avoid the evil consequences of the threatened excommunication, he placed a guard round the palace of the Archbishop, judging that the latter would not be so foolish as to launch out an anathema which would cause the city to be starved, and himself in it. The marketpeople would not have dared to come to the city with provisions, so long as it remained under the ban. There would have been too much inconvenience to himself and his ghostly brethren in such a measure; and, as the Viceroy anticipated, the good Cardinal reserved his thunders for some other occasion.

Still there was the populace. To quiet their clamour and avert the impending insurrection, the agents of the government adroitly mingled with the people, and spread abroad a report that Tophania had poisoned all the wells and fountains of the city. This was enough. The popular feeling turned against her immediately. Those who, but a moment before, had looked upon her as a saint, now reviled her as a devil, and were as eager for her punishment as they had before been for her escape. Tophania was then put to the torture. She confessed the long catalogue of her crimes, and named all the persons who had employed her. She was shortly afterwards strangled, and her corpse thrown over the wall into the garden of the convent, from whence she had been taken. This appears to have been done to conciliate the clergy, by allowing them, at least, the burial of one who had taken refuge within their precincts.

After her death the mania for poisoning seems to have abated; but we have yet to see what hold it took upon the French people at a somewhat earlier period. So rooted had it become in France between the years 1670 and 1680, that Madame de Sevigne, in one of her letters, expresses her fear that Frenchman and poisoner would become synonymous terms.

As in Italy, the first notice the government received of the prevalence of this crime was given by the clergy, to whom females of high rank, and some among the middle and lower classes, had avowed in the confessional that they had poisoned their husbands. In consequence of these disclosures, two Italians, named Exili and Glaser, were arrested, and thrown into the Bastille, on the charge of compounding and selling the drugs used for these murders. Glaser died in prison, but Exili remained without trial for several months; and there, shortly afterwards, he made the acquaintance of another prisoner, named Sainte Croix, by whose example the crime was still further disseminated among the French people.

The most notorious of the poisoners that derived their pernicious knowledge from this man was Madame de Brinvilliers, a young woman connected both by birth and marriage with some of the noblest families of France. She seems, from her very earliest years, to have been heartless and depraved; and, if we may believe her own confession, was steeped in wickedness ere she had well entered her teens. She was, however, beautiful and accomplished; and, in the eye of the world, seemed exemplary and kind. Guyot de Pitaval, in the "Causes Celebres," and Madame de Sevigne, in her Letters, represent her as mild and agreeable in her manners, and offering no traces on her countenance of the evil soul within. She was married in 1651 to the Marquis de Brinvilliers, with whom she lived unhappily for some years. He was a loose dissipated character, and was the means of introducing Sainte Croix to his wife, a man who cast a blight upon her life, and dragged her on from crime to crime till her offences became so great that the mind shudders to dwell upon them. For this man she conceived a guilty passion, to gratify which she plunged at once into the gulf of sin. She was drawn to its most loathsome depths ere retribution overtook her.

She had as yet shown a fair outside to the world, and found but little difficulty in effecting a legal separation from her husband, who had not the art to conceal his vices. The proceeding gave great offence to her family. She appears, after this, to have thrown off the mask completely, and carried on her intrigues so openly with her lover, Sainte Croix, that her father, M. D'Aubray, scandalised at her conduct, procured a lettre de cachet, and had him imprisoned in the Bastille for a twelvemonth.

Sainte Croix, who had been in Italy, was a dabbler in poisons. He knew something of the secrets of the detestable La Spara, and improved himself in them from the instructions of Exili, with whom he speedily contracted a sort of friendship. By him he was shown how to prepare, not only the liquid poisons employed in Italy, but that known as succession powder, which afterwards became so celebrated in France. Like his mistress, he appeared amiable, witty, and intelligent, and showed no signs to the world of the two fierce passions, revenge and avarice, which were gnawing at his heart. Both these passions were to be sated on the unfortunate family of D'Aubray; his revenge, because they had imprisoned him; and his avarice, because they were rich. Reckless and extravagant, he was always in want of money, and he had no one to supply him but Madame de Brinvilliers, whose own portion was far from sufficient to satisfy his need. Groaning to think that any impediment should stand between him and wealth, he conceived the horrid idea of poisoning M. D'Aubray her father, and her two brothers, that she might inherit the property. Three murders were nothing to such a villain. He communicated his plan to Madame de Brinvilliers; and she, without the slightest scruple, agreed to aid him: he undertook to compound the poisons, and she to administer them. The zeal and alacrity with which she set to work seem hardly credible. Sainte Croix found her an apt scholar; and she soon became as expert as himself in the manufacture of poisons. To try the strength of the first doses, she used to administer them to dogs, rabbits, and pigeons. Afterwards, wishing to be more certain of their effects, she went round to the hospitals, and administered them to the sick poor in the soups which she brought in apparent charity. [This is denied by Voltaire in his "Age of Louis XIV;" but he does not state for what reason. His words are, "Il est faux qu'elle eut essaye ses poisons dans les hopitaux, comme le disait le peuple et comme il est ecrit dans les 'Causes Celebres,' ouvrage d'un avocat sans cause et fait pour le peuple."] None of the poisons were intended to kill at the first dose; so that she could try them once upon an individual without fear of murder. She tried the same atrocious experiment upon the guests at her father's table, by poisoning a pigeon-pie! To be more certain still, she next poisoned herself! When convinced by this desperate essay of the potency of the draught, she procured an antidote from Sainte Croix, and all doubts being removed, commenced operations upon her grey-headed father. She administered the first dose with her own hands, in his chocolate. The poison worked well. The old man was taken ill, and his daughter, apparently full of tenderness and anxiety, watched by his bedside. The next day she gave him some broth, which she recommended as highly nourishing. This also was poisoned. In this manner she gradually wore out his frame, and in less than ten days he was a corpse! His death seemed so much the result of disease, that no suspicions were excited.

When the two brothers arrived from the provinces to render the last sad duties to their sire, they found their sister as grieved, to all outward appearance, as even filial affection could desire: but the young men only came to perish. They stood between Sainte Croix and the already half-clutched gold, and their doom was sealed. A man, named La Chaussee, was hired by Sainte Croix to aid in administering the poisons; and, in less than six weeks' time, they had both gone to their long home.

Suspicion was now excited; but so cautiously had all been done, that it found no one upon whom to attach itself. The Marquise had a sister, and she was entitled, by the death of her relatives, to half the property. Less than the whole would not satisfy Sainte Croix, and he determined that she should die the same death as her father and brothers. She was too distrustful, however; and, by quitting Paris, she escaped the destruction that was lurking for her.

The Marquise had undertaken these murders to please her lover. She was now anxious to perpetrate another on her own account. She wished to marry Sainte Croix; but, though separated from her husband, she was not divorced. She thought it would be easier to poison him than to apply to the tribunals for a divorce, which might, perhaps, be refused. But Salute Croix had no longer any love for his guilty instrument. Bad men do not admire others who are as bad as themselves. Though a villain himself, he had no desire to marry one, and was not at all anxious for the death of the Marquis. He seemed, however, to enter into the plot, and supplied her with poison for her husband: but he took care to provide a remedy. La Brinvilliers poisoned him one day, and Sainte Croix gave him an antidote the next. In this manner he was buffetted about between them for some time, and finally escaped with a ruined constitution and a broken heart.

But the day of retribution was at hand, and a terrible mischance brought the murders to light. The nature of the poisons compounded by Salute Croix was so deadly, that, when working in his laboratory, he was obliged to wear a mask, to preserve himself from suffocation. One day, the mask slipped off, and the miserable wretch perished in his crimes. His corpse was found, on the following morning, in the obscure lodging where he had fitted up his laboratory. As he appeared to be without friends or relatives, the police took possession of his effects. Among other things was found a small box, to which was affixed the following singular document:--

"I humbly beg, that those into whose hands this box may fall, will do me the favour to deliver it into the hands only of the Marchioness de Brinvilliers, who resides in the Rue Neuve St. Paul, as everything it contains concerns her, and belongs to her alone; and as, besides, there is nothing in it that can be of use to any person but her. In case she shall be dead before me, it is my wish that it be burned, with everything it contains, without opening or altering anything. In order that no one may plead ignorance, I swear by the God that I adore, and by all that is held most sacred, that I assert nothing but the truth: and if my intentions, just and reasonable as they are, be thwarted in this point by any persons, I charge their consciences with it, both in this world and that which is to come, in order that I may unload mine. I protest that this is my last will. Done at Paris, the 25th of May, 1672.

"(Signed) Sainte Croix."

This earnest solicitation, instead of insuring respect as was intended, excited curiosity. The box was opened, and found to contain some papers, and several vials and powders. The latter were handed to a chemist for analysis, and the documents were retained by the police, and opened. Among them was found a promissory note of the Marchioness de Brinvilliers, for thirty thousand francs, to the order of Sainte Croix. The other papers were of greater importance, as they implicated both her and her servant, La Chaussee, in the recent murders. As soon as she was informed of the death of Sainte Croix, she made an attempt to gain possession of his papers and the box; but, being refused, she saw that there was no time to be lost, and immediately quitted. Next morning the police were on her trail; but she succeeded in escaping to England. La Chaussee was not so fortunate. Altogether ignorant of the fatal mischance which had brought his villanies to light, he did not dream of danger. He was arrested and brought to trial: being put to the torture, he confessed that he had administered poison to the Messieurs d'Aubray, and that he had received a hundred pistoles, and the promise of an annuity for life, from Sainte Croix and Madame de Brinvilliers, for the job. He was condemned to be broken alive on the wheel, and the Marchioness was, by default, sentenced to be beheaded. He was executed accordingly, in March 1673, on the Place de Greve, in Paris.

La Brinvilliers appears to have resided for nearly three years in England. Early in 1676, thinking that the rigour of pursuit was over, and that she might venture to return to the Continent, she proceeded secretly to Liege. Notwithstanding her care, the French authorities were soon apprised of her return; and arrangements were promptly made with the municipality of that city, to permit the agents of the French police to arrest her within the limits of their jurisdiction. Desgrais, an officer of the marechaussee, accordingly left Paris for that purpose. On his arrival in Liege, he found that she had sought shelter within the walls of a convent. Here the arm of the law, long as it is said to be, could not reach her: but Desgrais was not a man to be baffled, and he resorted to stratagem to accomplish what force could not. Having disguised himself as a priest, he sought admission to the convent, and obtained an interview with La Brinvilliers. He said, that being a Frenchman, and passing through Liege, he could not leave that city without paying a visit to a lady whose beauty and misfortunes were so celebrated. Her vanity was flattered by the compliment. Desgrais saw, to use a vulgar but forcible expression, "that he had got on the blind side of her;" and he adroitly continued to pour out the language of love and admiration, till the deluded Marchioness was thrown completely off her guard. She agreed, without much solicitation, to meet him outside the walls of the convent, where their amorous intrigue might be carried on more conveniently than within. Faithful to her appointment with her supposed new lover, she came, and found herself, not in the embrace of a gallant, but in the custody of a policeman.

Her trial was not long delayed. The proofs against her were abundant. The dying declaration of La Chaussee would have been alone enough to convict her; but besides that, there were the mysterious document attached to the box of St. Croix; her flight from France; and, stronger and more damning proof than all, a paper, in her own handwriting, found among the effects of St. Croix, in which she detailed to him the misdeeds of her life, and spoke of the murder of her father and brothers, in terms that left no doubt of her guilt. During the trial, all Paris was in commotion. La Brinvilliers was the only subject of conversation. All the details of her crimes were published, and greedily devoured; and the idea of secret poisoning was first put into the heads of hundreds, who afterwards became guilty of it.

On the 16th of July 1676, the Superior Criminal Court of Paris pronounced a verdict of guilty against her, for the murder of her father and brothers, and the attempt upon the life of her sister. She was condemned to be drawn on a hurdle, with her feet bare, a rope about her neck, and a burning torch in her hand, to the great entrance of the cathedral of Notre Dame; where she was to make the amende honorable, in sight of all the people; to be taken from thence to the Place de Greve, and there to be beheaded. Her body was afterwards to be burned, and her ashes scattered to the winds.

After her sentence, she made a full confession of her guilt. She seems to have looked upon death without fear; but it was recklessness, not courage, that supported her. Madame de Sevigne says, that when on the hurdle, on her way to the scaffold, she entreated her confessor to exert his influence with the executioner to place himself next to her, that his body might hide from her view "that scoundrel, Desgrais, who had entrapped her." She also asked the ladies, who had been drawn to their windows to witness the procession, what they were looking at? adding, "a pretty sight you have come to see, truly!" She laughed when on the scaffold, dying as she had lived, impenitent and heartless. On the morrow, the populace came in crowds to collect her ashes, to preserve them as relics. She was regarded as a martyred saint, and her ashes were supposed to be endowed, by Divine grace, with the power of curing all diseases. Popular folly has often canonised persons whose pretensions to sanctity were extremely equivocal; but the disgusting folly of the multitude, in this instance, has never been surpassed.

Before her death, proceedings were instituted against M. de Penautier, treasurer of the province of Languedoc, and Receiver-general for the clergy, who was accused by a lady, named St. Laurent, of having poisoned her husband, the late Receiver-general, in order to obtain his appointment. The circumstances of this case were never divulged, and the greatest influence was exerted to prevent it from going to trial. He was known to have been intimate with Sainte Croix and Madame de Brinvilliers, and was thought to have procured his poisons from them. The latter, however, refused to say anything which might implicate him. The inquiry was eventually stifled, after Penautier had been several months in the Bastille.

The Cardinal de Bonzy was accused by the gossips of the day of being an accomplice of Penautier. The Cardinal's estates were burthened with the payment of several heavy annuities; but, about the time that poisoning became so fashionable, all the annuitants died off, one after the other. The Cardinal, in talking of these annuitants, afterwards used to say, "Thanks to my star, I have outlived them all!" A wit, seeing him and Penautier riding in the same carriage, cried out, in allusion to this expression, "There go the Cardinal de Bonzy and his star!"

It was now that the mania for poisoning began to take hold of the popular mind. From this time until the year 1682, the prisons of France teemed with persons accused of this crime; and it is very singular, that other offences decreased in a similar proportion. We have already seen the extent to which it was carried in Italy. It was, if possible, surpassed in France. The diabolical ease with which these murders could be effected, by means of these scentless and tasteless poisons, enticed the evil-minded. Jealousy, revenge, avarice, even petty spite, alike resorted to them. Those who would have been deterred, by fear of detection, from using the pistol or the dagger, or even strong doses of poison, which kill at once, employed slow poisons without dread. The corrupt Government of the day, although it could wink at the atrocities of a wealthy and influential courtier, like Penautier, was scandalised to see the crime spreading among the people. Disgrace was, in fact, entailed, in the eyes of Europe, upon the name of Frenchman. Louis XIV, to put a stop to the evil, instituted what was called the Chambre Ardente, or Burning Chamber, with extensive powers, for the trial and punishment of the prisoners.

Two women, especially, made themselves notorious at this time, and were instrumental to the deaths of hundreds of individuals. They both resided in Paris, and were named Lavoisin and Lavigoreux. Like Spars and Tophania, of whom they were imitators, they chiefly sold their poisons to women who wanted to get rid of their husbands; and, in some few instances, to husbands who wanted to get rid of their wives. Their ostensible occupation was that of midwives. They also pretended to be fortune-tellers, and were visited by persons of every class of society. The rich and poor thronged alike to their mansardes, to learn the secrets of the future. Their prophecies were principally of death. They foretold to women the approaching dissolution of husbands, and to needy heirs, the end of rich relatives, who had made them, as Byron expresses it, "wait too, too long already." They generally took care to be instrumental in fulfilling their own predictions. They used to tell their wretched employers, that some sign of the approaching death would take place in the house, such as the breaking of glass or china; and they paid servants considerable fees to cause a breakage, as if by accident, exactly at the appointed time. Their occupation as midwives made them acquainted with the secrets of many families, which they afterwards turned to dreadful account.

It is not known how long they had carried on this awful trade before they were discovered. Detection finally overtook them at the close of the year 1679. They were both tried, found guilty, and burned alive on the Place de Greve, on the 22nd of February, 1680, after their hands had been bored through with a red-hot iron, and then cut off. Their numerous accomplices in Paris and in the provinces were also discovered and brought to trial. According to some authors, thirty, and to others, fifty of them, chiefly women, were hanged in the principal cities.

Lavoisin kept a list of the visiters who came to her house to purchase poisons. This paper was seized by the police on her arrest, and examined by the tribunals. Among the names were found those of the Marshal de Luxembourg, the Countess de Soissons, and the Duchess de Bouillon. The Marshal seems only to have been guilty of a piece of discreditable folly in visiting a woman of this description, but the popular voice at the time imputed to him something more than folly. The author of the "Memoirs of the Affairs of Europe since the Peace of Utrecht," says, "The miserable gang who dealt in poison and prophecy alleged that he had sold himself to the devil, and that a young girl of the name of Dupin had been poisoned by his means. Among other stories, they said he had made a contract with the devil, in order to marry his son to the daughter of the Marquis of Louvois. To this atrocious and absurd accusation the Marshal, who had surrendered himself at the Bastille on the first accusation against him, replied with the mingled sentiment of pride and innocence, 'When Mathieu de Montmorenci, my ancestor, married the widow of Louis le Gros, he did not have recourse to the devil, but to the States-General, in order to obtain for the minor king the support of the house of Montmorenci.' This brave man was imprisoned in a cell six feet and a half long, and his trial, which was interrupted for several weeks, lasted altogether fourteen months. No judgment was pronounced upon him."

The Countess of Soissons fled to Brussels, rather than undergo the risk of a trial; and was never able to clear herself from the stigma that attached to her, of having made an attempt to poison the Queen of Spain by doses of succession powder. The Duchess of Bouillon was arrested, and tried by the Chambre Ardente. It would appear, however, that she had nothing to do with the slow poisons, but had merely endeavoured to pry into the secrets of futurity, and gratify her curiosity with a sight of the devil. One of the presidents of the Chambre, La Reynie, an ugly little old man, very seriously asked her whether she had really seen the devil; to which the lady replied, looking him full in the face, "Oh yes! I see him now. He is in the form of a little ugly old man, exceedingly illnatured, and is dressed in the robes of a counsellor of State." M. la Reynie prudently refrained from asking any more questions of a lady with so sharp and ready a tongue. The Duchess was imprisoned for several months in the Bastile; and nothing being proved against her, she was released at the intercession of her powerful friends. The severe punishment of criminals of this note might have helped to abate the fever of imitation among the vulgar; -- their comparative impunity had a contrary tendency. The escape of Penautier, and the wealthy Cardinal de Bonzy his employer, had the most pernicious effect. For two years longer the crime continued to rage, and was not finally suppressed till the stake had blazed, or the noose dangled, for upwards of a hundred individuals.

Haunted Houses

Here's a knocking indeed! . . . . Knock! knock! knock . . . . Who's there, i' the name o' Beelzebub? . . . .
Who's there, i' the devil's name? Knock! knock! knock! -- Never at quiet? --*Macbeth.*

Who has not either seen or heard of some house, shut up and uninhabitable, fallen into decay, and looking dusty and dreary, from which, at midnight, strange sounds have been heard to issue -- aerial knockings -- the rattling of chains, and the groaning of perturbed spirits? -- a house that people have thought it unsafe to pass after dark, and which has remained for years without a tenant, and which no tenant would occupy, even were he paid to do so? There are hundreds of such houses in England at the present day; hundreds in France, Germany, and almost every country of Europe, which are marked with the mark of fear -- places for the timid to avoid, and the pious to bless themselves at, and ask protection from, as they pass -- the abodes of ghosts and evil spirits. There are many such houses in London; and if any vain boaster of the march of intellect would but take the trouble to find them out and count them, he would be convinced that intellect must yet make some enormous strides before such old superstitions can be eradicated.

The idea that such houses exist is a remnant of the witch creed, which merits separate notice from its comparative harmlessness, and from its being not so much a madness as a folly of the people. Unlike other notions that sprang from the belief in witchcraft, and which we have already dwelt upon at sufficient length, it has sent no wretches to the stake or the gibbet, and but a few to the pillory only.

Many houses have been condemned as haunted, and avoided by the weak and credulous, from circumstances the most trifling in themselves, and which only wanted a vigorous mind to clear up, at once, and dissipate all alarm. A house in Aix-la-Chapelle, a large desolate-looking building, remained uninhabited for five years, on account of the mysterious knockings that there were heard within it at all hours of the day and night. Nobody could account for the noises; and the fear became at last so excessive, that the persons who inhabited the houses on either side relinquished their tenancy, and went to reside in other quarters of the town, where there was less chance of interruption from evil spirits. From being so long without an inhabitant the house at last grew so ruinous, so dingy, and so miserable in its outward appearance, and so like the place that ghosts might be supposed to haunt, that few persons cared to go past it after sunset. The knocking that was heard in one of the upper rooms was not very loud, but it was very regular. The gossips of the neighbourhood asserted that they often heard groans from the cellars, and saw lights moved about from one window to another immediately after the midnight bell had tolled. Spectres in white habiliments were reported to have gibed and chattered from the windows; but all these stories could bear no investigation. The knocking, however, was a fact which no one could dispute, and several ineffectual attempts were made by the proprietor to discover the cause. The rooms were sprinkled with holy water -- the evil spirits were commanded in due form, by a priest, to depart thence to the Red Sea; but the knockings still continued, in spite of all that could be done in that way. Accident at last discovered the cause, and restored tranquillity to the neighbourhood. The proprietor, who suffered not only in his mind but in his pocket, had sold the building at a ruinously small price, to get rid of all future annoyance. The new proprietor was standing in a room on the first floor when he heard the door driven to at the bottom with a considerable noise, and then fly open immediately, about two inches and no more. He stood still a minute and watched, and the same thing occurred a second and a third time. He examined the door attentively, and all the mystery was unravelled. The latch of the door was broken so that it could not be fastened, and it swung chiefly upon the bottom hinge. Immediately opposite was a window, in which one pane of glass was broken; and when the wind was in a certain quarter, the draught of air was so strong that it blew the door to with some violence. There being no latch, it swung open again; and when there was a fresh gust, was again blown to. The new proprietor lost no time in sending for a glazier, and the mysterious noises ceased for ever. The house was replastered and repainted, and once more regained its lost good name. It was not before two or three years, however, that it was thoroughly established in popular favour; and many persons, even then, would always avoid passing it, if they could reach their destination by any other street.

A similar story is narrated by Sir Walter Scott, in his Letters on Demonology and Witchcraft, the hero of which was a gentleman of birth and distinction, well known in the political world. Shortly after he succeeded to his title and estates, there was a rumour among the servants concerning a strange noise that used to be heard at night in the family mansion, and the cause of which no one could ascertain. The gentleman resolved to discover it himself, and to watch for that purpose with a domestic who had grown old in the family, and who, like the rest, had whispered strange things about the knocking having begun immediately upon the death of his old master. These two watched until the noise was heard, and at last traced it to a small store-room, used as a place for keeping provisions of various kinds for the family, and of which the old butler had the key. They entered this place, and remained for some time, without hearing the noises which they had traced thither. At length the sound was heard, but much lower than it seemed to be while they were further off, and their imaginations were more excited. They then discovered the cause without difficulty. A rat, caught in an old-fashioned trap, had occasioned the noise by its efforts to escape, in which it was able to raise the trap-door of its prison to a certain height, but was then obliged to drop it. The noise of the fall resounding through the house had occasioned the mysterious rumours, which, but for the investigation of the proprietor, would, in all probability, have acquired so bad a name for the dwelling that no servants would have inhabited it. The circumstance was told to Sir Walter Scott by the gentleman to whom it happened.

But, in general, houses that have acquired this character, have been more indebted for it, to the roguery of living men, than to accidents like these. Six monks played off a clever trick of the kind upon that worthy King, Louis, whose piety has procured him, in the annals of his own country, the designation of "the Saint." Having heard his confessor speak in terms of warm eulogy of the goodness and learning of the monks of the order of Saint Bruno, he expressed his wish to establish a community of them near Paris. Bernard de la Tour, the superior, sent six of the brethren, and the King gave them a handsome house to live in, in the village of Chantilly. It so happened that, from their windows, they had a very fine view of the ancient palace of Vauvert, which had been built for a royal residence by King Robert, but deserted for many years. The worthy monks thought the palace would just suit them, but their modesty was so excessive that they were ashamed to ask the King for a grant of it in due form. This difficulty was not to be overcome, and the monks set their ingenuity to work to discover another plan. The palace of Vauvert had never laboured under any imputation upon its character until they became its neighbours; but, somehow or other, it almost immediately afterwards began to acquire a bad name. Frightful shrieks were heard to proceed from it at night -- blue, red, and green lights were suddenly observed to glimmer from the windows, and as suddenly to disappear: the clanking of chains was heard, and the howling as of persons in great pain. These disturbances continued for several months, to the great terror of all the country round, and even of the pious King Louis, to whom, at Paris, all the rumours were regularly carried, with whole heaps of additions, that accumulated on the way. At last a great spectre, clothed all in pea-green, with a long white beard and a serpent's tail, took his station regularly at midnight in the principal window of the palace, and howled fearfully and shook his fists at the passengers. The six monks of Chantilly, to whom all these things were duly narrated, were exceedingly wroth that the devil should play such antics right opposite their dwelling, and hinted to the commissioners, sent down by Saint Louis to investigate the matter, that, if they were allowed to inhabit the palace, they would very soon make a clearance of the evil spirits. The King was quite charmed with their piety, and expressed to them how grateful he felt for their disinterestedness. A deed was forthwith drawn up -- the royal sign-manual was affixed to it, and the palace of Vauvert became the property of the monks of Saint Bruno. The deed is dated in 1259. [Garinet. Histoire de la Magie en France, page 75.] The disturbances ceased immediately -- the lights disappeared, and the green ghost (so said the monks) was laid at rest for ever under the waves of the Red Sea.

In the year 1580, one Gilles Blacre had taken the lease of a house in the suburbs of Tours, but repenting him of his bargain with the landlord, Peter Piquet, he endeavoured to prevail upon him to cancel the agreement. Peter, however, was satisfied with his tenant and his terms, and would listen to no compromise. Very shortly afterwards, the rumour was spread all over Tours that the house of Gilles Blacre was haunted. Gilles himself asserted that he verily believed his house to be the general rendezvous of all the witches and evil spirits of France. The noise they made was awful, and quite prevented him from sleeping. They knocked against the wall -- howled in the chimneys -- broke his window-glass -- scattered his pots and pans all over his kitchen, and set his chairs and tables a dancing the whole night through. Crowds of persons assembled around the house to hear the mysterious noises; and the bricks were observed to detach themselves from the wall and fall into the streets upon the heads of those who had not said their paternoster before they came out in the morning. These things having continued for some time, Gilles Blacre made his complaint to the Civil Court of Tours, and Peter Piquet was summoned to show cause why the lease should not be annulled. Poor Peter could make no defence, and the court unanimously agreed that no lease could hold good under such circumstances, and annulled it accordingly, condemning the unlucky owner to all the expenses of the suit. Peter appealed to the Parliament of Paris; and, after a long examination, the Parliament confirmed the lease. "Not," said the judge, "because it bas not been fully and satisfactorily proved that the house is troubled by evil spirits, but that there was an informality in the proceedings before the Civil Court of Tours, that rendered its decision null and of no effect."

A similar cause was tried before the Parliament of Bordeaux, in the year 1595, relative to a house in that city which was sorely troubled by evil spirits. The Parliament appointed certain ecclesiastics to examine and report to them, and on their report in the affirmative that the house was haunted, the lease was annulled, and the tenant absolved from all payment of rent and taxes. [Garinet. Histoire de la Magie en France, page 156.]

One of the best stories of a haunted house is that of the royal palace of Woodstock, in the year 1649, when the commissioners sent from London by the Long Parliament to take possession of it, and efface all the emblems of royalty about it, were fairly driven out by their fear of the devil and the annoyances they suffered from a roguish cavalier, who played the imp to admiration. The commissioners, dreading at that time no devil, arrived at Woodstock on the 13th of October, 1649. They took up their lodgings in the late King's apartments-turned the beautiful bedrooms and withdrawing-rooms into kitchens and sculleries -- the council-hall into a brew-house, and made the dining-room a place to keep firewood in. They pulled down all the insignia of royal state, and treated with the utmost indignity everything that recalled to their memory the name or the majesty of Charles Stuart. One Giles Sharp accompanied them in the capacity of clerk, and seconded their efforts, apparently with the greatest zeal. He aided them to uproot a noble old tree, merely because it was called the King's Oak, and tossed the fragments into the dining-room to make cheerful fires for the commissioners. During the first two days, they heard some strange noises about the house, but they paid no great attention to them. On the third, however, they began to suspect they had got into bad company; for they heard, as they thought, a supernatural dog under their bed, which gnawed their bedclothes. On the next day, the chairs and tables began to dance, apparently of their own accord. On the fifth day, something came into the bedchamber and walked up and down, and fetching the warming-pan out of the withdrawing-room, made so much noise with it that they thought five church-bells were ringing in their ears. On the sixth day, the plates and dishes were thrown up and down the dining-room. On the seventh, they penetrated into the bedroom in company with several logs of wood, and usurped the soft pillows intended for the commissioners. On the eighth and ninth nights, there was a cessation of hostilities; but on the tenth, the bricks in the chimneys became locomotive, and rattled and danced about the floors, and round the heads of the commissioners, all the night long. On the eleventh, the demon ran away with their breeches, and on the twelfth filled their beds so full of pewter-platters that they could not get into them. On the thirteenth night, the glass became unaccountably seized with a fit of cracking, and fell into shivers in all parts of the house. On the fourteenth, there was a noise as if forty pieces of artillery had been fired off, and a shower of pebble-stones, which so alarmed the commissioners that, "struck with great horror, they cried out to one another for help."

They first of all tried the efficacy of prayers to drive away the evil spirits; but these proving unavailing, they began seriously to reflect whether it would not be much better to leave the place altogether to the devils that inhabited it. They ultimately resolved, however, to try it a little longer; and having craved forgiveness of all their sins, betook themselves to bed. That night they slept in tolerable comfort, but it was merely a trick of their tormentor to lull them into false security. When, on the succeeding night, they heard no noises, they began to flatter themselves that the devil was driven out, and prepared accordingly to take up their quarters for the whole winter in the palace. These symptoms on their part became the signal for renewed uproar among the fiends. On the 1st of November, they heard something walking with a slow and solemn pace up and down the withdrawing-room, and immediately afterwards a shower of stones, bricks, mortar, and broken glass pelted about their ears. On the 2nd the steps were again heard in the withdrawing-room, sounding to their fancy very much like the treading of an enormous bear, which continued for about a quarter of an hour. This noise having ceased, a large warming-pan was thrown violently upon the table, followed by a number of stones and the jawbone of a horse. Some of the boldest walked valiantly into the withdrawing-room, armed with swords, and pistols; but could discover nothing. They were afraid that night to go to sleep, and sat up, making fires in every room, and burning candles and lamps in great abundance; thinking that, as the fiends loved darkness, they would not disturb a company surrounded with so much light. They were deceived, however: buckets of water came down the chimneys and extinguished the fires, and the candles were blown out, they knew not how. Some of the servants who had betaken themselves to bed were drenched with putrid ditch-water as they lay, and arose in great fright, muttering incoherent prayers, and exposing to the wondering eyes of the commissioners their linen all dripping with green moisture, and their knuckles red with the blows they had at the same time received from some invisible tormentors. While they were still speaking, there was a noise like the loudest thunder, or the firing of a whole park of artillery, upon which they all fell down upon their knees and implored the protection of the Almighty. One of the commissioners then arose, the others still kneeling, and asked in a courageous voice, and in the name of God, who was there, and what they had done that they should be troubled in that manner. No answer was returned, and the noises ceased for a while. At length, however, as the commissioners said, "the devil came again, and brought with it seven devils worse than itself." Being again in darkness, they lighted a candle and placed it in the doorway, that it might throw a light upon the two chambers at once; but it was suddenly blown out, and one commissioner said that he had "seen the similitude of a horse's hoof striking the candle and candlestick into the middle of the chamber, and afterwards making three scrapes on the snuff to put it out." Upon this, the same person was so bold as to draw his sword; but he asserted positively that he had hardly withdrawn it from the scabbard before an invisible hand seized hold of it and tugged with him for it, and prevailing, struck him so violent a blow with the pommel that he was quite stunned. Then the noises began again; upon which, with one accord, they all retired into the presence-chamber, where they passed the night, praying and singing psalms.

They were by this time convinced that it was useless to struggle any longer with the powers of evil, that seemed determined to make Woodstock their own. These things happened on the Saturday night; and, being repeated on the Sunday, they determined to leave the place immediately, and return to London. By Tuesday morning early, all their preparations were completed; and, shaking the dust off their feet, and devoting Woodstock and all its inhabitants to the infernal gods, they finally took their departure. [Dr. H. More's Continuation of Glanvil's Collection of Relations in proof of Witchcraft.]

Many years elapsed before the true cause of these disturbances was discovered. It was ascertained, at the Restoration, that the whole was the work of Giles Sharp, the trusty clerk of the commissioners. This man, whose real name was Joseph Collins, was a concealed royalist, and had passed his early life within the bowers of Woodstock; so that he knew every hole and corner of the place, and the numerous trap-doors and secret passages that abounded in the building. The commissioners, never suspecting the true state of his opinions, but believing him to be revolutionary to the back-bone, placed the utmost reliance upon him; a confidence which he abused in the manner above detailed, to his own great amusement, and that of the few cavaliers whom he let into the secret.

Quite as extraordinary and as cleverly managed was the trick played off at Tedworth, in 1661, at the house of Mr. Mompesson, and which is so circumstantially narrated by the Rev. Joseph Glanvil, under the title of "The Demon of Tedworth," and appended, among other proofs of witchcraft, to his noted work, called "Sadducismus Triumphatus." About the middle of April, in the year above mentioned, Mr. Mompesson, having returned to his house, at Tedworth, from a journey he had taken to London, was informed by his wife, that during his absence they had been troubled with the most extraordinary noises. Three nights afterwards he heard the noise himself; and it appeared to him to be that of "a great knocking at his doors, and on the outside of his walls." He immediately arose, dressed himself, took down a pair of pistols, and walked valiantly forth to discover the disturber, under the impression that it must be a robber: but, as he went, the noise seemed to travel before or behind him; and, when he arrived at the door from which he thought it proceeded, he saw nothing, but still heard "a strange hollow sound." He puzzled his brains for a long time, and searched every corner of the house; but, discovering nothing, he went to bed again. He was no sooner snug under the clothes, than the noise began again more furiously than ever, sounding very much like a "thumping and drumming on the top of his house, and then by degrees going off into the air."

These things continued for several nights, when it came to the recollection of Mr. Mompesson that some time before, he had given orders for the arrest and imprisonment of a wandering drummer, who went about the country with a large drum, disturbing quiet people and soliciting alms, and that he had detained the man's drum, and that, probably, the drummer was a wizard, and had sent evil spirits to haunt his house, to be revenged of him. He became strengthened in his opinion every day, especially when the noises assumed, to his fancy, a resemblance to the beating of a drum, "like that at the breaking up of a guard." Mrs. Mompesson being brought to bed, the devil, or the drummer, very kindly and considerately refrained from making the usual riot; but, as soon as she recovered strength, began again "in a ruder manner than before, following and vexing the young children, and beating their bedsteads with so much violence that every one expected they would fall in pieces." For an hour together, as the worthy Mr. Mompesson repeated to his wondering neighbours, this infernal drummer "would beat 'Roundheads and Cuckolds,' the 'Tat-too,' and several other points of war, as cleverly as any soldier." When this had lasted long enough, he changed his tactics, and scratched with his iron talons under the children's bed. "On the 5th of November," says the Rev. Joseph Glanvil, "it made a mighty noise; and a servant, observing two boards in the children's room seeming to move, he bid it give him one of them. Upon which the board came (nothing moving it, that he saw), within a yard of him. The man added, 'Nay, let me have it in my hand ;' upon which the spirit, devil, or drummer pushed it towards him so

285

close, that he might touch it. "This," continues Glanvil, "was in the day-time, and was seen by a whole room full of people. That morning it left a sulphureous smell behind it, which was very offensive. At night the minister, one Mr. Cragg, and several of the neighbours, came to the house, on a visit. Mr. Cragg went to prayers with them, kneeling at the children's bedside, where it then became very troublesome and loud. During prayer time, the spirit withdrew into the cock-loft, but returned as soon as prayers were done; and then, in sight of the company, the chairs walked about the room of themselves, the children's shoes were hurled over their heads, and every loose thing moved about the chamber. At the same time, a bed-staff was thrown at the minister, which hit him on the leg, but so favourably, that a lock of wool could not have fallen more softly." On another occasion, the blacksmith of the village, a fellow who cared neither for ghost nor devil, slept with John, the footman, that he also might hear the disturbances, and be cured of his incredulity, when there "came a noise in the room, as if one had been shoeing a horse, and somewhat came, as it were, with a pair of pincers," snipping and snapping at the poor blacksmith's nose the greater part of the night. Next day it came, panting like a dog out of breath; upon which some woman present took a bed-staff to knock at it, "which was caught suddenly out of her hand, and thrown away; and company coming up, the room was presently filled with a bloomy noisome smell, and was very hot, though without fire, in a very sharp and severe winter. It continued in the bed, panting and scratching for an hour and a half, and then went into the next room, where it knocked a little, and seemed to rattle a chain."

The rumour of these wonderful occurrences soon spread all over the country, and people from far and near flocked to the haunted house of Tedworth, to believe or doubt, as their natures led them, but all filled with intense curiosity. It appears, too, that the fame of these events reached the royal ear, and that some gentlemen were sent by the King to investigate the circumstances, and draw up a report of what they saw or heard. Whether the royal commissioners were more sensible men than the neighbours of Mr. Mompesson, and required more clear and positive evidence than they, or whether the powers with which they were armed to punish anybody who might be found carrying on this deception, frightened the evil-doers, is not certain; but Glanvil himself reluctantly confesses, that all the time they were in the house, the noises ceased, and nothing was heard or seen. "However," says he, "as to the quiet of the house when the courtiers were there, the intermission may have been accidental, or perhaps the demon was not willing to give so public a testimony of those transactions which might possibly convince those who, he had rather, should continue in unbelief of his existence."

As soon as the royal commissioners took their departure, the infernal drummer re-commenced his antics, and hundreds of persons were daily present to hear and wonder. Mr. Mompesson's servant was so fortunate as not only to hear, but to see this pertinacious demon; for it came and stood at the foot of his bed. "The exact shape and proportion of it he could not discover; but he saw a great body, with two red and glaring eyes, which, for some time, were fixed steadily on him, and at length disappeared." Innumerable were the antics it played. Once it purred like a cat; beat the children's legs black and blue; put a long spike into Mr. Mompesson's bed, and a knife into his mother's; filled the porrengers with ashes; hid a Bible under the grate; and turned the money black in people's pockets. "One night," said Mr. Mompesson, in a letter to Mr. Glanvil, "there were seven or eight of these devils in the shape of men, who, as soon as a gun was fired, would shuffle away into an arbour;" a circumstance which might have convinced Mr. Mompesson of the mortal nature of his persecutors, if he had not been of the number of those worse than blind, who shut their eyes and refuse to see.

In the mean time the drummer, the supposed cause of all the mischief, passed his time in Gloucester gaol, whither he had been committed as a rogue and a vagabond. Being visited one day by some person from the neighbourhood of Tedworth, he asked what was the news in Wiltshire, and whether people did not talk a great deal about a drumming in a gentleman's house there? The visiter replied, that he heard of nothing else; upon which the drummer observed, "I have done it; I have thus plagued him; and he shall never be quiet until he hath made me satisfaction for taking away my drum." No doubt the fellow, who seems to have been a gipsy, spoke the truth, and that the gang of which he was a member knew more about the noises at Mr. Mompesson's house than anybody else. Upon these words, however, he was brought to trial at Salisbury, for witchcraft; and, being found guilty, was sentenced to transportation; a sentence which, for its leniency, excited no little wonder in that age, when such an accusation, whether proved or not, generally insured the stake or the gibbet. Glanvil says, that the noises ceased immediately the drummer was sent beyond the seas; but that, some how or other, he managed to return from transportation; "by raising storms and affrighting the seamen, it was said;" when the disturbances were forthwith renewed, and continued at intervals for several years. Certainly, if the confederates of this roving gipsy were so pertinacious in tormenting poor weak Mr. Mompesson, their pertinacity is a most extraordinary instance of what revenge is capable of. It was believed by many, at the time, that Mr. Mompesson himself was privy to the whole matter, and permitted and encouraged these tricks in his house for the sake of notoriety; but it seems more probable that the gipsies were the real delinquents, and that Mr. Mompesson was as much alarmed and bewildered as his credulous neighhours, whose excited imaginations conjured up no small portion of these stories,

"Which rolled, and as they rolled, grew larger every hour."

Many instances, of a similar kind, during the seventeenth century, might be gleaned from Glanvil and other writers of that period; but they do not differ sufficiently from these to justify a detail of them. The most famous of all haunted houses acquired its notoriety much nearer our own time; and the circumstances connected with it are so curious, and afford so fair a specimen of the easy credulity even of well-informed and sensible people, as to merit a little notice in this chapter. The Cock Lane Ghost, as it was called, kept London in commotion for a considerable time, and was the theme of conversation among the learned and the illiterate, and in every circle, from that of the prince to that of the peasant.

At the commencement of the year 1760, there resided in Cock Lane, near West Smithfield, in the house of one Parsons, the parish clerk of St. Sepulchre's, a stockbroker, named Kent. The wife of this gentleman had died in child-bed during the previous year, and his sister-in-law, Miss Fanny, had arrived from Norfolk to keep his house for him. They soon conceived a mutual affection, and each of them made a will in the other's favour. They lived some months in the house of Parsons, who, being a needy man, borrowed money of his lodger. Some difference arose betwixt them, and Mr. Kent left the house, and instituted legal proceedings against the parish clerk for the recovery of his money.

While this matter was yet pending, Miss Fanny was suddenly taken ill of the small-pox; and, notwithstanding every care and attention, she died in a few days, and was buried in a vault under Clerkenwell church. Parsons now began to hint that the poor lady had come unfairly by her death, and that Mr. Kent was accessory to it, from his too great eagerness to enter into possession of the property she had bequeathed him. Nothing further was said for nearly two years; but it would appear that Parsons was of so revengeful a character, that he had never forgotten or forgiven his differences with Mr. Kent, and the indignity of having been sued for the borrowed money. The strong passions of pride and avarice were silently at work during all that interval, hatching schemes of revenge, but dismissing them one after the other as impracticable, until, at last, a notable one suggested itself. About the beginning of the year 1762, the alarm was spread over all the neighbourhood of Cock Lane, that the house of Parsons was haunted by the ghost of poor Fanny, and that the daughter of Parsons, a girl about twelve years of age, had several times seen and conversed with the spirit, who had, moreover, informed her, that she had not died of the smallpox, as was currently reported, but of poison, administered by Mr. Kent. Parsons, who originated, took good care to countenance these reports; and, in answer to numerous inquiries, said his house was every night, and had been for two years, in fact, ever since the death of Fanny, troubled by a loud knocking at the doors and in the walls. Having thus prepared the ignorant and credulous neighbours to believe or exaggerate for themselves what he had told them, he sent for a gentleman of a higher class in life, to come and witness these extraordinary occurrences. The gentleman came accordingly, and found the daughter of Parsons, to whom the spirit alone appeared, and whom alone it answered, in bed, trembling violently, having just seen the ghost, and been again informed that she had died from poison. A loud knocking was also heard from every part of the chamber, which so mystified the not very clear understanding of the visiter, that he departed, afraid to doubt and ashamed to believe, but with a promise to bring the clergyman of the parish and several other gentlemen on the following day, to report upon the mystery.

On the following night he returned, bringing with him three clergymen, and about twenty other persons, including two negroes, when, upon a consultation with Parsons, they resolved to sit up the whole night, and await the ghost's arrival. It was then explained by Parsons, that although the ghost would never render itself visible to anybody but his daughter, it had no objection to answer the questions that might be put to it, by any person present, and that it expressed an affirmation by one knock, a negative by two, and its displeasure by a kind of scratching. The child was then put into bed along with her sister, and the clergymen examined the bed and bed-clothes to satisfy themselves that no trick was played, by knocking upon any substance concealed among the clothes. As on the previous night, the bed was observed to shake violently.

After some hours, during which they all waited with exemplary patience, the mysterious knocking was heard in the wall, and the child declared that she saw the ghost of poor Fanny. The following questions were then gravely put by the clergyman, through the medium of one Mary Frazer, the servant of Parsons, and to whom it was said the deceased lady had been much attached. The answers were in the usual fashion, by a knock or knocks:--

"Do you make this disturbance on account of the ill usage you received from Mr. Kent ?" -- "Yes."

"Were you brought to an untimely end by poison ?" -- "Yes."

"How was the poison administered, in beer or in purl ?" -- "In purl."

"How long was that before your death?" -- "About three hours."

"Can your former servant, Carrots, give any information about the poison?" -- "Yes."

"Are you Kent's wife's sister ?" -- "Yes."

"Were you married to Kent after your sister's death?" -- "No."

"Was anybody else, besides Kent, concerned in your murder?" -- "No."

"Can you, if you like, appear visibly to anyone?" -- "Yes."

"Will you do so?" -- "Yes."

"Can you go out of this house?" -- "Yes."

"Is it your intention to follow this child about everywhere?" -- "Yes."

"Are you pleased in being asked these questions?" -- "Yes."

"Does it ease your troubled soul?" -- "Yes."

[Here there was heard a mysterious noise, which some wiseacre present compared to the fluttering of wings.]

"How long before your death did you tell your servant, Carrots, that you were poisoned? -- An hour?" -- "Yes."

[Carrots, who was present, was appealed to; but she stated positively that such was not the fact, as the deceased was quite speechless an hour before her death. This shook the faith of some of the spectators, but the examination was allowed to continue.]

"How long did Carrots live with you?" -- "Three or four days."

[Carrots was again appealed to, and said that this was true.]

"If Mr. Kent is arrested for this murder, will he confess?" -- "Yes."

"Would your soul be at rest if he were hanged for it?" -- "Yes."

"Will he be hanged for it?" -- "Yes."

"How long a time first?" -- "Three years."

"How many clergymen are there in this room?" -- "Three."

"How many negroes?" -- "Two."

"Is this watch (held up by one of the clergymen) white?" -- "No."

"Is it yellow?" -- "No."

"Is it blue?" -- "No."

"Is it black?" -- "Yes."

[The watch was in a black shagreen case.]

"At what time this morning will you take your departure?"

The answer to this question was four knocks, very distinctly heard by every person present; and accordingly, at four o'clock precisely, the ghost took its departure to the Wheatsheaf public-house, close by, where it frightened mine host and his lady almost out of their wits by knocking in the ceiling right above their bed.

The rumour of these occurrences very soon spread over London, and every day Cock Lane was rendered impassable by the crowds of people who assembled around the house of the parish clerk, in expectation of either seeing the ghost or of hearing the mysterious knocks. It was at last found necessary, so clamorous were they for admission within the haunted precincts, to admit those only who would pay a certain fee, an arrangement which was very convenient to the needy and money-loving Mr. Parsons. Indeed, things had taken a turn greatly to his satisfaction; he not only had his revenge, but he made a profit out of it. The ghost, in consequence, played its antics every night, to the great amusement of many hundreds of people and the great perplexity of a still greater number.

Unhappily, however, for the parish clerk, the ghost was induced to make some promises which were the means of utterly destroying its reputation. It promised, in answer to the questions of the Reverend Mr. Aldritch of Clerkenwell, that it would not only follow the little Miss Parsons wherever she went, but would also attend him, or any other gentleman, into the vault under St. John's Church, where the body of the murdered woman was deposited, and would there give notice of its presence by a distinct knock upon the coffin. As a preliminary, the girl was conveyed to the house of Mr. Aldritch near the church, where a large party of ladies and gentlemen, eminent for their acquirements, their rank, or their wealth, had assembled. About ten o'clock on the night of the 1st of February, the girl having been brought from Cock Lane in a coach, was put to bed by several ladies in the house of Mr. Aldritch; a strict examination having been previously made that nothing was hidden in the bedclothes. While the gentlemen,. in an adjoining chamber, were deliberating whether they should proceed in a body to the vault, they were summoned into the bedroom by the ladies, who affirmed, in great alarm, that the ghost was come, and that they heard the knocks and scratches. The gentlemen entered accordingly, with a determination to suffer no deception. The little girl, on being asked whether she saw the ghost, replied, "No; but she felt it on her back like a mouse." She was then required to put her hands out of bed, and they being held by some of the ladies, the spirit was summoned in the usual manner to answer, if it were in the room. The question was several times put with great solemnity; but the customary knock was not heard in reply in the walls, neither was there any scratching. The ghost was then asked to render itself visible, but it did not choose to grant the request. It was next solicited to give some token of its presence by a sound of any sort, or by touching the hand or cheek of any lady or gentleman in the room; but even with this request the ghost would not comply.

There was now a considerable pause, and one of the clergymen went downstairs to interrogate the father of the girl, who was waiting the result of the experiment. He positively denied that there was any deception, and even went so far as to say that he himself, upon one occasion, had seen and conversed with the awful ghost. This having been communicated to the company, it was unanimously resolved to give the ghost another trial; and the clergyman called out in a loud voice to the supposed spirit that the gentleman to whom it had promised to appear in the vault, was about to repair to that place, where he claimed the fulfilment of its promise. At one hour after midnight they all proceeded to the church, and the gentleman in question, with another, entered the vault alone, and took up their position alongside of the coffin of poor Fanny. The ghost was then summoned to appear, but it appeared not; it was summoned to knock, but it knocked not; it was summoned to scratch, but it scratched not; and the two retired from the vault, with the firm belief that the whole business was a deception practised by Parsons and his daughter. There were others, however, who did not wish to jump so hastily to a conclusion, and who suggested that they were, perhaps, trifling with this awful and supernatural being, which, being offended with them for their presumption, would not condescend to answer them. Again, after a serious consultation, it was agreed on all hands that, if the ghost answered anybody at all, it would answer Mr. Kent, the supposed murderer; and he was accordingly requested to go down into the vault. He went with several others, and summoned the ghost to answer whether he had indeed poisoned her. There being no answer, the question was put by Mr. Aldritch, who conjured it, if it were indeed a spirit, to end their doubts-make a sign of its presence, and point out the guilty person. There being still no answer for the space of half an hour, during which time all these boobies waited with the most praiseworthy perseverance, they returned to the house of Mr. Aldritch, and ordered the girl to get up and dress herself. She was strictly examined, but persisted in her statement that she used no deception, and that the ghost had really appeared to her.

So many persons had, by their openly expressed belief of the reality of the visitation, identified themselves with it, that Parsons and his family were far from being the only persons interested in the continuance of the delusion. The result of the experiment convinced most people; but these were not to be convinced by any evidence, however positive, and they, therefore, spread abroad the rumour, that the ghost had not appeared in the vault because Mr. Kent had taken care beforehand to have the coffin removed. That gentleman, whose position was a very painful one, immediately procured competent witnesses, in whose presence the vault was entered and the coffin of poor Fanny opened. Their deposition was then published; and Mr. Kent indicted Parsons and his wife, his daughter, Mary Frazer the servant, the Reverend Mr. Moor, and a tradesman, two of the most prominent patrons of the deception, for a conspiracy. The trial came on in the Court of King's Bench, on the 10th of July, before Lord Chief-Justice Mansfield, when, after an investigation which lasted twelve hours, the whole of the conspirators were found guilty. The Reverend Mr. Moor and his friend were severely reprimanded in open court, and recommended to make some pecuniary compensation to the prosecutor for the aspersions they had been instrumental in throwing upon his character. Parsons was sentenced to stand three times in the pillory, and to be imprisoned for two years: his wife to one year's, and his servant to six months' imprisonment in the Bridewell. A printer, who had been employed by them to publish an account of the proceedings for their profit, was also fined fifty pounds, and discharged.

The precise manner in which the deception was carried on has never been explained. The knocking in the wall appears to have been the work of Parsons' wife, while the scratching part of the business was left to the little girl. That any contrivance so clumsy could have deceived anybody, cannot fail to excite our wonder. But thus it always is. If two or three persons can only be found to take the lead in any absurdity, however great, there is sure to be plenty of imitators. Like sheep in a field, if one clears the stile, the rest will follow.

About ten years afterwards, London was again alarmed by the story of a haunted house. Stockwell, near Vauxhall, the scene of the antics of this new ghost, became almost as celebrated in the annals of superstition as Cock Lane. Mrs. Golding, an elderly lady, who resided alone with her servant, Anne Robinson, was sorely surprised on the evening of Twelfth-Day, 1772, to observe a most extraordinary commotion among her crockery. Cups and saucers rattled down the chimney -- pots and pans were whirled down stairs, or through the windows; and hams, cheeses, and loaves of bread disported themselves upon the floor as if the devil were in them. This, at least, was the conclusion that Mrs. Golding came to; and being greatly alarmed, she invited some of her neighbours to stay with her, and protect her from the evil one. Their presence, however, did not put a stop to the insurrection of china, and every room in the house was in a short time strewed with the fragments. The chairs and tables joined, at last, in the tumults, and things looked altogether so serious and inexplicable, that the neighbours, dreading that the house itself would next be seized with a fit of motion, and tumble about their ears, left poor Mrs. Golding to bear the brunt of it by herself. The ghost in this case was solemnly remonstrated with, and urged to take its departure; but the demolition continuing as great as before, Mrs. Golding finally made up her mind to quit the house altogether. She took refuge with Anne Robinson in the house of a neighbour; but his glass and crockery being immediately subjected to the same persecution, he was reluctantly compelled to give her notice to quit. The old lady thus forced back to her own house, endured the disturbance for some days longer, when suspecting that Anne Robinson was the cause of all the mischief, she dismissed her from her service. The extraordinary appearances immediately ceased, and were never afterwards renewed; a fact which is of itself sufficient to point out the real disturber. A long time afterwards, Anne Robinson confessed the whole matter to the Reverend Mr. Bray field. This gentleman confided the story to Mr. Hone, who has published an explanation of the mystery. Anne, it appears, was anxious to have a clear house, to carry on an intrigue with her lover, and resorted to this trick to effect her purpose. She placed the china on the shelves in such a manner that it fell on the slightest motion, and attached horse-hairs to other articles, so that she could jerk them down from an adjoining room without being perceived by any one. She was exceedingly dexterous at this sort of work, and would have proved a formidable rival to many a juggler by profession. A full explanation of the whole affair may be found in the "Every-day Book."

The latest instance of the popular panic occasioned by a house supposed to be haunted, occurred in Scotland, in the winter of the year 1838. On the 5th of December, the inmates of the farm-house of Baldarroch, in the district of Banchory, Aberdeenshire, were alarmed by observing a great number of sticks, pebble-stones, and clods of earth flying about their yard and premises. They endeavoured, but in vain, to discover who was the delinquent; and the shower of stones continuing for five days in succession, they came at last to the conclusion that the devil and his imps were alone the cause of it. The rumour soon spread over all that part of the country, and hundreds of persons came from far and near to witness the antics of the devils of Baldarroch. After the fifth day, the shower of clods and stones ceased on the outside of the premises, and the scene shifted to the interior. Spoons, knives, plates, mustard-pots, rolling-pins, and flat-irons appeared suddenly endued with the power of self-motion, and were whirled from room to room, and rattled down the chimneys in a manner which nobody could account for. The lid of a mustard-pot was put into a cupboard by the servant-girl in the presence of scores of people, and in a few minutes afterwards came bouncing down the chimney to the consternation of everybody. There was also a tremendous knocking at the doors and on the roof, and pieces of stick and pebble-stones rattled against the windows and broke them. The whole neighbourhood was a scene of alarm; and not only the vulgar, but persons of education, respectable farmers, within a circle of twenty miles, expressed their belief in the supernatural character of these events, and offered up devout prayers to be preserved from the machinations of the Evil One. The note of fear being once sounded, the visiters, as is generally the case in all tales of wonder, strove with each other who should witness the most extraordinary occurrences; and within a week, it was generally believed in the parishes of Banchory-Ternan, Drumoak, Durris, Kincardine-O'Neil, and all the circumjacent districts of Mearns and Aberdeenshire, that the devil had been seen in the act of hammering upon the house-top of Baldarroch. One old man asserted positively that, one night, after having been to see the strange gambols of the knives and mustard-pots, he met the phantom of a great black man, "who wheeled round his head with a whizzing noise, making a wind about his ears that almost blew his bonnet off," and that he was haunted by him in this manner for three miles. It was also affirmed and believed, that all horses and dogs that approached this enchanted ground, were immediately affected -- that a gentleman, slow of faith, had been cured of his incredulity by meeting the butter-churn jumping in at the door as he himself was going out -- that the roofs of houses had been torn off, and that several ricks in the corn-yard had danced a quadrille together, to the sound of the devil's bagpipes re-echoing from the mountain-tops. The women in the family of the persecuted farmer of Baldarroch also kept their tongues in perpetual motion; swelling with their strange stories the tide of popular wonder. The good wife herself, and all her servants, said that, whenever they went to bed, they were attacked with stones and other missiles, some of which came below the blankets and gently tapped their toes. One evening, a shoe suddenly darted across a garret where some labourers were sitting, and one of the men, who attempted to catch it, swore positively that it was so hot and heavy he was unable to hold it. It was also said that the bearbeater (a sort of mortar used to bruise barley in) -- an object of such weight that it requires several men to move it -- spontaneously left the barn and flew over the house-top, alighting at the feet of one of the servant maids, and hitting her, but without hurting her in the least, or even causing her any alarm; it being a fact well known to her, that all objects thus thrown about by the devil lost their specific gravity, and could harm nobody, even though they fell upon a person's head.

Among the persons drawn to Baldarroch by these occurrences were the heritor, the minister, and all the elders of the Kirk, under whose superintendence an investigation was immediately commenced. Their proceedings were not promulgated for some days; and, in the mean time, rumour continued to travel through all the Highlands, magnifying each mysterious incident the further it got from home. It was said, that when the goodwife put her potato-pot on the fire, each potato, as the water boiled, changed into a demon, and grinned horribly at her as she lifted the lid; that not only chairs and tables, but carrots and turnips, skipped along the floor in the merriest manner imaginable; that shoes and boots went through all the evolutions of the Highland fling without any visible wearers directing their motions; and that a piece of meat detached itself from the hook on which it hung in the pantry, and placed itself before the fire, whence all the efforts of the people of the house were unable to remove it until it was thoroughly roasted; and that it then flew up the chimney with a tremendous bang. At Baldarroch itself the belief was not quite so extravagant; but the farmer was so convinced that the devil and his imps were alone the cause of all the disturbance, that he travelled a distance of forty miles to an old conjuror, named Willie Foreman, to induce him, for a handsome fee, to remove the enchantment from his property. There were, of course, some sensible and educated people, who, after stripping the stories circulated of their exaggeration, attributed all the rest to one or other of two causes; first, that some gipsies, or strolling mendicants, hidden in the neighbouring plantation, were amusing themselves by working on the credulity of the country people; or, secondly, that the inmates of Baldarroch carried on this deception themselves, for some reason or other, which was not very clear to anybody. The last opinion gained but few believers, as the farmer and his family were much respected; and so many persons had, in the most open manner, expressed their belief in the supernatural agency, that they did not like to stultify themselves by confessing that they had been deceived.

At last, after a fortnight's continuance of the noises, the whole trick was discovered. The two servant lasses were strictly examined, and then committed to prison. It appeared that they were alone at the bottom of the whole affair, and that the extraordinary alarm and credulity of their master and mistress, in the first instance, and of the neighbours and country people afterwards, made their task comparatively easy. A little common dexterity was all they had used; and, being themselves unsuspected, they swelled the alarm by the wonderful stories they invented. It was they who loosened the bricks in the chimneys, and placed the dishes in such a manner on the shelves, that they fell on the slightest motion. In short, they played the same tricks as those used by the servant girl at Stockwell, with the same results, and for the same purpose -- the gratification of a love of mischief. They were no sooner secured in the county gaol than the noises ceased, and most people were convinced that human agency alone had worked all the wonder. Some few of the most devoutly superstitious still held out in their first belief, and refused to listen to any explanation.

These tales of haunted houses, especially those of the last and present century, however they may make us blush for popular folly, are yet gratifying in their results; for they show that society has made a vast improvement. Had Parsons and his wife, and the other contrivers of the Cock Lane deception, lived two hundred years earlier, they would not, perhaps, have found a greater number of dupes, but they would have been hanged as witches, instead of being imprisoned as vagabonds. The ingenious Anne Robinson and the sly lasses of Baldarroch would, doubtless, have met a similar fate. Thus it is pleasant to reflect, that though there may be as much folly and credulity in the world as ever, in one class of society, there is more wisdom and mercy in another than ever were known before. Lawgivers, by blotting from the statute-book the absurd or sanguinary enactments of their predecessors, have made one step towards teaching the people. It is to be hoped that the day is not far distant when lawgivers will teach the people by some more direct means, and prevent the recurrence of delusions like these, and many worse, which might be cited, by securing to every child born within their dominions an education in accordance with the advancing state of civilization. If ghosts and witches are not yet altogether exploded, it is the fault, not so much of the ignorant people, as of the law and the government that have neglected to enlighten them.

The Alchymists; or Searchers for the Philosopher's Stone and the Water of Life

"*Mercury (loquitur).* The mischief a secret any of them know, above the consuming of coals and drawing of usquebaugh! Howsoever they may pretend, under the specious names of Geber, Arnold, Lulli, or bombast of Hohenheim, to commit miracles in art, and treason against nature! As if the title of philosopher, that creature of glory, were to be fetched out of a furnace! I am their crude, and their sublimate, their precipitate, and their unctions; their male and their female, sometimes their hermaphrodite -- what they list to style me! They will calcine you a grave matron, as it might be a mother of the maids, and spring up a young virgin out of her ashes, as fresh as a phoenix; lay you an old courtier on the coals, like a sausage or a bloat-herring, and, after they have broiled him enough, blow a soul into him, with a pair of bellows! See! they begin to muster again, and draw their forces out against me!   The   genius   of   the   place   defend   me!"
-- Ben Jonson's Masque "Mercury vindicated from the Alchymists."

Dissatisfaction with his lot seems to be the characteristic of man in all ages and climates. So far, however, from being an evil, as at first might be supposed, it has been the great civiliser of our race; and has tended, more than anything else, to raise us above the condition of the brutes. But the same discontent which has been the source of all improvement, has been the parent of no small progeny of follies and absurdities; to trace these latter is the object of the present volume. Vast as the subject appears, it is easily reducible within such limits as will make it comprehensive without being wearisome, and render its study both instructive and amusing.

Three causes especially have excited our discontent; and, by impelling us to seek for remedies for the irremediable, have bewildered us in a maze of madness and error. These are death, toil, and ignorance of the future -- the doom of man upon this sphere, and for which he shows his antipathy by his love of life, his longing for abundance, and his craving curiosity to pierce the secrets of the days to come. The first has led many to imagine that they might find means to avoid death, or, failing in this, that they might, nevertheless, so prolong existence as to reckon it by centuries instead of units. From this sprang the search, so long continued and still pursued, for the elixir vitae, or water of life, which has led thousands to pretend to it and millions to believe in it. From the second sprang the absurd search for the philosopher's stone, which was to create plenty by changing all metals into gold; and from the third, the false sciences of astrology, divination, and their divisions of necromancy, chiromancy, augury, with all their train of signs, portents, and omens.

In tracing the career of the erring philosophers, or the wilful cheats, who have encouraged or preyed upon the credulity of mankind, it will simplify and elucidate the subject, if we divide it into three classes: -- the first comprising alchymists, or those in general who have devoted themselves to the discovering of the philosopher's stone and the water of life; the second comprising astrologers, necromancers, sorcerers, geomancers, and all those who pretended to discover futurity; and the third consisting of the dealers in charms, amulets, philters, universal-panacea mongers, touchers for the evil, seventh sons of a seventh son, sympathetic powder compounders, homeopathists, animal magnetizers, and all the motley tribe of quacks, empirics, and charlatans.

But, in narrating the career of such men, it will be found that many of them united several or all of the functions just mentioned; that the alchymist was a fortune-teller, or a necromancer -- that he pretended to cure all maladies by touch or charm, and to work miracles of every kind. In the dark and early ages of European history, this is more especially the case. Even as we advance to more recent periods, we shall find great difficulty in separating the characters. The alchymist seldom confined himself strictly to his pretended science -- the sorcerer and necromancer to theirs, or the medical charlatan to his. Beginning with alchymy, some confusion of these classes is unavoidable; but the ground will clear for us as we advance.

Let us not, in the pride of our superior knowledge, turn with contempt from the follies of our predecessors. The study of the errors into which great minds have fallen in the pursuit of truth can never be uninstructive. As the man looks back to the days of his childhood and his youth, and recalls to his mind the strange notions and false opinions that swayed his actions at that time, that he may wonder at them, so should society, for its edification, look back to the opinions which governed the ages fled. He is but a superficial thinker who would despise and refuse to hear of them merely because they are absurd. No man is so wise but that he may learn some wisdom from his past errors, either of thought or action, and no society has made such advances as to be capable of no improvement from the retrospect of its past folly and credulity. And not only is such a study instructive: he who reads for amusement only, will find no chapter in the annals of the human mind more amusing than this. It opens out the whole realm of fiction -- the wild, the fantastic, and the wonderful, and all the immense variety of things "that are not, and cannot be; but that have been imagined and believed."

For more than a thousand years the art of alchymy captivated many noble spirits, and was believed in by millions. Its origin is involved in obscurity. Some of its devotees have claimed for it an antiquity coeval with the creation of man himself; others, again, would trace it no further back than the time of Noah. Vincent de Beauvais argues, indeed, that all the antediluvians must have possessed a knowledge of alchymy; and particularly cites Noah as having been acquainted with the elixir vitae, or he could not have lived to so prodigious an age, and have begotten children when upwards of five hundred. Lenglet du Fresnoy, in his "History of the Hermetic Philosophy," says, "Most of them pretended that Shem, or Chem, the son of Noah, was an adept in the art, and thought it highly probable that the words chemistry and alchymy were both derived from his name." Others say, the art was derived from the Egyptians, amongst whom it was first founded by Hermes Trismegistus. Moses, who is looked upon as a first-rate alchymist, gained his knowledge in Egypt; but he kept it all to himself, and would not instruct the children of Israel in its mysteries. All the writers upon alchymy triumphantly cite the story of the golden calf, in the 32nd chapter of Exodus, to prove that this great lawgiver was an adept, and could make or unmake gold at his pleasure. It is recorded, that Moses was so wroth with the Israelites for their idolatry, "that he took the calf which they had made, and burned it in the fire, and ground it to powder, and strewed it upon the water, and made the children of Israel drink of it." This, say the alchymists, he never could have done, had he not been in possession of the philosopher's stone; by no other means could he have made the powder of gold float upon the water. But we must leave this knotty point for the consideration of the adepts in the art, if any such there be, and come to more modern periods of its history. The Jesuit, Father Martini, in his "Historia Sinica," says, it was practised by the Chinese two thousand five hundred years before the birth of Christ; but his assertion, being unsupported, is worth nothing. It would appear, however, that pretenders to the art of making gold and silver existed in Rome in the first centuries after the Christian era, and that, when discovered, they were liable to punishment as knaves and impostors. At Constantinople, in the fourth century, the transmutation of metals was very generally believed in, and many of the Greek ecclesiastics wrote treatises upon the subject. Their names are preserved, and some notice of their works given, in the third volume of Lenglet du Fresnoy's "History of the Hermetic Philosophy." Their notion appears to have been, that all metals were composed of two substances; the one, metallic earth; and the other, a red inflammable matter, which they called sulphur. The pure union of these substances formed gold; but other metals were mixed with and contaminated by various foreign ingredients. The object of the philosopher's stone was to dissolve or neutralize all these ingredients, by which iron, lead, copper, and all metals would be transmuted into the original gold. Many learned and clever men wasted their time, their health, and their energies, in this vain pursuit; but for several centuries it took no great hold upon the imagination of the people. The history of the delusion appears, in a manner, lost from this time till the eighth century, when it appeared amongst the Arabians. From this period it becomes easier to trace its progress. A master then appeared, who was long looked upon as the father of the science, and whose name is indissolubly connected with it.

Geber

Of this philosopher, who devoted his life to the study of alchymy, but few particulars are known. He is thought to have lived in the year 730. His true name was Abou Moussah Djafar, to which was added Al Soft, or "The Wise," and he was born at Hauran, in Mesopotamia. ["Biographie Universelle."] Some have thought he was a Greek, others a Spaniard, and others, a prince of Hindostan: but, of all the mistakes which have been made respecting him, the most ludicrous was that made by the French translator of Sprenger's "History of Medicine," who thought, from the sound of his name, that he was a German, and rendered it as the "Donnateur," or Giver. No details of his life are known; but it is asserted, that he wrote more than five hundred works upon the philosopher's stone and the water of life. He was a great enthusiast in his art, and compared the incredulous to little children shut up in a narrow room, without windows or aperture, who, because they saw nothing beyond, denied the existence of the great globe itself. He thought that a preparation of gold would cure all maladies, not only in man, but in the inferior animals and plants. He also imagined that all the metals laboured under disease, with the exception of gold, which was the only one in perfect health. He affirmed, that the secret of the philosopher's stone had been more than once discovered; but that the ancient and wise men who had hit upon it, would never, by word or writing, communicate it to men, because of their unworthiness and incredulity. [His "sum of perfection," or instructions to students to aid them in the laborious search for the stone and elixir, has been translated into most of the languages of Europe. An English translation, by a great enthusiast in alchymy, one Richard Russell, was published in London in 1686. The preface is dated eight years previously, from the house of the alchymist, "at the Star, in Newmarket, in Wapping, near the Dock." His design in undertaking the translation was, as he informs us, to expose the false pretences of the many ignorant pretenders to the science who abounded in his day.] But the life of Geber, though spent in the pursuit of this vain chimera, was not altogether useless. He stumbled upon discoveries which he did not seek, and science is indebted to him for the first mention of corrosive sublimate, the red oxide of mercury, nitric acid, and the nitrate of silver. [Article, Geber, "Biographie Universelle."]

For more than two hundred years after the death of Geber, the Arabian philosophers devoted themselves to the study of alchymy, joining with it that of astrology. Of these the most celebrated was

Alfarabi

Alfarabi flourished at the commencement of the tenth century, and enjoyed the reputation of being one of the most learned men of his age. He spent his life in travelling from country to country, that he might gather the opinions of philosophers upon the great secrets of nature. No danger dismayed him; no toil wearied him of the pursuit. Many sovereigns endeavoured to retain him at their courts; but he refused to rest until he had discovered the great object of his life -- the art of preserving it for centuries, and of making gold as much as he needed. This wandering mode of life at last proved fatal to him. He had been on a visit to Mecca, not so much for religious as for philosophical purposes, when, returning through Syria, he stopped at the court of the Sultan Seifeddoulet, who was renowned as the patron of learning. He presented himself in his travelling attire, in the presence of that monarch and his courtiers; and, without invitation, coolly sat himself down upon the sofa, beside the Prince. The courtiers and wise men were indignant; and the Sultan, who did not know the intruder, was at first inclined to follow their example. He turned to one of his officers, and ordered him to eject the presumptuous stranger from the room; but Alfarabi, without moving, dared them to lay hands upon him; and, turning himself calmly to the prince, remarked, that he did not know who was his guest, or he would treat him with honour, not with violence. The Sultan, instead of being still further incensed, as many potentates would have been, admired his coolness; and, requesting him to sit still closer to him on the sofa, entered into a long conversation with him upon science and divine philosophy. All the court were charmed with the stranger. Questions for discussion were propounded, on all of which he showed superior knowledge. He convinced every one that ventured to dispute with him; and spoke so eloquently upon the science of alchymy, that he was at once recognised as only second to the great Geber himself. One of the doctors present inquired whether a man who knew so many sciences was acquainted with music? Alfarabi made no reply, but merely requested that a lute should be brought him. The lute was brought; and he played such ravishing and tender melodies, that all the court were melted into tears. He then changed his theme, and played airs so sprightly, that he set the grave philosophers, Sultan and all, dancing as fast as their legs could carry them. He then sobered them again by a mournful strain, and made them sob and sigh as if broken-hearted. The Sultan, highly delighted with his powers, entreated him to stay, offering him every inducement that wealth, power, and dignity could supply; but the alchymist resolutely refused, it being decreed, he said, that he should never repose till he had discovered the philosopher's stone. He set out accordingly the same evening, and was murdered by some thieves in the deserts of Syria. His biographers give no further particulars of his life beyond mentioning, that he wrote several valuable treatises on his art, all of which, however, have been lost. His death happened in the year 954.

Avicenna

Avicenna, whose real name was Ebn Cinna, another great alchymist, was born at Bokhara, in 980. His reputation as a physician and a man skilled in all sciences was so great, that the Sultan Magdal Douleth resolved to try his powers in the great science of government. He was accordingly made Grand Vizier of that Prince, and ruled the state with some advantage: but, in a science still more difficult, he failed completely. He could not rule his own passions, but gave himself up to wine and women, and led a life of shameless debauchery. Amid the multifarious pursuits of business and pleasure, he nevertheless found time to write seven treatises upon the philosopher's stone, which were for many ages looked upon as of great value by pretenders to the art. It is rare that an eminent physician, as Avicenna appears to have been, abandons himself to sensual gratification; but so completely did he become enthralled in the course of a few years, that he was dismissed from his high office, and died shortly afterwards, of premature old age and a complication of maladies, brought on by debauchery. His death took place in the year 1036. After his time, few philosophers of any note in Arabia are heard of as devoting themselves to the study of alchymy; but it began shortly afterwards to attract greater attention in Europe. Learned men in France, England, Spain, and Italy expressed their belief in the science, and many devoted their whole energies to it. In the twelfth and thirteenth centuries especially, it was extensively pursued, and some of the brightest names of that age are connected with it. Among the most eminent of them are

Albertus Magnus and Thomas Aquina

The first of these philosophers was born in the year 1193, of a noble family at Lawingen, in the duchy of Neuburg, on the Danube. For the first thirty years of his life, he appeared remarkably dull and stupid, and it was feared by every one that no good could come of him. He entered a Dominican monastery at an early age; but made so little progress in his studies, that he was more than once upon the point of abandoning them in despair; but he was endowed with extraordinary perseverance. As he advanced to middle age, his mind expanded, and he learned whatever he applied himself to with extreme facility. So remarkable a change was not, in that age, to be accounted for but by a miracle. It was asserted and believed that the Holy Virgin, touched with his great desire to become learned and famous, took pity upon his incapacity, and appeared to him in the cloister where he sat, almost despairing, and asked him whether he wished to excel in philosophy or divinity. He chose philosophy, to the chagrin of the Virgin, who reproached him in mild and sorrowful accents that he had not made a better choice. She, however, granted his request that he should become the most excellent philosopher of the age; but set this drawback to his pleasure, that he should relapse, when at the height of his fame, into his former incapacity and stupidity. Albertus never took the trouble to contradict the story, but prosecuted his studies with such unremitting zeal that his reputation speedily spread over all Europe. In the year 1244, the celebrated Thomas Aquinas placed himself under his tuition. Many extraordinary stories are told of the master and his pupil. While they paid all due attention to other branches of science, they never neglected the pursuit of the philosopher's stone and the elixir vitae. Although they discovered neither, it was believed that Albert had seized some portion of the secret of life, and found means to animate a brazen statue, upon the formation of which, under proper conjunctions of the planets, he had been occupied many years of his life. He and Thomas Aquinas completed it together, endowed it with the faculty of speech, and made it perform the functions of a domestic servant. In this capacity it was exceedingly useful; but, through some defect in the machinery, it chattered much more than was agreeable to either philosopher. Various remedies were tried to cure it of its garrulity, but in vain; and one day Thomas Aquinas was so enraged at the noise it made, when he was in the midst of a mathematical problem, that he seized a ponderous hammer and smashed it to pieces. [Naude, "Apologie des Grands Hommes accuses de Magie ;" chap. xviii.] He was sorry afterwards for what he had done, and was reproved by his master for giving way to his anger, so unbecoming in a philosopher. They made no attempt to re-animate the statue.

Such stories as these show the spirit of the age. Every great man who attempted to study the secrets of nature was thought a magician; and it is not to be wondered at that, when philosophers themselves pretended to discover an elixir for conferring immortality, or a red stone which was to create boundless wealth, that popular opinion should have enhanced upon their pretensions, and have endowed them with powers still more miraculous. It was believed of Albertus Magnus that he could even change the course of the seasons; a feat which the many thought less difficult than the discovery of the grand elixir. Albertus was desirous of obtaining a piece of ground on which to build a monastery, in the neighbourhood of Cologne. The ground belonged to William, Count of Holland and King of the Romans, who, for some reason or other, did not wish to part with it. Albertus is reported to have gained it by the following extraordinary method: -- He invited the Prince, as he was passing through Cologne, to a magnificent entertainment prepared for him and all his court. The Prince accepted it, and repaired with a lordly retinue to the residence of the sage. It was in the midst of winter; the Rhine was frozen over, and the cold was so bitter that the knights could not sit on horseback without running the risk of losing their toes by the frost. Great, therefore, was their surprise, on arriving at Albert's house, to find that the repast was spread in his garden, in which the snow had drifted to the depth of several feet. The Earl,in high dudgeon, remounted his steed; but Albert at last prevailed upon him to take his seat at the table. He had no sooner done so, than the dark clouds rolled away from the sky -- a warm sun shone forth -- the cold north wind veered suddenly round, and blew a mild breeze from the south -- the snows melted away -- the ice was unbound upon the streams, and the trees put forth their green leaves and their fruit -- flowers sprang up beneath their feet, while larks, nightingales, blackbirds, cuckoos, thrushes, and every sweet song-bird, sang hymns from every tree. The Earl and his attendants wondered greatly; but they ate their dinner, and in recompence for it, Albert got his piece of ground to build a convent on. He had not, however, shown them all his power. Immediately that the repast was over, he gave the word, and dark clouds obscured the sun -- the snow fell in large flakes -- the singing-birds fell dead -- the leaves dropped from the trees, and the winds blew so cold, and howled so mournfully, that the guests wrapped themselves up in their thick cloaks, and retreated into the house to warm themselves at the blazing fire in Albert's kitchen. [Lenglet, "Histoire de la Philosophie Hermetique." See also, Godwin's "Lives of the Necromancers."]

Thomas Aquinas also could work wonders as well as his master. It is related of him, that he lodged in a street at Cologne, where he was much annoyed by the incessant clatter made by the horses' hoofs, as they were led through it daily to exercise by their grooms. He had entreated the latter to select some other spot where they might not disturb a philosopher, but the grooms turned a deaf ear to all his solicitations. In this emergency he had recourse to the aid of magic. He constructed a small horse of bronze, upon which he inscribed certain cabalistic characters, and buried it at midnight in the midst of the highway. The next morning, a troop of grooms came riding along as usual; but the horses, as they arrived at the spot where the magic horse was buried, reared and plunged violently -- their nostrils distended with terror -- their manes grew erect, and the perspiration ran down their sides in streams. In vain the riders applied the spur -- in vain they coaxed or threatened, the animals would not pass the spot. On the following day, their success was no better. They were at length compelled to seek another spot for their exercise, and Thomas Aquinas was left in peace. [Naude, "Apologie des Grands Hommes accuses de Magie;" chap. xvii.]

Albertus Magnus was made Bishop of Ratisbon in 1259; but he occupied the See only four years, when he resigned, on the ground that its duties occupied too much of the time which he was anxious to devote to philosophy. He died in Cologne in 1280, at the advanced age of eighty-seven. The Dominican writers deny that he ever sought the philosopher's stone, but his treatise upon minerals sufficiently proves that he did.

Artephius

Artephius, a name noted in the annals of alchymy, was born in the early part of the twelfth century. He wrote two famous treatises; the one upon the philosopher's stone, and the other on the art of prolonging human life. In the latter he vaunts his great qualifications for instructing mankind on such a matter, as he was at that time in the thousand and twenty-fifth year of his age! He had many disciples who believed in his extreme age, and who attempted to prove that he was Apollonius of Tyana, who lived soon after the advent of Jesus Christ, and the particulars of whose life and pretended miracles have been so fully described by Philostratus. He took good care never to contradict a story, which so much increased the power he was desirous of wielding over his fellow-mortals. On all convenient occasions, he boasted of it; and having an excellent memory, a fertile imagination, and a thorough knowledge of all existing history, he was never at a loss for an answer when questioned as to the personal appearance, the manners, or the character of the great men of antiquity. He also pretended to have found the philosopher's stone; and said that, in search of it, he had descended to hell, and seen the devil sitting on a throne of gold, with a legion of imps and fiends around him. His works on alchymy have been translated into French, and were published in Paris in 1609 or 1610.

Alain de Lisle

Contemporary with Albertus Magnus was Alain de Lisle, of Flanders, who was named, from his great learning, the "universal doctor." He was thought to possess a knowledge of all the sciences, and, like Artephius, to have discovered the elixir vitae. He became one of the friars of the abbey of Citeaux, and died in 1298, aged about one hundred and ten years. It was said of him, that he was at the point of death when in his fiftieth year; but that the fortunate discovery of the elixir enabled him to add sixty years to his existence. He wrote a commentary on the prophecies of Merlin.

Arnold de Villeneuve

This philosopher has left a much greater reputation. He was born in the year 1245, and studied medicine with great success in the University of Paris. He afterwards travelled for twenty years in Italy and Germany, where he made acquaintance with Pietro d'Apone; a man of a character akin to his own, and addicted to the same pursuits. As a physician, he was thought, in his own lifetime, to be the most able the world had ever seen. Like all the learned men of that day, he dabbled in astrology and alchymy, and was thought to have made immense quantities of gold from lead and copper. When Pietro d'Apone was arrested in Italy, and brought to trial as a sorcerer, a similar accusation was made against Arnold; but he managed to leave the country in time and escape the fate of his unfortunate friend. He lost some credit by predicting the end of the world, but afterwards regained it. The time of his death is not exactly known; but it must have been prior to the year 1311, when Pope Clement V. wrote a circular letter to all the clergy of Europe who lived under his obedience, praying them to use their utmost efforts to discover the famous treatise of Arnold on "The Practice of Medicine." The author had promised, during his lifetime, to make a present of the work to the Holy See, but died without fulfilling it.

In a very curious work by Monsieur Longeville Harcouet, entitled "The History of the Persons who have lived several centuries, and then grown young again," there is a receipt, said to have been given by Arnold de Villeneuve, by means of which any one might prolong his life for a few hundred years or so. In the first place, say Arnold and Monsieur Harcouet, "the person intending so to prolong his life must rub himself well, two or three times a week, with the juice or marrow of cassia (moelle de la casse). Every night, upon going to bed, he must put upon his heart a plaster, composed of a certain quantity of Oriental saffron, red rose-leaves, sandal-wood, aloes, and amber, liquified in oil of roses and the best white wax. In the morning, he must take it off, and enclose it carefully in a leaden box till the next night, when it must be again applied. If he be of a sanguine temperament, he shall take sixteen chickens -- if phlegmatic, twenty-five -- and if melancholy, thirty, which he shall put into a yard where the air and the water are pure. Upon these he is to feed, eating one a day; but previously the chickens are to be fattened by a peculiar method, which will impregnate their flesh with the qualities that are to produce longevity in the eater. Being deprived of all other nourishment till they are almost dying of hunger, they are to be fed upon broth made of serpents and vinegar, which broth is to be thickened with wheat and bran." Various ceremonies are to be performed in the cooking of this mess, which those may see in the book of M. Harcouet, who are at all interested in the matter; and the chickens are to be fed upon it for two months. They are then fit for table, and are to be washed down with moderate quantities of good white wine or claret. This regimen is to be followed regularly every seven years, and any one may live to be as old as Methuselah! It is right to state, that M. Harcouet has but little authority for attributing this precious composition to Arnold of Villeneuve. It is not to be found in the collected works of that philosopher; but was first brought to light by a M. Poirier, at the commencement of the sixteenth century, who asserted that he had discovered it in MS. in the undoubted writing of Arnold.

Pietro d'Apone

This unlucky sage was born at Apone, near Padua, in the year 1250. Like his friend Arnold de Villeneuve, he was an eminent physician, and a pretender to the arts of astrology and alchymy. He practised for many years in Paris, and made great wealth by killing and curing, and telling fortunes. In an evil day for him, he returned to his own country, with the reputation of being a magician of the first order. It was universally believed that he had drawn seven evil spirits from the infernal regions, whom he kept enclosed in seven crystal vases, until he required their services, when he sent them forth to the ends of the earth to execute his pleasure. One spirit excelled in philosophy; a second, in alchymy; a third, in astrology; a fourth, in physic; a fifth, in poetry; a sixth, in music; and the seventh, in painting: and whenever Pietro wished for information or instruction in any of these arts, he had only to go to his crystal vase, and liberate the presiding spirit. Immediately, all the secrets of the art were revealed to him; and he might, if it pleased him, excel Homer in poetry, Apelles in painting, or Pythagoras himself in philosophy. Although he could make gold out of brass, it was said of him, that he was very sparing of his powers in that respect, and kept himself constantly supplied with money by other and less creditable means. Whenever he disbursed gold, he muttered a certain charm, known only to himself; and next morning the gold was safe again in his own possession. The trader to whom he gave it, might lock it in his strong box, and have it guarded by a troop of soldiers; but the charmed metal flew back to its old master. Even if it were buried in the earth, or thrown into the sea, the dawn of the next morning would behold it in the pockets of Pietro. Few people, in consequence, liked to have dealings with such a personage, especially for gold. Some, bolder than the rest, thought that his power did not extend over silver; but, when they made the experiment, they found themselves mistaken. Bolts and bars could not restrain it, and it sometimes became invisible in their very hands, and was whisked through the air to the purse of the magician. He necessarily acquired a very bad character; and, having given utterance to some sentiments regarding religion which were the very reverse of orthodox, he was summoned before the tribunals of the Inquisition to answer for his crimes as a heretic and a sorcerer. He loudly protested his innocence, even upon the rack, where he suffered more torture than nature could support. He died in prison ere his trial was concluded, but was afterwards found guilty. His bones were ordered to be dug up, and publicly burned. He was also burned in effigy in the streets of Padua.

Raymond Lulli

While Arnold de Villeneuve and Pietro d'Apone flourished in France and Italy, a more celebrated adept than either appeared in Spain. This was Raymond Lulli, a name which stands in the first rank among the alchymists. Unlike many of his predecessors, he made no pretensions to astrology or necromancy; but, taking Geber for his model, studied intently the nature and composition of metals, without reference to charms, incantations, or any foolish ceremonies. It was not, however, till late in life that he commenced his study of the art. His early and middle age were spent in a different manner, and his whole history is romantic in the extreme. He was born of an illustrious family, in Majorca, in the year 1235. When that island was taken from the Saracens by James I, King of Aragon, in 1230, the father of Raymond, who was originally of Catalonia, settled there, and received a considerable appointment from the Crown. Raymond married at an early age; and, being fond of pleasure, he left the solitudes of his native isle, and passed over with his bride into Spain. He was made Grand Seneschal at the court of King James, and led a gay life for several years. Faithless to his wife, he was always in the pursuit of some new beauty, till his heart was fixed at last by the lovely, but unkind Ambrosia de Castello. This lady, like her admirer, was married; but, unlike him, was faithful to her vows, and treated all his solicitations with disdain. Raymond was so enamoured, that repulse only increased his flame; he lingered all night under her windows, wrote passionate verses in her praise, neglected his affairs, and made himself the butt of all the courtiers. One day, while watching under her lattice, he by chance caught sight of her bosom, as her neckerchief was blown aside by the wind. The fit of inspiration came over him, and he sat down and composed some tender stanzas upon the subject, and sent them to the lady. The fair Ambrosia had never before condescended to answer his letters; but she replied to this. She told him, that she could never listen to his suit; that it was unbecoming in a wise man to fix his thoughts, as he had done, on any other than his God; and entreated him to devote himself to a religious life, and conquer the unworthy passion which he had suffered to consume him. She, however, offered, if he wished it, to show him the fair bosom which had so captivated him. Raymond was delighted. He thought the latter part of this epistle but ill corresponded with the former, and that Ambrosia, in spite of the good advice she gave him, had, at last, relented, and would make him as happy as he desired. He followed her about from place to place, entreating her to fulfil her promise: but still Ambrosia was cold, and implored him with tears to importune her no longer; for that she never could be his, and never would, if she were free to-morrow. "What means your letter, then?" said the despairing lover. "I will show you!" replied Ambrosia, who immediately uncovered her bosom, and exposed to the eyes of her horror-stricken admirer, a large cancer, which had extended to both breasts. She saw that he was shocked; and, extending her hand to him, she prayed him once more to lead a religious life, and set his heart upon the Creator, and not upon the creature. He went home an altered man. He threw up, on the morrow, his valuable appointment at the court, separated from his wife, and took a farewell of his children, after dividing one-half of his ample fortune among them. The other half he shared among the poor. He then threw himself at the foot of a crucifix, and devoted himself to the service of God, vowing, as the most acceptable atonement for his errors, that he would employ the remainder of his days in the task of converting the Mussulmans to the Christian religion. In his dreams he saw Jesus Christ, who said to him, "Raymond! Raymond! follow me!" The vision was three times repeated, and Raymond was convinced that it was an intimation direct from Heaven. Having put his affairs in order, he set out on a pilgrimage to the shrine of St. James of Compostello, and afterwards lived for ten years in solitude amid the mountains of Aranda. Here he learned the Arabic, to qualify himself for his mission of converting the Mahometans. He also studied various sciences, as taught in the works of the learned men of the East, and first made acquaintance with the writings of Geber, which were destined to exercise so much influence over his future life.

At the end of this probation, and when he had entered his fortieth year, he emerged from his solitude into more active life. With some remains of his fortune, which had accumulated during his retirement, he founded a college for the study of Arabic, which was approved of by the Pope, with many commendations upon his zeal and piety. At this time he narrowly escaped assassination from an Arabian youth whom he had taken into his service. Raymond had prayed to God, in some of his accesses of fanaticism, that he might suffer martyrdom in his holy cause. His servant had overheard him; and, being as great a fanatic as his master, he resolved to gratify his wish, and punish him, at the same time, for the curses which he incessantly launched against Mahomet and all who believed in him, by stabbing him to the heart. He, therefore, aimed a blow at his master, as he sat one day at table; but the instinct of self-preservation being stronger than the desire of martyrdom, Raymond grappled with his antagonist, and overthrew him. He scorned to take his life himself; but handed him over to the authorities of the town, by whom he was afterwards found dead in his prison.

After this adventure Raymond travelled to Paris, where he resided for some time, and made the acquaintance of Arnold de Villeneuve. From him he probably received some encouragement to search for the philosopher's stone, as he began from that time forth to devote less of his attention to religious matters, and more to the study of alchymy. Still he never lost sight of the great object for which he lived -- the conversion of the Mahometans -- and proceeded to Rome, to communicate personally with Pope John XXI, on the best measures to be adopted for that end. The Pope gave him encouragement in words, but failed to associate any other persons with him in the enterprise which he meditated. Raymond, therefore, set out for Tunis alone, and was kindly received by many Arabian philosophers, who had heard of his fame as a professor of alchymy. If he had stuck to alchymy while in their country, it would have been well for him; but he began cursing Mahomet, and got himself into trouble. While preaching

303

the doctrines of Christianity in the great bazaar of Tunis, he was arrested and thrown into prison. He was shortly afterwards brought to trial, and sentenced to death. Some of his philosophic friends interceded hard for him, and he was pardoned, upon condition that he left Africa immediately, and never again set foot in it. If he was found there again, no matter what his object might be, or whatever length of time might intervene, his original sentence would be carried into execution. Raymond was not at all solicitous of martyrdom when it came to the point, whatever he might have been when there was no danger, and he gladly accepted his life upon these conditions, and left Tunis with the intention of proceeding to Rome. He afterwards changed his plan, and established himself at Milan, where, for a length of time, he practised alchymy, and some say astrology, with great success.

Most writers who believed in the secrets of alchymy, and who have noticed the life of Raymond Lulli, assert, that while in Milan, he received letters from Edward King of England, inviting him to settle in his states. They add, that Lulli gladly accepted the invitation, and had apartments assigned for his use in the Tower of London, where he refined much gold; superintended the coinage of "rose-nobles;" and made gold out of iron, quicksilver, lead, and pewter, to the amount of six millions. The writers in the "Biographie Universelle," an excellent authority in general, deny that Raymond was ever in England, and say, that in all these stories of his wondrous powers as an alchymist, he has been mistaken for another Raymond, a Jew, of Tarragona. Naude, in his "Apologie," says, simply, "that six millions were given by Raymond Lulli to King Edward, to make war against the Turks and other infidels:" not that he transmuted so much metal into gold; but, as he afterwards adds, that he advised Edward to lay a tax upon wool, which produced that amount. To show that Raymond went to England, his admirers quote a work attributed to him, "De Transmutatione Animae Metallorum," in which he expressly says, that he was in England at the intercession of the King. [Vidimus omnia ista dum ad Angliam transiimus, propter intercessionem Domini Regis Edoardi illustrissimi.] The hermetic writers are not agreed whether it was Edward I, or Edward II, who invited him over; but, by fixing the date of his journey in 1312, they make it appear that it was Edward II. Edmond Dickenson, in his work on the "Quintessences of the Philosophers," says, that Raymond worked in Westminster Abbey, where, a long time after his departure, there was found in the cell which he had occupied, a great quantity of golden dust, of which the architects made a great profit. In the biographical sketch of John Cremer, Abbot of Westminster, given by Lenglet, it is said, that it was chiefly through his instrumentality that Raymond came to England. Cremer had been himself for thirty years occupied in the vain search for the philosopher's stone, when he accidentally met Raymond in Italy, and endeavoured to induce him to communicate his grand secret. Raymond told him that he must find it for himself, as all great alchymists had done before him. Cremer, on his return to England, spoke to King Edward in high terms of the wonderful attainments of the philosopher, and a letter of invitation was forthwith sent him. Robert Constantinus, in the "Nomenclatore Scriptorum Medicorum," published in 1515, says, that after a great deal of research, be found that Raymond Lulli resided for some time in London, and that he actually made gold, by means of the philosopher's stone, in the Tower; that he had seen the golden pieces of his coinage, which were still named in England the nobles of Raymond, or rose-nobles. Lulli himself appears to have boasted that he made gold; for, in his well-known "Testamentum," he states, that he converted no less than fifty thousand pounds weight of quicksilver, lead, and pewter into that metal. [Converti una vice in aurum ad L millia pondo argenti vivi, plumbi, et stanni. -- Lullii Testamentum.] It seems highly probable that the English King, believing in the extraordinary powers of the alchymist, invited him to England to make test of them, and that he was employed in refining gold and in coining. Camden, who is not credulous in matters like these, affords his countenance to the story of his coinage of nobles; and there is nothing at all wonderful in the fact of a man famous for his knowledge of metals being employed in such a capacity. Raymond was, at this time, an old man, in his seventy-seventh year, and somewhat in his dotage. He was willing enough to have it believed that he had discovered the grand secret, and supported the rumour rather than contradicted it. He did not long remain in England; but returned to Rome, to carry out the projects which were nearer to his heart than the profession of alchymy. He had proposed them to several successive Popes with little or no success. The first was a plan for the introduction of the

304

Oriental languages into all the monasteries of Europe; the second, for the reduction into one of all the military orders, that, being united, they might move more efficaciously against the Saracens; and, the third, that the Sovereign Pontiff should forbid the works of Averroes to be read in the schools, as being more favourable to Mahometanism than to Christianity. The Pope did not receive the old man with much cordiality; and, after remaining for about two years in Rome, he proceeded once more to Africa, alone and unprotected, to preach the Gospel of Jesus. He landed at Bona in 1314; and so irritated the Mahometans by cursing their prophet, that they stoned him, and left him for dead on the sea-shore. He was found some hours afterwards by a party of Genoese merchants, who conveyed him on board their vessel, and sailed towards Majorca. The unfortunate man still breathed, but could not articulate. He lingered in this state for some days, and expired just as the vessel arrived within sight of his native shores. His body was conveyed with great pomp to the church of St. Eulalia, at Palma, where a public funeral was instituted in his honour. Miracles were afterwards said to have been worked at his tomb.

Thus ended the career of Raymond Lulli, one of the most extraordinary men of his age; and, with the exception of his last boast about the six millions of gold, the least inclined to quackery of any of the professors of alchymy. His writings were very numerous, and include nearly five hundred volumes, upon grammar, rhetoric, morals, theology, politics, civil and canon law, physics, metaphysics, astronomy, medicine, and chemistry.

Roger Bacon

The powerful delusion of alchymy seized upon a mind still greater than that of Raymond Lulli. Roger Bacon firmly believed in the philosopher's stone, and spent much of his time in search of it. His example helped to render all the learned men of the time more convinced of its practicability, and more eager in the pursuit. He was born at Ilchester, in the county of Somerset, in the year 1214. He studied for some time in the university of Oxford, and afterwards in that of Paris, in which he received the degree of doctor of divinity. Returning to England in 1240, he became a monk of the order of St. Francis. He was by far the most learned man of his age; and his acquirements were so much above the comprehension of his contemporaries, that they could only account for them by supposing that he was indebted for them to the devil. Voltaire has not inaptly designated him "De l'or encroute de toutes les ordures de son siecle;" but the crust of superstition that enveloped his powerful mind, though it may have dimmed, could not obscure the brightness of his genius. To him, and apparently to him only, among all the inquiring spirits of the time, were known the properties of the concave and convex lens. He also invented the magic-lantern; that pretty plaything of modern days, which acquired for him a reputation that embittered his life. In a history of alchymy, the name of this great man cannot be omitted, although, unlike many others of whom we shall have occasion to speak, he only made it secondary to other pursuits. The love of universal knowledge that filled his mind, would not allow him to neglect one branch of science, of which neither he nor the world could yet see the absurdity. He made ample amends for his time lost in this pursuit by his knowledge in physics and his acquaintance with astronomy. The telescope, burning-glasses, and gunpowder, are discoveries which may well carry his fame to the remotest time, and make the world blind to the one spot of folly -- the diagnosis of the age in which he lived, and the circumstances by which he was surrounded. His treatise on the "Admirable Power of Art and Nature in the Production of the Philosopher's Stone" was translated into French by Girard de Tormes, and published at Lyons in 1557. His "Mirror of Alchymy" was also published in French in the same year, and in Paris in 1612, with some additions from the works of Raymond Lulli. A complete list of all the published treatises upon the subject may be seen in Lenglet du Fresnoy.

Pope John XXII

This Prelate is said to have been the friend and pupil of Arnold de Villeneuve, by whom he was instructed in all the secrets of alchymy. Tradition asserts of him, that he made great quantities of gold, and died as rich as Croesus. He was born at Cahors, in the province of Guienne, in the year 1244. He was a very eloquent preacher, and soon reached high dignity in the Church. He wrote a work on the transmutation of metals, and had a famous laboratory at Avignon. He issued two Bulls against the numerous pretenders to the art, who had sprung up in every part of Christendom; from which it might be inferred that he was himself free from the delusion. The alchymists claim him, however, as one of the most distinguished and successful professors of their art, and say that his Bulls were not directed against the real adepts, but the false pretenders. They lay particular stress upon these words in his Bull, "Spondent, quas non exhibent, divitias, pauperes alchymistae." These, it is clear, they say, relate only to poor alchymists, and therefore false ones. He died in the year 1344, leaving in his coffers a sum of eighteen millions of florins. Popular belief alleged that he had made, and not amassed, this treasure; and alchymists complacently cite this as a proof that the philosopher's stone was not such a chimera as the incredulous pretended. They take it for granted that John really left this money, and ask by what possible means he could have accumulated it. Replying to their own question, they say triumphantly, "His book shows it was by alchymy, the secrets of which he learned from Arnold de Villeneuve and Raymond Lulli. But he was as prudent as all other hermetic philosophers. Whoever would read his book to find out his secret, would employ all his labour in vain; the Pope took good care not to divulge it." Unluckily for their own credit, all these gold-makers are in the same predicament; their great secret loses its worth most wonderfully in the telling, and therefore they keep it snugly to themselves. Perhaps they thought that, if everybody could transmute metals, gold would be so plentiful that it would be no longer valuable, and that some new art would be requisite to transmute it back again into steel and iron. If so, society is much indebted to them for their forbearance.

Jean de Meung

All classes of men dabbled in the art at this time; the last mentioned was a Pope, the one of whom we now speak was a poet. Jean de Meung, the celebrated author of the "Roman de la Rose," was born in the year 1279 or 1280, and was a great personage at the courts of Louis X, Philip the Long, Charles IV, and Philip de Valois. His famous poem of the "Roman de la Rose," which treats of every subject in vogue at that day, necessarily makes great mention of alchymy. Jean was a firm believer in the art, and wrote, besides his, "Roman," two shorter poems, the one entitled, "The Remonstrance of Nature to the wandering Alchymist," and "The Reply of the Alchymist to Nature." Poetry and alchymy were his delight, and priests and women were his abomination. A pleasant story is related of him and the ladies of the court of Charles IV. He had written the following libellous couplet upon the fair sex :--

"Toutes etes, serez, ou futes
De fait ou de volonte, putains,
Et qui, tres bien vous chercherait
Toutes putains, vous trouverait."

[These verses are but a coarser expression of the slanderous line of Pope, that "every woman is at heart a rake."]

This naturally gave great offence; and being perceived one day, in the King's antechamber, by some ladies who were waiting for an audience, they resolved to punish him. To the number of ten or twelve, they armed themselves with canes and rods; and surrounding the unlucky poet, called upon the gentlemen present to strip him naked, that they might wreak just vengeance upon him, and lash him through the streets of the town. Some of the lords present were in no wise loth, and promised themselves great sport from his punishment. But Jean de Meung was unmoved by their threats, and stood up calmly in the midst of them, begging them to hear him first, and then, if not satisfied, they might do as they liked with him. Silence being restored, he stood upon a chair, and entered on his defence. He acknowledged that he was the author of the obnoxious verses, but denied that they bore reference to all womankind. He only meant to speak of the vicious and abandoned, whereas those whom he saw around him, were patterns of virtue, loveliness, and modesty. If, however, any lady present thought herself aggrieved, he would consent to be stripped, and she might lash him till her arms were wearied. It is added, that by this means Jean escaped his flogging, and that the wrath of the fair ones immediately subsided. The gentlemen present were, however, of opinion, that if every lady in the room, whose character corresponded with the verses, had taken him at his word, the poet would, in all probability, have been beaten to death. All his life long he evinced a great animosity towards the priesthood, and his famous poem abounds with passages reflecting upon their avarice, cruelty, and immorality. At his death he left a large box, filled with some weighty material, which he bequeathed to the Cordeliers, as a peace-offering, for the abuse he had lavished upon them. As his practice of alchymy was well-known, it was thought the box was filled with gold and silver, and the Cordeliers congratulated each other on their rich acquisition. When it came to be opened, they found to their horror that it was filled only with slates, scratched with hieroglyphic and cabalistic characters. Indignant at the insult, they determined to refuse him Christian burial, on pretence that he was a sorcerer. He was, however, honourably buried in Paris, the whole court attending his funeral.

Nicholas Flamel

The story of this alchymist, as handed down by tradition, and enshrined in the pages of Lenglet du Fresnoy, is not a little marvellous. He was born at Pontoise of a poor but respectable family, at the end of the thirteenth, or beginning of the fourteenth, century. Having no patrimony, he set out for Paris at an early age, to try his fortune as a public scribe. He had received a good education, was well skilled in the learned languages, and was an excellent penman. He soon procured occupation as a letter-writer and copyist, and used to sit at the corner of the Rue de Marivaux, and practise his calling: but he hardly made profits enough to keep body and soul together. To mend his fortunes he tried poetry; but this was a more wretched occupation still. As a transcriber he had at least gained bread and cheese; but his rhymes were not worth a crust. He then tried painting with as little success; and as a last resource, began to search for the philosopher's stone, and tell fortunes. This was a happier idea; he soon increased in substance, and had wherewithal to live comfortably. He, therefore, took unto himself his wife Petronella, and began to save money; but continued to all outward appearance as poor and miserable as before. In the course of a few years, he became desperately addicted to the study of alchymy, and thought of nothing but the philosopher's stone, the elixir of life, and the universal alkahest. In the year 1257, he bought by chance an old book for two florins, which soon became the sole study and object of his life. It was written with a steel instrument upon the bark of trees, and contained twenty-one, or as he himself always expressed it, three times seven, leaves. The writing was very elegant and in the Latin language. Each seventh leaf contained a picture and no writing. On the first of these was a serpent swallowing rods; on the second, a cross with a serpent crucified; and on the third, the representation of a desert, in the midst of which was a fountain with serpents crawling from side to side. It purported to be written by no less a personage than "Abraham, patriarch, Jew, prince, philosopher, priest, Levite, and astrologer;" and invoked curses upon any one who should cast eyes upon it, without being a sacrificer or a scribe. Nicholas Flamel never thought it extraordinary that Abraham should have known Latin, and was convinced that the characters on his book had been traced by the hands of that great patriarch himself. He was at first afraid to read it, after he became aware of the curse it contained; but he got over that difficulty by recollecting that, although he was not a sacrificer, he had practised as a scribe. As he read he was filled with admiration, and found that it was a perfect treatise upon the transmutation of metals. All the process was clearly explained; the vessels, the retorts, the mixtures, and the proper times and seasons for the experiment. But as ill-luck would have it, the possession of the philosopher's stone or prime agent in the work was presupposed. This was a difficulty which was not to be got over. It was like telling a starving man how to cook a beefsteak, instead of giving him the money to buy one. But Nicholas did not despair; and set about studying the hieroglyphics and allegorical representations with which the book abounded. He soon convinced himself that it had been one of the sacred books of the Jews, and that it was taken from the temple of Jerusalem on its destruction by Titus. The process of reasoning by which he arrived at this conclusion is not stated.

From some expression in the treatise, he learned that the allegorical drawings on the fourth and fifth leaves, enshrined the secret of the philosopher's stone, without which all the fine Latin of the directions was utterly unavailing. He invited all the alchymists and learned men of Paris to come and examine them, but they all departed as wise as they came. Nobody could make anything either of Nicholas or his pictures; and some even went so far as to say that his invaluable book was not worth a farthing. This was not to be borne; and Nicholas resolved to discover the great secret by himself, without troubling the philosophers. He found on the first page, of the fourth leaf, the picture of Mercury, attacked by an old man resembling Saturn or Time. The latter had an hourglass on his head, and in his hand a scythe, with which he aimed a blow at Mercury's feet. The reverse of the leaf represented a flower growing on a mountain top, shaken rudely by the wind, with a blue stalk, red and white blossoms, and leaves of pure gold. Around it were a great number of dragons and griffins. On the first page of the fifth leaf was a fine garden, in the midst of which was a rose tree in full bloom, supported against the trunk of a gigantic oak. At the foot of this there bubbled up a fountain of milk-white water, which forming a small stream, flowed through the garden, and was afterwards lost in the sands. On the second page was a King, with a sword in his hand, superintending a number of soldiers, who, in execution of his orders, were killing a great multitude of young children, spurning the prayers and tears of their mothers, who tried to save them from destruction. The blood of the children was carefully collected by another party of soldiers, and put into a large vessel, in which two allegorical figures of the Sun and Moon were bathing themselves.

For twenty-one years poor Nicholas wearied himself with the study of these pictures, but still he could make nothing of them. His wife Petronella at last persuaded him to find out some learned Rabbi; but there was no Rabbi in Paris learned enough to be of any service to him. The Jews met but small encouragement to fix their abode in France, and all the chiefs of that people were located in Spain. To Spain accordingly Nicholas Flamel repaired. He left his book in Paris for fear, perhaps, that he might be robbed of it on the road; and telling his neighbours that he was going on a pilgrimage to the shrine of St. James of Compostello, he trudged on foot towards Madrid in search of a Rabbi. He was absent two years in that country, and made himself known to a great number of Jews, descendants of those who had been expelled from France in the reign of Philip Augustus. The believers in the philosopher's stone give the following account of his adventures: -- They say that at Leon he made the acquaintance of a converted Jew, named Cauches, a very learned physician, to whom he explained the title and the nature of his little book. The Doctor was transported with joy as soon as he heard it named, and immediately resolved to accompany Nicholas to Paris, that he might have a sight of it. The two set out together; the Doctor on the way entertaining his companion with the history of his book, which, if the genuine book he thought it to be, from the description he had heard of it, was in the handwriting of Abraham himself, and had been in the possession of personages no less distinguished than Moses, Joshua, Solomon, and Esdras. It contained all the secrets of alchymy and of many other sciences, and was the most valuable book that had ever existed in this world. The Doctor was himself no mean adept, and Nicholas profited greatly by his discourse, as in the garb of poor pilgrims they wended their way to Paris, convinced of their power to turn every old shovel in that capital into pure gold. But, unfortunately, when they reached Orleans, the Doctor was taken dangerously ill. Nicholas watched by his bedside, and acted the double part of a physician and nurse to him; but he died after a few days, lamenting with his last breath that he had not lived long enough to see the precious volume. Nicholas rendered the last honours to his body; and with a sorrowful heart, and not one sous in his pocket, proceeded home to his wife Petronella. He immediately recommenced the study of his pictures; but for two whole years he was as far from understanding them as ever. At last, in the third year, a glimmer of light stole over his understanding. He recalled some expression of his friend, the Doctor, which had hitherto escaped his memory, and he found that all his previous experiments had been conducted on a wrong basis. He recommenced them now with renewed energy, and at the end of the year had the satisfaction to see all his toils rewarded. On the 13th January 1382, says Lenglet, he made a projection on mercury, and had some very excellent silver. On the 25th April following, he converted a large quantity of mercury into gold, and the great secret was his.

Nicholas was now about eighty years of age, and still a hale and stout old man. His friends say that, by the simultaneous discovery of the elixir of life, he found means to keep death at a distance for another quarter of a century; and that he died in 1415, at the age of 116. In this interval he had made immense quantities of gold, though to all outward appearance he was as poor as a mouse. At an early period of his changed fortune, he had, like a worthy man, taken counsel with his old wife Petronella, as to the best use he could make of his wealth. Petronella replied, that as unfortunately they had no children, the best thing he could do, was to build hospitals and endow churches. Nicholas thought so too, especially when he began to find that his elixir could not keep off death, and that the grim foe was making rapid advances upon him. He richly endowed the church of St. Jacques de la Boucherie, near the Rue de Marivaux, where he had all his life resided, besides seven others in different parts of the kingdom. He also endowed fourteen hospitals, and built three chapels.

The fame of his great wealth and his munificent benefactions soon spread over all the country, and he was visited, among others, by the celebrated Doctors of that day, Jean Gerson, Jean de Courtecuisse, and Pierre d'Ailli. They found him in his humble apartment, meanly clad, and eating porridge out of an earthen vessel; and with regard to his secret, as impenetrable as all his predecessors in alchymy. His fame reached the ears of the King, Charles VI, who sent M. de Cramoisi, the Master of Requests, to find out whether Nicholas had indeed discovered the philosopher's stone. But M. de Cramoisi took nothing by his visit; all his attempts to sound the alchymist were unavailing, and he returned to his royal master no wiser than he came. It was in this year, 1414, that he lost his faithful Petronella. He did not long survive her; but died in the following year, and was buried with great pomp by the grateful priests of St. Jacques de la Boucherie.

The great wealth of Nicholas Flamel is undoubted, as the records of several churches and hospitals in France can testify. That he practised alchymy is equally certain, as he left behind several works upon the subject.

Those who knew him well, and who were incredulous about the philosopher's stone, give a very satisfactory solution of the secret of his wealth. They say that he was always a miser and a usurer; that his journey to Spain was undertaken with very different motives from those pretended by the alchymists; that, in fact, he went to collect debts due from Jews in that country to their brethren in Paris, and that he charged a commission of fully cent. per cent. in consideration of the difficulty of collecting and the dangers of the road; that when he possessed thousands, he lived upon almost nothing; and was the general money-lender, at enormous profits, of all the dissipated young men at the French court.

Among the works written by Nicholas Flamel on the subject of alchymy, is "The Philosophic Summary," a poem, reprinted in 1735, as an appendix to the third volume of the "Roman de la Rose." He also wrote three treatises upon natural philosophy, and an alchymic allegory, entitled "Le Desir desire." Specimens of his writing, and a fac-simile of the drawings in his book of Abraham, may be seen in Salmon's "Bibliotheque des Philosophes Chimiques." The writer of the article, "Flamel," in the "Biographie Universelle," says that, for a hundred years after the death of Flamel, many of the adepts believed that he was still alive, and that he would live for upwards of six hundred years. The house he formerly occupied, at the corner of the Rue de Marivaux, has been often taken by credulous speculators, and ransacked from top to bottom, in the hopes that gold might be found. A report was current in Paris, not long previous to the year 1816, that some lodgers had found in the cellars several jars filled with a dark-coloured ponderous matter. Upon the strength of the rumour, a believer in all the wondrous tales told of Nicholas Flamel bought the house, and nearly pulled it to pieces in ransacking the walls and wainscotting for hidden gold. He got nothing for his pains, however, and had a heavy bill to pay to restore his dilapidations.

George Ripley

While alchymy was thus cultivated on the continent of Europe, it was not neglected in the isles of Britain. Since the time of Roger Bacon, it had fascinated the imagination of many ardent men in England. In the year 1404, an act of parliament was passed, declaring the making of gold and silver to be felony. Great alarm was felt at that time lest any alchymist should succeed in his projects, and perhaps bring ruin upon the state, by furnishing boundless wealth to some designing tyrant, who would make use of it to enslave his country. This alarm appears to have soon subsided; for, in the year 1455, King Henry VI, by advice of his council and parliament, granted four successive patents and commissions to several knights, citizens of London, chemists, monks, mass-priests, and others, to find out the philosopher's stone and elixir, "to the great benefit," said the patent, "of the realm, and the enabling of the King to pay all the debts of the Crown in real gold and silver." Prinn, in his "Aurum Reginae," observes, as a note to this passage, that the King's reason for granting this patent to ecclesiastics was, that they were such good artists in transubstantiating bread and wine in the Eucharist, and therefore the more likely to be able to effect the transmutation of baser metals into better. No gold, of course, was ever made; and, next year, the King, doubting very much of the practicability of the thing, took further advice, and appointed a commission of ten learned men, and persons of eminence, to judge and certify to him whether the transmutation of metals were a thing practicable or no. It does not appear whether the commission ever made any report upon the subject.

In the succeeding reign, an alchymist appeared who pretended to have discovered the secret. This was George Ripley, the canon of Bridlington, in Yorkshire. He studied for twenty years in the universities of Italy, and was a great favourite with Pope Innocent VIII, who made him one of his domestic chaplains, and master of the ceremonies in his household. Returning to England in 1477, he dedicated to King Edward IV. his famous work, "The Compound of Alchymy; or, the Twelve Gates leading to the Discovery of the Philosopher's Stone." These gates he described to be calcination, solution, separation, conjunction, putrefaction, congelation, cibation, sublimation, fermentation, exaltation, multiplication, and projection! to which he might have added botheration, the most important process of all. He was very rich, and allowed it to be believed that he could make gold out of iron. Fuller, in his "Worthies of England," says that an English gentleman of good credit reported that, in his travels abroad, he saw a record in the island of Malta, which declared that Ripley gave yearly to the knights of that island, and of Rhodes, the enormous sum of one hundred thousand pounds sterling, to enable them to carry on the war against the Turks. In his old age, he became an anchorite near Boston, and wrote twenty-five volumes upon the subject of alchymy, the most important of which is the "Duodecim Portarum," already mentioned. Before he died, he seems to have acknowledged that he had misspent his life in this vain study, and requested that all men, when they met with any of his books, would burn them, or afford them no credit, as they had been written merely from his opinion, and not from proof; and that subsequent trial had made manifest to him that they were false and vain. [Fuller's "Worthies of England."]

Basil Valentine

Germany also produced many famous alchymists in the fifteenth century, the chief of whom are Basil Valentine, Bernard of Treves, and the Abbot Trithemius. Basil Valentine was born at Mayence, and was made prior of St. Peter's, at Erfurt, about the year 1414. It was known, during his life, that he diligently sought the philosopher's stone, and that he had written some works upon the process of transmutation. They were thought, for many years, to be lost; but were, after his death, discovered enclosed in the stone work of one of the pillars in the Abbey. They were twenty-one in number, and are fully set forth in the third volume of Lenglet's "History of the Hermetic Philosophy." The alchymists asserted, that Heaven itself conspired to bring to light these extraordinary works; and that the pillar in which they were enclosed was miraculously shattered by a thunderbolt; and that, as soon as the manuscripts were liberated, the pillar closed up again of its own accord!

Bernard of Treves

The life of this philosopher is a remarkable instance of talent and perseverance misapplied. In the search of his chimera nothing could daunt him. Repeated disappointment never diminished his hopes; and, from the age of fourteen to that of eighty-five, he was incessantly employed among the drugs and furnaces of his laboratory, wasting his life with the view of prolonging it, and reducing himself to beggary in the hopes of growing rich.

He was born at either Treves or Padua, in the year 1406. His father is said by some to have been a physician in the latter city; and by others, to have been Count of the Marches of Treves, and one of the most wealthy nobles of his country. At all events, whether noble or physician, he was a rich man, and left his son a magnificent estate. At the age of fourteen he first became enamoured of the science of alchymy, and read the Arabian authors in their own language. He himself has left a most interesting record of his labours and wanderings, from which the following particulars are chiefly extracted: -- The first book which fell into his hands, was that of the Arabian philosopher, Rhazes, from the reading of which he imagined that he had discovered the means of augmenting gold a hundred fold. For four years he worked in his laboratory, with the book of Rhazes continually before him. At the end of that time, he found that he had spent no less than eight hundred crowns upon his experiment, and had got nothing but fire and smoke for his pains. He now began to lose confidence in Rhazes, and turned to the works of Geber. He studied him assiduously for two years; and, being young, rich, and credulous, was beset by all the chymists of the town, who kindly assisted him in spending his money. He did not lose his faith in Geber, or patience with his hungry assistants, until he had lost two thousand crowns - a very considerable sum in those days.

Among all the crowd of pretended men of science who surrounded him, there was but one as enthusiastic and as disinterested as himself. With this man, who was a monk of the order of St. Francis, he contracted an intimate friendship, and spent nearly all his time. Some obscure treatises of Rupecissa and Sacrobosco having fallen into their hands, they were persuaded, from reading them, that highly rectified spirits of wine was the universal alkahest, or dissolvent, which would aid them greatly in the process of transmutation. They rectified the alcohol thirty times, till they made it so strong as to burst the vessels which contained it. After they had worked three years, and spent three hundred crowns in the liquor, they discovered that they were on the wrong track. They next tried alum and copperas; but the great secret still escaped them. They afterwards imagined that there was a marvellous virtue in all excrement, especially the human, and actually employed more than two years in experimentalizing upon it, with mercury, salt, and molten lead! Again the adepts flocked around him from far and near, to aid him with their counsels. He received them all hospitably, and divided his wealth among them so generously and unhesitatingly, that they gave him the name of the "good Trevisan," by which he is still often mentioned in works that treat on alchymy. For twelve years he led this life, making experiments every day upon some new substance, and praying to God night and morning that he might discover the secret of transmutation.

In this interval he lost his friend the monk, and was joined by a magistrate of the city of Treves, as ardent as himself in the search. His new acquaintance imagined that the ocean was the mother of gold, and that sea-salt would change lead or iron into the precious metals. Bernard resolved to try; and, transporting his laboratory to a house on the coast of the Baltic, he worked upon salt for more than a year, melting it, sublimating it, crystalizing it, and occasionally drinking it, for the sake of other experiments. Still the strange enthusiast was not wholly discouraged, and his failure in one trial only made him the more anxious to attempt another.

He was now approaching the age of fifty, and had as yet seen nothing of the world. He, therefore, determined to travel through Germany, Italy, France, and Spain. Wherever he stopped he made inquiries whether there were any alchymists in the neighbourhood. He invariably sought them out; and, if they were poor, relieved, and, if affluent, encouraged them. At Citeaux he became acquainted with one Geoffrey Leuvier, a monk of that place, who persuaded him that the essence of egg-shells was a valuable ingredient. He tried, therefore, what could be done; and was only prevented from wasting a year or two on the experiment by the opinions of an attorney, at Berghem, in Flanders, who said that the great secret resided in vinegar and copperas. He was not convinced of the absurdity of this idea until he had nearly poisoned himself. He resided in France for about five years, when, hearing accidentally that one Master Henry, confessor to the Emperor Frederic III, had discovered the philosopher's stone, he set out for Germany to pay him a visit. He had, as usual, surrounded himself with a set of hungry dependants, several of whom determined to accompany him. He had not heart to refuse them, and he arrived at Vienna with five of them. Bernard sent a polite invitation to the confessor, and gave him a sumptuous entertainment, at which were present nearly all the alchymists of Vienna. Master Henry frankly confessed that he had not discovered the philosopher's stone, but that he had all his life been employed in searching for it, and would so continue, till he found it; -- or died. This was a man after Bernard's own heart, and they vowed with each other an eternal friendship. It was resolved, at supper, that each alchymist present should contribute a certain sum towards raising forty-two marks of gold, which, in five days, it was confidently asserted by Master Henry, would increase, in his furnace, five fold. Bernard, being the richest man, contributed the lion's share, ten marks of gold, Master Henry five, and the others one or two a piece, except the dependants of Bernard, who were obliged to borrow their quota from their patron. The grand experiment was duly made; the golden marks were put into a crucible, with a quantity of salt, copperas, aquafortis, egg-shells, mercury, lead, and dung. The alchymists watched this precious mess with intense interest, expecting that it would agglomerate into one lump of pure gold. At the end of three weeks they gave up the trial, upon some excuse that the crucible was not strong enough, or that some necessary ingredient was wanting. Whether any thief had put his hands into the crucible is not known, but it is certain that the gold found therein at the close of the experiment was worth only sixteen marks, instead of the forty-two, which were put there at the beginning.

Bernard, though he made no gold at Vienna, made away with a very considerable quantity. He felt the loss so acutely, that he vowed to think no more of the philosopher's stone. This wise resolution he kept for two months; but he was miserable. He was in the condition of the gambler, who cannot resist the fascination of the game while he has a coin remaining, but plays on with the hope of retrieving former losses, till hope forsakes him, and he can live no longer. He returned once more to his beloved crucibles, and resolved to prosecute his journey in search of a philosopher who had discovered the secret, and would communicate it to so zealous and persevering an adept as himself. From Vienna he travelled to Rome, and from Rome to Madrid. Taking ship at Gibraltar, he proceeded to Messina; from Messina to Cyprus; from Cyprus to Greece; from Greece to Constantinople; and thence into Egypt, Palestine, and Persia. These wanderings occupied him about eight years. From Persia he made his way back to Messina, and from thence into France. He afterwards passed over into England, still in search of his great chimera; and this occupied four years more of his life. He was now growing both old and poor; for he was sixty-two years of age, and had been obliged to sell a great portion of his patrimony to provide for his expenses. His journey to Persia had cost upwards of thirteen thousand crowns, about one-half of which had been fairly melted in his all-devouring furnaces: the other half was lavished upon the sycophants that he made it his business to search out in every town he stopped at.

On his return to Treves he found, to his sorrow, that, if not an actual beggar, he was not much better. His relatives looked upon him as a madman, and refused even to see him. Too proud to ask for favours from any one, and still confident that, some day or other, he would be the possessor of unbounded wealth, he made up his mind to retire to the island of Rhodes, where he might, in the mean time, hide his poverty from the eyes of all the world. Here he might have lived unknown and happy; but, as ill luck would have it, he fell in with a monk as mad as himself upon the subject of transmutation. They were, however, both so poor that they could not afford to buy the proper materials to work with. They kept up each other's spirits by learned discourses on the Hermetic Philosophy, and in the reading of all the great authors who had written upon the subject. Thus did they nurse their folly, as the good wife of Tam O'Shanter did her wrath, "to keep it warm." After Bernard had resided about a year in Rhodes, a merchant, who knew his family, advanced him the sum of eight thousand florins, upon the security of the last-remaining acres of his formerly large estate. Once more provided with funds, he recommenced his labours with all the zeal and enthusiasm of a young man. For three years he hardly stepped out of his laboratory: he ate there, and slept there, and did not even give himself time to wash his hands and clean his beard, so intense was his application. It is melancholy to think that such wonderful perseverance should have been wasted in so vain a pursuit, and that energies so unconquerable should have had no worthier field to strive in. Even when he had fumed away his last coin, and had nothing left in prospective to keep his old age from starvation, hope never forsook him. He still dreamed of ultimate success, and sat down a greyheaded man of eighty, to read over all the authors on the hermetic mysteries, from Geber to his own day, lest he should have misunderstood some process, which it was not yet too late to recommence. The alchymists say, that he succeeded at last, and discovered the secret of transmutation in his eighty-second year. They add, that he lived three years afterwards to enjoy his wealth. He lived, it is true, to this great age, and made a valuable discovery - more valuable than gold or gems. He learned, as he himself informs us, just before he had attained his eighty-third year, that the great secret of philosophy was contentment with our lot. Happy would it have been for him if he had discovered it sooner, and before he became decrepit, a beggar, and an exile!

He died at Rhodes, in the year 1490, and all the alchymists of Europe sang elegies over him, and sounded his praise as the "good Trevisan." He wrote several treatises upon his chimera, the chief of which are, the "Book of Chemistry," the "Verbum dimissum," and an essay "De Natura Ovi."

Trithemius

The name of this eminent man has become famous in the annals of alchymy, although he did but little to gain so questionable an honour. He was born in the year 1462, at the village of Trittheim, in the electorate of Treves. His father was John Heidenberg, a vine-grower, in easy circumstances, who, dying when his son was but seven years old, left him to the care of his mother. The latter married again very shortly afterwards, and neglected the poor boy, the offspring of her first marriage. At the age of fifteen he did not even know his letters, and was, besides, half starved, and otherwise ill-treated by his step-father; but the love of knowledge germinated in the breast of the unfortunate youth, and he learned to read at the house of a neighbour. His father-in-law set him to work in the vineyards, and thus occupied all his days; but the nights were his own. He often stole out unheeded, when all the household were fast asleep, poring over his studies in the fields, by the light of the moon; and thus taught himself Latin and the rudiments of Greek. He was subjected to so much ill-usage at home, in consequence of this love of study, that he determined to leave it. Demanding the patrimony which his father had left him, he proceeded to Treves; and, assuming the name of Trithemius, from that of his native village of Trittheim, lived there for some months, under the tuition of eminent masters, by whom he was prepared for the university. At the age of twenty, he took it into his head that he should like to see his mother once more; and he set out on foot from the distant university for that purpose. On his arrival near Spannheim, late in the evening of a gloomy winter's day, it came on to snow so thickly, that he could not proceed onwards to the town. He, therefore, took refuge for the night in a neighbouring monastery; but the storm continued several days, the roads became impassable, and the hospitable monks would not hear of his departure. He was so pleased with them and their manner of life, that he suddenly resolved to fix his abode among them, and renounce the world. They were no less pleased with him, and gladly received him as a brother. In the course of two years, although still so young, he was unanimously elected their Abbot. The financial affairs of the establishment had been greatly neglected, the walls of the building were falling into ruin, and everything was in disorder. Trithemius, by his good management and regularity, introduced a reform in every branch of expenditure. The monastery was repaired, and a yearly surplus, instead of a deficiency, rewarded him for his pains. He did not like to see the monks idle, or occupied solely between prayers for their business, and chess for their relaxation. He, therefore, set them to work to copy the writings of eminent authors. They laboured so assiduously, that, in the course of a few years, their library, which had contained only about forty volumes, was enriched with several hundred valuable manuscripts, comprising many of the classical Latin authors, besides the works of the early fathers, and the principal historians and philosophers of more modern date. He retained the dignity of Abbot of Spannheim for twenty-one years, when the monks, tired of the severe discipline he maintained, revolted against him, and chose another abbot in his place. He was afterwards made Abbot of St. James, in Wurtzburg, where he died in 1516.

During his learned leisure at Spannheim, he wrote several works upon the occult sciences, the chief of which are an essay on geomancy, or divination by means of lines and circles on the ground; another upon sorcery; a third upon alchymy; and a fourth upon the government of the world by its presiding angels, which was translated into English, and published by the famous William Lilly in 1647.

It has been alleged by the believers in the possibility of transmutation, that the prosperity of the abbey of Spannheim, while under his superintendence, was owing more to the philosopher's stone than to wise economy. Trithemius, in common with many other learned men, has been accused of magic; and a marvellous story is told of his having raised from the grave the form of Mary of Burgundy, at the intercession of her widowed husband, the Emperor Maximilian. His work on steganographia, or cabalistic writing, was denounced to the Count Palatine, Frederic II, as magical and devilish; and it was by him taken from the shelves of his library and thrown into the fire. Trithemius is said to be the first writer who makes mention of the wonderful story of the devil and Dr. Faustus, the truth of which he firmly believed. He also recounts the freaks of a spirit, named Hudekin, by whom he was at times tormented. [Biographie Universelle]

The Marechal de Rays

One of the greatest encouragers of alchymy in the fifteenth century was Gilles de Laval, Lord of Rays and a Marshal of France. His name and deeds are little known; but in the annals of crime and folly, they might claim the highest and worst pro-eminence. Fiction has never invented anything wilder or more horrible than his career; and were not the details but too well authenticated by legal and other documents which admit no doubt, the lover of romance might easily imagine they were drawn to please him from the stores of the prolific brain, and not from the page of history.

He was born about the year 1420, of one of the noblest families of Brittany. His father dying when Gilles had attained his twentieth year, he came into uncontrolled possession, at that early age, of a fortune which the monarchs of France might have envied him. He was a near kinsman of the Montmorencys, the Roncys, and the Craons; possessed fifteen princely domains, and had an annual revenue of about three hundred thousand livres. Besides this, he was handsome, learned, and brave. He distinguished himself greatly in the wars of Charles VII, and was rewarded by that monarch with the dignity of a marshal of France. But he was extravagant and magnificent in his style of living, and accustomed from his earliest years to the gratification of every wish and passion; and this, at last, led him from vice to vice, and from crime to crime, till a blacker name than his is not to be found in any record of human iniquity.

In his castle of Champtoce, he lived with all the splendour of an Eastern Caliph. He kept up a troop of two hundred horsemen to accompany him wherever he went; and his excursions for the purposes of hawking and hunting were the wonder of all the country around, so magnificent were the caparisons of his steeds and the dresses of his retainers. Day and night, his castle was open all the year round to comers of every degree. He made it a rule to regale even the poorest beggar with wine and hippocrass. Every day an ox was roasted whole in his spacious kitchens, besides sheep, pigs, and poultry sufficient to feed five hundred persons. He was equally magnificent in his devotions. His private chapel at Champtoce was the most beautiful in France, and far surpassed any of those in the richly-endowed cathedrals of Notre Dame in Paris, of Amiens, of Beauvais, or of Rouen. It was hung with cloth of gold and rich velvet. All the chandeliers were of pure gold, curiously inlaid with silver. The great crucifix over the altar was of solid silver, and the chalices and incense-burners were of pure gold. He had, besides, a fine organ, which he caused to be carried from one castle to another, on the shoulders of six men, whenever he changed his residence. He kept up a choir of twenty-five young children of both sexes, who were instructed in singing by the first musicians of the day. The master of his chapel he called a bishop, who had under him his deans, archdeacons, and vicars, each receiving great salaries; the bishop four hundred crowns a year, and the rest in proportion.

He also maintained a whole troop of players, including ten dancing-girls and as many ballad-singers, besides morris-dancers, jugglers, and mountebanks of every description. The theatre on which they performed was fitted up without any regard to expense; and they played mysteries, or danced the morris-dance, every evening, for the amusement of himself and household, and such strangers as were sharing his prodigal hospitality.

315

At the age of twenty-three, he married Catherine, the wealthy heiress of the house of Touars, for whom he refurnished his castle at an expense of a hundred thousand crowns. His marriage was the signal for new extravagance, and he launched out more madly than ever he had done before; sending for fine singers or celebrated dancers from foreign countries to amuse him and his spouse, and instituting tilts and tournaments in his great court-yard almost every week for all the knights and nobles of the province of Brittany. The Duke of Brittany's court was not half so splendid as that of the Marechal de Rays. His utter disregard of wealth was so well known that he was made to pay three times its value for everything he purchased. His castle was filled with needy parasites and panderers to his pleasures, amongst whom he lavished rewards with an unsparing hand. But the ordinary round of sensual gratification ceased at last to afford him delight: he was observed to be more abstemious in the pleasures of the table, and to neglect the beauteous dancing-girls who used formerly to occupy so much of his attention. He was sometimes gloomy and reserved; and there was an unnatural wildness in his eye which gave indications of incipient madness. Still, his discourse was as reasonable as ever; his urbanity to the guests that flocked from far and near to Champtoce suffered no diminution; and learned priests, when they conversed with him, thought to themselves that few of the nobles of France were so well-informed as Gilles de Laval. But dark rumours spread gradually over the country; murder, and, if possible, still more atrocious deeds were hinted at; and it was remarked that many young children, of both sexes, suddenly disappeared, and were never afterwards heard of. One or two had been traced to the castle of Champtoce, and had never been seen to leave it; but no one dared to accuse openly so powerful a man as the Marechal de Rays. Whenever the subject of the lost children was mentioned in his presence, he manifested the greatest astonishment at the mystery which involved their fate, and indignation against those who might be guilty of kidnapping them. Still the world was not wholly deceived; his name became as formidable to young children as that of the devouring ogre in fairy tales; and they were taught to go miles round, rather than pass under the turrets of Champtoce.

In the course of a very few years, the reckless extravagance of the Marshal drained him of all his funds, and he was obliged to put up some of his estates for sale. The Duke of Brittany entered into a treaty with him for the valuable seignory of Ingrande; but the heirs of Gilles implored the interference of Charles VII. to stay the sale. Charles immediately issued an edict, which was confirmed by the Provincial Parliament of Brittany, forbidding him to alienate his paternal estates. Gilles had no alternative but to submit. He had nothing to support his extravagance but his allowance as a Marshal of France, which did not cover the one-tenth of his expenses. A man of his habits and character could not retrench his wasteful expenditure and live reasonably; he could not dismiss without a pang his horsemen, his jesters, his morris-dancers, his choristers, and his parasites, or confine his hospitality to those who really needed it. Notwithstanding his diminished resources, he resolved to live as he had lived before, and turn alchymist, that he might make gold out of iron, and be still the wealthiest and most magnificent among the nobles of Brittany.

In pursuance of this determination he sent to Paris, Italy, Germany, and Spain, inviting all the adepts in the science to visit him at Champtoce. The messengers he despatched on this mission were two of his most needy and unprincipled dependants, Gilles de Sille and Roger de Bricqueville. The latter, the obsequious panderer to his most secret and abominable pleasures, he had intrusted with the education of his motherless daughter, a child but five years of age, with permission, that he might marry her at the proper time to any person he chose, or to himself if he liked it better. This man entered into the new plans of his master with great zeal, and introduced to him one Prelati, an alchymist of Padua, and a physician of Poitou, who was addicted to the same pursuits. The Marshal caused a splendid laboratory to be fitted up for them, and the three commenced the search for the philosopher's stone. They were soon afterwards joined by another pretended philosopher, named Anthony of Palermo, who aided in their operations for upwards of a year. They all fared sumptuously at the Marshal's expense, draining him of the ready money he possessed, and leading him on from day to day with the hope that they would succeed in the object of their search. From time to time new aspirants from the remotest parts of Europe arrived at his castle, and for months he had upwards of twenty alchymists at work - trying to transmute copper into gold, and wasting the gold, which was still his own, in drugs and elixirs.

But the Lord of Rays was not a man to abide patiently their lingering processes. Pleased with their comfortable quarters, they jogged on from day to day, and would have done so for years, had they been permitted. But he suddenly dismissed them all, with the exception of the Italian Prelati, and the physician of Poitou. These he retained to aid him to discover the secret of the philosopher's stone by a bolder method. The Poitousan had persuaded him that the devil was the great depositary of that and all other secrets, and that he would raise him before Gilles, who might enter into any contract he pleased with him. Gilles expressed his readiness, and promised to give the devil anything but his soul, or do any deed that the arch-enemy might impose upon him. Attended solely by the physician, he proceeded at midnight to a wild-looking place in a neighbouring forest; the physician drew a magic circle around them on the sward, and muttered for half an hour an invocation to the Evil Spirit to arise at his bidding, and disclose the secrets of alchymy. Gilles looked on with intense interest, and expected every moment to see the earth open, and deliver to his gaze the great enemy of mankind. At last the eyes of the physician became fixed, his hair stood on end, and he spoke, as if addressing the fiend. But Gilles saw nothing except his companion. At last the physician fell down on the sward as if insensible. Gilles looked calmly on to see the end. After a few minutes the physician arose, and asked him if he had not seen how angry the devil looked? Gilles replied, that he had seen nothing; upon which his companion informed him that Beelzebub had appeared in the form of a wild leopard, growled at him savagely, and said nothing; and that the reason why the Marshal had neither seen nor heard him, was that he hesitated in his own mind as to devoting himself entirely to the service. De Rays owned that he had indeed misgivings, and inquired what was to be done to make the devil speak out, and unfold his secret? The physician replied, that some person must go to Spain and Africa to collect certain herbs which only grew in those countries, and offered to go himself, if De Rays would provide the necessary funds. De Rays at once consented; and the physician set out on the following day with all the gold that his dupe could spare him. The Marshal never saw his face again.

But the eager Lord of Champtoce could not rest. Gold was necessary for his pleasures; and unless, by supernatural aid, he had no means of procuring many further supplies. The physician was hardly twenty leagues on his journey, before Gilles resolved to make another effort to force the devil to divulge the art of gold making. He went out alone for that purpose, but all his conjurations were of no effect. Beelzebub was obstinate, and would not appear. Determined to conquer him if he could, he unbosomed himself to the Italian alchymist, Prelati. The latter offered to undertake the business, upon condition that De Rays did not interfere in the conjurations, and consented besides to furnish him with all the charms and talismans that might be required. He was further to open a vein in his arm, and sign with his blood a contract that he would work the devil's will in all things, and offer up to him a sacrifice of the heart, lungs, hands, eyes, and blood of a young child. The grasping monomaniac made no hesitation; but agreed at once to the disgusting terms proposed to him. On the following night, Prelati went out alone; and after having been absent for three or four hours, returned to Gilles, who sat anxiously awaiting him. Prelati then informed him that he had seen the devil in the shape of a handsome youth of twenty. He further said, that the devil desired to be called Barron in all future invocations; and had shown him a great number of ingots of pure gold, buried under a large oak in the neighbouring forest, all of which, and as many more as he desired, should become the property of the Marechal de Rays if he remained firm, and broke no condition of the contract. Prelati further showed him a small casket of black dust, which would turn iron into gold; but as the process was very troublesome, he advised that they should be contented with the ingots they found under the oak tree, and which would more than supply all the wants that the most extravagant imagination could desire. They were not, however, to attempt to look for the gold till a period of seven times seven weeks, or they would find nothing but slates and stones for their

317

pains. Gilles expressed the utmost chagrin and disappointment, and at once said that he could not wait for so long a period; if the devil were not more prompt, Prelati might tell him, that the Marechal de Rays was not to be trifled with, and would decline all further communication with him. Prelati at last persuaded him to wait seven times seven days. They then went at midnight with picks and shovels to dig up the ground under the oak, where they found nothing to reward them but a great quantity of slates, marked with hieroglyphics. It was now Prelati's turn to be angry; and he loudly swore that the devil was nothing but a liar and a cheat. The Marshal joined cordially in the opinion, but was easily persuaded by the cunning Italian to make one more trial. He promised at the same time that he would endeavour, on the following night, to discover the reason why the devil had broken his word. He went out alone accordingly, and on his return informed his patron that he had seen Barron, who was exceedingly angry that they had not waited the proper time ere they looked for the ingots. Barron had also said, that the Marechal de Rays could hardly expect any favours from him, at a time when he must know that he had been meditating a pilgrimage to the Holy Land, to make atonement for his sins. The Italian had doubtless surmised this, from some incautious expression of his patron, for De Rays frankly confessed that there were times when, sick of the world and all its pomps and vanities, he thought of devoting himself to the service of God.

In this manner the Italian lured on from month to month his credulous and guilty patron, extracting from him all the valuables he possessed, and only waiting a favourable opportunity to decamp with his plunder. But the day of retribution was at hand for both. Young girls and boys continued to disappear in the most mysterious manner; and the rumours against the owner of Champtoce grew so loud and distinct, that the Church was compelled to interfere. Representations were made by the Bishop of Nantes to the Duke of Brittany, that it would be a public scandal if the accusations against the Marechal de Rays were not inquired into. He was arrested accordingly in his own castle, along with his accomplice Prelati, and thrown into a dungeon at Nantes to await his trial.

The judges appointed to try him were the Bishop of Nantes Chancellor of Brittany, the Vicar of the Inquisition in France, and the celebrated Pierre l'Hopital, the President of the Provincial Parliament. The offences laid to his charge were sorcery, sodomy, and murder. Gilles, on the first day of his trial, conducted himself with the utmost insolence. He braved the judges on the judgment seat, calling them simoniacs and persons of impure life, and said he would rather be hanged by the neck like a dog without trial, than plead either guilty or not guilty to such contemptible miscreants. But his confidence forsook him as the trial proceeded, and he was found guilty on the clearest evidence of all the crimes laid to his charge. It was proved that he took insane pleasure in stabbing the victims of his lust, and in observing the quivering of their flesh, and the fading lustre of their eyes as they expired. The confession of Prelati first made the judges acquainted with this horrid madness, and Gilles himself confirmed it before his death. Nearly a hundred children of the villagers around his two castles of Champtoce and Machecoue, had been missed within three years the greater part, if not all, of whom were immolated to the lust or the cupidity of this monster. He imagined that he thus made the devil his friend, and that his recompence would be the secret of the philosopher's stone.

Gilles and Prelati were both condemned to be burned alive. At the place of execution they assumed the air of penitence and religion. Gilles tenderly embraced Prelati, saying, "Farewell, friend Francis! In this world we shall never meet again; but let us place our hopes in God; we shall see each other in Paradise." Out of consideration for his high rank and connections, the punishment of the Marshal was so far mitigated, that he was not burned alive like Prelati. He was first strangled, and then thrown into the flames: his body, when half consumed, was given over to his relatives for interment; while that of the Italian was burned to ashes, and then scattered in the winds. [For full details of this extraordinary trial, see "Lobineau's Nouvelle Histoire de Bretagne;" and D'Argentre's work on the same subject.]

Jacques Coeur

This remarkable pretender to the secret of the philosopher's stone, was contemporary with the last mentioned. He was a great personage at the court of Charles VII, and in the events of his reign played a prominent part. From a very humble origin he rose to the highest honours of the state, and amassed enormous wealth, by peculation and the plunder of the country which he should have served. It was to hide his delinquencies in this respect, and to divert attention from the real source of his riches, that he boasted of having discovered the art of transmuting the inferior metals into gold and silver.

His father was a goldsmith in the city of Bourges; but so reduced in circumstances towards the latter years of his life, that he was unable to pay the necessary fees to procure his son's admission into the guild. Young Jacques became, however, a workman in the Royal Mint of Bourges, in 1428, and behaved himself so well, and showed so much knowledge of metallurgy, that he attained rapid promotion in that establishment. He had also the good fortune to make the acquaintance of the fair Agnes Sorel, by whom he was patronized and much esteemed. Jacques had now three things in his favour - ability, perseverance, and the countenance of the King's mistress. Many a man succeeds with but one of these to help him forward: and it would have been strange indeed, if Jacques Coeur, who had them all, should have languished in obscurity. While still a young man he was made Master of the Mint, in which he had been a journeyman, and installed at the same time into the vacant office of Grand Treasurer of the royal household.

He possessed an extensive knowledge of finance, and turned it wonderfully to his own advantage as soon as he became intrusted with extensive funds. He speculated in articles of the first necessity, and made himself very unpopular by buying up grain, honey, wines, and other produce, till there was a scarcity, when he sold it again at enormous profit. Strong in the royal favour, he did not hesitate to oppress the poor by continual acts of forestalling and monopoly. As there is no enemy so bitter as the estranged friend, so of all the tyrants and tramplers upon the poor, there is none so fierce and reckless as the upstart that sprang from their ranks. The offensive pride of Jacques Coeur to his inferiors was the theme of indignant reproach in his own city, and his cringing humility to those above him was as much an object of contempt to the aristocrats into whose society he thrust himself. But Jacques did not care for the former, and to the latter he was blind. He continued his career till he became the richest man in France, and so useful to the King that no important enterprise was set on foot until he had been consulted. He was sent in 1446 on an embassy to Genoa, and in the following year to Pope Nicholas V. In both these missions he acquitted himself to the satisfaction of his sovereign, and was rewarded with a lucrative appointment, in addition to those which he already held.

In the year 1449, the English in Normandy, deprived of their great general, the Duke of Bedford, broke the truce with the French King, and took possession of a small town belonging to the Duke of Brittany. This was the signal for the recommencemerit of a war, in which the French regained possession of nearly the whole province. The money for this war was advanced, for the most part, by Jacques Coeur. When Rouen yielded to the French, and Charles made his triumphal entry into that city, accompanied by Dunois and his most famous generals, Jacques was among the most brilliant of his cortege. His chariot and horses vied with those of the King in the magnificence of their trappings; and his enemies said of him that he publicly boasted that he alone had driven out the English, and that the valour of the troops would would have been nothing without his gold.

Dunois appears, also, to have been partly of the same opinion. Without disparaging the courage of the army, he acknowledged the utility of the able financier, by whose means they had been fed and paid, and constantly afforded him his powerful protection.

When peace returned, Jacques again devoted himself to commerce, and fitted up several galleys to trade with the Genoese. He also bought large estates in various parts of France; the chief of which were the baronies of St. Fargeau, Meneton, Salone, Maubranche, Meaune, St. Gerant de Vaux, and St. Aon de Boissy; the earldoms or counties of La Palisse, Champignelle, Beaumont, and Villeneuve la Genet, and the marquisate of Toucy. He also procured for his son, Jean Coeur, who had chosen the Church for his profession, a post no less distinguished than that of Archbishop of Bourges.

Everybody said that so much wealth could not have been honestly acquired; and both rich and poor longed for the day that should humble the pride of the man, whom the one class regarded as an upstart and the other as an oppressor. Jacques was somewhat alarmed at the rumours that were afloat respecting him, and of dark hints that he had debased the coin of the realm and forged the King's seal to an important document, by which he had defrauded the state of very considerable sums. To silence these rumours, he invited many alchymists from foreign countries to reside with him, and circulated a counter-rumour, that he had discovered the secret of the philosopher's stone. He also built a magnificent house in his native city, over the entrance of which he caused to be sculptured the emblems of that science. Some time afterwards, he built another, no less splendid, at Montpellier, which he inscribed in a similar manner. He also wrote a treatise upon the hermetic philosophy, in which he pretended that he knew the secret of transmuting metals.

But all these attempts to disguise his numerous acts of peculation proved unavailing; and he was arrested in 1452, and brought to trial on several charges. Upon one only, which the malice of his enemies invented to ruin him, was he acquitted; which was, that he had been accessory to the death, by poison, of his kind patroness, Agnes Sorel. Upon the others, he was found guilty; and sentenced to be banished the kingdom, and to pay the enormous fine of four hundred thousand crowns. It was proved that he had forged the King's seal; that, in his capacity of Master of the Mint of Bourges, he had debased, to a very great extent, the gold and silver coin of the realm; and that he had not hesitated to supply the Turks with arms and money to enable them to carry on war against their Christian neighbours, for which service he had received the most munificent recompences. Charles VII. was deeply grieved at his condemnation, and believed to the last that he was innocent. By his means the fine was reduced within a sum which Jacques Coeur could pay. After remaining for some time in prison, he was liberated, and left France with a large sum of money, part of which, it was alleged, was secretly paid him by Charles out of the produce of his confiscated estates. He retired to Cyprus, where he died about 1460, the richest and most conspicuous personage of the island.

The writers upon alchymy all claim Jacques Coeur as a member of their fraternity, and treat as false and libellous the more rational explanation of his wealth which the records of his trial afford. Pierre Borel, in his "Antiquites Gauloises," maintains the opinion that Jacques was an honest man, and that he made his gold out of lead and copper by means of the philosopher's stone. The alchymic adepts in general were of the same opinion; but they found it difficult to persuade even his contemporaries of the fact. Posterity is still less likely to believe it.

Inferior Adepts of the Fourteenth and Fifteenth Centuries

Many other pretenders to the secrets of the philosopher's stone appeared in every country in Europe, during the fourteenth and fifteenth centuries. The possibility of transmutation was so generally admitted, that every chemist was more or less an alchymist. Germany, Holland, Italy, Spain, Poland, France, and England produced thousands of obscure adepts, who supported themselves, in the pursuit of their chimera, by the more profitable resources of astrology and divination. The monarchs of Europe were no less persuaded than their subjects of the possibility of discovering the philosopher's stone. Henry VI. and Edward IV. of England encouraged alchymy. In Germany, the Emperors Maximilian, Rodolph, and Frederic II. devoted much of their attention to it; and every inferior potentate within their dominions imitated their example. It was a common practice in Germany, among the nobles and petty sovereigns, to invite an alchymist to take up his residence among them, that they might confine him in a dungeon till he made gold enough to pay millions for his ransom. Many poor wretches suffered perpetual imprisonment in consequence. A similar fate appears to have been intended by Edward II. for Raymond Lulli, who, upon the pretence that he was thereby honoured, was accommodated with apartments in the Tower of London. He found out in time the trick that was about to be played him, and managed to make his escape, some of his biographers say, by jumping into the Thames, and swimming to a vessel that lay waiting to ceive him. In the sixteenth century, the same system was pursued, as will be shown more fully in the life of Seton the Cosmopolite, in the succeeding chapter.

The following is a catalogue of the chief authors upon alchymy, who flourished during this epoch, and whose lives and adventures are either unknown or are unworthy of more detailed notice. John Dowston, an Englishman, lived in 1315, and wrote two treatises on the philosopher's stone. Richard, or, as some call him, Robert, also an Englishman, lived in 1330, and wrote a work entitled "Correctorium Alchymiae," which was much esteemed till the time of Paracelsus. In the same year lived Peter of Lombardy, who wrote what he called a "Complete Treatise upon the Hermetic Science," an abridgement of which was afterwards published by Lacini, a monk of Calabria. In 1330 the most famous alchymist of Paris was one Odomare, whose work "De Practica Magistri" was, for a long time, a hand-book among the brethren of the science. John de Rupecissa, a French monk of the order of St. Francis, flourished in 1357, and pretended to be a prophet as well as an alchymist. Some of his prophecies were so disagreeable to Pope Innocent VI, that the Pontiff determined to put a stop to them, by locking up the prophet in the dungeons of the Vatican. It is generally believed that he died there, though there is no evidence of the fact. His chief works are the "Book of Light," the "Five Essences," the "Heaven of Philosophers," and his grand work "De Confectione Lapidis." He was not thought a shining light among the adepts. Ortholani was another pretender, of whom nothing is known, but that he exercised the arts of alchymy and astrology at Paris, shortly before the time of Nicholas Flamel. His work on the practice of alchymy was written in that city in 1358. Isaac of Holland wrote, it is supposed, about this time; and his son also devoted himself to the science. Nothing worth repeating is known of their lives. Boerhaave speaks with commendation of many passages in their works, and Paracelsus esteemed them highly: the chief are "De Triplici Ordine Elixiris et Lapidis Theoria," printed at Berne in 1608; and "Mineralia Opera, seu de Lapide Philosophico," printed at Middleburg in 1600. They also wrote eight other works upon the same subject. Koffstky, a Pole, wrote an alchymical treatise, entitled "The Tincture of Minerals," about the year 1488. In this list of authors a royal name must not be forgotten. Charles VI. of France, one of the most credulous princes of the day, whose court absolutely swarmed with alchymists, conjurers, astrologers, and quacks of every description, made several attempts to discover the philosopher's stone, and thought he knew so much about it, that he determined to enlighten the world with a treatise. It is called the "Royal Work of Charles VI. of France, and the Treasure of Philosophy." It is said to be the original from which Nicholas Flamel took the idea of his "Desir Desire." Lenglet du Fresnoy says it is very allegorical, and utterly incomprehensible. For a more complete list of the hermetic philosophers of the fourteenth and fifteenth centuries, the reader is referred to the third volume of Lenglet's History already quoted.

Progress of the Infatuation During the Sixteenth and Seventeenth Centuries--Present State of the Science

During the sixteenth and seventeenth centuries, the search for the philosopher's stone was continued by thousands of the enthusiastic and the credulous; but a great change was introduced during this period. The eminent men who devoted themselves to the study, totally changed its aspect, and referred to the possession of their wondrous stone and elixir, not only the conversion of the base into the precious metals, but the solution of all the difficulties of other sciences. They pretended that by its means man would be brought into closer communion with his Maker; that disease and sorrow would be banished from the world; and that "the millions of spiritual beings who walk the earth unseen" would be rendered visible, and become the friends, companions, and instructors of mankind. In the seventeenth century more especially, these poetical and fantastic doctrines excited the notice of Europe; and from Germany, where they had been first disseminated by Rosencreutz, spread into France and England, and ran away with the sound judgment of many clever, but too enthusiastic, searchers for the truth. Paracelsus, Dee, and many others of less note, were captivated by the grace and beauty of the new mythology, which was arising to adorn the literature of Europe. Most of the alchymists of the sixteenth century, although ignorant of the Rosicrucians as a sect, were, in some degree, tinctured with their fanciful tenets: but before we speak more fully of these poetical visionaries, it will be necessary to resume the history of the hermetic folly where we left off in the former chapter, and trace the gradual change that stole over the dreams of the adepts. It will be seen that the infatuation increased rather than diminished as the world grew older.

Augurello

Among the alchymists who were born in the fifteenth, and distinguished themselves in the sixteenth century, the first, in point of date, is John Aurelio Augurello. He was born at Rimini in 1441, and became Professor of the belles lettres at Venice and Trevisa. He was early convinced of the truth of the hermetic science, and used to pray to God that he might be happy enough to discover the philosopher's stone. He was continually surrounded by the paraphernalia of chemistry, and expended all his wealth in the purchase of drugs and metals. He was also a poet, but of less merit than pretensions. His "Chrysopeia," in which he pretended to teach the art of making gold, he dedicated to Pope Leo X, in the hope that the Pontiff would reward him handsomely for the compliment; but the Pope was too good a judge of poetry to be pleased with the worse than mediocrity of his poem, and too good a philosopher to approve of the strange doctrines which it inculcated: he was, therefore, far from gratified at the dedication. It is said, that when Augurello applied to him for a reward, the Pope, with great ceremony and much apparent kindness and cordiality, drew an empty purse from his pocket, and presented it to the alchymist, saying, that since he was able to make gold, the most appropriate present that could be made him, was a purse to put it in. This scurvy reward was all that the poor alchymist ever got either for his poetry or his alchymy. He died in a state of extreme poverty, in the eighty-third year of his age.

Cornelius Agrippa

This alchymist has left a more distinguished reputation. The most extraordinary tales were told and believed of his powers. He could turn iron into gold by his mere word. All the spirits of the air, and demons of the earth, were under his command, and bound to obey him in everything. He could. raise from the dead the forms of the great men of other days, and make them appear "in their habit as they lived," to the gaze of the curious who had courage enough to abide their presence.

322

He was born at Cologne in 1486, and began, at an early age, the study of chemistry and philosophy. By some means or other which have never been very clearly explained, he managed to impress his contemporaries with a great idea of his wonderful attainments. At the early age of twenty, so great was his reputation as an alchymist, that the principal adepts of Paris wrote to Cologne, inviting him to settle in France, and aid them with his experience in discovering the philosopher's stone. Honours poured upon him in thick succession; and he was highly esteemed by all the learned men of his time. Melancthon speaks of him with respect and commendation. Erasmus also bears testimony in his favour; and the general voice of his age proclaimed him a light of literature and an ornament to philosophy. Some men, by dint of excessive egotism, manage to persuade their contemporaries that they are very great men indeed: they publish their acquirements so loudly in people's ears, and keep up their own praises so incessantly, that the world's applause is actually taken by storm. Such seems to have been the case with Agrippa. He called himself a sublime theologian, an excellent jurisconsult, an able physician, a great philosopher, and a successful alchymist. The world, at last, took him at his word; and thought that a man who talked so big, must have some merit to recommend him -- that it was, indeed, a great trumpet which sounded so obstreperous a blast. He was made secretary to the Emperor Maximilian, who conferred upon him the title of Chevalier, and gave him the honorary command of a regiment. He afterwards became Professor of Hebrew and the belles lettres, at the University of Dole, in France; but quarrelling with the Franciscan monks upon some knotty point of divinity, he was obliged to quit the town. He took refuge in London, where he taught Hebrew and cast nativities, for about a year. From London he proceeded to Pavia, and gave lectures upon the writings, real or supposed, of Hermes Trismegistus; and might have lived there in peace and honour, had he not again quarrelled with the clergy. By their means his position became so disagreeable, that he was glad to accept an offer made him by the magistracy of Metz, to become their Syndic and Advocate-General. Here, again, his love of disputation made him enemies: the theological wiseacres of that city asserted, that St. Anne had three husbands, in which opinion they were confirmed by the popular belief of the day. Agrippa needlessly ran foul of this opinion, or prejudice as he called it, and thereby lost much of his influence. Another dispute, more creditable to his character, occurred soon after, and sank him for ever in the estimation of the Metzians. Humanely taking the part of a young girl who was accused of witchcraft, his enemies asserted, that he was himself a sorcerer, and raised such a storm over his head, that he was forced to fly the city. After this, he became physician to Louisa de Savoy, mother of King Francis I. This lady was curious to know the future, and required her physician to cast her nativity. Agrippa replied, that he would not encourage such idle curiosity. The result was, he lost her confidence, and was forthwith dismissed. If it had been through his belief in the worthlessness of astrology, that he had made his answer, we might admire his honest and fearless independence; but, when it is known that, at the very same time, he was in the constant habit of divination and fortunetelling; and that he was predicting splendid success, in all his undertakings, to the Constable of Bourbon, we can only wonder at his thus estranging a powerful friend through mere petulance and perversity.

He was, about this time, invited both by Henry VIII. of England, and Margaret of Austria, Governess of the Low Countries, to fix his residence in their dominions. He chose the service of the latter, by whose influence he was made historiographer to the Emperor Charles V. Unfortunately for Agrippa, he never had stability enough to remain long in one position, and offended his patrons by his restlessness and presumption. After the death of Margaret, he was imprisoned at Brussels, on a charge of sorcery. He was released after a year; and, quitting the country, experienced many vicissitudes. He died in great poverty in 1534, aged forty-eight years.

While in the service of Margaret of Austria, he resided principally at Louvain, in which city he wrote his famous work on the Vanity and Nothingness of human Knowledge. He also wrote, to please his Royal Mistress, a treatise upon the Superiority of the Female Sex, which be dedicated to her, in token of his gratitude for the favours she had heaped upon him. The reputation he left behind him in these provinces was anything but favourable. A great number of the marvellous tales that are told of him, relate to this period of his life. It was said, that the gold which he paid to the traders with whom he dealt, always looked remarkably bright, but invariably turned into pieces of slate and stone in the course of four-and-twenty hours. Of this spurious gold he was believed to have made large quantities by the aid of the devil, who, it would appear from this, had but a very superficial knowledge of alchymy, and much less than the Marechal de Rays gave him credit for. The Jesuit Delrio, in his book on Magic and Sorcery, relates a still more extraordinary story of him. One day, Agrippa left his house, at Louvain; and, intending to be absent for some time, gave the key of his study to his wife, with strict orders that no one should enter it during his absence. The lady herself, strange as it may appear, had no curiosity to pry into her husband's secrets, and never once thought of entering the forbidden room: but a young student, who had been accommodated with an attic in the philosopher's house, burned with a fierce desire to examine the study; hoping, perchance, that he might purloin some book or implement which would instruct him in the art of transmuting metals. The youth, being handsome, eloquent, and, above all, highly complimentary to the charms of the lady, she was persuaded, without much difficulty, to lend him the key, but gave him strict orders not to remove anything. The student promised implicit obedience, and entered Agrippa's study. The first object that caught his attention, was a large grimoire, or book of spells, which lay open on the philosopher's desk. He sat himself down immediately, and began to read. At the first word he uttered, he fancied he heard a knock at the door. He listened; but all was silent. Thinking that his imagination had deceived him, he read on, when immediately a louder knock was heard, which so terrified him, that he started to his feet. He tried to say, "come in;" but his tongue refused its office, and he could not articulate a sound. He fixed his eyes upon the door, which, slowly opening, disclosed a stranger of majestic form, but scowling features, who demanded sternly, why he was summoned? "I did not summon you," said the trembling student. "You did!" said the stranger, advancing, angrily; "and the demons are not to be invoked in vain." The student could make no reply; and the demon, enraged that one of the uninitiated should have summoned him out of mere presumption, seized him by the throat and strangled him. When Agrippa returned, a few days afterwards, he found his house beset with devils. Some of them were sitting on the chimneypots, kicking up their legs in the air; while others were playing at leapfrog, on the very edge of the parapet. His study was so filled with them that he found it difficult to make his way to his desk. When, at last, he had elbowed his way through them, he found his book open, and the student lying dead upon the floor. He saw immediately how the mischief had been done; and, dismissing all the inferior imps, asked the principal demon how he could have been so rash as to kill the young man. The demon replied, that he had been needlessly invoked by an insulting youth, and could do no less than kill him for his presumption. Agrippa reprimanded him severely, and ordered him immediately to reanimate the dead body, and walk about with it in the market-place for the whole of the afternoon. The demon did so: the student revived; and, putting his arm through that of his unearthly murderer, walked very lovingly with him, in sight of all the people. At sunset, the body fell down again, cold and lifeless as before, and was carried by the crowd to the hospital, it being the general opinion that he had expired in a fit of apoplexy. His conductor immediately disappeared. When the body was examined, marks of strangulation were found on the neck, and prints of the long claws of the demon on various parts of it. These appearances, together with a story, which soon obtained currency, that the companion of the young man had vanished in a cloud of flame and smoke, opened people's eyes to the truth. The magistrates of Louvain instituted inquiries; and the result was, that Agrippa was obliged to quit the town.

Other authors besides Delrio relate similar stories of this philosopher. The world in those days was always willing enough to believe in tales of magic and sorcery; and when, as in Agrippa's case, the alleged magician gave himself out for such, and claimed credit for the wonders he worked, it is not surprising that the age should have allowed his pretensions. It was dangerous boasting, which sometimes led to the stake or the gallows, and therefore was thought to be not without foundation. Paulus Jovius, in his "Eulogia Doctorum Virorum," says, that the devil, in the shape of a large black dog, attended Agrippa wherever he went. Thomas Nash, in his adventures of Jack Wilton, relates, that at the request of Lord Surrey, Erasmus, and some other learned men, Agrippa called up from the grave many of the great philosophers of antiquity; among others, Tully, whom he caused to re-deliver his celebrated oration for Roscius. He also showed Lord Surrey, when in Germany, an exact resemblance in a glass of his mistress the fair Geraldine. She was represented on her couch weeping for the absence of her lover. Lord Surrey made a note of the exact time at which he saw this vision, and ascertained afterwards that his mistress was actually so employed at the very minute. To Thomas Lord Cromwell, Agrippa represented King Henry VIII. hunting in Windsor Park, with the principal lords of his court; and to please the Emperor Charles V. he summoned King David and King Solomon from the tomb.

Naude, in his "Apology for the Great Men who have been falsely suspected of Magic," takes a great deal of pains to clear Agrippa from the imputations cast upon him by Delrio, Paulus Jovius, and other such ignorant and prejudiced scribblers. Such stories demanded refutation in the days of Naude, but they may now be safely left to decay in their own absurdity. That they should have attached, however, to the memory of a man, who claimed the power of making iron obey him when he told it to become gold, and who wrote such a work as that upon magic, which goes by his name, is not at all surprising.

Paracelsus

This philosopher, called by Naude, "the zenith and rising sun of all the alchymists," was born at Einsiedeln, near Zurich, in the year 1493. His true name was Hohenheim; to which, as he himself informs us, were prefixed the baptismal names of Aureolus Theophrastus Bombastes Paracelsus. The last of these he chose for his common designation while he was yet a boy; and rendered it, before he died, one of the most famous in the annals of his time. His father, who was a physician, educated his son for the same pursuit. The latter was an apt scholar, and made great progress. By chance the work of Isaac Hollandus fell into his hands, and from that time he became smitten with the mania of the philosopher's stone. All his thoughts henceforth were devoted to metallurgy; and he travelled into Sweden that he might visit the mines of that country, and examine the ores while they yet lay in the bowels of the earth. He also visited Trithemius at the monastery of Spannheim, and obtained instructions from him in the science of alchymy. Continuing his travels, he proceeded through Prussia and Austria into Turkey, Egypt, and Tatary, and thence returning to Constantinople, learned, as he boasted, the art of transmutation, and became possessed of the elixir vitae. He then established himself as a physician in his native Switzerland at Zurich, and commenced writing works upon alchymy and medicine, which immediately fixed the attention of Europe. Their great obscurity was no impediment to their fame; for the less the author was understood, the more the demonologists, fanatics, and philosopher's-stone-hunters seemed to appreciate him. His fame as a physician kept pace with that which he enjoyed as an alchymist, owing to his having effected some happy cures by means of mercury and opium; drugs unceremoniously condemned by his professional brethren. In the year 1526, he was chosen Professor of Physics and Natural Philosophy in the University of Basle, where his lectures attracted vast numbers of students. He denounced the writings of all former physicians as tending to mislead; and publicly burned the works of Galen and Avicenna, as quacks and impostors. He exclaimed, in presence of the admiring and half-bewildered crowd, who assembled to witness the ceremony, that there was more knowledge in his shoestrings than in the writings of these physicians. Continuing in the same strain, he said all the universities in the world were full of ignorant quacks; but that he, Paracelsus, over flowed with wisdom. "You will all follow my new system," said he, with furious gesticulations, "Avicenna, Galen, Rhazis, Montagnana, Meme -- you will all follow me, ye professors of Paris, Montpellier, Germany, Cologne, and Vienna! and all ye that dwell on the Rhine and the Danube -- ye that inhabit the isles of the sea; and ye also, Italians, Dalmatians, Athenians, Arabians, Jews -- ye will all follow my doctrines, for I am the monarch of medicine!"

But he did not long enjoy the esteem of the good citizens of Basle. It is said that he indulged in wine so freely, as not unfrequently to be seen in the streets in a state of intoxication. This was ruinous for a physician, and his good fame decreased rapidly. His ill fame increased in still greater proportion, especially when he assumed the airs of a sorcerer. He boasted of the legions of spirits at his command; and of one especially, which he kept imprisoned in the hilt of his sword. Wetterus, who lived twenty-seven months in his service, relates that he often threatened to invoke a whole army of demons, and show him the great authority which he could exercise over them. He let it be believed, that the spirit in his sword had custody of the elixir of life, by means of which he could make any one live to be as old as the antediluvians. He also boasted that he had a spirit at his command, called "Azoth," whom he kept imprisoned in a jewel; and in many of the old portraits he is represented with a jewel, inscribed with the word "Azoth," in his hand.

If a sober prophet has little honour in his own country, a drunken one has still less. Paracelsus found it at last convenient to quit Basle, and establish himself at Strasbourg. The immediate cause of this change of residence was as follows: -- A citizen lay at the point of death, and was given over by all the physicians of the town. As a last resource Paracelsus was called in, to whom the sick man promised a magnificent recompence, if by his means he were cured. Paracelsus gave him two small pills, which the man took and rapidly recovered. When he was quite well, Paracelsus sent for his fee; but the citizen had no great opinion of the value of a cure which had been so speedily effected. He had no notion of paying a handful of gold for two pills, although they had saved his life, and he refused to pay more than the usual fee for a single visit. Paracelsus brought an action against him, and lost it. This result so exasperated him, that he left Basle in high dudgeon. He resumed his wandering life, and travelled in Germany and Hungary, supporting himself as he went on the credulity and infatuation of all classes of society. He cast nativities -- told fortunes -- aided those who had money to throw away upon the experiment, to find the philosopher's stone -- prescribed remedies for cows and pigs, and aided in the recovery of stolen goods. After residing successively at Nuremburg, Augsburg, Vienna, and Mindelheim, he retired in the year 1541 to Saltzbourg, and died in a state of abject poverty in the hospital of that town.

If this strange charlatan found hundreds of admirers during his life, he found thousands after his death. A sect of Paracelsists sprang up in France and Germany, to perpetuate the extravagant doctrines of their founder upon all the sciences, and upon alchymy in particular. The chief leaders were Bodenstein and Dorneus. The following is a summary of his doctrine, founded upon supposed existence of the philosopher's stone; it is worth preserving from its very absurdity, and altogether unparalleled in the history of philosophy:-- First of all, he maintained that the contemplation of the perfection of the Deity sufficed to procure all wisdom and knowledge; that the Bible was the key to the theory of all diseases, and that it was necessary to search into the Apocalypse to know the signification of magic medicine. The man who blindly obeyed the will of God, and who succeeded in identifying himself with the celestial intelligences, possessed the philosopher's stone -- he could cure all diseases, and prolong life to as many centuries as he pleased; it being by the very same means that Adam and the antediluvian patriarchs prolonged theirs. Life was an emanation from the stars -- the sun governed the heart, and the moon the brain. Jupiter governed the liver, Saturn the gall, Mercury the lungs, Mars the bile, and Venus the loins. In the stomach of every human being there dwelt a demon, or intelligence, that was a sort of alchymist in his way, and mixed, in their due proportions, in his crucible, the various aliments that were sent into that grand laboratory the belly.[See the article "Paracelsus," by the learned Renaudin, in the "Biographie Universelle."] He was proud of the title of magician, and boasted that he kept up a regular correspondence with Galen from hell; and that he often summoned Avicenna from the same regions to dispute with him on the false notions he had promulgated respecting alchymy, and especially regarding potable gold and the elixir of life. He imagined that gold could cure ossification of the heart, and, in fact, all diseases, if it were gold which had been transmuted from an inferior metal by means of the philosopher's stone, and if it were applied under certain conjunctions of the planets. The mere list of the works in which he advances these frantic imaginings, which he called a doctrine, would occupy several

George Agricola

This alchymist was born in the province of Misnia, in 1494. His real name was Bauer, meaning a husbandman, which, in accordance with the common fashion of his age, he Latinized into Agricola. From his early youth, he delighted in the visions of the hermetic science. Ere he was sixteen, he longed for the great elixir which was to make him live for seven hundred years, and for the stone which was to procure him wealth to cheer him in his multiplicity of days. He published a small treatise upon the subject at Cologne, in 1531, which obtained him the patronage of the celebrated Maurice, Duke of Saxony. After practising for some years as a physician at Joachimsthal, in Bohemia, he was employed by Maurice as superintendent of the silver mines of Chemnitz. He led a happy life among the miners, making various experiments in alchymy while deep in the bowels of the earth. He acquired a great knowledge of metals, and gradually got rid of his extravagant notions about the philosopher's stone. The miners had no faith in alchymy; and they converted him to their way of thinking, not only in that but in other respects. From their legends, he became firmly convinced that the bowels of the earth were inhabited by good and evil spirits, and that firedamp and other explosions sprang from no other causes than the mischievous propensities of the latter. He died in the year 1555, leaving behind him the reputation of a very able and intelligent man.

Denis Zachaire

Autobiography, written by a wise man who was once a fool, is not only the most instructive, but the most delightful of reading. Denis Zachaire, an alchymist of the sixteenth century, has performed this task, and left a record of his folly and infatuation in pursuit of the philosopher's stone, which well repays perusal. He was born in the year 1510, of an ancient family in Guienne, and was early sent to the university of Bordeaux, under the care of a tutor to direct his studies. Unfortunately, his tutor was a searcher for the grand elixir, and soon rendered his pupil as mad as himself upon the subject. With this introduction, we will allow Denis Zachaire to speak for himself, and continue his narrative in his own words :--" I received from home," says he, "the sum of two hundred crowns for the expenses of myself and master; but before the end of the year, all our money went away in the smoke of our furnaces. My master, at the same time, died of a fever, brought on by the parching heat of our laboratory, from which he seldom or never stirred, and which was scarcely less hot than the arsenal of Venice. His death was the more unfortunate for me, as my parents took the opportunity of reducing my allowance, and sending me only sufficient for my board and lodging, instead of the sum I required to continue my operations in alchymy.

"To meet this difficulty and get out of leading-strings, I returned home at the age of twenty-five, and mortgaged part of my property for four hundred crowns. This sum was necessary to perform an operation of the science, which had been communicated to me by an Italian at Toulouse, and who, as he said, had proved its efficacy. I retained this man in my service, that we might see the end of the experiment. I then, by means of strong distillations, tried to calcinate gold and silver; but all my labour was in vain. The weight of the gold I drew out of my furnace was diminished by one-half since I put it in, and my four hundred crowns were very soon reduced to two hundred and thirty. I gave twenty of these to my Italian, in order that he might travel to Milan, where the author of the receipt resided, and ask him the explanation of some passages which we thought obscure. I remained at Toulouse all the winter, in the hope of his return; but I might have remained there till this day if I had waited for him, for I never saw his face again.

"In the succeeding summer there was a great plague, which forced me to quit the town. I did not, however, lose sight of my work. I went to Cahors, where I remained six months, and made the acquaintance of an old man, who was commonly known to the people as 'the Philosopher;' a name which, in country places, is often bestowed upon people whose only merit is, that they are less ignorant than their neighbours. I showed him my collection of alchymical receipts, and asked his opinion upon them. He picked out ten or twelve of them, merely saying that they were better than the others. When the plague ceased, I returned to Toulouse, and recommenced my experiments in search of the stone. I worked to such effect that my four hundred crowns were reduced to one hundred and seventy.

"That I might continue my work on a safer method, I made acquaintance, in 1537, with a certain Abbe, who resided in the neighbourhood. He was smitten with the same mania as myself, and told me that one of his friends, who had followed to Rome in the retinue of the Cardinal d'Armagnac, had sent him from that city a new receipt, which could not fail to transmute iron and copper, but which would cost two hundred crowns. I provided half this money, and the Abbe the rest; and we began to operate at our joint expense. As we required spirits of wine for our experiment, I bought a tun of excellent vin de Gaillac. I extracted the spirit, and rectified it several times. We took a quantity of this, into which we put four marks of silver, and one of gold, that had been undergoing the process of calcination for a month. We put this mixture cleverly into a sort of horn-shaped vessel, with another to serve as a retort; and placed the whole apparatus upon our furnace, to produce congelation. This experiment lasted a year; but, not to remain idle, we amused ourselves with many other less important operations. We drew quite as much profit from these as from our great work.

The whole of the year 1537 passed over without producing any change whatever: in fact, we might have waited till doomsday for the congelation of our spirits of wine. However, we made a projection with it upon some heated quicksilver; but all was in vain. Judge of our chagrin, especially of that of the Abbe, who had already boasted to all the monks of his monastery, that they had only to bring the large pump which stood in a corner of the cloister, and he would convert it into gold; but this ill luck did not prevent us from persevering. I once more mortgaged my paternal lands for four hundred crowns, the whole of which I determined to devote to a renewal of my search for the great secret. The Abbe contributed the same sum; and, with these eight hundred crowns, I proceeded to Paris, a city more abounding with alchymists than any other in the world, resolved never to leave it until I had either found the philosopher's stone, or spent all my money. This journey gave the greatest offence to all my relations and friends, who, imagining that I was fitted to be a great lawyer, were anxious that I should establish myself in that profession. For the sake of quietness, I pretended, at last, that such was my object.

"After travelling for fifteen days, I arrived in Paris, on the 9th of January 1539. I remained for a month, almost unknown; but I had no sooner begun to frequent the amateurs of the science, and visited the shops of the furnace-makers, than I had the acquaintance of more than a hundred operative alchymists, each of whom had a different theory and a different mode of working. Some of them preferred cementation; others sought the universal alkahest, or dissolvent; and some of them boasted the great efficacy of the essence of emery. Some of them endeavoured to extract mercury from other metals to fix it afterwards; and, in order that each of us should be thoroughly acquainted with the proceedings of the others, we agreed to meet somewhere every night, and report progress. We met sometimes at the house of one, and sometimes in the garret of another; not only on week days, but on Sundays, and the great festivals of the Church. 'Ah!' one used to say, 'if I had the means of recommencing this experiment, I should do something.' ' Yes,' said another, 'if my crucible had not cracked, I should have succeeded before now :' while a third exclaimed, with a sigh, 'If I had but had a round copper vessel of sufficient strength, I would have fixed mercury with silver.' There was not one among them who had not some excuse for his failure; but I was deaf to all their speeches. I did not want to part with my money to any of them, remembering how often I had been the dupe of such promises.

"A Greek at last presented himself; and with him I worked a long time uselessly upon nails, made of cinabar, or vermilion. I was also acquainted with a foreign gentleman newly arrived in Paris, and often accompanied him to the shops of the goldsmiths, to sell pieces of gold and silver, the produce, as he said, of his experiments. I stuck closely to him for a long time, in the hope that he would impart his secret. He refused for a long time, but acceded, at last, on my earnest entreaty, and I found that it was nothing more than an ingenious trick. I did not fail to inform my friend, the Abbe, whom I had left at Toulouse, of all my adventures; and sent him, among other matters, a relation of the trick by which this gentleman pretended to turn lead into gold. The Abbe still imagined that I should succeed at last, and advised me to remain another year in Paris, where I had made so good a beginning. I remained there three years; but, notwithstanding all my efforts, I had no more success than I had had elsewhere.

"I had just got to the end of my money, when I received a letter from the Abbe, telling me to leave everything, and join him immediately at Toulouse. I went accordingly, and found that he had received letters from the King of Navarre (grandfather of Henry IV). This Prince was a great lover of philosophy, full of curiosity, and had written to the Abbe, that I should visit him at Pau; and that he would give me three or four thousand crowns, if I would communicate the secret I had learned from the foreign gentleman. The Abbe's ears were so tickled with the four thousand crowns, that he let me have no peace, night or day, until he had fairly seen me on the road to Pau. I arrived at that place in the month of May 1542. I worked away, and succeeded, according to the receipt I had obtained. When I had finished, to the satisfaction of the King, he gave me the reward that I expected. Although he was willing enough to do me further service, he was dissuaded from it by the lords of his court; even by many of those who had been most anxious that I should come. He sent me then about my business, with many thanks; saying, that if there was anything in his kingdom which he could give me -- such as the produce of confiscations, or the like -- he should be most happy. I thought I might stay long enough for these prospective confiscations, and never get them at last; and I therefore determined to go back to my friend, the Abbe.

"I learned, that on the road between Pau and Toulouse, there resided a monk, who was very skilful in all matters of natural philosophy. On my return, I paid him a visit. He pitied me very much, and advised me, with much warmth and kindness of expression, not to amuse myself any longer with such experiments as these, which were all false and sophistical; but that I should read the good books of the old philosophers, where I might not only find the true matter of the science of alchymy, but learn also the exact order of operations which ought to be followed. I very much approved of this wise advice; but, before I acted upon it, I went back to my Abbe, of Toulouse, to give him an account of the eight hundred crowns, which we had had in common; and, at the same time, share with him such reward as I had received from the King of Navarre. If he was little satisfied with the relation of my adventures since our first separation, he appeared still less satisfied when I told him I had formed a resolution to renounce the search for the philosopher's stone. The reason was, that he thought me a good artist. Of our eight hundred crowns, there remained but one hundred and seventy-six. When I quitted the Abbe, I went to my own house, with the intention of remaining there, till I had read all the old philosophers, and of then proceeding to Paris.

"I arrived in Paris on the day after All Saints, of the year 1546, and devoted another year to the assiduous study of great authors. Among others, the 'Turba Philosophorum' of the 'Good Trevisan,' ' The Remonstance of Nature to the wandering Alchymist,' by Jean de Meung; and several others of the best books: but, as I had no right' principles, I did not well know what course to follow.

"At last I left my solitude; not to see my former acquaintances, the adepts and operators, but to frequent the society of true philosophers. Among them I fell into still greater uncertainties; being, in fact, completely bewildered by the variety of operations which they showed me. Spurred on, nevertheless, by a sort of frenzy or inspiration, I threw myself into the works of Raymond Lulli and of Arnold de Villeneuve. The reading of these, and the reflections I made upon them, occupied me for another year, when I finally determined on the course I should adopt. I was obliged to wait, however, until I had mortgaged another very considerable portion of my patrimony. This business was not settled until the beginning of Lent, 1549, when I commenced my operations. I laid in a stock of all that was necessary, and began to work the day after Easter. It was not, however, without some disquietude and opposition from my friends who came about me; one asking me what I was going to do, and whether I had not already spent money enough upon such follies. Another assured me that, if I bought so much charcoal, I should strengthen the suspicion already existing, that I was a coiner of base money. Another advised me to purchase some place in the magistracy, as I was already a Doctor of Laws. My relations spoke in terms still more annoying to me, and even threatened that, if I continued to make such a fool of myself, they would send a posse of police-officers into my house, and break all my furnaces and crucibles into atoms. I was wearied almost to death by this continued persecution; but I found comfort in my work and in the progress of my experiment, to which I was very attentive, and which went on bravely from day to day. About this time, there was a dreadful plague in Paris, which interrupted all intercourse between man and man, and left me as much to myself as I could desire. I soon had the satisfaction to remark the progress and succession of the three colours which, according to the philosophers, always prognosticate the approaching perfection of the work. I observed them distinctly, one after the other; and next year, being Easter Sunday, 1550, I made the great trial. Some common quicksilver, which I put into a small crucible on the fire, was, in less than an hour, converted into very good gold. You may judge how great was my joy, but I took care not to boast of it. I returned thanks to God for the favour he had shown me, and prayed that I might only be permitted to make such use of it as would redound to his glory.

"On the following day, I went towards Toulouse to find the Abbe, in accordance with a mutual promise that we should communicate our discoveries to each other. On my way, I called in to see the sage monk who had assisted me with his counsels; but I had the sorrow to learn that they were both dead. After this, I would not return to my own home, but retired to another place, to await one of my relations whom I had left in charge of my estate. I gave him orders to sell all that belonged to me, as well movable as immovable -- to pay my debts with the proceeds, and divide all the rest among those in any way related to me who might stand in need of it, in order that they might enjoy some share of the good fortune which had befallen me. There was a great deal of talk in the neighbourhood about my precipitate retreat; the wisest of my acquaintance imagining that, broken down and ruined by my mad expenses, I sold my little remaining property that I might go and hide my shame in distant countries.

"My relative already spoken of rejoined me on the 1st of July, after having performed all the business I had intrusted him with. We took our departure together, to seek a land of liberty. We first retired to Lausanne, in Switzerland, when, after remaining there for some time, we resolved to pass the remainder of our days in some of the most celebrated cities of Germany, living quietly and without splendour."

Thus ends the story of Denis Zachaire, as written by himself. He has not been so candid at its conclusion as at its commencement, and has left the world in doubt as to his real motives for pretending that he had discovered the philosopher's stone. It seems probable that the sentence he puts into the months of his wisest acquaintances was the true reason of his retreat; that he was, in fact, reduced to poverty, and hid his shame in foreign countries. Nothing further is known of his life, and his real name has never yet been discovered. He wrote a work on alchymy, entitled "The true Natural Philosophy of Metals."

Dr. Dee and Edward Kelly

John Dee and Edward Kelly claim to be mentioned together, having been so long associated in the same pursuits, and undergone so many strange vicissitudes in each other's society. Dee was altogether a wonderful man, and had he lived in an age when folly and superstition were less rife, he would, with the same powers which he enjoyed, have left behind him a bright and enduring reputation. He was born in London, in the year 1527, and very early manifested a love for study. At the age of fifteen he was sent to Cambridge, and delighted so much in his books, that he passed regularly eighteen hours every day among them. Of the other six, he devoted four to sleep and two for refreshment. Such intense application did not injure his health, and could not fail to make him one of the first scholars of his time. Unfortunately, however, he quitted the mathematics and the pursuits of true philosophy to indulge in the unprofitable reveries of the occult sciences. He studied alchymy, astrology, and magic, and thereby rendered himself obnoxious to the authorities at Cambridge. To avoid persecution, he was at last obliged to retire to the university of Louvain; the rumours of sorcery that were current respecting him rendering his longer stay in England not altogether without danger. He found at Louvain many kindred spirits who had known Cornelius Agrippa while he resided among them, and by whom he was constantly entertained with the wondrous deeds of that great master of the hermetic mysteries. From their conversation he received much encouragement to continue the search for the philosopher's stone, which soon began to occupy nearly all his thoughts.

He did not long remain on the Continent, but returned to England in 1551, being at that time in the twenty-fourth year of his age. By the influence of his friend, Sir John Cheek, he was kindly received at the court of King Edward VI, and rewarded (it is difficult to say for what) with a pension of one hundred crowns. He continued for several years to practise in London as an astrologer; casting nativities, telling fortunes, and pointing out lucky and unlucky days. During the reign of Queen Mary he got into trouble, being suspected of heresy, and charged with attempting Mary's life by means of enchantments. He was tried for the latter offence, and acquitted; but was retained in prison on the former charge, and left to the tender mercies of Bishop Bonner. He had a very narrow escape from being burned in Smithfield, but he, somehow or other, contrived to persuade that fierce bigot that his orthodoxy was unimpeachable, and was set at liberty in 1555.

On the accession of Elizabeth, a brighter day dawned upon him. During her retirement at Woodstock, her servants appear to have consulted him as to the time of Mary's death, which Circumstance, no doubt, first gave rise to the serious charge for which he was brought to trial. They now came to consult him more openly as to the fortunes of their mistress; and Robert Dudley, the celebrated Earl of Leicester, was sent by command of the Queen herself to know the most auspicious day for her coronation. So great was the favour he enjoyed that, some years afterwards, Elizabeth condescended to pay him a visit at his house in Mortlake, to view his museum of curiosities, and, when he was ill, sent her own physician to attend upon him.

Astrology was the means whereby he lived, and he continued to practise it with great assiduity; but his heart was in alchymy. The philosopher's stone and the elixir of life haunted his daily thoughts and his nightly dreams. The Talmudic mysteries, which he had also deeply studied, impressed him with the belief, that he might hold converse with spirits and angels, and learn from them all the mysteries of the universe. Holding the same idea as the then obscure sect of the Rosicrucians, some of whom he had perhaps encountered in his travels in Germany, he imagined that, by means of the philosopher's stone, he could summon these kindly spirits at his will. By dint of continually brooding upon the subject, his imagination became so diseased, that he at last persuaded himself that an angel appeared to him, and promised to be his friend and companion as long as he lived. He relates that, one day, in November 1582, while he was engaged in fervent prayer, the window of his museum looking towards the west suddenly glowed with a dazzling light, in the midst of which, in all his glory, stood the great angel Uriel. Awe and wonder rendered him speechless; but the angel smiling graciously upon him, gave him a crystal, of a convex form, and told him that, whenever he wished to hold converse with the beings of another sphere, he had only to gaze intently upon it, and they would appear in the crystal and unveil to him all the secrets of futurity. [The "crystal" alluded to appears to have been a black stone, or piece of polished coal. The following account of it is given in the Supplement to Granger's "Biographical History." -- "The black stone into which Dee used to call his spirits was in the collection of the Earls of Peterborough, from whence it came to Lady Elizabeth Germaine. It was next the property of the late Duke of Argyle, and is now Mr. Walpole's. It appears upon examination to be nothing more than a polished piece of cannel coal; but this is what Butler means when he says, 'Kelly did all his feats upon The devil's looking-glass -- a stone.'"] This saying, the angel disappeared. Dee found from experience of the crystal that it was necessary that all the faculties of the soul should be concentrated upon it, otherwise the spirits did not appear. He also found that he could never recollect the conversations he had with the angels. He therefore determined to communicate the secret to another person, who might converse with the spirits while he (Dee) sat in another part of the room, and took down in writing the revelations which they made.

He had at this time in his service, as his assistant, one Edward Kelly, who, like himself, was crazy upon the subject of the philosopher's stone. There was this difference, however, between them, that, while Dee was more of an enthusiast than an impostor, Kelly was more of an impostor than an enthusiast. In early life he was a notary, and had the misfortune to lose both his ears for forgery. This mutilation, degrading enough in any man, was destructive to a philosopher; Kelly, therefore, lest his wisdom should suffer in the world's opinion, wore a black skull-cap, which, fitting close to his head, and descending over both his cheeks, not only concealed his loss, but gave him a very solemn and oracular appearance. So well did he keep his secret, that even Dee, with whom he lived so many years, appears never to have discovered it. Kelly, with this character, was just the man to carry on any piece of roguery for his own advantage, or to nurture the delusions of his master for the same purpose. No sooner did Dee inform him of the visit he had received from the glorious Uriel, than Kelly expressed such a fervour of belief that Dee's heart glowed with delight. He set about consulting his crystal forthwith, and on the 2nd of December 1581, the spirits appeared, and held a very extraordinary discourse with Kelly, which Dee took down in writing. The curious reader may see this farrago of nonsense among the Harleian MSS. in the British Museum. The later consultations were published in a folio volume, in 1659, by Dr. Meric Casaubon, under the title of "A True and Faithful Relation of what passed between Dr. John Dee and some Spirits; tending, had it succeeded, to a general Alteration of most States and Kingdoms in the World." [Lilly, the astrologer, in his Life written by himself, frequently tells of prophecies delivered by the angels in a manner similar to the angels of Dr. Dee. He says, "The prophecies were not given vocally by the angels, but by inspection of the crystal in types and figures, or by apparition the circular way; where, at some distance, the angels appear, representing by forms, shapes, and creatures what is demanded. It is very rare, yea, even in our days," quoth that wiseacre, "for any operator or master to hear the angels speak articulately: when they do speak, it is like the Irish, much in the throat!"]

The fame of these wondrous colloquies soon spread over the country, and even reached the Continent. Dee, at the same time, pretended to be in possession of the elixir vitae, which he stated he had found among the ruins of Glastonbury Abbey, in Somersetshire. People flocked from far and near to his house at Mortlake to have their nativities cast, in preference to visiting astrologers of less renown. They also longed to see a man who, according to his own account, would never die. Altogether, he carried on a very profitable trade, but spent so much in drugs and metals to work out some peculiar process of transmutation, that he never became rich.

About this time there came into England a wealthy Polish nobleman, named Albert Laski, Count Palatine of Siradz. His object was principally, he said, to visit the court of Queen Elizabeth, the fame of whose glory and magnificence had reached him in distant Poland. Elizabeth received this flattering stranger with the most splendid hospitality, and appointed her favourite Leicester to show him all that was worth seeing in England. He visited all the curiosities of London and Westminster, and from thence proceeded to Oxford and Cambridge, that he might converse with some of the great scholars whose writings shed lustre upon the land of their birth. He was very much disappointed at not finding Dr. Dee among them, and told the Earl of Leicester that he would not have gone to Oxford if he had known that Dee was not there. The Earl promised to introduce him to the great alchymist on their return to London, and the Pole was satisfied. A few days afterwards, the Earl and Laski being in the antechamber of the Queen, awaiting an audience of her Majesty, Dr. Dee arrived on the same errand, and was introduced to the Pole. [Albert Laski, son of Jaroslav, was Palatine of Siradz, and afterwards of Sendomir, and chiefly contributed to the election of Henry of Valois, the Third of France, to the throne of Poland, and was one of the delegates who went to France in order to announce to the new monarch his elevation to the sovereignty of Poland. After the deposition of Henry, Albert Laski voted for Maximilian of Austria. In 1585 he visited England, when Queen Elizabeth received him with great distinction. The honours which were shown him during his visit to Oxford, by the especial command of the Queen, were equal to those rendered to sovereign princes. His extraordinary prodigality rendered his enormous wealth insufficient to defray his expenses, and he therefore became a zealous adept in alchymy, and took from England to Poland with him two known alchymists. -- Count Valerian Krasinski's "Historical Sketch of the Reformation in Poland."] An interesting conversation ensued, which ended by the stranger inviting himself to dine with the astrologer at his house at Mortlake. Dee returned home in some tribulation, for he found he had not money enough, without pawning his plate, to entertain Count Laski and his retinue in a manner becoming their dignity. In this emergency he sent off an express to the Earl of Leicester, stating frankly the embarrassment he laboured under, and praying his good offices in representing the matter to her Majesty. Elizabeth immediately sent him a present of twenty pounds.

On the appointed day, Count Laski came, attended by a numerous retinue, and expressed such open and warm admiration of the wonderful attainments of his host, that Dee turned over, in his own mind, how he could bind irretrievably to his interests a man who seemed so well inclined to become his friend. Long acquaintance with Kelly had imbued him with all the roguery of that personage; and he resolved to make the Pole pay dearly for his dinner. He found out, before many days, that he possessed great estates in his own country, as well as great influence; but that an extravagant disposition had reduced him to temporary embarrassment. He also discovered, that he was a firm believer in the philosopher's stone and the water of life. He was, therefore, just the man upon whom an adventurer might fasten himself. Kelly thought so too; and both of them set to work, to weave a web, in the meshes of which they might firmly entangle the rich and credulous stranger. They went very cautiously about it; first throwing out obscure hints of the stone and the elixir; and, finally, of the spirits, by means of whom they could turn over the pages of the Book of Futurity, and read the awful secrets inscribed therein. Laski eagerly implored that he might be admitted to one of their mysterious interviews with Uriel and the angels; but they knew human nature too well to accede at once to the request. To the Count's entreaties they only replied by hints of the difficulty or impropriety of summoning the spirits in the presence of a stranger; or of one who might, perchance, have no other motive than the gratification of a vain curiosity: but they only meant to whet the edge of his appetite by this delay, and would have been sorry indeed if the Count had been discouraged. To show how exclusively the thoughts both of Dee and Kelly were fixed upon their dupe, at this time, it is only necessary to read the introduction to their first interview with the spirits, related in the volume of Dr. Casaubon. The entry made by Dee, under the date of the 25th of May 1583, says, that when the spirit appeared to them, "I, [John Dee], and E. K. [Edward Kelly], sat together, conversing of that noble Polonian Albertus Laski, his great honour here with us obtained, and of his great liking among all sorts of the people." No doubt they were discussing how they might make the most of the "noble Polonian," and concocting the fine story with which they afterwards excited his curiosity, and drew him firmly within their toils. "Suddenly," says Dee, as they were thus employed, "there seemed to come out of the oratory, a spiritual creature, like a pretty girl, of seven or nine years of age, attired on her head, with her hair rolled up before, and hanging down behind; with a gown of silk, of changeable red and green, and with a train. She seemed to play up and down, and seemed to go in and out behind the books; and, as she seemed to go between them, the books displaced themselves, and made way for her."

With such tales as these they lured on the Pole from day to day; and at last persuaded him to be a witness of their mysteries. Whether they played off any optical delusions upon him; or whether, by the force of a strong imagination, he deluded himself, does not appear; but certain it is, that he became a complete tool in their hands, and consented to do whatever they wished him. Kelly, at these interviews, placed himself at a certain distance from the wondrous crystal, and gazed intently upon it; while Dee took his place in corner, ready to set down the prophecies as they were uttered by the spirits. In this manner they prophesied to the Pole, that he should become the fortunate possessor of the philosopher's stone; that he should live for centuries, and be chosen King of Poland; in which capacity he should gain many great victories over the Saracens, and make his name illustrious over all the earth. For this pose it was necessary, however, that Laski should leave England, and take them with him, together with their wives and families; that he should treat them all sumptuously, and allow them to want for nothing. Laski at once consented; and very shortly afterwards they were all on the road to Poland.

It took them upwards of four months to reach the Count's estates, in the neighbourhood of Cracow. In the mean time, they led a pleasant life, and spent money with an unsparing hand. When once established in the Count's palace, they commenced the great hermetic operation of transmuting iron into gold. Laski provided them with all necessary materials, and aided them himself with his knowledge of alchymy: but, somehow or other, the experiment always failed at the very moment that it ought to have succeeded; and they were obliged to recommence operations on a grander scale. But the hopes of Laski were not easily extinguished. Already, in idea, the possessor of countless millions, he was not to be cast down for fear of present expenses. He thus continued from day to day, and from month to month, till he was, at last, obliged to sell a portion of his deeply-mortgaged estates, to find aliment for the hungry crucibles of Dee and Kelly, and the no less hungry stomachs of their wives and families. It was not till ruin stared him in the face, that he awoke from his dream of infatuation -- too happy, even then, to find that he had escaped utter beggary. Thus restored to his senses, his first thought was how to rid himself of his expensive visiters. Not wishing to quarrel with them, he proposed that they should proceed to Prague, well furnished with letters of recommendation to the Emperor Rudolph. Our alchymists too plainly saw that nothing more was to be made of the almost destitute Count Laski. Without hesitation, therefore, they accepted the proposal, and set out forthwith to the Imperial residence. They had no difficulty, on their arrival at Prague, in obtaining an audience of the Emperor. They found him willing enough to believe that such a thing as the philosopher's stone existed, and flattered themselves that they had made a favourable impression upon him; but, from some cause or other -- perhaps the look of low cunning and quackery upon the face of Kelly -- the Emperor conceived no very high opinion of their abilities. He allowed them, however, to remain for some months at Prague, feeding themselves upon the hope that he would employ them: but the more he saw of them, the less he liked them; and, when the Pope's Nuncio represented to him, that he ought not to countenance such heretic magicians, he gave orders that they should quit his dominions within four-and-twenty hours. It was fortunate for them that so little time was given them; for, had they remained six hours longer, the Nuncio had received orders to procure a perpetual dungeon, or the stake, for them.

Not knowing well where to direct their steps, they resolved to return to Cracow, where they had still a few friends; but, by this time, the funds they had drawn from Laski were almost exhausted; and they were many days obliged to go dinnerless and supperless. They had great difficulty to keep their poverty a secret from the world; but they managed to bear privation without murmuring, from a conviction that if the fact were known, it would militate very much against their pretensions. Nobody would believe that they were possessors of the philosopher's stone, if it were once suspected that they did not know how to procure bread for their subsistence. They still gained a little by casting nativities, and kept starvation at arm's length, till a new dupe, rich enough for their purposes, dropped into their toils, in the shape of a royal personage. Having procured an introduction to Stephen, King of Poland, they predicted to him, that the Emperor Rudolph would shortly be assassinated, and that the Germans would look to Poland for his successor. As this prediction was not precise enough to satisfy the King, they tried their crystal again; and a spirit appeared, who told them that the new sovereign of Germany would be Stephen of Poland. Stephen was credulous enough to believe them, and was once present when Kelly held his mystic conversations with the shadows of his crystal. He also appears to have furnished them with money to carry on their experiments in alchymy: but he grew tired, at last, of their broken promises, and their constant drains upon his pocket; and was on the point of discarding them with disgrace, when they met with another dupe, to whom they eagerly transferred their services. This was Count Rosenberg, a nobleman of large estates, at Trebona, in Bohemia. So comfortable did they find themselves in the palace of this munificent patron, that they remained nearly four years with him, faring sumptuously, and having an almost unlimited command of his money. The Count was more ambitious than avaricious: he had wealth enough, and did not care for the philosopher's stone on account of the gold, but of the length of days it would bring him. They had their predictions, accordingly, all ready framed to suit his character. They prophesied that he should be chosen King of Poland; and promised, moreover, that he should live for five hundred years to enjoy his dignity; provided always, that he found them sufficient money to carry on their experiments.

But now, while fortune smiled upon them; while they revelled in the rewards of successful villany, retributive justice came upon them in a shape they had not anticipated. Jealousy and mistrust sprang up between the two confederates, and led to such violent and frequent quarrels, that Dee was in constant fear of exposure. Kelly imagined himself a much greater personage than Dee; measuring, most likely, by the standard of impudent roguery; and was displeased that on all occasions, and from all persons, Dee received the greater share of honour and consideration. He often threatened to leave Dee to shift for himself; and the latter, who had degenerated into the mere tool of his more daring associate, was distressed beyond measure at the prospect of his desertion. His mind was so deeply imbued with superstition, that he believed the rhapsodies of Kelly to be, in a great measure, derived from his intercourse with angels; and he knew not where, in the whole world, to look for a man of depth and wisdom enough to succeed him. As their quarrels every day became more and more frequent, Dee wrote letters to Queen Elizabeth, to secure a favourable reception on his return to England; whither he intended to proceed, if Kelly forsook him. He also sent her a round piece of silver, which he pretended he had made of a portion of brass cut out of a warming-pan. He afterwards sent her the warming-pan also, that she might convince herself that the piece of silver corresponded exactly with the hole which was cut into the brass. While thus preparing for the worst, his chief desire was to remain in Bohemia with Count Rosenberg, who treated him well, and reposed much confidence in him. Neither had Kelly any great objection to remain; but a new passion had taken possession of his breast, and he was laying deep schemes to gratify it. His own wife was ill-favoured and ill-natured; Dee's was comely and agreeable: and he longed to make an exchange of partners, without exciting the jealousy or shocking the morality of Dee. This was a difficult matter; but, to a man like Kelly, who was as deficient in rectitude and right feeling as he was full of impudence and ingenuity, the difficulty was not insurmountable. He had also deeply studied the character and the foibles of Dee; and he took his measures accordingly. The next time they consulted the spirits, Kelly pretended to be shocked at their language, and refused to tell Dee what they had said. Dee insisted, and was informed that they were henceforth to have their wives in common. Dee, a little startled, inquired whether the spirits might not mean that they were to live in common harmony and good-will? Kelly tried again, with apparent reluctance, and said the spirits insisted upon the literal interpretation. The poor fanatic, Dee, resigned himself to their will; but it suited Kelly's purpose to appear coy a little longer. He declared that the spirits must be spirits, not of good, but of evil; and refused to consult them any more. He thereupon took his departure, saying that he would never return.

Dee, thus left to himself, was in sore trouble and distress of mind. He knew not on whom to fix as the successor to Kelly for consulting the spirits; but at last chose his son Arthur, a boy of eight years of age. He consecrated him to this service with great ceremony, and impressed upon the child's mind the dignified and awful nature of the duties he was called upon to perform; but the poor boy had neither the imagination, the faith, nor the artifice of Kelly. He looked intently upon the crystal, as he was told; but could see nothing and hear nothing. At last, when his eyes ached, he said he could see a vague indistinct shadow; but nothing more. Dee was in despair. The deception had been carried on so long, that he was never so happy as when he fancied he was holding converse with superior beings; and he cursed the day that had put estrangement between him and his dear friend Kelly. This was exactly what Kelly had foreseen; and, when he thought the Doctor had grieved sufficiently for his absence, he returned unexpectedly, and entered the room where the little Arthur was in vain endeavouring to distinguish something in the crystal. Dee, in entering this circumstance in his journal, ascribes this sudden return to a "miraculous fortune," and a "divine fate;" and goes on to record that Kelly immediately saw the spirits, which had remained invisible to little Arthur. One of these spirits reiterated the previous command, that they should have their wives in common. Kelly bowed his head, and submitted; and Dee, in all humility, consented to the arrangement.

This was the extreme depth of the wretched man's degradation. In this manner they continued to live for three or four months, when, new quarrels breaking out, they separated once more. This time their separation was final. Kelly, taking the elixir which he had found in Glastonbury Abbey, proceeded to Prague, forgetful of the abrupt mode in which he had previously been expelled from that city. Almost immediately after his arrival, he was seized by order of the Emperor Rudolph, and thrown into prison. He was released after some months' confinement, and continued for five years to lead a vagabond life in Germany, telling fortunes at one place, and pretending to make gold at another. He was a second time thrown into prison, on a charge of heresy and sorcery; and he then resolved, if ever he obtained his liberty, to return to England. He soon discovered that there was no prospect of this, and that his imprisonment was likely to be for life. He twisted his bed-clothes into a rope, one stormy night in February 1595, and let himself down from the window of his dungeon, situated at the top of a very high tower. Being a corpulent man, the rope gave way, and he was precipitated to the ground. He broke two of his ribs, and both his legs; and was otherwise so much injured, that he expired a few days afterwards.

Dee, for a while, had more prosperous fortune. The warming-pan he had sent to Queen Elizabeth was not without effect. He was rewarded, soon after Kelly had left him, with an invitation to return to England. His pride, which had been sorely humbled, sprang up again to its pristine dimensions; and he set out for Bohemia with a train of attendants becoming an ambassador. How he procured the money does not appear, unless from the liberality of the rich Bohemian Rosenberg, or perhaps from his plunder. He travelled with three coaches for himself and family, and three waggons to carry his baggage. Each coach had four horses, and the whole train was protected by a guard of four and twenty soldiers. This statement may be doubted; but it is on the authority of Dee himself, who made it on oath before the commissioners appointed by Elizabeth to inquire into his circumstances. On his arrival in England he had an audience of the Queen, who received him kindly as far as words went, and gave orders that he should not be molested in his pursuits of chemistry and philosophy. A man who boasted of the power to turn baser metals into gold, could not, thought Elizabeth, be in want of money; and she, therefore, gave him no more substantial marks of her approbation than her countenance and protection.

Thrown thus unexpectedly upon his own resources, Dee began in earnest the search for the philosopher's stone. He worked incessantly among his furnaces, retorts, and crucibles, and almost poisoned himself with deleterious fumes. He also consulted his miraculous crystal; but the spirits appeared not to him. He tried one Bartholomew to supply the place of the invaluable Kelly; but he being a man of some little probity, and of no imagination at all, the spirits would not hold any communication with him. Dee then tried another pretender to philosophy, of the name of Hickman; but had no better fortune. The crystal had lost its power since the departure of its great high-priest. From this quarter then Dee could get no information on the stone or elixir of the alchymists, and all his efforts to discover them by other means were not only fruitless but expensive. He was soon reduced to great distress, and wrote piteous letters to the Queen, praying relief. He represented that, after he left England with Count Laski, the mob had pillaged his house at Mortlake, accusing him of being a necromancer and a wizard; and had broken all his furniture, burned his library, consisting of four thousand rare volumes, and destroyed all the philosophical instruments and curiosities in his museum. For this damage he claimed compensation; and furthermore stated, that, as he had come to England by the Queen's command, she ought to pay the expenses of his journey. Elizabeth sent him small sums of money at various times; but, Dee still continuing his complaints, a commission was appointed to inquire into his circumstances. He finally obtained a small appointment as Chancellor of St. Paul's cathedral, which he exchanged, in 1595, for the wardenship of the college at Manchester. He remained in this capacity till 1602 or 1603, when, his strength and intellect beginning to fail him, he was compelled to resign. He retired to his old dwelling at Mortlake, in a state not far removed from actual want, supporting himself as a common fortune-teller, and being often obliged to sell or pawn his books to procure a dinner. James I. was often applied to on his behalf, but he refused to do anything for him. It may be said to the discredit of this King, that the only reward he would grant the indefatigable Stowe, in his days of old age and want, was the royal permission to beg; but no one will blame him for neglecting such a quack as John Dee. He died in 1608, in the eighty-first year of his age, and was buried at Mortlake.

The Cosmopolite

Many disputes have arisen as to the real name of the alchymist who wrote several works under the above designation. The general opinion is that he was a Scotsman, named Seton; and that by a fate very common to alchymists, who boasted too loudly of their powers of transmutation, he ended his days miserably in a dungeon, into which he was thrown by a German potentate until he made a million of gold to pay his ransom. By some he has been confounded with Michael Sendivog, or Sendivogius, a Pole, a professor of the same art, who made a great noise in Europe at the commencement of the seventeenth century. Lenglet du Fresnoy, who is in general well-informed with respect to the alchymists, inclines to the belief that these personages were distinct; and gives the following particulars of the Cosmopolite, extracted from George Morhoff, in his "Epistola ad Langelottum," and other writers.

About the year 1600, one Jacob Haussen, a Dutch pilot, was shipwrecked on the coast of Scotland. A gentleman, named Alexander Seton, put off in a boat, and saved him from drowning, and afterwards entertained him hospitably for many weeks at his house on the shore. Haussen saw that he was addicted to the pursuits of chemistry, but no conversation on the subject passed between them at the time. About a year and a half afterwards, Haussen being then at home at Enkhuysen, in Holland, received a visit from his former host. He endeavoured to repay the kindness that had been shown him; and so great a friendship arose between them, that Seton, on his departure, offered to make him acquainted with the great secret of the philosopher's stone. In his presence the Scotsman transmuted a great quantity of base metal into pure gold, and gave it him as a mark of his esteem. Seton then took leave of his friend, and travelled into Germany. At Dresden he made no secret of his wonderful powers; having, it is said, performed transmutation successfully before a great assemblage of the learned men of that city. The circumstance coming to the ears of the Duke or Elector of Saxony, he gave orders for the arrest of the alchymist. He caused him to be imprisoned in a high tower, and set a guard of forty men to watch that he did not escape, and that no strangers were admitted to his presence. The unfortunate Seton received several visits from the Elector, who used every art of persuasion to make him divulge his secret. Seton obstinately refused either to communicate his secret, or to make any gold for the tyrant; on which he was stretched upon the rack, to see if the argument of torture would render him more tractable. The result was still the same, - neither hope of reward nor fear of anguish could shake him. For several months he remained in prison, subjected alternately to a sedative and a violent regimen, till his health broke, and he wasted away almost to a skeleton.

There happened at that time to be in Dresden a learned Pole, named Michael Sendivogius, who had wasted a good deal of his time and substance in the unprofitable pursuits of alchymy. He was touched with pity for the hard fate, and admiration for the intrepidity of Seton; and determined, if possible, to aid him in escaping from the clutch of his oppressor. He requested the Elector's permission to see the alchymist, and obtained it with some difficulty. He found him in a state of great wretchedness, -- shut up from the light of day in a noisome dungeon, and with no better couch or fare than those allotted to the worst of criminals. Seton listened eagerly to the proposal of escape, and promised the generous Pole that he would make him richer than an Eastern monarch if by his means he were liberated. Sendivogius immediately commenced operations. He sold some property which he possessed near Cracow, and with the proceeds led a merry life at Dresden. He gave the most elegant suppers, to which he regularly invited the officers of the guard, and especially those who did duty at the prison of the alchymist. He insinuated himself at last into their confidence, and obtained free ingress to his friend as often as he pleased; pretending that he was using his utmost endeavours to conquer his obstinacy and worm his secret out of him. When their project was ripe, a day was fixed upon for the grand attempt; and Sendivogius was ready with a postchariot to convey him with all speed into Poland. By drugging some wine which he presented to the guards of the prison, he rendered them so drowsy that he easily found means to scale a wall unobserved, with Seton, and effect his escape. Seton's wife was in the chariot awaiting him, having safely in her possession a small packet of a black powder, which was, in fact, the philosopher's stone, or ingredient for the transmutation of iron and copper into gold. They all arrived in safety at Cracow; but the frame of Seton was so wasted by torture of body and starvation, to say nothing of the anguish of mind he had endured, that he did not long survive. He died in Cracow in 1603 or 1604, and was buried under the cathedral church of that city. Such is the story related of the author of the various works which bear the name of the Cosmopolite. A list of them may be found in the third volume of the "History of the Hermetic Philosophy."

Sendivogius

On the death of Seton, Sendivogius married his widow, hoping to learn from her some of the secrets of her deceased lord in the art of transmutation. The ounce of black powder stood him, however, in better service; for the alchymists say that, by its means, he converted great quantities of quicksilver into the purest gold. It is also said that he performed this experiment successfully before the Emperor Rudolph II, at Prague; and that the Emperor, to commemorate the circumstance, caused a marble tablet to be affixed to the wall of the room in which it was performed, bearing this inscription, "Faciat hoc quispiam alius, quod fecit Sendivogius Polonus." M. Desnoyers, secretary to the Princess Mary of Gonzaga, Queen of Poland, writing from Warsaw in 1651, says that he saw this tablet, which existed at that time, and was often visited by the curious.

The after-life of Sendivogius is related in a Latin memoir of him by one Brodowski, his steward; and is inserted by Pierre Borel in his "Treasure of Gaulish Antiquities." The Emperor Rudolph, according to this authority, was so well pleased with his success, that he made him one of his counsellors of state, and invited him to fill a station in the royal household and inhabit the palace. But Sendivogius loved his liberty, and refused to become a courtier. He preferred to reside on his own patrimonial estate of Gravarna, where, for many years, he exercised a princely hospitality. His philosophic powder, which, his steward says, was red, and not black, he kept in a little box of gold; and with one grain of it he could make five hundred ducats, or a thousand rix-dollars. He generally made his projection upon quicksilver. When he travelled, he gave this box to his steward, who hung it round his neck by a gold chain next his skin. But the greatest part of the powder he used to hide in a secret place cut into the step of his chariot. He thought that, if attacked at any time by robbers, they would not search such a place as that. When he anticipated any danger, he would dress himself in his valet's clothes, and, mounting the coach-box, put the valet inside. He was induced to take these precautions, because it was no secret that he possessed the philosopher's stone; and many unprincipled adventurers were on the watch for an opportunity to plunder him. A German Prince, whose name Brodowski has not thought fit to chronicle, served him a scurvy trick, which ever afterwards put him on his guard. This prince went on his knees to Sendivogius, and entreated him in the most pressing terms to satisfy his curiosity by converting some quicksilver into gold before him. Sendivogius, wearied by his importunity, consented, upon a promise of inviolable secrecy. After his departure, the Prince called a German alchymist, named Muhlenfels, who resided in his house, and told him all that had been done. Muhlenfels entreated that he might have a dozen mounted horsemen at his command, that he might instantly ride after the philosopher, and either rob him of all his powder or force from him the secret of making it. The Prince desired nothing better; and Muhlenfels, being provided with twelve men well mounted and armed, pursued Sendivogius in hot haste. He came up with him at a lonely inn by the road-side, just as he was sitting down to dinner. He at first endeavoured to persuade him to divulge the secret; but, finding this of no avail, he caused his accomplices to strip the unfortunate Sendivogius and tie him naked to one of the pillars of the house. He then took from him his golden box, containing a small quantity of the powder; a manuscript book on the philosopher's stone; a golden medal with its chain, presented to him by the Emperor Rudolph; and a rich cap ornamented with diamonds, of the value of one hundred thousand rix-dollars. With this booty he decamped, leaving Sendivogius still naked and firmly bound to the pillar. His servants had been treated in a similar manner; but the people of the inn released them all as soon as the robbers were out of sight.

Sendivogius proceeded to Prague, and made his complaint to the Emperor. An express was instantly sent off to the Prince, with orders that he should deliver up Muhlenfels and all his plunder. The Prince, fearful of the Emperor's wrath, caused three large gallows to be erected in his court-yard; on the highest of which he hanged Muhlenfels, with another thief on each side of him. He thus propitiated the Emperor, and got rid of an ugly witness against himself. He sent back, at the same time, the bejewelled hat, the medal and chain, and the treatise upon the philosopher's stone, which had been stolen from Sendivogius. As regarded the powder, he said he had not seen it, and knew nothing about it.

This adventure made Sendivogius more prudent; he would no longer perform the process of transmutation before any strangers, however highly recommended. He pretended, also, to be very poor; and sometimes lay in bed for weeks together, that people might believe he was suffering from some dangerous malady, and could not therefore by any possibility be the owner of the philosopher's stone. He would occasionally coin false money, and pass it off as gold; preferring to be esteemed a cheat rather than a successful alchymist.

Many other extraordinary tales are told of this personage by his steward Brodowski, but they are not worth repeating. He died in 1636, aged upwards of eighty, and was buried in his own chapel at Gravarna. Several works upon alchymy have been published under his name.

The Rosicrucians

It was during the time of the last-mentioned author that the sect of the Rosicrucians first began to create a sensation in Europe. The influence which they exercised upon opinion during their brief career, and the permanent impression which they have left upon European literature, claim for them especial notice. Before their time, alchymy was but a grovelling delusion; and theirs is the merit of having spiritualised and refined it. They also enlarged its sphere, and supposed the possession of the philosopher's stone to be, not only the means of wealth, but of health and happiness; and the instrument by which man could command the services of superior beings, control the elements to his will, defy the obstructions of time and space, and acquire the most intimate knowledge of all the secrets of the universe. Wild and visionary as they were, they were not without their uses; if it were only for having purged the superstitions of Europe of the dark and disgusting forms with which the monks had peopled it, and substituted, in their stead, a race of mild, graceful, and beneficent beings.

They are said to have derived their name from Christian Rosencreutz, or "Rose-cross," a German philosopher, who travelled in the Holy Land towards the close of the fourteenth century. While dangerously ill at a place called Damcar, he was visited by some learned Arabs, who claimed him as their brother in science, and unfolded to him, by inspiration, all the secrets of his past life, both of thought and of action. They restored him to health by means of the philosopher's stone, and afterwards instructed him in all their mysteries. He returned to Europe in 1401, being then only twenty-three years of age; and drew a chosen number of his friends around him, whom he initiated into the new science, and bound by solemn oaths to keep it secret for a century. He is said to have lived eighty-three years after this period, and to have died in 1484.

Many have denied the existence of such a personage as Rosencreutz, and have fixed the origin of this sect at a much later epoch. The first dawning of it, they say, is to be found in the theories of Paracelsus, and the dreams of Dr. Dee, who, without intending it, became the actual, though never the recognised founders of the Rosicrucian philosophy. It is now difficult, and indeed impossible, to determine whether Dee and Paracelsus obtained their ideas from the then obscure and unknown Rosicrucians, or whether the Rosicrucians did but follow and improve upon them. Certain it is, that their existence was never suspected till the year 1605, when they began to excite attention in Germany. No sooner were their doctrines promulgated, than all the visionaries, Paracelsists, and alchymists, flocked around their standard, and vaunted Rosencreutz as the new regenerator of the human race. Michael Mayer, a celebrated physician of that day, and who had impaired his health and wasted his fortune in searching for the philosopher's stone, drew up a report of the tenets and ordinances of the new fraternity, which was published at Cologne, in the year 1615. They asserted, in the first place, "that the meditations of their founders surpassed everything that had ever been imagined since the creation of the world, without even excepting the revelations of the Deity; that they were destined to accomplish the general peace and regeneration of man before the end of the world arrived; that they possessed all wisdom and piety in a supreme degree; that they possessed all the graces of nature, and could distribute them among the rest of mankind according to their pleasure; that they were subject to neither hunger, nor thirst, nor disease, nor old age, nor to any other inconvenience of nature; that they knew by inspiration, and at the first glance, every one who was worthy to be admitted into their society; that they had the same knowledge then which they would have possessed if they had lived from the beginning of the world, and had been always acquiring it; that they had a volume in which they could read all that ever was or ever would be written in other books till the end of time; that they could force to, and retain in their service the most powerful spirits and demons; that, by the virtue of their songs, they could attract pearls and precious stones from the depths of the sea or the bowels of the earth; that God had covered them with a thick cloud, by means of which they could shelter themselves from the malignity of their enemies, and that they could thus render themselves invisible from all eyes; that the eight first brethren of the "Rose-cross" had power to cure all maladies; that, by means of the fraternity, the triple diadem of the Pope would be reduced into dust; that they only admitted two sacraments, with the ceremonies of the primitive Church, renewed by them; that they recognised the Fourth Monarchy and the Emperor of the Romans as their chief and the chief of all Christians; that they would provide him with more gold, their treasures being inexhaustible, than the King of Spain had ever drawn from the golden regions of Eastern and Western Ind." This was their confession of faith. Their rules of conduct were six in number, and as follow:--

First. That, in their travels, they should gratuitously cure all diseases.

Secondly. That they should always dress in conformity to the fashion of the country in which they resided.

Thirdly. That they should, once every year, meet together in the place appointed by the fraternity, or send in writing an available excuse.

Fourthly. That every brother, whenever he felt inclined to die, should choose a person worthy to succeed him.

Fifthly. That the words "Rose-cross" should be the marks by which they should recognise each other.

Sixthly. That their fraternity should be kept secret for six times twenty years.

They asserted that these laws had been found inscribed in a golden book in the tomb of Rosencreutz, and that the six times twenty years from his death expired in 1604. They were consequently called upon, from that time forth, to promulgate their doctrine for the welfare of mankind. [The following legend of the tomb of Rosencreutz, written by Eustace Budgell, appears in No. 379 of the Spectator:-- "A certain person, having occasion to dig somewhat deep in the ground where this philosopher lay interred, met with a small door, having a wall on each side of it. His curiosity, and the hope of finding some hidden treasure, soon prompted him to force open the door. He was immediately surprised by a sudden blaze of light, and discovered a very fair vault. At the upper end of it was a statue of a man in armour, sitting by a table, and leaning on his left arm. He held a truncheon in his right hand, and had a lamp burning before him. The man had no sooner set one foot within the vault, than the statue, erecting itself from its leaning posture, stood bolt upright; and, upon the fellow's advancing another step, lifted up the truncheon in his right hand. The man still ventured a third step; when the statue, with a furious blow, broke the lamp into a thousand pieces, and left his guest in sudden darkness. Upon the report of this adventure, the country people came with lights to the sepulchre, and discovered that the statue, which was made of brass, was nothing more than a piece of clock-work; that the floor of the vault was all loose, and underlaid with several springs, which, upon any man's entering, naturally produced that which had happened. Rosicreucius, say his disciples, made use of this method to show the world that he had re-invented the ever-burning lamps of the ancients, though he was resolved no one should reap any advantage from the discovery."]

For eight years these enthusiasts made converts in Germany; but they excited little or no attention in other parts of Europe. At last they made their appearance in Paris, and threw all the learned, all the credulous, and all the lovers of the marvellous into commotion. In the beginning of March 1623, the good folks of that city, when they arose one morning, were surprised to find all their walls placarded with the following singular manifesto:--

"We, the deputies of the principal College of the Brethren of the Rose-cross, have taken up our abode, visible and invisible, in this city, by the grace of the Most High, towards whom are turned the hearts of the just. We show and teach without books or signs, and speak all sorts of languages in the countries where we dwell, to draw mankind, our fellows, from error and from death."

For a long time this strange placard was the sole topic of conversation in all public places. Some few wondered; but the greater number only laughed at it. In the course of a few weeks two books were published, which raised the first alarm respecting this mysterious society, whose dwelling-place no one knew, and no members of which had ever been seen. The first was called a history of "The frightful Compacts entered into between the Devil and the pretended 'Invisibles;' with their damnable Instructions, the deplorable Ruin of their Disciples, and their miserable End." The other was called an "Examination of the new and unknown Cabala of the Brethren of the Rose-cross, who have lately inhabited the City of Paris; with the History of their Manners, the Wonders worked by them, and many other Particulars."

These books sold rapidly. Every one was anxious to know something of this dreadful and secret brotherhood. The badauds of Paris were so alarmed that they daily expected to see the arch-enemy walking in propria persona among them. It was said in these volumes, that the Rosicrucian society consisted of six-and-thirty persons in all, who had renounced their baptism and hope of resurrection. That it was not by means of good angels, as they pretended, that they worked their prodigies; but that it was the devil who gave them power to transport themselves from one end of the world to the other with the rapidity of thought; to speak all languages; to have their purses always full of money, however much they might spend; to be invisible, and penetrate into the most secret places, in spite of fastenings of bolts and bars; and to be able to tell the past and future. These thirty-six brethren were divided into bands or companies:- six of them only had been sent on the mission to Paris, six to Italy, six to Spain, six to Germany, four to Sweden, and two into Switzerland; two into Flanders, two into Lorraine, and two into Franche Comte. It was generally believed that the missionaries to France resided somewhere in the Marais du Temple. That quarter of Paris soon acquired a bad name; and people were afraid to take houses in it, lest they should be turned out by the six invisibles of the Rose-cross. It was believed by the populace, and by many others whose education should have taught them better, that persons of a mysterious aspect used to visit the inns and hotels of Paris, and eat of the best meats and drink of the best wines, and then suddenly melt away into thin air when the landlord came with the reckoning. That gentle maidens, who went to bed alone, often awoke in the night and found men in bed with them, of shape more beautiful than the Grecian Apollo, who immediately became invisible when an alarm was raised. It was also said that many persons found large heaps of pure gold in their houses, without knowing from whence they came. All Paris was in alarm. No man thought himself secure of his goods, no maiden of her virginity, or wife of her chastity, while these Rosicrucians were abroad. In the midst of the commotion, a second placard was issued to the following effect:--

"If any one desires to see the brethren of the Rose-cross from curiosity only, he will never communicate with us. But if his will really induces him to inscribe his name in the register of our brotherhood, we, who can judge of the thoughts of all men, will convince him of the truth of our promises. For this reason we do not publish to the world the place of our abode. Thought alone, in unison with the sincere will of those who desire to know us, is sufficient to make us known to them, and them to us."

Though the existence of such a society as that of the Rose-cross was problematical, it was quite evident that somebody or other was concerned in the promulgation of these placards, which were stuck up on every wall in Paris. The police endeavoured in vain to find out the offenders, and their want of success only served to increase the perplexity of the public. The church very soon took up the question; and the Abbe Gaultier, a Jesuit, wrote a book to prove that, by their enmity to the Pope, they could be no other than disciples of Luther, sent to promulgate his heresy. Their very name, he added, proved that they were heretics; a cross surmounted by a rose being the heraldic device of the arch-heretic Luther. One Garasse said they were a confraternity of drunken impostors; and that their name was derived from the garland of roses, in the form of a cross, hung over the tables of taverns in Germany as the emblem of secrecy, and from whence was derived the common saying, when one man communicated a secret to another, that it was said "under the rose." Others interpreted the letters F. R. C. to mean, not Brethren of the Rose-cross, but Fratres Roris Cocti, or Brothers of Boiled Dew; and explained this appellation by alleging that they collected large quantities of morning dew, and boiled it, in order to extract a very valuable ingredient in the composition of the philosopher's stone and the water of life.

The fraternity thus attacked defended themselves as well as they were able. They denied that they used magic of any kind, or that they consulted the devil. They said they were all happy; that they had lived more than a century, and expected to live many centuries more; and that the intimate knowledge which they possessed of all nature was communicated to them by God himself as a reward for their piety and utter devotion to his service. Those were in error who derived their name from a cross of roses, or called them drunkards. To set the world right on the first point, they reiterated that they derived their name from Christian Rosencreutz, their founder; and, to answer the latter charge, they repeated that they knew not what thirst was, and had higher pleasures than those of the palate. They did not desire to meddle with the politics or religion of any man or set of men, although they could not help denying the supremacy of the Pope, and looking upon him as a tyrant. Many slanders, they said, had been repeated respecting them; the most unjust of which was, that they indulged in carnal appetites, and, under the cloak of their invisibility, crept into the chambers of beautiful maidens. They asserted, on the contrary, that the first vow they took on entering the society was a vow of chastity; and that any one among them who transgressed in that particular would immediately lose all the advantages he enjoyed, and be exposed once more to hunger, woe, disease, and death, like other men. So strongly did they feel on the subject of chastity, that they attributed the fall of Adam solely to his want of this virtue. Besides defending themselves in this manner, they entered into a further confession of their faith. They discarded for ever all the old tales of sorcery and witchcraft, and communion with the devil. They said there were no such horrid, unnatural, and disgusting beings as the incubi and succubi, and the innumerable grotesque imps that men had believed in for so many ages. Man was not surrounded with enemies like these, but with myriads of beautiful and beneficent beings, all anxious to do him service. The air was peopled with sylphs, the water with undines or naiads, the bowels of the earth with gnomes, and the fire with salamanders. All these beings were the friends of man, and desired nothing so much as that men should purge themselves of all uncleanness, and thus be enabled to see and converse with them. They possessed great power, and were unrestrained by the barriers of space or the obstructions of matter. But man was in one particular their superior. He had an immortal soul, and they had not. They might, however, become sharers in man's immortality, if they could inspire one of that race with the passion of love towards them. Hence it was the constant endeavour of the female spirits to captivate the admiration of men; and of the male gnomes, sylphs, salamanders, and undines, to be beloved by a woman. The object of this passion, in returning their love, imparted a portion of that celestial fire the soul; and from that time forth the beloved became equal to the lover, and both, when their allotted course was run, entered together into the mansions of felicity. These spirits, they said, watched constantly over mankind by night and day. Dreams, omens, and presentiments were all their works, and the means by which they gave warning of the approach of danger. But, though so well inclined to befriend man for their own sakes, the want of a soul rendered them at times capricious and revengeful: they took offence on slight causes, and heaped injuries instead of benefits on the heads of those who extinguished the light of reason that was in them, by gluttony, debauchery, and other appetites of the body.

The excitement produced in Paris by the placards of the brotherhood, and the attacks of the clergy, wore itself away after a few months. The stories circulated about them became at last too absurd even for that age of absurdity, and men began to laugh once more at those invisible gentlemen and their fantastic doctrines. Gabriel Naude at that conjuncture brought out his "Avis a la France sur les Freres de la Rose-croix," in which he very successfully exposed the folly of the new sect. This work, though not well written, was well timed. It quite extinguished the Rosicrucians of France; and, after that year, little more was heard of them. Swindlers, in different parts of the country, assumed the name at times to cloak their depredations; and now and then one of them was caught, and hanged for his too great ingenuity in enticing pearls and precious stones from the pockets of other people into his own, or for passing off lumps of gilded brass for pure gold, made by the agency of the philosopher's stone. With these exceptions, oblivion shrouded them.

The doctrine was not confined to a sphere so narrow as France alone; it still flourished in Germany, and drew many converts in England. The latter countries produced two great masters, in the persons of Jacob Bohmen and Robert Fludd; pretended philosophers, of whom it is difficult to say which was the more absurd and extravagant. It would appear that the sect was divided into two classes,-- the brothers Roseae Crucis, who devoted themselves to the wonders of this sublunary sphere; and the brothers Aureae Crucis, who were wholly occupied in the contemplation of things Divine. Fludd belonged to the first class, and Bohmen to the second. Fludd may be called the father of the English Rosicrucians, and as such merits a conspicuous niche in the temple of Folly.

He was born in the year 1574, at Milgate, in Kent; and was the son of Sir Thomas Fludd, Treasurer of War to Queen Elizabeth. He was originally intended for the army; but he was too fond of study, and of a disposition too quiet and retiring to shine in that sphere. His father would not, therefore, press him to adopt a course of life for which he was unsuited, and encouraged him in the study of medicine, for which he early manifested a partiality. At the age of twenty-five he proceeded to the Continent; and being fond of the abstruse, the marvellous, and the incomprehensible, he became an ardent disciple of the school of Paracelsus, whom he looked upon as the regenerator, not only of medicine, but of philosophy. He remained six years in Italy, France, and Germany; storing his mind with fantastic notions, and seeking the society of enthusiasts and visionaries. On his return to England, in 1605, he received the degree of Doctor of Medicine from the University of Oxford, and began to practice as a physician in London.

He soon made himself conspicuous. He Latinized his name from Robert Fludd into Robertus a Fluctibus, and began the promulgation of many strange doctrines. He avowed his belief in the philosopher's stone, the water of life, and the universal alkahest; and maintained that there were but two principles of all things, -- which were, condensation, the boreal or northern virtue; and rarefaction, the southern or austral virtue. A number of demons, he said, ruled over the human frame, whom he arranged in their places in a rhomboid. Every disease had its peculiar demon who produced it, which demon could only be combated by the aid of the demon whose place was directly opposite to his in the rhomboidal figure. Of his medical notions we shall have further occasion to speak in another part of this book, when we consider him in his character as one of the first founders of the magnetic delusion, and its offshoot, animal magnetism, which has created so much sensation in our own day.

As if the doctrines already mentioned were not wild enough, he joined the Rosicrucians as soon as they began to make a sensation in Europe, and succeeded in raising himself to high consideration among them. The fraternity having been violently attacked by several German authors, and among others by Libavius, Fludd volunteered a reply, and published, in 1616, his defence of the Rosicrucian philosophy, under the title of the "Apologia, compendiaria, Fraternitatem de Rosea-cruce, Suspicionis et Infamiae maculis aspersam, abluens." This work immediately procured him great renown upon the Continent, and he was henceforth looked upon as one of the high-priests of the sect. Of so much importance was he considered, that Keppler and Gassendi thought it necessary to refute him; and the latter wrote a complete examination of his doctrine. Mersenne also, the friend of Descartes, and who had defended that philosopher when accused of having joined the Rosicrucians, attacked Dr. a Fluctibus, as he preferred to be called, and showed the absurdity of the brothers of the Rose-cross in general, and of Dr. a Fluctibus in particular. Fluctibus wrote a long reply, in which he called Mersenne an ignorant calumniator, and reiterated that alchymy was a profitable science, and the Rosicrucians worthy to be the regenerators of the world. This book was published at Frankfort, and was entitled "Summum Bonum, quod est Magiae, Cabalae, Alchimiae, Fratrum Roseae-Crucis verorum, et adversus Mersenium Calumniatorem." Besides this, he wrote several other works upon alchymy, a second answer to Libavius upon the Rosicrucians, and many medical works. He died in London in 1637.

After his time there was some diminution of the sect in England. They excited but little attention, and made no effort to bring themselves into notice. Occasionally, some obscure and almost incomprehensible work made its appearance, to show the world that the folly was not extinguished. Eugenius Philalethes, a noted alchymist, who has veiled his real name under this assumed one, translated "The Fame and Confession of the Brethren of the Rosie Cross," which was published in London in 1652. A few years afterwards, another enthusiast, named John Heydon, wrote two works on the subject: the one entitled "The Wise Man's Crown, or the Glory of the Rosie Cross ;" and the other, "The Holy Guide, leading the way to unite Art and Nature, with the Rosie Crosse uncovered." Neither of these attracted much notice. A third book was somewhat more successful: it was called "A New Method of Rosicrucian Physic; by John Heydon, the servant of God and the secretary of Nature." A few extracts will show the ideas of the English Rosicrucians about this period. Its author was an attorney, "practising (to use his own words) at Westminster Hall all term times as long as he lived, and in the vacations devoting himself to alchymical and Rosicrucian meditation." In his preface, called by him an Apologue for an Epilogue, he enlightens the public upon the true history and tenets of his sect. Moses, Elias, and Ezekiel were, he says, the most ancient masters of the Rosicrucian philosophy. Those few then existing in England and the rest of Europe, were as the eyes and ears of the great King of the universe, seeing and hearing all things; seraphically illuminated; companions of the holy company of unbodied souls and immortal angels; turning themselves, Proteus-like, into any shape, and having the power of working miracles. The most pious and abstracted brethren could slack the plague in cities, silence the violent winds and tempests, calm the rage of the sea and rivers, walk in the air, frustrate the malicious aspect of witches, cure all diseases, and turn all metals into gold. He had known in his time two famous brethren of the Rosie Cross, named Walfourd and Williams, who had worked miracles in his sight, and taught him many excellent predictions of astrology and earthquakes. "I desired one of these to tell me," says he, "whether my complexion were capable of the society of my good genius. 'When I see you again,' said he, (which was when he pleased to come to me, for I knew not where to go to him,) 'I will tell you.' When I saw him afterwards, he said, 'You should pray to God; for a good and holy man can offer no greater or more acceptable service to God than the oblation of himself -- his soul.' He said, also, that the good genii were the benign eyes of God, running to and fro in the world, and with love and pity beholding the innocent endeavours of harmless and single-hearted men, ever ready to do them good and to help them."

Heydon held devoutly true that dogma of the Rosicrucians which said that neither eating nor drinking was necessary to men. He maintained that any one might exist in the same manner as that singular people dwelling near the source of the Ganges, of whom mention was made in the travels of his namesake, Sir Christopher Heydon, who had no mouths, and therefore could not eat, but lived by the breath of their nostrils; except when they took a far journey, and then they mended their diet with the smell of flowers. He said that in really pure air "there was a fine foreign fatness," with which it was sprinkled by the sunbeams, and which was quite sufficient for the nourishment of the generality of mankind. Those who had enormous appetites he had no objection to see take animal food, since they could not do without it; but he obstinately insisted that there was no necessity why they should eat it. If they put a plaster of nicely-cooked meat upon their epigastrium, it would be sufficient for the wants of the most robust and voracious! They would by that means let in no diseases, as they did at the broad and common gate, the mouth, as any one might see by example of drink; for, all the while a man sat in water, he was never athirst. He had known, he said, many Rosicrucians, who, by applying wine in this manner, had fasted for years together. In fact, quoth Heydon, we may easily fast all our life, though it be three hundred years, without any kind of meat, and so cut off all danger of disease.

This "sage philosopher" further informed his wondering contemporaries that the chiefs of the doctrine always carried about with them to their place of meeting their symbol, called the R.C. which was an ebony cross, flourished and decked with roses of gold; the cross typifying Christ's sufferings upon the Cross for our sins, and the roses of gold the glory and beauty of his Resurrection. This symbol was carried alternately to Mecca, Mount Calvary, Mount Sinai, Haran, and to three other places, which must have been in mid-air, called Cascle, Apamia, and Chaulateau Virissa Caunuch, where the Rosicrucian brethren met when they pleased, and made resolution of all their actions. They always took their pleasures in one of these places, where they resolved all questions of whatsoever had been done, was done, or should be done, in the world, from the beginning to the end thereof. "And these," he concludes, "are the men called Rosicrucians

Towards the end of the seventeenth century, more rational ideas took possession of the sect, which still continued to boast of a few members. They appear to have considered that contentment was the true philosopher's stone, and to have abandoned the insane search for a mere phantom of the imagination. Addison, in "The Spectator," [No. 574. Friday, July 30th, 1714.] gives an account of his conversation with a Rosicrucian; from which it may be inferred that the sect had grown wiser in their deeds, though in their talk they were as foolish as ever. "I was once," says he, "engaged in discourse with a Rosicrucian about the great secret. He talked of the secret as of a spirit which lived within an emerald, and converted everything that was near it to the highest perfection that it was capable of. 'It gives a lustre,' says he, 'to the sun, and water to the diamond. It irradiates every metal, and enriches lead with all the properties of gold. It heightens smoke into flame, flame into light, and light into glory.' He further added 'that a single ray of it dissipates pain, and care, and melancholy from the person on whom it falls. In short,' says he, 'its presence naturally changes every place into a kind of heaven.' After he had gone on for some time in this unintelligible cant, I found that he jumbled natural and moral ideas together into the same discourse, and that his great secret was nothing else but content."

Jacob Bohmen

It is now time to speak of Jacob Bohmen, who thought he could discover the secret of the transmutation of metals in the Bible, and who invented a strange heterogeneous doctrine of mingled alchymy and religion, and founded upon it the sect of the Aurea-crucians. He was born at Gorlitz, in Upper Lusatia, in 1575; and followed, till his thirtieth year, the occupation of a shoemaker. In this obscurity he remained, with the character of a visionary and a man of unsettled mind, until the promulgation of the Rosicrucian philosophy in his part of Germany, toward the year 1607 or 1608. From that time he began to neglect his leather, and buried his brain under the rubbish of metaphysics. The works of Paracelsus fell into his hands; and these, with the reveries of the Rosicrucians, so completely engrossed his attention that be abandoned his trade altogether, sinking, at the same time, from a state of comparative independence into poverty and destitution. But he was nothing daunted by the miseries and privations of the flesh; his mind was fixed upon the beings of another sphere, and in thought he was already the new apostle of the human race. In the year 1612, after a meditation of four years, he published his first work, entitled "Aurora; or, The Rising of the Sun;" embodying the ridiculous notions of Paracelsus, and worse confounding the confusion of that writer. The philosopher's stone might, he contended, be discovered by a diligent search of the Old and New Testaments, and more especially of the Apocalypse, which alone contained all the secrets of alchymy. He contended that the Divine Grace operated by the same rules, and followed the same methods, that the Divine Providence observed in the natural world; and that the minds of men were purged from their vices and corruptions in the very same manner that metals were purified from their dross, namely, by fire.

Besides the sylphs, gnomes, undines, and salamanders, he acknowledged various ranks and orders of demons. He pretended to invisibility and absolute chastity. He also said that, if it pleased him, he could abstain for years from meat and drink, and all the necessities of the body. It is needless, however, to pursue his follies any further. He was reprimanded for writing this work by the magistrates of Gorlitz, and commanded to leave the pen alone and stick to his wax, that his family might not become chargeable to the parish. He neglected this good advice, and continued his studies; burning minerals and purifying metals one day, and mystifying the Word of God on the next. He afterwards wrote three other works, as sublimely ridiculous as the first. The one was entitled "Metallurgia," and has the slight merit of being the least obscure of his compositions. Another was called "The Temporal Mirror of Eternity ;" and the last his "Theosophy revealed," full of allegories and metaphors,

"All strange and geason,
Devoid of sense and ordinary reason."

Bohmen died in 1624, leaving behind him a considerable number of admiring disciples. Many of them became, during the seventeenth century, as distinguished for absurdity as their master; amongst whom may be mentioned Gifftheil, Wendenhagen, John Jacob Zimmermann, and Abraham Frankenberg. Their heresy rendered them obnoxious to the Church of Rome; and many of them suffered long imprisonment and torture for their faith. One, named Kuhlmann, was burned alive at Moscow, in 1684, on a charge of sorcery. Bohmen's works were translated into English, and published, many years afterwards by an enthusiast, named William Law.

Mormius

Peter Mormius, a notorious alchymist, and contemporary of Bohmen, endeavoured, in 1630, to introduce the Rosicrucian philosophy into Holland. He applied to the States-General to grant him a public audience, that he might explain the tenets of the sect, and disclose a plan for rendering Holland the happiest and richest country on the earth, by means of the philosopher's' stone and the service of the elementary spirits. The States-General wisely resolved to have nothing to do with him. He thereupon determined to shame them by printing his book, which he did at Leyden the same year. It was entitled "The Book of the most Hidden Secrets of Nature," and was divided into three parts; the first treating of "perpetual motion," the second of the "transmutation of metals," and the third of the "universal medicine." He also published some German works upon the Rosicrucian philosophy, at Frankfort, in 1617.

Poetry and Romance are deeply indebted to the Rosicrucians for many a graceful creation. The literature of England, France, and Germany contains hundreds of sweet fictions, whose machinery has been borrowed from their day-dreams. The "delicate Ariel" of Shakspeare stands pre-eminent among the number. From the same source Pope drew the airy tenants of Belinda's dressing-room, in his charming "Rape of the Lock;" and La Motte Fouque, the beautiful and capricious water-nymph, Undine, around whom he has thrown more grace and loveliness, and for whose imaginary woes he has excited more sympathy, than ever were bestowed on a supernatural being. Sir Walter Scott also endowed the White Lady of Avenel with many of the attributes of the undines, or water-sprites. German romance and lyrical poetry teem with allusions to sylphs, gnomes, undines, and salamanders; and the French have not been behind in substituting them, in works of fiction, for the more cumbrous mythology of Greece and Rome. The sylphs, more especially, have been the favourites of the bards, and have become so familiar to the popular mind as to be, in a manner, confounded with that other race of ideal beings, the fairies, who can boast of an antiquity much more venerable in the annals of superstition. Having these obligations to the Rosicrucians, no lover of poetry can wish, however absurd they were, that such a sect of philosophers had never existed.

Borri

Just at the time that Michael Mayer was making known to the world the existence of such a body as the Rosicrucians, there was born in Italy a man who was afterwards destined to become the most conspicuous member of the fraternity. The alchymic mania never called forth the ingenuity of a more consummate or more successful impostor than Joseph Francis Borri. He was born in 1616 according to some authorities, and in 1627 according to others, at Milan; where his father, the Signor Branda Borri, practised as a physician. At the age of sixteen, Joseph was sent to finish his education at the Jesuits' College in Rome, where he distinguished himself by his extraordinary memory. He learned everything to which he applied himself with the utmost ease. In the most voluminous works no fact was too minute for his retention, and no study was so abstruse but that he could master it; but any advantages he might have derived from this facility, were neutralized by his ungovernable passions and his love of turmoil and debauchery. He was involved in continual difficulty, as well with the heads of the college as with the police of Rome, and acquired so bad a character that years could not remove it. By the aid of his friends he established himself as a physician in Rome, and also obtained some situation in the Pope's household. In one of his fits of studiousness he grew enamoured of alchymy, and determined to devote his energies to the discovery of the philosopher's stone. Of unfortunate propensities he had quite sufficient, besides this, to bring him to poverty. His pleasures were as expensive as his studies, and both were of a nature to destroy his health and ruin his fair fame. At the age of thirty-seven he found that he could not live by the practice of medicine, and began to look about for some other employment. He became, in 1653, private secretary to the Marquis di Mirogli, the minister of the Archduke of Innspruk at the court of Rome. He continued in this capacity for two years; leading, however, the same abandoned life as heretofore, frequenting the society of gamesters, debauchees, and loose women, involving himself in disgraceful street quarrels, and alienating the patrons who were desirous to befriend him.

All at once a sudden change was observed in his conduct. The abandoned rake put on the outward sedateness of a philosopher; the scoffing sinner proclaimed that he had forsaken his evil ways, and would live thenceforth a model of virtue. To his friends this reformation was as pleasing as it was unexpected; and Borri gave obscure hints that it had been brought about by some miraculous manifestation of a superior power. He pretended that he held converse with beneficent spirits; that the secrets of God and nature were revealed to him; and that he had obtained possession of the philosopher's stone. Like his predecessor, Jacob Bohmen, he mixed up religious questions with his philosophical jargon, and took measures for declaring himself the founder of a new sect. This, at Rome itself, and in the very palace of the Pope, was a hazardous proceeding; and Borri just awoke to a sense of it in time to save himself from the dungeons of the Castle of St. Angelo. He fled to Innspruck, where he remained about a year, and then returned to his native city of Milan.

The reputation of his great sanctity had gone before him; and he found many persons ready to attach themselves to his fortunes. All who were desirous of entering into the new communion took an oath of poverty, and relinquished their possessions for the general good of the fraternity. Borri told them that he had received from the archangel Michael a heavenly sword, upon the hilt of which were engraven the names of the seven celestial Intelligences. "Whoever shall refuse," said he, "to enter into my new sheepfold, shall be destroyed by the papal armies, of whom God has predestined me to be the chief. To those who follow me, all joy shall be granted. I shall soon bring my chemical studies to a happy conclusion by the discovery of the philosopher's stone, and by this means we shall all have as much gold as we desire. I am assured of the aid of the angelic hosts, and more especially of the archangel Michael's. When I began to walk in the way of the spirit, I had a vision of the night, and was assured by an angelic voice that I should become a prophet. In sign of it I saw a palm-tree, surrounded with all the glory of Paradise. The angels come to me whenever I call, and reveal to me all the secrets of the universe. The sylphs and elementary spirits obey me, and fly to the uttermost ends of the world to serve me, and those whom I delight to honour." By force of continually repeating such stories as these, Borri soon found himself at the head of a very considerable number of adherents. As he figures in these pages as an alchymist, and not as a religious sectarian, it will be unnecessary to repeat the doctrines which he taught with regard to some of the dogmas of the Church of Rome, and which exposed him to the fierce resentment of the papal authority. They were to the full as ridiculous as his philosophical pretensions. As the number of his followers increased, he appears to have cherished the idea of becoming one day a new Mahomet, and of founding, in his native city of Milan, a monarchy and religion of which he should be the king and the prophet. He had taken measures, in the year 1658, for seizing the guards at all the gates of that city, and formally declaring himself the monarch of the Milanese. Just as he thought the plan ripe for execution, it was discovered. Twenty of his followers were arrested, and he himself managed, with the utmost difficulty, to escape to the neutral territory of Switzerland, where the papal displeasure could not reach him.

The trial of his followers commenced forthwith, and the whole of them were sentenced to various terms of imprisonment. Borri's trial proceeded in his absence, and lasted for upwards of two years. He was condemned to death as a heretic and sorcerer in 1661, and was burned in effigy in Rome by the common hangman.

Borri, in the mean time, lived quietly in Switzerland, indulging himself in railing at the Inquisition and its proceedings. He afterwards went to Strasbourg, intending to fix his residence in that town. He was received with great cordiality, as a man persecuted for his religious opinions, and withal a great alchymist. He found that sphere too narrow for his aspiring genius, and retired in the same year to the more wealthy city of Amsterdam. He there hired a magnificent house, established an equipage which eclipsed in brilliancy those of the richest merchants, and assumed the title of Excellency. Where he got the money to live in this expensive style was long a secret: the adepts in alchymy easily explained it, after their fashion. Sensible people were of opinion that be had come by it in a less wonderful manner; for it was remembered that, among his unfortunate disciples in Milan, there were many rich men, who, in conformity with one of the fundamental rules of the sect, had given up all their earthly wealth into the hands of their founder. In whatever manner the money was obtained, Borri spent it in Holland with an unsparing hand, and was looked up to by the people with no little respect and veneration. He performed several able cures, and increased his reputation so much that he was vaunted as a prodigy. He continued diligently the operations of alchymy, and was in daily expectation that he should succeed in turning the inferior metals into gold. This hope never abandoned him, even in the worst extremity of his fortunes;

and in his prosperity it led him into the most foolish expenses: but he could not long continue to live so magnificently upon the funds he had brought from Italy; and the philosopher's stone, though it promised all for the wants of the morrow, never brought anything for the necessities of to-day. He was obliged in a few months to retrench, by giving up his large house, his gilded coach, and valuable blood-horses, his liveried domestics, and his luxurious entertainments. With this diminution of splendour came a diminution of renown. His cures did not appear so miraculous, when he went out on foot to perform them, as they had seemed when "his Excellency" had driven to a poor man's door in his carriage with six horses. He sank from a prodigy into an ordinary man. His great friends showed him the cold shoulder, and his humble flatterers carried their incense to some other shrine. Borri now thought it high time to change his quarters. With this view he borrowed money wherever he could get it, and succeeded in obtaining two hundred thousand florins from a merchant, named De Meer, to aid, as he said, in discovering the water of life. He also obtained six diamonds, of great value, on pretence that he could remove the flaws from them without diminishing their weight. With this booty he stole away secretly by night, and proceeded to Hamburgh.

On his arrival in that city, he found the celebrated Christina, the ex-Queen of Sweden. He procured an introduction to her, and requested her patronage in his endeavour to discover the philosopher's stone. She gave him some encouragement; but Borri, fearing that the merchants of Amsterdam, who had connexions in Hamburgh, might expose his delinquencies if he remained in the latter city, passed over to Copenhagen, and sought the protection of Frederic III, the King of Denmark.

This Prince was a firm believer in the transmutation of metals. Being in want of money, he readily listened to the plans of an adventurer who had both eloquence and ability to recommend him. He provided Borri with the means to make experiments, and took a great interest in the progress of his operations. He expected every month to possess riches that would buy Peru; and, when he was disappointed, accepted patiently the excuses of Borri who, upon every failure, was always ready with some plausible explanation. He became, in time, much attached to him; and defended him from the jealous attacks of his courtiers, and the indignation of those who were grieved to see their monarch the easy dupe of a charlatan. Borri endeavoured, by every means in his power, to find aliment for this good opinion. His knowledge of medicine was useful to him in this respect, and often stood between him and disgrace. He lived six years in this manner at the court of Frederic; but that monarch dying in 1670, he was left without a protector.

As he had made more enemies than friends in Copenhagen, and had nothing to hope from the succeeding sovereign, he sought an asylum in another country. He went first to Saxony; but met so little encouragement, and encountered so much danger from the emissaries of the Inquisition, that he did not remain there many months. Anticipating nothing but persecution in every country that acknowledged the spiritual authority of the Pope, he appears to have taken the resolution to dwell in Turkey, and turn Mussulman. On his arrival at the Hungarian frontier, on his way to Constantinople, he was arrested on suspicion of being concerned in the conspiracy of the Counts Nadasdi and Frangipani, which had just been discovered. In vain he protested his innocence, and divulged his real name and profession. He was detained in prison, and a letter despatched to the Emperor Leopold to know what should be done with him. The star of his fortunes was on the decline. The letter reached Leopold at an unlucky moment. The Pope's Nuncio was closeted with his Majesty; and he no sooner heard the name of Joseph Francis Borri, than he demanded him as a prisoner of the Holy See. The request was complied with; and Borri, closely manacled, was sent under an escort of soldiers to the prison of the Inquisition at Rome. He was too much of an impostor to be deeply tinged with fanaticism, and was not unwilling to make a public recantation of his heresies if he could thereby save his life. When the proposition was made to him, he accepted it with eagerness. His punishment was to be commuted into the hardly less severe one of perpetual imprisonment; but he was too happy to escape the clutch of the executioner at any price, and he made the amende honorable in face of the assembled multitudes of Rome on the 27th of October 1672. He was then transferred to the prisons of the Castle of St. Angelo, where he remained till his death, twenty-three years afterwards. It is said that, towards the close of his life, considerable indulgence was granted him; that he was allowed to have a laboratory, and to cheer the solitude of his dungeon by searching for the philosopher's stone. Queen Christina, during her residence at Rome, frequently visited the old man, to converse with him upon chemistry and the doctrines of the Rosicrucians. She even obtained permission that he should leave his prison occasionally for a day or two, and reside in her palace, she being responsible for his return to captivity. She encouraged him to search for the great secret of the alchymists, and provided him with money for the purpose. It may well be supposed that Borri benefited most by this acquaintance, and that Christina got nothing but experience. It is not sure that she gained even that; for, until her dying day, she was convinced of the possibility of finding the philosopher's stone, and ready to assist any adventurer either zealous or impudent enough to pretend to it.

After Borri had been about eleven years in confinement, a small volume was published at Cologne, entitled "The Key of the Cabinet of the Chevalier Joseph Francis Borri; in which are contained many curious Letters upon Chemistry and other Sciences, written by him; together with a Memoir of his Life." This book contained a complete exposition of the Rosicrucian philosophy, and afforded materials to the Abbe de Villars for his interesting "Count de Gabalis," which excited so much attention at the close of the seventeenth century.

Borri lingered in the prison of St. Angelo till 1695, when he died in his eightieth year. Besides "The Key of the Cabinet," written originally in Copenhagen, in 1666, for the edification of King Frederic III, he published a work upon alchymy and the secret sciences, under the title of "The Mission of Romulus to the Romans."

Inferior Alchymists of the Seventeenth Century

Besides the pretenders to the philosopher's stone whose lives have been already narrated, this and the preceding century produced a great number of writers, who inundated literature with their books upon the subject. In fact, most of the learned men of that age had some faith in it. Van Helmont, Borrichius, Kirchen, Boerhaave, and a score of others, though not professed alchymists, were fond of the science, and countenanced its professors. Helvetius, the grandfather of the celebrated philosopher of the same name, asserts that he saw an inferior metal turned into gold by a stranger, at the Hague, in 1666. He says that, sitting one day in his study, a man, who was dressed as a respectable burgher of North Holland, and very modest and simple in his appearance, called upon him, with the intention of dispelling his doubts relative to the philosopher's stone. He asked Helvetius if he thought he should know that rare gem if he saw it. To which Helvetius replied, that he certainly should not. The burgher immediately drew from his pocket a small ivory box, containing three pieces of metal, of the colour of brimstone, and extremely heavy; and assured Helvetius, that of them he could make as much as twenty tons of gold. Helvetius informs us, that he examined them very attentively; and seeing that they were very brittle, he took the opportunity to scrape off a very small portion with his thumb-nail. He then returned them to the stranger, with an entreaty that he would perform the process of transmutation before him. The stranger replied, that he was not allowed to do so, and went away. After his departure, Helvetius procured a crucible and a portion of lead, into which, when in a state of fusion, he threw the stolen grain from the philosopher's stone. He was disappointed to find that the grain evaporated altogether, leaving the lead in its original state.

Some weeks afterwards, when he had almost forgotten the subject, he received another visit from the stranger. He again entreated him to explain the processes by which he pretended to transmute lead. The stranger at last consented, and informed him, that one grain was sufficient; but that it was necessary to envelope it in a ball of wax before throwing it on the molten metal; otherwise its extreme volatility would cause it to go off in vapour. They tried the experiment, and succeeded to their heart's content. Helvetius repeated the experiment alone, and converted six ounces of lead into very pure gold.

The fame of this event spread all over the Hague, and all the notable persons of the town flocked to the study of Helvetius to convince themselves of the fact. Helvetius performed the experiment again, in the presence of the Prince of Orange, and several times afterwards, until he exhausted the whole of the powder he had received from the stranger, from whom, it is necessary to state, he never received another visit; nor did he ever discover his name or condition. In the following year Helvetius published his "Golden Calf," ["Vitulus Aureus quem Mundus adorat et orat, in quo tractatur de naturae miraculo transmutandi metalla."--Hagae, 1667.] in which he detailed the above circumstances.

About the same time, the celebrated Father Kircher published his "Subterranean World," in which he called the alchymists a congregation of knaves and impostors, and their science a delusion. He admitted that he had himself been a diligent labourer in the field, and had only come to this conclusion after mature consideration and repeated fruitless experiments. All the alchymists were in arms immediately, to refute this formidable antagonist. One Solomon de Blauenstein was the first to grapple with him, and attempted to convict him of wilful misrepresentation, by recalling to his memory the transmutations by Sendivogius, before the Emperor Frederic III. and the Elector of Mayence; all performed within a recent period. Zwelfer and Glauber also entered into the dispute, and attributed the enmity of Father Kircher to spite and jealousy against adepts who had been more successful than himself.

It was also pretended that Gustavus Adolphus transmuted a quantity of quicksilver into pure gold. The learned Borrichius relates, that he saw coins which had been struck of this gold; and Lenglet du Fresnoy deposes to the same circumstance. In the Travels of Monconis the story is told in the following manner:-- "A merchant of Lubeck, who carried on but little trade, but who knew how to change lead into very good gold, gave the King of Sweden a lingot which he had made, weighing, at least, one hundred pounds. The King immediately caused it to be coined into ducats; and because he knew positively that its origin was such as had been stated to him, he had his own arms graven upon the one side, and emblematical figures of Mercury and Venus on the other. "I," continued Monconis, "have one of these ducats in my possession; and was credibly informed, that, after the death of the Lubeck merchant, who had never appeared very rich, a sum of no less than one million seven hundred thousand crowns was found in his coffers." [Voyages de Monconis, tome ii. p. 379.]

Such stories as these, confidently related by men high in station, tended to keep up the infatuation of the alchymists in every country of Europe. It is astonishing to see the number of works which were written upon the subject during the seventeenth century alone, and the number of clever men who sacrificed themselves to the delusion. Gabriel de Castaigne, a monk of the order of St. Francis, attracted so much notice in the reign of Louis XIII, that that monarch secured him in his household, and made him his Grand Almoner. He pretended to find the elixir of life; and Louis expected, by his means, to have enjoyed the crown for a century. Van Helmont also pretended to have once performed with success the process of transmuting quicksilver; and was, in consequence, invited by the Emperor Rudolph II. to fix his residence at the court of Vienna. Glauber, the inventor of the salts which still bear his name, and who practised as a physician at Amsterdam about the middle of the seventeenth century, established a public school in that city for the study of alchymy, and gave lectures himself upon the science. John Joachim

Becher, of Spire, acquired great reputation at the same period; and was convinced that much gold might be made out of flint stones by a peculiar process, and the aid of that grand and incomprehensible substance, the philosopher's stone. He made a proposition to the Emperor Leopold of Austria, to aid him in these experiments; but the hope of success was too remote, and the present expense too great to tempt that monarch; and he therefore gave Becher much of his praise, but none of his money. Becher afterwards tried the States-General of Holland, with no better success.

With regard to the innumerable tricks by which impostors persuaded the world that they had succeeded in making gold, and of which so many stories were current about this period, a very satisfactory report was read by M. Geoffroy, the elder, at the sitting of the Royal Academy of Sciences, at Paris, on the 15th of April, 1722. As it relates principally to the alchymic cheats of the sixteenth and seventeenth centuries, the following abridgment of it may not be out of place in this portion of our history:-- The instances of successful transmutation were so numerous, and apparently so well authenticated, that nothing short of so able an exposure as that of M. Geoffroy could disabuse the public mind. The trick to which they oftenest had recourse, was to use a double-bottomed crucible, the under surface being of iron or copper, and the upper one of wax, painted to resemble the same metal. Between the two they placed as much gold or silver dust as was necessary for their purpose. They then put in their lead, quicksilver, or other ingredients, and placed their pot upon the fire. Of course, when the experiment was concluded, they never failed to find a lump of gold at the bottom. The same result was produced in many other ways. Some of them used a hollow wand, filled with gold or silver dust, and stopped at the ends with wax or butter. With this they stirred the boiling metal in their crucibles, taking care to accompany the operation with many ceremonies, to divert attention from the real purpose of the manoeuvre. They also drilled holes in lumps of lead, into which they poured molten gold, and carefully closed the aperture with the original metal. Sometimes they washed a piece of gold with quicksilver. When in this state they found no difficulty in palming it off upon the uninitiated as an inferior metal, and very easily transmuted it into fine sonorous gold again, with the aid of a little aquafortis.

Others imposed by means of nails, half iron and half gold or silver. They pretended that they really transmuted the precious half from iron, by dipping it in a strong alcohol. M. Geoffroy produced several of these nails to the Academy of Sciences, and showed how nicely the two parts were soldered together. The golden or silver half was painted black to resemble iron, and the colour immediately disappeared when the nail was dipped into aquafortis. A nail of this description was, for a long time, in the cabinet of the Grand Duke of Tuscany. Such also, said M. Geoffroy, was the knife presented by a monk to Queen Elizabeth of England; the blade of which was half gold and half steel. Nothing at one time was more common than to see coins, half gold and half silver, which had been operated upon by alchymists, for the same purposes of trickery. In fact, says M. Geoffroy, in concluding his long report, there is every reason to believe that all the famous histories which have been handed down to us, about the transmutation of metals into gold or silver, by means of the powder of projection, or philosophical elixirs, are founded upon some successful deception of the kind above narrated. These pretended philosophers invariably disappeared after the first or second experiment, or their powders or elixirs have failed to produce their effect, either because attention being excited they have found no opportunity to renew the trick without being discovered, or because they have not had sufficient gold dust for more than one trial.

The disinterestedness of these would-be philosopher looked, at first sight, extremely imposing. Instances were not rare, in which they generously abandoned all the profits of their transmutations - even the honour of the discovery! But this apparent disinterestedness was one of the most cunning of their manoeuvres. It served to keep up the popular expectation; it showed the possibility of discovering the philosopher's stone, and provided the means of future advantages, which they were never slow to lay hold of -- such as entrances into royal households, maintenance at the public expense, and gifts from ambitious potentates, too greedy after the gold they so easily promised.

It now only remains to trace the progress of the delusion from the commencement of the eighteenth century until the present day. It will be seen, that until a very recent period, there were but slight signs of a return to reason.

Jean Delisle

In the year 1705, there was much talk in France of a blacksmith, named Delisle, who had discovered the philosopher's stone, and who went about the country turning lead into gold. He was a native of Provence, from which place his fame soon spread to the capital. His early life is involved in obscurity; but Longlet du Fresnoy has industriously collected some particulars of his later career, which possess considerable interest. He was a man without any education, and had been servant in his youth to an alchymist, from whom he learned many of the tricks of the fraternity. The name of his master has never been discovered; but it is pretended that he rendered himself in some manner obnoxious to the government of Louis XIV, and was obliged, in consequence, to take refuge in Switzerland. Delisle accompanied him as far as Savoy, and there, it is said, set upon him in a solitary mountain-pass, and murdered and robbed him. He then disguised himself as a pilgrim, and returned to France. At a lonely inn, by the road-side, where he stopped for the night, he became acquainted with a woman, named Aluys; and so sudden a passion was enkindled betwixt them, that she consented to leave all, follow him, and share his good or evil fortune wherever he went. They lived together for five or six years in Provence, without exciting any attention, apparently possessed of a decent independence. At last, in 1706, it was given out that he was the possessor of the philosopher's stone; and people, from far and near, came flocking to his residence, at the Chateau de la Palu, at Sylanez, near Barjaumont, to witness the wealth he could make out of pumps and fire shovels. The following account of his operations is given in a letter addressed by M. de Cerisy, the Prior of Chateauneuf, in the Diocese of Riez, in Provence, to the Vicar of St. Jacques du Hautpas, at Paris, and dated the 18th of November 1706:--

"I have something to relate to you, my dear cousin, which will be interesting to you and your friends. The philosopher's stone, which so many persons have looked upon as a chimera, is at last found. It is a man named Delisle, of the parish of Sylanez, and residing within a quarter of a league of me, that has discovered this great secret. He turns lead into gold, and iron into silver, by merely heating these metals red hot, and pouring upon them, in that state, some oil and powder he is possessed of; so that it would not be impossible for any man to make a million a day, if he had sufficient of this wondrous mixture. Some of the pale gold which he had made in this manner, he sent to the jewellers of Lyons, to have their opinion on its quality. He also sold twenty pounds weight of it to a merchant of Digne, named Taxis. All the jewellers say they never saw such fine gold in their lives. He makes nails, part gold, part iron, and part silver. He promised to give me one of them, in a long conversation which I had with him the other day, by order of the Bishop of Sends, who saw his operations with his own eyes, and detailed all the circumstances to me.

"The Baron and Baroness de Rheinwald showed me a lingot of gold made out of pewter before their eyes by M. Delisle. My brother-in-law Sauveur, who has wasted fifty years of his life in this great study, brought me the other day a nail which he had seen changed into gold by Delisle, and fully convinced me that all his previous experiments were founded on an erroneous principle. This excellent workman received, a short time ago, a very kind letter from the superintendent of the royal household, which I read. He offered to use all his influence with the ministers to prevent any attempts upon his liberty, which has twice been attacked by the agents of government. It is believed that the oil he makes use of, is gold or silver reduced to that state. He leaves it for a long time exposed to the rays of the sun. He told me that it generally took him six months to make all his preparations. I told him that, apparently, the King wanted to see him. He replied that he could not exercise his art in every place, as a certain climate and temperature were absolutely necessary to his success. The truth is, that this man appears to have no ambition. He only keeps two horses and two men-servants. Besides, he loves his liberty, has no politeness, and speaks very bad French; but his judgment seems to be solid. He was formerly no more than a blacksmith, but excelled in that trade without having been taught it. All the great lords and seigneurs from far and near come to visit him, and pay such court to him, that it seems more like idolatry than anything else. Happy would France be if this man would discover his secret to the King, to whom the superintendent has already sent some lingots! But the happiness is too great to be hoped for; for I fear that the workman and his secret will expire together. There is no doubt that this discovery will make a great noise in the kingdom, unless the character of the man, which I have just depicted to you, prevent it. At all events, posterity will hear of him."

In another letter to the same person, dated the 27th of January 1707, M. de Cerisy says, "My dear cousin, I spoke to you in my last letter of the famous alchymist of Provence, M. Delisle. A good deal of that was only hearsay, but now I am enabled to speak from my own experience. I have in my possession a nail, half iron and half silver, which I made myself. That great and admirable workman also bestowed a still greater privilege upon me -- he allowed me to turn a piece of lead which I had brought with me into pure gold, by means of his wonderful oil and powder. All the country have their eyes upon this gentleman: some deny loudly, others are incredulous; but those who have seen acknowledge the truth. I have read the passport that has been sent to him from Court, with orders that he should present himself at Paris early in the spring. He told me that he would go willingly, and that it was himself who fixed the spring for his departure; as he wanted to collect his materials, in order that, immediately on his introduction to the King, he might make an experiment worthy of his Majesty, by converting a large quantity of lead into the finest gold. I sincerely hope that he will not allow his secret to die with him, but that he will communicate it to the King. As I had the honour to dine with him on Thursday last, the 20th of this month, being seated at his side, I told him in a whisper that he could, if he liked, humble all the enemies of France. He did not deny it, but began to smile. In fact, this man is the miracle of art. Sometimes he employs the oil and powder mixed, sometimes the powder only, but in so small a quantity that, when the lingot which I made was rubbed all over with it, it did not show at all."

This soft-headed priest was by no means the only person in the neighbourhood who lost his wits in hopes of the boundless wealth held out by this clever impostor. Another priest, named De Lions, a chanter in the cathedral of Grenoble, writing on the 30th January 1707, says, -- "M. Mesnard, the curate of Montier, has written to me, stating that there is a man, about thirty-five years of age, named Delisle, who turns lead and iron into gold and silver; and that this transmutation is so veritable and so true, that the goldsmiths affirm that his gold and silver are the purest and finest they ever saw. For five years, this man was looked upon as a madman or a cheat; but the public mind is now disabused with respect to him. He now resides with M. de la Palu, at the chateau of the same name. M. de la Palu is not very easy in his circumstances, and wants money to portion his daughters, who have remained single till middle age, no man being willing to take them without a dowry. M. Delisle has promised to make them the richest girls in the province before he goes to Court, having been sent for by the King. He has asked for a little time before his departure, in order that he may collect powder enough to make several quintals of gold before the eyes of his Majesty, to whom he intends to present them. The principal matter of his wonderful powder is composed of simples, principally the herbs Lunaria major and minor. There is a good deal of the first planted by him in the gardens of La Palu; and he gets the other from the mountains, that stretch about two leagues from Montier. What I tell you now is not a mere story invented for your diversion: M. Mesnard can bring forward many witnesses to its truth; among others, the Bishop of Senes, who saw these surprising operations performed; and M. de Cerisy, whom you know well. Delisle transmutes his metals in public. He rubs the lead or iron with his powder, and puts it over burning charcoal. In a short time it changes colour; the lead becomes yellow, and is found to be converted into excellent gold: the iron becomes white, and is found to be pure silver. Delisle is altogether an illiterate person. M. de St. Auban endeavoured to teach him to read and write, but he profited very little by his lessons. He is unpolite, fantastic, and a dreamer, and acts by fits and starts."

Delisle, it would appear, was afraid of venturing to Paris. He knew that his sleight of hand would be too narrowly watched in the royal presence; and upon some pretence or other, he delayed the journey for more than two years. Desmarets, the Minister of Finance to Louis XIV, thinking the "philosopher" dreaded foul play, twice sent him a safe conduct under the King's seal; but Delisle still refused. Upon this, Desmarets wrote to the Bishop of Sends for his real opinion as to these famous transmutations. The following was the answer of that prelate:--

"Copy of a report addressed to M. Desmarets, Comptroller-General of the Finances to His Majesty Louis XIV, by the Bishop of Senes, dated March 1709.

"SIR,--- A twelvemonth ago, or a little more, I expressed to you my joy at hearing of your elevation to the ministry; I have now the honour to write you my opinion of the Sieur Delisle, who has been working at the transmutation of metals in my diocese. I have, during the last two years, spoken of him several times to the Count de Pontchartrain, because he asked me; but I have not written to you, sir, or to M. de Chamillart, because you neither of you requested my opinion upon the subject. Now, however, that you have given me to understand that you wish to know my sentiments on the matter, I will unfold myself to you in all sincerity, for the interests of the King and the glory of your ministry.

"There are two things about the Sieur Delisle which, in my opinion, should be examined without prejudice: the one relates to his secret; the other, to his person; that is to say, whether his transmutations are real, and whether his conduct has been regular. As regards the secret of the philosopher's stone, I deemed it impossible, for a long time; and for more than three years, I was more mistrustful of the pretensions of this Sieur Delisle than of any other person. During this period I afforded him no countenance; I even aided a person, who was highly recommended to me by an influential family of this province, to prosecute Delisle for some offence or other which it was alleged he had committed. But this person, in his anger against him, having told me that he had himself been several times the bearer of gold and silver to the goldsmiths of Nice, Aix, and Avignon, which had been transmuted by Delisle from lead and iron, I began to waver a little in my opinions respecting him. I afterwards met Delisle at the house of one of my friends. To please me, the family asked Delisle to operate before me, to which he immediately consented. I offered him some iron nails, which he changed into silver in the chimney-place before six or seven credible witnesses. I took the nails thus transmuted, and sent them by my almoner to Irabert, the jeweller of Aix, who, having subjected them to the necessary trial, returned them to me, saying they were very good silver. Still, however, I was not quite satisfied. M. de Pontchartrain having hinted to me, two years previously, that I should do a thing agreeable to his Majesty if I examined into this business of Delisle, I resolved to do so now. I therefore summoned the alchymist to come to me at Castellane. He came; and I had him escorted by eight or ten vigilant men, to whom I had given notice to watch his hands strictly. Before all of us he changed two pieces of lead into gold and silver. I sent them both to M. de Pontchartrain; and he afterwards informed me by a letter, now lying before me, that he had shown them to the most experienced goldsmiths of Paris, who unanimously pronounced them to be gold and silver of the very purest quality, and without alloy. My former bad opinion of Delisle was now indeed shaken. It was much more so when he performed transmutation five or six times before me at

Senes, and made me perform it myself before him without his putting his hand to anything. You have seen, sir, the letter of my nephew, the Pere Berard, of the Oratoire at Paris, on the experiment that he performed at Castellane, and the truth of which I hereby attest. Another nephew of mine, the Sieur Bourget, who was here three weeks ago, performed the same experiment in my presence, and will detail all the circumstances to you personally at Paris. A hundred persons in my diocese have been witnesses of these things. I confess to you, sir, that, after the testimony of so many spectators and so many goldsmiths, and after the repeatedly successful experiments that I saw performed, all my prejudices vanished. My reason was convinced by my eyes; and the phantoms of impossibility which I had conjured up were dissipated by the work of my own hands.

"It now only remains for me to speak to you on the subject of his person and conduct. Three suspicions have been excited against him: the first, that he was implicated in some criminal proceeding at Cisteron, and that he falsified the coin of the realm; the second, that the King sent him two safe-conducts without effect; and the third, that he still delays going to court to operate before the King. You may see, sir, that I do not hide or avoid anything. As regards the business at Cisteron, the Sieur Delisle has repeatedly assured me that there was nothing against him which could reasonably draw him within the pale of justice, and that he had never carried on any calling injurious to the King's service. It was true that, six or seven years ago, he had been to Cisteron to gather herbs necessary for his powder, and that he had lodged at the house of one Pelouse, whom he thought an honest man. Pelouse was accused of clipping Louis d'ors; and as he had lodged with him, he was suspected of being his accomplice. This mere suspicion, without any proof whatever, had caused him to be condemned for contumacy; a common case enough with judges, who always proceed with much rigour against those who are absent. During my own sojourn at Aix, it was well known that a man, named Andre Aluys, had spread about reports injurious to the character of Delisle, because he hoped thereby to avoid paying him a sum of forty Louis that he owed him. But permit me, sir, to go further, and to add that, even if there were well-founded supicions against Delisle, we should look with some little indulgence on the faults of a man who possesses a secret so useful to the state. As regards the two safe-conducts sent him by the King, I think I can answer certainly that it was through no fault of his that he paid so little attention to them. His year, strictly speaking, consists only of the four summer months; and when by any means he is prevented from making the proper use of them, he loses a whole year. Thus the first safe-conduct became useless by the irruption of the Duke of Savoy in 1707; and the second had hardly been obtained, at the end of June 1708, when the said Delisle was insulted by a party of armed men, pretending to act under the authority of the Count de Grignan, to whom he wrote several letters of complaint, without receiving any answer, or promise that his safety would be attended to. What I have now told you, sir, removes the third objection, and is the reason why, at the present time, he cannot go to Paris to the King, in fulfilment of his promises made two years ago. Two, or even three, summers have been lost to him, owing to the continual inquietude he has laboured under. He has, in consequence, been unable to work, and has not collected a sufficient quantity of his oil and powder, or brought what he has got to the necessary degree of perfection. For this reason also he could not give the Sieur de Bourget the portion he promised him for your inspection. If the other day he changed some lead into gold with a few grains of his powder, they were assuredly all he had; for he told me that such was the fact long before he knew my nephew was coming. Even if he had preserved this small quantity to operate before the King, I am sure that, on second thoughts, he would never have adventured with so little; because the slightest obstacles in the metals (their being too hard or too soft, which is only discovered in operating) would have caused him to be looked upon as an impostor, if, in case his first powder had proved ineffectual, he had not been possessed of more to renew the experiment and surmount the difficulty.

"Permit me, sir, in conclusion, to repeat that such an artist as this should not be driven to the last extremity, nor forced to seek an asylum offered to him in other countries, but which he has despised, as much from his own inclinations as from the advice I have given him. You risk nothing in giving him a little time, and in hurrying him you may lose a great deal. The genuineness of his gold can no longer be doubted, after the testimony of so many jewellers of Aix, Lyons, and Paris in its favour. As it is not his fault that the previous safe-conducts sent to him have been of no service, it will be necessary to send him another; for the success of which I will be answerable, if you will confide the matter to me, and trust to my zeal for the service of his Majesty, to whom I pray you to communicate this letter, that I may be spared the just reproaches he might one day heap upon me if he remained ignorant of the facts I have now written to you. Assure him, if you please, that, if you send me such a safe-conduct, I will oblige the Sieur Delisle to depose with me such precious pledges of his fidelity, as shall enable me to be responsible myself to the King. These are my sentiments, and I submit them to your superior knowledge; and have the honour to remain, with much respect, &c.

"* JOHN, Bishop of Senes."

"To M. Desmarets, Minister of State, and "Comptroller-General of the Finances, at Paris."

That Delisle was no ordinary impostor, but a man of consummate cunning and address, is very evident from this letter. The Bishop was fairly taken in by his clever legerdemain, and when once his first distrust was conquered, appeared as anxious to deceive himself as even Delisle could have wished. His faith was so abundant that he made the case of his protege his own, and would not suffer the breath of suspicion to be directed against him. Both Louis and his minister appear to have been dazzled by the brilliant hopes he had excited, and a third pass, or safe-conduct, was immediately sent to the alchymist, with a command from the King that he should forthwith present himself at Versailles, and make public trial of his oil and powder. But this did not suit the plans of Delisle: in the provinces he was regarded as a man of no small importance; the servile flattery that awaited him wherever he went was so grateful to his mind that he could not willingly relinquish it and run upon certain detection at the court of the Monarch. Upon one pretext or another he delayed his journey, notwithstanding the earnest solicitations of his good friend the Bishop. The latter had given his word to the minister, and pledged his honour that he would induce Delisle to go, and he began to be alarmed when he found he could not subdue the obstinacy of that individual. For more than two years he continued to remonstrate with him, and was always met by some excuse, that there was not sufficient powder, or that it had not been long enough exposed to the rays of the sun. At last his patience was exhausted; and fearful that he might suffer in the royal estimation by longer delay, he wrote to the King for a lettre de cachet, in virtue of which the alchymist was seized at the castle of La Palu, in the month of June 1711, and carried off to be imprisoned in the Bastille.

The gendarmes were aware that their prisoner was supposed to be the lucky possessor of the philosopher's stone, and on the road they conspired to rob and murder him. One of them pretended to be touched with pity for the misfortunes of the philosopher, and offered to give him an opportunity of escape whenever he could divert the attention of his companions. Delisle was profuse in his thanks, little dreaming of the snare that was laid for him. His treacherous friend gave notice of the success of the stratagem so far; and it was agreed that Delisle should be allowed to struggle with and overthrow one of them while the rest were at some distance. They were then to pursue him and shoot him through the heart; and after robbing the corpse of the philosopher's stone, convey it to Paris on a cart, and tell M. Desmarets that the prisoner had attempted to escape, and would have succeeded, if they had not fired after him and shot him through the body. At a convenient place the scheme was executed. At a given signal from the friendly gendarme Delisle fled, while another gendarme took aim and shot him through the thigh. Some peasants arriving at the instant, they were prevented from killing him as they intended; and he was transported to Paris, maimed and bleeding. He was thrown into a dungeon in the Bastille, and obstinately tore away the bandages which the surgeons applied to his wound. He never afterwards rose from his bed.

The Bishop of Senes visited him in prison, and promised him his liberty if he would transmute a certain quantity of lead into gold before the King. The unhappy man had no longer the means of carrying on the deception; he had no gold, and no double-bottomed crucible or hollow wand to conceal it in, even if he had. He would not, however, confess that he was an impostor; but merely said he did not know how to make the powder of projection, but had received a quantity from an Italian philosopher, and had used it all in his various transmutations in Provence. He lingered for seven or eight months in the Bastille, and died from the effects of his wound, in the forty-first year of his age.

Albert Aluys

This pretender to the philosopher's stone, was the son, by a former husband, of the woman Aluys, with whom Delisle became acquainted at the commencement of his career, in the cabaret by the road side, and whom he afterwards married. Delisle performed the part of a father towards him, and thought he could show no stronger proof of his regard, than by giving him the necessary instructions to carry on the deception which had raised himself to such a pitch of greatness. The young Aluys was an apt scholar, and soon mastered all the jargon of the alchymists. He discoursed learnedly upon projections, cimentations, sublimations, the elixir of life, and the universal alkahest; and on the death of Delisle gave out that the secret of that great adept had been communicated to him, and to him only. His mother aided in the fraud, with the hope they might both fasten themselves, in the true alchymical fashion, upon some rich dupe, who would entertain them magnificently while the operation was in progress. The fate of Delisle was no inducement for them to stop in France. The Provencals, it is true, entertained as high an opinion as ever of his skill, and were well inclined to believe the tales of the young adept on whom his mantle had fallen; but the dungeons of the Bastille were yawning for their prey, and Aluys and his mother decamped with all convenient expedition. They travelled about the Continent for several years, sponging upon credulous rich men, and now and then performing successful transmutations by the aid of double-bottomed crucibles and the like. In the year 1726, Aluys, without his mother, who appears to have died in the interval, was at Vienna, where he introduced himself to the Duke de Richelieu, at that time ambassador from the court of France. He completely deceived this nobleman; he turned lead into gold (apparently) on several occasions, and even made the ambassador himself turn an iron nail into a silver one. The Duke afterwards boasted to Lenglet du Fresnoy of his achievements as an alchymist, and regretted that be had not been able to discover the secret of the precious powder by which he performed them.

Aluys soon found that, although he might make a dupe of the Duke de Richelieu, he could not get any money from him. On the contrary, the Duke expected all his pokers and fire shovels to be made silver, and all his pewter utensils gold; and thought the honour of his acquaintance was reward sufficient for a roturier, who could not want wealth since he possessed so invaluable a secret. Aluys seeing that so much was expected of him, bade adieu to his Excellency, and proceeded to Bohemia, accompanied by a pupil, and by a young girl who had fallen in love with him in Vienna. Some noblemen in Bohemia received him kindly, and entertained him at their houses for months at a time. It was his usual practice to pretend that he possessed only a few grains of his powder, with which he would operate in any house where he intended to fix his quarters for the season. He would make the proprietor a present of the piece of gold thus transmuted, and promise him millions, if he could only be provided with leisure to gather his lunaria major and minor on their mountain tops, and board, lodging, and loose cash for himself, his wife, and his pupil in the interval.

He exhausted in this manner the patience of some dozen of people, when, thinking that there was less danger for him in France, under the young king Louis XV, than under his old and morose predecessor, he returned to Provence. On his arrival at Aix, he presented himself before M. le Bret, the President of the province, a gentleman who was much attached to the pursuits of alchymy, and had great hopes of being himself able to find the philosopher's stone. M. le Bret, contrary to his expectation, received him very coolly, in consequence of some rumours that were spread abroad respecting him; and told him to call upon him on the morrow. Aluys did not like the tone of the voice, or the expression of the eye of the learned President, as that functionary looked down upon him. Suspecting that all was not right, he left Aix secretly the same evening, and proceeded to Marseilles. But the police were on the watch for him; and he had not been there four-and-twenty hours, before he was arrested on a charge of coining, and thrown into prison.

As the proofs against him were too convincing to leave him much hope of an acquittal, he planned an escape from durance. It so happened that the gaoler had a pretty daughter, and Aluys soon discovered that she was tender-hearted. He deavoured to gain her in his favour, and succeeded. The damsel, unaware that he was a married man, conceived and encouraged a passion for him, and generously provided him with the means of escape. After he had been nearly a year in prison he succeeded in getting free, leaving the poor girl behind, to learn that be was already married, and to lament in solitude that she had given her heart to an ungrateful vagabond.

When he left Marseilles, he had not a shoe to his foot, or a decent garment to his back, but was provided with some money and clothes by his wife in a neighbouring town. They then found their way to Brussels, and by dint of excessive impudence, brought themselves into notice. He took a house, fitted up a splendid laboratory, and gave out that he knew the secret of transmutation. In vain did M. Percel, the brother-in-law of Lenglet du Fresnoy, who resided in that city, expose his pretensions, and hold him up to contempt as an ignorant impostor: the world believed him not. They took the alchymist at his word, and besieged his doors, to see and wonder at the clever legerdemain by which he turned iron nails into gold and silver. A rich greffier paid him a large sum of money that he might be instructed in the art, and Aluys gave him several lessons on the most common principles of chemistry. The greffier studied hard for a twelvemonth, and then discovered that his master was a quack. He demanded his money back again; but Aluys was not inclined to give it him, and the affair was brought before the civil tribunal of the province. In the mean time, however, the greffier died suddenly; poisoned, according to the popular rumour, by his debtor, to avoid repayment. So great an outcry arose in the city, that Aluys, who may have been innocent of the crime, was nevertheless afraid to remain and brave it. He withdrew secretly in the night, and retired to Paris. Here all trace of him is lost. He was never heard of again; but Lenglet du Fresnoy conjectures, that he ended his days in some obscure dungeon, into which he was cast for coining, or other malpracticcs.

The Count de St. Germain

This adventurer was of a higher grade than the last, and played a distinguished part at the court of Louis XV. He pretended to have discovered the elixir of life, by means of which he could make any one live for centuries; and allowed it to be believed that his own age was upwards of two thousand years. He entertained many of the opinions of the Rosicrucians; boasted of his intercourse with sylphs and salamanders; and of his power of drawing diamonds from the earth, and pearls from the sea, by the force of his incantations. He did not lay claim to the merit of having discovered the philosopher's stone; but devoted so much of his time to the operations of alchymy, that it was very generally believed, that, if such a thing as the philosopher's stone had ever existed, or could be called into existence, he was the man to succeed in finding it.

It has never yet been discovered what was his real name, or in what country he was born. Some believed, from the Jewish cast of his handsome countenance, that he was the "wandering Jew;" others asserted, that he was the issue of an Arabian princess, and that his father was a salamander; while others, more reasonable, affirmed him to be the son of a Portuguese Jew, established at Bourdeaux. He first carried on his imposture in Germany, where he made considerable sums by selling an elixir to arrest the progress of old age. The Marechal de Belle-Isle purchased a dose of it; and was so captivated with the wit, learning, and good manners of the charlatan, and so convinced of the justice of his most preposterous pretensions, that he induced him to fix his residence in Paris. Under the Marshal's patronage, he first appeared in the gay circles of that capital. Every one was delighted with the mysterious stranger; who, at this period of his life, appears to have been about seventy years of age, but did not look more than forty-five. His easy assurance imposed upon most people. His reading was extensive, and his memory extraordinarily tenacious of the slightest circumstances. His pretension to have lived for so many centuries naturally exposed him to some puzzling questions, as to the appearance, life, and conversation of the great men of former days; but he was never at a loss for an answer. Many who questioned him for the purpose of scoffing at him, refrained in perplexity, quite bewildered by his presence of mind, his ready replies, and his astonishing accuracy on every point mentioned in history. To increase the mystery by which he was surrounded, he permitted no person to know how he lived. He dressed in a style of the greatest magnificence; sported valuable diamonds in his hat, on his fingers, and in his shoe-buckles; and sometimes made the most costly presents to the ladies of the court. It was suspected by many that he was a spy, in the pay of the English ministry; but there never was a tittle of evidence to support the charge. The King looked upon him with marked favour, was often closeted with him for hours together, and would not suffer anybody to speak disparagingly of him. Voltaire constantly turned him into ridicule; and, in one of his letters to the King of Prussia, mentions him as "un comte pour fire;" and states, that he pretended to have dined with the holy fathers, at the Council of Trent!

In the "Memoirs of Madame du Hausset," chamber-woman to Madame du Pompadour, there are some amusing anecdotes of this personage. Very soon after his arrival in Paris, he had the entree of her dressing-room; a favour only granted to the most powerful lords at the court of her royal lover. Madame was fond of conversing with him; and, in her presence, he thought fit to lower his pretensions very considerably: but he often allowed her to believe that he had lived two or three hundred years, at least. "One day," says Madame du Hausset, "Madame said to him, in my presence, 'What was the personal appearance of Francis I? He was a King I should have liked.' 'He was, indeed, very captivating,' replied St. Germain; and he proceeded to describe his face and person, as that of a man whom he had accurately observed. 'It is a pity he was too ardent. I could have given him some good advice, which would have saved him from all his misfortunes: but he would not have followed it; for it seems as if a fatality attended princes, forcing them to shut their ears to the wisest counsel.' 'Was his court very brilliant?' inquired Madame du Pompadour. 'Very,' replied the Count; 'but those of his grandsons surpassed it. In the time of Mary Stuart and Margaret of Valois, it was a land of enchantment -- a temple sacred to pleasures of every kind.' Madame said, laughing, 'You seem to have seen all this.' 'I have an excellent memory,' said he, 'and have read the history of France with great care. I sometimes amuse myself, not by making, but by letting, it be believed that I lived in old times.'

"'But you do not tell us your age,' said Madame du Pompadour to him on another occasion; 'and yet you pretend you are very old. The Countess de Gergy, who was, I believe, ambassadress at Vienna some fifty years ago, says she saw you there, exactly the same as you now appear.'

"'It is true, Madam,' replied St. Germain; 'I knew Madame de Gergy many years ago.'

"'But, according to her account, you must be more than a hundred years old?'

"'That is not impossible,' said he, laughing; 'but it is much more possible that the good lady is in her dotage.'

"'You gave her an elixir, surprising for the effects it produced; for she says, that during a length of time, she only appeared to be eighty-four; the age at which she took it. Why don't you give it to the King ?'

"'O Madam !' he exclaimed, 'the physicians would have me broken on the wheel, were I to think of drugging his Majesty.'"

When the world begins to believe extraordinary things of an individual, there is no telling where its extravagance will stop. People, when once they have taken the start, vie with each other who shall believe most. At this period all Paris resounded with the wonderful adventures of the Count de St. Germain; and a company of waggish young men tried the following experiment upon its credulity:- A clever mimic, who, on account of the amusement he afforded, was admitted into good society, was taken by them, dressed as the Count de St. Germain, into several houses in the Rue du Marais. He imitated the Count's peculiarities admirably, and found his auditors open-mouthed to believe any absurdity he chose to utter. No fiction was too monstrous for their all-devouring credulity. He spoke of the Saviour of the world in terms of the greatest familiarity; said he had supped with him at the marriage in Canaan of Galilee, where the water was miraculously turned into wine. In fact, he said he was an intimate friend of his, and had often warned him to be less romantic and imprudent, or he would finish his career miserably. This infamous blasphemy, strange to say, found believers; and, ere three days had elapsed, it was currently reported that St. Germain was born soon after the deluge, and that he would never die!

St. Germain himself was too much a man of the world to assert anything so monstrous; but he took no pains to contradict the story. In all his conversations with persons of rank and education, he advanced his claims modestly, and as if by mere inadvertency; and seldom pretended to a longevity beyond three hundred years; except when he found he was in company with persons who would believe anything. He often spoke of Henry VIII, as if he had known him intimately; and of the Emperor Charles V, as if that monarch had delighted in his society. He would describe conversations which took place with such an apparent truthfulness, and be so exceedingly minute and particular as to the dress and appearance of the individuals, and even the weather at the time, and the furniture of the room, that three persons out of four were generally inclined to credit him. He had constant applications from rich old women for an elixir to make them young again; and, it would appear, gained large sums in this manner. To those whom he was pleased to call his friends, he said, his mode of living and plan of diet were far superior to any elixir; and that anybody might attain a patriarchal age, by refraining from drinking at meals, and very sparingly at any other time. The Baron de Gleichen followed this system, and took great quantities of senna leaves, expecting to live for two hundred years. He died, however, at seventy-three. The Duchess de Choiseul was desirous of following the same system; but the Duke her husband, in much wrath, forbade her to follow any system prescribed by a man who had so equivocal a reputation as M. de St. Germain.

Madame du Hausset says, she saw St. Germain, and conversed with him several times. He appeared to her to be about fifty years of age, was of the middle size, and had fine expressive features. His dress was always simple, but displayed much taste. He usually wore diamond rings of great value; and his watch and snuff-box were ornamented with a profusion of precious stones. One day, at Madame du

Pompadour's apartments, where the principal courtiers were assembled, St. Germain made his appearance in diamond knee and shoe buckles, of so fine a water, that Madame said, she did not think the King had any equal to them. He was entreated to pass into the antechamber, and undo them; which he did, and brought them to Madame, for closer inspection. M. de Gontant, who was present, said their value could not be less than two hundred thousand livres, or upwards of eight thousand pounds sterling. The Baron de Gleichen, in his "Memoirs," relates, that the Count one day showed him so many diamonds, that he thought he saw before him all the treasures of Aladdin's lamp; and adds, that he had had great experience in precious stones, and was convinced that all those possessed by the Count were genuine. On another occasion, St. Germain showed Madame du Pompadour a small box, containing topazes, emeralds, and diamonds, worth half a million of livres. He affected to despise all this wealth, to make the world more easily believe that he could, like the Rosicrucians, draw precious stones out of the earth by the magic of his song. He gave away a great number of these jewels to the ladies of the court; and Madame du Pompadour was so charmed with his generosity, that she gave him a richly-enamelled snuff-box, as a token of her regard; on the lid of which was beautifully painted a portrait of Socrates, or some other Greek sage, to whom she compared him. He was not only lavish to the mistresses, but to the maids. Madame du Hausset says, -- "The Count came to see Madame du Pompadour, who was very ill, and lay on the sofa. He showed her diamonds enough to furnish a king's treasury. Madame sent for me to see all those beautiful things. I looked at them with an air of the utmost astonishment; but I made signs to her, that I thought them all false. The Count felt for something in a pocket-book about twice as large as a spectacle-case; and, at length, drew out two or three little paper packets, which he unfolded, and exhibited a superb ruby. He threw on the table, with a contumptuous air, a little cross of green and white stones. I looked at it, and said it was not to be despised. I then put it on, and admired it greatly. The Count begged me to accept it. I refused. He urged me to take it. At length, he pressed so warmly, that Madame, seeing it could not be worth more than a thousand livres, made me a sign to accept it. I took the cross, much pleased with the Count's politeness."

How the adventurer obtained his wealth remains a secret. He could not have made it all by the sale of his elixir vitae in Germany; though, no doubt, some portion of it was derived from that source. Voltaire positively says, he was in the pay of foreign governments; and in his letter to the King of Prussia, dated the 5th of April 1758, says, that he was initiated in all the secrets of Choiseul, Kaunitz, and Pitt. Of what use he could be to any of those ministers, and to Choiseul especially, is a mystery of mysteries.

There appears no doubt that he possessed the secret of removing spots from diamonds; and, in all probability, he gained considerable sums by buying, at inferior prices, such as had flaws in them, and afterwards disposing of them at a profit of cent. per cent. Madame du Hausset relates the following anecdote on this particular:-- "The King," says she, "ordered a middling-sized diamond, which had a flaw in it, to be brought to him. After having it weighed, his Majesty said to the Count, 'The value of this diamond, as it is, and with the flaw in it, is six thousand livres; without the flaw, it would be worth, at least, ten thousand. Will you undertake to make me a gainer of four thousand livres?' St. Germain examined it very attentively, and said, 'It is possible; it may be done. I will bring it you again in a month.' At the time appointed, the Count brought back the diamond, without a spot, and gave it to the King. It was wrapped in a cloth of amianthos, which he took off. The King had it weighed immediately, and found it very little diminished. His Majesty then sent it to his jeweller, by M. de Gonrant, without telling him of anything that had passed. The jeweller gave nine thousand six hundred livres for it. The King, however, sent for the diamond back again, and said he would keep it as a curiosity. He could not overcome his surprise; and said M. de St. Germain must be worth millions; especially if he possessed the secret of making large diamonds out of small ones. The Count neither said that he could, or could not; but positively asserted, that he knew how to make pearls grow, and give them the finest water. The King paid him great attention, and so did Madame du Pompadour. M. du Quesnoy once said, that St. Germain was a quack; but the King reprimanded him. In fact, his Majesty appears infatuated by him; and sometimes talks of him as if his descent were illustrious."

St. Germain had a most amusing vagabond for a servant, to whom he would often appeal for corrobation, when relating some wonderful event that happened centuries before. The fellow, who was not without ability, generally corroborated him in a most satisfactory manner. Upon one occasion, his master was telling a party of ladies and gentlemen, at dinner, some conversation he had had in Palestine, with King Richard I. of England, whom he described as a very particular friend of his. Signs of astonishment and incredulity were visible on the faces of the company; upon which St. Germain very coolly turned to his servant, who stood behind his chair, and asked him if he had not spoken truth? "I really cannot say," replied the man, without moving a muscle; "you forget, sir, I have only been five hundred years in your service!" "Ah! true," said his master; "I remember now; it was a little before your time!" Occasionally, when with men whom he could not so easily dupe, he gave utterance to the contempt with which he could scarcely avoid regarding such gaping credulity. "These fools of Parisians," said he, to the Baron de Gleichen, "believe me to be more than five hundred years old; and, since they will have it so, I confirm them in their idea. Not but that I really am much older than I appear."

Many other stories are related of this strange impostor; but enough have been quoted to show his character and pretensions. It appears that he endeavoured to find the philosopher's stone; but never boasted of possessing it. The Prince of Hesse Cassel, whom he had known years before, in Germany, wrote urgent letters to him, entreating him to quit Paris, and reside with him. St. Germain at last consented. Nothing further is known of his career. There were no gossipping memoir-writers at the court of Hesse Cassel to chronicle his sayings and doings. He died at Sleswig, under the roof of his friend the Prince, in the year 1784.

Cagliostro

This famous charlatan, the friend and successor of St. Germain, ran a career still more extraordinary. He was the arch-quack of his age, the last of the great pretenders to the philosopher's stone and the water of life, and during his brief season of prosperity one of the most conspicuous characters of Europe.

His real name was Joseph Balsamo. He was born at Palermo about the year 1743, of humble parentage. He had the misfortune to lose his father during his infancy, and his education was left in consequence to some relatives of his mother, the latter being too poor to afford him any instruction beyond mere reading and writing. He was sent in his fifteenth year to a monastery, to be taught the elements of chemistry and physic; but his temper was so impetuous, his indolence so invincible, and his vicious habits so deeply rooted, that he made no progress. After remaining some years, he left it with the character of an uninformed and dissipated young man, with good natural talents but a bad disposition. When he became of age, he abandoned himself to a life of riot and debauchery, and entered himself, in fact, into that celebrated fraternity, known in France and Italy as the "Knights of Industry," and in England as the "Swell Mob." He was far from being an idle or unwilling member of the corps. The first way in which he distinguished himself was by forging orders of admission to the theatres. He afterwards robbed his uncle, and counterfeited a will. For acts like these, he paid frequent compulsory visits to the prisons of Palermo. Somehow or other he acquired the character of a sorcerer - of a man who had failed in discovering the secrets of alchymy, and had sold his soul to the devil for the gold which he was not able to make by means of transmutation. He took no pains to disabuse the popular mind on this particular, but rather encouraged the belief than otherwise. He at last made use of it to cheat a silversmith, named Marano, of about sixty ounces of gold, and was in consequence obliged to leave Palermo. He persuaded this man that he could show him a treasure hidden in a cave, for which service he was to receive the sixty ounces of gold, while the silversmith was to have all the treasure for the mere trouble of digging it up. They went together at midnight to an excavation in the vicinity of Palermo, where Balsamo drew a magic circle, and invoked the devil to show his treasures. Suddenly there appeared half a dozen fellows, the accomplices of the swindler, dressed to represent devils, with horns on their heads, claws to their fingers, and vomiting apparently red and blue flame. They were armed with pitchforks, with which they belaboured poor Marano till he was almost dead, and robbed him of his sixty ounces of gold and all the valuables he carried about his person. They then made off, accompanied by Balsamo, leaving the unlucky silversmith to recover or die at his leisure. Nature chose the former course; and soon after daylight he was restored to his senses, smarting in body from his blows and in spirit for the deception of which he had been the victim. His first impulse was to denounce Balsamo to the magistrates of the town; but on further reflection he was afraid of the ridicule that a full exposure of all the circumstances would draw upon him: he therefore took the truly Italian resolution of being revenged on Balsamo by murdering him at the first convenient opportunity. Having given utterance to this threat in the hearing of a friend of Balsamo, it was reported to the latter, who immediately packed up his valuables and quitted Europe.

He chose Medina, in Arabia, for his future dwelling-place, and there became acquainted with a Greek named Altotas, a man exceedingly well versed in all the languages of the East, and an indefatigable student of alchymy. He possessed an invaluable collection of Arabian manuscripts on his favourite science, and studied them with such unremitting industry that he found he had not sufficient time to attend to his crucibles and furnaces without neglecting his books. He was looking about for an assistant when Balsamo opportunely presented himself, and made so favourable an impression that he was at once engaged in that capacity. But the relation of master and servant did not long subsist between them; Balsamo was too ambitious and too clever to play a secondary part, and within fifteen days of their first acquaintance they were bound together as friends and partners. Altotas, in the course of a long life devoted to alchymy, had stumbled upon some valuable discoveries in chemistry, one of which was an ingredient for improving the manufacture of flax, and imparting to goods of that material a gloss and softness almost equal to silk. Balsamo gave him the good advice to leave the philosopher's stone for the present undiscovered, and make gold out of their flax. The advice was taken, and they proceeded together to Alexandria to trade, with a large stock of that article. They stayed forty days in Alexandria, and gained a considerable sum by their venture. They afterwards visited other cities in Egypt, and were equally successful. They also visited Turkey, where they sold drugs and amulets. On their return to Europe, they were driven by stress of weather into Malta, and were hospitably received by Pinto, the Grand Master of the Knights, and a famous alchymist. They worked in his laboratory for some months, and tried hard to change a pewter-platter into a silver one. Balsamo, having less faith than his companions, was sooner wearied; and obtaining from his host many letters of introduction to Rome and Naples, he left him and Altotas to find the philosopher's stone and transmute the pewter-platter without him.

He had long since dropped the name of Balsamo on account of the many ugly associations that clung to it; and during his travels had assumed at least half a score others, with titles annexed to them. He called himself sometimes the Chevalier de Fischio, the Marquis de Melissa, the Baron de Belmonte, de Pelligrini, d'Anna, de Fenix, de Harat, but most commonly the Count de Cagliostro. Under the latter title he entered Rome, and never afterwards changed it. In this city he gave himself out as the restorer of the Rosicrucian philosophy; said he could transmute all metals into gold; that he could render himself invisible, cure all diseases, and administer an elixir against old age and decay. His letters from the Grand Master Pinto procured him an introduction into the best families. He made money rapidly by the sale of his elixir vitae; and, like other quacks, performed many remarkable cures by inspiring his patients with the most complete faith and reliance upon his powers; an advantage which the most impudent charlatans often possess over the regular practitioner.

While thus in a fair way of making his fortune he became acquainted with the beautiful Lorenza Feliciana, a young lady of noble birth, but without fortune. Cagliostro soon discovered that she possessed accomplishments that were invaluable. Besides her ravishing beauty, she had the readiest wit, the most engaging manners, the most fertile imagination, and the least principle of any of the maidens of Rome. She was just the wife for Cagliostro, who proposed himself to her, and was accepted. After their marriage, he instructed his fair Lorenza in all the secrets of his calling - taught her pretty lips to invoke angels, and genii, sylphs, salamanders, and undines, and, when need required, devils and evil spirits. Lorenza was an apt scholar: she soon learned all the jargon of the alchymists and all the spells of the enchanters; and thus accomplished the hopeful pair set out on their travels, to levy contributions on the superstitious and the credulous.

They first went to Sleswig on a visit to the Count de St. Germain, their great predecessor in the art of making dupes, and were received by him in the most magnificent manner. They no doubt fortified their minds for the career they had chosen, by the sage discourse of that worshipful gentleman; for immediately after they left him, they began their operations. They travelled for three or four years in Russia, Poland, and Germany, transmuting metals, telling fortunes, raising spirits, and selling the elixir vitae wherever they went; but there is no record of their doings from whence to draw a more particular detail. It was not until they made their appearance in England in 1776, that the names of the Count and Countess di Cagliostro began to acquire a European reputation. They arrived in London in the July of that year, possessed of property in plate, jewels, and specie to the amount of about three thousand pounds. They hired apartments in Whitcombe-street, and lived for some months quietly. In the same house there lodged a Portuguese woman named Blavary, who, being in necessitous circumstances, was engaged by the Count as interpreter. She was constantly admitted into his laboratory, where he spent much of his time in search of the philosopher's stone. She spread abroad the fame of her entertainer in return for his hospitality, and laboured hard to impress everybody with as full a belief in his extraordinary powers as she felt herself. But as a female interpreter of the rank and appearance of Madame Blavary did not exactly correspond with the Count's notions either of dignity or decorum, he hired a person named Vitellini, a teacher of languages, to act in that capacity. Vitellini was a desperate gambler; a man who had tried almost every resource to repair his ruined fortunes, including among the rest the search for the philosopher's stone. Immediately that he saw the Count's operations, he was convinced that the great secret was his, and that the golden gates of the palace of fortune were open to let him in. With still more enthusiasm than Madame Blavary, he held forth to his acquaintance, and in all public places, that the Count was an extraordinary man, a true adept, whose fortune was immense, and who could transmute into pure and solid gold, as much lead, iron, and copper as he pleased. The consequence was, that the house of Cagliostro was besieged by crowds of the idle, the credulous, and the avaricious, all eager to obtain a sight of the "philosopher," or to share in the boundless wealth which he could call into existence.

Unfortunately for Cagliostro, he had fallen into evil hands; instead of duping the people of England as he might have done, he became himself the victim of a gang of swindlers, who, with the fullest reliance on his occult powers, only sought to make money of him. Vitellini introduced to him a ruined gambler like himself, named Scot, whom he represented as a Scottish nobleman, attracted to London solely by his desire to see and converse with the extraordinary man whose fame had spread to the distant mountains of the north. Cagliostro received him with great kindness and cordiality; and "Lord" Scot thereupon introduced a woman named Fry, as Lady Scot, who was to act as chaperone to the Countess di Cagliostro, and make her acquainted with all the noble families of Britain. Thus things went swimmingly. "His lordship," whose effects had not arrived from Scotland, and who had no banker in

London, borrowed two hundred pounds of the Count; they were lent without scruple, so flattered was Cagliostro by the attentions they paid him, the respect, nay, veneration they pretended to feel for him, and the complete deference with which they listened to every word that fell from his lips.

Superstitious, like all desperate gamesters, Scot had often tried magical and cabalistic numbers, in the hope of discovering lucky numbers in the lottery, or at the roulette tables. He had in his possession a cabalistic manuscript, containing various arithmetical combinations of the kind, which he submitted to Cagliostro, with an urgent request that he would select a number. Cagliostro took the manuscript and studied it; but, as he himself informs us, with no confidence in its truth. He however predicted twenty as the successful number for the 6th of November following. Scot ventured a small sum upon this number, out of the two hundred pounds he had borrowed, and won. Cagliostro, incited by this success, prognosticated number twenty-five for the next drawing. Scot tried again, and won a hundred guineas. The numbers fifty-five and fifty-seven were announced with equal success for the 18th of the same month, to the no small astonishment and delight of Cagliostro, who thereupon resolved to try fortune for himself, and not for others. To all the entreaties of Scot and his lady that he would predict more numbers for them, he turned a deaf ear, even while he still thought him a lord and a man of honour. But when he discovered that he was a mere swindler, and the pretended Lady Scot an artful woman of the town, he closed his door upon them and on all their gang.

Having complete faith in the supernatural powers of the Count, they were in the deepest distress at having lost his countenance. They tried by every means their ingenuity could suggest, to propitiate him again; they implored, they threatened, and endeavoured to bribe him. But all was vain. Cagliostro would neither see nor correspond with them. In the mean time they lived extravagantly; and in the hope of future, exhausted all their present gains. They were reduced to the last extremity, when Miss Fry obtained access to the Countess, and received a guinea from her on the representation that she was starving. Miss Fry, not contented with this, begged her to intercede with her husband, that for the last time he would point out a lucky number in the lottery. The Countess promised to exert her influence, and Cagliostro thus entreated, named the number eight, at the same time reiterating his determination to have no more to do with any of them. By an extraordinary hazard, which filled Cagliostro with surprise and pleasure, number eight was the greatest prize in the lottery. Miss Fry and her associates cleared fifteen hundred guineas by the adventure; and became more than ever convinced of the occult powers of Cagliostro, and strengthened in their determination never to quit him until they had made their fortunes. Out of the proceeds, Miss Fry bought a handsome necklace at a pawnbrokers for ninety guineas. She then ordered a richly chased gold box, having two compartments, to be made at a jeweller's, and putting the necklace in the one, filled the other with a fine aromatic snuff. She then sought another interview with Madame di Cagliostro, and urged her to accept the box as a small token of her esteem and gratitude, without mentioning the valuable necklace that was concealed in it. Madame di Cagliostro accepted the present, and was from that hour exposed to the most incessant persecution from all the confederates, Blavary, Vitellini, and the pretended Lord and Lady Scot. They flattered themselves they had regained their lost footing in the house, and came day after day to know lucky numbers in the lottery; sometimes forcing themselves up the stairs, and into the Count's laboratory, in spite of the efforts of the servants to prevent them. Cagliostro, exasperated at their pertinacity, threatened to call in the assistance of the magistrates; and taking Miss Fry by the shoulders, pushed her into the street.

From that time may be dated the misfortunes of Cagliostro. Miss Fry, at the instigation of her paramour, determined on vengeance. Her first act was to swear a debt of two hundred pounds against Cagliostro, and to cause him to be arrested for that sum. While he was in custody in a sponging house, Scot, accompanied by a low attorney, broke into his laboratory, and carried off a small box, containing, as they believed, the powder of transmutation, and a number of cabalistic manuscripts and treatises upon alchymy. They also brought an action against him for the recovery of the necklace; and Miss Fry accused both him and his Countess of sorcery and witchcraft, and of foretelling numbers in the lottery by the aid of the devil. This latter charge was actually heard before Mr. Justice Miller. The action of trover for the necklace was tried before the Lord Chief Justice of the Common Pleas, who recommended the parties to submit to arbitration. In the mean time Cagliostro remained in prison for several weeks, till having procured bail, he was liberated. He was soon after waited upon by an attorney named Reynolds, also deep in the plot, who offered to compromise all the actions upon certain conditions. Scot, who had accompanied him, concealed himself behind the door, and suddenly rushing out, presented a pistol at the heart of Cagliostro, swearing he would shoot him instantly, if he would not tell him truly the art of predicting lucky numbers, and of transmuting metals. Reynolds pretending to be very angry, disarmed his accomplice, and entreated the Count to satisfy them by fair means, and disclose his secrets, promising that if he would do so, they would discharge all the actions, and offer him no further molestation. Cagliostro replied, that threats and entreaties were alike useless; that he knew no secrets; and that the powder of transmutation of which they had robbed him, was of no value to anybody but himself. He offered, however, if they would discharge the actions, and return the powder and the manuscripts, he would forgive them all the money they had swindled him out of. These conditions were refused; and Scot and Reynolds departed, swearing vengeance against him.

Cagliostro appears to have been quite ignorant of the forms of law in England, and to have been without a friend to advise him as to the best course he should pursue. While he was conversing with his Countess on the difficulties that beset them, one of his bail called, and invited him to ride in a hackney coach to the house of a person who would see him righted. Cagliostro consented, and was driven to the King's Bench prison, where his friend left him. He did not discover for several hours that he was a prisoner, or in fact understand the process of being surrendered by one's bail.

He regained his liberty in a few weeks; and the arbitrators between him and Miss Fry, made their award against him. He was ordered to pay the two hundred pounds she had sworn against him, and to restore the necklace and gold box which had been presented to the Countess. Cagliostro was so disgusted, that he determined to quit England. His pretensions, besides, had been unmercifully exposed by a Frenchman, named Morande, the Editor of the Courier de l'Europe, published in London. To add to his distress, he was recognised in Westminster Hall, as Joseph Balsamo, the swindler of Palermo. Such a complication of disgrace was not to be borne. He and his Countess packed up their small effects, and left England with no more than fifty pounds, out of the three thousand they had brought with them.

They first proceeded to Brussels, where fortune was more auspicious. They sold considerable quantities of the elixir of life, performed many cures, and recruited their finances. They then took their course through Germany to Russia, and always with the same success. Gold flowed into their coffers faster than they could count it. They quite forgot all the woes they had endured in England, and learned to be more circumspect in the choice of their acquaintance.

In the year 1780, they made their appearance in Strasbourg. Their fame had reached that city before them. They took a magnificent hotel, and invited all the principal persons of the place to their table. Their wealth appeared to be boundless, and their hospitality equal to it. Both the Count and Countess acted as physicians, and gave money, advice, and medicine to all the necessitous and suffering of the town. Many of the cures they performed, astonished those regular practitioners who did not make sufficient allowance for the wonderful influence of imagination in certain cases. The Countess, who at this time was not more than five-and-twenty, and all radiant with grace, beauty, and cheerfulness, spoke openly of her eldest son as a fine young man of eight-and-twenty, who had been for some years a captain in the Dutch service. The trick succeeded to admiration. All the ugly old women in Strasbourg, and for miles around, thronged the saloon of the Countess to purchase the liquid which was to make them as blooming as their daughters; the young women came in equal abundance that they might preserve their charms, and when twice as old as Ninon de L'Enclos, be more captivating than she; while men were not wanting fools enough to imagine, that they might keep off the inevitable stroke of the grim foe, by a few drops of the same incomparable elixir. The Countess, sooth to say, looked like an incarnation of immortal loveliness, a very goddess of youth and beauty; and it is possible that the crowds of young men and old, who at all convenient seasons haunted the perfumed chambers of this enchantress, were attracted less by their belief in her occult powers than from admiration of her languishing bright eyes and sparkling conversation. But amid all the incense that was offered at her shrine, Madame di Cagliostro was ever faithful to her spouse. She encouraged hopes, it is true, but she never realised them; she excited admiration, yet kept it within bounds; and made men her slaves, without ever granting a favour of which the vainest might boast.

In this city they made the acquaintance of many eminent persons, and among others, of the Cardinal Prince de Rohan, who was destined afterwards to exercise so untoward an influence over their fate. The Cardinal, who seems to have had great faith in him as a philosopher, persuaded him to visit Paris in his company, which he did, but remained only thirteen days. He preferred the society of Strasbourg, and returned thither, with the intention of fixing his residence far from the capital. But he soon found that the first excitement of his arrival had passed away. People began to reason with themselves, and to be ashamed of their own admiration. The populace, among whom he had lavished his charity with a bountiful hand, accused him of being the Antichrist, the Wandering Jew, the man of fourteen hundred years of age, a demon in human shape, sent to lure the ignorant to their destruction; while the more opulent and better informed called him a spy in the pay of foreign governments, an agent of the police, a swindler, and a man of evil life. The outcry grew at last so strong, that he deemed it prudent to try his fortune elsewhere.

He went first to Naples, but that city was too near Palermo; he dreaded recognition from some of his early friends, and after a short stay, returned to France. He chose Bordeaux as his next dwelling-place, and created as great a sensation there as he had done in Strasbourg. He announced himself as the founder of a new school of medicine and philosophy, boasted of his ability to cure all diseases, and invited the poor and suffering to visit him, and he would relieve the distress of the one class, and cure the ailings of the other. All day long the street opposite his magnificent hotel was crowded by the populace; the halt and the blind, women with sick babes in their arms, and persons suffering under every species of human infirmity flocked to this wonderful doctor. The relief he afforded in money more than counterbalanced the failure of his nostrums; and the affluence of people from all the surrounding country became so great, that the jurats of the city granted him a military guard, to be stationed day and night before his door, to keep order. The anticipations of Cagliostro were realised. The rich were struck with admiration of his charity and benevolence, and impressed with a full conviction of his marvellous powers. The sale of the elixir went on admirably. His saloons were thronged with wealthy dupes who came to purchase immortality. Beauty, that would endure for centuries, was the attraction for the fair sex; health and strength for the same period were the baits held out to the other. His charming Countess in the meantime brought grist to the mill, by telling fortunes and casting nativities, or granting attendant sylphs to any ladies who would pay sufficiently for their services. What was still better, as tending to keep up the credit of her husband, she gave the most magnificent parties in Bordeaux.

But as at Strasbourg the popular delusion lasted for a few months only, and burned itself out; Cagliostro forgot, in the intoxication of success, that there was a limit to quackery, which once passed, inspired distrust. When he pretended to call spirits from the tomb, people became incredulous. He was accused of

369

being an enemy to religion - of denying Christ, and of being the Wandering Jew. He despised these rumours as long as they were confined to a few; but when they spread over the town -- when he received no more fees -- when his parties were abandoned, and his acquaintance turned away when they met him in the street, he thought it high time to shift his quarters.

He was by this time wearied of the provinces, and turned his thoughts to the capital. On his arrival, he announced himself as the restorer of Egyptian Freemasonry and the founder of a new philosophy. He immediately made his way into the best society by means of his friend the Cardinal de Rohan. His success as a magician was quite extraordinary: the most considerable persons of the time visited him. He boasted of being able, like the Rosicrucians, to converse with the elementary spirits; to invoke the mighty dead from the grave, to transmute metals, and to discover occult things, by means of the special protection of God towards him. Like Dr. Dee, he summoned the angels to reveal the future; and they appeared, and conversed with him in crystals and under glass bells. [See the Abbe Fiard, and "Anecdotes of the Reign of Louis XVI." p. 400.] "There was hardly," says the Biographie des Contemporains, "a fine lady in Paris who would not sup with the shade of Lucretius in the apartments of Cagliostro -- a military officer who would not discuss the art of war with Cesar, Hannibal, or Alexander; or an advocate or counsellor who would not argue legal points with the ghost of Cicero." These interviews with the departed were very expensive; for, as Cagliostro said, the dead would not rise for nothing. The Countess, as usual, exercised all her ingenuity to support her husband's credit. She was a great favourite with her own sex; to many a delighted and wondering auditory of whom she detailed the marvellous powers of Cagliostro. She said he could render himself invisible, traverse the world with the rapidity of thought, and be in several places at the same time. ["Biographie des Contemporains," article "Cagliostro." See also "Histoire de la Magie en France," par M. Jules Garinet, p. 284.]

He had not been long at Paris before he became involved in the celebrated affair of the Queen's necklace. His friend, the Cardinal de Rohan, enamoured of the charms of Marie Antoinette, was in sore distress at her coldness, and the displeasure she had so often manifested against him. There was at that time a lady, named La Motte, in the service of the Queen, of whom the Cardinal was foolish enough to make a confidant. Madame de la Motte, in return, endeavoured to make a tool of the Cardinal, and succeeded but too well in her projects. In her capacity of chamber-woman, or lady of honour to the Queen, she was present at an interview between her Majesty and M. Boehmer, a wealthy jeweller of Paris, when the latter offered for sale a magnificent diamond necklace, valued at 1,600,000 francs, or about 64,000 pounds sterling. The Queen admired it greatly, but dismissed the jeweller, with the expression of her regret that she was too poor to purchase it. Madame de la Motte formed a plan to get this costly ornament into her own possession, and determined to make the Cardinal de Rohan the instrument by which to effect it. She therefore sought an interview with him, and pretending to sympathise in his grief for the Queen's displeasure, told him she knew a way by which he might be restored to favour. She then mentioned the necklace, and the sorrow of the Queen that she could not afford to buy it. The Cardinal, who was as wealthy as he was foolish, immediately offered to purchase the necklace, and make a present of it to the Queen. Madame de la Motte told him by no means to do so, as he would thereby offend her Majesty. His plan would be to induce the jeweller to give her Majesty credit, and accept her promissory note for the amount at a certain date, to be hereafter agreed upon. The Cardinal readily agreed to the proposal, and instructed the jeweller to draw up an agreement, and he would procure the Queen's signature. He placed this in the hands of Madame de la Motte, who returned it shortly afterwards, with the words, "Bon, bon - approuve -- Marie Antoinette," written in the margin. She told him at the same time that the Queen was highly pleased with his conduct in the matter, and would appoint a meeting with him in the gardens of Versailles, when she would present him with a flower, as a token of her regard. The Cardinal showed the forged document to the jeweller, obtained the necklace, and delivered it into the hands of Madame de la Motte. So far all was well. Her next object was to satisfy the Cardinal, who awaited impatiently the promised interview with his royal mistress.

There was at that time in Paris a young woman named D'Oliva, noted for her resemblance to the Queen; and Madame de la Motte, on the promise of a handsome reward, found no difficulty in persuading her to personate Marie Antoinette, and meet the Cardinal de Rohan at the evening twilight in the gardens of Versailles. The meeting took place accordingly. The Cardinal was deceived by the uncertain light, the great resemblance of the counterfeit, and his own hopes; and having received the flower from Mademoiselle D'Oliva, went home with a lighter heart than had beat in his bosom for many a day. [The enemies of the unfortunate Queen of France, when the progress of the Revolution embittered their animosity against her. maintained that she was really a party in this transaction; that she, and not Mademoiselle D'Oliva, met the Cardinal and rewarded him with the flower; and that the story above related was merely concocted between her, La Motte, and others to cheat the jeweller of his 1,600,000 francs.]

In the course of time the forgery of the Queen's signature was discovered. Boehmer the jeweller immediately named the Cardinal de Rohan and Madame de la Motte as the persons with whom he had negotiated, and they were both arrested and thrown into the Bastille. La Motte was subjected to a rigorous examination, and the disclosures she made implicating Cagliostro, he was seized, along with his wife, and also sent to the Bastille, A story involving so much scandal necessarily excited great curiosity. Nothing was to be heard of in Paris but the Queen's necklace, with surmises of the guilt or innocence of the several parties implicated. The husband of Madame de la Motte escaped to England, and in the opinion of many took the necklace with him, and there disposed of it to different jewellers in small quantities at a time. But Madame de la Motte insisted that she had entrusted it to Cagliostro, who had seized and taken it to pieces, to "swell the treasures of his immense unequalled fortune." She spoke of him as "an empiric, a mean alchymist, a dreamer on the philosopher's stone, a false prophet, a profaner of the true worship, the self-dubbed Count Cagliostro!" She further said that he originally conceived the project of ruining the Cardinal de Rohan; that he persuaded her, by the exercise of some magic influence over her mind, to aid and abet the scheme; and that he was a robber, a swindler, and a sorcerer!

After all the accused parties had remained for upwards of six months in the Bastille, the trial commenced. The depositions of the witnesses having been heard, Cagliostro, as the principal culprit, was first called upon for his defence. He was listened to with the most breathless attention. He put himself into a theatrical attitude, and thus began:-- "I am oppressed! -- I am accused! -- I am calumniated! Have I deserved this fate? I descend into my conscience, and I there find the peace that men refuse me! I have travelled a great deal -- I am known over all Europe, and a great part of Asia and Africa. I have everywhere shown myself the friend of my fellow-creatures. My knowledge, my time, my fortune have ever been employed in the relief of distress! I have studied and practised medicine, but I have never degraded that most noble and most consoling of arts by mercenary speculations of any kind. Though always giving, and never receiving, I have preserved my independence. I have even carried my delicacy so far as to refuse the favours of kings. I have given gratuitously my remedies and my advice to the rich: the poor have received from me both remedies and money. I have never contracted any debts, and my manners are pure and uncorrupted." After much more self-laudation of the same kind, he went on to complain of the great hardships he had endured in being separated for so many months from his innocent and loving wife, who, as he was given to understand, had been detained in the Bastille, and perhaps chained in an unwholesome dungeon. He denied unequivocally that he had the necklace, or that he had ever seen it; and to silence the rumours and accusations against him, which his own secrecy with regard to the events of his life had perhaps originated, he expressed himself ready to satisfy the curiosity of the public, and to give a plain and full account of his career. He then told a romantic and incredible tale, which imposed upon no one. He said he neither knew the place of his birth nor the name of his parents, but that he spent his infancy in Medina in Arabia, and was brought up under the name of Acharat. He lived in the palace of the Great Muphti in that city, and always had three servants to wait upon him, besides his preceptor, named Althotas. This Althotas was very fond of him, and told him that his father and mother, who were Christians and nobles, died when he was three months old, and left him in the care of the Muphti. He could never, he said, ascertain their names, for whenever he asked Althotas the question, he was told that it would be dangerous for him to know. Some incautious expressions dropped by his preceptor gave him reason to think they were from Malta. At the age of twelve he began his travels, and learned the various languages of the East. He remained three years in Mecca, where the Cherif, or governor, showed him so much kindness, and spoke to him so tenderly and affectionately, that he sometimes thought that personage was his father. He quitted this good man with tears in his eyes, and never saw him afterwards; but he was convinced that he was, even at that moment, indebted to his care for all the advantages he enjoyed. Whenever he arrived in any city, either of Europe or Asia, he found an account opened for him at the principal bankers' or merchants'. He could draw upon them to the amount of thousands and hundreds of thousands; and no questions were ever asked beyond his name. He had only to mention the word Acharat, and all his wants were supplied. He firmly believed that the Cherif of Mecca was the friend to whom all was owing. This was the secret of his wealth, and he had no occasion to resort to swindling for a livelihood. It was not worth his while to steal a diamond necklace when he had wealth enough to purchase as many as he pleased, and more magnificent ones than had ever been worn by a Queen of France. As to the other charges brought against him by Madame de la Motte, he had but a short answer to give. She had called him an empiric. He was not unfamiliar with the word. If it meant a man who, without being a physician, had some knowledge of medicine, and took no fees -- who cured both rich and poor, and took no money from either, he confessed that he was such a man, that he was an empiric. She had also called him a mean alchymist. Whether he were an alchymist or not, the epithet mean could only be applied to those who begged and cringed, and he had never done either. As regarded his being a dreamer about the philosopher's stone, whatever his opinions upon that subject might be, he had been silent, and had never troubled the public with his dreams. Then, as to his being a false prophet, he had not always been so; for he had prophesied to the Cardinal de Rohan that Madame de la Motte would prove a dangerous woman, and the result had verified the prediction. He denied that he was a profaner of the true worship, or that he had ever striven to bring religion into contempt; on the contrary, he respected every man's religion, and never meddled with it. He also denied that he was a Rosicrucian, or that he had ever pretended to be three hundred years of age, or to have had one man in his service for a hundred and fifty years. In conclusion, he said every statement that Madame de la Motte had made regarding him was false, and that she was mentiris impudentissime, which two words he begged her counsel to translate for her, as it was not polite to tell her so in French.

Such was the substance of his extraordinary answer to the charges against him; an answer which convinced those who were before doubtful that he was one of the most impudent impostors that had ever run the career of deception. Counsel were then heard on behalf of the Cardinal de Rohan and Madame de la Motte. It appearing clearly that the Cardinal was himself the dupe of a vile conspiracy; and there being no evidence against Cagliostro, they were both acquitted. Madame de la Motte was found guilty, and sentenced to be publicly whipped, and branded with a hot iron on the back.

Cagliostro and his wife were then discharged from custody. On applying to the officers of the Bastille for the papers and effects which had been seized at his lodgings, he found that many of them had been abstracted. He thereupon brought an action against them for the recovery of his MSS. and a small portion of the powder of transmutation. Before the affair could be decided, he received orders to quit Paris within four-and-twenty hours. Fearing that if he were once more inclosed in the dungeons of the Bastille he should never see daylight again, he took his departure immediately and proceeded to England. On his arrival in London he made the acquaintance of the notorious Lord George Gordon, who espoused his cause warmly, and inserted a letter in the public papers, animadverting upon the conduct of the Queen of France in the affair of the necklace, and asserting that she was really the guilty party. For this letter Lord George was exposed to a prosecution at the instance of the French Ambassador - found guilty of libel, and sentenced to fine and a long imprisonment.

Cagliostro and the Countess afterwards travelled in Italy, where they were arrested by the Papal Government in 1789, and condemned to death. The charges against him were, that he was a freemason, a heretic, and a sorcerer. This unjustifiable sentence was afterwards commuted into one of perpetual imprisonment in the Castle of St. Angelo. His wife was allowed to escape severer punishment by immuring herself in a nunnery. Cagliostro did not long survive. The loss of liberty preyed upon his mind -- accumulated misfortunes had injured his health and broken his spirit, and he died early in 1790. His fate may have been no better than he deserved, but it is impossible not to feel that his sentence for the crimes assigned was utterly disgraceful to the government that pronounced it.

Present State of Alchymy

We have now finished the list of the persons who have most distinguished themselves in this foolish and unprofitable pursuit. Among them are men of all ranks, characters, and conditions; the truthseeking, but erring philosopher; the ambitious prince and the needy noble, who have believed in it; as well as the designing charlatan, who has not believed in it, but has merely made the pretension to it the means of cheating his fellows, and living upon their credulity. One or more of all these classes will be found in the foregoing pages. It will be seen, from the record of their lives, that the delusion, humiliating as it was to human intellect, was not altogether without its uses. Men, in striving to gain too much, do not always overreach themselves: if they cannot arrive at the inaccessible mountain-top, they may, perhaps, get half way towards it, and pick up some scraps of wisdom and knowledge on the road. The useful science of chemistry is not a little indebted to its spurious brother of alchymy. Many valuable discoveries have been made in that search for the impossible, which might otherwise have been hidden for centuries yet to come. Roger Bacon, in searching for the philosopher's stone, discovered gunpowder, a still more extraordinary substance. Van Helmont, in the same pursuit, discovered the properties of gas; Geber made discoveries in chemistry which were equally important; and Paracelsus, amidst his perpetual visions of the transmutation of metals, found that mercury was a remedy for one of the most odious and excruciating of all the diseases that afflict humanity.

In our day, no mention is made in Europe of any new devotees of the science. The belief in witchcraft, which is scarcely more absurd, still lingers in the popular mind: but none are so credulous as to believe that any elixir could make man live for centuries, or turn all our iron and pewter into gold. Alchymy, in Europe, may be said to be wholly exploded; but in the East it still flourishes in as great repute as ever. Recent travellers make constant mention of it, especially in China, Hindostan, Persia, Tartary, Egypt, and Arabia.

Fortune Telling

And men still grope t' anticipate
The cabinet designs of Fate;
Apply to wizards to foresee
What shall and what shall never be.
-- *Hudibras*, part iii. canto 3.

In accordance with the plan laid down, we proceed to the consideration of the follies into which men have been led by their eager desire to pierce the thick darkness of futurity. God himself, for his own wise purposes, has more than once undrawn the impenetrable veil which shrouds those awful secrets; and, for purposes just as wise, he has decreed that, except in these instances, ignorance shall be our lot for ever. It is happy for man that he does not know what the morrow is to bring forth; but, unaware of this great blessing, he has, in all ages of the world, presumptuously endeavoured to trace the events of unborn centuries, and anticipate the march of time. He has reduced this presumption into a study. He has divided it into sciences and systems without number, employing his whole life in the vain pursuit. Upon no subject has it been so easy to deceive the world as upon this. In every breast the curiosity exists in a greater or less degree, and can only be conquered by a long course of self-examination, and a firm reliance that the future would not be hidden from our sight, if it were right that we should be acquainted with it.

An undue opinion of our own importance in the scale of creation is at the bottom of all our unwarrantable notions in this respect. How flattering to the pride of man to think that the stars in their courses watch over him, and typify, by their movements and aspects, the joys or the sorrows that await him! He, less in proportion to the universe than the all but invisible insects that feed in myriads on a summer's leaf, are to this great globe itself, fondly imagines that eternal worlds were chiefly created to prognosticate his fate. How we should pity the arrogance of the worm that crawls at our feet, if we knew that it also desired to know the secrets of futurity, and imagined that meteors shot athwart the sky to warn it that a tom-tit was hovering near to gobble it up; that storms and earthquakes, the revolutions of empires, or the fall of mighty monarchs, only happened to, predict its birth, its progress, and its decay! Not a whit less presuming has man shown himself; not a whit less arrogant are the sciences, so called, of astrology, augury, necromancy, geomancy, palmistry, and divination of every kind.

Leaving out of view the oracles of pagan antiquity and religious predictions in general, and confining ourselves solely to the persons who, in modern times, have made themselves most conspicuous in foretelling the future, we shall find that the sixteenth and seventeenth centuries were the golden age of these impostors. Many of them have been already mentioned in their character of alchymists. The union of the two pretensions is not at all surprising. It was to be expected that those who assumed a power so preposterous as that of prolonging the life of man for several centuries, should pretend, at the same time, to foretell the events which were to mark that preternatural span of existence. The world would as readily believe that they had discovered all secrets, as that they had only discovered one. The most celebrated astrologers of Europe, three centuries ago, were alchymists. Agrippa, Paracelsus, Dr. Dee, and the Rosicrucians, all laid as much stress upon their knowledge of the days to come, as upon their pretended possession of the philosopher's stone and the elixir of life. In their time, ideas of the wonderful, the diabolical, and the supernatural, were rifer than ever they were before. The devil or the stars were universally believed to meddle constantly in the affairs of men; and both were to be consulted with proper ceremonies. Those who were of a melancholy and gloomy temperament betook themselves to necromancy and sorcery; those more cheerful and aspiring, devoted themselves to astrology. The latter science was encouraged by all the monarchs and governments of that age. In England, from the time of Elizabeth to that of William and Mary, judicial astrology was in high repute. During that period flourished Drs. Dee, Lamb, and Forman; with Lilly, Booker, Gadbury, Evans, and scores of nameless impostors in every considerable town and village in the country, who made it their business to cast nativities, aid in the recovery of stolen goods, prognosticate happy or unhappy marriages, predict whether journeys would be prosperous, and note lucky moments for the commencement of any enterprise, from the setting up of a cobler's shop to the marching of an army. Men who, to use the words of Butler, did

"Deal in Destiny's dark counsel,
And sage opinion of the moon sell;
To whom all people far and near
On deep importance did repair,
When brass and pewter pots did stray,
And linen slunk out of the way."

In Lilly's Memoirs of his Life and Times, there are many notices of the inferior quacks who then abounded, and upon whom he pretended to look down with supreme contempt; not because they were astrologers, but because they debased that noble art by taking fees for the recovery of stolen property. From Butler's Hudibras and its curious notes, we may learn what immense numbers of these fellows lived upon the credulity of mankind in that age of witchcraft and diablerie. Even in our day how great is the reputation enjoyed by the almanac-makers, who assume the name of Francis Moore. But in the time of Charles I. and the Commonwealth, the most learned, the most noble, and the most conspicuous characters did not hesitate to consult astrologers in the most open manner. Lilly, whom Butler has immortalized under the name of Sydrophel, relates, that he proposed to write a work called "An Introduction to Astrology," in which he would satisfy the whole kingdom of the lawfulness of that art. Many of the soldiers were for it, he says, and many of the Independent party, and abundance of worthy men in the House of Commons, his assured friends, and able to take his part against the Presbyterians, who would have silenced his predictions if they could. He afterwards carried his plan into execution, and when his book was published, went with another astrologer named Booker to the headquarters of the parliamentary army at Windsor, where they were welcomed and feasted in the garden where General Fairfax lodged. They were afterwards introduced to the general, who received them very kindly, and made allusion to some of their predictions. He hoped their art was lawful and agreeable to God's word; but he did not understand it himself. He did not doubt, however, that the two astrologers feared God, and therefore he had a good opinion of them. Lilly assured him that the art of astrology was quite consonant to the Scriptures; and confidently predicted from his knowledge of the stars, that the parliamentary army would overthrow all its enemies. In Oliver's Protectorate, this quack informs us that he wrote freely enough. He became an Independent, and all the soldiery were his friends. When he went to Scotland, he saw a soldier standing in front of the army, with a book of prophecies in his hand, exclaiming to the several companies as they passed by him, "Lo! hear what Lilly saith: you are in this month promised victory! Fight it out, brave boys! and then read that month's prediction!"

After the great fire of London, which Lilly said he had foretold, he was sent for by the committee of the House of Commons appointed to inquire into the causes of the calamity. In his "Monarchy or no Monarchy," published in 1651, he had inserted an hieroglyphical plate, representing on one side persons in winding sheets digging graves; and on the other a large city in flames. After the great fire some sapient member of the legislature bethought him of Lilly's book, and having mentioned it in the house, it was agreed that the astrologer should be summoned. Lilly attended accordingly, when Sir Robert Brooke told him the reason of his summons, and called upon him to declare what he knew. This was a rare opportunity for the vain-glorious Lilly to vaunt his abilities; and he began a long speech in praise of himself and his pretended science. He said, that after the execution of Charles I, he was extremely desirous to know what might from that time forth happen to the parliament and to the nation in general. He, therefore, consulted the stars and satisfied himself. The result of his judgment he put into emblems and hieroglyphics, without any commentary, so that the true meaning might be concealed from the vulgar, and made manifest only to the wise; imitating in this the example of many wise philosophers who had done the like.

"Did you foresee the year of the fire?" said a member. "No!" quoth Lilly, "nor was I desirous: of that I made no scrutiny." After some further parley the house found they could make nothing of the astrologer, and dismissed him with great civility.

One specimen of the explanation of a prophecy given by Lilly, and related by him with much complacency, will be sufficient to show the sort of trash by which he imposed upon the million. "In the year 1588," says he, "there was a prophecy printed in Greek characters, exactly deciphering the long troubles of the English nation from 1641 to 1660;" and it ended thus:-- "And after him shall come a dreadful dead man, and with him a royal G, of the best blood in the world, and he shall have the crown, and shall set England on the right way, and put out all heresies." The following is the explanation of this oracular absurdity:--

"Monkery being extinguished above eighty or ninety years, and the Lord General's name being Monk, is the dead man. The royal G. or C, [it is gamma in the Greek, intending C. in the Latin, being the third letter in the Alphabet] is Charles II, who for his extraction may be said to be of the best blood of the world."

In France and Germany astrologers met even more encouragement than they received in England. In very early ages, Charlemagne and his successors fulminated their wrath against them in common with sorcerers. Louis XI, that most superstitious of men, entertained great numbers of them at his court; and Catherine de Medicis, that most superstitious of women, hardly ever took any affair of importance without consulting them. She chiefly favoured her own countrymen; and during the time she governed France, the land was overrun by Italian conjurors, necromancers, and fortune-tellers of every kind. But the chief astrologer of that day, beyond all doubt, was the celebrated Nostradamus, physician to her husband, King Henry II. He was born in 1503, at the town of St. Remi, in Provence, where his father was a notary. He did not acquire much fame till he was past his fiftieth year, when his famous "Centuries," a collection of verses, written in obscure and almost unintelligible language, began to excite attention. They were so much spoken of in 1556, that Henry II. resolved to attach so skilful a man to his service, and appointed him his physician. In a biographical notice of him prefixed to the edition of his "Vraies Centuries," published at Amsterdam in 1668, we are informed that he often discoursed with his royal master on the secrets of futurity, and received many great presents as his reward, besides his usual allowance for medical attendance. After the death of Henry, he retired to his native place, where Charles IX. paid him a visit in 1564, and was so impressed with veneration for his wondrous knowledge of the things that were to be, not in France only, but in the whole world for hundreds of years to come, that he made him a counsellor of state, and his own physician, besides treating him in other matters with a royal liberality. "In fine," continues his biographer, "I should be too prolix were I to tell all the honours conferred upon him, and all the great nobles and learned men that arrived at his house, from the very ends of the earth, to see and converse with him as if he had been an oracle. Many strangers, in fact, came to France for no other purpose than to consult him."

The prophecies of Nostradamus consist of upwards of a thousand stanzas, each of four lines, and are to the full as obscure as the oracles of old. They take so great a latitude, both as to time and space, that they are almost sure to be fulfilled somewhere or other in the course of a few centuries; A little ingenuity like that evinced by Lilly, in his explanation about General Monk and the dreadful dead man, might easily make events to fit some of them.

Let us try. In his second century, prediction 66, he says,-- '

"From great dangers the captive is escaped.
A little time, great fortune changed.
In the palace the people are caught.
By good augury the city is besieged."

"What is this," a believer might exclaim, "but the escape of Napoleon from Elba -- his changed fortune, and the occupation of Paris by the allied armies?" -- Let us try again. In his third century, prediction 98, he says,--

"Two royal brothers will make fierce war on each other;
So mortal shall be the strife between them,
That each one shall occupy a fort against the other;
For their reign and life shall be the quarrel."

Some Lillius Redivivus would find no difficulty in this prediction. To use a vulgar phrase, it is as clear as a pikestaff. Had not the astrologer in view Don Miguel and Don Pedro when he penned this stanza, so much less obscure and oracular than the rest?

He is to this day extremely popular in France and the Walloon country of Belgium, where old farmer-wives consult him with great confidence and assiduity.

Catherine di Medicis was not the only member of her illustrious house who entertained astrologers. At the beginning of the fifteenth century, there was a man named Basil, residing in Florence, who was noted over all Italy for his skill in piercing the darkness of futurity. It is said that he foretold to Cosmo di Medicis, then a private citizen, that he would attain high dignity, inasmuch as the ascendant of his nativity was adorned with the same propitious aspects as those of Augustus Caesar and the Emperor Charles V. [Hermippus Redivivus, p. 142.] Another astrologer foretold the death of Prince Alexander di Medicis; and so very minute and particular was be in all the circumstances, that he was suspected of being chiefly instrumental in fulfilling his own prophecy; a very common resource with these fellows, to keep up their credit. He foretold confidently that the Prince should die by the hand of his own familiar friend, a person of a slender habit of body, a small face, a swarthy complexion, and of most remarkable taciturnity. So it afterwards happened; Alexander having been murdered in his chamber by his cousin Lorenzo, who corresponded exactly with the above description. [Jovii Elog. p. 320.] The author of Hermippus Redivivus, in relating this story, inclines to the belief that the astrologer was guiltless of any

378

participation in the crime, but was employed by some friend of Prince Alexander, to warn him of his danger.

A much more remarkable story is told of an astrologer, who lived in Romagna, in the fifteenth century, and whose name was Antiochus Tibertus. [Les Anecdotes de Florence ou l'Histoire secrete de la Maison di Medicis, p. 318.] At that time nearly all the petty sovereigns of Italy retained such men in their service; and Tibertus having studied the mathematics with great success at Paris, and delivered many predictions, some of which, for guesses, were not deficient in shrewdness, was taken into the household of Pandolfo di Malatesta, the sovereign of Rimini. His reputation was so great, that his study was continually thronged, either with visitors who were persons of distinction, or with clients who came to him for advice, and in a short time he acquired a considerable fortune. Notwithstanding all these advantages he passed his life miserably, and ended it on the scaffold. The following story afterwards got into circulation, and has been often triumphantly cited by succeeding astrologers as an irrefragable proof of the truth of their science. It was said, that long before he died he uttered three remarkable prophecies; one relating to himself, another to his friend, and the third to his patron, Pandolfo di Malatesta. The first delivered was that relating to his friend, Guido di Bogni, one of the greatest captains of the time. Guido was exceedingly desirous to know his fortune, and so importuned Tibertus, that the latter consulted the stars, and the lines on his palm, to satisfy him. He afterwards told him with a sorrowful face, that according to all the rules of astrology and palmistry, he should be falsely suspected by his best friend, and should lose his life in consequence. Guido then asked the astrologer if he could foretell his own fate; upon which Tibertus again consulted the stars, and found that it was decreed from all eternity that he should end his days on the scaffold. Malatesta, when he heard these predictions, so unlikely, to all present appearance, to prove true, desired his astrologer to predict his fate also; and to hide nothing from him, however unfavourable it might be. Tibertus complied, and told his patron, at that time one of the most flourishing and powerful princes of Italy, that he should suffer great want, and die at last, like a beggar, in the common hospital of Bologna: and so it happened in all three cases. Guido di Bogni was accused by his own father-in-law, the Count di Bentivoglio, of a treasonable design to deliver up the city of Rimini to the papal forces, and was assassinated afterwards, by order of the tyrant Malatesta, as he sat at the supper-table, to which he had been invited in all apparent friendship. The astrologer was, at the same time, thrown into prison, as being concerned in the treason of his friend. He attempted to escape, and had succeeded in letting himself down from his dungeon window into a moat, when he was discovered by the sentinels. This being reported to Malatesta, he gave orders for his execution on the following morning.

Malatesta had, at this time, no remembrance of the prophecy; and his own fate gave him no uneasiness: but events were silently working its fulfilment. A conspiracy had been formed, though Guido di Bogni was innocent of it, to deliver up Rimini to the Pope; and all the necessary measures having been taken, the city was seized by the Count de Valentinois. In the confusion, Malatesta had barely time to escape from his palace in disguise. He was pursued from place to place by his enemies, abandoned by all his former friends, and, finally, by his own children. He at last fell ill of a languishing disease, at Bologna; and, nobody caring to afford him shelter, he was carried to the hospital, where he died. The only thing that detracts from the interest of this remarkable story is the fact, that the prophecy was made after the event.

For some weeks before the birth of Louis XIV, an astrologer from Germany, who had been sent for by the Marshal de Bassompierre and other noblemen of the court, had taken up his residence in the palace, to be ready, at a moment's notice, to draw the horoscope of the future sovereign of France. When the Queen was taken in labour, he was ushered into a contiguous apartment, that he might receive notice of the very instant the child was born. The result of his observations were the three words, diu, dure, feliciter; meaning, that the new-born Prince should live and reign long, with much labour, and with great glory. No prediction less favourable could have been expected from an astrologer, who had his bread to get, and who was at the same time a courtier. A medal was afterwards struck in commemoration of the event; upon one side of which was figured the nativity of the Prince, representing him as driving the chariot of Apollo, with the inscription "Ortus solis Gallici," -- the rising of the Gallic sun.

The best excuse ever made for astrology was that offered by the great astronomer, Keppler, himself an unwilling practiser of the art. He had many applications from his friends to cast nativities for them, and generally gave a positive refusal to such as he was not afraid of offending by his frankness. In other cases he accommodated himself to the prevailing delusion. In sending a copy of his "Ephemerides" to Professor Gerlach, he wrote that they were nothing but worthless conjectures; but he was obliged to devote himself to them, or he would have starved. "Ye overwise philosophers," he exclaimed, in his "Tertius Interveniens;" "ye censure this daughter of astronomy beyond her deserts! Know ye not that she must support her mother by her charms? The scanty reward of an astronomer would not provide him with bread, if men did not entertain hopes of reading the future in the heavens."

NECROMANCY was, next to astrology, the pretended science most resorted to, by those who wished to pry into the future. The earliest instance upon record is that of the Witch of Endor and the spirit of Samuel. Nearly all the nations of antiquity believed in the possibility of summoning departed ghosts to disclose the awful secrets that God made clear to the disembodied. Many passages in allusion to this subject, will at once suggest themselves to the classical reader; but this art was never carried on openly in any country. All governments looked upon it as a crime of the deepest dye. While astrology was encouraged, and its professors courted and rewarded, necromancers were universally condemned to the stake or the gallows. Roger Bacon, Albertus Magnus, Arnold of Villeneuve, and many others, were accused, by the public opinion of many centuries, of meddling in these unhallowed matters. So deep-rooted has always been the popular delusion with respect to accusations of this kind, that no crime was ever disproved with such toil and difficulty. That it met great encouragement, nevertheless, is evident from the vast numbers of pretenders to it; who, in spite of the danger, have existed in all ages and countries.

GEOMANCY, or the art of foretelling the future by means of lines and circles, and other mathematical figures drawn on the earth, is still extensively practised in Asiatic countries, but is almost unknown in Europe.

AUGURY, from the flight or entrails of birds, so favourite a study among the Romans, is, in like manner, exploded in Europe. Its most assiduous professors, at the present day, are the abominable Thugs of India.

DIVINATION, of which there are many kinds, boasts a more enduring reputation. It has held an empire over the minds of men from the earliest periods of recorded history, and is, in all probability, coeval with time itself. It was practised alike by the Jews, the Egyptians, the Chaldeans, the Persians, the Greeks, and the Romans; is equally known to all modern nations, in every part of the world; and is not unfamiliar to the untutored tribes that roam in the wilds of Africa and America. Divination, as practised in civilized Europe at the present day, is chiefly from cards, the tea-cup, and the lines on the palm of the hand. Gipsies alone make a profession of it; but there are thousands and tens of thousands of humble families in which the good-wife, and even the good-man, resort to the grounds at the bottom of their teacups, to know whether the next harvest will be abundant, or their sow bring forth a numerous litter; and in which the young maidens look to the same place to know when they are to be married, and whether the man of their choice is to be dark or fair, rich or poor, kind or cruel. Divination by cards, so great a favourite among the moderns, is, of course, a modern science; as cards do not yet boast an antiquity of much more than four hundred years. Divination by the palm, so confidently believed in by half the village lasses in Europe, is of older date, and seems to have been known to the Egyptians in the time of the patriarchs; as well as divination by the cup, which, as we are informed in Genesis, was practised by Joseph. Divination by the rod was also practised by the Egyptians. In comparatively recent times, it was pretended that by this means hidden treasures could be discovered. It now appears to be altogether exploded in Europe. Onomancy, or the foretelling a man's fate by the letters of his name, and the various transpositions of which they are capable, is a more modern sort of divination; but it reckons comparatively few believers.

The following list of the various species of Divination formerly in use, is given by Gaule, in his "Magastromancer," and quoted in Hone's "Year Book," p. 1517.

Stareomancy, or divining by the elements.
Aeromancy, or divining by the air.
Pyromancy, by fire.
Hydromancy, by water.
Geomancy, by earth.
Theomancy, pretending to divine by the revelation of the Spirit, and by the Scriptures, or word of God.
Demonomancy, by the aid of devils and evil spirits.
Idolomancy, by idols, images, and figures.
Psychomancy, by the soul, affections, or dispositions of men.
Antinopomancy, by the entrails of human beings.
Theriomancy, by beasts.
Ornithomancy, by birds.
Icthyomancy, by fishes.
Botanomancy, by herbs.
Lithomancy, by stones.
Kleromancy, by lots.
Oneiromancy, by dreams.
Onomancy, by names.
Arithmancy, by numbers.
Logarithmancy, by logarithms.
Sternomancy, by the marks from the breast to the belly.
Gastromancy, by the sound of, or marks upon, the belly.
Omphelomancy, by the navel.
Chiromancy, by the hands.
Paedomancy, by the feet.
Onchyomancy, by the nails.
Cephaleonomancy, by asses' heads.
Tuphramancy, by ashes.
Kapnomancy, by smoke.
Livanomancy, by the burning of incense.
Keromancy, by the melting of wax.
Lecanomancy, by basins of water.
Katoxtromancy, by looking-glasses.
Chartomancy, by writing in papers, and by Valentines.
Macharomancy, by knives and swords.
Crystallomancy, by crystals.

Dactylomancy, by rings.
Koseinomancy, by sieves.
Axinomancy, by saws.
Kaltabomancy, by vessels of brass, or other metal.
Spatalamancy, by skins, bones, &c.
Roadomancy, by stars.
Sciomancy, by shadows.
Astragalomancy, by dice.
Oinomancy, by the lees of wine.
Sycomancy, by figs.
Typomancy, by cheese.
Alphitomancy, by meal, flour, or bran.
Krithomancy, by corn or grain.
Alectromancy, by cocks.
Gyromancy, by circles.
Lampadomancy, by candles and lamps.

ONEIRO-CRITICISM, or the art of interpreting dreams, is a relic of the most remote ages, which has subsisted through all the changes that moral or physical revolutions have operated in the world. The records of five thousand years bear abundant testimony to the universal diffusion of the belief, that the skilful could read the future in dreams. The rules of the art, if any existed in ancient times, are not known; but in our day, one simple rule opens the whole secret. Dreams, say all the wiseacres in Christendom, are to be interpreted by contraries. Thus, if you dream of filth, you will acquire something valuable; if you dream of the dead, you will hear news of the living; if you dream of gold and silver, you run a risk of being without either; and if you dream you have many friends, you will be persecuted by many enemies. The rule, however, does not hold good in all cases. It is fortunate to dream of little pigs, but unfortunate to dream of big bullocks. If you dream you have lost a tooth, you may be sure that you will shortly lose a friend; and if you dream that your house is on fire, you will receive news from a far country. If you dream of vermin, it is a sign that there will be sickness in your family; and if you dream of serpents, you will have friends who, in the course of time, will prove your bitterest enemies; but, of all dreams, it is most fortunate if you dream that you are wallowing up to your neck in mud and mire. Clear water is a sign of grief; and great troubles, distress, and perplexity are predicted, if you dream that you stand naked in the public streets, and know not where to find a garment to shield you from the gaze of the multitude.

In many parts of Great Britain, and the continents of Europe and America, there are to be found elderly women in the villages and country-places whose interpretations of dreams are looked upon with as much reverence as if they were oracles. In districts remote from towns it is not uncommon to find the members of a family regularly every morning narrating their dreams at the breakfast-table, and becoming happy or miserable for the day according to their interpretation. There is not a flower that blossoms, or fruit that ripens, that, dreamed of, is not ominous of either good or evil to such people. Every tree of the field or the forest is endowed with a similar influence over the fate of mortals, if seen in the night-visions. To dream of the ash, is the sign of a long journey; and of an oak, prognosticates long life and prosperity. To dream you strip the bark off any tree, is a sign to a maiden of an approaching loss of a character; to a married woman, of a family bereavement; and to a man, of an accession of fortune. To dream of a leafless tree, is a sign of great sorrow; and of a branchless trunk, a sign of despair and suicide. The elder-tree is more auspicious to the sleeper; while the fir-tree, better still, betokens all manner of comfort and prosperity. The lime-tree predicts a voyage across the ocean; while the yew and the alder are ominous of sickness to the young and of death to the old.

It is quite astonishing to see the great demand there is, both in England and France, for dream-books, and other trash of the same kind. Two books in England enjoy an extraordinary popularity, and have run through upwards of fifty editions in as many years in London alone, besides being reprinted in Manchester, Edinburgh, Glasgow, and Dublin. One is "Mother Bridget's Dream-book and Oracle of Fate;" the other is the "Norwood Gipsy." It is stated on the authority of one who, is curious in these matters, that there is a demand for these works, which are sold at sums varying from a penny to sixpence, chiefly to servant-girls and imperfectly-educated people, all over the country, of upwards of eleven thousand annually; and that at no period during the last thirty years has the average number sold been less than this. The total number during this period would thus amount to 330,000.

Among the flowers and fruits charged with messages for the future, the following is a list of the most important, arranged from approved sources, in alphabetical order:-

Asparagus, gathered and tied up in bundles, is an omen of tears. If you see it growing in your dreams, it is a sign of good fortune.

Aloes, without a flower, betoken long life: in flower, betoken a legacy.

Artichokes. This vegetable is a sign that you will receive, in a short time, a favour from the hands of those from whom you would least expect it.

Agrimony. This herb denotes that there will be sickness in your house.

Anemone, predicts love.

Auriculas, in beds, denote luck; in pots, marriage: while to gather them, foretells widowhood.

Bilberries, predict a pleasant excursion.

Broom-flowers, an increase of family.

Cauliflowers, predict that all your friends will slight you, or that you will fall into poverty and find no one to pity you.

Dock-leaves, a present from the country.

Daffodils. Any maiden who dreams of daffodils is warned by her good angel to avoid going into a wood with her lover, or into any dark or retired place where she might not be able to make people hear her if she cried out. Alas! for her if she pay no attention to the warning! She shall be rifled of the precious flower of chastity, and shall never again have right to wear the garland of virginity.

"Never again shall she put garland on;
Instead of it, she'll wear sad cypress now,
And bitter elder broken from the bough."

Figs, if green, betoken embarrassment; if dried, money to the poor and mirth to the rich.

Heart's-ease, betokens heart's pain.

Lilies, predict joy; water-lilies, danger from the sea.

Lemons, betoken a separation.

Pomegranates, predict happy wedlock to those who are single, and reconciliation to those who are married and have disagreed.

Quinces, prognosticate pleasant company.

Roses, denote happy love, not unmixed with sorrow from other sources.

Sorrel, To dream of this herb is a sign that you will shortly have occasion to exert all your prudence to overcome some great calamity.

Sunflowers, show that your pride will be deeply wounded.

Violets, predict evil to the single and joy to the married.

Yellow-flowers of any kind predict jealousy.

Yew-berries, predict loss of character to both sexes.

It should be observed that the rules for the interpretation of dreams are far from being universal. The cheeks of the peasant girl of England glow with pleasure in the morning after she has dreamed of a rose, while the paysanne of Normandy dreads disappointment and vexation for the very same reason. The Switzer who dreams of an oaktree does not share in the Englishman's joy; for he imagines that the vision was a warning to him that, from some trifling cause, an overwhelming calamity will burst over him. Thus do the ignorant and the credulous torment themselves; thus do they spread their nets to catch vexation, and pass their lives between hopes which are of no value and fears which are a positive evil.

OMENS. -- Among the other means of self-annoyance upon which men have stumbled, in their vain hope of discovering the future, signs and omens hold a conspicuous place. There is scarcely an occurrence in nature which, happening at a certain time, is not looked upon by some persons as a prognosticator either of good or evil. The latter are in the greatest number, so much more ingenious are we in tormenting ourselves than in discovering reasons for enjoyment in the things that surround us. We go out of our course to make ourselves uncomfortable; the cup of life is not bitter enough to our palate, and we distil superfluous poison to put into it, or conjure up hideous things to frighten ourselves at, which would never exist if we did not make them. "We suffer," says Addison, ["Spectator," No. 7, March 8th, 1710-11.] "as much from trifling accidents as from real evils. I have known the shooting of a star spoil a night's rest, and have seen a man in love grow pale and lose his appetite upon the plucking of a merrythought. A screech-owl at midnight has alarmed a family more than a band of robbers; nay, the voice of a cricket has struck more terror than the roaring of a lion. There is nothing so inconsiderable which may not appear dreadful to an imagination that is filled with omens and prognostics. A rusty nail or a crooked pin shoot up into prodigies."

The century and a quarter that has passed away since Addison wrote has seen the fall of many errors. Many fallacies and delusions have been crushed under the foot of time since then; but this has been left unscathed, to frighten the weakminded and embitter their existence. A belief in omens is not confined to the humble and uninformed. A general, who led an army with credit, has been known to feel alarmed at a winding-sheet in the candle; and learned men, who had honourably and fairly earned the highest honours of literature, have been seen to gather their little ones around them, and fear that one would be snatched away, because,

"When stole upon the time the dead of night,
And heavy sleep had closed up mortal eyes,"

a dog in the street was howling at the moon. Persons who would acknowledge freely that the belief in omens was unworthy of a man of sense, have yet confessed at the same time that, in spite of their reason, they have been unable to conquer their fears of death when they heard the harmless insect called the death-watch ticking in the wall, or saw an oblong hollow coal fly out of the fire.

Many other evil omens besides those mentioned above alarm the vulgar and the weak. If a sudden shivering comes over such people, they believe that, at that instant, an enemy is treading over the spot that will one day be their grave. If they meet a sow when they first walk abroad in the morning, it is an omen of evil for that day. To meet an ass, is in like manner unlucky. It is also very unfortunate to walk under a ladder; to forget to eat goose on the festival of St. Michael; to tread upon a beetle, or to eat the twin nuts that are sometimes found in one shell. Woe, in like manner, is predicted to that wight who inadvertently upsets the salt; each grain that is overthrown will bring to him a day of sorrow. If thirteen persons sit at table, one of them will die within the year; and all of them will be unhappy. Of all evil omens, this is the worst. The facetious Dr. Kitchener used to observe that there was one case in which he believed that it was really unlucky for thirteen persons to sit down to dinner, and that was when there was only dinner enough for twelve. Unfortunately for their peace of mind, the great majority of people do not take this wise view of the matter. In almost every country of Europe the same superstition prevails, and some carry it so far as to look upon the number thirteen as in every way ominous of evil; and if they find thirteen coins in their purse, cast away the odd one like a polluted thing. The philosophic Beranger, in his exquisite song, "Thirteen at Table," has taken a poetical view of this humiliating superstition, and mingled, as is his wont, a lesson of genuine wisdom in his lay. Being at dinner, he overthrows the salt, and, looking round the room, discovers that he is the thirteenth guest. While he is mourning his unhappy fate, and conjuring up visions of disease and suffering, and the grave, he is suddenly startled by the apparition of Death herself, not in the shape of a grim foe, with skeleton ribs and menacing dart, but of an angel of light, who shows the folly of tormenting ourselves with the dread of her approach, when she is the friend, rather than the enemy, of man, and frees us from the fetters which bind us to the dust.

If men could bring themselves to look upon Death in this manner, living well and wisely till her inevitable approach, how vast a store of grief and vexation would they spare themselves!

Among good omens, one of the most conspicuous is to meet a piebald horse. To meet two of these animals is still more fortunate; and if on such an occasion you spit thrice, and form any reasonable wish, it will be gratified within three days. It is also a sign of good fortune if you inadvertently put on your stocking wrong side out. If you wilfully wear your stocking in this fashion, no good will come of it. It is very lucky to sneeze twice; but if you sneeze a third time, the omen loses its power, and your good fortune will be nipped in the bud. If a strange dog follow you, and fawn on you, and wish to attach itself to you, it is a sign of very great prosperity. Just as fortunate is it if a strange male cat comes to your house and manifests friendly intentions towards your family. If a she eat, it is an omen, on the contrary, of very great misfortune. If a swarm of bees alight in your garden, some very high honour and great joys await you.

Besides these glimpses of the future, you may know something of your fate by a diligent attention to every itching that you may feel in your body. Thus, if the eye or the nose itches, it is a sign you will be shortly vexed; if the foot itches you will tread upon strange ground; and if the elbow itches, you will change your bedfellow. Itching of the right-hand prognosticates that you will soon have a sum of money; and of the left, that you will be called upon to disburse it.

These are but a few of the omens which are generally credited in modern Europe. A complete list of them would fatigue from its length, and sicken from its absurdity. It would be still more unprofitable to attempt to specify the various delusions of the same kind which are believed among Oriental nations. Every reader will remember the comprehensive formula of cursing preserved in "Tristram Shandy:" -- curse a man after any fashion you remember or can invent, you will be sure to find it there. The Oriental creed of omens is not less comprehensive. Every movement of the body, every emotion of the mind, is at certain times an omen. Every form and object in nature, even the shape of the clouds and the changes of the weather; every colour, every sound, whether of men or animals, or birds or insects, or inanimate things, is an omen. Nothing is too trifling or inconsiderable to inspire a hope which is not worth cherishing, or a fear which is sufficient to embitter existence.

From the belief in omens springs the superstition that has, from very early ages, set apart certain days, as more favourable than others, for prying into the secrets of futurity. The following, copied verbatim from the popular "Dream and Omen Book" of Mother Bridget, will show the belief of the people of England at the present day. Those who are curious as to the ancient history of these observances, will find abundant aliment in the "Every-day Book."

"The 1st of January. -- If a young maiden drink, on going to bed, a pint of cold spring-water, in which is beat up an amulet, composed of the yolk of a pullet's egg, the legs of a spider, and the skin of an eel pounded, her future destiny will be revealed to her in a dream. This charm fails of its effect if tried any

386

other day of the year.

"Valentine Day. -- Let a single woman go out of her own door very early in the morning, and if the first person she meets be a woman, she will not be married that year: if she meet a man, she will be married within three months.

"Lady Day. -- The following charm may be tried this day with certain success: -- String thirty-one nuts on a string, composed of red worsted mixed with blue silk, and tie it round your neck on going to bed, repeating these lines --

'Oh, I wish ! oh, I wish to see
Who my true love is to be !'

Shortly after midnight, you will see your lover in a dream, and be informed at the same time of all the principal events of your future life.

"St. Swithin's Eve. -- Select three things you most wish to know; write them down with a new pen and red ink on a sheet of fine-wove paper, from which you must previously cut off all the corners and burn them. Fold the paper into a true-lover's knot, and wrap round it three hairs from your head. Place the paper under your pillow for three successive nights, and your curiosity to know the future will be satisfied.

"St. Mark's Eve. -- Repair to the nearest churchyard as the clock strikes twelve, and take from a grave on the south-side of the church three tufts of grass (the longer and ranker the better), and on going to bed place them under your pillow, repeating earnestly three several times,

'The Eve of St. Mark by prediction is blest,
Set therefore my hopes and my fears all to rest:
Let me know my fate, whether weal or woe;
Whether my rank's to be high or low;
Whether to live single, or be a bride,
And the destiny my star doth provide.'

Should you have no dream that night, you will be single and miserable all your life. If you dream of thunder and lightning, your life will be one of great difficulty and sorrow.

"Candlemas Eve. -- On this night (which is the purification of the Virgin Mary), let three, five, seven, or nine, young maidens assemble together in a square chamber. Hang in each corner a bundle of sweet herbs, mixed with rue and rosemary. Then mix a cake of flour, olive-oil, and white sugar; every maiden having an equal share in the making and the expense of it. Afterwards, it must be cut into equal pieces, each one marking the piece as she cuts it with the initials of her name. It is then to be baked one hour before the fire, not a word being spoken the whole time, and the maidens sitting with their arms and knees across. Each piece of cake is then to be wrapped up in a sheet of paper, on which each maiden

387

shall write the love part of Solomon's Songs. If she put this under her pillow, she will dream true. She will see her future husband and every one of her children, and will know, besides, whether her family will be poor or prosperous -- a comfort to her, or the contrary.

"Midsummer. -- Take three roses, smoke them with sulphur, and exactly at three in the day, bury one of the roses under a yew tree; the second in a newly-made grave, and put the third under your pillow for three nights, and at the end of that period burn it in a fire of charcoal. Your dreams during that time will be prophetic of your future destiny, and, what is still more curious and valuable (Mother Bridget loquitur), the man whom you are to wed, will know no peace till he comes and visits you. Besides this, you will perpetually haunt his dreams.

"St. John's Eve. -- Make a new pincushion of the very best black velvet (no inferior quality will answer the purpose), and on one side stick your name in full length with the very smallest pins that can be bought (none other will do). On the other side, make a cross with some very large pins, and surround it with a circle. Put this into your stocking when you take it off at night, and hang it up at the foot of the bed. All your future life will pass before you in a dream.

"First New Moon of the Year. -- On the first new moon in the year, take a pint of clear springwater and infuse into it the white of an egg laid by a white hen, a glass of white wine, three almonds peeled white, and a tablespoonful of white rose-water. Drink this on going to bed, not making more nor less than three draughts of it; repeating the following verses three several times in a clear distinct voice, but not so loud as to be overheard by anybody:--

' If I dream of water pure
Before the coming morn,
'Tis a sign I shall be poor,
And unto wealth not born.
If I dream of tasting beer,
Middling then will be my cheer-
Chequer'd with the good and bad,
Sometimes joyful, sometimes sad;
But should I dream of drinking wine,
Wealth and pleasure will be mine.
The stronger the drink, the better the cheer-
Dreams of my destiny, appear, appear!'

"Twenty-ninth of February. -- This day, as it only occurs once in four years, is peculiarly auspicious to those who desire to have a glance at futurity, especially to young maidens burning with anxiety to know the appearance and complexion of their future lords. The charm to be adopted is the following: Stick twenty-seven of the smallest pins that are made, three by three, into a tallow candle. Light it up at the wrong end, and then place it in a candlestick made out of clay, which must be drawn from a virgin's grave. Place this on the chimney-place, in the left-hand corner, exactly as the clock strikes twelve, and go to bed immediately. When the candle is burnt out, take the pins and put them into your left-shoe; and before nine nights have elapsed your fate will be revealed to you."

We have now taken a hasty review of the various modes of seeking to discover the future, especially as

388

practised in modern times. The main features of the folly appear essentially the same in all countries. National character and peculiarities operate some difference of interpretation. The mountaineer makes the natural phenomena which he most frequently witnesses prognosticative of the future. The dweller in the plains, in a similar manner, seeks to know his fate among the signs of the things that surround him, and tints his superstition with the hues of his own clime. The same spirit animates them all -- the same desire to know that which Infinite Mercy has concealed. There is but little probability that the curiosity of mankind in this respect will ever be wholly eradicated. Death and ill-fortune are continual bugbears to the weak-minded, the irreligious, and the ignorant; and while such exist in the world, divines will preach upon its impiety and philosophers discourse upon its absurdity in vain. Still, it is evident that these follies have greatly diminished. Soothsayers and prophets have lost the credit they formerly enjoyed, and skulk in secret now where they once showed their faces in the blaze of day. So far there is manifest improvement.

The Magnetisers

THE MAGNETISERS.

Some deemed them wondrous wise,
and some believed them mad.

Beattie's Minstrel.

The wonderful influence of imagination in the cure of diseases is well known. A motion of the hand, or a glance of the eye, will throw a weak and credulous patient into a fit; and a pill made of bread, if taken with sufficient faith, will operate a cure better than all the drugs in the pharmacopoeia. The Prince of Orange, at the siege of Breda, in 1625, cured all his soldiers who were dying of the scurvy, by a philanthropic piece of quackery, which he played upon them with the knowledge of the physicians, when all other means had failed. [See Van der Mye's account of the siege of Breda. The garrison, being afflicted with scurvy, the Prince of Orange sent the physicians two or three small phials, containing a decoction of camomile, wormwood, and camphor, telling them to pretend that it was a medicine of the greatest value and extremest rarity, which had been procured with very much danger and difficulty from the East; and so strong, that two or three drops would impart a healing virtue to a gallon of water. The soldiers had faith in their commander; they took the medicine with cheerful faces, and grew well rapidly. They afterwards thronged about the Prince in groups of twenty and thirty at a time, praising his skill, and loading him with protestations of gratitude.] Many hundreds of instances, of a similar kind, might be related, especially from the history of witchcraft. The mummeries, strange gesticulations, and barbarous jargon of witches and sorcerers, which frightened credulous and nervous women, brought on all those symptoms of hysteria and other similar diseases, so well understood now, but which were then supposed to be the work of the devil, not only by the victims and the public in general, but by the operators themselves.

In the age when alchymy began to fall into some disrepute, and learning to lift up its voice against it, a new delusion, based upon this power of imagination, suddenly arose, and found apostles among all the alchymists. Numbers of them, forsaking their old pursuits, made themselves magnetisers. It appeared first in the shape of mineral, and afterwards of animal, magnetism, under which latter name it survives to this day, and numbers its dupes by thousands.

The mineral magnetisers claim the first notice, as the worthy predecessors of the quacks of the present day. The honour claimed for Paracelsus of being the first of the Rosicrucians has been disputed; but his claim to be considered the first of the magnetisers can scarcely be challenged. It has been already mentioned of him, in the part of this work which treats of alchymy, that, like nearly all the distinguished adepts, he was a physician; and pretended, not only to make gold and confer immortality, but to cure all diseases. He was the first who, with the latter view, attributed occult and miraculous powers to the magnet. Animated apparently by a sincere conviction that the magnet was the philosopher's stone, which, if it could not transmute metals, could soothe all human suffering and arrest the progress of decay, he travelled for many years in Persia and Arabia, in search of the mountain of adamant, so famed in oriental fables. When he practised as a physician at Basle, he called one of his nostrums by the name of azoth -- a stone or crystal, which, he said, contained magnetic properties, and cured epilepsy, hysteria, and spasmodic affections. He soon found imitators. His fame spread far and near; and thus were sown the first seeds of that error which has since taken root and flourished so widely. In spite of the denial of modern practitioners, this must be considered the origin of magnetism; for we find that, beginning with Paracelsus, there was a regular succession of mineral magnetisers until Mesmer appeared, and gave a new feature to the delusion.

Paracelsus boasted of being able to transplant diseases from the human frame into the earth, by means of the magnet. He said there were six ways by which this might be effected. One of them will be quite sufficient, as a specimen. "If a person suffer from disease, either local or general, let the following remedy be tried. Take a magnet, impregnated with mummy [Mummies were of several kinds, and were all of great use in magnetic medicines. Paracelsus enumerates six kinds of mummies; the first four only differing in the composition used by different people for preserving their dead, are the Egyptian, Arabian, Pisasphaltos, and Lybian. The fifth mummy of peculiar power was made from criminals that had been hanged; "for from such there is a gentle siccation, that expungeth the watery humour, without destroying the oil and spirituall, which is cherished by the heavenly luminaries, and strengthened continually by the affluence and impulses of the celestial spirits; whence it may be properly called by the name of constellated or celestial mummie." The sixth kind of mummy was made of corpuscles, or spiritual effluences, radiated from the living body; though we cannot get very clear ideas on this head, or respecting the manner in which they were caught. -- "Medicina Diatastica; or, Sympathetical Mummie, abstracted from the Works of Paracelsus, and translated out of the Latin, by Fernando Parkhurst, Gent." London, 1653. pp. 2.7. Quoted by the "Foreign Quarterly Review," vol. xii. p. 415.] and mixed with rich earth. In this earth sow some seeds that have a congruity or homogeneity with the disease: then let this earth, well sifted and mixed with mummy, be laid in an earthen vessel; and let the seeds committed to it be watered daily with a lotion in which the diseased limb or body has been washed. Thus will the disease be transplanted from the human body to the seeds which are in the earth. Having done this, transplant the seeds from the earthen vessel to the ground, and wait till they begin to sprout into herbs: as they increase, the disease will diminish; and when they have arrived at their full growth, it will disappear altogether."

Kircher the Jesuit, whose quarrel with the alchymists was the means of exposing many of their impostures, was a firm believer in the efficacy of the magnet. Having been applied to by a patient afflicted with hernia, he directed the man to swallow a small magnet reduced to powder, while he applied, at the same time, to the external swelling a poultice, made of filings of iron. He expected that by this means the magnet, when it got to the corresponding place inside, would draw in the iron, and with it the tumour; which would thus, he said, be safely and expeditiously reduced.

As this new doctrine of magnetism spread, it was found that wounds inflicted with any metallic substance could be cured by the magnet. In process of time the delusion so increased, that it was deemed sufficient to magnetise a sword, to cure any hurt which that sword might have inflicted! This was the origin of the celebrated "weapon-salve," which excited so much attention about the middle of the seventeenth century. The following was the recipe given by Paracelsus for the cure of any wounds inflicted by a sharp weapon, except such as had penetrated the heart, the brain, or the arteries. "Take of moss growing on the head of a thief who has been hanged and left in the air; of real mummy; of human blood, still warm -- of each, one ounce; of human suet, two ounces; of linseed oil, turpentine, and Armenian bole -- of each, two drachms. Mix all well in a mortar, and keep the salve in an oblong, narrow urn." With this salve the weapon, after being dipped in the blood from the wound, was to be carefully anointed, and then laid by in a cool place. In the mean time, the wound was to be duly washed with fair clean water, covered with a clean, soft, linen rag, and opened once a day to cleanse off purulent or other matter. Of the success of this treatment, says the writer of the able article on Animal Magnetism, in the twelfth volume of the "Foreign Quarterly Review," there cannot be the least doubt;

"for surgeons at this moment follow exactly the same method, except anointing the weapon!

The weapon salve continued to be much spoken of on the Continent, and many eager claimants appeared for the honour of the invention. Dr. Fludd, or A Fluctibus, the Rosicrucian, who has been already mentioned in a previous part of this volume, was very zealous in introducing it into England. He tried it with great success in several cases; and no wonder; for, while he kept up the spirits of his patients by boasting of the great efficacy of the salve, he never neglected those common, but much more important remedies, of washing, bandaging, &c. which the experience of all ages had declared sufficient for the purpose. Fludd, moreover, declared, that the magnet was a remedy for all diseases, if properly applied; but that man having, like the earth, a north and a south pole, magnetism could only take place when his body was in a boreal position! In the midst of his popularity, an attack was made upon him and his favourite remedy, the salve; which, however, did little or nothing to diminish the belief in its efficacy. One "Parson Foster" wrote a pamphlet, entitled "Hyplocrisma Spongus; or, a Spunge to wipe away the Weapon-Salve ;" in which he declared, that it was as bad as witchcraft to use or recommend such an unguent; that it was invented by the devil, who, at the last day, would seize upon every person who had given it the slightest encouragement. "In fact," said Parson Foster, "the devil himself gave it to Paracelsus; Paracelsus to the Emperor; the Emperor to the courtier; the courtier to Baptista Porta; and Baptista Porta to Dr. Fludd, a doctor of physic, yet living and practising in the famous city of London, who now stands tooth and nail for it." Dr. Fludd, thus assailed, took up the pen in defence of his unguent, in a reply called "The Squeezing of Parson Foster's Spunge; wherein the Spunge-Bearer's immodest Carriage and Behaviour towards his Brethren is detected; the bitter Flames of his slanderous Reports are, by the sharp Vinegar of Truth, corrected and quite extinguished; and, lastly, the virtuous Validity of his Spunge in wiping away the Weapon-Salve, is crushed out and clean abolished."

Shortly after this dispute a more distinguished believer in the weapon-salve made his appearance, in the person of Sir Kenelm Digby, the son of Sir Everard Digby, who was executed for his participation in the Gunpowder Plot. This gentleman, who, in other respects, was an accomplished scholar and an able man, was imbued with all the extravagant notions of the alchymists. He believed in the philosopher's stone, and wished to engage Descartes to devote his energies to the discovery of the elixir of life, or some other means by which the existence of man might be prolonged to an indefinite period. He gave his wife, the beautiful Venetia Anastasia Stanley, a dish of capons, fed upon vipers, according to the plan supposed to have been laid down by Arnold of Villeneuve, in the hope that she might thereby preserve her loveliness for a century. If such a man once took up the idea of the weapon-salve, it was to be expected that he would make the most of it. In his hands, however, it was changed from an unguent into a powder, and was called the powder of sympathy. He pretended that he had acquired the knowledge of it from a Carmelite friar, who had learned it in Persia or Armenia, from an oriental philosopher of great renown. King James, the Prince of Wales, the Duke of Buckingham, and many other noble personages, believed in its efficacy. The following remarkable instance of his mode of cure was read by Sir Kenelm to a society of learned men at Montpellier. Mr. James Howell, the well-known author of the "Dendrologia," and of various letters, coming by chance as two of his best friends were fighting a duel, rushed between them, and endeavoured to part them. He seized the sword of one of the combatants by the hilt, while, at the same time, he grasped the other by the blade. Being transported with fury one against the other, they struggled to rid themselves of the hindrance caused by their friend; and in so doing, the one whose sword was held by the blade by Mr. Howell, drew it away roughly, and nearly cut his hand off, severing the nerves and muscles, and penetrating to the bone. The other, almost at the same instant, disengaged his sword, and aimed a blow at the head of his antagonist, which Mr. Howell observing, raised his wounded hand with the rapidity of thought, to prevent the blow. The sword fell on the back of his already wounded hand, and cut it severely. "It seemed," said Sir Kenelm Digby, "as if some unlucky star raged over them, that they should have both shed the blood of that dear friend, for whose life they would have given their own, if they had been in their proper mind at the time." Seeing Mr. Howell's face all

393

besmeared with blood from his wounded hand, they both threw down their swords and embraced him, and bound up his hand with a garter, to close the veins, which were cut, and bled profusely. They then conveyed him home, and sent for a surgeon. King James, who was much attached to Mr. Howell, afterwards sent his own surgeon to attend him. We must continue the narrative in the words of Sir Kenelm Digby:- "It was my chance," says he, "to be lodged hard by him: and, four or five days after, as I was making myself ready, he came to my house, and prayed me to view his wounds; 'for I understand,' said he, 'that you have extraordinary remedies on such occasions; and my surgeons apprehend some fear, that it may grow to a gangrene, and so the hand must be cut off.' In effect, his countenance discovered that he was in much pain, which, he said, was insupportable, in regard of the extreme inflammation. I told him I would willingly serve him; but if, haply, he knew the manner how I could cure him, without touching or seeing him, it might be that he would not expose himself to my manner of curing; because he would think it, peradventure, either ineffectual or superstitious. He replied, 'The many wonderful things which people have related unto me of your way of medicinement, makes me nothing doubt at all of its efficacy; and all that I have to say unto you is comprehended in the Spanish proverb, Hagase el milagro y hagalo Mahoma -- Let the miracle be done, though Mahomet do it.'

"I asked him then for anything that had the blood upon it: so he presently sent for his garter, wherewith his hand was first bound; and, as I called for a basin of water, as if I would wash my hands, I took a handful of powder of vitriol, which I had in my study, and presently dissolved it. As soon as the bloody garter was brought me, I put it in the basin, observing, in the interim, what Mr. Howell did, who stood talking with a gentleman in a corner of my chamber, not regarding at all what I was doing. He started suddenly, as if he had found some strange alteration in himself. I asked him what he ailed? 'I know not what ails me; but I find that I feel no more pain. Methinks that a pleasing kind of freshness, as it were a wet cold napkin, did spread over my hand, which hath taken away the inflammation that tormented me before.' I replied, 'Since, then, you feel already so much good of my medicament, I advise you to cast away all your plasters; only keep the wound clean, and in a moderate temper, betwixt heat and cold.' This was presently reported to the Duke of Buckingham, and a little after, to the King, who were both very curious to know the circumstances of the business; which was, that after dinner, I took the garter out of the water, and put it to dry before a great fire. It was scarce dry before Mr. Howell's servant came running, and saying that his master felt as much burning as ever he had done, if not more; for the heat was such as if his hand were betwixt coals of fire. I answered, that although that had happened at present, yet he should find ease in a short time; for I knew the reason of this new accident, and would provide accordingly; for his master should be free from that inflammation, it might be, before he could possibly return to him: but, in case he found no ease, I wished him to come presently back again; if not, he might forbear coming. Thereupon he went; and, at the instant, I did put the garter again into the water; thereupon he found his master without any pain at all. To be brief, there was no sense of pain afterwards; but within five or six days, the wounds were cicatrised and entirely healed."

Such is the marvellous story of Sir Kenelm Digby. Other practitioners of that age were not behind him in absurdity. It was not always necessary to use either the powder of sympathy, or the weapon-salve, to effect a cure. It was sufficient to magnetise the sword with the hand (the first faint dawn of the animal theory), to relieve any pain the same weapon had caused. They pretended, that if they stroked the sword upwards with their fingers, the wounded person would feel immediate relief; but if they stroked it downwards, he would feel intolerable pain.[Reginald Scott, quoted by Sir Walter Scott, in the notes to the "Lay of the Last Minstrel," c. iii. v. xxiii.]

Another very strange notion of the power and capabilities of magnetism was entertained at the same time. It was believed that a sympathetic alphabet could be made on the flesh, by means of which persons could correspond with each other, and communicate all their ideas with the rapidity of volition, although thousands of miles apart. From the arms of two persons a piece of flesh was cut, and mutually transplanted, while still warm and bleeding. The piece so severed grew to the new arm on which it was placed; but still retained so close a sympathy with its native limb, that its old possessor was always sensible of any injury done to it. Upon these transplanted pieces were tattooed the letters of the alphabet; so that, when a communication was to be made, either of the persons, though the wide Atlantic rolled between them, had only to prick his arm with a magnetic needle, and straightway his friend received intimation that the telegraph was at work. Whatever letter he pricked on his own arm pained the same letter on the arm of his correspondent. ["Foreign Quarterly Review," vol. xii. p. 417.] Who knows but this system, if it had received proper encouragement, might not have rendered the Post-Office unnecessary, and even obviated much of the necessity for railroads? Let modern magnetisers try and bring it to perfection. It is not more preposterous than many of their present notions; and, if carried into effect, with the improvement of some stenographical expedient for diminishing the number of punctures, would be much more useful than their plan of causing persons to read with their great toes, [Wirth's "Theorie des Somnambulismes," p. 79.] or seeing, with their eyes shut, into other people's bodies, and counting the number of arteries therein. ["Report of the Academic Royale de Medicine," -- case of Mademoiselle Celine Sauvage, p. 186.]

Contemporary with Sir Kenelm Digby, was the no less famous Mr. Valentine Greatraks who, without mentioning magnetism, or laying claim to any theory, practised upon himself and others a deception much more akin to the animal magnetism of the present day, than the mineral magnetism it was then so much the fashion to study. He was the son of an Irish gentleman, of good education and property, in the county of Cork. He fell, at an early age, into a sort of melancholy derangement. After some time, he had an impulse, or strange persuasion in his mind, which continued to present itself, whether he were sleeping or waking, that God had given him the power of curing the king's evil. He mentioned this persuasion to his wife, who very candidly told him that he was a fool! He was not quite sure of this, notwithstanding the high authority from which it came, and determined to make trial of the power that was in him. A few days afterwards, he went to one William Maher, of Saltersbridge, in the parish of Lismore, who was grievously afflicted with the king's evil in his eyes, cheek, and throat. Upon this man, who was of abundant faith, he laid his hands, stroked him, and prayed fervently. He had the satisfaction to see him heal considerably in the course of a few days; and, finally, with the aid of other remedies, to be quite cured. This success encouraged him in the belief that he had a divine mission. Day after day he had further impulses from on high, that he was called upon to cure the ague also. In the course of time he extended his powers to the curing of epilepsy, ulcers, aches, and lameness. All the county of Cork was in a commotion to see this extraordinary physician, who certainly operated some very great benefit in cases where the disease was heightened by hypochondria and depression of spirits. According to his own account, [Greatraks' Account of himself, in a letter to the Honourable Robert Boyle.] such great multitudes resorted to him from divers places, that he had no time to follow his own business, or enjoy the company of his family and friends. He was obliged to set aside three days in the week, from six in the morning till six at night, during which time only he laid hands upon all that came. Still the crowds which thronged around him were so great, that the neighbouring towns were not able to accommodate them. He thereupon left his house in the country, and went to Youghal, where the resort of sick people, not only from all parts of Ireland, but from England, continued so great, that the magistrates were afraid they would infect the place by their diseases. Several of these poor credulous people no sooner saw him than they fell into fits, and he restored them by waving his hand in their faces, and praying over them. Nay, he affirmed, that the touch of his glove had driven pains away, and, on one occasion, cast out from a woman several devils, or evil spirits, who tormented her day and night. "Every one of these devils," says Greatraks, "was like to choke her, when it came up into her throat." It is evident, from this, that the woman's complaint was nothing but hysteria.

The clergy of the diocese of Lismore, who seem to have had much clearer notions of Greatraks' pretensions than their parishioners, set their faces against the new prophet and worker of miracles. He was cited to appear in the Dean's Court, and prohibited from laying on his hands for the future: but he cared nothing for the church. He imagined that he derived his powers direct from Heaven, and continued to throw people into fits, and bring them to their senses again, as usual, almost exactly after the fashion of modern magnetisers. His reputation became, at last, so great, that Lord Conway sent to him from London, begging-that he would come over immediately, to cure a grievous head-ache which his lady had suffered for several years, and which the principal physicians of England had been unable to relieve.

Greatraks accepted the invitation, and tried his manipulations and prayers upon Lady Conway. He failed, however, in affording any relief. The poor lady's head-ache was excited by causes too serious to allow her any help, even from faith and a lively imagination. He lived for some months in Lord Conway's house, at Ragley, in Warwickshire, operating cures similar to those he had performed in Ireland. He afterwards removed to London, and took a house in Lincoln's Inn Fields, which soon became the daily resort of all the nervous and credulous women of the metropolis. A very amusing account of Greatraks at this time (1665), is given in the second volume of the "Miscellanies of St. Evremond," under the title of the Irish prophet. It is the most graphic sketch ever made of this early magnetiser. Whether his pretensions were more or less absurd than those of some of his successors, who have lately made their appearance among us, would be hard to say.

"When M. de Comminges," says St. Evremond, "was ambassador from his most Christian Majesty to the King of Great Britain, there came to London an Irish prophet, who passed himself off as a great worker of miracles. Some persons of quality having begged M. de Comminges to invite him to his house, that they might be witnesses of some of his miracles, the ambassador promised to satisfy them, as much from his own curiosity as from courtesy to his friends; and gave notice to Greatraks that he would be glad to see him.

"A rumour of the prophet's coming soon spread all over the town, and the hotel of M. de Comminges was crowded by sick persons, who came full of confidence in their speedy cure. The Irishman made them wait a considerable time for him, but came at last, in the midst of their impatience, with a grave and simple countenance, that showed no signs of his being a cheat. Monsieur de Comminges prepared to question him strictly, hoping to discourse with him on the matters that he had read of in Van Helmont and Bodinus; but he was not able to do so, much to his regret, for the crowd became so great, and cripples and others pressed around so impatiently to be the first cured, that the servants were obliged to use threats, and even force, before they could establish order among them, or place them in proper ranks.

"The prophet affirmed that all diseases were caused by evil spirits. Every infirmity was with him a case of diabolical possession. The first that was presented to him was a man suffering from gout and rheumatism, and so severely that the physicians had been unable to cure him. 'Ah,' said the miracle-worker, 'I have seen a good deal of this sort of spirits when I was in Ireland. They are watery spirits, who bring on cold shivering, and excite an overflow of aqueous humours in our poor bodies.' Then addressing the man, he said, 'Evil spirit, who hast quitted thy dwelling in the waters to come and afflict this miserable body, I command thee to quit thy new abode, and to return to thine ancient habitation!' This said, the sick man was ordered to withdraw, and another was brought forward in his place. This new comer said he was tormented by the melancholy vapours. In fact, he looked like a hypochondriac; one of those persons diseased in imagination, and who but too often become so in reality. 'Aerial spirit,' said the Irishman, 'return, I command thee, into the air! -- exercise thy natural vocation of raising tempests, and do not excite any more wind in this sad unlucky body!' This man was immediately turned away to make room for a third patient, who, in the Irishman's opinion, was only tormented by a little bit of a sprite, who could not withstand his command for an instant. He Pretended that he recognized this sprite by some marks which were invisible to the company, to whom he turned with a smile, and said, 'This sort of spirit does not often do much harm, and is always very diverting.' To hear him talk, one would have imagined that he knew all about spirits -- their names, their rank, their numbers, their employment, and all the functions they were destined to; and he boasted of being much better acquainted with the intrigues of demons than he was with the affairs of men. You can hardly imagine what a reputation he gained in a short time. Catholics and Protestants visited him from every part, all believing that power from Heaven was in his hands."

After relating a rather equivocal adventure of a husband and wife, who implored Greatraks to cast out the devil of dissension which had crept in between them, St. Evremond thus sums up the effect he produced on the popular mind: -- "So great was the confidence in him, that the blind fancied they saw the light which they did not see -- the deaf imagined that they heard -- the lame that they walked straight, and the paralytic that they had recovered the use of their limbs. An idea of health made the sick forget for a while their maladies; and imagination, which was not less active in those merely drawn by curiosity than in the sick, gave a false view to the one class, from the desire of seeing, as it operated a false cure on the other from the strong desire of being healed. Such was the power of the Irishman over the mind, and such was the influence of the mind upon the body. Nothing was spoken of in London but his prodigies; and these prodigies were supported by such great authorities, that the bewildered multitude believed them almost without examination, while more enlightened people did not dare to reject them from their own knowledge. The public opinion, timid and enslaved, respected this imperious and, apparently, well-authenticated error. Those who saw through the delusion kept their opinion to themselves, knowing how useless it was to declare their disbelief to a people filled with prejudice and admiration."

About the same time that Valentine Greatraks was thus magnetising the people of London, an Italian enthusiast, named Francisco Bagnone, was performing the same tricks in Italy, and with as great success. He had only to touch weak women with his hands, or sometimes (for the sake of working more effectively upon their fanaticism)with a relic, to make them fall into fits and manifest all the symptoms of magnetism.

Besides these, several learned men, in different parts of Europe, directed their attention to the study of the magnet, believing it might he rendered efficacious in many diseases. Van Helmont, in particular, published a work on the effects of magnetism on the human frame; and Balthazar Gracian, a Spaniard, rendered himself famous for the boldness of his views on the subject. "The magnet," said the latter, "attracts iron; iron is found everywhere; everything, therefore, is under the influence of magnetism. It is only a modification of the general principle, which establishes harmony or foments divisions among men. It is the same agent which gives rise to sympathy, antipathy, and the passions." ["Introduction to the Study of Animal Magnetism," by Baron Dupotet de Sennevoy, p. 315.]

Baptista Porta, who, in the whimsical genealogy of the weapon-salve, given by Parson Foster in his attack upon Dr. a Fluctibus, is mentioned as one of its fathers, had also great faith in the efficacy of the magnet, and operated upon the imagination of his patients in a manner which was then considered so extraordinary that he was accused of being a magician, and prohibited from practising by the Court of Rome. Among others who distinguished themselves by their faith in magnetism, Sebastian Wirdig and William Maxwell claim especial notice. Wirdig was professor of medicine at the University of Rostock in Mecklenburgh, and wrote a treatise called "The New Medicine of the Spirits," which he presented to the Royal Society of London. An edition of this work was printed in 1673, in which the author maintained that a magnetic influence took place, not only between the celestial and terrestrial bodies, but between all living things. The whole world, he said, was under the influence of magnetism: life was preserved by magnetism; death was the consequence of magnetism!

Maxwell, the other enthusiast, was an admiring disciple of Paracelsus, and boasted that he had irradiated the obscurity in which too many of the wonder-working recipes of that great philosopher were enveloped. His works were printed at Frankfort, in 1679. It would seem, from the following passage, that he was aware of the great influence of imagination, as well in the production as in the cure of diseases. "If you wish to work prodigies," says he, "abstract from the materiality of beings -- increase the sum of spirituality in bodies -- rouse the spirit from its slumbers. Unless you do one or other of these things -- unless you can bind the idea, you can never perform anything good or great." Here, in fact, lies the whole secret of magnetism, and all delusions of a similar kind: increase the spirituality -- rouse the spirit from its slumbers, or in other words, work upon the imagination -- induce belief and blind confidence, and you may do anything. This passage, which is quoted with approbation by M. Dupotet in a recent work ["Introduction to the Study of Animal Magnetism," p. 318.] as strongly corroborative of the theory now advanced by the animal-magnetists, is just the reverse. If they believe they can work all their wonders by the means so dimly shadowed forth by Maxwell, what becomes of the universal fluid pervading all nature, and which they pretend to pour into weak and diseased bodies from the tips of their fingers?

Early in the eighteenth century, the attention of Europe was directed to a very remarkable instance of fanaticism, which has been claimed by the animal magnetists, as a proof of their science. The convulsionaries of St. Medard, as they were called, assembled in great numbers round the tomb of their favourite saint, the Jansenist priest Paris, and taught one another how to fall into convulsions. They believed that St. Paris would cure all their infirmities; and the number of hysterical women and weak-minded persons of all descriptions that flocked to the tomb from far and near was so great, as daily to block up all the avenues leading to the spot. Working themselves up to a pitch of excitement, they went off one after the other into fits, while some of them, still in apparent possession of all their faculties, voluntarily exposed themselves to sufferings, which on ordinary occasions would have been sufficient to deprive them of life. The scenes that occurred were a scandal to civilization and to religion -- a strange mixture of obscenity, absurdity, and superstition. While some were praying on bended knees at the shrine of St. Paris, others were shrieking and making the most hideous noises. The women especially exerted themselves. On one side of the chapel there might be seen a score of them, all in convulsions, while at another as many more, excited to a sort of frenzy, yielded themselves up to gross indecencies. Some of them took an insane delight in being beaten and trampled upon. One in particular, according to Montegre, whose account we quote [Dictionnaire des Sciences Medicales -- Article "Convulsionnaires," par Montegre.] was so enraptured with this ill usage, that nothing but the hardest blows would satisfy her. While a fellow of herculean strength was beating her with all his might with a heavy bar of iron, she kept continually urging him to renewed exertion. The harder he struck the better she liked it, exclaiming all the while, "Well done, brother; well done; oh, how pleasant it is! what good you are doing me! courage, my brother, courage; strike harder; strike harder still!" Another of these fanatics had, if possible, a still greater love for a beating. Carre de Montgeron, who relates the circumstance, was unable to satisfy her with sixty blows of a large sledge hammer. He afterwards used the same weapon, with the same degree of strength, for the sake of experiment, and succeeded in battering a hole in a stone wall at the twenty-fifth stroke. Another woman, named Sonnet, laid herself down on a red-hot brazier without flinching, and acquired for herself the nickname of the salamander; while others, desirous of a more illustrious martyrdom, attempted to crucify themselves. M. Deleuze, in his critical history of Animal Magnetism, attempts to prove that this fanatical frenzy was produced by magnetism, and that these mad enthusiasts magnetised each other without being aware of it. As well might he insist that the fanaticism which tempts the Hindoo bigot to keep his arms stretched in a horizontal position till the sinews wither, or his fingers closed upon his palms till the nails grow out of the backs of his hands, is also an effect of magnetism!

For a period of sixty or seventy years, magnetism was almost wholly confined to Germany. Men of sense and learning devoted their attention to the properties of the loadstone; and one Father Hell, a jesuit, and professor of astronomy at the University of Vienna, rendered himself famous by his magnetic cures. About the year 1771 or 1772, he invented steel plates of a peculiar form, which he applied to the naked body, as a cure for several diseases. In the year 1774, he communicated his system to Anthony Mesmer. The latter improved upon the ideas of Father Hell, constructed a new theory of his own, and became the founder of ANIMAL MAGNETISM.

It has been the fashion among the enemies of the new delusion to decry Mesmer as an unprincipled adventurer, while his disciples have extolled him to the skies as a regenerator of the human race. In nearly the same words, as the Rosicrucians applied to their founders, he has been called the discoverer of the secret which brings man into more intimate connexion with his Creator; the deliverer of the soul from the debasing trammels of the flesh; the man who enables us to set time at defiance, and conquer the obstructions of space. A careful sifting of his pretensions -- and examination of the evidence brought forward to sustain them, will soon show which opinion is the more correct. That the writer of these pages considers him in the light of a man, who deluding himself, was the means of deluding others, may be inferred from his finding a place in these volumes, and figuring among the Flamels, the Agrippas, the Borris, the Boehmens, and the Cagliostros.

He was born in May 1734, at Mersburg, in Swabia, and studied medicine at the University of Vienna. He took his degrees in 1766, and chose the influence of the planets on the human body as the subject of his inaugural dissertation. Having treated the matter quite in the style of the old astrological physicians, he was exposed to some ridicule both then and afterwards. Even at this early period some faint ideas of his great theory were germinating in his mind. He maintained in his dissertation, "that the sun, moon, and fixed stars mutually affect each other in their orbits; that they cause and direct in our earth a flux and reflux not only in the sea, but in the atmosphere, and affect in a similar manner all organized bodies through the medium of a subtile and mobile fluid, which pervades the universe and associates all things together in mutual intercourse and harmony." This influence, he said, was particularly exercised on the nervous system, and produced two states which he called intension and remission, which seemed to him to account for the different periodical revolutions observable in several maladies. When in after-life he met with Father Hell, he was confirmed by that person's observations in the truth of many of his own ideas. Having caused Hell to make him some magnetic plates, he determined to try experiments with them himself for his further satisfaction.

He tried accordingly, and was astonished at his success. The faith of their wearers operated wonders with the metallic plates. Mesmer made due reports to Father Hell of all he had done, and the latter published them as the results of his own happy invention, and speaking of Mesmer as a physician whom he had employed to work under him. Mesmer took offence at being thus treated, considering himself a far greater personage than Father Hell. He claimed the invention as his own, accused Hell of a breach of confidence, and stigmatized him as a mean person, anxious to turn the discoveries of others to his own account. Hell replied, and a very pretty quarrel was the result, which afforded small talk for months to the literati of Vienna. Hell ultimately gained the victory. Mesmer, nothing daunted, continued to promulgate his views, till he stumbled at last upon the animal theory.

One of his patients was a young lady named Oesterline, who suffered under a convulsive malady. Her attacks were periodical, and attended by a rush of blood to the head, followed by delirium and syncope. These symptoms he soon succeeded in reducing under his system of planetary influence, and imagined he could foretell the periods of accession and remission. Having thus accounted satisfactorily to himself for the origin of the disease, the idea struck him that he could operate a certain cure, if he could ascertain beyond doubt what he had long believed, that there existed between the bodies which compose our globe, an action equally reciprocal and similar to that of the heavenly bodies, by means of which he could imitate artificially the periodical revolutions of the flux and reflux beforementioned. He soon convinced himself that this action did exist. When trying the metallic plates of Father Hell, he thought their efficacy depended on their form; but he found afterwards that he could produce the same effects without using them at all, merely by passing his hands downwards towards the feet of the patient -- even when at a considerable distance.

This completed the theory of Mesmer. He wrote an account of his discovery to all the learned societies of Europe, soliciting their investigation. The Academy of Sciences at Berlin was the only one that answered him, and their answer was anything but favourable to his system or flattering to himself. Still he was not discouraged. He maintained to all who would listen to him that the magnetic matter, or fluid, pervaded all the universe -- that every human body contained it, and could communicate the superabundance of it to another by an exertion of the will. Writing to a friend from Vienna, he said, "I have observed that the magnetic is almost the same thing as the electric fluid, and that it may be propagated in the same manner, by means of intermediate bodies. Steel is not the only substance adapted to this purpose. I have rendered paper, bread, wool, silk, stones, leather, glass, wood, men, and dogs -- in short, everything I touched, magnetic to such a degree that these substances produced the same effects as the loadstone on diseased persons. I have charged jars with magnetic matter in the same way as is done with electricity."

Mesmer did not long find his residence at Vienna as agreeable as he wished. His pretensions were looked upon with contempt or indifference, and the case of Mademoiselle Oesterline brought him less fame than notoriety. He determined to change his sphere of action, and travelled into Swabia and Switzerland. In the latter country he met with the celebrated Father Gassner, who, like Valentine Greatraks, amused himself by casting out devils, and healing the sick by merely laying hands upon them. At his approach puling girls fell into convulsions, and the hypochondriac fancied themselves cured. His house was daily besieged by the lame, the blind, and the hysteric. Mesmer at once acknowledged the efficacy of his cures, and declared that they were the obvious result of his own newly-discovered power of magnetism. A few of the Father's patients were forthwith subjected to the manipulations of Mesmer, and the same symptoms were induced. He then tried his hand upon some paupers in the hospitals of Berne and Zurich, and succeeded, according to his own account, but no other person's, in curing an opththalmia and a gutta serena. With memorials of these achievements he returned to Vienna, in the hope of silencing his enemies, or at least forcing them to respect his newly-acquired reputation, and to examine his system more attentively.

His second appearance in that capital was not more auspicious than the first. He undertook to cure a Mademoiselle Paradis, who was quite blind, and subject to convulsions. He magnetised her several times, and then declared that she was cured; at least, if she was not, it was her fault, and not his. An eminent oculist of that day, named Birth, went to visit her, and declared that she was as blind as ever; while her family said she was as much subject to convulsions as before. Mesmer persisted that she was cured. Like the French philosopher, he would not allow facts to interfere with his theory. [An enthusiastic philosopher, of whose name we are not informed, had constructed a very satisfactory theory on some subject or other, and was not a little proud of it. "But the facts, my dear fellow," said his friend, "the facts do not agree with your theory." -- "Don't they," replied the philosopher, shrugging his shoulders, "then, taut pis pour les faits;" -- so much the worse for the facts.] He declared that there was a conspiracy against him; and that Mademoiselle Paradis, at the instigation of her family, feigned blindness in order to injure his reputation!

The consequences of this pretended cure taught Mesmer that Vienna was not the sphere for him. Paris, the idle, the debauched, the pleasure-hunting, the novelty-loving, was the scene for a philosopher like him, and thither he repaired accordingly. He arrived at Paris in 1778, and began modestly, by making himself and his theory known to the principal physicians. At first, his encouragement was but slight; he found people more inclined to laugh at than to patronise him. But he was a man who had great confidence in himself, and of a perseverance which no difficulties could overcome. He hired a sumptuous apartment, which he opened to all comers who chose to make trial of the new power of nature. M. D'Eslon, a physician of great reputation, became a convert; and from that time, Animal Magnetism, or, as some called it, Mesmerism, became the fashion in Paris. The women were quite enthusiastic about it, and their admiring tattle wafted its fame through every grade of society. Mesmer was the rage; and high and low, rich and poor, credulous and unbelieving, all hastened to convince themselves of the power of this mighty magician, who made such magnificent promises. Mesmer, who knew as well as any man living the influence of the imagination, determined that, on that score, nothing should be wanting to heighten the effect of the magnetic charm. In all Paris, there was not a house so charmingly furnished as Monsieur Mesmer's. Richly-stained glass shed a dim religious light on his spacious saloons, which were almost covered with mirrors. Orange blossoms scented all the air of his corridors; incense of the most expensive kinds burned in antique vases on his chimney-pieces; aeolian harps sighed melodious music from distant chambers; while sometimes a sweet female voice, from above or below, stole softly upon the mysterious silence that was kept in the house, and insisted upon from all visitors. "Was ever anything so delightful?" cried all the Mrs. Wittitterley's of Paris, as they thronged to his house in search of pleasant excitement; "so wonderful!" said the pseudo-philosophers, who would believe anything if it were the fashion; "so amusing!" said the worn-out debauchees, who had drained the cup of sensuality to its dregs, and who longed to see lovely women in convulsions, with the hope that they might gain some new emotions from the sight.

The following was the mode of operation: -- In the centre of the saloon was placed an oval vessel, about four feet in its longest diameter, and one foot deep. In this were laid a number of wine-bottles, filled with magnetised water, well corked-up, and disposed in radii, with their necks outwards. Water was then poured into the vessel so as just to cover the bottles, and filings of iron were thrown in occasionally to heighten the magnetic effect. The vessel was then covered with an iron cover, pierced through with many holes, and was called the baquet. From each hole issued a long moveable rod of iron, which the patients were to apply to such parts of their bodies as were afflicted. Around this baquet the patients were directed to sit, holding each other by the hand, and pressing their knees together as closely as possible to facilitate the passage of the magnetic fluid from one to the other.

Then came in the assistant magnetisers, generally strong, handsome young men, to pour into the patient from their finger-tips fresh streams of the wondrous fluid. They embraced the patients between the knees, rubbed them gently down the spine and the course of the nerves, using gentle pressure upon the breasts of the ladies, and staring them out of countenance to magnetise them by the eye! All this time the most rigorous silence was maintained, with the exception of a few wild notes on the harmonica or the piano-forte, or the melodious voice of a hidden opera-singer swelling softly at long intervals. Gradually the cheeks of the ladies began to glow, their imaginations to become inflamed; and off they went, one after the other, in convulsive fits. Some of them sobbed and tore their hair, others laughed till the tears ran from their eyes, while others shrieked and screamed and yelled till they became insensible altogether.

This was the crisis of the delirium. In the midst of it, the chief actor made his appearance, waving his wand, like Prospero, to work new wonders. Dressed in a long robe of lilac-coloured silk, richly embroidered with gold flowers, bearing in his hand a white magnetic rod; and, with a look of dignity which would have sat well on an eastern caliph, he marched with solemn strides into the room. He awed the still sensible by his eye, and the violence of their symptoms diminished. He stroked the insensible with his hands upon the eyebrows and down the spine; traced figures upon their breast and abdomen with his long white wand, and they were restored to consciousness. They became calm, acknowledged his power, and said they felt streams of cold or burning vapour passing through their frames, according as he waved his wand or his fingers before them.

"It is impossible," says M. Dupotet, "to conceive the sensation which Mesmer's experiments created in Paris. No theological controversy, in the earlier ages of the Catholic Church, was ever conducted with greater bitterness." His adversaries denied the discovery; some calling him a quack, others a fool, and others, again, like the Abbe Fiard, a man who had sold himself to the devil! His friends were as extravagant in their praise, as his foes were in their censure. Paris was inundated with pamphlets upon the subject, as many defending as attacking the doctrine. At court, the Queen expressed herself in favour of it, and nothing else was to be heard of in society.

By the advice of M. D'Eslon, Mesmer challenged an examination of his doctrine by the Faculty of Medicine. He proposed to select twenty-four patients, twelve of whom he would treat magnetically, leaving the other twelve to be treated by the faculty according to the old and approved methods. He also stipulated, that to prevent disputes, the government should nominate certain persons who were not physicians, to be present at the experiments; and that the object of the inquiry should be, not how these effects were produced, but whether they were really efficacious in the cure of any disease. The faculty objected to limit the inquiry in this manner, and the proposition fell to the ground.

Mesmer now wrote to Marie Antoinette, with the view of securing her influence in obtaining for him the protection of government. He wished to have a chateau and its lands given to him, with a handsome yearly income, that he might be enabled to continue his experiments at leisure, untroubled by the persecution of his enemies. He hinted the duty of governments to support men of science, and expressed his fear, that if he met no more encouragement, he should be compelled to carry his great discovery to some other land more willing to appreciate him. "In the eyes of your Majesty," said he, "four or five hundred thousand francs, applied to a good purpose, are of no account. The welfare and happiness of your people are everything. My discovery ought to be received and rewarded with a munificence worthy of the monarch to whom I shall attach myself." The government at last offered him a pension of twenty thousand francs, and the cross of the order of St. Michael, if he had made any discovery in medicine, and would communicate it to physicians nominated by the King. The latter part of the proposition was not agreeable to Mesmer. He feared the unfavourable report of the King's physicians; and, breaking off the negotiation, spoke of his disregard of money, and his wish to have his discovery at once recognised by the government. He then retired to Spa, in a fit of disgust, upon pretence of drinking the waters for the benefit of his health.

After he had left Paris, the Faculty of Medicine called upon M. D'Eslon, for the third and last time, to renounce the doctrine of animal magnetism, or be expelled from their body. M. D'Eslon, so far from doing this, declared that he had discovered new secrets, and solicited further examination. A royal commission of the Faculty of Medicine was, in consequence, appointed on the 12th of March 1784, seconded by another commission of the Academie des Sciences, to investigate the phenomena and report upon them. The first commission was composed of the principal physicians of Paris; while, among the eminent men comprised in the latter, were Benjamin Franklin, Lavoisier, and Bailly, the historian of astronomy. Mesmer was formally invited to appear before this body, but absented himself from day to day, upon one pretence or another. M. D'Eslon was more honest, because he thoroughly believed in the phenomena, which it is to be questioned if Mesmer ever did, and regularly attended the sittings and performed experiments.

Bailly has thus described the scenes of which he was a witness in the course of this investigation. "The sick persons, arranged in great numbers and in several rows around the baquet, receive the magnetism by all these means: by the iron rods which convey it to them from the baquet -- by the cords wound round their bodies -- by the connection of the thumb, which conveys to them the magnetism of their neighbours -- and by the sounds of a pianoforte, or of an agreeable voice, diffusing the magnetism in the air. The patients were also directly magnetised by means of the finger and wand of the magnetiser moved slowly before their faces, above or behind their heads, and on the diseased parts, always observing the direction of the holes. The magnetiser acts by fixing his eyes on them. But above all, they are magnetised by the application of his hands and the pressure of his fingers on the hypochondres and on the regions of the abdomen; an application often continued for a long time-sometimes for several hours.

"Meanwhile the patients in their different conditions present a very varied picture. Some are calm, tranquil, and experience no effect. Others cough, spit, feel slight pains, local or general heat, and have sweatings. Others again are agitated and tormented with convulsions. These convulsions are remarkable in regard to the number affected with them, to their duration and force. As soon as one begins to be convulsed, several others are affected. The commissioners have observed some of these convulsions last more than three hours. They are accompanied with expectorations of a muddy viscous water, brought away by violent efforts. Sometimes streaks of blood have been observed in this fluid. These convulsions are characterized by the precipitous, involuntary motion of all the limbs, and of the whole body: by the construction of the throat -- by the leaping motions of the hypochondria and the epigastrium -- by the dimness and wandering of the eyes -- by piercing shrieks, tears, sobbing, and immoderate laughter. They are preceded or followed by a state of languor or reverie, a kind of depression, and sometimes drowsiness. The smallest sudden noise occasions a shuddering; and it was remarked, that the change of measure in the airs played on the piano-forte had a great influence on the patients. A quicker motion, a livelier melody, agitated them more, and renewed the vivacity of their convulsions.

"Nothing is more astonishing than the spectacle of these convulsions. One who has not seen them can form no idea of them. The spectator is as much astonished at the profound repose of one portion of the patients as at the agitation of the rest - at the various accidents which are repeated, and at the sympathies which are exhibited. Some of the patients may be seen devoting their attention exclusively to one another, rushing towards each other with open arms, smiling, soothing, and manifesting every symptom of attachment and affection. All are under the power of the magnetiser; it matters not in what state of drowsiness they may be, the sound of his voice -- a look, a motion of his hand -- brings them out of it. Among the patients in convulsions there are always observed a great many women, and very few men." [Rapport des Commissaires, redige par M. Bailly. -- Paris, 1784.]

These experiments lasted for about five months. They had hardly commenced, before Mesmer, alarmed at the loss both of fame and profit, determined to return to Paris. Some patients of rank and fortune, enthusiastic believers in his doctrine, had followed him to Spa. One of them named Bergasse, proposed to open a subscription for him, of one hundred shares, at one hundred louis each, on condition that he would disclose his secret to the subscribers, who were to be permitted to make whatever use they pleased of it. Mesmer readily embraced the proposal; and such was the infatuation, that the subscription was not only filled in a few days, but exceeded by no less a sum than one hundred and forty thousand francs.

With this fortune he returned to Paris, and recommenced his experiments, while the royal commission continued theirs. His admiring pupils, who had paid him so handsomely for his instructions, spread the delusion over the country, and established in all the principal towns of France, "Societies of Harmony," for trying experiments and curing all diseases by means of magnetism. Some of these societies were a scandal to morality, being joined by profligate men of depraved appetites, who took a disgusting delight in witnessing young girls in convulsions. Many of the pretended magnetisers were notorious libertines, who took that opportunity of gratifying their passions. An illegal increase of the number of French citizens was anything but a rare consequence in Strasburg, Nantes, Bourdeaux, Lyons, and other towns, where these societies were established.

At last the Commissioners published their report, which was drawn up by the illustrious and unfortunate Bailly. For clearness of reasoning and strict impartiality it has never been surpassed. After detailing the various experiments made, and their results, they came to the conclusion that the only proof advanced in support of Animal Magnetism was the effects it produced on the human body -- that those effects could be produced without passes or other magnetic manipulations - that all these manipulations, and passes, and ceremonies never produce any effect at all if employed without the patient's knowledge; and that therefore imagination did, and animal magnetism did not, account for the phenomena.

This report was the ruin of Mesmer's reputation in France. He quitted Paris shortly after, with the three hundred and forty thousand francs which had been subscribed by his admirers, and retired to his own country, where he died in 1815, at the advanced age of eighty-one. But the seeds he had sown fructified of themselves, nourished and brought to maturity by the kindly warmth of popular credulity. Imitators sprang up in France, Germany, and England, more extravagant than their master, and claiming powers for the new science which its founder had never dreamt of. Among others, Cagliostro made good use of the delusion in extending his claims to be considered a master of the occult sciences. But he made no discoveries worthy to be compared to those of the Marquis de Puysegur and the Chevalier Barbarin, honest men, who began by deceiving themselves before they deceived others.

The Marquis de Puysegur, the owner of a considerable estate at Busancy, was one of those who had entered into the subscription for Mesmer. After that individual had quitted France, he retired to Busancy with his brother to try Animal Magnetism upon his tenants, and cure the country people of all manner of diseases. He was a man of great simplicity and much benevolence, and not only magnetised but fed the sick that flocked around him. In all the neighbourhood, and indeed within a circumference of twenty miles, he was looked upon as endowed with a power almost Divine. His great discovery, as he called it, was made by chance. One day he had magnetised his gardener; and observing him to fall into a deep sleep, it occurred to him that he would address a question to him, as he would have done to a natural somnambulist. He did so, and the man replied with much clearness and precision. M. de Puysegur was agreeably surprised: he continued his experiments, and found that, in this state of magnetic somnambulism, the soul of the sleeper was enlarged, and brought into more intimate communion with all nature, and more especially with him, M. de Puysegur. He found that all further manipulations were unnecessary; that, without speaking or making any sign, he could convey his will to the patient; that he could, in fact, converse with him, soul to soul, without the employment of any physical operation whatever!

Simultaneously with this marvellous discovery he made another, which reflects equal credit upon his understanding. Like Valentine Greatraks, he found it hard work to magnetise all that came - that he had not even time to take the repose and relaxation which were necessary for his health. In this emergency he hit upon a clever expedient. He had heard Mesmer say that he could magnetise bits of wood -- why should he not be able to magnetise a whole tree? It was no sooner thought than done. There was a large elm on the village green at Busancy, under which the peasant girls used to dance on festive occasions, and the old men to sit, drinking their vin du pays on the fine summer evenings. M. de Puysegur proceeded to this tree and magnetised it, by first touching it with his hands and then retiring a few steps from it; all the while directing streams of the magnetic fluid from the branches toward the trunk, and from the trunk toward the root. This done, he caused circular seats to be erected round it, and cords suspended from it in all directions. When the patients had seated themselves, they twisted the cords round the diseased parts of their bodies, and held one another firmly by their thumbs to form a direct channel of communication for the passage of the fluid.

M. de Puysegur had now two hobbies - the man with the enlarged soul, and the magnetic elm. The infatuation of himself and his patients cannot be better expressed than in his own words. Writing to his brother, on the 17th of May 1784, he says, "If you do not come, my dear friend, you will not see my extraordinary man, for his health is now almost quite restored. I continue to make use of the happy power for which I am indebted to M. Mesmer. Every day I bless his name; for I am very useful, and produce many salutary effects on all the sick poor in the neighbourhood. They flock around my tree; there were more than one hundred and thirty of them this morning. It is the best baquet possible; not a leaf of it but communicates health! all feel, more or less, the good effects of it. You will be delighted to see the charming picture of humanity which this presents. I have only one regret - it is, that I cannot touch all who come. But my magnetised man -- my intelligence - sets me at ease. He teaches me what conduct I should adopt. According to him, it is not at all necessary that I should touch every one; a look, a gesture, even a wish, is sufficient. And it is one of the most ignorant peasants of the country that teaches me this! When he is in a crisis, I know of nothing more profound, more prudent, more clearsighted (clairvoyant) than he is."

In another letter, describing his first experiment with the magnetic tree, he says, "Yester evening I brought my first patient to it. As soon as I had put the cord round him he gazed at the tree; and, with an air of astonishment which I cannot describe, exclaimed, 'What is it that I see there?' His head then sunk down, and he fell into a perfect fit of somnambulism. At the end of an hour, I took him home to his house again, when I restored him to his senses. Several men and women came to tell him what he had been doing. He maintained it was not true; that, weak as he was, and scarcely able to walk, it would have been scarcely possible for him to have gone down stairs and walked to the tree. To-day I have repeated the experiment on him, and with the same success. I own to you that my head turns round with pleasure to think of the good I do. Madame de Puysegur, the friends she has with her, my servants, and, in fact, all who are near me, feel an amazement, mingled with admiration, which cannot be described; but they do not experience the half of my sensations. Without my tree, which gives me rest, and which will give me still more, I should be in a state of agitation, inconsistent, I believe, with my health. I exist too much, if I may be allowed to use the expression."

In another letter, he descants still more poetically upon his gardener with the enlarged soul. He says, "It is from this simple man, this tall and stout rustic, twenty-three years of age, enfeebled by disease, or rather by sorrow, and therefore the more predisposed to be affected by any great natural agent, -- it is from this man, I repeat, that I derive instruction and knowledge. When in the magnetic state, he is no longer a peasant who can hardly utter a single sentence; he is a being, to describe whom I cannot find a name. I need not speak; I have only to think before him, when he instantly understands and answers me. Should anybody come into the room, he sees him, if I desire it (but not else), and addresses him, and says what I wish him to say; not indeed exactly as I dictate to him, but as truth requires. When he wants to add more than I deem it prudent strangers should hear, I stop the flow of his ideas, and of his conversation in the middle of a word, and give it quite a different turn!"

Among other persons attracted to Busancy by the report of these extraordinary occurrences was M. Cloquet, the Receiver of Finance. His appetite for the marvellous being somewhat insatiable, he readily believed all that was told him by M. de Puysegur. He also has left a record of what he saw, and what he credited, which throws a still clearer light upon the progress of the delusion. ["Introduction to the Study of Animal Magnetism," by Baron Dupotet, p. 73.] He says that the patients he saw in the magnetic state had an appearance of deep sleep, during which all the physical faculties were suspended, to the advantage of the intellectual faculties. The eyes of the patients were closed; the sense of hearing was abolished, and they awoke only at the voice of their magnetiser. "If any one touched a patient during a crisis, or even the chair on which he was seated," says M. Cloquet, "it would cause him much pain and suffering, and throw him into convulsions. During the crisis, they possess an extraordinary and supernatural power, by which, on touching a patient presented to them, they can feel what part of his body is diseased, even by merely passing their hand over the clothes." Another singularity was, that these sleepers who could thus discover diseases -- see into the interior of other men's stomachs, and point out remedies, remembered absolutely nothing after the magnetiser thought proper to disenchant them. The time that elapsed between their entering the crisis and their coming out of it was obliterated. Not only had the magnetiser the power of making himself heard by the somnambulists, but he could make them follow him by merely pointing his finger at them from a distance, though they had their eyes the whole time completely closed.

Such was Animal Magnetism under the auspices of the Marquis de Puysegur. While he was hibiting these fooleries around his elm-tree, a magnetiser of another class appeared in Lyons, in the person of the Chevalier de Barbarin. This person thought the effort of the will, without any of the paraphernalia of wands or baquets, was sufficient to throw patients into the magnetic sleep. He tried it and succeeded. By sitting at the bedside of his patients, and praying that they might be magnetised, they went off into a state very similar to that of the persons who fell under the notice of M. de Puysegur. In the course of time, a very considerable number of magnetisers, acknowledging Barbarin for their model, and called after him Barbarinists, appeared in different parts, and were believed to have effected some remarkable cures. In Sweden and Germany, this sect of fanatics increased rapidly, and were called spiritualists, to distinguish them from the followers of M. de Puysegur, who were called experimentalists. They maintained that all the effects of Animal Magnetism, which Mesmer believed to be producible by a magnetic fluid dispersed through nature, were produced by the mere effort of one human soul acting upon another; that when a connexion had once been established between a magnetiser and his patient, the former could communicate his influence to the latter from any distance, even hundreds of miles, by the will! One of them thus described the blessed state of a magnetic patient: -- "In such a man animal instinct ascends to the highest degree admissible in this world. The clairvoyant is then a pure animal, without any admixture of matter. His observations are those of a spirit. He is similar to God. His eye penetrates all the secrets of nature. When his attention is fixed on any of the objects of this world -- on his disease, his death, his well-beloved, his friends, his relations, his enemies, -- in spirit he sees them acting; he penetrates into the causes and the consequences of their actions; he becomes a physician, a prophet, a divine!" [See "Foreign Review, Continental Miscellany," vol. v. 113.]

Let us now see what progress these mysteries made in England. In the year 1788, Dr. Mainauduc, who had been a pupil, first of Mesmer, and afterwards of D'Eslon, arrived in Bristol, and gave public lectures upon magnetism. His success was quite extraordinary. People of rank and fortune hastened from London to Bristol to be magnetised, or to place themselves under his tuition. Dr. George Winter, in his History of Animal Magnetism, gives the following list of them: -- "They amounted to one hundred and twenty-seven, among whom there were one duke, one duchess, one marchioness, two countesses, one earl, one baron, three baronesses, one bishop, five right honourable gentlemen and ladies, two baronets, seven members of parliament, one clergyman, two physicians, seven surgeons, besides ninety-two gentlemen and ladies of respectability." He afterwards established himself in London, where he performed with equal success.

He began by publishing proposals to the ladies for the formation of a Hygeian Society. In this paper he vaunted highly the curative effects of Animal Magnetism, and took great credit to himself for being the first person to introduce it into England, and thus concluded:-- "As this method of cure is not confined to sex, or college education, and the fair sex being in general the most sympathising part of the creation, and most immediately concerned in the health and care of its offspring, I think myself bound in gratitude to you, ladies, for the partiality you have shown me in midwifery, to contribute, as far as lies in my power, to render you additionally useful and valuable to the community. With this view, I propose forming my Hygeian Society, to be incorporated with that of Paris. As soon as twenty ladies have given in their names, the day shall be appointed for the first meeting at my house, when they are to pay fifteen guineas, which will include the whole expense."

Hannah More, in a letter addressed to Horace Walpole, in September 1788, speaks of the "demoniacal mummeries" of Dr. Mainauduc, and says he was in a fair way of gaining a hundred thousand pounds by them, as Mesmer had done by his exhibitions in Paris.

So much curiosity was excited by the subject that, about the same time, a man, named Holloway, gave a course of lectures on Animal Magnetism in London, at the rate of five guineas for each pupil, and realised a considerable fortune. Loutherbourg, the painter, and his wife followed the same profitable trade; and such was the infatuation of the people to be witnesses of their strange manipulations, that, at times, upwards of three thousand persons crowded around their house at Hammersmith, unable to gain admission. The tickets sold at prices varying from one to three guineas. Loutherbourg performed his cures by the touch, after the manner of Valentine Greatraks, and finally pretended to a Divine mission. An account of his miracles, as they were called, was published in 1789, entitled "A List of New Cures performed by Mr. and Mrs. de Loutherbourg of Hammersmith Terrace, without Medicine; by a Lover of the Lamb of God. Dedicated to his Grace the Archbishop of Canterbury."

This "Lover of the Lamb of God" was a half-crazy old woman, named Mary Pratt, who conceived for Mr. and Mrs. de Loutherbourg a veneration which almost prompted her to worship them. She chose for the motto of her pamphlet a verse in the thirteenth chapter of the Acts of the Apostles: "Behold, ye despisers, and wonder and perish! for I will work a work in your days which ye shall not believe though a man declare it unto you." Attempting to give a religious character to the cures of the painter, she thought a woman was the proper person to make them known, since the apostle had declared that a man should not be able to conquer the incredulity of the people. She stated that, from Christmas 1788 to July 1789, De Loutherbourg and his wife had cured two thousand people, "having been made proper recipients to receive Divine manuductions; which heavenly and Divine influx, coming from the radix God, his Divine Majesty had most graciously bestowed upon them to diffuse healing to all, be they deaf, dumb, blind, lame, or halt."

In her dedication to the Archbishop of Canterbury, she implored him to compose a new form of prayer to be used in all churches and chapels, that nothing might impede this inestimable gift from having its due course. She further entreated all the magistrates and men of authority in the land to wait on Mr. and Mrs. de Loutherbourg, to consult with them on the immediate erection of a large hospital, with a pool of Bethesda attached to it. All the magnetisers were scandalised at the preposterous jabber of this old woman, and De Loutherbourg appears to have left London to avoid her; continuing, however, in conjunction with his wife, the fantastic tricks which had turned the brain of this poor fanatic, and deluded many others who pretended to more sense than she had.

From this period until 1798, magnetism excited little or no attention in England. An attempt to revive the doctrine was made in that year, but it was in the shape of mineral rather than of animal magnetism. One Benjamin Douglas Perkins, an American, practising as a surgeon in Leicestersquare, invented and took out a patent for the celebrated "Metallic Tractors." He pretended that these tractors, which were two small pieces of metal strongly magnetised, something resembling the steel plates which were first brought into notice by Father Hell, would cure gout, rheumatism, palsy, and in fact, almost every disease the human frame was subject to, if applied externally to the afflicted part, and moved about gently, touching the surface only. The most wonderful stories soon obtained general circulation, and the press groaned with pamphlets, all vaunting the curative effects of the tractors, which were sold at five guineas the pair. Perkins gained money rapidly. Gouty subjects forgot their pains in the presence of this new remedy; the rheumatism fled at its approach; and toothache, which is often cured by the mere sight of a dentist, vanished before Perkins and his marvellous steel plates. The benevolent Quakers, of whose body he was a member, warmly patronised the invention. Desirous that the poor, who could not afford to pay Mr. Perkins five guineas, or even five shillings, for his tractors, should also share in the benefits of that sublime discovery, they subscribed a large sum, and built an hospital, called the "Perkinean Institution," in which all comers might be magnetised free of cost. In the course of a few months they were in very general use, and their lucky inventor in possession of five thousand pounds.

Dr. Haygarth, an eminent physician at Bath, recollecting the influence of imagination in the cure of disease, hit upon an expedient to try the real value of the tractors. Perkins's cures were too well established to be doubted; and Dr. Haygarth, without gainsaying them, quietly, but in the face of numerous witnesses, exposed the delusion under which people laboured with respect to the curative medium. He suggested to Dr. Falconer that they should make wooden tractors, paint them to resemble the steel ones, and see if the very same effects would not be produced. Five patients were chosen from the hospital in Bath, upon whom to operate. Four of them suffered severely from chronic rheumatism in the ankle, knee, wrist, and hip; and the fifth had been afflicted for several months with the gout. On the day appointed for the experiments, Dr. Haygarth and his friends assembled at the hospital, and with much solemnity brought forth the fictitious tractors. Four out of the five patients said their pains were immediately relieved; and three of them said they were not only relieved, but very much benefited. One felt his knee warmer, and said he could walk across the room. He tried and succeeded, although on the previous day he had not been able to stir. The gouty man felt his pains diminish rapidly, and was quite easy for nine hours, until he went to bed, when the twitching began again. On the following day the real tractors were applied to all the patients, when they described their symptoms in nearly the same terms.

To make still more sure, the experiment was tried in the Bristol Infirmary, a few weeks afterwards, on a man who had a rheumatic affection in the shoulder, so severe as to incapacitate him from lifting his hand from his knee. The fictitious tractors were brought and applied to the afflicted part, one of the physicians, to add solemnity to the scene, drawing a stop-watch from his pocket to calculate the time exactly, while another, with a pen in his hand, sat down to write the change of symptoms from minute to minute as they occurred. In less than four minutes the man felt so much relieved, that he lifted his hand several inches without any pain in the shoulder!

An account of these matters was published by Dr. Haygarth, in a small volume entitled, "Of the Imagination, as a Cause and Cure of Disorders, exemplified by fictitious Tractors." The exposure was a coup de grace to the system of Mr. Perkins. His friends and patrons, still unwilling to confess that they had been deceived, tried the tractors upon sheep, cows, and horses, alleging that the animals received benefit from the metallic plates, but none at all from the wooden ones. But they found nobody to believe them; the Perkinean Institution fell into neglect; and Perkins made his exit from England, carrying with him about ten thousand pounds, to soothe his declining years in the good city of Pennsylvania.

Thus was magnetism laughed out of England for a time. In France, the revolution left men no leisure for such puerilities. The "Societes de l'Harmonie," of Strasburg, and other great towns, lingered for a while, till sterner matters occupying men's attention, they were one after the other abandoned, both by pupils and professors. The system thus driven from the first two nations of Europe, took refuge among the dreamy philosophers of Germany. There the wonders of the magnetic sleep grew more and more wonderful every day; the patients acquired the gift of prophecy - their vision extended over all the surface of the globe -- they could hear and see with their toes and fingers, and read unknown languages, and understand them too, by merely having the book placed on their bellies. Ignorant clodpoles, when once entranced by the grand Mesmeric fluid, could spout philosophy diviner than Plato ever wrote, descant upon the mysteries of the mind with more eloquence and truth than the profoundest metaphysicians the world ever saw, and solve knotty points of divinity with as much ease as waking men could undo their shoe-buckles!

During the first twelve years of the present century, little was heard of Animal Magnetism in any country of Europe. Even the Germans forgot their airy fancies; recalled to the knowledge of this every-day world by the roar of Napoleon's cannon and the fall or the establishment of kingdoms. During this period, a cloud of obscurity hung over the science, which was not dispersed until M. Deleuze published, in 1813, his "Histoire Critique du Magnetisme Animal." This work gave a new impulse to the half-forgotten delusion; newspapers, pamphlets, and books again waged war upon each other on the question of its truth or falsehood; and many eminent men in the profession of medicine recommended inquiry, with an earnest design to discover the truth.

The assertions made in the celebrated treatise of Deleuze are thus summed up: [See the very calm, clear, and dispassionate article upon the subject in the fifth volume (1830) of "The Foreign Review," page 96, et seq.] -- "There is a fluid continually escaping from the human body," and "forming an atmosphere around us," which, as "it has no determined current," produces no sensible effects on surrounding individuals. It is, however, "capable of being directed by the will;" and, when so directed, "is sent forth in currents," with a force corresponding to the energy we possess. Its motion is "similar to that of the rays from burning bodies;" "it possesses different qualities in different individuals." It is capable of a high degree of concentration, "and exists also in trees." The will of the magnetiser, "guided by a motion of the hand, several times repeated in the same direction," can fill a tree with this fluid. Most persons, when this fluid is poured into them, from the body and by the will of the magnetiser, "feel a sensation of heat or cold" when he passes his hand before them, without even touching them. Some persons, when sufficiently charged with this fluid, fall into a state of somnambulism, or magnetic ecstasy; and, when in this state, "they see the fluid encircling the magnetiser like a halo of light, and issuing in luminous streams from his mouth and nostrils, his head, and hands; possessing a very agreeable smell, and communicating a particular taste to food and water."

One would think that these absurdities were quite enough to be insisted upon by any physician who wished to be considered sane, but they only form a small portion of the wondrous things related by M. Deleuze. He further said, "When magnetism produces somnambulism, the person who is in this state acquires a prodigious extension of all his faculties. Several of his external organs, especially those of sight and hearing, become inactive; but the sensations which depend upon them take place internally. Seeing and hearing are carried on by the magnetic fluid, which transmits the impressions immediately, and without the intervention of any nerves or organs directly to the brain. Thus the somnambulist, though his eyes and ears are closed, not only sees and hears, but sees and hears much better than he does when awake. In all things he feels the will of the magnetiser, although that will be not expressed. He sees into the interior of his own body, and the most secret organization of the bodies of all those who may be put en rapport, or in magnetic connexion, with him. Most commonly, he only sees those parts which are diseased and disordered, and intuitively prescribes a remedy for them. He has prophetic visions and sensations, which are generally true, but sometimes erroneous. He expresses himself with astonishing eloquence and facility. He is not free from vanity. He becomes a more perfect being of his own accord for a certain time, if guided wisely by the magnetiser, but wanders if he is ill-directed."

According to M. Deleuze, any person could become a magnetiser and produce these effects, by conforming to the following conditions, and acting upon the following rules:--

Forget for a while all your knowledge of physics and metaphysics.

Remove from your mind all objections that may occur.

Imagine that it is in your power to take the malady in hand, and throw it on one side.

Never reason for six weeks after you have commenced the study.

Have an active desire to do good; a firm belief in the power of magnetism, and an entire confidence in employing it. In short, repel all doubts; desire success, and act with simplicity and attention.

That is to say, "be very credulous; be very persevering; reject all past experience, and do not listen to reason," and you are a magnetiser after M. Deleuze's own heart.

Having brought yourself into this edifying state of fanaticism, "remove from the patient all persons who might be troublesome to you: keep with you only the necessary witnesses -- a single person, if need be; desire them not to occupy themselves in any way with the processes you employ and the effects which result from them, but to join with you in the desire of doing good to your patient. Arrange yourself so as neither to be too hot nor too cold, and in such a manner that nothing may obstruct the freedom of your motions; and take precautions to prevent interruption during the sitting. Make your patient then sit as commodiously as possible, and place yourself opposite to him, on a seat a little more elevated, in such a manner that his knees may be betwixt yours, and your feet at the side of his. First, request him to resign himself; to think of nothing; not to perplex himself by examining the effects which may be produced; to banish all fear; to surrender himself to hope, and not to be disturbed or discouraged if the action of magnetism should cause in him momentary pains. After having collected yourself, take his thumbs between your fingers in such a way that the internal part of your thumbs may be in contact with the internal part of his, and then fix your eyes upon him! You must remain from two to five minutes in this situation, or until you feel an equal heat between your thumbs and his. This done, you will withdraw your hands, removing them to the right and left; and at the same time turning them till their internal surface be outwards, and you will raise them to the height of the head. You will now place them upon the two shoulders, and let them remain there about a minute; afterwards drawing them gently along the arms to the extremities of the fingers, touching very slightly as you go. You will renew this pass five or six times, always turning your hands, and removing them a little from the body before you lift them. You will then place them above the head; and, after holding them there for an instant, lower them, passing them before the face, at the distance of one or two inches, down to the pit of the stomach. There you will stop them two minutes also, putting your thumbs upon the pit of the stomach and the rest of your fingers below the ribs. You will then descend slowly along the body to the knees, or rather, if you can do so without deranging yourself, to the extremity of the feet. You will repeat the same processes several times during the remainder of the sitting. You will also occasionally approach your patient, so as to place your hands behind his shoulders, in order to descend slowly along the spine of the back and the thighs, down to the knees or the feet. After the first passes, you may dispense with putting your hands upon the head, and may make the subsequent passes upon the arms, beginning at the shoulders, and upon the body, beginning at the stomach."

Such was the process of magnetising recommended by Deleuze. That delicate, fanciful, and nervous women, when subjected to it, should have worked themselves into convulsions will be readily believed by the sturdiest opponent of Animal Magnetism. To sit in a constrained posture -- be stared out of countenance by a fellow who enclosed her knees between his, while he made passes upon different parts of her body, was quite enough to throw any weak woman into a fit, especially if she were predisposed to hysteria, and believed in the efficacy of the treatment. It is just as evident that those of stronger minds and healthier bodies should be sent to sleep by the process. That these effects have been produced by these means there are thousands of instances to show. But are they testimony in favour of Animal Magnetism? - do they prove the existence of the magnetic fluid? Every unprejudiced person must answer in the negative. It needs neither magnetism, nor ghost from the grave, to tell us that silence, monotony, and long recumbency in one position must produce sleep, or that excitement, imitation, and a strong imagination, acting upon a weak body, will bring on convulsions. It will be seen hereafter that magnetism produces no effects but these two; that the gift of prophecy - supernatural eloquence - the transfer of the senses, and the power of seeing through opaque substances, are pure fictions, that cannot be substantiated by anything like proof.

M. Deleuze's book produced quite a sensation in France; the study was resumed with redoubled vigour. In the following year, a journal was established devoted exclusively to the science, under the title of "Annales du Magnetisme Animal;" and shortly afterwards appeared the "Bibliotheque du Magnetisme Animal," and many others. About the same time, the Abbe Faria, "the man of wonders," began to magnetise; and the belief being that he had more of the Mesmeric fluid about him, and a stronger will, than most men, he was very successful in his treatment. His experiments afford a convincing proof that imagination can operate all, and the supposed fluid none, of the resuits so confidently claimed as evidence of the new science. He placed his patients in an arm-chair; told them to shut their eyes; and then, in a loud commanding voice, pronounced the single word, "Sleep!" He used no manipulations whatever -- had no baquet, or conductor of the fluid; but he nevertheless succeeded in causing sleep in hundreds of patients. He boasted of having in his time produced five thousand somnambulists by this method. It was often necessary to repeat the command three or four times; and if the patient still remained awake, the Abbe got out of the difficulty by dismissing him from the chair, and declaring that he was incapable of being acted on. And here it should be remarked that the magnetisers do not lay claim to a universal efficacy for their fluid; the strong and the healthy cannot be magnetised; the incredulous cannot be magnetised; those who reason upon it cannot be magnetised; those who firmly believe in it can be magnetised; the weak in body can be magnetised, and the weak in mind can be magnetised. And lest, from some cause or other, individuals of the latter classes should resist the magnetic charm, the apostles of the science declare that there are times when even they cannot be acted upon; the presence of one scorner or unbeliever may weaken the potency of the fluid and destroy its efficacy. In M. Deleuze's instructions to a magnetiser, he expressly says, "Never magnetise before inquisitive persons!" ["Histoire Critique du Magnetisme Animal," p. 60.] Yet the followers of this delusion claim for it the rank of a science!

The numerous writings that appeared between the years 1813 and 1825 show how much attention was excited in France. With every succeeding year some new discovery was put forth, until at last the magnetisers seemed to be very generally agreed that there were six separate and distinct degrees of magnetisation. They have been classed as follow:-

In the first stage, the skin of the patient becomes slightly reddened; and there is a feeling of heat, comfort, and lightness all over the body; but there is no visible action on the senses.

In the second stage, the eye is gradually abstracted from the dominion of the will (or, in other words, the patient becomes sleepy). The drooping eyelids cannot be raised; the senses of hearing, smelling, feeling, and tasting are more than usually excited. In addition, a variety of nervous sensations are felt, such as spasms of the muscles and prickings of the skin, and involuntary twitchings in various parts of the body.

In the third stage, which is that of magnetic sleep, all the senses are closed to external impressions; and sometimes fainting, and cataleptic or apoplectic attacks may occur.

In the fourth stage, the patient is asleep to all the world; but he is awake within his own body, and consciousness returns. While in this state, all his senses are transferred to the skin. He is in the perfect crisis, or magnetic somnambulism; a being of soul and mind -- seeing without eyes -- hearing without ears, and deadened in body to all sense of feeling.

In the fifth stage, which is that of lucid vision, the patient can see his own internal organisation, or that of others placed in magnetic communication with him. He becomes, at the same time, possessed of the instinct of remedies. The magnetic fluid, in this stage, unites him by powerful attraction to others, and establishes between them an impenetration of thought and feeling so intense as to blend their different natures into one.

In the sixth stage, which is at the same time the rarest and the most perfect of all, the lucid vision is not obstructed by opaque matter, or subject to any barriers interposed by time or space. The magnetic fluid, which is universally spread in nature, unites the individual with all nature, and gives him cognizance of coming events by its universal lucidity.

So much was said and written between the years 1820 and 1825, and so many converts were made, that the magnetisers became clamorous for a new investigation. M. de Foissac, a young physician, wrote to the Academie Royale du Medicine a letter, calling for inquiry, in which he complained of the unfairness of the report of Messrs. Bailly and Franklin in 1784, and stating that, since that time, the science had wholly changed by the important discovery of magnetic somnambulism. He informed the Academy that he had under his care a young woman, whose powers of divination when in the somnambulic state were of the most extraordinary character. He invited the members of that body to go into any hospital, and choose persons afflicted with any diseases, acute or chronic, simple or complex, and his somnambulist, on being put en rapport, or in magnetic connexion, with them, would infallibly point out their ailings and name the remedies. She, and other somnambulists, he said, could, by merely laying the hand successively on the head, the chest, and the abdomen of a stranger, immediately discover his maladies, with, the pains and different alterations thereby occasioned. They could indicate, besides, whether the cure were possible, and, if so, whether it were easy or difficult, near or remote, and what means should be employed to attain this result by the surest and readiest way. In this examination they never departed from the sound principles of medicine. "In fact," added M. de Foissac, "I go further, and assert that their inspirations are allied to the genius which animated Hippocrates!"

In the mean time experiments were carried on in various hospitals of Paris. The epileptic patients at the Salpetriere were magnetised by permission of M. Esquirol. At the Bicetre also the same resuits were obtained. M. de Foissac busied himself with the invalids at the Hospice de la Charite, and M. Dupotet was equally successful in producing sleep or convulsions at Val de Grace. Many members of the Chamber of Deputies became converts, and M. Chardel, the Comte de Gestas, M. de Laseases, and others, opened their saloons to those who were desirous of being instructed in animal magnetism. [Dupotet's Introduction to the Study of Animal Magnetism, page 23.] Other physicians united with M. de Foissac in calling for an inquiry; and ultimately the Academy nominated a preliminary committee of five of its members, namely, Messrs Adelon, Burdin, Marc, Pariset, and Husson, to investigate the alleged facts, and to report whether the Academy, without any compromise of its dignity, could appoint a new commission.

Before this committee, M. de Foissac produced his famous somnambulist; but she failed in exhibiting any one of the phenomena her physician had so confidently predicted: she was easily thrown into the state of sleep, by long habit and the monotony of the passes and manipulations of her magnetiser; but she could not tell the diseases of persons put en rapport with her. The committee of five framed excuses for this failure, by saying, that probably the magnetic fluid was obstructed, because they were "inexperienced, distrustful, and perhaps impatient." After this, what can be said for the judgment or the impartiality of such a committee? They gave at last their opinion, that it would be advisable to appoint a new commission. On the 13th of December 1825, they presented themselves to the Academie to deliver their report. A debate ensued, which occupied three days, and in which all the most distinguished members took part. It was finally decided by a majority of ten, that the commission should be appointed, and the following physicians were chosen its members:-- They were eleven in number, viz. Bourdois de la Motte, the President; Fouquier, Gueneau de Mussy, Guersent, Husson, Itard, Marc, J. J. Leroux, Thillay, Double, and Majendie.

These gentlemen began their labours by publishing an address to all magnetisers, inviting them to come forward and exhibit in their presence the wonders of animal magnetism. M. Dupotet says that very few answered this amicable appeal, because they were afraid of being ridiculed when the report should be published. Four magnetisers, however, answered their appeal readily, and for five years were busily engaged in bringing proofs of the new science before the commission. These were M. de Foissac, M. Dupotet, M. Chapelain, and M. de Geslin. It would be but an unprofitable, and by no means a pleasant task to follow the commissioners in their erratic career, as they were led hither and thither by the four lights of magnetism above mentioned; the four "Wills-o'-the-Wisp" which dazzled the benighted and bewildered doctors on that wide and shadowy region of metaphysical inquiry -- the influence of mind over matter. It will be better to state at once the conclusion they came to after so long and laborious an investigation, and then examine whether they were warranted in it by the evidence brought before them.

The report, which is exceedingly voluminous, is classed under thirty different heads, and its general tenor is favourable to magnetism. The reporters expressly state their belief in the existence of the magnetic fluid, and sum up the result of their inquiries in the four assertions which follow:--

1. Magnetism has no effect upon persons in a sound state of health, nor upon some diseased persons.

2. In others its effects are slight.

3. These effects are sometimes produced by weariness or ennui, by monotony, and by the imagination.

4. We have seen these effects developed independently of the last causes, most probably as the effects of magnetism alone.

It will be seen that the first and second of these sentences presuppose the existence of that magnetic power, which it is the object of the inquiry to discover. The reporters begin, by saying, that magnetism exists, when after detailing their proofs, they should have ended by affirming it. For the sake of lucidity, a favourite expression of their own, let us put the propositions into a new form and new words, without altering the sense.

1. Certain effects, such as convulsions, somnambulism, &c. are producible in the human frame, by the will of others, by the will of the patient himself, or by both combined, or by some unknown means, we wish to discover, perhaps by magnetism.

2. These effects are not producible upon all bodies. They cannot be produced upon persons in a sound state of health, nor upon some diseased persons; while in other eases, the effects are very slight.

3. These effects were produced in many cases that fell under our notice, in which the persons operated on were in a weak state of health, by weariness or ennui, by monotony, and by the power of imagination.

4. But in many other eases these effects were produced, and were clearly not the result of weariness or ennui, of monotony, or of the power of the imagination. They were, therefore, produced by the magnetic processes we employed: -- ergo -- Animal Magnetism exists.

Every one, whether a believer or disbeliever in the doctrine, must see that the whole gist of the argument will be destroyed, if it be proved that the effects which the reporters claimed as resulting from a power independent of weariness, monotony, and the imagination, did, in fact, result from them, and from nothing else. The following are among the proofs brought forward to support the existence of the magnetic fluid, as producing those phenomena:--

414

"A child, twenty-eight months old, was magnetised by M. Foissac, at the house of M. Bourdois. The child, as well as its father, was subject to attacks of epilepsy. Almost immediately after M. Foissac had begun his manipulations and passes, the child rubbed its eyes, bent its head to one side, supported it on one of the cushions of the sofa where it was sitting, yawned, moved itself about, scratched its head and its ears, appeared to strive against the approach of sleep, and then rose, if we may be allowed the expression, grumbling. Being taken away to satisfy a necessity of nature, it was again placed on the sofa, and magnetised for a few moments. But as there appeared no decided symptoms of somnolency this time, we terminated the experiment."

And this in all seriousness and sobriety was called a proof of the existence of the magnetic fluid! That these effects were not produced by the imagination may be granted; but that they were not produced by weariness and monotony is not so clear. A child is seated upon a sofa, a solemn looking gentleman, surrounded by several others equally grave, begins to play various strange antics before it, moving his hands mysteriously, pointing at his head, all the while preserving a most provoking silence. And what does the child? It rubs its eyes, appears restless, yawns, scratches its head, grumbles, and makes an excuse to get away. Magnetism, forsooth! 'Twas a decided case of botheration!

The next proof (so called), though not so amusing, is equally decisive of the mystification of the Commissioners. A deaf and dumb lad, eighteen years of age, and subject to attacks of epilepsy, was magnetised fifteen times by M. Foissac. The phenomena exhibited during the treatment were a heaviness of the eyelids, a general numbness, a desire to sleep, and sometimes vertigo:-- the epileptic attacks were entirely suspended, and did not return till eight months afterwards. Upon this case and the first mentioned, the Committee reasoned thus:-- "These cases appear to us altogether worthy of remark. The two individuals who formed the subject of the experiment, were ignorant of what was done to them. The one, indeed, was not in a state capable of knowing it; and the other never had the slightest idea of magnetism. Both, however, were insensible of its influence; and most certainly it is impossible in either case to attribute this sensibility to the imagination." The first case has been already disposed of. With regard to the second, it is very possible to attribute all the results to imagination. It cannot be contended, that because the lad was deaf and dumb he had no understanding, that he could not see the strange manipulations of the magnetiser, and that he was unaware that his cure was the object of the experiments that were thus made upon him. Had he no fancy merely because he was dumb? and could he, for the same reason, avoid feeling a heaviness in his eyelids, a numbness, and a sleepiness, when he was forced to sit for two or three hours while M. Foissac pointed his fingers at him? As for the amelioration in his health, no argument can be adduced to prove that he was devoid of faith in the remedy; and that, having faith, he should not feel the benefit of it as well as thousands of others who have been cured by means wholly as imaginary.

The third case is brought forward with a still greater show of authority. Having magnetised the child and the dumb youth with results so extraordinary, M. Foissac next tried his hand upon a Commissioner. M. Itard was subjected to a course of manipulations; the consequences were a flow of saliva, a metallic savour in the mouth, and a severe headach. These symptoms, say the reporters, cannot be accounted for by the influence of imagination. M. Itard, it should be remarked, was a confirmed valetudinarian; and a believer, before the investigation commenced, in the truth of magnetism. He was a man, therefore, whose testimony cannot be received with implicit credence upon this subject. He may have repeated, and so may his brother Commissioners, that the results above stated were not produced by the power of the imagination. The patients of Perkins, of Valentine Greatraks, of Sir Kenelm Digby, of Father Gassner, were all equally positive: but what availed their assertions? Experience soon made it manifest, that no other power than that of imagination worked the wonders in their case. M. Itard's is not half so extraordinary; the only wonder is, that it should ever have been insisted upon.

The Commissioners having, as they thought, established beyond doubt the existence of the magnetic fluid, (and these are all their proofs,) next proceeded to investigate the more marvellous phenomena of the science; such as the transfer of the senses; the capability of seeing into one's own or other people's insides, and of divining remedies; and the power of prophecy. A few examples will suffice.

M. Petit was magnetised by M. Dupotet, who asserted that the somnambulist would be able to choose, with his eyes shut, a mesmerised coin out of twelve others. The experiment was tried, and the somnambulist chose the wrong one. [Report of the Commissioners, p. 153.]

Baptiste Chamet was also magnetised by M. Dupotet, and fell into the somnambulic state after eight minutes. As he appeared to be suffering great pain, he was asked what ailed him, when he pointed to his breast, and said he felt pain there. Being asked what part of his body that was, he said his liver. [Ibid, p. 137.]

Mademoiselle Martineau was magnetised by M. Dupotet, and it was expected that her case would prove not only the transfer of the senses, but the power of divining remedies. Her eyes having been bandaged, she was asked if she could not see all the persons present? She replied, no; but she could hear them talking. No one was speaking at the time. She said she would awake after five or ten minutes sleep. She did not awake for sixteen or seventeen minutes. She announced that on a certain day she would be able to tell exactly the nature of her complaint, and prescribe the proper remedies. On the appointed day she was asked the question, and could not answer. [Report of the Commissioners, p. 139.]

Mademoiselle Couturier, a patient of M. de Geslin, was thrown into the state of somnambulism, and M. de Geslin said she would execute his mental orders. One of the Committee then wrote on a slip of paper the words "Go and sit down on the stool in front of the piano." He handed the paper to M. de Geslin, who having conceived the words mentally, turned to his patient, and told her to do as he required of her. She rose up, went to the clock, and said it was twenty minutes past nine. She was tried nine times more, and made as many mistakes. [Idem, p. 139.]

Pierre Cazot was an epileptic patient, and was said to have the power of prophecy. Being magnetised on the 22nd of April, he said that in nine weeks he should have a fit, in three weeks afterwards go mad, abuse his wife, murder some one, and finally recover in the month of August. After which he should never have an attack again. [Idem, p. 180] In two days after uttering this prophecy, he was run over by a cabriolet and killed. [Foreign Quarterly Review, vol. xii. p. 439] A post mortem examination was made of his body, when it was ascertained beyond doubt, that even had he not met with this accident, he could never have recovered. [At the extremity of the plexus choroides was found a substance, yellow within, and white without, containing small hydatids. -- Report oltre Commissioners, p. 186.]

The inquest which had been the means of eliciting these, along with many other facts, having sat for upwards of five years, the magnetisers became anxious that the report should be received by the solemn conclave of the Academie. At length a day (the 20th of June 1831) was fixed for the reading. All the doctors of Paris thronged around the hall to learn the result; the street in front of the building was crowded with medical students; the passages were obstructed by philosophers. "So great was the sensation," says M. Dupotet, "that it might have been supposed the fate of the nation depended on the result." M. Husson, the reporter, appeared at the bar and read the report, the substance of which we have just extracted. He was heard at first with great attention, but as he proceeded signs of impatience and dissent were manifested on all sides. The unreasonable inferences of the Commissioners -- their false conclusions - their too positive assertions, were received with repeated marks of disapprobation. Some of the academicians started from their seats, and apostrophising the Commissioners, accused them of partiality or stolidity. The Commissioners replied; until, at last, the uproar became so violent that an adjournment of the sitting was moved and carried. On the following day the report was concluded. A stormy discussion immediately ensued, which certainly reflected no credit upon the opponents of Animal Magnetism. Both sides lost temper - the anti-magnetists declaring that the whole was a fraud and a delusion; the pro-magnetists reminding the Academy that it was too often the fate of truth to be scorned and disregarded for a while, but that eventually her cause would triumph. "We do not care for your disbelief," cried one, "for in this very hall your predecessors denied the circulation of the blood!" - "Yes," cried another, "and they denied the falling of meteoric stones!" while a third exclaimed "Grande est veritas et praevalebit!" Some degree of order being at last restored, the question whether the report should be received and published was decided in the negative. It was afterwards agreed that a limited number of copies should be lithographed, for the private use of such members as wished to make further examination.

As might have been expected, magnetism did not suffer from a discussion which its opponents had conducted with so much intemperance. The followers of magnetism were as loud as ever in vaunting its efficacy as a cure, and its value, not only to the science of medicine, but to philosophy in general. By force of repeated outcries against the decision of the Academie, and assertions that new facts were discovered day after day, its friends, six years afterwards, prevailed upon that learned and influential body to institute another inquiry. The Academie, in thus consenting to renew the investigation after it had twice solemnly decided (once in conjunction with, and once in opposition to a committee of its own appointment) that Animal Magnetism was a fraud or a chimera, gave the most striking proof of its own impartiality and sincere desire to arrive at the truth.

The new Commission was composed of M. Roux, the President; and Messieurs Bouillard, Cloquet, Emery, Pelletier, Caventon, Oudet, Cornac, and Dubois d'Amiens. The chief magnetiser upon the occasion was M. Berna, who had written to the Academie on the 12th of February 1837, offering to bring forward the most convincing proofs of the truth of the new "science." The Commissioners met for the first time on the 27th of February, and delivered their report, which was drawn up by M. Dubois d'Amiens, on the 22nd of August following. After a careful examination of all the evidence, they decided, as Messieurs Bailly and Franklin had done in 1784, that the touchings, imagination, and the force of imitation would account satisfactorily for all the phenomena; that the supposed Mesmeric fluid would not; that M. Berna, the magnetiser, laboured under a delusion; and that the facts brought under their notice were anything but conclusive in favour of the doctrine of Animal Magnetism, and could have no relation either with physiology or with therapeutics.

The following abridgment of the report will show that the Commissioners did not thus decide without abundant reason. On the 3rd of March they met at the house of M. Roux, the President, when M. Berna introduced his patient, a young girl of seventeen, of a constitution apparently nervous and delicate, but with an air sufficiently cool and self-sufficient. M. Berna offered eight proofs of Animal Magnetism, which he would elicit in her case, and which he classed as follow:--

1. He would throw her into the state of somnambulism.

2. He would render her quite insensible to bodily pain.

3. He would restore her to sensibility by his mere will, without any visible or audible manifestation of it.

4. His mental order should deprive her of motion.

5. He would cause her, by a mental order, to cease answering in the midst of a conversation, and by a second mental order would make her begin again.

6. He would repeat the same experiment, separated from his patient by a door.

7. He would awake her.

8. He would throw her again into the somnambulic state, and by his will successively cause her to lose and recover the sensibility of any part of her body.

Before any attempt at magnetisation was made by M. Berna, the Commissioners determined to ascertain how far, in her ordinary state, she was sensible to pricking. Needles of a moderate size were stuck into her hands and neck, to the depth of half a line, and she was asked by Messieurs Roux and Caventon whether she felt any pain. She replied that she felt nothing; neither did her countenance express any pain. The Commissioners, somewhat surprised at this, repeated their question, and inquired whether she was absolutely insensible. Being thus pressed, she acknowledged that she felt a little pain.

These preliminaries having been completed, M. Berna made her sit close by him. He looked steadfastly at her, but made no movements or passes whatever. After the lapse of about two minutes she fell back asleep, and M. Berna told the Commissioners that she was now in the state of magnetic somnambulism. He then arose, and again looking steadfastly at her from a short distance, declared, after another minute, that she was struck with general insensibility.

To ascertain this, the girl's eyes having been previously bandaged, Messieurs Bouillard, Emery, and Dubois pricked her one after the other with needles. By word she complained of no pain; and her features, where the bandage allowed them to be seen, appeared calm and unmoved. But M. Dubois having stuck his needle rather deep under her chin, she immediately made with much vivacity a movement of deglutition.

This experiment having failed, M. Berna tried another, saying that he would, by the sole and tacit intervention of his will, paralyze any part of the girl's body the Commissioners might mention. To avoid the possibility of collusion, M. Dubois drew up the following conditions:-- " That M. Berna should maintain the most perfect silence, and should receive from the hands of the Commissioners papers, on which should be written the parts to be deprived of motion and sensibility, and that M. Berna should let them know when he had done it by closing one of his eyes, that they might verify it. The parts to be deprived of sensibility were the chin, the right thumb, the region of the left deltoid, and that of the right patella." M. Berna would not accept these conditions, giving for his reason that the parts pointed out by the Commissioners were too limited; that, besides, all this was out of his programme, and he did not understand why such precautions should be taken against him.

M. Berna had written in his programme that he would deprive the whole body of sensibility, and then a part only. He would afterwards deprive the two arms of motion -- then the two legs -- then a leg and an arm - then the neck, and lastly the tongue. All the evidence he wished the Commissioners to have was after a very unsatisfactory fashion. He would tell the somnambulist to raise her arm, and if she did not raise it, the limb was to be considered paralyzed. Besides this, the Commissioners were to make haste with their observations. If the first trials did not succeed, they were to be repeated till paralysis was produced. "These," as the Commissioners very justly remarked, "were not such conditions as men of science, who were to give an account of their commission, could exactly comply with." After some time spent in a friendly discussion of the point, M. Berna said he could do no more at that meeting. Then placing himself opposite the girl, he twice exclaimed, "Wake!" She awakened accordingly, and the sitting terminated.

At the second meeting, M. Berna was requested to paralyze the right arm only of the girl by the tacit intervention of his will, as he had confidently assured the Commissioners he could. M. Berna, after a few moments, made a sign with his eye that he had done so, when M. Bouillard proceeded to verify the fact. Being requested to move her left arm, she did so. Being then requested to move her right leg, she said the whole of her right side was paralyzed -- she could neither move arm nor leg. On this experiment the Commissioners remark: "M. Berna's programme stated that he had the power of paralyzing either a single limb or two limbs at once, we chose a single limb, and there resulted, in spite of his will, a paralysis of two limbs." Some other experiments, equally unsatisfactory, were tried with the same girl. M. Berna was soon convinced that she had not studied her part well, or was not clever enough to reflect any honour upon the science, and he therefore dismissed her. Her place was filled by a woman, aged about thirty, also of very delicate health; and the following conclusive experiments were tried upon her:-

The patient was thrown into the somnambulic state, and her eyes covered with a bandage. At the invitation of the magnetiser, M. Dubois d'Amiens wrote several words upon a card, that the somnambule might read them through her bandages, or through her occiput. M. Dubois wrote the word Pantagruel, in perfectly distinct roman characters; then placing himself behind the somnambule, he presented the card close to her occiput. The magnetiser was seated in front of the woman and of M. Dubois, and could not see the writing upon the card. Being asked by her magnetiser what was behind her head, she answered, after some hesitation, that she saw something white -- something resembling a card -- a visiting-card. It should be remembered that M. Berna had requested M. Dubois aloud to take a card and write upon it, and that the patient must have heard it, as it was said in her presence. She was next asked if she could distinguish what there was on this card. She replied "Yes; there was writing on it." -- "Is it small or large, this writing?" inquired the magnetiser. "Pretty large," replied she. "What is written on it?" continued the magnetiser. "Wait a little-I cannot see very plain. Ah! there is first an M. Yes, it is a word beginning with an M." [The woman thought it was a visiting-card, and guessed that doubtless it would begin with the words Monsieur or Madame.] M. Cornac, unknown to the magnetiser, who alone put the questions, passed a perfectly blank card to M. Dubois, who substituted it quietly for the one on which he had written the word Pantagruel. The somnambule still persisted that she saw a word beginning with an M. At last, after some efforts, she added doubtingly that she thought she could see two lines of writing. She was still thinking of the visiting-card, with a name in one line and the address on the other.

Many other experiments of the same kind, and with a similar result, were tried with blank cards; and it was then determined to try her with playing-cards. M. Berna had a pack of them on his table, and addressing M. Dubois aloud, he asked him to take one of them and place it at the occiput of the somnambule. M. Dubois asked him aloud whether he should take a court card. "As you please," replied the magnetiser. As M. Dubois went towards the table, the idea struck him that he would not take either a court or a common card, but a perfectly blank card of the same size. Neither M. Berna nor the somnambule was aware of the substitution. He then placed himself behind her as before, and held the card to her occiput so that M. Berna could not see it. M. Berna then began to magnetise her with all his force, that he might sublimate her into the stage of extreme lucidity, and effectually transfer the power of vision to her occiput. She was interrogated as to what she could see. She hesitated; appeared to struggle with herself, and at last said she saw a card. "But what do you see on the card?" After a little hesitation, she said she could see black and red (thinking of the court card).

The Commissioners allowed M. Berna to continue the examination in his own way. After some fruitless efforts to get a more satisfactory answer from the somnambule, he invited M. Dubois to pass his card before her head, close against the bandage covering her eyes. This having been done, the somnambule said she could see better. M. Berna then began to put some leading questions, and she replied that she could see a figure. Hereupon, there were renewed solicitations from M. Berna. The somnambule, on her part, appeared to be making great efforts to glean some information from her magnetiser, and at last said that she could distinguish the Knave. But this was not all; it remained for her to say which of the four knaves. In answer to further inquiries, she said there was black by the side of it. Not being contradicted at all, she imagined that she was in the right track; and made, after much pressing, her final guess, that it was the Knave of Clubs.

M. Berna, thinking the experiment finished, took the card from the hands of M. Dubois, and in presence of all the Commissioners saw that it was entirely blank. Blank was his own dismay.

As a last experiment, she was tried with a silver medal. It was with very great difficulty that any answers could be elicited from her. M. Cornac held the object firmly closed in his hand close before the bandage over her eyes. She first said she saw something round; she then said it was flesh-coloured -- then yellow -- then the colour of gold. It was as thick as an onion: and, in answer to incessant questions, she said it was yellow on one side, white on the other, and had black above it. She was thinking, apparently, of a gold watch, with its white dial and black figures for the hours. Solicited, for the last time, to explain herself clearly -- to say, at least, the use of the object and its name, she appeared to be anxious to collect all her energies, and then uttered only the word "hour." Then, at last, as if suddenly illumined, she cried out that "it was to tell the hour."

Thus ended the sitting. Some difficulties afterwards arose between the Commissioners and M. Berna, who wished that a copy of the proces verbal should be given him. The Commissioners would not agree; and M. Berna, in his turn, refused to make any fresh experiments. It was impossible that any investigation could have been conducted more satisfactorily than this. The report of the Commissioners was quite conclusive; and Animal Magnetism since that day lost much of its repute in France. M. Dupotet, with a perseverance and ingenuity worthy a better cause, has found a satisfactory excuse for the failure of M. Berna. Having taken care in his work not to publish the particulars, he merely mentions, in three lines, that M. Berna failed before a committee of the Royal Academy of Medicine in an endeavour to produce some of the higher magnetic phenomena. "There are a variety of incidental circumstances," says that shining light of magnetism, "which it is difficult even to enumerate. An over-anxiety to produce the effects, or any incidental suggestions that may disturb the attention of the magnetiser, will often be sufficient to mar the successful issue of the experiment." ["Introduction to the Study of Animal Magnetism," by Baron Dupotet de Sennevoy, London, 1838, p. 159.] Such are the miserable shifts to which error reduces its votaries!

While Dupotet thus conveniently forbears to dwell upon the unfavourable decision of the committee of

1837, let us hear how he dilates upon the favourable report of the previous committee of 1835, and how he praises the judgment and the impartiality of its members. "The Academie Royale de Medicine," says he, "put upon record clear and authenticated evidence in favour of Animal Magnetism. The Comissioners detailed circumstantially the facts which they witnessed, and the methods they adopted to detect every possible source of deception. Many of the Commissioners, when they entered on the investigation, were not only unfavourable to magnetism, but avowedly unbelievers; so that their evidence in any court of justice would be esteemed the most unexceptionable that could possibly be desired. They were inquiring too, not into any speculative or occult theory, upon which there might be a chance of their being led away by sophistical representations, but they were inquiring into the existence of facts only -- plain demonstrable facts, which were in their own nature palpable to every observer." ["Introduction to the Study of Animal Magnetism," p. 27.] M. Dupotet might not unreasonably be asked whether the very same arguments ought not to be applied to the unfavourable report drawn up by the able M. Dubois d'Amiens and his coadjutors in the last inquiry. If the question were asked, we should, in all probability, meet some such a reply as this: -- "True, they might; but then you must consider the variety of incidental circumstances, too numerous to mention! M. Berna may have been over anxious; in fact, the experiments must have been spoiled by an incidental suggestion!"

A man with a faith so lively as M. Dupotet was just the person to undertake the difficult mission of converting the English to a belief in magnetism. Accordingly we find that, very shortly after the last decision of the Academie, M. Dupotet turned his back upon his native soil and arrived in England, loaded with the magnetic fluid, and ready to re-enact all the fooleries of his great predecessors, Mesmer and Puysegur. Since the days of Perkinism and metallic tractors, until 1833, magnetism had made no progress, and excited no attention in England. Mr. Colquhoun, an advocate at the Scottish bar, published in that year the, till then, inedited report of the French commission of 1831, together with a history of the science, under the title of "Isis Revelata; or, an Inquiry into the Origin, Progress, and present State of Animal Magnetism." Mr. Colquhoun was a devout believer, and his work was full of enthusiasm. It succeeded in awakening some interest upon a subject certainly very curious, but it made few or no converts. An interesting article, exposing the delusion, appeared in the same year in the "Foreign Quarterly Review;" and one or two medical works noticed the subject afterwards, to scout it and turn it into ridicule. The arrival of M. Dupotet, in 1837, worked quite a revolution, and raised Animal Magnetism to a height of favour, as great as it had ever attained even in France.

He began by addressing letters of invitation to the principal philosophers and men of science, physicians, editors of newspapers, and others, to witness the experiments, which were at first carried on at his own residence, in Wigmore-street, Cavendish-square. Many of them accepted the invitation; and, though not convinced, were surprised and confounded at the singular influence which he exercised over the imagination of his patients. Still, at first, his success was not flattering. To quote his own words, in the dedication of his work to Earl Stanhope, "he spent several months in fruitless attempts to induce the wise men of the country to study the phenomena of magnetism. His incessant appeals for an examination of these novel facts remained unanswered, and the press began to declare against him." With a saddened heart, he was about to renounce the design he had formed of spreading magnetism in England, and carry to some more credulous people the important doctrines of which he had made himself the apostle. Earl Stanhope, however, encouraged him to remain; telling him to hope for a favourable change in public opinion, and the eventual triumph of that truth of which he was the defender. M. Dupotet remained. He was not so cruel as to refuse the English people a sight of his wonders. Although they might be ungrateful, his kindness and patience should be long enduring.

In the course of time his perseverance met its reward. Ladies in search of emotions -- the hysteric, the idle, the puling, and the ultra-sentimental crowded to his saloons, as ladies similarly predisposed had crowded to Mesmer's sixty years before. Peers, members of the House of Commons, philosophers, men of letters, and physicians came in great numbers -- some to believe, some to doubt, and a few to scoff. M. Dupotet continued his experiments, and at last made several important converts. Most important of all for a second Mesmer, he found a second D'Eslon.

Dr. Elliotson, the most conspicuous among the converts of Dupotet, was, like D'Eslon, a physician in extensive practice -- a thoroughly honest man, but with a little too much enthusiasm. The parallel holds good between them in every particular; for, as D'Eslon had done before him, Dr. Elliotson soon threw his master into the shade, and attracted all the notice of the public upon himself. He was at that time professor of the principles and practice of medicine at the University College, London, and physician to the hospital. In conjunction with M. Dupotet, he commenced a course of experiments upon some of the patients in that institution. The reports which were published from time to time, partook so largely of the marvellous, and were corroborated by the evidence of men whose learning, judgment, and integrity it was impossible to call in question, that the public opinion was staggered. Men were ashamed to believe, and yet afraid to doubt; and the subject at last became so engrossing that a committee of some of the most distinguished members of the medical profession undertook to investigate the phenomena, and report upon them.

In the mean time, Dr. Elliotson and M. Dupotet continued the public exhibition at the hospital; while the credulous gaped with wonder, and only some few daring spirits had temerity enough to hint about quackery and delusion on the part of the doctors, and imposture on the part of the patients. The phenomena induced in two young women, sisters, named Elizabeth and Jane Okey, were so extraordinary that they became at last the chief, if not the only proofs of the science in London. We have not been able to meet with any reports of these experiments from the pen of an unbeliever, and are therefore compelled to rely solely upon the reports published under the authority of the magnetisers themselves, and given to the world in "The Lancet" and other medical journals.

Elizabeth Okey was an intelligent girl, aged about seventeen, and was admitted into the University College hospital, suffering under attacks of epilepsy. She was magnetised repeatedly by M. Dupotet in the autumn of 1837, and afterwards by Dr. Elliotson at the hospital, during the spring and summer of 1838. By the usual process, she was very easily thrown into a state of deep unconscious sleep, from which she was aroused into somnambulism and delirium. In her waking state she was a modest well-behaved girl, and spoke but little. In the somnambulic state, she appeared quite another being; evinced considerable powers of mimicry; sang comic songs; was obedient to every motion of her magnetiser; and was believed to have the power of prophesying the return of her illness -- the means of cure, and even the death or recovery of other patients in the ward.

Mesmer had often pretended in his day that he could impart the magnetic power to pieces of metal or wood, strings of silk or cord, &c. The reader will remember his famous battery, and the no less famous tree of M. de Puysegur. During the experiments upon Okey, it was soon discovered that all the phenomena could be produced in her, if she touched any object that had been previously mesmerised by the will or the touch of her magnetiser. At a sitting, on the 5th of July 1838, it was mentioned that Okey, some short time previously, and while in the state of magnetic lucidity, had prophesied that, if mesmerised tea were placed in each of her hands, no power in nature would be able to awake her until after the lapse of a quarter of an hour. The experiment was tried accordingly. Tea which had been touched by the magnetiser was placed in each hand, and she immediately fell asleep. After ten minutes, the customary means to awaken her were tried, but without effect. She was quite insensible to all external impressions. In a quarter of an hour, they were tried with redoubled energy, but still in vain. She was left alone for six minutes longer; but she still slept, and it was found quite impossible to wake her. At last some one present remarked that this wonderful sleep would, in all probability, last till the tea was removed from her bands. The suggestion was acted upon, the tea was taken away, and she awoke in a few seconds. ["Lancet," vol. ii. 1837-8, p. 585.]

On the 12th of July, just a week afterwards, numerous experiments as to the capability of different substances for conveying the magnetic influence were tried upon her. A slip of crumpled paper, magnetised by being held in the hand, produced no effect. A penknife magnetised her immediately. A piece of oilskin had no influence. A watch placed on her palm sent her to sleep immediately, if the metal part were first placed in contact with her; the glass did not affect her so quickly. As she was leaving the room, a sleeve-cuff made of brown-holland, which had been accidentally magnetised by a spectator, stopped her in mid career, and sent her fast to sleep. It was also found that, on placing the point of her finger on a sovereign which had been magnetised, she was immediately stupefied. A pile of sovereigns produced sleep; but if they were so placed that she could touch the surface of each coin, the sleep became intense and protracted.

Still more extraordinary circumstances were related of this patient. In her state of magnetic sleep, she said that a tall black man, or negro, attended her, and prompted the answers she was to give to the various perplexing questions that were put to her. It was also asserted that she could use the back of her hand as an organ of vision. The first time this remarkable phenomenon was said to have been exhibited was a few days prior to the 5th of July. On the latter day, being in what was called a state of loquacious somnambulism, she was asked by Dr. Elliotson's assistant whether she had an eye in her hand. She replied that "it was a light there, and not an eye." "Have you got a light anywhere else?" -- "No, none anywhere else." -- "Can you see with the inside as well as the out?" -- "Yes; but very little with the inside."

On the 9th of July bread with butter was given to her, and while eating it she drank some magnetised water, and falling into a stupor dropped her food from her hand and frowned. The eyes, partially closed, had the abstracted aspect that always accompanies stupefaction. The right-hand was open, the palm upwards; the left, with its back presented anteriorly, was relaxed and curved. The bread being lost, she moved her left-hand about convulsively until right over the bread, when a clear view being obtained, the hand turned suddenly round and clutched it eagerly. Her hand was afterwards wrapped in a handkerchief; but then she could not see with it, and laid it on her lap with an expression of despair.

These are a few only of the wonderful feats of Elizabeth Okey. Jane was not quite so clever; but she nevertheless managed to bewilder the learned men almost as much as her sister. A magnetised sovereign having been placed on the floor, Jane, then in the state of delirium, was directed to stoop and pick it up. She stooped, and having raised it about three inches, was fixed in a sound sleep in that constrained position. Dr. Elliotson pointed his finger at her, to discharge some more of the mesmeric fluid into her, when her hand immediately relaxed its grasp of the coin, and she re-awoke into the state of delirium, exclaiming, "God bless my soul!"

It is now time to mention the famous gold-chain experiment which was performed at the hospital upon Elizabeth Okey, in the presence of Count Flahault, Dr. Lardner, Mr. Knatchbull the professor of Arabic in the University of Oxford, and many other gentlemen. The object of the experiment was to demonstrate that, when Okey held one end of a gold chain, and Dr. Elliotson, or any other magnetiser, the other, the magnetic fluid would travel through the chain, and, after the lapse of a minute, stupify the patient. A long gold chain having been twice placed around her neck, Dr. Elliotson at once threw her into a state of stupor. It was then found that, if the intermediate part of the chain were twisted around a piece of wood, or a roll of paper, the passage of the fluid would be checked, and stupor would not so speedily ensue. If the chain were removed, she might be easily thrown into the state of delirium; when she would sing at the request of her magnetiser; and, if the chain were then unrolled, her voice would be arrested in the most gradual manner; its loudness first diminishing -- the tune then becoming confused, and finally lost altogether. The operations of her intellect could be checked, while the organs of sound would still continue to exert themselves. For instance, while her thoughts were occupied on the poetry and air of Lord Byron's song, "The Maid of Athens," the chain was unrolled; and when she had reached the line, "My life, I love you!" the stupor had increased; a cold statue-like aspect crept over the face -- the voice sank -- the limbs became rigid -- the memory was gone -- the faculty of forecasting the thoughts had departed, and but one portion of capacity remained -- that of repeating again and again, perhaps twenty times, the line and music which had last issued from her lips, without pause, and in the proper time, until the magnetiser stopped her voice altogether, by further unrolling the chain and stupifying her. On another trial, she was stopped in the comic song, "Sir Frog he would a wooing go," when she came to the line,

"Whether his mother would let him or no;"

while her left hand outstretched, with the chain in it, was moving up and down, and the right toe was tapping the time on the floor; and with these words and actions she persevered for fifty repetitions, until the winding of the chain re-opened her faculties, when she finished the song. ["Lancet," vol. ii. 1837-8, p.617.]

The report from which we have extracted the above passage further informed the public and the medical profession, and expected them to believe, that, when this species of stupefaction was produced while she was employed in any action, the action was repeated as long as the mesmeric influence lasted. For instance, it was asserted that she was once deprived of the motion of every part of her body, except the right forefinger, with which she was rubbing her chin; and that, when thrown into the trance, she continued rubbing her chin for several minutes, until she was unmagnetised, when she ceased. A similar result was obtained when she was smoothing down her hair; and at another time when she was imitating the laughter of the spectators, excited beyond control by her clever mimicry. At another time she was suddenly thrown into the state of delirious stupor while pronouncing the word "you," of which she kept prolonging the sound for several minutes, with a sort of vibrating noise, until she was awakened. At another time, when a magnetised sovereign was given to her, wrapped up in paper, she caught it in her hand, and turned it round flatwise between her fingers, saying that it was wrapped up "very neatly indeed." The mesmeric influence caught her in the remark, which she kept repeating over and over again, all the while twirling the sovereign round and round until the influence in the coin had evaporated.

We are also told of a remarkable instance of the force of the magnetic power. While Elizabeth Okey was one day employed in writing, a sovereign which had been imbued with the fluid was placed upon her boot. In half a minute her leg was paralyzed -- rooted to the floor -- perfectly immovable at the joints, and visited, apparently, with pain so intense that the girl writhed in agony. "The muscles of the leg were found," says the report, "as rigid and stiff as if they had been carved in wood. When the sovereign was removed, the pain left her in a quarter of a minute. On a subsequent day, a mesmerised sovereign was placed in her left hand as it hung at her side, with the palm turned slightly outwards. The hand and arm were immediately paralyzed -- fixed with marble-like firmness." No general stupor having occurred, she was requested to move her arm; but she could not lift it a hair's-breadth from her side. On another occasion, when in a state of delirium, in which she had remained three hours, she was asked to describe her feelings when she handled any magnetised object and went off into the stupor. She had never before, although several times asked, given any information upon the subject. She now replied that, at the moment of losing her senses through any manipulations, she experienced a sensation of opening in the crown of her head; that she never knew when it closed again; but that her eyes seemed to become exceedingly large; -- three times as big as before. On recovering from this state, she remembered nothing that had taken place in the interval, whether that interval were hours or days; her only sensation was that of awakening, and of something being lifted from her eyes.

The regular publication of these marvellous experiments, authenticated as they were by many eminent names, naturally excited the public attention in an extreme degree. Animal Magnetism became the topic of discussion in every circle -- politics and literature were for a time thrown into the shade, so strange were the facts, or so wonderful was the delusion. The public journals contented themselves in many instances with a mere relation of the results, without giving any opinion as to the cause. One of them which gave a series of reports upon the subject, thus described the girl, and avowed its readiness to believe all that was related of her. [Morning Post, March 2, 1838.] "Her appearance as she sits, as pale and almost as still as a corpse, is strangely awful. She whistles to oblige Dr. Elliotson: an incredulous bystander presses his fingers upon her lips; she does not appear conscious of the nature of the interruption; but when asked to continue, replies in childish surprise, 'it can't.' This state of magnetic semi-existence will continue we know not how long. She has continued in it for twelve days at a time, and when awakened to real life forgets all that has occurred in the magnetic one. Can this be deception? We have conversed with the poor child her ordinary state as she sat by the fire in her ward, suffering from the headach, which persecutes her almost continually when not under the soothing fluence of the magnetic operation, and we confess we never beheld anybody less likely to prove an impostor. We have seen Professor Faraday exerting his acute and sagacious powers for an hour together, in the endeavour to detect some physical discrepancy in her performance, or elicit some blush of mental confusion by his naive and startling remarks. But there was nothing which could be detected, and the professor candidly confessed that the matter was beyond his philosophy to unravel."

Notwithstanding this sincere, and on the point of integrity, unimpeachable evidence in her favour; notwithstanding that she appeared to have no motives for carrying on so extraordinary and long-continued a deception, the girl was an impostor, and all these wise, learned, and contemplative men her dupes. It was some time, however, before this fact was clearly established, and the delusion dissipated by the clear light of truth. In the mean time various other experiments on the efficacy of the supposed magnetic power were tried in various parts of England; but the country did not furnish another epileptic girl so clever as Elizabeth Okey. An exhibition of the kind was performed on a girl named Sarah Overton, at the workhouse of the parish of St. Martin's-in-the-Fields. The magnetiser on this occasion was Mr. Bainbridge, the parish surgeon. It is but justice to him to state, that he conducted the experiments with the utmost fairness, and did not pretend to produce any of the wondrous and incredible phenomena of other practitioners. This girl, whose age was about twenty, had long been subject to epileptic fits, and appeared remarkably simple and modest in her manners and appearance. She was brought into the room and placed in a chair. About twenty gentlemen were present. Mr. Bainbridge stationed himself behind, and pointed his fingers at her brain, while his assistant in front made the magnetic passes before her eyes, and over her body. It cannot be said that her imagination was not at work; for she had been previously magnetised, and was brought in with her eyes open, and in complete possession of all her faculties. No means had been taken to prevent interruption during the sitting; new visiters continually arrived, and the noise of the opening and shutting of the door repeatedly called from Mr. Bainbridge a request that all should be kept silent. The girl herself constantly raised her head to see who was coming in; but still, in direct contradiction to M. Dupotet, and, indeed, all the magnetisers, who have repeated over and over again, that interruption destroys the magnetic power, she fell into a deep sleep at the end of about twelve minutes. In this state, which is that called "Mesmeric Coma," she was quite insensible. Though pulled violently by the hair, and pricked on the arm with a pin, she showed no signs of consciousness or feeling. In a short time afterwards, she was awakened into the somnambulic or delirious state, when she began to converse freely with the persons around her, but more especially with her magnetiser. She would sing if required, and even dance in obedience to his command, and pretended to see him although her eyes were closely blindfolded with a handkerchief. She seemed to have a constant tendency to fall back into the state of coma, and had to be aroused with violence every two or three minutes to prevent a relapse. A motion of the hand before her face was sufficient to throw her, in the middle of a song, into this insensible state; but it was observed particularly that she fell at regular intervals, whether any magnetic passes were made at her or not. It was hinted aloud to a person present that be should merely bend his body before her, and she would become insensible, and fall to the ground. The pass was made, and she fell accordingly into the arms of a medical gentleman, who stood behind ready to receive her. The girl having been again aroused into the state of delirium, another person, still audibly, was requested to do the same. He did not; but the girl fell as before. The experiments were sufficient to convince the author that one human being could indubitably exercise a very wonderful influence over another; but that imagination only, and not the mesmeric fluid, was the great agent by which these phenomena could be produced in persons of strong faith and weak bodies.

Some gentlemen present were desirous of trying whether any of the higher mesmeric states, such as that of lucidity and clairvoyance could be produced. Mr. Bainbridge was willing to allow the experiment to be made, but previously expressed his own doubts upon the subject. A watch was then put into her bosom, the dial plate and glass against her skin, to ascertain whether she could see without the intervention of the organs of sight. She was asked what hour it was; and was promised a shilling if she would tell by the watch which had been placed in her bosom. She held out her hand for the shilling, and received it with great delight. She was then asked if she could see the watch? She said "no -- not a watch; she could see something -- something that was very pretty indeed." "Come, come, Sally," said Mr. Bainbridge, "you must not be so stupid; rouse up, girl, and tell us what o'clock it is, and I'll give you another shilling!" The girl at this time seemed to be relapsing into a deep sleep; but on being shaken, aroused herself with a convulsive start. In reply to further questions, she said, "she could see a clock, a very pretty clock, indeed!" She was again asked, five or six times, what the hour was: she at last replied that "it was ten minutes to two." The watch being then taken out of her bosom, it was found to be on the stroke of two. Every one present, including the magnetiser, confessed that there was nothing wonderful in the conjecture she had hazarded. She knew perfectly well what hour it was before she was brought into the ward, as there was a large clock in the workhouse, and a bell which rang at dinner time; she calculated mentally the interval that had since elapsed, and guessed accordingly. The same watch was afterwards advanced four or five hours, and put into her bosom without a word being said in her hearing. On being again asked what o'clock it was by that watch, and promised another shilling if she would tell, she still replied that it was near two -- the actual time. Thus, as Mr. Bainbridge had predicted, the experiment came to nothing. The whole case of this girl offered a striking instance of the power of imagination, but no proof whatever of the supposed existence of the magnetic fluid.

The Medical Committee of the University College Hospital took alarm at a very early period at the injury which might be done to that Institution, by the exhibitions of Okey and her magnetisers. A meeting was held in June 1838, at which Dr. Elliotson was not present, to take into consideration the reports of the experiments that had been published in the Medical Journals. Resolutions were then passed to the effect, that Dr. Elliotson should be requested to refrain from further public exhibitions of mesmerism; and, at the same time, stating the wish of the Committee not to interfere with its private employment as a remedial agent, if he thought it would be efficacious upon any of the patients of the Institution. Dr. Elliotson replied, that no consideration should prevent him from pursuing the investigation of Animal Magnetism; but that he had no desire to make a public exhibition of it. He had only given lectures and demonstrations when numbers of scientific gentlemen were present; he still continued to receive numerous letters from learned and eminent men, entreating permission to witness the phenomena; but if the Committee willed it, he should admit no person without their sanction. He shortly afterwards sent a list of the names of individuals who were anxious to witness the experiments. The Committee returned it to him unread, with the reply that they could not sanction any exhibition that was so entirely foreign to the objects of the Hospital. In answer to this, Dr. Elliotson reiterated his full belief in the doctrines of Animal Magnetism, and his conviction that his experiments would ultimately throw a light upon the operations of nature, which would equal, if not exceed, that elicited by the greatest discoveries of by-gone ages. The correspondence dropped here; and the experiments continued as usual.

The scene, however, was drawing to a close. On the 25th of August, a notice was published in the Lancet, to the effect, that some experiments had been performed on the girls Elizabeth and Jane Okey, at the house of Mr. Wakley, a report of which was only withheld in the hope that the Committee of Members of the Medical Profession, then sitting to investigate the phenomena of mesmerism, would publish their report of what they had witnessed. It was further stated, that whether that Committee did or did not publish their report, the result of the experiments at Mr. Wakley's house should certainly be made known in the next number of that journal. Accordingly, on the 1st of September appeared a statement, which overthrew, in the most complete manner, the delusion of mesmerism. Nothing could have been better conducted than these experiments; nothing could be more decisive of the fact, that all the phenomena were purely the results of the excited imaginations of the girls, aided in no slight degree by their wilful deception.

The first experiments were performed on the 16th of August, in the presence of Mr. Wakley, M. Dupotet, Dr. Elliotson, Dr. Richardson, Mr. Herring, Mr. Clarke, and Mr. G. Mills the writer of the published reports of the experiments at the University College Hospital. Dr. Elliotson had said, that nickel was capable of retaining and transmitting the magnetic fluid in an extraordinary degree; but that lead possessed no such virtues. The effects of the nickel, he was confident, would be quite astounding; but that lead might always be applied with impunity. A piece of nickel was produced by the Doctor, about three quarters of an ounce in weight, together with a piece of lead of the same shape and smoothness, but somewhat larger. Elizabeth Okey was seated in a chair; and, by a few passes and manipulations, was thrown into the state of "ecstatic delirium." A piece of thick pasteboard was then placed in front of her face, and held in that situation by two of the spectators, so that she could not see what was passing either below or in front of her. Mr. Wakley having received both the nickel and the lead, seated himself opposite the girl, and applied the lead to each hand alternately, but in such a manner as to lead her to believe that both metals had been used. No effect was produced. The nickel magnetised by Dr. Elliotson was, after a pause, applied in a similar manner. No results followed. After another pause, the lead was several times applied, and then again the nickel. After the last application of the nickel, the face of the patient became violently flushed, the eyes were convulsed into a startling squint, she fell back in the chair, her breathing was hurried, her limbs rigid, and her back bent in the form of a bow. She remained in this state for a quarter of an hour.

This experiment was not considered a satisfactory proof of the magnetic powers of the nickel; and Dr. Elliotson suggested that, in the second experiment, that metal should alone be tried. Mr. Wakley was again the operator; but, before commencing, he stated privately to Mr. Clarke, that instead of using nickel only, he would not employ the nickel at all. Mr. Clarke, unseen by any person present, took the piece of nickel; put it into his waistcoat pocket; and walked to the window, where he remained during the whole of the experiment. Mr. Wakley again sat down, employing both hands, but placing his fingers in such a manner, that it was impossible for any person to see what substance he held. Presently, on applying his left hand, the girl's vision being still obstructed by the pasteboard, Mr. Herring, who was standing near, said in a whisper, and with much sincerity, "Take care, don't apply the nickel too strongly." Immediately the face of the girl became violently red, her eyes were fixed in an intense squint, she fell back convulsively in her chair, and all the previous symptoms were produced more powerfully than before. Dr. Elliotson observed that the effects were most extraordinary; that no other metal than nickel could produce them, and that they presented a beautiful series of phenomena. This paroxysm lasted half an hour. Mr. Wakley retired with Dr. Elliotson and the other gentlemen into an adjoining room, and convinced them that he had used no nickel at all, but a piece of lead and a farthing.

This experiment was twice repeated with the same results. A third trial was made with the nickel, but no effect was produced.

On the succeeding day the experiments were repeated upon both the sisters, chiefly with mesmerised water and sovereigns. The investigation occupied about five hours, and the following were the results:--

1. Six wine glasses, filled with water unmesmerised, were placed on a table, and Jane Okey being called in, was requested to drink from each of them successively. She did so, and no effect was produced.

2. The same six glasses stood on the table, the water in the fourth having been subjected for a long time to the supposed magnetic influence. She was requested in like manner to drink of these. She did so, and again no effect was produced, although, according to the doctrine of the magnetisers, she ought to have been immediately fixed on drinking of the fourth.

3. In this experiment the position of the glasses was changed. There was no result.

4. Was a repetition of the foregoing. No result.

5. The water in all the glasses was subjected to the supposed magnetic influence from the fingers of Dr. Elliotson, until, in his opinion, it was strongly magnetised. Still no result.

6. The glasses were filled up with fresh water unmesmerised. No result.

7. The water was strongly magnetised in each glass, and the girl emptied them all. No result.

It would be needless to go through the whole series of experiments. The results may be briefly stated. Sovereigns unmesmerised threw the girls into convulsions, or fixed them. Mesmerised sovereigns sometimes did and sometimes did not produce these symptoms. Elizabeth Okey became repeatedly fixed when drinking unmagnetised water; while that which had been subjected to the powers of a supposed magnetic battery, produced no results. Altogether twenty-nine experiments were tried, which convinced every one present, except Dr. Elliotson, that Animal Magnetism was a delusion, that the girls were of very exciteable imaginations, and arrant impostors.

Their motives for carrying on so extraordinary a deception have often been asked. The question is easily answered. Poor girls, unknown and unnoticed, or, if noticed, perhaps despised, they found themselves all at once the observed of all observers, by the really remarkable symptoms of their disease, which it required no aid from magnetism to produce. Flattered by the oft-repeated experiments and constant attentions of doctors and learned men, who had begun by deluding themselves, they imagined themselves persons of vast importance, and encouraged by degrees the whims of their physicians, as the means of prolonging the consideration they so unexpectedly enjoyed. Constant practice made them at last all but perfect in the parts they were performing; and they failed at last, not from a want of ingenuity, or of a most wonderful power over their own minds, and by their minds upon their bodies, but from the physical impossibility of seeing through a thick pasteboard, or into the closed hands of Mr. Wakley. The exposure that was made was complete and decisive. From that day forth, magnetism in England has hid its diminished head, and affronted no longer the common sense of the age. M. Dupotet is no more heard of, the girls Okey afford no more either wonder or amusement by their clever acting, and reason has resumed her sway in the public mind.

A few more circumstances remain to be stated. Elizabeth Okey left the hospital; but was re-admitted some weeks afterwards, labouring under ischuria, a fresh complaint, unconnected with her former malady. As experiments in magnetism were still tried upon her privately, notwithstanding the recent exposure and the all but universal derision of the public, the House Committee of the hospital, early in December, met to consider the expediency of expelling the girl. Dr. Elliotson, on that occasion, expressed his opinion that it was necessary to retain her in the hospital, as she was too ill to be discharged. It was then elicited from the nurse, who was examined by the Committee, that Okey, when in the state of "magnetic delirium," was in the habit of prophesying the death or recovery of the patients in the ward; that, with the consent of Dr. Elliotson, she had been led in the twilight into the men's ward, and had prophesied in a similar manner; her predictions being taken down in writing, and given in a sealed paper to the apothecary, to be opened after a certain time, that it might be seen whether they were verified. Dr. Elliotson did not deny the fact. The nurse also stated more particularly the manner in which the prophecies were delivered. She said that, on approaching the bed of a certain patient, Okey gave a convulsive shudder, exclaiming that "Great Jacky was sitting on the bedclothes!" On being asked to explain herself, she said that Great Jacky was the angel of death. At the bedside of another patient she shuddered slightly, and said "Little Jacky was there!" Dr. Elliotson did not altogether discredit the predictions; but imagined they might ultimately be verified by the death or recovery of the patient. Upon the minds of the patients themselves, enfeebled as they were by disease and suffering, the worst effects were produced. One man's death was accelerated by the despondency it occasioned, and the recovery of others was seriously impeded.

When these facts became known, the Council of the College requested the Medical Committee to discharge Okey and prevent any further exhibitions of Animal Magnetism in the wards. The latter part of this request having been communicated to Dr. Elliotson, he immediately sent in his resignation. A successor was afterwards appointed in the person of Dr. Copland. At his inaugural lecture the students of the college manifested a riotous disposition, called repeatedly for their old instructor, and refused to allow the lecture to proceed; but it appears the disturbance was caused by their respect and affection for Dr. Elliotson individually, and not from any participation in his ideas about magnetism.

Extravagant as the vagaries of the English professors of magnetism may appear, they are actual common sense in comparison with the aberrations of the Germans. The latter have revived all the exploded doctrines of the Rosicrucians; and in an age which is called enlightened, have disinterred from the rubbish of antiquity, the wildest superstitions of their predecessors, and built upon them theories more wild and startling than anything before attempted or witnessed among mankind. Paracelsus and Bohmen,

Borri and Meyer, with their strange heterogeneous mixture of alchymy and religion, but paved the way for the stranger, and even more extravagant mixture of magnetism and religion, as now practised in Germany. Magnetism, it is believed, is the key of all knowledge, and opens the door to those forbidden regions where all the wonders of God's works are made clear to the mind of man. The magnetic patient is possessed of all gifts -- can converse with myriads of spirits, and even with God himself -- be transported with greater rapidity than the lightning's flash to the moon or the stars, and see their inhabitants, and hold converse with them on the wonders and beauties of their separate spheres, and the power and goodness of the God who made them. Time and space are to them as if annihilated -- nothing is hidden from them -- past, present, or future. They divine the laws by which the universe is upheld, and snatch the secrets of the Creator from the darkness in which, to all other men, it is enveloped. For the last twenty or thirty years these daring and blasphemous notions have flourished in rank luxuriance; and men of station in society, learning, and apparent good sense in all the usual affairs of life, have publicly given in their adhesion, and encouraged the doctrine by their example, or spread it abroad by their precepts. That the above summary of their tenets may not he deemed an exaggeration we enter into particulars, and refer the incredulous that human folly in the present age could ever be pushed so far, to chapter and verse for every allegation.

In a work published in Germany in 1817, by J. A. L. Richter, entitled "Considerations on Animal Magnetism," the author states that in magnetism is to be found the solution of the enigmas of human existence, and particularly the enigmas of Christianity, on the mystic and obscure parts of which it throws a light which permits us to gaze clearly on the secrets of the mystery. Wolfart's "Annals of Animal Magnetism" abound with similar passages; and Kluge's celebrated work is written in the same spirit. "Such is the wonderful sympathy," says the latter, "between the magnetiser and the somnambulist that he has known the latter to vomit and be purged in consequence of medicine which the former had taken. Whenever he put pepper on his tongue, or drank wine, the patient could taste these things distinctly on her palate." But Kerner's history of the case of Madame Hauffe, the famous magnetic woman, "Seer" or "Prophetess of Prevorst," Will give a more complete and melancholy proof of the sad wanderings of these German "men of science," than any random selections we might make from their voluminous works. This work was published in two volumes, and the authenticity of its details supported by Gorres, Eschenmeyer, and other men of character and reputation in Germany: it is said to have had an immense sale. She resided in the house of Kerner, at Weinsberg; and being weak and sickly, was very easily thrown into a state of somnambulism. "She belonged," says Kerner, "to a world of spirits; she was half spirit herself; she belonged to the region beyond death, in which she already half existed. * * * Her body clothed her spirit like a thin veil. * * * She was small and slightly made, had an Oriental expression of countenance, and the piercing eyes of a prophet, the gleams of which were increased in their power and beauty by her long dark eyebrows and eyelashes. She was a flower of light, living upon sunbeams. * * * Her spirit often seemed to be separated from her frame. The spirits of all things, of which mankind in general have no perception, were perceptible to and operated upon her, more particularly the spirits of metals, herbs, men, and animals. All imponderable matters, even the rays of light, had an effect upon her when she was magnetised." The smell of flint was very agreeable to her. Salt laid on her hand caused a flow of saliva: rock crystal laid on the pit of her stomach produced rigidity of the whole body. Red grapes produced certain effects, if placed in her hands; white grapes produced different effects. The bone of an elk would throw her into an epileptic fit. The tooth of a mammoth produced a feeling of sluggishness. A spider's web rolled into a ball produced a prickly feeling in the hands, and a restlessness in the whole body. Glow-worms threw her into the magnetic sleep. Music somnambulised her. When she wanted to be cheerful, she requested Kerner to magnetise the water she drank, by playing the Jew's-harp. She used to say in her sleep, "Magnetise the water by seven vibrations of the harp." If she drank water magnetised in this manner, she was constrained involuntarily to pour forth her soul in song. The eyes of many men threw her into the state of somnambulism. She said that in those eyes there was a spiritual spark, which was the mirror of the soul. If a magnetised rod were laid on her right eye, every object on which she gazed appeared magnified.

It was by this means that she was enabled to see the inhabitants of the moon. She said, that on the left side of the moon, the inhabitants were great builders, and much happier than those on the right side. "I often see," said she to her magnetiser, "many spirits with whom I do not come into contact. Others come to me, and I speak to them; and they often spend months in my company. I hear and see other things at the same time; but I cannot turn my eyes from the spirits; they are in magnetic rapport with me. They look like clouds, thin, but not transparent; though, at first, they seem so. Still, I never saw one which cast a shadow. Their form is similar to that which they possessed when alive; but colourless, or grey. They wear clothing; and it appears as if made of clouds, also colourless and misty grey. The brighter and better spirits wear long garments, which hang in graceful folds, with belts around their waists. The expression of their features is sad and solemn. Their eyes are bright, like fire; but none of them that I ever saw had hair upon their heads. They make noises when they wish to excite the attention of those who have not the gift of seeing them. These noises consist of sounds in the air, sometimes sudden and sharp, and causing a shock. Sometimes the sounds are plaintive and musical; at other times they resemble the rustling of silk, the falling of sand, or the rolling of a ball. The better spirits are brighter than the bad ones, and their voice is not so strong. Many, particularly the dark, sad spirits, when I uttered words of religious consolation, sucked them in, as it were; and I saw them become brighter and quite glorious in consequence: but I became weaker. Most of the spirits who come to me are of the lowest regions of the spiritual world, which are situated just above our atmosphere. They were, in their life, grovelling and low-minded people, or such as did not die in the faith of Jesus; or else such as, in expiring, clung to some earthly thought or affection, which now presses upon them, and prevents them from soaring up to heaven. I once asked a spirit whether children grew after death? 'Yes,' replied the spirit,' the soul gradually expands, until it becomes as large as it would have been on earth. I cannot effect the salvation of these spirits; I am only their mediator. I pray ardently with them, and so lead them by degrees to the great Saviour of the world. It costs an infinity of trouble before such a soul turns again to the Lord.'"

It would, however, serve no good purpose to extend to greater length the reveries of this mad woman, or to set down one after the other the names of the magnetisers who encouraged her in her delusions -- being themselves deluded. To wade through these volumes of German mysticism is a task both painful and disgusting -- and happily not necessary. Enough has been stated to show how gross is the superstition even of the learned; and that errors, like comets, run in one eternal cycle -- at their apogee in one age, at their perigee in the next, but returning in one phase or another for men to wonder at.

In England the delusion of magnetism may for the present be considered as fairly exploded. Taking its history from the commencement, and tracing it to our own day, it can hardly be said, delusion though it was, that it has been wholly without its uses. To quote the words of Bailly, in 1784, "Magnetism has not been altogether unavailing to the philosophy which condemns it: it is an additional fact to record among the errors of the human mind, and a great experiment on the strength of the imagination." Over that vast inquiry of the influence of mind over matter, -- an inquiry which the embodied intellect of mankind will never be able to fathom completely, -- it will, at least, have thrown a feeble and imperfect light. It will have afforded an additional proof of the strength of the unconquerable will, and the weakness of matter as compared with it; another illustration of the words of the inspired Psalmist, that "we are fearfully and wonderfully made." If it serve no other purpose than this, its history will prove useful. Truth ere now has been elicited by means of error; and Animal Magnetism, like other errors, may yet contribute its quota towards the instruction and improvement of mankind.

THE END

BN Publishing

www.bnpublishing.com

CPSIA information can be obtained
at www.ICGtesting.com
Printed in the USA
LVHW060552270921
698790LV00012B/504